Jan Zacharias van Rookhuijzen
Herodotus and the Topography of Xerxes' Invasion

Jan Zacharias van Rookhuijzen

Herodotus and the Topography of Xerxes' Invasion

DE GRUYTER

This book was based on the dissertation titled "Where Xerxes' Throne Once Stood: Gazing with Herodotus at the Persian Invasion in the Landscapes of Greece and Anatolia", defended on 1 February 2018 at Radboud University, Nijmegen, the Netherlands. The project's supervisors were Prof. dr. M.J.G.M. De Pourcq, Prof. dr. A.P.M.H. Lardinois and Prof. dr. E.M. Moormann.

ISBN 978-3-11-071017-5
e-ISBN (PDF) 978-3-11-061253-0
e-ISBN (EPUB) 978-3-11-061151-9

Library of Congress Cataloging-in-Publication Data
Names: Rookhuijzen, Jan Zacharias van, 1988- author.
Title: Herodotus and the topography of Xerxes' invasion : place and memory in
   Greece and Anatolia / Jan Zacharias van Rookhuijzen.
Other titles: Where Xerxes throne once stood
Description: Berlin ; Boston : De Gruyter, [2018] | Revision of author's
   thesis (doctoral)--Radboud University, 2018, titled Where Xerxes throne
   once stood: gazing with Herodotus at the Persian invasion in the
   landscapes of Greece and Anatolia. | Includes bibliographical references
   and index.
Identifiers: LCCN 2018030915 (print) | LCCN 2018043255 (ebook) | ISBN
   9783110612530 (electronic Portable Document Format (pdf) | ISBN
   9783110610208 | ISBN 9783110610208print : paper) | ISBN
   9783110612530e-book pdf) | ISBN 9783110611519e-book epub)
Subjects: LCSH: Greece--History--Persian Wars, 500-449 B.C. | Herodotus.
   History.
Classification: LCC DF225 (ebook) | LCC DF225 .R67 2018 (print) | DDC
   938/.03--dc23
LC record available at https://lccn.loc.gov/2018030915

Bibliographic information published by the Deutsche Nationalbibliothek
The Deutsche Nationalbibliothek lists this publication in the Deutsche Nationalbibliografie;
detailed bibliographic data are available on the Internet at http://dnb.dnb.de.

© 2020 Walter de Gruyter GmbH, Berlin/Boston
This volume is text- and page-identical with the hardback published in 2019.
Typesetting: Integra Software Services Pvt. Ltd.
Printing and binding: CPI books GmbH, Leck

www.degruyter.com

For my parents and sisters.

"Circumstances of climate and situation, otherwise trivial, become interesting from that connection with great men, and great actions, which history and poetry have given them: the life of Miltiades or Leonidas could never be read with so much pleasure, as on the plains of Marathon or at the Streights of Thermopylae; the Iliad has new beauties on the banks of the Scamander, and the Odyssey is most pleasing in the countries where Ulysses travelled and Homer sung.

The particular pleasure, it is true, which an imagination warmed on the spot receives from those scenes of heroick actions, the traveller can only feel, nor is it to be communicated by description. But the classical ground not only makes us always relish the poet, or historian more, but sometimes helps us to understand them better."

Preface of The Ruins of Palmyra, otherwise Tedmore, in the desart
by Robert Wood (1753), London.

Preface

Travelling to the lands of the ancient world often feels like time travel. Here we can tread in the footsteps of our textual heroes and observe the same landscapes and buildings that were part of their world; whether in reality or in our imagination. This can be an emotional, almost overwhelming experience, with sentiments ranging from delight and surprise, to frustration and confusion (when reality challenges our expectations). This book is the result of my personal fascination with these experiences.

I found in Herodotus' *Histories* the ideal companion to exploring them.

I am grateful to my supervisors Maarten De Pourcq, André Lardinois, and Eric Moormann for their fantastic input, support, and patience. I owe special thanks to Josine Blok who read and commented on the entire manuscript before its final submission.

Apart from my supervisors, the following colleagues at Nijmegen (and many others) have made this research an enormously enjoyable experience: Lucien van Beek, Sven Betjes, Luuk de Blois, Bé Breij, Esmée Bruggink, Diederik Burgersdijk, Vanessa Cazzato, Maarten van Deventer, Chris Dickenson, Roald Dijkstra, Lien Foubert, Lisenka Fox, Nathalie de Haan, Olivier Hekster, Eveline van Hilten, Rens de Hond, Vincent Hunink, Raphael Hunsucker, Janneke de Jong, Suzanne van de Liefvoort, Stéphane Martin, Stephan Mols, Floris Overduin, Marc van der Poel, Aurora Raimondi-Cominesi, René Reijnen, Willeon Slenders, Daniëlle Slootjes, Lydia Spielberg, Claire Stocks, Christel Veen, Martje de Vries, Marenne Zandstra.

The following non-exhaustive, alphabetical list consists of names of further persons who I also owe gratitude for their feedback, conversations and support during my research: Selim Adalı, Antiopi Argyriou, Mathieu de Bakker, Daniël Bartelds, Koen Blok, Deborah Boedeker, Gerard Boter, Jan Brouwe, Amber Brüsewitz, Liesbeth Claes, Tamara Dijkstra, Marc Domingo Gygax, Floris van den Eijnde, David van Eijndhoven, Gunnel Ekroth, Thomas Figueira, Edith Foster, Michael Flower, Therese Fuhrer, Hans-Joachim Gehrke, Marc Gehrmann, Fokke Gerritsen, Ulrich Gotter, Vasilis Gravanis, Ulf Hailer, Rianne Hermans, Kerstin Hofmann, Marietta Horster, Martin Hose, Pieter Houten, Irene de Jong, Sjoukje Kamphorst, Nino Luraghi, Marian Makins, Richard Martin, Jeremy McInerney, Daniel Mendelsohn, Anna Michaelidou, Elizabeth Minchin, Astrid Möller, Onno van Nijf, Arjan Nijk, Robert Parker, Giacomo Pedini, Jeremiah Pelgrom, Gloria Pinney-Ferrari, Timothy Power, Giorgia Proietti, Nicholas Purcell, Winfred van de Put, Kurt Raaflaub, Reinder Reinders, Bettina Reitz-Joosse, Albert Rijksbaron, Ineke Sluiter, Peter Stork, Siward Tacoma, Muriël van Teeseling, Nino Vallen, Miguel-John Versluys, Daan Viergever, Jan Vonk, Willemijn Waal, Christian Wendt, Gert Jan van Wijngaarden, Clem Wood, Greg Woolf.

I was very happy to find Steven Clark, Claire Stocks and Clem Wood willing to help with the English.

Finally, I am grateful to the editorial team at De Gruyter for their support, and to Caroline van Toor for her help in making the index.

This research has benefited from grants and/or institutional support from: the Institute for Historical, Literary and Cultural Studies, Radboud University (the PhD position); OIKOS, National Research School in Classical Studies (travel grant 2017); the Netherlands Institute in Athens; Netherlands Institute in Istanbul, fellowship (October–November 2013); Freie Universität, Berlin (fellowship at the TOPOI Exzellenzkluster, May 2015); Princeton University, Visiting Scholar Research Collaborator (September–December 2016); Stichting Philologisch Studiefonds, travel grant (June 2017).

Names of ancient authors, gods, mythological figures, famous historical persons, well-known regions, cities, rivers mountains have sometimes been latinised or anglicised. Other names are original (or have been transliterated). Names of ancient works are latinised, with the exception of Herodotus' *Histories* and Homer's *Iliad* and *Odyssey*. Names of medieval and later date are original (or transliterated) or anglicised. Modern Greek names have been transliterated according to pronunciation, except where a different rendering is more familiar. Turkish names follow current spelling.

References to ancient authors follow the editions as given in the list of primary sources (§5.1). References to works which are the only work of an author are not mentioned. References to Herodotus' *Histories* are only indicated by book and paragraph numbers (for example: 7.192), except where this practise could give rise to confusion. Internal references are preceded by the sign §. First names of modern authors have been given in the bibliography where available.

Some standard works (for example *LSJ* and *IG*) have been abbreviated; full references are given in the bibliography. For the sake of clarity, names of ancient authors, works and journals have not been abbreviated.

Contents

Preface —— IX

List of maps and figures —— XV

1   Introduction —— 1
1.1   Topic —— 1
1.2   Hypothesis & scope —— 2
1.3   Mnemotopes —— 5
1.3.1   The choice of a term —— 5
1.3.2   Forms and limits of mnemotopes —— 7
1.3.3   Collectivity and symbolism —— 9
1.3.4   Tourism —— 11
1.3.5   Spatial densification —— 13
1.3.6   Mnemotopes and historicity —— 15
1.3.7   Summary —— 19
1.4   Mnemotopes and Herodotus —— 20
1.4.1   Herodotus' *Histories* as a source of mnemotopes —— 20
1.4.2   Mnemotopes of eastern kings in the *Histories* —— 24
1.4.3   Mnemotopes of the Persian Wars: a new and controversial perspective —— 28
1.4.4   Summary —— 38

2   Topographical Case Studies —— 39
2.1   The march through Anatolia —— 39
2.1.1   The Halys river —— 40
2.1.2   The waterfall and cave at Kelainai —— 42
2.1.3   Croesus' stele at Kydrara —— 48
2.1.4   The plane tree of Kallatebos —— 51
2.1.5   Sardis —— 56
2.1.6   Summary —— 60
2.2   The Troad and the Hellespont —— 61
2.2.1   Mount Ida —— 62
2.2.2   The Scamander river —— 65
2.2.3   Troy: the temple of Athena Ilias and the tombs of the heroes —— 67
2.2.4   Abydos: Xerxes' throne (I) and the Hellespont bridges —— 78
2.2.5   Agore and Helle's grave —— 86
2.2.6   Summary —— 89

2.3	The march through northern Greece —— 89	
2.3.1	The 'Royal Road' through Thrace —— 91	
2.3.2	The cape of Sarpedon and lake Stentoris —— 92	
2.3.3	Doriskos —— 93	
2.3.4	The Strymon river and Ennea Hodoi —— 95	
2.3.5	The canal through the Athos peninsula —— 101	
2.3.6	The tomb of Artachaies —— 105	
2.3.7	The Tempe valley —— 107	
2.3.8	The Macedonian mountain —— 110	
2.3.9	The temple of Zeus Laphystios at Halos —— 113	
2.3.10	Summary —— 117	
2.4	The advance of the armada and the battle of Artemision —— 118	
2.4.1	The Myrmex reef —— 120	
2.4.2	The beach where the Persian armada moored and Sepias —— 122	
2.4.3	Artemision —— 136	
2.4.4	Aphetai —— 140	
2.4.5	The Koila of Euboea —— 143	
2.4.6	Summary —— 148	
2.5	The battle of Thermopylae —— 148	
2.5.1	The pass, the Persian base at Trachis and Xerxes' throne (II) —— 150	
2.5.2	The Phocian wall —— 156	
2.5.3	The Anopaia path —— 158	
2.5.4	The hill of the last stance of the three hundred Spartans —— 162	
2.5.5	Summary —— 169	
2.6	The march through Phocis —— 169	
2.6.1	The destruction of Phocis; Abai —— 170	
2.6.2	Tithorea —— 175	
2.6.3	The sanctuary of Athena Pronaia at Delphi —— 177	
2.6.4	The Korykian cave —— 186	
2.6.5	Summary —— 188	
2.7	The destructions of Athens and Eleusis —— 189	
2.7.1	The Areopagus —— 191	
2.7.2	The sanctuary of Aglauros —— 197	
2.7.3	The μέγαρον —— 201	
2.7.4	The temple of Erechtheus and Athena's olive tree —— 207	
2.7.5	The Anaktoron of Demeter in Eleusis —— 210	
2.7.6	Summary —— 214	
2.8	The battle of Salamis and Xerxes' escape —— 214	
2.8.1	Psyttaleia —— 216	
2.8.2	Artemis' coast and Mounichia: the trophy and the tomb —— 222	
2.8.3	Xerxes' throne (III) —— 228	
2.8.4	The temple of Athena Skiras —— 231	

2.8.5	The beach of Kolias —— **233**	
2.8.6	Xerxes' causeway and ship bridge —— **234**	
2.8.7	Cape Zoster —— **237**	
2.8.8	Xerxes' flight to Abdera —— **239**	
2.8.9	The siege of Potidaia —— **240**	
2.8.10	Summary —— **243**	
2.9	The battle of Plataea —— **244**	
2.9.1	The Persian fort —— **246**	
2.9.2	Erythrai; the pass of the 'Oak Heads' —— **249**	
2.9.3	The shrine of Androkrates and the Gargaphie spring —— **250**	
2.9.4	The 'island' —— **257**	
2.9.5	The temple of Hera —— **259**	
2.9.6	Argiopion and the temple of Demeter —— **262**	
2.9.7	The necropolis —— **269**	
2.9.8	Summary —— **272**	
2.10	The battle of Mykale and the fall of Sestos —— **273**	
2.10.1	Kalamoi and the temple of Hera at Samos —— **274**	
2.10.2	Skolopoeis and the temple of Demeter —— **275**	
2.10.3	The landing place of the Athenians and the route of the Spartans —— **281**	
2.10.4	Protesilaos' grave —— **282**	
2.10.5	Sestos and the place of Artaÿktes' crucifixion —— **286**	
2.10.6	Summary —— **288**	
3	**A Typology of Mnemotopes —— 290**	
3.1	General mnemotopical processes —— **290**	
3.1.1	Speaking toponyms —— **290**	
3.1.2	Accumulation —— **291**	
3.1.3	Infrastructural mnemotopes —— **294**	
3.2	Temple mnemotopes —— **295**	
3.2.1	Persian vandalism —— **296**	
3.2.2	Divine intervention —— **298**	
3.2.3	Persian participation in Greek cult —— **301**	
3.3	Military mnemotopes —— **302**	
3.3.1	Usual battle sites —— **302**	
3.3.2	Concatenation; vantage points —— **303**	
3.3.3	Monumentalisation and tombs —— **304**	
3.3.4	Places of refuge —— **305**	
3.3.5	Pass lore: The enemy's bypass and blockades —— **306**	
3.3.6	Thrones —— **308**	

4   Conclusion —— 309

Bibliography —— 310
    Literature and scholia —— **310**
    Inscriptions —— **315**
    Secondary sources —— **317**

Index Locorum —— 351

General Index —— 365

List of maps and figures

Maps were drawn in outline by René Reijnen and labelled by the author. Photographs were taken by the author, unless otherwise indicated.

Map 1	Overview of most important sites associated with the Persian invasion —— 21	
Map 2	Anatolia —— 39	
Map 3	The Troad and the Hellespont —— 60	
Map 4	Central Greece —— 118	
Map 5	Plan of Acropolis —— 189	
Map 6	Salamis and a part of Attica —— 215	
Map 7	The battlefield of Plataea —— 244	

Fig. 1	The Karabel A inscription —— 26	
Fig. 2	Suçikan Parkı, Dinar, the source of Herodotus' Katarrektes —— 44	
Fig. 3	The cave behind the waterfall at Kelainai (Dinar) —— 46	
Fig. 4	Acı Göl, the lake where salt is produced —— 49	
Fig. 5	Kolossai —— 50	
Fig. 6	Hierapolis (Pamukkale), looking north towards the Kogamos Valley —— 53	
Fig. 7	The temple of Artemis at Sardis with the acropolis of Sardis in the background —— 58	
Fig. 8	The Gargaron peak of Mount Ida —— 64	
Fig. 9	The Scamander shortly before debouching into the Hellespont —— 66	
Fig. 10	The Hellenistic foundations of the temple of Athena at Hisarlık —— 70	
Fig. 11	Sivri Tepe —— 72	
Fig. 12	Mal Tepe —— 80	
Fig. 13	The Hellespont from the European bridgehead (Bigalı Kalesi) —— 81	
Fig. 14	A striking mound-like hill southeast of Koruköy (Helle's grave?) —— 88	
Fig. 15	The Saraya hill, believed to be the location of ancient Doriskos —— 94	
Fig. 16	The hill of Amphipolis and the Strymon river. The site of the bridge is approximately where the bottom of the hill meets the river —— 96	
Fig. 17	A remnant of the Athos canal at its southwestern end —— 103	
Fig. 18	A tumulus near the Athos canal, believed to be that of Artachaies —— 107	
Fig. 19	The Tempe valley near its eastern end —— 109	
Fig. 20	Remains of Gonnoi, looking east towards the Tempe valley, with foothills of Mount Olympus to the left —— 112	
Fig. 21	Magoula Plataniotiki, the site of Pre-Hellenistic Halos —— 115	
Fig. 22	Keramidi, in whose vicinity the town of Kasthanaia has been surmised —— 124	
Fig. 23	The beach of Kamari —— 126	
Fig. 24	Several of the 'Ovens' on the coast of Sepias —— 130	
Fig. 25	Remains of the temple of Artemis at the hill of Agios Giorgios —— 138	
Fig. 26	The central square of Afissos with the fountain water issuing into the Pagasetic Gulf —— 142	
Fig. 27	The environs of Cape Kymi (Cape Kaphereus?) —— 146	
Fig. 28	The pass of Thermopylae —— 151	
Fig. 29	The hot spring at Thermopylae —— 153	
Fig. 30	Part of the defensive structure usually identified as the Phocian wall —— 157	
Fig. 31	The gorge of the Asopos river —— 159	
Fig. 32	The Bastion rock, identified with the Melampygos rock —— 160	

Fig. 33	The hill of the last stance of the Greeks with the modern epigram of Simonides —— 164
Fig. 34	Remains of Drymos, a Phocian city destroyed by Xerxes' army —— 171
Fig. 35	The site of Kalapodi, believed by some to be the oracle of Abai —— 174
Fig. 36	Mavri Troupa, the 'Cave of Odysseas Androutsos' near Tithorea —— 176
Fig. 37	The tholos in the sanctuary of Athena Pronaia —— 180
Fig. 38	A rock in the temenos of Athena Pronaia —— 183
Fig. 39	The Korykian cave on Mount Parnassos —— 187
Fig. 40	The Areopagus (right) in relation to the Acropolis —— 193
Fig. 41	The cave on the east side of the Acropolis: the shrine of Aglauros —— 199
Fig. 42	The fundament of the Old Temple of Athena Polias —— 203
Fig. 43	The 'Periclean' Erechtheion and the olive tree —— 209
Fig. 44	Remains of the Telesterion at Eleusis —— 212
Fig. 45	Psyttaleia —— 219
Fig. 46	The block on the tip of the Kynosoura peninsula —— 225
Fig. 47	The alleged burial mound of the Greeks who fell during the battle of Salamis —— 226
Fig. 48	The Aigaleos ridge —— 229
Fig. 49	The cape of Vouliagmeni, which has been identified with cape Zoster —— 238
Fig. 50	Remains of the fortress city of Zone near modern Mesimvria —— 241
Fig. 51	Remains of fortifications near Potidaia. The ancient city was located on the coast visible in the background —— 243
Fig. 52	The three hills marking the pass of the 'Oak Heads' —— 250
Fig. 53	The spring Kiafa Retsi (Gargaphie?) —— 252
Fig. 54	The church of Agios Dimitrios, which may occupy the site of the shrine of Androkrates —— 253
Fig. 55	The hill of the Analipsi chapel, believed to be Herodotus' island —— 258
Fig. 56	The old fortification walls of Plataea as seen from the approximate location of the temple of Hera —— 261
Fig. 57	The approximate location of the temple of Demeter —— 265
Fig. 58	New Priene and its acropolis —— 276
Fig. 59	The temple of Demeter and Kore at New Priene —— 281
Fig. 60	Karaağaç Tepe (Protesilaos' grave?) —— 284

1 Introduction

1.1 Topic

The world is full of places which invite a passer-by to pause his errands for a moment, and to remember that, right where he is standing, once upon a time something very important happened. In Sarajevo, a plaque points out the place where Franz Ferdinand of Austria was shot, and the First World War began; the Hougoumont farm in the Belgian town of Braine-l'Alleud marks the epicentre of the battle of Waterloo and the downfall of Napoleon; and the September 11 Memorial in New York marks the place where the two towers of the World Trade Center once stood.

Such contemporary examples are part of an old and widespread phenomenon. The holy sites of many religions mark places where significant religious events were thought to have occurred. Followers of various faiths make their way to the top of the mountain Sri Pada or 'Holy Foot' in Sri Lanka, where they revere a footprint, variously said to be of Buddha, Shiva, Adam or Saint Thomas. The Holy Land has for centuries been a destination for Christian pilgrims eager to behold with their own eyes Jesus' birthplace at Bethlehem and the site of his crucifixion at the Calvary. And in Greece, one could, with the help of Pausanias' work, gaze at Nestor's house and Agamemnon's plane tree.[1] We make ordinary places more special and evocative by pointing out their roles in history, religion and fiction, and in the process, our world becomes more meaningful.

The desire of people to imagine the past at significant locations may safely be thought of as universal.[2] To the above examples of the 'tourist gaze' and the 'pilgrim gaze' we can add many other gazes: that of the local, and even that of the archaeologist.[3] This book argues for the existence of such gazes in the 'founding' work of history itself: as it turns out, the world on which Herodotus of Halicarnassus has given us a window was one in which the question 'Where did it happen?' was often asked, and in which answers to that question were easily found.

A clear example appears in the following excerpt from the *Histories* (7.31), in which Herodotus indicates a very specific place associated with Xerxes' march from Persia to Greece in the early fifth century BCE. He reports a plane tree on the route of the Persian king, where he performed a kind of 'tree worship'.[4]

---

[1] On Pausanias as a constructor of memorial landscapes, see Alcock 1994.
[2] Cf. Ingold 2012, 2: "All seeing [...] is imagining. To perceive a landscape is therefore to imagine it."
[3] The term 'tourist gaze' is coined by John Urry (2002, first edition 1990). For an example of the ways in which historical imagination is central within archaeological practise, see Vergunst 2012.
[4] All translations from the Greek and Latin are by the author unless stated otherwise. Throughout the present project, the words 'Herodotus' and '*Histories*' have been omitted from textual references to them.

> ὡς δὲ ἐκ τῆς Φρυγίης ἐσέβαλε ἐς τὴν Λυδίην, σχιζομένης τῆς ὁδοῦ καὶ τῆς μὲν ἐς ἀριστερὴν ἐπὶ Καρίης φερούσης τῆς δὲ ἐς δεξιὴν ἐς Σάρδις, τῇ καὶ πορευομένῳ διαβῆναι τὸν Μαίανδρον ποταμὸν πᾶσα ἀνάγκη γίνεται καὶ ἰέναι παρὰ Καλλάτηβον πόλιν, ἐν τῇ ἄνδρες δημιουργοὶ μέλι ἐκ μυρίκης τε καὶ πυροῦ ποιεῦσι, ταύτην ἰὼν ὁ Ξέρξης τὴν ὁδὸν εὗρε πλατάνιστον, τὴν κάλλεος εἵνεκα δωρησάμενος κόσμῳ χρυσέῳ καὶ μελεδωνῷ ἀθανάτῳ ἀνδρὶ ἐπιτρέψας δευτέρῃ ἡμέρῃ ἀπίκετο ἐς τῶν Λυδῶν τὸ ἄστυ.

> And when Xerxes entered Lydia from Phrygia, at the point where the road splits with the left one leading to Caria and the right one to Sardis, along which one cannot avoid crossing the Maeander and to go past the city of Kallatebos, in which the craftsmen make a sweet from tamarisk and wheat, while going that way, he found a plane tree. Because of its beauty he decorated it with gold and made one of the Immortals guard it, and he arrived at the city of the Lydians on the second day.

As will be discussed in §2.1.4, Herodotus probably based this anecdote on Anatolian folklore, in which stories about the visit of the Persian king had become attached to one or more real plane trees. I propose to call this kind of place a *mnemotope*, or 'place of memory' (§1.3). This concept describes how communities come to associate particular historical or mythical narratives with particular places.

Although historical narratives often feature places like the plane tree of Kallatebos, there has been surprisingly little recognition, let alone understanding of the processes by which ancient authors may have come up with them. The perspective has also been lacking in scholarship on Herodotus. Investigating this topography as a collection of mnemotopes therefore offers a new perspective on an important text about an important event.

1.2 Hypothesis & scope

This book will apply the concept of mnemotope to the Persian invasion of Greece, which consists of Xerxes' march from Persia to Greece and the subsequent encounters of the Persian and Greek armies until the siege of Sestos (480–479 BCE). It is my hypothesis that the framework of mnemotopes is a useful heuristic tool to understand the topography of Xerxes' invasion as recounted in Herodotus' *Histories*.

To explore this hypothesis, I will first try to arrive at a general understanding of mnemotopes in §1.3. In §1.4 we will then see that there is much scope for exploring mnemotopes in Herodotus' work, and that this exploration offers new insights that complement previous research on Herodotus' work and the Persian Wars.

Part 2 features a full discussion of the individual mnemotopes within the topography of Xerxes' invasion. These places have been grouped into ten case studies. Within each case study, the relevant sites are addressed, as far as possible, individually. For every mnemotope the following questions, where applicable, will be answered:
- What is being remembered at the mnemotope?
- Where was the mnemotope located?

- What other narratives were localised here?
- Is there reason to doubt the historicity of the narratives or their localisation?[5]
- Are there any alternative traditions about the localisation of the narrative?
- Does the narrative adhere to a common place?

It could be argued that the physical context of mnemotopes is irrelevant as the concept revolves around the ideas embodied by these places. However, as indicated above, places may become mnemotopes because their form sometimes inspires or influences the story. Furthermore, knowledge about the physical environment of a mnemotope is a requirement to comment on its prominence, visibility and visitability, parameters which are important in the formation of mnemotopes. Moreover, in some cases there are correlations between two or more different places, which are only perceptible when these are properly mapped. In some cases the physical environment gives reason to doubt the historical accuracy of our sources. Finally, the identification of the place is a requirement to unlock access to archaeological sources that may provide a deeper understanding of it.

For reasons of feasibility the research topic is limited along several lines. First, it will only be concerned with Xerxes' invasion of Greece and it will therefore not include a study of the battle of Marathon, which happened during the reign of Darius. This battle probably was the most 'remembered' Persian War battle for the Athenians[6]; nevertheless, it is justifiable to exclude it from this study, because Xerxes' campaign is the only real invasion of Greece, and the narrative about it is a self-contained, independent section within the *Histories*, with only few digressions.[7] Second, only those mnemotopes of Xerxes' invasion that occur in the *Histories* will be discussed. While other, mainly later, sources will be used where necessary to elucidate the questions presented above,[8] they are hardly ever securely independent

---

[5] The historicity of the Persian Wars as such is not at stake in this study. However, this question of historicity is still relevant because it is more obvious to explain a place as a mnemotope when the historicity is problematic (on this issue see §1.3.6).

[6] On the memory of the battle of Marathon see e.g. Gehrke 2003; Proietti 2012a; 2014.

[7] For this idea cf. Macan 1908, I xv; Myres 1953, 215 ("After the string of footnotes to Marathon [...] the curtain falls at the end of Book VI, and rises forthwith on the third act of the Herodotean trilogy, the story of the expedition of Xerxes."); Pohlenz 1961, 19; Immerwahr 1966, 126. But see also de Jong 2001, who argues that there is much integration of the two parts through prolepses and analepses.

[8] A good overview of the other sources for the Persian Wars can be found in Hignett 1963, 7–25. These may help to 'confirm' Herodotus' mnemotopes and in localising the places. They may also reveal alternative traditions for the site in question, or preserve mythical traditions which help to understand how a mnemotope came into existence.

of Herodotus' account,[9] and usually to be placed in a different memory context.[10] At any rate, the number of mnemotopes which do not appear in Herodotus is rather limited, as Herodotus' work is by far the richest account, the 'master narrative', of the Persian Wars. While Pausanias is the most important source for sites associated with this event after Herodotus,[11] they are also found in other ancient authors, and the process of identifying such places has been reactivated in modern times.[12] Third, there will be no extensive discussion of objects or relics of Xerxes' invasion. As will be explained (§1.3.2), these are not included in my definition of mnemotope and have already been studied elsewhere.[13] Finally, because mnemotopes signify events cast in narratives, only those places where Herodotus localises specific events of the Persian Wars will be studied; places that merely function as geographical markers will not be considered.

---

9 Herodotus has been a popular author throughout antiquity and the Byzantine period and knowledge of his work can be assumed for all authors after him (see in general Stephanie West in Bowie 2007, 33–34; Hornblower 2006; Murray 1972 and Priestley 2014, 157–158 for the Hellenistic period; Hart 1982, 174–175 for the playwrights).
10 Commemoration of the Persian Wars in later times was of a different nature: in the Roman period, early Greek history was viewed through the lens of nostalgia: see Alcock 2002, 74–86; Ziegler 2007 (for an overview of the role of the memory of the Persian Wars during the Second Sophistic); Proietti 2012a, 108–110; Miles 2014, 137–138.
11 Pausanias had a great interest in identifying mnemotopes of the Persian Wars (cf. Alcock 1994, 252–254; Jacquemin 2006; Pretzler 2007, 100; Miles 2014, 136–137); he indicated himself that he only discusses details of the wars which Herodotus does not mention (2.30.4). Notable examples include the story of the last Persian soldiers who had jumped into the sea, after having been driven into a frenzy by the gods upon entering the sanctuary of the Kabeiroi at Thebes (9.25.9); a rock (1.44.4) on the road to the Attic town of Pagai where the Persians would have shot all their arrows in vain, driven into a frenzy by Artemis (the rock apparently still exists near modern Alepochori; cf. Papachatzi 1974, 510–511; Gauer 1968, 124–125; Green 1996, 234); and the Hellenion at Sparta was the place where military actions in the Trojan War and Persian War were planned (3.12.6, cf. Arafat 2013, 213). Pausanias also mentions various statues in the Greek world that had allegedly been returned from Persia, after having been stolen by Xerxes (e.g. Pausanias 1.16.3; 8.46.3).
12 Strabo (10.2.9) mentions that a small hill near Chalkis in Boeotia was the grave of Salganeos, who showed the way to the Persians. Modern examples include the 'Thronos tou Xerxi' in Perama (see §2.8.3) and the town of Vasilika in Euboea (see §2.4) which claims to be the site where Xerxes' fleet anchored.
13 Gauer 1968 is the most elaborate work on these monuments and lists extensive literature. Among the more notable monuments which he mentions as dedications after the war are Pheidias' sculpture of Zeus in Olympia (pages 19–20) and the Athena Promachos on the Acropolis (pages 38–39; 103–105). On the Athenian Agora as a repository for such monuments, see pages 14–15, 38 (and cf. Shrimpton 1997, 186; Miller 1999, 29–62). For the symbolic role of objects in Herodotus see Hollmann 2011, 176–207.

1.3 Mnemotopes

1.3.1 The choice of a term

This book is positioned at the crossroads of the major research themes of 'space' and 'memory', which have left their mark on the study of the ancient world. The spatial turn has taught us that textual space may have a thematic function, can mirror or contrast themes of the work, expose symbolic functions, characterise characters, and psychologise them.[14] The field of memory studies has highlighted that "memory is the present past",[15] and that we must accordingly approach the past from the perspective of the people who engaged with and (sometimes) created that past.[16]

The approach presented here is more specific and concerns the overlap of these domains: the role of space in ancient memory. In recent years, studies have appeared which demonstrate that this relationship can be successfully explored in the Graeco-Roman world,[17] and the ancients themselves had developed a mnemonic system in which memories could be tied to specific locations in the memoriser's spatial memory (the method of loci; cf. Cicero, *De Oratore* 2.350–360). But the more specific process of localisation as described in the introduction does not have a well-defined theoretical basis, nor does it have a commonly accepted term. In what follows, I will explain my choice of the term 'mnemotope', and make an attempt at defining and explaining it by resorting to observations in previous scholarship.

From the mid-twentieth century onwards studies have appeared in which the kind of places discussed in this book are recognised and explored as cultural phenomena. A pioneering book by Maurice Halbwachs from 1941, *La topographie légendaire des évangiles en Terre Sainte*, attempted to discover to what 'laws' "les lieux où

---

[14] De Jong 2012, 13–17; she also draws an important distinction between fabula-space (the theoretically complete depiction of the locations) and story-space (the space actually presented by the text) in narrative literature (pages 2–3).
[15] Terdiman 1993, 8. See also Ankersmit 1994, 125–130 for a contrast between old historiography (the text as a window onto the past) and new historiography (the text as a window onto the author); Rothberg 2009, 3–4.
[16] For approaches to space in Greek literature, see e.g. De Jong 2012 and the other contributions in that volume. For a thorough overview of the field of memory studies, with a rich bibliography, see Franchi & Proietti 2015, 40–59 (about the field's foundational works) and 59–78 (recent studies). For a short but instructive overview about the history of the conceptual field of memory, see Neumann & Zierold 2012.
[17] Such approaches are found in Mayor 2000 (regarding fossils); Alcock 2002; Boardman 2002; Hartmann 2010; Zwingmann 2012; Ambühl 2016 (on Thessaly as a landscape of war); Minchin 2016 (on the landscape of the Troad); Reitz-Joosse 2016 (on memory of the battlefield of Actium). See generally Van Dyke & Alcock 2003, 5–6 with further references. See also Steinbock 2013, 10 (with literature) on the need for semantic memory to be accompanied by visual imagery, and pages 84–94 on monuments and inscriptions in the construction of this memory.

se sont passés les événements" obey.[18] By studying medieval travel accounts about the Holy Land, Halbwachs arrived at a theoretical model for what he called the *cadre matériel*, which is still in its essence useful, as we will see below. Halbwachs stressed the 'sacred' character of these places by calling them *lieux saints*.[19] However, as outlined above, the concept is much broader than the religious sphere.

A related concept is *lieu de mémoire*, which was coined by the French historian Pierre Nora in the 1980s, in a time characterised by increased efforts to conserve and to canonise both tangible and intangible heritage. Nora employed the term not only to describe physical places, buildings (such as the Eiffel Tower), but also persons (Jeanne d'Arc), objects (the French tricolour), and events (Bastille day), the main criterion being that the 'object' has symbolic value for French society.[20] Although Nora designed the concept for France, it has become an important term in several European national canon efforts in the past decades and has gained acceptance in its French disguise in several other linguistic communities. The study of the ancient world has also embraced the concept, with numerous publications using the term to enshrine wide-ranging instances of Graeco-Roman heritage and accomplishments.[21] Although this 'inclusive' understanding of the term *lieu de mémoire* is predominant, some writers have restricted their definitions to physical places, describing a process very similar to that set out in this study.[22] However, because the term *lieu de mémoire* is used so divergently, both in origin and in later practise, it is potentially confusing and will therefore not be employed in this book.

A more precise alternative for the French *lieu de mémoire* is available: the Greek calque *mnemotope*. This term has been used by Jan Assmann to describe physical

---

18 Halbwachs 1941, 1–3.
19 Halbwachs 1941, 156–160, 164: the *lieux saints* would help the pilgrim to reinforce his faith; cf. ibidem, 1: "du jour où ces souvenirs se sont posés sur certains lieux, ils les ont transfigurés. D'autant plus qu'il ne s'agit pas de faits historiques ordinaires, mais d'événements surnaturels. Le cadre local où on les replace est aussi en partie surnaturel, et c'est avec les yeux de la foi qu'au delà des apparences sensibles on croit saisir un autre monde, qui n'est plus tout à fait dans l'espace et qui est le seul véritable pour un chrétien." Cf. Halbwachs 1997, first edition 1950, 227–232.
20 Nora 1984–1992.
21 The application of the concept of *lieu de mémoire* in antiquity has been as diverse as in Nora's work. Exemplary in this respect is the series *Erinnerungsorte der Antike* by Elke Stein-Hölkeskamp and Karl-Joachim Hölkeskamp, in which the material covered by the term is divided into six different categories: concrete geographical places, monuments and material culture, literary texts, mythical and historical persons, ideas and ideals, and Meistererzählungen (see Hölkeskamp & Stein-Hölkeskamp 2010, 14–15). At least one scholar (Boter 2007, 343) has employed the term *non-lieu de mémoire* with reference to utopia-like places such as Atlantis; as these places are fictional, or at least, do not have a well-defined identification in the real world, they do not fall under the definition used in this study.
22 Such approaches are found in Hölscher 2010; Hartmann 2010 (especially 141–159); Zwingmann 2012. For a succinct discussion of the drift in the use of spatial terms from places to objects and concepts in modern scholarship, see Günzel 2012.

places where people may have (pseudo-)historical experiences,[23] and thereby encompasses one specific case of Nora's *lieu de mémoire*. It has not, to my best knowledge at the time of writing, been adopted by other scholars in this sense. It does not carry the same canon-describing associations as the term *lieu de mémoire*, but it is readily applicable in archaeological, historical and anthropological studies. It allows the inclusion of both mythical and historical places.

In recent years, many more studies have appeared which explore the relation between place and memory. Instead of giving an overview of these here, I will discuss them where relevant in the rest of §1.3. I will sometimes make recourse to examples from the ancient world; however, the application of the concept in that field of study will be developed specifically in §1.4. Throughout this discussion, I will refer to the places under study as *mnemotopes* when I find that the author's approach to the material is similar to that of my definition of the term.

1.3.2 Forms and limits of mnemotopes

Mnemotopes may take any form. They can be man-made structures and natural landmarks,[24] and even empty spaces (the phenomenon of *damnatio memoriae* may, paradoxically, lead to mnemotope formation).[25] It therefore seems more worthwhile to define mnemotopes by indicating what they *cannot* be. First, places where objects are

---

23 E.g. Assmann 1992, 59–60. Note that he follows Halbwachs, but does not distinguish between tradition and memory (page 45).
24 Vansina (1985, 45–46) mentions abandoned towns, battlefields, grave sites and house estates of ruling elites. Hartmann (2010, 145–159) indicates that man-made mnemotopes may also include architecture, sculptures, and textual evidence. Natural mnemotopes were already studied by Halbwachs (1941); e.g. a rock in Jerusalem where Salomo combatted demons (pages 27–28), or the fountain where Jesus healed a blind man (pages 31–33). Another example is the almond tree near Betthar, where Jacob was said to have slept and an angel appeared (page 17). Vansina (1985, 46) stresses that impressive natural phenomena may have iconatrophic power (i.e. the power to evoke etiological stories). Cf. Evans 1991, 130: "Local traditions that centered around monuments [...] could be purely fictional. An isolated monument without a legible inscription is a mythopoeic catalyst. For that matter, myths could gather around natural phenomena, such as rock formations." See also Schama 1995 for various examples of how elements of natural landscapes could become 'recognised' as connected to particular historical moments.
25 See Nelson & Olin 2003, 4; Hartmann 2010, 142–145; Price 2012, 28. As Halbwachs noted (1941, 162–165), even when there is a conscious effort to efface a mnemotope, the *cadre matériel* remains. The rock chambers of the Bamiyan Buddhas which were blown down by the Taliban in 2001 are still there; they therefore imply that their contents have been destroyed, i.e. that Islam has prevailed over Buddhism. The place has remained relevant, even for the Taliban, but for entirely different reasons. A historical example is the Beeldenstorm, which refers to the destruction by Calvinists of Catholic religious images in various parts of Europe (particularly Switzerland and the Low Countries) in the sixteenth century (cf. the analysis by Elsner 2003, 223–225). Catholic art was not annihilated; it was

kept are not by themselves mnemotopes. Admittedly, there is some overlap between these concepts, as objects may carry memories with them.[26] Well-known examples are the relics of saints kept in shrines and venerated by pilgrims. However, such objects may be regarded as different from mnemotopes because they are transportable,[27] not embedded in a surrounding landscape, and less persistent. They may, however, help as additional 'evidence' that a particular event occurred at that place.

Second, mnemotopes should be distinguished from monuments. Tonio Hölscher has contrasted them in an enlightening way.[28] For him, mnemotopes are places, varying from a simple rock to an edifice, which are salient because of their physical permanence. Their attraction lies in the assumption by visitors that one can re-experience 'historical' (or mythical) events, or follow in the footsteps of famous persons.[29] By contrast, monuments are meant to emphasise and commemorate a certain aspect of a historical event or person. The monument may be placed in an associated place, but is usually set up at a place where more people can see it; mnemotopes, on the other hand, may sometimes need effort to be reached.[30] Another important difference is that mnemotopes, while sometimes intentionally created, are not experienced as such; monuments, on the other hand, never pretend to be unintentional, nor are they perceived as such. This is not to say that the two distinct processes of memory never intermingle: a mnemotope can be enhanced with monuments exactly because it *is* a mnemotope. Conversely, given enough time, a monument can also become a *mnemotope* when people start associating it with certain stories, for example about later interactions with the monument.

Finally, a distinction should be made between mnemotopes and landscapes.[31] Mnemotopes are specific landmarks; a landscape is a much broader and vaguer category, which may encompass different kinds of places and nature. While events like battles may be vaguely situated in a general area, this area should be confined in some way to be classified as a mnemotope. Only when there are multiple mnemotopes in a particular area, may this area be called a memory landscape.[32] However, there is

---

replaced by a new memory: the 'headlessness' of sculptures of saints testified to the superiority of the new religious order.

26 For a monumental work on relics in antiquity, see Hartmann 2010. On the ways in which objects may have memories attached to them, see Tonkin 1992, 94–95.

27 In rare instances, an entire mnemotope can be transported. An example is the Santa Casa, the purported house of Mary, allegedly transported to Loreto in Italy in the 1290s (the house is also claimed to be in Ephesus).

28 Hölscher 2010, 131; note that he uses the term *lieu de mémoire* in the sense of mnemotope. Cf. Riegl 1928, 144–151 on the difference between intentional and unintentional monuments.

29 Hölscher 2010, 137.

30 Hölscher 2010, 131–132.

31 See Alcock 2002, 28–32 for a contrast of monuments (including unfixed objects) and landscapes.

32 Cf. Assmann 1992, 60.

a grey area: certain larger elements of landscapes may be considered mnemotopes, such as rivers and mountains.

1.3.3 Collectivity and symbolism

Memories of historical events are known to be thoroughly shaped by contemporary social concerns and are a way of fostering group ties and, thereby, collective identities.[33] Likewise, mnemotopes are assumed to play a role in the collective mind of certain groups.[34] Halbwachs, for example, supposed that *lieux saints* could only be born from ideas that are subject to a doctrine in a large, durable group which observes certain cults and religious festivals.[35] Assmann similarly suggested that the past is part of a connective structure binding individuals into a common 'we'.[36] The collective aspect of mnemotopes is most apparent in the fact that they can become valuable 'possessions'[37]: they may be used to invent local pasts which emphasise unity,[38] can play a role during the founding of cities,[39] and may be politically appropriated.[40] Additionally, the mere act of visiting a mnemotope can be a status-enhancing experience.[41]

The collectivity of mnemotopes is also apparent in the observation that they may play a role in the designation of a particular event as 'important', and thus have a

---

[33] Halbwachs 1997 (first edition 1950), 51–96 first made a distinction between individual and collective memory. See also Fentress & Wickham 1992; Gehrke 2001. On the social relevance of memory within the context of oral traditions, see Vansina 1985, 95–123. It has even been argued that "there is no such thing as individual memory" (Schudson 1995, 346).
[34] E.g. Halbwachs 1941, 2; 1997, first edition 1950, 193–236 (argueing that the stable character of space gives the illusion of retrieving the past in the present); Assmann 1992, 37; Hartmann 2010, 141.
[35] Halbwachs 1941, 159–160, 189.
[36] Assmann 1988, 12–16; 1992, 16–17; 38–39: "Diese Tendenz zur Lokalisierung gilt für jegliche Art von Gemeinschaften. Jede Gruppe, die sich als solche konsolidieren will, ist bestrebt, sich Orte zu schaffen und zu sichern, die nicht nur Schauplätze ihrer Interaktionsformen abgeben, sondern Symbole ihrer Identität und Anhaltspunkte ihrer Erinnerung."
[37] Alcock 2002, 16; Steinbock 2013, 17–18; Hölscher 2010, 130; Bowie 2012, 286: "[...] stories are not innocent tradition, but weapons in the selective creation of an identity, the claiming of a privilege, or the justification of an act."
[38] Shrimpton 1997, 29; 149 (smaller objects).
[39] Malkin 2011, 131–132.
[40] Cf. de Haan 2007, 376 on the 'repossession' of the Forum Romanum by the popes from Avignon in a ritual procession.
[41] As most people in the developed world now engage in travel, it is thought that they lose status if they do not travel (Urry 2002, 5). The reverse is arguably also true: the more one travels, the more one sees, and the higher one's status. Travel is often a form of conspicuous consumption (Urry 2002, 23). Redfield 1985, 100: "The greater the difference, the more the journey is worth the trip and the more worth collecting are the images, memories and souvenirs that the tourist takes home with him."

symbolic meaning that transcends the locality itself. For example, the Israeli desert fortress of Masada has developed into a collection of mnemotopes for the famous story of the Roman siege of the fortress that culminated in the collective suicide of a group of Jewish rebels: individual mnemotopes, such as 'the army camps', 'the ramp', and the 'living quarters' allow one to re-experience the narrative on the spot. Together, these mnemotopes tell a story of Jewish resistance and heroism, and thereby turn Masada into a symbol in the collective identity (or, one might argue, mythology) of the modern state of Israel. Places like Masada are what one may term a *lieu de mémoire* in Nora's sense.

However, there are two problems with the view that collectivity is a criterion for classifying a place as a mnemotope. The term 'collective' might suggest very large communities, such as the Christians, the Dutch or the Greeks. However, mnemotopes may be exclusively relevant to much smaller communities. Peasants of the Cévennes mountains in France (at least until the late 1960s) had rich local, oral, and often completely unhistorical traditions about the Camisard revolts of 1702–1704, which cemented a tradition of resistance within their group identity, and were often topographically motivated in the local landscape.[42] In this case, it has been observed that these communities in their oral traditions completely omitted important events which historians would perhaps expect to find, such as the French Revolution.[43] The meaning of the associated event may also shift over time. We may ask ourselves, for example, whether the Hermannsdenkmal which commemorates the battle of the Teutoburg Forest, the location of a battle between the Romans and some Germanic tribes in 9 CE, still symbolises German resistance against invading forces for the Germans of today as much as it did for Germans of the Romantic era. The important realisation is that mnemotopes may or may not have symbolic meanings that transcend the locality itself.

Another, more fundamental problem is that it remains vague what a collective mind actually is.[44] Groups and group identities are fluid, and even when a mnemotope retains its appeal over time, different groups may have different associations to it (cf. the example of the Sri Pada in Sri Lanka in §1.1). At any rate, the creation of a mnemotope cannot, in most cases, be traced to a particular person or group.[45]

---

[42] Fentress & Wickham 1992, 92–93.
[43] Fentress & Wickham 1992, 95–96.
[44] On the problems of understanding memory in 'collective' terms, see Steinbock 2013, 8–9 (opting for the term 'social' instead). We should be careful not to understand 'collective' in a Greek context as 'Panhellenic', especially with respect to myths. Price (2012, 23) points out that the study of Greek mythology cannot forego local myths despite the emphasis normally placed on the 'collectivity' of mythology. In fact, local myths are more prone to be 'played out' when the occasion arises, as they are better suited to enhance local identities (as opposed to Panhellenic myths). Local stories can be just as collective as 'blockbuster' myths, albeit at a more modest level (i.e. in the polis).
[45] In most cases it is impossible to indicate who designated a place as a mnemotope for some event, as the whole point of a mnemotope is that the event simply happened there (Hölscher 2010, 135).

Thus, while collectivity can be an important aspect of mnemotopes, it is a malleable term and is not useful as a criterion for retrieving mnemotopes. This is, at any rate, not how our material should be approached. We may rather assume from the outset that most mnemotopes exist in collective identities. For example, for the purpose of this book, the places associated with the Persian Wars featured (and often still feature) in collective memory as sites of Panhellenic or polis-centred heroism, because the Persian Wars very soon after the war turned into the prime historical event that symbolised the struggle between Greeks and Barbarians, and the supremacy of freedom.[46] They also retained this status for a very long time, as evidenced by the accounts of later Greek authors such as Plutarch and Pausanias.[47]

1.3.4 Tourism

Many modern mnemotopes attract visitors, and it has even been argued that one of the reasons for people to engage in tourism is to experience such sites.[48] At the same time, mnemotopes may be invented in order to attract visitors to certain sites. As mnemotopes create travel, and travel creates mnemotopes, the link between mnemotopes and travel (or 'tourism') is important. The applicability of the concept to the ancient world is therefore partly dependent on the existence of this phenomenon there.

The scale of travel in ancient Greece was much smaller than it is today, although certain activities which may be described using the term tourism certainly existed, as has been expounded in recent studies.[49] Such tourism could take place in many

---

46 See Gehrke 2001 301–304; 2003, 19–29 (within the context of the battle of Marathon).
47 For Plutarch as a source for the Persian Wars see Pelling 2007, 150–162, who points out that Plutarch had an interest in traces of the Persian Wars. His account is largely complementary to that of Herodotus: he only adds new information, assuming that his readers knew Herodotus' account. He was probably not as critical of Herodotus as sometimes thought on the basis of *De Herodoti malignitate*.
48 It has been suggested that the concept of *lieu de mémoire* itself is now being defined in such a way to make it more compatible with tourism, by restricting its application to physical places (Nauta 2007, 260–261).
49 The literature on the history of tourism acknowledges its limited existence in premodern societies (e.g. Feifer 1985, 7–24; Urry 2002, 4). One's potential of going away depended, as it does now, on one's time and resources. With constant struggles to fulfil basic needs, unfair income distributions, travelling surely was not on everybody's mind. Moreover, it was potentially very hazardous, with a lack of transport possibilities (although sea trade networks covered vast areas), communication infrastructure and the threat of brigandry. It is safe to say that traveling was in antiquity much more an elite phenomenon than it is today: only those who could bear these high costs would make a trip (it should, however, be noted that non-elite persons such as slaves will also have embarked on such trips). The importance of tourism in Antiquity has been given a new impulse by Hartmann (2010, 191–245) for

different contexts, including professional, state, educational, pilgrim, festive, purely touristic and various other ones, which are often difficult to separate from each other; it was not only limited to the elite population.⁵⁰ It is a given that many ancient Greeks engaged in travel: commercial ships plied routes across the Aegean, military action ensured the movement of soldiers, slaves were shipped and aoidoi and other artists roamed around the region's cities. Great distances were covered for specific reasons: journeys to important sanctuaries such as Delphi and Olympia happened out of religious and athletic motivations. Accordingly, literature gives us examples of men who prided themselves in having travelled far and wide.⁵¹ Already in Herodotus' work the word θεωρίη is used in contexts where it may be translated as 'sightseeing' or 'tourism' (1.29; 1.30).⁵²

In these instances, there is rarely an explicit reference to the interaction of travellers with mnemotopes, but the potential was large. Mnemotopes could be part of the religious experience at sanctuaries, such as the place where Poseidon planted his trident on the Athenian Acropolis (see §2.7.4). In other cases interaction with mnemotopes may also be regarded as a 'byproduct' of travelling: the *periploi* are full of mythical mnemotopes on coasts that are readily interpretable as convenient anchorage points. Likewise, a roadside rock with a specific association could hardly be the aim of a trip, but if it lay on a busy route, it could function as an important landmark along the way. Thus many Greeks engaged in some sort of travelling during which mnemotopes were visible and visitable; when not as an aim in itself, as a 'byproduct' of the journey.

Egypt, Greece and Rome, and by Zwingmann (2012), who has collected the evidence relating to ancient tourism in Asia Minor. She argues that although the ancients did not have a term for tourism, the term tourism is readily applicable to antiquity, as far as sightseeing is concerned, and that there are clear indications that a touristic infrastructure existed, including tourist guides, the sale of souvenirs, hotels and even heritage management (see especially pages 15–16; 374–391). The impact of pilgrimage in ancient Greece is analysed in Dillon 1997.
50 Zwingmann 2012, 16–25.
51 Travel has been called a "[p]eculiarly Greek way of being in the world" (Redfield 1985, 118). An old example is fifth-century BCE philosopher Democritus of Abdera, who congratulated himself with the following words (fragment 299): "ἐγὼ δὲ τῶν κατ' ἐμαυτὸν ἀνθρώπων γῆν πλείστην ἐπεπλανησάμην ἱστορέων τὰ μήκιστα καὶ ἀέρας τε καὶ γέας πλείστας εἶδον [...]" 'I, of all men of my time, have travelled farthest, getting to know the most, and I have seen most skies and lands'. By Democritus' time, apparently, it had become a prerequisite for anyone who wanted to say something about the world to be well-travelled. For another example, on the prestige which the possibility to travel bestowed upon the great archaic lawgivers, see Szegedy-Maszak 1978, 202–204. In the Hellenistic period some travel literature existed, such as the work of Heraclides Criticus, which was mainly concerned with the visual splendour of Athens (Hölscher 2010, 128–130). We also know that various emperors and wealthy persons took part in tourist trips to Greece (cf. Boardman 2002, 61).
52 Also compare the word θεωρός, which can be translated as 'tourist' (e.g. Plato, *Leges* 12.953).

1.3.5 Spatial densification

It has been observed that memories are often associated with particular important events or persons, while minor events or persons are forgotten.[53] The same holds true for prominent places: they may become a mnemotope for more than one story. I propose to call this process *spatial densification*. There are two different ways in which this process occurs.

The first type of spatial densification is *clustering*. This was noted already by Halbwachs in the case of the Church of the Holy Sepulchre in Jerusalem. In addition to the sepulchre itself and the Calvary, dozens of other mnemotopes can be found here, including the place of Jesus' anointment, the appearance of an angel to Mary, Jesus' revelation to Mary of Magdalen and Mary, the prison where he waited while his cross was being put up, the place where he was stripped of his clothes, the place where he was crowned with thorns, and where he was nailed to the cross. Some of the stories concern the later legends about the church: there is, for instance, a chapel which marks the spot where Helen, who came to Jerusalem to find places connected to Jesus' life, prayed.[54] Similar descriptions can be given for the Cenacle Church and the Via Dolorosa.[55] At such places, we witness the existence of chains of mnemotopes, where one could literally have 'a trip down memory lane'. The same principle applies, on a somewhat larger scale, to rural areas, where we see that events are localised in proximity to another one. For example, the site of Jesus' feeding miracle is situated on the Lake of Tiberias, along the road and close to the traditional site of the Sermon on the Mount.[56] Halbwachs attributed the demand for localising events in a single space to convenience,[57] an explanation to which we will turn in 1.3.6 when we discuss the relation of mnemotopes to historicity.

In a more recent study, Azaryahu and Foote argue that what they call 'historical spaces' (and which I would name mnemotopes) are arranged into three broad categories based on the scale of the area: (1) single points and places, (2) routes and paths, and (3) large areas.[58] Category 1 is relatively straightforward; in category 2 narratives are simplified into a collection of particular anecdotes, while the narratives are often enhanced using pre-existing dominant buildings and landmarks.[59] In category 3, which also applies to large battles and military campaigns, even more simplification is required: "time or space is shortened, concatenated, compressed, lengthened, embellished, straightened, or smoothed", which is often done by selecting individual

---

[53] This is what Assmann 1997, 7 calls 'constellative myths'. See also Alcock 2002, 17.
[54] Halbwachs 1941, 41–42; cf. Pococke 1745, II.1 15–19.
[55] Halbwachs 1941, 81–83 and 102–112, respectively.
[56] Halbwachs 1941, 137.
[57] Halbwachs 1941, 186–187.
[58] Azaryahu & Foote 2008, 183.
[59] Azaryahu & Foote 2008, 185–187.

locations and claiming that actions took place nearby.[60] Azaryahu and Foote also argue that "some historical events, especially those that conflate linear progression in both space and time, can easily be configured as a spatial narrative of history that dramatises successive events."[61] When complex historical events are traced in or projected onto the landscape, it is likely that they crystallise around individual sites, which may be 'concatenated' into spatial narratives. A clear example of this phenomenon in a (quasi-)historical text is the fifth book of the twelfth-century *Liber Sancti Jacobi*, which is a pilgrim's guide allowing pilgrims on the Saint James Route to visit sites allegedly connected to the battle of Roncesvalles (778 CE), including the Roland hospice (built on the site of Roland's death), situated close to a rock which the hero miraculously split, the meadow of a 'spear miracle', and the site of the battle itself at Roncesvalles.[62] Other good examples are found on more modern battle fields, such as that of Waterloo.[63]

A related, but distinct phenomenon is *accumulation*, which occurs when a mnemotope has more than one narrative associated with it. Halbwachs noted many of these accumulations; for example, Martha would have met Jesus on the same spot where Jesus allegedly mounted a donkey.[64] He also noted the phenomenon that Jewish mnemotopes acquire an additional Christian one. For instance, Jesus' place of birth, Bethlehem, is also the site of the tomb of the matriarch of Judaism, Rachel; the Cenacle, the traditional site of the last supper, as well as the house of Caiaphas, are very close to the purported tomb of David[65]; and a fountain in Jerusalem where Jesus cured the blind (*Evangelium secundum Joannem* 9.7) was also connected to the prescription of washing cow's ash in a well, known from the Old Testament (*Numeri* 19.17).[66] Halbwachs pointed out that, while these accumulations may be coincidental because there were holy Jewish sites everywhere, in some cases a connection between the events was sought. This connection may consist of the shared convenience or the physical prominence of the location. For example, the pool of Bethesda acquired both Jewish and Christian associations because it is such a remarkable structure. These explanations are particularly successful for stories without a symbolic connection.[67] In other cases, symbolic explanations are also possible: for example, the Calvary was both the site of Jesus' death and the offering of Isaac because they are examples of

---

[60] Azaryahu & Foote 2008, 187; the examples mentioned are the fortress of Masada in Israel and the battlefield of Gettysburg in the United States. See also Vansina 1985, 167–176 on the ways in which narratives are structured in memory.
[61] Azaryahu & Foote 2008, 193. See also Fentress & Wickham 1992, 49–51 on the need for memory to rely on stories; Schudson 1995, 355–358 on the narrativisation of the past in collective memory.
[62] Brall-Tuchel 2003, 44–45.
[63] Pelzer 2003, 149–150.
[64] Halbwachs 1941, 49–50.
[65] Halbwachs 1941, 74; 90–91.
[66] Halbwachs 1941, 31–33.
[67] Halbwachs 1941, 185.

human sacrifice. Such links may have been inspired by a wish to lend more credence to the stories, or more significance to the site.[68] In the end, the correspondences are not unsurprising because mnemotopes are at once part of the distant past, the recent past, and the present; as Crang & Travlou say: "Places of memory stand inserted simultaneously in a past order and the present, and are thus doubly located through (at least) two different sets of coordinates. In doing this they offer cracks in the surface of the present where time can be otherwise."[69]

1.3.6 Mnemotopes and historicity

As we have already seen in some of the examples discussed above, mnemotopes are usually more revealing of the time in which they were created than of the time of the commemorated event. This leads to a paradoxical situation, because empirical studies show that locations are a prerequisite for memories and function as verification tools. The anthropologist Jan Vansina notes that "When Trobrianders (New Guinea) hear assertions that run counter to their everyday ideas about natural laws, the words of their ancestors, while true, should still be backed up by a trace of the event visible in the landscape. Otherwise the tradition is true, but not factual."[70] By making a story graphical, a mnemotope helps visitors to re-experience the story on the spot. It thereby helps in making a story credible: if one sees where something happened, one no longer needs proof that it happened. There is an affinity of this observation with Roland Barthes' *effet de réel*, the 'reality effect' produced by seemingly redundant but graphic ecphrastic information in novelistic literature, as well as in historical writing.[71] I suggest that mnemotopes are important producers of this effect: pointing out the place of an event releases an author from the obligation to show that it happened in the first place. As such, mnemotopes may play a role as a rhetorical argument in political debates.[72] A striking example from ancient Greece is a rock in the harbour of Corfu (Kerkyra), which was said to be the petrified ship of the Phaeacians, mentioned in the *Odyssey*, and 'evidence' that Kerkyra was actually the elusive mythical island of Scheria; it was on this basis that the locals claimed naval leadership (Thucydides 1.25). Along similar lines, it is recognised that the presence of mnemotopes in the landscape leads to their use as moral guidance within local communities.[73]

---

[68] Halbwachs 1941, 175–180 (with more examples of coincidence of Christian and Jewish mnemotopes).
[69] Crang & Travlou 2001, 175.
[70] Vansina 1985, 129–130 (quote); Immerwahr 1960; Vansina 1961, 145; Shrimpton 1997, 60; Flower 2013, 141–142.
[71] Barthes 1984, 167–174; see also Ankersmit 1994, 139–147.
[72] Ferrari 2002, 28–29.
[73] Tonkin 1992, 127–128.

Yet, while mnemotopes are presented as authentic, or even as evidence for the historicity of the event, such claims are often problematic. A frequent type of 'error' is the wrong location of an event. For example, the Teutoburg forest was identified by nineteenth-century scholarship with a prominent, forested hill near Bielefeld; subsequently, it became an important mnemotope, as testified by the erection of the Hermannsdenkmal and the renaming of the forest to Teutoburger Wald. Meanwhile, countless other identifications have been proffered. Another frequent 'mistake' is the association between place and story, or that between place and person. For example, in medieval Iran, the legacy of the Achaemenid dynasty was forgotten and the ruined palace city of Persepolis became known as the 'Throne of Jamshid' (Takht-e-Jamshid), and the main Achaemenid burial site is now called 'Image of Rostam' (Nashq-e Rostam): Jamshid and Rostam were both mythical kings. Possibly the most famous figure from antiquity whose name was and is still used freely to explain anomalous or spectacular features and places is Alexander the Great.[74]

In such discussions, the word 'mistake' is only valid for those who seek historical authenticity. But within the context of memory, the word is, in fact, a misnomer: the truth is only relatively relevant to the process of remembering.[75] Moreover, as laid out in the introduction, even fictional works inspire the creation of mnemotopes, where people come to re-experience events which only happened in their imagination.

Although it is difficult to prove that a mnemotope represents a historically authentic story when there is only one site, it is certain that at least one place is inauthentic when there are two or more alternative mnemotopes.[76] A case in point is the prison of Socrates in Athens, situated variously in a cave on Philopappos Hill, the Tower of the Winds or on the Agora.[77] The fluidity of such identifications appears in a Christian example: a cave near Jerusalem was indicated in one account as the place where Jesus was betrayed by Judas, and the garden of Gethsemane was the supposed scene of Jesus' agony. In a later tradition, the sites were switched.[78]

While the phenomenon of historically inauthentic mnemotopes is easy to illustrate, the reasons for their existence are multi-faceted. Halbwachs attributed the

---

[74] Examples of structures attributed to Alexander the Great are the 'Caspian Gates' at Derbent in the Caucasus (in reality built by the Sassanids) and many forts in Afghanistan, such as the one at Qarat.
[75] On the problematic relationship between oral traditions (or local folklore) and historicity, see Fentress & Wickham 1992, 75–86; 92–114; Tonkin 1992, 119–121 (argueing that a sharp distinction between history and memory cannot be made).
[76] On competition between claims of relics and mnemotopes, see Hartmann 2010, 101–105.
[77] Schrijvers 2007. The rape of Persephone was also contested by various sites; the Asian city of Nysa, near a sanctuary marking the entrance to the underworld, was particularly vocal about it, as the theme featured on coins and on a theatrical frieze (Price 2012, 21). Another case is the Grotto of the Nymphs at Ithaca (known from the *Odyssey*) which was recreated in Hellenistic times, although other sites have also been identified as such (Antonaccio 1995, 152–155; Boardman 2002, 67–70).
[78] Halbwachs 1941, 120–125.

occurrence of 'inauthentic' mnemotopes related to Jesus' life to people's decreasing familiarity with the original events.[79] He explained the coexistence of multiple mnemotopes in the same collective memory by pointing out not only that people may use different sources for their localisations, but also that there is a certain tolerance for it: people do not want to lose any potential trace of the event.[80] Another reason identified by Halbwachs is convenience. For example, the place where John the Baptist would have conducted his work was situated on the inhabited site of the Jordan river, while earlier traditions placed it on the other, uninhabited side.[81] Similarly, when the material correlate of a mnemotope is destroyed, the memory may be absorbed by another site. For example, the repentance of Peter was first localised on the site of a basilica in the Kidron Valley. After this basilica was destroyed, the memory was moved to the alleged house of Caiaphas on Mount Zion.[82]

Halbwachs' points about decreasing familiarity and convenience are relevant, but they offer only a partial explanation because mnemotopes may also arise by invented traditions, or, in other words, mark events which never occurred in the first place, but arose *ex post facto*. In some cases, we may hope to find a 'culprit' who tried to 'alter history'. Politically loaded mnemotopes were especially liable to become the subject of historical 'fraud'. A similar process can be observed at modern historical sites. Much tourism takes place around such sites, which has spurred a great supply of 'historical' places, not just by history and archaeology enthusiasts and academics, but more revealingly also by those who directly benefit financially from tourism: local individuals, companies and authorities.[83] For example, the modern archaeological site of Knossos owes at least part of its position as Crete's foremost tourist site to its being the mnemotope of king Minos. Another example is the modern city of Nazareth, which attracts Christian pilgrims, although the location of the town is actually unknown.[84] At such places, authenticity is sold and bought, but only rarely obtained.

Much more often, the process is subconscious: we now know that memory is often factually wrong, even when it records recent events in vivid detail,[85] and that historical events can be 'narrativised' into simple, but dramatic stories.[86] It is recognised that people who were not born at the time of an event may, through the mediation of stories and images, remember that event very vividly, as if they were there. This is

---

79 Halbwachs 1941, 153.
80 Halbwachs 1941, 188, 191.
81 Halbwachs 1941, 56.
82 Halbwachs 1941, 187.
83 Urry 2002, 95; 103–110.
84 Halbwachs 1941, 150.
85 For the many ways in which oral traditions reshape the memory of historical events, Vansina 1985 remains authoritative; see also Fentress & Wickham 1992, 1–7; 75–86; 92–114; Tonkin 1992, 113–136. See Shrimpton 1997, 55–62 for examples of this process following the Second World War.
86 Steinbock 2013, 17.

especially the case for traumatic events such as the Holocaust.[87] Memory distortion is called *confabulation* by psychologists, and is known to be stronger when recollection depends on reconstruction, and when the source is not known; temporal or thematic confabulation is common in memories of experienced events, as the brain does not 'tag' them accordingly.[88] Perhaps most revealingly, empirical research has shown a strong correlation between the suggestion of an event to test persons and their subsequent belief that they truly experienced that event.[89] Similar observations apply to collective memory: it is recognised that collective memory gets distorted with time, contains cognitive biases of success, narrativises the past into interesting stories that stress the action of certain individuals, and is socially 'conventionalised'.[90]

As regards mnemotopes, we know that traditions may arise in reaction to striking objects or natural features. This was already noted by Halbwachs.[91] In a classic anthropological study on oral traditions, and their creation and transformation among African peoples, Jan Vansina showed that the physical world is an important catalyst of such traditions, and termed this process *iconatrophy*[92]; and various other scholars have paid attention to the phenomenon.[93] In an interesting example from ancient Greece, we now know that a mysterious battle between Argos and Sparta, fought at Hysiai and only known from Pausanias (2.24.7) is an invented tradition based on a monument that related not to city of Argos, but to the mythical figure of the same name.[94] Yet we cannot say that somebody consciously altered history in this case (although this was, in the end, the effect). The monument simply inspired the story and was at the same time the best proof one could have imagined.

Even though the claims made at mnemotopes are often at odds with the historical reality of the events which they commemorate, this is, of course, not necessarily always

---

87 See Hirsch 2012, especially 4–6; 31–36 on the phenomenon of *postmemory*. In an example from Modern Greece, memories of the civil war were not available among villagers; instead they talked about events from the Ottoman period, which they could not have experienced (Tonkin 1992, 116–117).
88 Moscovitch 1995, 245–247.
89 Lotfu, Feldman & Dashiell 1995.
90 Schudson 1995.
91 Halbwachs 1941, 157 noted that "Les lieux sacrés commémorent donc, non pas des faits certifiés par des témoins contemporains, mais des croyances nées peut-être non loin de ces lieux, et qui se sont fortifiées en s'y enracinant."
92 Vansina (1961, 145) noted that archaeological objects may inspire traditions but that these rarely have any historical value. In his later study (1985, 10–11) he states: "It is therefore necessary to treat all stories tied to archaeological sites with some caution." He also (1985, 46) points out that impressive natural phenomena have iconatrophic power (i.e. the power to evoke etiological stories).
93 Cf. Proietti 2012c, 186–187 with note 18; Flower 2013 (a case study of Herodotean traditions about Croesus, which were often connected to votive offerings at Delphi). Assmann (1992, 40–42; 65) describes a similar phenomenon. It is also known biologically that the link between memory and perception is strong (cf. Squire 1995, 198–200).
94 Robertson 1992, xiii-xiv (focusing especially on festivals); 208–216.

the case. It is possible that an event happened at a site and that this site subsequently developed into a mnemotope, which thereby commemorated a story with an 'absolute' historical truth. But even the mere process of selection of mnemotopes gives prominence to the narratives commemorated at them; and it thereby already (re)shapes history.

If the relation between mnemotopes and the historicity of the commemorated event is sometimes inexact, we may ask ourselves: does the question of historicity pertain to the identification of mnemotopes in a historical work at all, and if yes, how? I propose that we envision the relation between historical sites and mnemotopes as partly overlapping: some mnemotopes are truly the sites of the commemorated events, others are not. Therefore, the identification of a place as a mnemotope and the tracing of its development (as will be done in this book) do not prove that the event commemorated at the mnemotope did not happen, or that it happened at a different place, for the simple reason that the analysis does not bring us back to the time of the alleged events, but only helps us to envisage how the mnemotope functioned in its own time.[95] Nevertheless, the reverse is true: when we can establish with reasonable certainty, through other means, that a place in a historical work *cannot* be the historical site of a particular event, there only exists scope to view the place as a mnemotope. In that case, alternative ways to explain the relevance of the place must be sought. If Herodotus had pointed out the moon as a significant site that Xerxes had visited, the best explanation is not that the Persian king had successfully launched a space program, but that the moon had somehow developed into a mnemotope for Xerxes' visit. Thus, establishing whether an event may historically have taken place at a site, while not the aim of the present study, can be helpful in understanding why a certain community localised the event at that specific place. In addition, the observation that a certain event cannot in reality have taken place gives more weight to the identification of the site as a mnemotope.

1.3.7 Summary

The topic of this book, for which Herodotus' account of Xerxes' invasion will be analysed, is the process by which narratives are localised. For a place where one or more events allegedly happened the term *mnemotope* will be employed. Mnemotopes are different from objects, as well as from monuments and landscapes, although these categories may be closely associated with them. Reasons for interaction with mnemotopes are varied. They function as a source of local and civic pride and status, and as a verification tool for the event. We can often observe a process of *spatial densification*, which may take the shape of *clustering* of mnemotopes which are close to each other, or *accumulation* of narratives at a single site. While mnemotopes sometimes function as proof for certain stories, there are many examples which show that the relation

---

95 This idea is already found in Halbwachs 1941, 2; 9.

between historical fact and mnemotope is, in fact, problematic. The aim of this study is not to prove that certain stories related by Herodotus did or did not happen, but testing the historicity of the event is instrumental in understanding the development of the mnemotope, as it gives more credence to alternative processes by which the mnemotope might have arisen.

1.4 Mnemotopes and Herodotus

1.4.1 Herodotus' *Histories* as a source of mnemotopes

Herodotus' *Histories* are, for several reasons, particularly fruitful ground to study the concept of mnemotopes. First, the *terminus post quem* of the *Histories* is traditionally given around 430 BCE on various internal and external grounds[96]; and Xerxes' invasion is believed to have occurred in 480 BCE.[97] This means that Herodotus wrote some fifty years after the events, a period which is long enough for a memory tradition about the wars to have come into full force. As James Romm points out, his work "is tinged with nostalgia and looks back on the Greco-Persian conflict in something of the same spirit – and from much the same distance – as we today look back on World War II".[98] In Herodotus' time, moreover, commemoration of the Persian Wars was relevant and widespread, because they had affected the lives of people's direct ancestors, and also because the Achaemenid Empire remained the great power of western Asia.[99]

A second reason why the concept of mnemotopes works so well for the *Histories* is that it is universally recognised that Herodotus relied primarily on oral

---

[96] A terminus post quem is offered by Herodotus' mention of the capture of Spartan envoys by Athenians (7.137), the date of which is secured to 430 BCE by the reference in Thucydides (2.67). A terminus ante quem could be 424 BCE, when the Athenians assailed Aegina (Thucydides 4.57); the assumption is that Herodotus would have surely mentioned this if his work had been written later. On these matters see Jacoby 1913, 231–232; Stephanie West in Bowie 2007, 28. It also seems that Aristophanes' *Acharnenses* (425 BCE) was influenced by the *Histories*, as some coincidences regarding Persian customs cannot be explained otherwise (line 85 and 1.133, line 82 and 1.192; cf. Jacoby 1913, 232).
[97] Herodotus himself (8.51) and Diodorus Siculus (11.1.2) dated Xerxes' invasion to the archonship of Kalliades, in the 75th Olympiad.
[98] Romm 1998, 195.
[99] See Evans 1991, 89–92 for a possible context in which Herodotus wrote, characterised by sentiments of both Panhellenism, polis pride and an obsession with important leaders during the war. See Thomas 1989, 221–226 for the role of the Persian Wars in the Athenian epitaphios. See Hölscher 2010, 136 for the idea that the fifth century BCE saw politicisation and identity-building in many parts of the Greek world. For many examples of the role of the Persian Wars in Athenian social memory see Steinbock 2013, 20, 100–154.

Map 1: Overview of most important sites associated with the Persian invasion.

history, which he often sourced locally.¹⁰⁰ As we have seen, local stories are likely to revolve around local landmarks; they are subject to local memory, traditions and

---

100 On the role of oral traditions in Herodotus and their complex relation to historical fact, see already Wecklein 1876, who stressed the degree to which Herodotus' traditions about the Persian Wars were shaped by folk traditions. He marked a significant number of Herodotus' anecdotes as unhistorical. On (local) oral traditions see further How & Wells 1912, I 30–31; Momigliano 1966; Thomas 1989; Evans 1991, 93–132 (on "epichoric traditions"); Lang 1984, 1–17 (suggesting that Herodotus' narrative itself also shows that it is shaped by techniques similar to oral narrative); Murray 1987; 2001; Cartledge 2002 (first published 1993), 21–33 (pointing out that Herodotus had only access to myths for his research on the Persian Wars); Christ 1994, 197–198; Osborne 1996, 5 (describing Herodotus as "an excellent guide to what the Greeks and others to whom he talked thought worth telling in the middle of the fifth century BC" and suggesting that (page 7) "The value of tradition [...] is as good as "the last person" speaking to Herodotus"); Luraghi 2001 (arguing that local oral history was Herodotus' main type of source, even when he does not explicitly say so); Porciani 2001, especially 13–63; 68–100; Steinbock 2013, 21–23; Luraghi 2013 (stressing that Herodotus organised material that was already narrativised in local folklore); Flower 2013, 125–127 (drawing a comparison between Herodotus and modern anthropologists). Franchi & Proietti 2015, 19–20. For the relation of Herodotus to Delphic oracles, see Maurizio 1997, arguing that oral traditions about these oracles intervened.

folklore,[101] and are liable to be biased or distorted.[102] At the same time, it is likely that those interviewed by Herodotus were prone to confirm his views, and that Herodotus was not likely to problematise their stories very much.[103] This notion accords well with the observation that the *Histories*, and in particular the battle narratives, consist mainly of juxtaposed anecdotes.[104] Herodotus, of course, also used written sources,[105] but this information may equally have been biased or distorted. For example, we know that Herodotus used poetry, such as Aeschylus' *Persae* (§2.8) and Simonides' war poems (e.g. §2.4.2, §2.5.4, §2.9.7), in which battles easily acquired a mythical sense and mnemotopes sometimes appear as historical places.

A third reason why the *Histories* are a good case study for the concept is that Herodotus himself was a remarkable traveller. While the exact extent of his journeys is a matter of debate,[106] there is not much reason to doubt that he was reasonably familiar with the areas of Greece and Anatolia where the Persian Wars were fought, or that he

---

101 Cf. Luraghi 2001, 150.
102 For the ways in which oral traditions in Herodotus could be distorted, see e.g. Bowie 2007, 22; Marincola 2007, 106: "Herodotus' narrative, however reliable, is already a 'deformation', in that it has synthesized, accepted, rejected, modified, and adapted what must have been many oral traditions about the Persian Wars." Regarding oracular texts in Herodotus, Maurizio 1997 argues that it is pointless to try to filter historically authentic information from them, as they are all structurally similar and owed their tradition to being miracle stories. Waters 2014, 124 points out that political tensions between different Greek cities at the time of Herodotus' research would have impacted the ways in which the wars were remembered.
103 See Waters 1985, 27; 89; 91 for the idea that Herodotus' sources would tend to be affirmative of his inquiries. See Rösler 2013 for the idea that Herodotus was rather credulous about these sources. It seems that Herodotus copied Aeschylus' numbers and geographical references; but cf. e.g. Kienast 1996, 301 who suggests that Herodotus tried to correct Aeschylus with his description of the army inspection at Doriskos.
104 Immerwahr 1966, 46–78; 238–241 (on battle narratives).
105 On the role of written sources in Herodotus, cf. Obst 1913, 28–29; Drews 1973; Marincola 2012, 3–5.
106 The bibliography on the 'autopsy' dimension of Herodotus is, as expected, huge. How & Wells (1912, I 18–20) discerned six different journeys, reflecting the areas treated by Herodotus. The most detailed exploration of this topic remains Jacoby 1913, who discussed the mention of ἐπιχώριοι (400, 403) and the phrases μέχρι ἐμεῦ, ἔτι καὶ νῦν, ἔτι καὶ ἐς ἐμέ, ἐπ' ἐμέο (249) and other indications as evidence for a real visit. His conclusion was that the extent of Herodotus' travels was "nicht gerade überwaltigend" (276). He stayed in settled, mostly coastal areas, and was not a true explorer. There is, in fact, some evidence to suggest that Herodotus travelled around the shores of the eastern Mediterranean using merchant ships: he mentions commercial items, methods of transport and their freight capacity, vessels, the navigability of rivers and trade routes (How & Wells 1912, I 17). Cf. Burn 1962, 339: "He writes as though he had been (sticking always to the coast) along the line of Xerxes' route [...]" It has even been suggested that the nautical parts of Herodotus' work are much more reliable than the land parts (Wallinga 2005, 6). On the extent of Herodotus' travels, see also Hauvette 1894, 16–37; Hignett 1963, 29; von Fritz 1967, 408–409; Armayor 1980 (on the autospy of the Sesostris monuments); Redfield 1985; Thomas 2000, 11–12; Müller 2004; Stephanie West in Bowie 2007, 27–28.

could at least rely on good eye-witness reports about these areas.[107] He was particularly interested in monuments, infrastructural projects, and inscriptions[108]; many of which are described digressively, as if from the perspective of a tourist (cf. the relation of mnemotopes and tourism in §1.3.4).[109] In addition, it has been suggested that many characters in the *Histories* seem to engage in tourism as a proxy for Herodotus' own research method.[110]

The reasons for Herodotus to include 'touristic' information may have been varied. These passages are usually entertaining, and the delight Herodotus must have had when seeing these places appears from his frequent announcements that a monument or object was still present in his own days; this quality of entertainment may have been important for his audience.[111] Such references may also have been useful for Herodotus as a rhetorical tool to substantiate claims within his milieu (cf. §1.3.6 on the rhetorical function of mnemotopes).[112] Several scholars have observed that a process of 'attribution', i.e. the matching of a story to a source is typical of Herodotus'

---

107 Immerwahr 1960, 290.
108 Rood 2012, 123–124 points out that Herodotus offers most spatial detail when describing large monuments. In his introduction Herodotus claims to be interested in ἔργα μεγάλα, and he makes mention of many θώματα and θωμαστά in his work, which are thought to refer to great sights (cf. Jacoby 1913, 331–334; Immerwahr 1960, 264–271; Barth 1968; Hartog 1980, 244–245; 248–249; 259–268; Redfield 1985, 97). For the role of objects in Herodotus, see Hedrick 1993; Dewald 1993; Hartmann, 2010, 423–431. On Herodotus' treatment of inscriptions, see West 1985; Osborne 2002, 511–512; Hartmann 2010, 68–70. Vandiver (1991, 75–82) devotes a chapter in her book about the association of heroes to landmarks in Herodotus' work, stating that "the association of heroes' names with landmarks served to link the heroic past with the human present through visible, public reference points."
109 Herodotus gives much information "in answer to the presumed question 'What is worth seeing now we're here?'" (Waters 1985, 42). He sometimes explicitly gives more information about an area because it has so many impressive sights (e.g. 2.35 for Egypt); see also Rood 2006, 292. The similarity of Pausanias' style to that of Herodotus is often noted (e.g. Pritchett 1993, 84, 342–343; Pretzler 2007, 55–56). This is not unexpected, as Herodotus is repeatedly explicit about his own practice of interlacing his work with digressions that are of only limited use for the 'big picture'.
110 In 1.29–30 Herodotus mentions that Solon, after making laws for the Athenians, stayed abroad for ten years for sightseeing (θεωρίη). In 4.76, he relates how the Scythian philosopher Anacharsis returned to Scythia after having seen much of the world and how he had become a wise man in the process. Even more crucially, Herodotus says that Persians travelled around the coasts of Greece to see famous places (3.136) and that Greeks did the same in Egypt (3.139). We will see in individual case studies that Xerxes was sometimes also depicted as a tourist.
111 Rood 2006, 292.
112 For the idea that (spatial) concretisation was a way for Herodotus to substantiate his claims, see Hartog 1980, 272–279, 346–349; Flory 1987, 40–41; Shrimpton 1997, 18–19; 69; Alonso-Núñez 2003, 145–146; Thomas 2006, 64 ("on one level a *thōma*, is also a test for successive writers to come up with a rational explanation"); Gehrke 2010, 25; Price 2012, 24–25. See Rosenmeyer 1982, 253 for the view that this concretisation did not have much historical significance. Cf. Polybius (12.26–27), who wrote that visiting important places is crucial for being a historian.

method.¹¹³ This was not necessarily a conscious process: Herodotus himself may well have been persuaded by his sources who told him a particular story in relation to a monument. In addition, seemingly digressive mentions may have had important narrative effects, such as symbolism.¹¹⁴

1.4.2 Mnemotopes of eastern kings in the *Histories*

A final factor for the density of mnemotopes in Herodotus' work is that it is in its essence a work about eastern kings.¹¹⁵ As such, the work is a treasure trove for 'celebrity' mnemotopes. These mnemotopes are often connected to objects, such as booty or dedications in Greek sanctuaries; for example, Phrygian king Midas had a throne in Delphi (1.14), Croesus donated columns to the temple of Artemis at Ephesus (1.92), and the general Datis had allegedly returned a stolen statue of Apollo to Delos (6.118).¹¹⁶ Another frequent occurrence is the association of kings with large (often infrastructural) monuments. These include bridges, such as the one built by the Babylonian queen Nitocris over the Euphrates (1.186), that of Cyrus over the Araxes (1.205), and those of Darius over the Bosporus (4.83) and the Danube (4.89).¹¹⁷ Darius is said to have built eight forts along the Oaros river (sometimes identified with the Volga) which, Herodotus informs us, were still extant in his time (4.123–124).¹¹⁸ Darius is also said to have left behind enormous stone heaps at the

---

113 Shrimpton 1997, 109–112; Ferrari 2002, 28–29; Fowler 2003, 308. Herodotus himself says (1.8) that "ὦτα γὰρ τυγχάνει ἀνθρώποισι ἐόντα ἀπιστότερα ὀφθαλμῶν" ('ears happen to be less reliable to people than eyes').
114 Rood (2012, 125–126) points out that this is often the case.
115 Much of Herodotus' work consists of tracing the exploits of oriental leaders, including the Lydian and Achaemenid kings (cf. Immerwahr 1966, 25–34). Herodotus, his sources, and his intellectual milieu seem to have been fascinated by their lineages, families, personalities, successes and mistakes, and regarded them as pivotal to the rise and fall of their kingdoms or empires (Singor 2007, 417–418); a similar interest is seen in the Egyptian pharaohs and their imperialist expansions, their founding of temples and cities and their personalities; only rarely does Herodotus give attention to other agents (Lloyd 2002, 422–424). The focus on these kings is so pervasive that the theme runs like a red string through the *Histories*, starting with the relatively hellenophile Croesus, and ending with the imperious Xerxes (Walter 2010, 407). This phenomenon is, of course, not limited to Herodotus. Xenophon's *Cyropaedia* is an attempt to establish what makes a good ruler, and in his *Vitae parallelae*, Plutarch investigated the influence of important 'personalities' on history.
116 For discussions of the relation of eastern kings to Greek oracles, see Rosenberger 2003, 42–50; Hutton 2005, 50; Flower 2013.
117 Further examples can be found in Xenophon, *Anabasis* 1.2.5, 2.4.13 and 2.4.24.
118 It is possible that Herodotus confused the geography of modern Romania with that of Ukraine and Russia (Bury 1897; Hignett 1963, 84). The forts, moreover, may have been built as fortifications against the peoples of the steppes by some earlier power from the south (Burn 1962, 132). Alternatively, they may well have been seen in any kind of ancient structures, such as burial mounds (kurgans).

Arteskos river (4.92).[119] Although it is possible that Darius passed such sites, the story about the rock piles more likely reflects a local tradition in which Darius' expedition was erroneously associated with them.[120] Impressive natural features could also inspire stories about the visit of a king[121]: examples include Darius' gazing over the Black Sea at the Symplegades (4.85),[122] and his admiration of the Tearos river in Thrace (4.91).[123]

These stories deserve special scrutiny because we know that Herodotus treated his eastern monarchs in stereotypical ways and that traditions about them regularly originate in folktale.[124] These insights can readily be applied to mnemotopes about these kings. When Herodotus talks about the actions of a specific king at a specific site, the tradition may be wrong about the identity of the king, or even wholly 'off the map'. The best example concerns Herodotus' description of several rock carvings near Smyrna featuring a warrior king and an inscription (2.106). One of the figures still exists; it is today known as the Karabel A inscription, and is situated on the modern road from Kemalpaşa to Torbalı, Turkey (see Figure 1 and Map 1). Herodotus points out that while others believed that the depicted king was the Ethiopian king Memnon, the correct identification was Sesostris. But Herodotus was also misguided: the surviving figure does not represent an Egyptian pharaoh, but Tarkasnawa, king of Mira, a Bronze Age state of western Anatolia. The carving featured Luwian hieroglyphs,

---

119 The location of this event has been elusive, but a good candidate is the modern Bulgarian village of Huhla at the Arda river (whose name may be derived from the ancient Arteskos); here, the river banks are covered with rocks, and at several places these have been piled up.
120 We may compare the Plaine de la Crau near Marseilles, an alluvial plain covered with stones, which, according to one of the traditions recorded by Strabo (4.1.7), originated as ammunition given to Heracles (cf. Boardman 2002, 110). Alternative locations include the Golyama (Danov 1976, 121–122; 265, note 118); megalithic tombs in the Sakar and Strandja (Archibald 1998, 82). On the symbolic role of such monuments as a marker of the strengths and weaknesses of kings, see Hollmann 2011, 203–207.
121 Christ 1994 lists all the examples; see particularly 178–179.
122 The place where Darius gazed at the Black Sea is now the lighthouse hill of Rumeli Feneri at the north entrance to the Bosporus, north of Istanbul; here, the Cyaneai or dark-blue rocks, whose pedigree as the Symplegads evaded by the Argo goes back to Homer (*Odyssey* 12.61), can still be seen; cf. Müller 1997, 859–863.
123 The Tearos river is probably to be identified with the modern Kaynarca Dere in Turkish Thrace; see Müller 1997, 942–948. The thirty-eight springs here (cf. 4.90) can also be found here. An 'Assyrian' cuneiform inscription was reported at a local monastery, but had already disappeared by 1847 (Jochmus 1854, 44). Unger & Weißbach 1915 reported an ancient pedestal with a slot for a stele. Cawkwell (2005, 55, note 10) doubts whether this is the original stele. Herodotus' story may well be authentic: West (1985, 296) points out that the contents of Tearos inscription are not unlikely, as they are similar to the Sousa statue inscription; cf. Danov 1976, 264. In 1937, a Persian inscription was found at Gherla in Romania, mentioning Darius, son of Hytaspes.
124 On this topic see Mantel 1976; Waters 1985, 136–149; Gammie 1986; Evans 1991, 41–88; Hansen 1996 (comparing stories about Gyges and Croesus to international folk tales); Wiesehöfer 2004, 212–214.

Fig. 1: The Karabel A inscription.

which resemble Egyptian ones.[125] It now seems that the Greek figures of Memnon and Sesostris are probably conflations of multiple historical kings, or may be completely imaginary.[126]

We have similar, though less equivocal, material from mainland Greece. Herodotus tells us that the Lydian king Croesus once came to the temple of Apollo in Thebes, and left behind a golden shield as a votive offering to the hero Amphiaraos for his arete (1.52) after the oracle had given a correct prediction (1.49). In 2005 an inscribed column drum was found in Thebes (dated to c. 500 BCE) recording a

---

[125] The inscription was deciphered by Hawkins 1998. For the relation between Herodotus and the inscription see Myres 1953, 6; Fehling 1971, 100–101; Danov 1976, 270; Armayor 1980 67–73; West 1985, 300–302; West 1992; Ivantchik 1999, especially 401–405; van Wees 2002, 331–332; Dalley 2003, 174, 176; Zwingmann 2012, 237–250; 2013 (pointing out that nineteenth-century scholarship failed to realise that the figures are not Egyptian because they assumed Herodotus' infallibility). Memnon was also popularly identified with monuments, but mainly in Egypt (sometimes erroneously, as with those of Amenophis III at Luxor; cf. Boardman 2002, 118–122).

[126] On Sesostris see Ivantchik 1999, in which the traditions about this king in ancient literature are analysed and from which it appears that Sesostris became a 'scapegoat' for many foreign exploits of the Egyptians.

rededication of a 'shiny shield', which if it was not the very inscription seen by Herodotus, is indicative of what he might have seen.[127] Peter Thonemann has suggested that the inscription not only shows that Herodotus misunderstood the dedication, which was probably set up as a memorial for Croesus' own arete (not only that of Amphiaraos), but that he may also have confused the Lydian king with an Attic nobleman with the same name (and whose grave marker survives as the famous Anavyssos kouros).[128]

Xerxes, the main character of the Persian invasion of Greece, was treated in a fashion similar to other eastern kings. Xerxes was known as the archetypical hubristic tyrant in later periods.[129] It has been argued that Herodotus' depiction of the king is more complex than that given by other authors: he is not only portrayed as hubristic but also, at least occasionally, as a more sympathetic figure.[130] It has even been felt that Xerxes' activities throughout the final three books of the *Histories* mirror those of Herodotus himself.[131] However, this 'complex Xerxes' is only partly attributable to Herodotus' literary agency; he also featured widely in folklore in the years after the invasion as a historical celebrity. As we will see, many of the stories told about him were grounded in mnemotopes.

---

127 The inscription was first published by Papazarkadas 2014, 233–247. He indicated that it may be possible that the inscription was seen by Herodotus, although his wording is not entirely similar.

128 Thonemann 2014. For the view that Delphian 'Croesus objects' may have yielded fanciful traditions, but that we should not go as far as to detach them from the historical Croesus because the Delphian traditions would have been reliable, see Flower 2013, 140–143. See Bassi 2014 for the view that Herodotus' account of Croesus' dedications is analogous to Croesus' rise and downfall.

129 For an overview of the relatively negative reputation of Xerxes in Greek literature, see Vandiver 1991, 203–205; Wiesehöfer 1993, 76–89. For Aeschylus' (and other playwrights') treatment of Xerxes, see Tracy 2008, 3; Bridges 2015, 11–43; for the role of Xerxes in fourth-century BCE Greek rhetoric, see Bridges 2015, 100–112; on Strabo's engagement with Xerxes, see Bridges 2015, 177–179; on Pausanias' engagement with Xerxes, see Bridges 2015, 179–182. On the problematic historicity of anecdotes about Xerxes, see Erbse 1992, 74–92.

130 On Herodotus' Xerxes as a complex character, see e.g. Burn 1962, 313–314; Immerwahr 1966, 176–183 (argueing that Xerxes' conflicting traits destroy him); Mayrhofer 1974, 113–115. For the view that Herodotus sometimes portrays Xerxes as ignorant, see Flory 1987, 45 (on omina); 104 (on ignoring the wisdom of advisors); 110 (on underestimating the Spartans). For the view that Herodotus sometimes emphasises Xerxes' prudence, see Bowie 2007, 9; Baragwanath 2008, 240–288. For the idea that Herodotus makes us want to sympathise with Xerxes, see Waters 1985, 146; Flory 1987, 76; Evans 1991, 60–67; Schulz 2013; Bridges 2015, 45–71. It is possible that the adduced examples of a more positive Xerxes were perceived by a contemporary audience as ironical or even comical. See Waters 1985, 170–171 and Shrimpton 1997, 199–200 for examples of Herodotean humour; and cf. Flory (1987), who has emphasised Herodotus' "Mozartean" (i.e. both comical and serious) tone (quote at page 20).

131 Grethlein 2009, 211: "Xerxes' gaze is carried by the desire to freeze the present, give it the final status of the past, and thus deprive it of all the insecurity that threatens human life." More fanciful is Grethlein's suggestion (pages 213–215) that Herodotus gives a meta-historical discourse through the character of Xerxes because he does not learn from history, even when he tries to record himself.

1.4.3 Mnemotopes of the Persian Wars: a new and controversial perspective

The perspective of mnemotopes has little precedent in the study of Greek historiography, and especially not in Herodotus' treatment of the Persian Wars. The above discussion shows that the potential for discussing mnemotopes in Herodotus' world is large. This accords with trends in Herodotean scholarship: a large body of literature has brought to the fore insights departing from the *Histories* as a purely historical text,[132] and various studies have appeared which complicate Herodotus' relation to space.[133] Recently, it has also been remarked that the perspective of memory studies is crucial in understanding Herodotus and the Persian Wars.[134] Nevertheless, it seems

---

[132] A selection of important insights: Aly (1969, first edition 1921) identified folkloristic tales throughout Herodotus' work, including books 6 to 9; de Sélincourt (1967, 244–245) argued that Herodotus put much literary drama (e.g. digressions, fables) into Xerxes' campaign, underlying Xerxes' defeat; von Fritz (1967, 275–279) highlighted the similarities between Xerxes' war and Lydian history; Flory (1987, 67) pointed out that the stories which Herodotus marks as false but still mentions, do have a theme relevant to the *Histories*; even one of the most staunch supporters of Herodotus reliability, Hammond (1988, 535–536) accepted that the exaggerations about the army (drinking rivers dry, sheep-pen method etc.) should not be taken factually but that they are all part of "a drama of religious and human significance which was moving towards a predestined tragic end." Evans (1991, 9–40) explore the thematic relations of Persian imperialism in the Herodotean worldview; Maurizio 1997 argued that while previous scholarship had naively tried to filter the 'authentic' from the 'inauthentic' Delphic oracles in Herodotus, they can never be taken as the *ipsissima verba* of the Pythia, but that a process of oral tradition underlies them in which they were reshaped; she showed that they all follow a pattern: crisis – consultation – interpretation – action – confirmation/refutation; Mikalson (2003, 10–11) described Herodotus' account of the Persian Wars as a "construction"; it was recognised by Forsdyke (2006, 226) that Herodotus drew information from sources which had remembered the past in ways that suited their contemporary needs and promoted their societal interests; Kuhrt (2007, 7) explained that the *Histories* were shaped by didactic motives; Bridges (2015) has explored Xerxes as a literary figure in Herodotus and other ancient literature.
[133] Notable studies are Janni 1984; Purves 2010, 118–158 (pointing out that Herodotus' conception of the world was schematic and that his work should be understood in hodological terms, i.e. as following pathways); Rood 2012 (a general appraisal).
[134] See e.g. Luraghi 2001, 149–150 for the idea that the information Herodotus' local informants would have conveyed should be understood in terms of memory. Especially notable is the work of Giorgia Proietti, whose work highlights that the perspective of memory is a crucial instrument for understanding the account of the Persian Wars as recounted by Herodotus; see in general Proietti 2012c. The same goes for archaeological phenomena: Proietti (2012a; 2014) discusses the stele of the Marathonomachoi which was found in the year 2000 in a villa of Herodes Atticus in the Peloponnese. According to Proietti, it does not reflect an actual epitaph from 490 BCE, but an attempt at memorialising the battle, perhaps by Herodes Atticus himself. Proietti 2015a discusses the evidence for trophies of the Persian Wars and argues that they are most successfully explained as re-memoralisation efforts of later date. See also Franchi & Proietti 2015 on previous work that has characterised war as a cultural phenomenon and has brought it within the realm of memory studies; Proietti 2012b on the role of memory in the creation of Greek identity; and Proietti 2015b on the memory about the fight on Psyttaleia.

that there has been a certain reluctance to pursue this avenue of study. I identify three factors that may have played a role in the continuation of this reluctance.

First, the sheer size of the Persian Wars as a topic seems to have prevented the appearance of comprehensive studies that could offer an understanding of the topographical layer of the account at large. An important exception is the *Topographischer Bildkommentar* in which Dietram Müller has tried to identify and to illustrate all geographical entities in Greece and Anatolia mentioned by Herodotus.[135] But this work has been criticised,[136] and although it remains useful as a starting point for those interested in the topography of Herodotus' world, it assumes that the events which Herodotus records are historical.[137] In a more concise manner, *The Landmark Herodotus: The Histories* (2007) also envisages to map all places mentioned by Herodotus. Presently, the *HESTIA project* run by various universities aims to carry out a spatial analysis of places mentioned in the *Histories*.[138] Apart from these projects, the topography of the *Histories* has usually been studied fragmentarily or as a byproduct of other questions.

A second reason is the divided nature of fields relevant to the question (classics, ancient history, archaeology, and iranology), which sometimes impedes cross-fertilisation of ideas and debates. There are indications that Iranologists, for example, are not always aware of the great strides in the understanding of the *Histories* made by literary scholars,[139] and some classicists have explicitly distanced themselves from the archaeological layer, which they consider irrelevant to understanding the text.[140] Meanwhile, archaeologists frequently mine information from the *Histories* without considering the narrative aspects of the work. A case in point is the army of Cambyses which, Herodotus says, disappeared in a sandstorm in the Egyptian desert (3.26). While countless attempts have been made to localise remains of the army, we should first ask ourselves whether the army went into the desert in the first place.[141] Both those who look at the topography of the work from a historical point of view and those

---

[135] Müller 1987 (Greece) and 1997 (Asia Minor).
[136] The *Topographischer Bildkommentar* was said to suffer from its titanic scope: the review by Gehrke (1990, 393) classifies it as "ein ziemlicher Fehlschlag", arguing that the latest literature at the time was not fully employed, and that the quality of presentation of the places is uneven, and does not offer any sort of interpretation. A favourable view of this work is found in Mikalson 2003, 14.
[137] As will appear in the case studies, I often found reason to disagree with locations given by Müller.
[138] See http://www.open.ac.uk/Arts/hestia/ (last consulted on 12 July 2017).
[139] On this, see Harrison 2011, 28–37.
[140] Hartog 1980, 24.
[141] See on this topic the TedX Talk by Olaf Kaper, who claims that the army was not lost, but defeated (2015): https://www.youtube.com/watch?v=41TPZWAgPoM&feature=youtu.be (last consulted on 12 July 2017). However, not even this is necessary: we may also group this case together with the many other examples of lost army stories in the *Histories* (e.g. §2.8.9).

who explain it as a literary construct often position themselves in different arenas; but both groups could benefit from each other's expertise.

The third reason for the reluctance among scholars to offer a mnemotopical reading of Herodotus' account, is a demand, both popular and academic, for the topography of the Persian Wars to be a direct and unproblematic reflection of the historical events. This demand has two causes. First, Herodotus is our only source for these events, as various scholars have stressed[142]; this has made it hard to relinquish the idea that the *Histories* are essentially trustworthy. Second, the demand that Herodotus' account of the Persian Wars is accurate may also be rooted in the philhellene paradigm prevalent in western thinking: the Persian Wars offer the prime example of a victory of the West over the East, and they are sometimes (still) believed to have heralded the Golden Age of Athens.[143] For example, in 1896, Ernest Arthur Gardner proclaimed that "It was Marathon, Salamis, and Plataea that first taught the Greek his true superiority over the "barbarian"."[144] In 1915, Colonel Arthur Boucher could remark at the start of his study of the battle of Plataea (with dramatic irony): "La victoire de Platées a sauvé notre civilisation du danger asiatique, comme les événements qui se déroulent actuellement sauveront le monde de la barbarie germanique."[145] Book titles such as *Persia and the Greeks: the Defence of the West, c. 546–478 B.C.* (Burn 1962), *The battle of Salamis: the naval encounter that saved Greece – and western civilization* (Strauss 2004) and *Thermopylae: The Battle that Changed the World* (Cartledge 2006) illustrate how canonical the Persian Wars have become for the history of Greece and the 'West' in general, even to this day.[146]

---

142 E.g. Burn 1962, 5: "[...] 'what really happened' usually appears deceptively clear when we have only one witness [...]". Immerwahr (1966, 6) noted that the "myth of the great struggle between East and West" was accepted by western scholars; Lewis (1985, 101–102): "Historians are not unaware that Herodotus' truthfulness has been challenged from time to time, but on the whole they take no notice. To speak frankly, they have to ignore such criticisms or be put out of business, particularly when dealing with Persian history." Vandiver (1991, 11): "Since Herodotus is our primary historical source for the Persian War, the assertion that artistic choice and design were at work in shaping the *Histories* may at first seem troubling." Lazenby (1993, 13): "In the end it is arguable that there is not much point in discussing the credibility of Herodotos, since, if what he says is not in general true, we might as well stop studying the Persian Wars."
143 See Harrison 2011, 91–108; Samiei 2014, 179–234 for the 'hellenist' perspective by which much of western scholarship has studied Ancient Persia, and on the ways in which scholars have responded to the insight from the end of the eighteenth century onwards that the East vs. West paradigm was problematic.
144 Gardner 1896, 215.
145 Boucher 1915, 17.
146 For further examples of this view see Gehrke 2001, 310–311 (underlining that this way of thinking had repercussions for the shaping of a western collective identity vis-à-vis eastern ones, including the Jewish); Samiei 2014 (e.g. 1–7, noting a more favourable attitude of Western scholars to Iranian culture from the 1850s to the 1930s, coinciding with the development of Indo-European studies and interest

Within this paradigm, it can be hard to accept that our only full source for the Persian Wars, Herodotus, is not (save for some details) trustworthy. It is not the case that today everyone adheres to this view; nevertheless, it underlies even some scholarly accounts of the Persian Wars.[147]

A case in point of the perceived trustworthiness of Herodotus is the scholarly treatment of the Themistocles decree (*SEG* 22.274). This inscription, discovered in the 1950s, challenges Herodotus' narrative about the Persian Wars because it reveals that the plan to evacuate Athens was made before the battles of Artemision and Thermopylae (which were then perhaps only delaying operations), whereas Herodotus portrays the evacuation as a last resort (8.41). It thereby also problematises such famous notions as the 'last stand' of Leonidas at Thermopylae (§2.5.4). After its discovery, the decree sparked a vehement debate. Some scholars pleaded for its usefulness as a supplement to Herodotus' account,[148] while others pointed at various textual anachronisms and argued that the text was a forgery from the fourth century BCE.[149] While today nobody doubts that the extant inscription dates indeed to the fourth century BCE, to qualify it as a 'forgery' neither does justice to the contents,[150] nor to the insight that Herodotus' account may be just as biased as the decree.[151] As scholarship focused on the date of the inscription, an important implication has gone unnoticed: accounts of the wars that significantly differed from Herodotus, even at the macro-level of strategy, were circulating not much later than, and probably before his work.[152] The fate of the

---

in the 'Aryans'). See Harrison 2011, 109–127 for heterogenous views of the Greek-Persian conflict in the modern world.
147 Cf. e.g. Waters 2014, 120: "Despite all the necessary caveats and qualifications […] there is no doubt that Xerxes' invasion of Greece and the Greeks' reaction to it marked a turning point in the history of the western world." For the ways in which the battle of Marathon was respected as a milestone of the victory of the West against oriental barbarians, and therefore of western freedom in general, and criticism of such assertions, see Hölkeskamp 2001, 229–331. See also Flower & Marincola 2002, 20–22 on the impossibility of fully rationalising Herodotus' account, as many historians do.
148 On the potential implications of the inscription, see Jameson 1960 (editio princeps), 203–206; 1961; de Sélincourt 1967, 249–250; Evans 1969; Hammond 1988, 558–563; Green 1996, xvi; 98–103.
149 Habicht 1961; Burn 1962, 364–377; Pritchett 1962; Hignett 1963, 458–468; Bengtson 1965, 58; Georges 1986 (alleging that Herodotus himself was responsible for the 'false' tradition recorded by the decree); Thomas 1989, 84–93 (on the use of such decrees by orators against the background of increased respect for written documents).
150 Green 1996, xvi.
151 On the structuring of the battles in Herodotus' work, see Immerwahr 1966 (254–267; 287–303), who notes the schematic way in which Herodotus subordinates the land battles to the accounts of naval action, their adherences to themes of Persian simultaneous combination of land and sea forces and of their overconfidence, and the parallelism in the descriptions of Thermopylae-Artemision, and Plataea-Mykale.
152 Cf. Georges 1986, who argues that the tradition recorded by the decree can be found in Herodotus' own work (7.139–144 and 8.40–41).

Themistocles decree is shared by 'conflicting' traditions preserved in other sources, such as the work of Ctesias.[153]

This does not mean that other, more critical views of Herodotus' account of the Persian Wars have not appeared among classical scholars, even at an early date. Edward Eastwick noted already in 1864: "Greece put on her poetical spectacles", and "The real fact is, young Europe is whipped and schooled into admiration of Greece, till no one dares give a candid opinion. Otherwise, how can men in their senses affect to believe all that stuff about the invasion of Xerxes?".[154] The studies cited in §1.4.1 also suggest that the historicity of the Persian Wars is often unclear.

More skeptical approaches are also found among Iranologists. They not only stress that Herodotus' account of the Persian Wars is often studied uncritically by classical scholars,[155] but they also offer radically different takes on certain subjects, such as the historical importance of the Greek victory. There is reason to believe that the Persians could not be bothered much by the situation in Greece,[156] and

---

[153] Ctesias has surprisingly different versions of certain anecdotes (as will appear in the individual case studies). It is difficult to explain how these different versions arose, but the mere fact that they existed is significant in itself. That said, Ctesias is often seen as unreliable (cf. Obst 1913, 32–33; Burn 1962, 11–12; Bigwood 1978; Bleckmann 2007). For a recent vindication see Kuhrt 2007, 8, stressing the different (Persian) perspective of Ctesias' material. On the romantic imagery of Xerxes found in Ctesias' work, see Bridges 2015, 128–132. On alternative traditions in Hellenistic sources, see Priestley 2014, 161–162.

[154] Eastwick 1864, 26–28.

[155] E.g. Cuyler Young Jr. 1980, 218: "Herodotus has become part of our western sub-conscious. We are obliged to accept the proposition that the odds against Greece were almost overwhelming when Xerxes marched, even if the figures given for the Persian forces in Herodotus must be wrong, because (thanks to our Greek historical heritage), we believe in the "Great event"." Kuhrt & Sancisi-Weerdenburg (1987, ix-x) attacked previous scholarship of Herodotus by summarising: "if the monuments did not agree with Herodotus, so much the worse for the monuments. The Greeks could not have been too far wrong: they were first of all Greeks, and therefore almost infallible, and secondly, they had been contemporaries and thus had had first hand knowledge." Briant (1996, 532) aptly summarised the account: "[I]l s'agit d'un roman, marqué par toute une série de motifs répétitifs, à partir duquel toute extrapolation historique est d'une imprudence extrême." Meanwhile, the criticism from Iranologists of classical scholars for being too credulous of the Greek sources is no longer valid, cf. Harrison 2011, 29–30.

[156] Macan (1908, II 3–4) already noted that the Persians were probably more interested in the north and east of the empire. Kuhrt (2007, 238–239) points out that while the 'Greek war' is the only event of Xerxes that we can define, Sousa and Persepolis continued to flourish, so the failed invasion of Greece was not all-important. Moreover, Briant (1996, 547–548, 557–559) underlines that demographically, there was no major problem after the wars for the Persians and that the imperial army was largely intact. Wiesehöfer 2004 discusses the ways in which Herodotus' statements about what the Persians thought about the war are usually misrepresented in modern scholarship, claiming that the Persians may not have been concerned with 'world domination' as is usually assumed. Sancisi-Weerdenburg (1980, 11–12) and Cawkwell (2005, 1) ask whether Xerxes could even be bothered to launch a new invasion to Greece. However, Cartledge (2013, 73–74) points out that it is too easy to say that Greece did

that conflicts between 'medising' Greeks of the north and those of the south were aggrandised as, or fitted into, the war between Persia and Greece.[157] It has even been argued that from the Persian perspective, Xerxes' expedition was a success: Xerxes himself claimed in one of his inscriptions from Persepolis (XPh) to have subjected the Yaunā on both sides of the Aegean. Even though the historical value of that inscription is sometimes dismissed,[158] other scholars point out that there actually was some basis for Xerxes' allegation.[159] Nevertheless, even in the field of Iranology, Herodotus' words are sometimes taken at face value and the Iranian perspective, however important, cannot in every instance shed new light on issues within his account.[160]

This great body of both Classical and Iranological scholarship has not always had the impact on historical or material investigations of Herodotus' narrative of the wars that it deserves.[161] Traditionally, criticism of Herodotus' account of the Persian wars

---

not matter to the Persians. After all, Greece was a substantial naval power in the Mediterranean and there was certainly a great strategic reason to attack them.
157 Cartledge 2013, 86; cf. 7.6 for the position of the Thessalian Aleuads.
158 Sancisi-Weerdenburg 1980, 11–12.
159 Mayrhofer (1974, 115) and Briant (1996, 558) suggested that the destruction of buildings on the Athenian Acropolis may have been a symbolic victory for the Persians (cf. 8.55, 8.98, 9.140; and Cataudella 1998 for the view that it was Xerxes' historic aim to punish Greece, and not to add it to his empire), and large parts of Northern Greece (Thrace, Macedonia and possibly Thessaly and Boeotia; cf. 8.115) were still under Xerxes' 'command'. Likewise, Cuyler Young Jr. (1980) noted that to Artaxerxes II, the Greeks had been subjected. Dio Chrysostom (*Orationes* 11.149) preserves a tradition which said that Xerxes had won the war (the author himself did not agree that that was true); on this cf. Dandamaev 1989, 226; Briant 1996, 558–559; Wiesehöfer 2004, 209–210; Kuhrt 2007, 241; Ruberto 2012; Waters 2014, 119, 132. Kuhrt 2007, 240 points out that, whatever happened, the Persians did successfully divide the Greeks. Hammond 1988, 588 underlines that Xerxes still ruled the islands and his fleet was not completely destroyed. Perhaps Mardonios, the Persian leader during the battle of Plataea, may have been left in Greece by Xerxes as a permanent satrap with his base at Thebes (cf. 7.5, where Herodotus' mentions Mardonios' ambition to be ὕπαρχος of all of Greece). On this see Walser 1984, 47–48; Waters 2014, 130. Wiesehöfer (2004, 216–218; 2013, 281–282) believes that it was never Xerxes' intention to rule directly over Greece, and that Mardonios did not aim at becoming a satrap, but rather that the Persians aimed at controlling Greece indirectly.
160 On the limits of the Persian sources and misuse of Greek sources by Iranologists see Harrison 2011, 22–37. See Sancisi-Weerdenburg, 1980 32–34 for an example of the difficulty we encounter in reconciling the Greek material with the Persian material: she advocated that the traditional view of Xerxes as a barbaric despot was based on Greek sources such as Herodotus, and suggested that a more 'tolerant' Xerxes appears in the Persian material; however, she also took various Herodotean anecdotes that suited her 'new' Xerxes as historical truths, such as Xerxes' alleged tolerance of Athenians worshipping Greek gods at the Acropolis (page 7), without explaining why any credence should be given to them (cf. §2.7.4).
161 On this see Wiesehöfer 2004, 209–212. A notable exception is Lendering 2011, 49–52, who criticises modern (popular) treatment of the battle of Thermopylae as grounded in early modern and romantic notions of the Persian Wars as the liberation of the West from Asia.

has not extended much beyond details, with perhaps the single most discussed piece of information being the size of Xerxes' army.[162] Leake's statement that "With the sole exception of the amount of the enemy's land forces, there is no reason to question the statements of Herodotus, who in his narrative of the Persian invasion has left us one of the most cautious and accurate narratives that ever was written, not even excepting those of Thucydides and Polybius"[163] is still not sufficiently questioned. A factor underlying this notion is the sheer size of the *Histories*, which allows for selective mining of examples that confirm one's viewpoint. In the scholarly literature there appear really two different 'Herodoti': a fantastical Herodotus distilled mainly and *grosso modo* from books 1–5 (the ethnographical logoi), and a more trustworthy Herodotus in books 6–9 (the account of the Persian Wars).[164] Recent scholarship demonstrates that the first Herodotus, who was always looked upon with skepticism, has actually recorded more reliable information than originally thought, or at least some information that was grounded in reality.[165] By contrast, it is usually assumed that the record about the Persian Wars written by the second Herodotus is basically correct, and that it should only be amended when there is no other option.[166]

---

[162] Clearly, Herodotus' number of more than five million people in the army is incredible: it has been pointed out that this would require the army column to be stretched out over more than 2000 km (Cuyler Young Jr. 1980, 217, note 8). Estimates can be found in most monographs on the Persian Wars; for recent (but too high) estimates, see Hammond 1988, 523–534, Ray 2009, 70; see Cuyler Young Jr. 1980, 221–229 for convincing calculations of the original force, and pages 230–232 for Mardonios' forces at Plataea; scholars of the Achaemenid Empire give much lower numbers (e.g. 60,000: Briant 1996, 543–544; Kuhrt 2007, 240). For the idea that it is unlikely that there were so many foreign contingents in the Persian armada as Herodotus suggests, see Macan 1908, II 181–182; Wallinga 2005, 13; 40–41. See also Hignett 1963, 348–351 for more reasons to doubt Herodotus' numbers. Elsewhere, such as at Mykale, Herodotus also has inflated figures (cf. Burn 1962, 549; Müller 1997, 631; Cawkwell 2005, 100). On Xerxes' enormous army as a commonplace, see Bridges 2015, 52–54.
[163] Leake 1835, II 50–51.
[164] Cf. Luraghi 2013, 88–97, who points out that early scholarship on oral traditions in Herodotus assumed that these had no bearing towards Herodotus' account of the Persian Wars. The dichotomy is very striking in Aly (1969, first edition 1921), who, despite setting out to identify folkloric elements in Herodotus' work, proclaims, at the point of his commentary in which Xerxes' march starts (page 180): "Was nun folgt, ist Historie." He limits his commentary of the invasion to a limited number of anecdotes. See also Waters 1985, who upheld the idea that the Egyptian logos is unreliable (page 79), while Herodotus' treatment of the Persian Wars, in spite of having its shortcomings, is a reflection of mostly reliable individuals and therefore essentially accurate (pages 80–81; 163–164; 173–174). Regarding the speeches in this material he argued that they were not entirely fictional, being uttered "only fifty years at most before Herodotus wrote" (pages 65–66).
[165] Overviews of examples where archaeology has confirmed such accounts; Pritchett 1982, 234–285; 1993; cf. Momigliano 1966, 128–129.
[166] Pritchett (1993, 290) even uses the 'infallibility' of the second Herodotus as an argument to discredit those who criticise the first Herodotus: "In the light of Fehling's final judgment about the *History* as a sort of fictive Epic [...] one might expect a consistent display of alleged fiction in the record of the Persian Wars. One does not change horses in mid-stream. Indeed, until the study of structuralist

Two arguments underlie this assumption. First, it is generally believed, and sometimes explicitly stated, that Herodotus had to please an audience that could verify his claims about the Persian Wars, as veterans of the wars were still alive; ergo his narrative must be correct.[167] However, there are various reasons to be skeptical about this. First, it is unclear who formed part of Herodotus' (projected) audience. It has been taken as Panhellenic,[168] or as a learned community[169]; but Herodotus himself explicitly states at the beginning of his work that it is his intention to record something that would survive into later ages. Thus, even though contemporary criticism of Herodotus' work was possible, that does not necessarily mean that he was taking account of it. The argument also presumes that this audience would primarily be interested in hearing a purely historical account of what happened, whereas there may have existed a greater demand for mythical parallels, or simply for a 'good story'.[170] In addition, at the time when Herodotus wrote his work (approximately 430 BCE), the number of 'veterans' had probably dwindled to very low numbers. Even if we accept that Herodotus had access to survivors of the wars (some of whom Herodotus may indeed have known, see 8.65 and 9.16), it is unclear what could have been expected of them, because, as we have seen in §1.3.6, human memory is often factually incorrect.

The second 'staple' argument for trust in the historical value of Herodotus' account of the Persian Wars is the idea that Herodotus had access to Persian sources. This may be argued on the basis of the introduction to the *Histories* (1.1), and by the fact that Herodotus is surprisingly knowledgable about Persian history, parts of which

---

techniques became a predominant force in our discipline in recent years, the main thrust of Herodotean scholarship was concentrated on Books 5.25–9."

167 This idea is found or is implicit in nearly all studies of the Persian Wars; it is most elaborately expounded in Pritchett 1993, 328–332; see also Aly 1969 (first edition 1921), 180; Hammond 1956, 39; Burn 1962, 5: "what he heard was what young soldiers had believed about the high command thirty or forty years before, exacerbated in the light of subsequent quarrels between the former allies." The view is more recently found in van Wees 2004, 182.

168 Jacoby 1913, 409–210 suggested that the 'local' character of many passages seems to indicate Herodotus was the first to put them in a Panhellenic context. Redfield 1985, 102 maintained that the *Histories* are a work written for Greeks by a Greek, because it contains much reflection on what it means to be Greek. Shrimpton 1997, 27; 96 poins out that by adopting a Panhellenic guise, Herodotus was free of attack and something of a mediator between rivalling states; also, apparently, he only takes a controversial stance when discussing non-Greek lands (page 176). Friedman 2006, 175–176 argues that Herodotus tried to recreate the Greek 'homeland' at the time of the Peloponnesian War. Stadter 2006, 253–254 argues that Herodotus had the (possibly anachronistic) view that Greece could only stand to foreign invasions when Athens and Sparta were not fighting; also cf. 8.144. But note that Herodotus' attitude to the Greeks was attacked by Plutarch in *De Herodoti malignitate*.

169 For the idea that Herodotus was connected with the literature of his time and different kinds of (scientific) debates, in which Herodotus sometimes takes a firm stance see Flory 1987, 16; Evans 1991, 100–101; Thomas 2000. See Fowler 2006 and 2013 for Herodotus' complex relation to his predecessors and contemporaries.

170 Vandiver 1991, 12–13.

are 'confirmed' by the Behistun inscription, as well as of Persian military commands and routes.[171] In addition, information exchange between Greece and Persia in the classical period can be presumed on the basis of the ample evidence for cultural interaction between the areas in this period.[172] It has even been suggested that Herodotus' work shows traces of Near Eastern thought patterns.[173] However, the extent of Herodotus' access to Persian sources remains unclear. It is certain that any contact between Herodotus and monolingual Persians must have been indirect, because it is unlikely that he knew the Persian language.[174] One could presume that he interviewed Persians who spoke Greek, or made use of interpreters; and we know that Herodotus had access to the works of earlier writers who had written about Persia.[175] Nevertheless, we may ask ourselves what could have been expected from these Persian sources.[176] The information offered by them was not inherently more reliable than that of Greek sources.[177] Moreover, it has been pointed out that Herodotus regarded Persian memory as suspicious, and often offers conflicting alternatives to their stories.[178]

For those who are conscious of the dangers of this sea of uncertainty there has always been one island of refuge, embedded in Herodotus' account itself: the topographical layer. This data has widely been seen as the most trustworthy information in the narrative: the many scholars who question the historicity of parts of Herodotus' account, generally accept the topography.[179] The 'realness' of the topography is

---

171 On the identification of Herodotus' Persians, see Vignolo Munson 2009; on the function of Persian history in the *Histories*, see Pohlenz 1961, 21–24. On his knowledge of the purforoi see Wallinga 2005, 82–84; on his knowledge of Persian military routes, see Obst 1913, 58; Casson 1926, 263; Meyer 1954, 228; Pohlenz 1961, 130–131; Burn 1962, 339; Kienast 1996, 300–301. For the view that Herodotus instead used Greek sources, see Obst 1913, 76; Kienast 1996, 300, note 55.
172 Cf. Miller 1999, especially 3–28; Llewellyn-Jones 2012 (on the ample evidence for Greek engagement with the Persians in the fourth century BCE).
173 Haubold 2013, 98–126.
174 On Herodotus' knowledge of the Persian language (or rather the lack thereof), see Sancisi-Weerdenburg 1994a, 209–210; Brock 2003, 11. The best example is 1.139, where Herodotus claims to have found a major discovery about the Persian language: all their names would end in -s.
175 E.g. Charon of Lampsacus, Dionysius of Miletus and Hellanicus of Lesbos. On this issue, see Lewis 1985, 102–106.
176 On these issues, see Waters 1985, 77–78, 85; de Jong 1997, 78–83 (stressing that Herodotus may have had contact with Greeks working in the Persian Empire, or with Persians living there); Wiesehöfer 2004, 210–211.
177 Harrison 2011, 20–21.
178 Luraghi 2001, 155–156.
179 Hignett (1963, vi) explicitly stated that his "[...] main concern has been to establish, as far as it is possible to do so, what actually happened in 480 and 479 B.C. [...]." Macan 1908, II 349: "[t]he explicit, and still more the implicit, topography of the ancient historians is, as a rule, the most certain and reliable element in their works." Hammond 1956, 33–34 expresses this idea very clearly, among other things calling the descriptions of ancient authors of the Salamis area as "factual, unambiguous, and dependable". Pritchett 1993, 294: "Whereas Homer and archaeology part company, the reverse is the

sometimes even considered diagnostic for the trustworthiness of the rest of the narrative (Boucher uses the word "pierre de touche").[180] Exemplary for this approach is the essay *On the Possibility of Reconstructing Marathon and other Ancient Battles* by N. Whatley.[181] Although this was, as far as I know, the first paper to explicitly point out that the exact events of ancient battles are retrievable only to a very limited degree, Whatley concludes that the topography may be used as a means of distilling authentic from inauthentic details of ancient battles.[182] Similarly, Pritchett has argued that the topography of a site should be investigated before the events; doing it the other way round would result in making the facts fit the evidence: "A first-rate historian who knew the countryside of his day should be regarded as right until he is proved wrong."[183] And because Herodotus' topography in Greece is relatively detailed and usually well 'mappable', his account of the Persian Wars as a whole is often largely accepted.

It is certainly not the case that modern scholars unanimously take Herodotus' topography for granted, but doubts are seldom made explicit. There are some exceptions. Philip Sabin points out that the topographical indications preserved in ancient authors are so difficult and conflicting that they have given rise to lengthy discussions and even heated debates about their exact locations, "without casting anything like commensurate light on the battle itself."[184] Moreover, he points out that one first has to establish that the event really took place at the site.[185] As Karen Bassi rightfully states: "the equation of material existence with historical reality [...] exemplifies the appeal of 'looking through' the historical text at the expense of 'looking at' it."[186]

This book will continue these lines of thought and show that the perspective of mnemotopes accommodates a critical stance of Herodotus' presentation of the topography in his account of the Persian invasion of Greece.

---

case with Herodotus." Also cf. Marinatos 1951, 18; Flory 1987, 17; in addition, popular or semi-popular accounts of the war such as Lazenby 1993, Balcer 1995, 225–298 and Holland 2005 still accept Herodotus as an unproblematic source for historical topography.
180 Boucher 1915, 258–259. Further cf. Munro 1902, 325: "[...] the broad features of the topography are sufficient to check our literary authorities, and if they have not always had due weight in the estimation of the evidence, it has been rather from deficiency of imagination in the historian than from ignorance of the facts." Pritchett 1993, 291: "we could confirm the record (7.188) of the shipwreck of Xerxes' fleet at the Ipnoi ("Ovens") by offering identifications of the three topographical checkpoints [...]."
181 Whatley 1964.
182 Whatley 1964, 123–124.
183 Pritchett 1965, 136. A similar idea is found in Aly 1969 (first edition 1921), 180, who believed that a visit to a battle site allowed Herodotus to 'fit in' the stories which he had heard.
184 Sabin 2007, 6–7.
185 Tuplin (2003, 407) remarks that "The fact that [a] statement could, topographically speaking, be true does not, of course, mean that it *is* true", suggesting that topographical parameters hardly shed any light on the accuracy of *Herodotus'* statements (*in casu* the division of Persian forces in Thrace).
186 Bassi 2014, 185.

1.4.4 Summary

The concept of *mnemotope* is not just relevant for religious sites and writings, it is also applicable to historical writings. Herodotus' *Histories* are an especially fruitful case study, as they were written approximately fifty years after the purported events and were based mostly on locally sourced information. Moreover, there are constant reminders in this work that Herodotus (and many of his characters) travelled himself, with accounts of topography functioning as proof for his anecdotes. In addition, the *Histories* contain many mnemotopes where famous rulers were remembered, ranging from infrastructural projects to natural landmarks. At the same time, we know that the information about these kings which reached Herodotus was already distorted. The Karabel A and Croesus inscriptions show that material culture could give rise to fantastical stories. Given this background, we may expect that stories about Xerxes originated in a similar way. The analysis of mnemotopes of Xerxes' invasion is a new undertaking. It questions the circumstance that Herodotus' topography has usually been taken for granted, interpreted as the most reliable information of the account, and even used as a confirmation of the events.

We thus embark on our tour around the Aegean Sea, in search of the mnemotopes that, this book argues, form the backbone of Herodotus' topography of Xerxes' invasion. We will start as far east as the topography allows us to go: in inner Anatolia.

2 Topographical Case Studies

Map 2: Anatolia.

2.1 The march through Anatolia

Two and a half millennia ago, troops from all corners of the world were seen moving on the roads of the Anatolian steppes.[1] The largest army ever created assembled at the Cappadocian town of Tiralla in the shadow of the Taurus mountains (7.26).[2]

---

[1] A selection of places discussed in this chapter features on Map 2.
[2] For the identification of Herodotus' Kritalla as the town of Tiralla at modern Başmakçı, see van Rookhuijzen 2017d, where I argue that ἐκ Κριτάλλων in Herodotus' text may be read as ἐκ Τιράλλων. Tiralla may have been the precursor to Faustinopolis, which we know was located near modern Başmakçı on the Cappadocian side of the Cilician gates.

From here, it proceeded west along the royal highway to Sardis.³ Its sole aim was the conquest of Greece. Its lord was Xerxes, "king of countries containing many kinds of men, king in this great earth far and wide",⁴ and soon to be king of Greece, at least for some time.

Or so wrote Herodotus in book seven of the *Histories* half a century later. This account has often been taken as purely historical. But we may also think of it as reflecting the folklore that had arisen in Anatolia and Greece as a response to the campaign. This especially concerns its topography. The king and his army would have visited the Halys river, Kelainai, the Maeander valley, Kallatebos and Sardis.⁵ It has been argued that Herodotus mentions these stations, and not others, because he was able to recount specific trivia about them that had little to do with the invasion per se.⁶ However, as we will see, there are different reasons why these places were connected to the passing of the army.⁷ Some of them may hence be explained as mnemotopes.

2.1.1 The Halys river

The first site reached by Xerxes' army after its departure from Tiralla was the Halys river on the border (apparently) between Cappadocia and Phrygia (7.26):

> οἱ δὲ ἐπείτε διαβάντες τὸν Ἅλυν ποταμὸν ὡμίλησαν τῇ Φρυγίῃ [...]
> And when they had crossed the river Halys they entered Phrygia [...]

The Halys river is commonly identified with the modern Kızılırmak, Turkey's biggest river. But this raises an interesting problem: if Xerxes did, in fact, visit such places as Kelainai in southern Phrygia (§2.1.2), crossing the Halys would be a long and

---

3 While Herodotus never explicitly says that Xerxes took this road, there is no reason to doubt that Xerxes did. Herodotus presents the road as the only route from Sardis to Iran (in Herodotus' conception of the world, there was nothing directly east of Cappadocia but Cilicia, cf. 5.49 and 5.52), and as a prestigious infrastructural project for the Persian kings: he calls the road ἡ βασιληίη ὁδός, mentions βασιλήιοι σταθμοί 'royal stations' (5.52–53) and says that there was a royal courier service along it (8.98). If my identification of Xerxes' mustering point at Kritalla as the city of Tiralla is correct (van Rookhuijzen 2017d), this provides further evidence that Xerxes took the road. The equation of the routes is also asserted by French 1998, 15.
4 Xerxes' own words in an inscription from Persepolis (XPh).
5 The army's subsequent visit to the Troad and the Hellespont is the subject of §2.2, and the battle of Mykale is discussed in §2.10.
6 Aly 1969 (first edition 1921), 170.
7 While the problem of the historicity of these anecdotes is another question, they were already classified as "not history" by Grundy 1901, 217; Waters 1985, 85 described the Anatolian stories as marvels. On the practice of sightseeing of Persian relics (mostly graves) in Anatolia in antiquity, see Zwingmann 2012, 304–305.

unnecessary detour.⁸ Some scholars have remedied this by suggesting that the army took a northern route through Anatolia, and crossed the Kızılırmak before turning south towards Kelainai.⁹ However, other scholars have suggested that the Halys was never visited as the army took the shorter, southern route through the Cilician gates (and thus followed the Royal Road).¹⁰ Did Herodotus, perhaps, make a mistake? While Herodotus was probably born in Anatolia,¹¹ he seemingly never penetrated into the peninsula, as his indications of distances are often incorrect.¹² Herodotus' conception of the Halys was also flawed (cf. 1.72, where the Halys is said to run through regions which are hundreds of kilometres away, such as Cilicia).

This widens the scope for viewing the river as a mnemotope. Herodotus' discussion (1.75) of the existence of ship bridges across the Halys or the construction of a canal by Thales of Miletus here (as most Greeks believed) demonstrates that the Halys was a topic in fifth-century BCE intellectual circles.¹³ The main point of the Halys was that it was an important frontier: it is presented as the eastern border of Phrygia, part of the Lydian empire (1.6; 1.28; 5.52) and the western border of Cappadocia, ruled by

---

8 Müller (1994, 37–38), taking this zigzagging as historical, attributed it to Xerxes' personal desire to visit these places.
9 One argument for a northern route is Herodotus' mention of the city of Pteria. This city has been identified with Hattuša (e.g. Calder 1925, 9) or Kerkenes, although there are no compelling arguments for those identifications. Müller (1994, 38) suggests that Xerxes visited Pteria because Cyrus had defeated the Lydians here; but this is speculation.
10 Macan 1908, I 40; Ramsay 1920, 89–90; Munro 1926a, 268. See Calder 1925 and French 1998 for calculations of the length of the southern route, which is surprisingly similar to Herodotus' remarks (5.52–54), if it is admitted that Herodotus was wrong about the Halys river. The Royal Road (5.52–54) connected the imperial capital of Sousa to Sardis via 111 caravanserais. Herodotus does not say that Xerxes took the Royal Road or deviated from it, but French 1998, 15 is explicit about the equation of these routes. The Royal Road cannot be established with certainty. Herodotus' topographical indications of its course are so vague that reconstructions are mostly based on the geographical limitations posed by the terrain of modern Turkey. It seems that Herodotus did not know the Royal Road, or the area in general, very well: while he was apparently able to calculate the total distance of this route, it is nearly excluded that Herodotus had travelled the entire road himself. His limited knowledge of the area presupposes an itinerary as a source, although it is debated whether this was of Persian or local Greek origin; for a Persian perspective, see How & Wells 1912, I 27; Macan 1908, II 127 suggested that the Greeks themselves may have possessed such information.
11 It is usually assumed that Herodotus was a native of Halicarnassus, a Greek city with a Carian hinterland; based on the names of his father and uncle, some have asserted that Herodotus himself was from a mixed Carian-Greek family (Stadter 2006, 242). Based on Herodotus' particular interest in Samos, it is sometimes claimed that he spent some time there (cf. How & Wells 1912, I 3; Tölle-Kastenbein 1976, 9–12). Thomas (2000, 11) points out that a particular passage (8.132) sounds as if Herodotus reproaches Greeks from the mainland for their disinterest in or ignorance about the Greek cities of Anatolia. Being not from the Greek mainland, Herodotus has been described as an 'outside observer' of events there (Stadter 2006, 242–243).
12 See Jacoby 1913, 268; Myres 1953, 6; Müller 1994, 17–18.
13 Flory 1987, 55 suggests that this canal never existed.

the Medes and the Persians (1.72; 5.52). As such, the Greeks saw the crossing of Halys as a symbolic act. When Croesus did so in order to confront Cyrus (1.75), he brought about the fall of his own empire, as an oracle had predicted (1.53). It also seems relevant that we are told in Aeschylus' *Persae* (866) that Darius did not cross the river. It is therefore significant that Xerxes does cross the Halys, and it has been suggested that this act underlines the transgressive character of his expedition.[14] Even though the symbolic value of the river could, perhaps, have been a reason for a historical detour, it is equally possible that Xerxes never crossed the Halys at all.

2.1.2 The waterfall and cave at Kelainai

The next place visited by the army was the city of Kelainai (7.26):

> [...] δι' αὐτῆς πορευόμενοι παρεγένοντο ἐς Κελαινάς, ἵνα πηγαὶ ἀναδιδοῦσι Μαιάνδρου ποταμοῦ καὶ ἑτέρου οὐκ ἐλάσσονος ἢ Μαιάνδρου, τῷ οὔνομα τυγχάνει ἐὸν Καταρρήκτης, ὃς ἐξ αὐτῆς τῆς ἀγορῆς τῆς Κελαινέων ἀνατέλλων ἐς τὸν Μαίανδρον ἐκδιδοῖ· ἐν τῇ καὶ ὁ τοῦ Σιληνοῦ Μαρσύεω ἀσκὸς ἀνακρέμαται, τὸν Φρυγῶν λόγος ἔχει ὑπὸ Ἀπόλλωνος ἐκδαρέντα ἀνακρεμασθῆναι.

> Continuing their march [through Phrygia] they arrived at Kelainai, where the sources come to the surface of the Maeander river and of another one (which is not smaller than the Maeander), whose name happens to be Katarrektes. This river, rising from the marketplace of Kelainai itself, pours out into the Maeander. There also hangs the skin of the Silen Marsyas, which, according to a story of the Phrygians, was flayed and hung up by Apollo.

Remains of Kelainai, later known as Apameia, are located on the İçlerca or Üçlerce hill to the north of the modern city of Dinar.[15] It was one of the main cities of Phrygia during the Achaemenid period.[16] The idea that Kelainai was a muster point for Anatolian forces recruited by Xerxes finds comfort in the importance of the city in the fifth century BCE and in the appearance of Achaemenid material culture in the area, of which the most significant example is the fifth-century BCE tomb of Tatarlı, now in

---

14 Baragwanath (2008, 271) points out that the passing of the Halys is part of a chain of Xerxes' transgressions. For the topos of eastern kings crossing rivers, see recently e.g. Bridges 2015, 58. See also Calder 1925, 9: "If Xerxes crossed the Halys, as Herodotus states, he must have crossed it on the footsteps of Cyrus the Great; there was no other way." For the crossing of rivers in the Near East as a symbolic act, see Desnier 1995.
15 E.g. Pococke 1745, II.2 79–81; Leake 1824, 146–163; Macan 1908, I 40; Müller 1994, 31; Müller 1997, 129–131; Tuplin 2011, 82 (offering this location as an alternative for the ridge from which the Dinar Suyu springs).
16 See Summerer 2011, 35–36 for the archaeological evidence, which is reported to include Achaemenid pottery, arrowheads and coins. For archaeological material of the pre-Achaemenid period in Kelainai, see Nunn 2011; Summerer 2011, 35. On the role of Kelainai in Xenophon's work, and a description of the topography as described by him, see Tuplin 2011.

the Archaeological Museum of Istanbul.[17] Its wood furnishings feature painted depictions of the triumph of the Persian king over Scythian-looking people, and a military procession that is reminiscent of Herodotus' descriptions of Xerxes' convoy (7.40-41). The tomb seems to continue a local Anatolian (Lydian or Phrygian) tradition, but the iconography shows Persian influences.[18] In addition, we are told that Xerxes had retreated to Kelainai after the battle of Salamis and built the acropolis of the city and a palace at its foot, at the sources of the Katarrektes-Marsyas (Xenophon, *Anabasis* 1.2.7). Several locations for this palace have been suggested.[19] Nevertheless, it has never been found and the association with Xerxes may have existed only in touristic lore of Kelainai.[20]

While the identification of the rivers in this area is not easy,[21] the Katarrektes ('Waterfall'), which Xenophon and other writers knew as the Marsyas (1.2.7-8), is probably the Dinar Suyu in the Suçıkan Parkı at the northeast of the town, where a waterfall still issues from the rockface. This area is not far from the presumed ancient agora.[22]

---

[17] Summerer 2011, 34–35. For an overview of the city's prominence as a meeting point from the Achaemenid to the Roman period, see Zwingmann 2011, 94–95; as such it was used by Cyrus the Younger (Xenophon, *Anabasis* 1.2.9) and Eumenes during the War of the Diadochs (Plutarch, *Eumenes* 8.5).

[18] For an overview of the tomb and assessment of its iconography, see Summerer 2007; 2008; 2011, 36–52. Summerer explains the procession as funerary, albeit with military elements. Draycott 2011 argues more strongly in favour of a military and Achaemenid interpretation of the paintings, calling them "virtually an illustration of Herodotus' description of Xerxes' war train as it departed Sardis on way to Greece" (57). She further places the painting within a context of competition of local western Anatolian elites that was relevant during the military presence of the Achaemenids in this area.

[19] For a discussion of the possibilities, see Tuplin 2011, 85–86. Xenophon also reports a paradeisos of Cyrus here, as well as a palace built on the sources of the Maeander river. For a discussion of its location with extensive bibliography see Tuplin 2011, 78. That Kelainai had a strong Persian association for a Greek audience is shown by its appearance in Timotheus' *Persae* (141) with reference to the battle of Salamis (Tuplin 2011, 73).

[20] This is suggested by Zwingmann 2011, 95. Tuplin (2011, 86–87) after discussing potential reasons why Xerxes may have been interested in building a palace here, concludes: "the very fact that Xerxes was associated with Celaenae for other reasons could have prompted fanciful invention. A place that boasted possession of the skin of Marsyas was plainly not constrained by the requirements of mundane truth."

[21] The ancient references to the rivers are many. See Müller 1997, 134–143; Sementchenko 2011, who identifies two additional traditions about the river landscape: according to the first, the Marsyas was confused with the Maeander; according to the second, both the Marsyas and the Maeander had sprung from a lake called Aulokrene.

[22] On the hydrology see Hogarth 1888; Macan 1908, I 40; Müller 1997, 139–142; Thonemann 2011, 70–71; Tuplin 2011, 79–81, discussing several problems, such as the circumstance that the hydrology of the area may have changed in modern times, making it unclear whether there was a waterfall here and that a full-fledged agora here is difficult to imagine.

44 — 2 Topographical Case Studies

Fig. 2: Suçikan Parkı, Dinar, the source of Herodotus' Katarrektes.

It is not immediately clear why Herodotus mentions this tourist attraction. Perhaps he did so as a consequence of his digressive style and love for marvels. After all, the Marsyas myth was popular in fifth-century BCE Greece,[23] and was Kelainai's main claim to fame. In addition to the strong connection of the myth to the city observed in literature,[24] the myth is depicted on local coins, and appears prominently on the proskenion of the theatre of Hierapolis, another city in Phrygia.[25] As Herodotus

---

23 Tuplin 2011, 73; Zwingmann 2011, 96.
24 Strabo (12.8.15) also placed the story of Olympos and Marsyas at Kelainai. According to Pliny the Elder (*Naturalis Historia* 16.89), there was a plane tree at Aulotrene from where Marsyas was hung (cf. Nollé 2006, 81–82 for a coin depicting the tree). The myth is also referred to by Pseudo-Apollodorus (1.4.2) and Diodorus Siculus (3.58.3), but without mentioning Kelainai. Also cf. Statius, *Thebais* 4.186; Ovid, *Metamorphoses* 6.392–400; Pausanias 10.30.9.
25 On the coins see Nollé 2006, 79–82; Zwingmann 2011, 97; on the proskenion see Thonemann 2011, 63–67 (showing that in the Hierapolis scene Aulutrene was ignored, so that Hierapolis could claim that the myth took place there); Zwingmann 2011, 96. Having physical evidence for the Marsyas myth was important, because Kelainai was not the only city that claimed ownership of it For a discussion of the competition, with rich literature, see Zwingmann 2011, 107. Kelainos, Lityersis, Cybele and Midas all had cults in the city. Nunn (2011, 28) connects the cultic significance of Kelainai to the Hittite

himself says, the myth had its main mnemotope at the Katarrektes waterfall. In this area the crucial relic, the skin of Marsyas himself, was shown. The sources speak of a cave; it has been suggested that this amounted to a large cave around the Katarrektes waterfall, which is believed to have collapsed already in Antiquity during an earthquake. A remnant of the cave can still be seen behind the waterfall, but is currently inaccessible after various earthquakes and redevelopment.[26] The same landmark was probably the κιβωτός or 'chest' that was the origin for Kelainai's later name 'Apameia at the Kibotos',[27] and became a mnemotope for various other stories of local mythology, as becomes clear from the literary evidence and coins. This was probably the place where the city founder Kelainos had made the river appear, and it was also known as the 'Spring of Midas' because that king had created it by stamping on the ground. The water was initially golden, and Midas had to pray to Dionysos to make it potable (Pseudo-Plutarch, *De fluviis* 10).[28] It has also been suggested that this was the location of the story according to which Zeus Kelaineus had slept with the mother goddess of the city and later, according to some sources, where Noah's ark landed (by folk etymology, because κιβωτός is the word for 'ark' in the Greek translation of the Old Testament).[29]

---

and Phrygian periods, and explains the mythical associations of the city as the result of its rich water sources.

26 Xenophon, *Anabasis* 1.2.8–9; Philostratos, *Icones* 1.20. For ideas about the remains of the cave with many ancient references to earthquakes in Kelainai, see Nollé 2006, 83–84. On the role of the Marsyas myth as part of the local memory landscape, see Zwingmann 2011, 96–98; Zwingmann 2014. Another site associated with Marsyas was the Aulutrene lake (changed by folk etymology into Aulokrene, 'Flute Fountain'), which had allegedly furnished the reeds for Marsyas' flute. Aulotrene (Strabo 12.8.15) is to be identified with a reedy lake (Karakuyu Gölü), 15 km east of Dinar near Eldere (beyond the Sultan Dağ mountain), and the water goes towards the Dinar Suyu. Tuplin 2011, 78; Zwingmann 2011, 98 (mentioning inscriptional evidence). On the folk etymology, see Zgusta 1984, 109–111; Zwingmann 2011, 98. We may even suppose that the city's insistence on the myth was directly relevant for its income: the Aulokrene lake was full of reeds from which flutes like the one which Marsyas was believed to have played could be made and sold. Marsyas was also said to have appeared as a divine force stopping a Celtic invasion of the city (Ovid, *Metamorphoses* 6.382–400; Pausanias 10.30.9).
27 See Nollé 2006, 82–84 for numismatic and literary attestations of this name.
28 Similarly, Claudian (*In Eutropium* 2.257–263) mentions that the rivers at Kelainai carried gold particles because Midas bathed in them. The spring of Midas was alternatively sighted at Thymbrion (Xenophon, *Anabasis* 1.2.13). According to a story in Pseudo-Plutarch (*De fluviis* 10.1), the earth had opened in Kelainai; Midas threw in his gold and silver to close the gap, to no avail. Then his son Anchuros realised that human life was more precious than material wealth and rode with his wife and his father Midas into the gap. Note that there are obvious similarities between the myths of Midas and the Silen and that of Apollo and Marsyas (who was a Silen himself).
29 For the hero Kelainos see Nollé 2006, 84–89. For the traditions about Midas and his sons at Kelainai see Nollé 2006, 100–103. For Zeus Kelaineus, see Nollé 2006, 69–75. For Kelainai as the location of the Ararat see Nollé 2006, 89–95; Zwingmann 2011, 99–108.

Fig. 3: The cave behind the waterfall at Kelainai (Dinar).

Even though the mention of the Marsyas myth in Herodotus' brief account is detached from the army's passing, we may wonder whether the waterfall-kibotos area had also developed into a mnemotope for the visit of Xerxes. The observations that the mnemotope was a storehouse for local memories about Midas, a mad king, lends credence to the idea that the passing of Xerxes and his army was recorded here in local folklore, too.

That the traditions about Xerxes at Kelainai were not all purely historical is suggested by the story of Pythios. This local man was severely punished by the Persian king in Sardis, where his son was executed (7.38), in spite of his earlier generous hospitality in Kelainai (7.27–7.30). The story of Pythios, who had also given a golden plane tree and a golden vine to Darius, is almost identical to that of Oiobazos (4.84);[30] and it has been identified by Aly as a folktale that is not only found in the story of khalif Al-Hakim and the merchant in *Arabian Nights*, but also echoes the lore about the tragic king Midas, who was not coincidentally king of Phrygia.[31] The story of

---

30 Cf. Bischoff 1932, 61.
31 Aly 1969 (first edition 1921), 171–175.

Pythios and Xerxes is also told in Plutarch (*Mulierum virtutes* 27). Plutarch additionally details that the man had an insatiable hunger for gold to the detriment of his subjects; Pythios only realised his mistakes when his wife made him suffer hunger by only giving him golden food, a theme reminiscent of the Midas saga. In addition, as the name Pythios is an epithet of Apollo, there could, perhaps, be a link between this story and the Marsyas myth, because Apollo had flayed Marsyas after his challenge;[32] but the story lines are too different to truly make the case. The name used by Plutarch is not Pythios, but Pythes, which according to Aly shows that Plutarch did not make use of Herodotus, and that both authors relied independently on folkloric traditions. Aly's observations indicate that Xerxes' visit somehow got interwoven with a local myth.

The recurring theme in the Marsyas, Midas and Pythios stories is hubris. Xerxes, the megalomaniac king from the east, could easily be associated with these stories because the theme was also applicable to him, as appears from so many other stories about him in Herodotus.[33] We will see in §2.1.4 that the same process is probably also responsible for the story about Xerxes and the plane tree (!) of Kallatebos. Here in Kelainai, the theme of hubris may perhaps also be accentuated by locals toponyms: it has been suggested that the name of the city Kelainai marked Xerxes' visit as ill-omened, because the word κελαινός means 'black, dark', and it is often used to describe terms connected to the netherworld.[34]

---

[32] Macan (1908, II 132) interpreted the Pythios story as one of the "humours of the voyage", exemplifying Xerxes' ruthlessness; Hauvette 1894, 301–303 was undecided about the historicity; similarly Sancisi-Weerdenburg (1980, 159–161) saw the story as a 'potlatch' anecdote, but left open the possibility that it was historically authentic. Baragnawath (2008, 269–280) advocated a connection between Pythios and Apollo; but also cf. Tuplin 2011, 88 note 94: "Pythius' name evokes Apollo who was also the killer of Marsyas. But I hesitate to think we should think anything of that." In this context, it is important that Apollo himself was responsible for the failure of the Persian invasion of Delphi (§2.6.3). On the links of the golden presents to Near Eastern iconography, see Briant 1996, 248–249.

[33] Bowie (2012, 274–275) suggests that Herodotus' reference to the Marsyas myth underlines Xerxes' hubris, possibly because this myth gave a mythical precedent of hubris against the gods. In his interpretation, the complex hydrology of Kelainai would provide a further parallel to the transgressive character of Xerxes' expedition. A different view is found in Tuplin 2011, 87–89, who believes that the case is stronger for such a reading of Xenophon, but also problematises the degree to which Marsyas was already regarded a hubristic sinner in fifth-century BCE Athens. However, I am inclined to believe that the hubris element was always a feature of the fairy-tale, or at least could be understood as such by some recipients of Herodotus and/or Xenophon.

[34] Tuplin 2011, 89: "for those of imaginative turn of mind, the sense that Celaenae was an ill-omened starting point can stand". For examples of the meaning of κελαινός see *LSJ* s.v. The meaning of the word is an argument for the hypothesis that Kelainai was (directly or indirectly) related to a Hittite settlement Kuwaliya, which means 'dark, blue': Zgusta 1984, 244; Nunn 2011, 20; 28; Thonemann 2011, 67–68. For the general idea that places in Herodotus' work may prompt symbolism, see Rood 2012, 125–126.

Similarly, the name Katarrektes may have been regarded in folk etymology as meaning 'army dissolver'.[35] As in other stances (§2.1.3 and §2.3.2), these tantalising points of hubris are only be read between the lines of Herodotus' brief account, and therefore remain speculative.

2.1.3 Croesus' stele at Kydrara

In 7.30 we are told that Xerxes sets out from Kelainai to the borders of Lydia:

ταῦτα δὲ εἴπας καὶ ἐπιτελέα ποιήσας ἐπορεύετο τὸ πρόσω αἰεί. Ἄναυα δὲ καλεομένην Φρυγῶν πόλιν παραμειβόμενος καὶ λίμνην ἐκ τῆς ἅλες γίνονται, ἀπίκετο ἐς Κολοσσὰς πόλιν μεγάλην Φρυγίης: ἐν τῇ Λύκος ποταμὸς ἐς χάσμα γῆς ἐσβάλλων ἀφανίζεται, ἔπειτα διὰ σταδίων ὡς πέντε μάλιστά κη ἀναφαινόμενος ἐκδιδοῖ καὶ οὗτος ἐς τὸν Μαίανδρον. ἐκ δὲ Κολοσσέων ὁ στρατὸς ὁρμώμενος ἐπὶ τοὺς οὔρους τῶν Φρυγῶν καὶ Λυδῶν ἀπίκετο ἐς Κύδραρα πόλιν, ἔνθα στήλη καταπεπηγυῖα, σταθεῖσα δὲ ὑπὸ Κροίσου, καταμηνύει διὰ γραμμάτων τοὺς οὔρους.

Having said and fulfilled [his promise towards Pythios], he marched onwards without stopping. And passing a Phrygian city called Anaua, and a lake from which salt originates, he arrived in Kolossai, a great city of Phrygia. Here the Lykos river disappears flowing into a gap in the earth, and then, remerging after some five stades, this river also issues into the Maeander. Setting out from Kolossai to the border of Phrygia and Lydia, he arrived at the city of Kydrara, where a stele has been installed, put up by Croesus. It marks the borders by an inscription.

Compared to the previous route, it seems that from Kelainai onwards Herodotus had access to more detailed 'route descriptions', which also featured various local wonders. The places here are mostly well-established: Anaua (elsewhere known as Sanaos) has been identified with modern Sarıkavak; the salt lake must be the lake to the south of this town, the modern Acı Göl, which still is a source of salt.[36]

---

35 The name derives from καταράσσω, which means 'to fall down' when referring to water, but 'to break up' when referring to armies; Herodotus uses the verb in this meaning in 9.69 (for more examples see *LSJ* s.v.). Herodotus insists on the name Katarrektes, despite the fact that this river was elsewhere called Marsyas. He obviously found it interesting given his wording: τῷ οὔνομα τυγχάνει ἐὸν Καταρρήκτης 'of which the name happens to be Katarrektes', a construction also used for the town of Agore (§2.2.5). Tuplin (2011, 89–90) comments on the variety in names for the same river; he believes it is unlikely that the river had a Greek name, and that Herodotus confused the name of the river with the fact that it was a waterfall.
36 Müller 1997, 95–96; French 1998, 17.

Fig. 4: Acı Göl, the lake where salt is produced.

The unexcavated remains of Kolossai are situated at four kilometres north of Honaz;³⁷ the Lykos river is the modern Çürüksu Su, between Kolossai and modern Konyalılar.³⁸ The mountainous landscape requires that the splitting of the road must have referred to the area of modern Sarayköy, which means that Kydrara is to be sought in this area.³⁹ Herodotus' omission of the sinter terraces of Hierapolis (Pamukkale), one

---

37 Leake 1824, 254; Radet 1891, 376; Müller 1997, 163–165; French 1998, 17.
38 Müller 1997, 171–175 (this river runs in a deep gorge as Herodotus describes). See Ramsay 1887, 358–359 for a discussion of the disappearance of the river under the ground (allegedly called *duden* in Turkish).
39 Kydrara is presumably identical to the place Karoura mentioned by Strabo (5.8.17), a small town on the Maeander river with several inns and hot springs (cf. Leake 1824, 250–251). The town also appears in Stephanus Byzantinus (*Ethnica* s.v. Κύδραρα) as situated close to the borders of Phrygia, and perhaps in Livy (37.56) as Hydrela. Kavakbaşı: Müller 1994, 32; 1997, 168–170 (stating that one could also hypothesise that Kydrara was the 'ancestor' town of Hierapolis, which was founded in the second century BCE by Eumenes II; but no pre-Hellenistic archaeological evidence has been found at Hierapolis). Other identifications exist: Dereköy: Rayet & Thomas 1877–1880, I 6; Sarayköy: Radet 1891, 377; French 1998, 17; Laodikeia: Macan 1908, I 45 with further literature. Pococke 1745, II.2 71 and Leake 1824, 250–251 identified Kydrara with hot springs 12 miles west of Denizli, which points at the Sarayköy area.

of the most remarkable natural landmarks of Anatolia, is striking and suggests his lack of in-depth knowledge of the region.⁴⁰

From a mnemotopical perspective it seems relevant that Xerxes passes a border stele set up by Croesus. Whether it was truly Croesus is inherently uncertain: we may compare this stele to that of Sesostris, where Herodotus displays a similar 'archaeological' interest, but misidentifies the king (see §1.4.2). It has been suggested that he mentions the inscription because it is a marker of the downfall of a king, a theme which recurs at various points in the *Histories*,⁴¹ or that Xerxes' passing of Kydrara is part of a series of boundary transgressions.⁴² But it may also simply have featured in the itinerary used by Herodotus.

Fig. 5: Kolossai.

---

40 Today Pamukkale is one of the most visited sites of Anatolia. This was not different in the Roman period, when interest centred on the Charoneion and the Pamukkale terraces, cf. Zwingmann 2012, 314–336. In the Christian period, a tree was pointed out as the one from which Philip the Apostle, who supposedly lay buried in the city, was hanged (Zwingmann 2012, 336–337).
41 West 1985, 295, noting that the names in a Lydian border inscription may have been partly readable for Greeks, as the Lydian alphabet was based on the Greek one.
42 Baragwanath 2008, 271. For the general idea that places in Herodotus' work may prompt such symbolic interpretations, see Rood 2012, 125–126.

2.1.4 The plane tree of Kallatebos

Another mnemotope appears on the way past the town of Kallatebos (7.31):

ὡς δὲ ἐκ τῆς Φρυγίης ἐσέβαλε ἐς τὴν Λυδίην, σχιζομένης τῆς ὁδοῦ καὶ τῆς μὲν ἐς ἀριστερὴν ἐπὶ Καρίης φερούσης τῆς δὲ ἐς δεξιὴν ἐς Σάρδις, τῇ καὶ πορευομένῳ διαβῆναι τὸν Μαίανδρον ποταμὸν πᾶσα ἀνάγκη γίνεται καὶ ἰέναι παρὰ Καλλάτηβον πόλιν, ἐν τῇ ἄνδρες δημιοργοὶ μέλι ἐκ μυρίκης τε καὶ πυροῦ ποιεῦσι, ταύτην ἰὼν ὁ Ξέρξης τὴν ὁδὸν εὗρε πλατάνιστον, τὴν κάλλεος εἵνεκα δωρησάμενος κόσμῳ χρυσέῳ καὶ μελεδωνῷ ἀθανάτῳ ἀνδρὶ ἐπιτρέψας δευτέρῃ ἡμέρῃ ἀπίκετο ἐς τῶν Λυδῶν τὸ ἄστυ.

And when Xerxes entered Lydia from Phrygia, at the point where the road splits with the left one leading to Caria and the right one to Sardis, along which one cannot avoid crossing the Maeander and to go past the city of Kallatebos, in which the craftsmen make a sweet from tamarisk and wheat, while going that way, he found a plane tree. Because of its beauty he decorated it with gold and made one of the Immortals guard it, and he arrived at the city of the Lydians on the second day.

The locations of Kallatebos and the plane tree (which do not need to be identical) are elusive. The possibly corrupted toponym Καλλάτηβος is seemingly *hapax legomenon*. For its location, we therefore need to rely on Herodotus' text, which states that the place lay on the road from Kydrara (in the vicinity of modern Sarayköy) to Sardis, and that it was north of the Maeander. This points to the valley of the Kogamos river (Alaşehir Çay), which runs past the ancient road from Kydrara to Sardis. Although various locations have been put forward both inside and outside of this valley, none of them is particularly appealing.[43]

It is in itself strange that a city about which Herodotus gave a short digression would disappear without a trace.[44] The practise of renaming cities from the Hellenistic

---

[43] For Davaslı, see Buresch 1898, 290–210; Zgusta 1984, 39 note 2. At the end of the nineteenth century a Roman-period honorary inscription (*BCH* 15, 1891, 373–380) was found at this (now deserted) town of and restored to οἱ κά[τοικοι οἱ ἐ]ν Κ[αλλάτ]αβοις. While it was later shown that this restoration is not possible (not only is there too little space for the reconstruction given by Radet, the -αβοις ending is not specific enough), it could perhaps represent Tabai, a shortened version of the name (Thonemann 2003, 102–103). For Sarıgöl, see Hamilton 1842, II 374; Radet 1891, 373–375; Müller 1994, 32; Green 1996, 66. Sarıgöl was previously called İnegöl. It happens that there was a hill with an old oak that stood south-east of Sarıgöl which supposedly had been a pilgrimage site for Greeks living in Philadelphia (Alaşehir), cf. Radet 1891, 380. For Derbent, see Buresch 1898, 211: he suggested a hill with ancient remains west of the village Derbent, some ten kilometres south of Sarıgöl, as a possible location; the village was previously called Kırk Çınar Dervend 'Forty Plane Trees Dervend'. For Buldan, see French 1998, 17. Philadelphia, the modern town of Alaşehir which dominates the valley, may also be considered. This city was allegedly founded by Eumenes II of Pergamon, but it may have replaced an older city; it is possible that Kallatebos was its name, but this must remain speculative; cf. Rawlinson 1880, 32. For Hierapolis (Pamukkale), see Ramsay 1887, 349.
[44] The manuscripts of the *Histories* have the accusative Καλλατιον (SV) and Καλλατιβον (AD). The town Kallatebos appears only one more time in Greek literature, in Stephanus Byzantinus as Καλάτιβος or Καλάτιβα (*Ethnica* s.v.), a city of Lydia; but this mention is based on Herodotus.

period onward may be the cause of this, and it is possible that the name Kallatebos is buried 'under' that of Philadelphia, Laodikeia or Hierapolis. Nevertheless, I would like to point out that the name of the city seems to resound in that of the city Keretapa (Κερετάπα) in Phrygia. This name appears on various imperial-period coins (where it is given the epithet Diokaisareia),[45] in the Byzantine gazetteer *Synekdemos* by Hierocles (666.2), and as Χαιρετόπα or Χαιρετάπα in various other sources from the Byzantine period.[46] The locations proposed for this town, however, are difficult to reconcile with Herodotus' indications that Xerxes encountered Kallatebos northwest of the Maeander river between Kydrara and Sardis. Although the efforts to pinpoint Keretapa are inconclusive,[47] the topographical indications in our sources generally point to the area of Kolossai. Le Quien, in explaining that the Greek church celebrated the appearance of St. Michael of Khonai at Keretapa, noted: "*Chonis*, quæ juxta *Chæretapa*",[48] the *Synekdemos* mentions it between Kolossai and Themissonion (unlocated); the Martyrdom of Artemon may mention it as τὴν Καισαρέων πόλιν in the vicinity of Laodikeia (Denizli);[49] and Ptolemy's atlas (*Geographia* 5.2.26) presents Diokaisareia as situated just north of Sanis (which is Sanaos or Anaua, modern Sarıkavak, see §2.1.3). According to Ramsay, Keretapa also appears closely linked to Hierapolis on some coins.[50] Nevertheless, Herodotus may have worked with a garbled account of the area, which would not be surprising given his patchy and sometimes distorted view of Anatolia, as his topographically erroneous treatment of the Halys and Mount Ida shows. Perhaps the mysterious Phrygian town of Ἀρδαβαῦ, linked by Ramsay to Kallatebos,[51] is another manifestation of Keretapa. There are, unfortunately, no means to ascertain whether these resemblances are more than coincidences.

---

45 Robert 1935, 106–107 with literature.
46 Robert 1935, 105.
47 Ramsay first located Keretapa at modern Sarıkavak; he later (1887, 360–361; 1897, 275–278) revised his identification to the town of Yeşilova, formerly called Kayadibi, mainly on the basis of an inscription containing the words Διεὶ Καίσαρι, and the idea that Kayadibi, Turkish for 'under the rock', would echo the element *-tapa*, potentialy Lydian for 'rock'. Robert (1935, 106–121) argued that this reasoning was not convincing and instead proposed the town of Yeşilyuva, where he saw many archaeological remains from the Byzantine period. He reported that at the time of his visit, the locals still called the town Kayser, which was sometimes by folk etymology changed to Kayahisar. Robert proposed that this name echoed Keretapa's epithet Diokaisareia. However, it is difficult to maintain that the name Diokaisareia was retained throughout the Byzantine and Ottoman periods, especially as it was dropped from official texts.
48 Le Quien 1740, I 813.
49 *Elogium S. Artemonis M. Fabulosum Ex Menaeis ad diem XXIV Martii 2* in *Acta Sanctorum Octobris Tomus IV* (1780), 44–46.
50 Ramsay 1897, 277.
51 Ramsay (1897, 573 n. 5) speculated that this toponym, which appears in second or third century CE as a κώμη of Phrygian Mysia and the birthplace of Montanus, in *Ad Avircium Marcellum contra Cataphrygas* fragment 2, may be a wrong rendering of Κάρδαβα, in turn derived from a name Καλλάταβα. On the name Kallatebos, see also Zgusta 1984, 92.

Fig. 6: Hierapolis (Pamukkale), looking north towards the Kogamos Valley.

Although we can only hope that new discoveries in the area will give additional clues about the location of Kallatebos, it is likely that there was a conspicuous plane tree somewhere here which in Herodotus' time was associated with Xerxes' visit. Pliny the Elder (*Naturalis Historia* 17.38.2), too, reports that there was a real plane tree connected with Xerxes: it had turned into an olive tree upon a visit by the Persian king.[52] Whether this was the same plane tree that Herodotus referred to half a millennium earlier is possible, but not necessary: Pliny refers to the city of Laodikeia (modern Denizli), not to Kallatebos. An early traveller to the area, reports that he had seen "the half-ruined trunk of one of the most gigantic plane-trees I had ever seen" just before he crossed the Lykos river.[53] He did not want to claim that it was identical to Xerxes' plane tree, although he seemingly believed that this was possible.

---

[52] On this story see Demandt 2002, 44, who suggests that it may symbolise Athenian supremacy over the Persians. Note, however, that stories about tree metamorphoses are common: cf. Theophrastus, *Historia plantarum* 2.3.1 on shape-shifting trees and omens; underlying it may be actual trees that grow on existing ones (cf. a Turkish news article about a plane tree growing inside an olive tree in Sarıgöl at http://www.memurlar.net/haber/414101/, last consulted on 12 July 2017). Is Laodikeia the reincarnation of Kallatebos, or did Pliny only refer to the general region of Laodikeia?
[53] Hamilton 1842, I 517.

What led to the creation of this mnemotope? I would argue that a visit of Xerxes may have been imagined at a real, conspicuous plane tree in this part of Anatolia. But the episode is usually explained differently: scholars often place it within the context of the Persian appreciation of nature and gardens, which was sometimes religiously motivated.[54] It is true that golden plane trees allegedly appear in the *Avesta* (the holy text of Zoroastrianism) with regard to the 'end of times'.[55] Trees also feature often in Achaemenid art, some of which are directly connected with Xerxes: as illustrations of the Kallatebos plane tree story, Briant mentions a seal of Xerxes (SXe), where we can see the king offering a crown to a stylised tree, and one of the Persepolis seals (24) shows the king with two guards and palm trees.[56] Such depictions probably hearken back to cross-cultural depictions of the 'golden life tree'.[57] In the Persepolis reliefs we also find depictions of officials next to trees. Sancisi-Weerdenburg quotes an interesting modern parallel regarding the Nowruz (Iranian New Year) celebrations, in which the shah presented his people with gems, hanging on gold-plated cypress and date trees around the reception room.[58]

But the specificity of tree cults in Persian culture is easy to overstate. Conspicuous trees appear in folklore all around the world, even in modern times. Ancient Greece was no exception: holy trees and especially plane trees were a common sight at sanctuaries,[59] and there are many examples of plane trees which developed into

---

54 E.g. Hauvette 1894, 301; Green (1996, 66) calls Xerxes' admiration a "nice blend of Achaemenid ostentatiousness and the instinctive Persian feeling for natural beauty". On the relation between Achaemenid kings and nature and gardening, see Briant 1996, 244–250; 2003; cf. also the Herodotean examples of Darius' nature-loving tendencies as the Tearos river and the Bosporus. Stubbings (1946, 65) asserted that it is "highly probable" that the episode is a manifestation of Persian religion. Boyce (1982, 165) went as far as suggesting that Xerxes offered to Ameša Spenta Ameretāt, the Zoroastrian 'Lord of all plants', and believed that "Xerxes created a shrine at the foot of this majestic tree; and a priest would probably have been left there with the soldier, to worship and pray." Demandt 2002, 45, too, connects the story with oriental tree cults. Dusinberre 2013, 53 maintains: "Whether an instance of tree worship or an appreciation of beauty, the king's treatment of this plane tree and his establishment of its care made a strong statement of wealth and power to the ancient local populace, one that had a tremendous impact on the imagination of generations." For the importance of the plane tree in Persian gardens, poetry, and its frequency as a toponym see A'lam 1990 and Demandt 2002, 49–51. For examples of Zoroastrian tree worship (including a cypress allegedly planted by Zarathustra himself in Kashmar, Iran), see A'lam 1994 and Demandt 2002, 48–49.
55 Demandt 2002, 46–48.
56 Briant 1996, 248; Kuhrt 2007, 247.
57 Stories about and artefacts depicting golden 'life' trees abound in many Eurasian (including Mesopotamian) cultures, and had also reached Achaemenid Persia. For depictions of cult trees on Assyrian cylinder seals and monumental sculpture, see Porter 2003; Giovino 2006.
58 Sancisi-Weerdenburg 1994b, 227.
59 For many examples of tree cults in Greece, see Demandt 2002, 72–105; 87–90 (plane trees); 115–116. There was one in the sanctuary of Zeus Statios at Labraunda in Caria (Herodotus 5.119), and at Korone, Messenia (Pausanias 4.34.4), and there was a sacred wood with plane trees in Pharai, Achaia

mnemotopes for visits of legendary historical celebrities, including Agamemnon, Menelaos and Alexander the Great.[60] Xerxes' plane tree (or trees) in Kallatebos and Laodikeia can be added to this list; perhaps it was simply a local tradition which was somehow picked up by Herodotus.[61] Given these parallels, the anecdote can also be explained from a local mnemotopical perspective, and one that was not constrained by concerns of historicity.

The story may be considered together with Herodotus' story about the golden plane tree presented to Xerxes' father Darius by Pythios, whom Xerxes had met in Kelainai (7.27; cf. §2.1.2). This object was also mentioned by Xenophon (*Hellenica* 7.1.38), and the accompanying vine was found in Sousa according to Diodorus Siculus (19.48.6-7). Although there exist other instances of golden trees as gifts in various cultures,[62] the connection of a golden plane tree with a Persian king is so specific that it is, to me, virtually impossible to see the Pythios story as detached from the Kallatebos story.[63]

As long as it remains unclear how precisely the various stories about Xerxes and a plane tree interlock, we may instead ask ourselves why the 'genre' was so successful. By the time Herodotus wrote, Xerxes had become a historical figure liable to that kind of story, especially because it highlighted a tragicomical stereotype of irrational

---

(Pausanias 7.22.1). The tree in Kelainai from which Marsyas' skin hung was also a plane (Pliny the Elder, *Naturalis Historia* 16.44). Many more examples can be found in book 17 of *Naturalis Historia*.

60 A plane tree in Aulis already appears in the *Iliad* (2.303–329) in relation to the portent of a sparrow family eaten by a snake; Agamemnon sacrificed here to the winds. The tree was shown to Pausanias in addition to the bronze threshold of Agamemnon's tent (9.19.7). Papachatzi (1981, 132) identifies the area with a fountain immediately east of the entrance of the temple of Artemis. A specimen at a source in Kaphyai (Arcadia) was called Menelaïs because Menelaos had visited it as he was summoning his forces for the Trojan expedition (Pausanias 8.23.4). It is perhaps to be identified with a source northwest of the ancient city, which lay southeast of the village Chotousa (Papachatzi 1980, 267). Pliny the Elder (*Naturalis Historia* 16.88) maintained, however that it had been planted by Agamemnon, as had been a plane tree in Delphi. Alexander the Great fell asleep under a plane tree in Smyrna (Pausanias 7.5.2–3; the scene was depicted on local coins); and Roman statesman Licinus Mucianus dined inside a famous plane tree in Lycia (*Naturalis Historia* 12.5); on this tree as a tourist site see Zwingmann 2012, 354. For more general observations of trees as mnemotopes see Birge 1994; Boardman 2002, 111–112; Hartmann 2010, 87–90; Miles 2016, 170–176. A famous example from Greece is Hippocrates' plane tree in Kos, under whose branches the ancient medic would have given his lectures (van Opstall 2007, 314).

61 Pohlenz 1961, 130.

62 Demandt 2002, 46–48. The golden plane anecdotes may also be related to the common theme of the 'golden bough', which most famously appears in Virgil's *Aeneis* as part of the prophecy by Sibylla (6.124–155; 6.183–211). For the view that these objects were historical, see e.g. Macan 1908, I 42; Obst 1913, 56.

63 E.g. Stubbings 1946; Baragwanath 2008, 274.

and 'barbarian' luxury.⁶⁴ I noted above (§2.1.2) that there is reason to connect the lore about Pythios with the stories about king Midas, the legendary ruler of this part of Anatolia.⁶⁵ I suggest that similarly there may have existed traditions in Kallatebos in which lore about Midas' 'tragic golden touch' was projected onto Xerxes.⁶⁶

That there was a conspicuous plane tree on the route from Kydrara to Sardis is likely. The historical Xerxes may, of course, have stopped here, as Herodotus suggests. At the same time, the frequency of 'plane tree fantasies' is high. Xerxes' interaction with the plane tree is more likely a reflection of local and/or Greek imagination than of Persian piety. Like the stories about Pythios, it may have been inspired by official imagery that the Achaemenids were circulating on cylinder seals, which have been found in western Anatolia and may well have reached the Greek world. The image of Xerxes offering a crown to the life tree looks like something that could have inspired both legends. This story may subsequently have been associated with a great tree near Kallatebos.

2.1.5 Sardis

Xerxes' army halted at Sardis, the seat of the satrapy of Sparda, and formerly the capital of the Lydian empire, at the west-most point of the Royal Road. Xerxes allegedly waited here for several months while the Athos canal and the Hellespont

---

64 The stereotype is found in e.g. Aelian, *Varia historia* 2.14. For the view that the Kallatebos story illustrated that stereotype, see Macan 1908, II 132 (describing it as one of the "humours of the voyage"); Flory 1987, 87 suggesting that Herodotus shows Xerxes at Kallatebos in a sympathetic, tragic light, foreshadowing similar episodes at the Hellespont (see §2.2.4) and Doriskos (see §2.3.3); Briant 1996, 246–247; Harrison 2000, 239; Baragwanath 2008, 270–271 (contrasting this 'frivolous' passage to Xerxes' later anger with the Hellespont). While others have suggested that Herodotus' wording does not allow such inferences (Sancisi-Weerdenburg 1994b, 216–218; Bridges 2015, 58 note 36) the brevity of the story does not exclude that he was working with some other, more elaborate source, in which these overtones may have been present.
65 Aly 1969 (first edition 1921), 171–175.
66 Herodotus knew Midas as a historical king and claimed to have seen his throne in Delphi (1.14). The story about the tree's golden decoration could perhaps be a rationalisation of a pre-existing myth; that magic may have been part of the original version, is suggested by Pliny's story that Xerxes turned a plane tree into an olive tree. It also seems relevant that Xerxes' route through Anatolia and Greece connects with several 'Midean' mnemotopes: Kelainai, Mount Tmolos (5.100; 1.93) and the 'Garden of Midas' (8.138). Moreover, Xerxes' decision to invade Delphi was prompted because he knew about its riches, which included Midas' throne. This example of myth-history may be proven to have existed if we had evidence that Midas was also connected with a plane tree which he turned into gold. As far as I know, we do not have this evidence; but we do have stories in Ovid's *Metamorphoses* that the twig of an oak tree (11.108–109) and apples which he had just gathered from a tree (11.111–113) turned into gold; and Maximus (*Dissertationes* 5.1) summarised the Midas myth and also mentions trees among the things that he turned into gold.

bridges were being built (7.32). Various omens took place here, such as an eclipse (7.37),[67] the birth of a hare to a horse, and the birth of a hermaphrodite mule (7.57). The point of the portents is that Xerxes did not understand them.[68] It was also here that Xerxes punished Pythios, whom he had just rewarded at Kelainai, by killing his eldest son, enraged about a question whether this son could be exempt from military service (7.38, cf. §2.1.2).[69] In addition, Xerxes has many conversations and dreams in Sardis, and even a post-war romance (9.108).[70] Elsewhere in the *Histories*, Sardis is the site of a Persian siege (1.84; cf. §2.7.2), as well as of a Greek one during the Ionian revolt in 498 BCE (5.100-102). Herodotus' account does not connect the invasion of Xerxes to any specific mnemotopes in the city. Nevertheless, many events here resonate with themes of the *Histories* as a whole.

There are extensive remains of the city of Sardis at the modern town of Sart. Because Sardis was close to the Aegean and Herodotus' topography of the city is quite detailed, including the appearance of the houses, and the monuments of the Lydian necropolis at Bin Tepe a few kilometres north of the city (1.93), it is reasonable to think that Herodotus drew upon sources which were familiar with the city's topography.[71] Sardis had some appeal as a tourist attraction, as Herodotus (1.29-30) claims that the city was visited by Greek scholars, including Solon, with the purpose of seeing the sites (θεωρίη).

Two sieges of Sardis were mnemotopically motivated in the city landscape. The Persian siege of 547 BCE was connected to the impregnability of the Acropolis (§2.7.2). The Greek siege of 499 BCE had a strong association with the temple of Cybele. The Greeks believed that the destruction of this temple at the hands of the Athenians was the pretext for the Persians to set out to destroy the temples on the Acropolis, and con-

---

[67] The eclipse would be a local tradition of Sardis, but it certainly did not take place in 480 BCE (Burn 1962, 321; Hignett 1963, 448; Hammond 1988, 536). There was one on 16 February 478, but the one that 'inspired' the story (if this was the way the story arose) may also have been an earlier one; the point is that it shows the extent to which salient events were synchronised in the tradition which Herodotus wrote down (cf. Macan 1908, I 57).
[68] Hollmann 2011, 72–74.
[69] It is possible that traditions about Xerxes in Sardis were modelled on earlier traditions told at Sardis. These may have been considerably older: the cruel execution of Pythios' eldest son, by cutting his body in two, is sometimes labelled as unhistorical (Obst 1913, 56), but it also bears a striking resemblance to rituals of Bronze Age Anatolia (for an example in the Hittite world, see Kümmel 1967, 150–153; Robertson 1982, 130; Kienast 1996, 292, especially note 20, 21 and 22). Baragwanath (2008, 269–280) has argued that the Pythios episode is part of a theme of childless rich people, and that the name Pythios evokes the epithet of the god Apollo.
[70] Flory (1987, 86) has remarked that the anecdotes about Xerxes in Sardis display him in a sympathetic, tragic light.
[71] Myres (1953, 6) and Cawkwell (2005, 4) maintained that Herodotus visited Sardis.

Fig. 7: The temple of Artemis at Sardis with the acropolis of Sardis in the background.

quering European Greece in the process (5.97; 5.102; 5.105; 6.94; 7.8.β, where multiple temples and sacred groves are mentioned; 7.11).[72]

The temple's archaeological identification is uncertain. Given the similarities between Cybele and Artemis, it is possible that it should be identified with that of Artemis.[73] However, contrary to what has been suggested,[74] this temple dates only from the Hellenistic period.[75] No evidence has yet appeared for a pre-Hellenistic temple at Sardis, except for the marble model of a temple (540-530 BCE) found in the Byzantine synagogue, which may point to the existence of such a temple at Sardis.[76] In addition, two altars were excavated here. One belonged to Artemis and is said to

---

[72] This event has been associated with destruction layers in the stratigraphy at various places in the lower city; cf. Mierse 1983a, 101.
[73] Hanfmann 1960, 526–527; see also Butler 1925, 102–103: Lydian inscriptions refer to the goddess as Artemis. There is also a stele from c. 430–420 BCE depicting two goddesses, one holding a deer and the other holding a lion, presumably Artemis and Cybele side by side (Dusinberre 2003, 106–107). For an elaborate discussion of the remains, see Yegül 2010.
[74] Butler 1925, 101–102, reporting foundations of the pre-Persian building.
[75] Hanfmann 1960, 527; Mierse 1983b; Müller 1997, 711.
[76] Dusinberre 2003, 68–69.

date to the Achaemenid period. Its stepped pyramid form may indicate the influence of Achaemenid fire altars.⁷⁷ The other was for Cybele (as evidenced by a Lydian inscription) and was refined with gold and lion imagery. It showed traces of burning, which suggests that it was (also?) in use as a fire altar.⁷⁸

Herodotus' belief that the destruction of the temple was the reason for the Persians to invade Greece is sometimes given credence by positing that the Persians identified Cybele with the Persian goddess Anahitā (Anaïtis), who features in the *Avesta*.⁷⁹ Nevertheless, some scholars have pointed out that the idea that the Persians were truly bothered by the destruction of this temple is rather strange.⁸⁰ It is possible that the ruined temple of Cybele had become a mnemotope in the cityscape of Sardis around which stories had crystallised that explained the cause of the Persian Wars.

There is no hint that a specific mnemotope within the city underlies any of the other stories. It may be that the palace(s) of Sardis also functioned as a mnemotope for the Persian stories, but they are not specifically associated with Xerxes. Ancient authors do mention Croesus' palace (Herodotus 1.30; Vitruvius 2.8.10; Pliny the Elder, *Naturalis Historia* 35.172), and Cyrus allegedly had a palace with a paradeisos here (Xenophon, *Oeconomicus* 4.20).⁸¹ To date, no trace of any Achaemenid palace has been found, so it is presumed that the older palace which had belonged to the Lydian kings and whose fundaments are still visible on the acropolis was also used by the Achaemenid rulers.⁸² In addition, pavilions with columns are thought to indicate the presence of paradeisoi.⁸³ According to Strabo (13.4.5) there was a lookout point on the Tmolos with an ἐξέδρα of white stone built by the Persians; but no archaeological traces have been reported.⁸⁴ Such details are remarkably not found in Herodotus' description of Sardis.

---

77 Mierse 1983b, 120–121; Dusinberre 2003, 60–64 (about links to the Achaemenid style). That this is indeed the altar of Artemis may be inferred from its location in the Hellenistic sanctuary of Artemis and the importance of the Artemis cult as it appears from inscriptions.
78 Ramage 1983, 36–37; Müller 1997, 711–713; Dusinberre 2003, 64–68.
79 On Herodotus' representation of Anahitā, see de Jong 1997, 104–107; 269–270.
80 E.g. Waters 1985, 101 (underlining Xerxes' imperialist motives); Rosenberger 2003, 76; Funke 2007, 24–25. Scheer (2000, 202) is undecided. On the difficulty in interpreting the event see Harrison 2011, 47–49.
81 For Sardis as a tourist site see Zwingmann 2012, 300 (suggesting that the touristic value was rather limited, and that landmarks are only described out in military contexts).
82 Mierse 1983a, 102; Müller 1997, 704; 707–708. Achaemenid Sardis probably lay east of the excavated area of Sardis, and there is very little specific Achaemenid-period material (Dusinberre 2003, 13). Dusinberre (2003, 73–75) identifies the Lydian palace with a building on the north side of the acropolis with terrace walls; the palace was turned into a government building perhaps in the Hellenistic period. For an overview of Persian engagement with Sardis, see Mierse 1983a.
83 Dusinberre 2003, 71–72.
84 Müller 1997, 746.

2.1.6 Summary

Herodotus' treatment of inner Anatolia is limited, with relatively few topographical indications. Contrary to what Herodotus suggests, the Halys was probably never crossed (if the rest of the route is more or less historical), and its mention is a result of Herodotus' limited understanding of Anatolian geography. Herodotus' assertion that Xerxes' crossed the Halys, where Croesus and Cyrus had previously waged battle, is exemplary for the way in which the invasion was remembered as one breaching boundaries. Croesus' stele at Kydrara furnished another reminder that Xerxes crossed such boundaries.

Kelainai was the mnemotope of the Marsyas myth; whether this tale was symbolically connected to Xerxes' march remains an open question. At Kallatebos we encounter the mnemotope of a conspicuous plane tree, whose association with Xerxes highlighted his tragic 'golden touch'. At Sardis, fifth-century BCE visitors were reminded of the Persian invasion at various mnemotopes, such as the royal palace and the ruined sanctuary of Cybele (the destruction of which was said to be the casus belli); but Herodotus does not explicitly refer to any of these places. On the whole, it remains rather unclear whether the localisations in Herodotus' work are the result of his own ideas, or reflect Anatolian traditions.

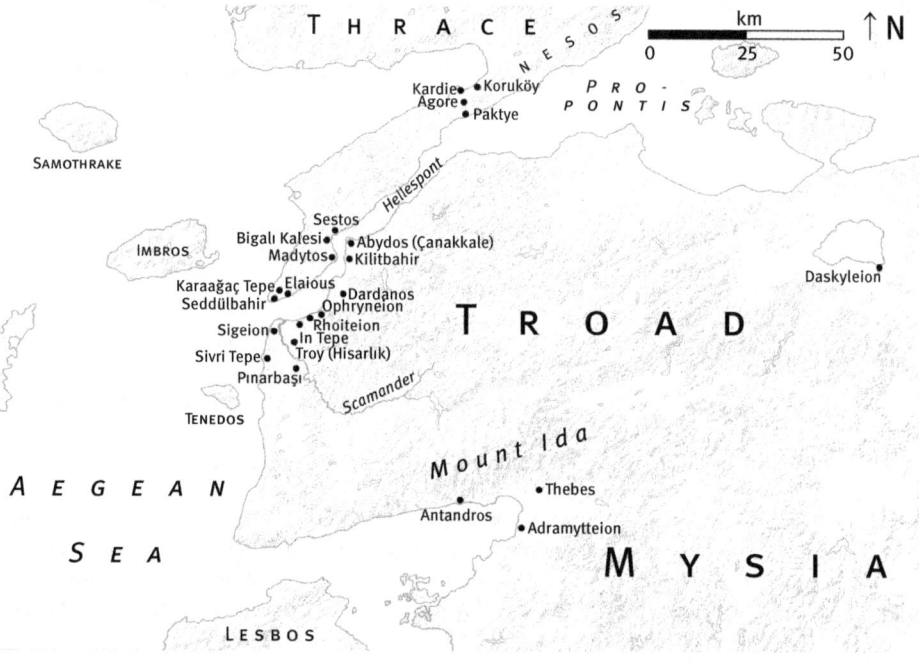

Map 3: The Troad and the Hellespont.

2.2 The Troad and the Hellespont

It is hard to overstate the importance of the Troad in ancient Graeco-Roman thought and culture, not only as a cultural symbol and fictional place, but also as a real-life landscape.[85] With the *Iliad* taking place nearly entirely within its confines, the Troad is a memory space par excellence. Unsurprisingly, the area was a touristic hotspot already in antiquity (complete with tour guides and souvenirs),[86] and in modern times.[87] Nearby, the Hellespont, presently known as Çanakkale Boğazı, is where the Thracian Chersonesos and the Troad, and thereby Europe and Asia, form their synapse. It was an important waterway linking the Aegean with the Sea of Marmara and the Black Sea. The Persians continued to control the area after the Persian Wars, even though it was also in touch with the Greek world.[88] As such, the Troad and the banks of the Hellespont featured many mnemotopes associated with the Argonautic and Trojan sagas.[89]

If Herodotus (7.42-43) is to be believed, the first recorded tourist to the Troad was none other than the king of the Persians himself. During the Persian invasion of Greece in 480 BCE, he allegedly guided his enormous army over Mount Ida and along the Scamander river, and climbed the citadel of Troy 'because he wanted to

---

[85] The part of this chapter that concerns the Troad has been the basis of a separate article in *Klio* (van Rookhuijzen 2017c). The present text (deviating from the text in the article on various points) has been included with kind permission from the editors. A selection of places mentioned in this chapter features on Map 3.
[86] For example, a quarter of Strabo's writings on the whole of Asia Minor is devoted to the relatively small Troad, because his readers "yearn for knowledge about famous and ancient matters" (13.1.1). Luce (1998, 132) remarks that "If one reads between the lines in Strabo, one can get some insight into contemporary tourism". Marcus Lucanus (*Pharsalia* 9.973) described the Troad as a land where *nullum est sine nomine saxum* ('no stone lacks a name'). For various other mnemotopes in the Troad beside the ones mentioned in this chapter, see Zwingmann 2012, 74–76. For tour guides in the Troad, see Minchin 2016, 267–270.
[87] Minchin 2016, 263–266.
[88] From 510 BCE, the Troad was mostly Persian territory. However, parts were controlled by Athens, Sparta and Mytilene (Rose 2006, 190). This ended with the battle of Mykale, after which all Greek cities joined the Delian confederation; still, the Persians controlled various parts at various points (Bieg 2006, 368). After Aigospotamoi the Troad fell into Spartan hands, but until Alexander's conquest Athens and Persia made attempts to expand their influence once more. It has been shown that there were Achaemenid magistrates living (Sekunda 1988), and that the elite of northwestern Asia Minor gradually adopted Persian customs and symbols during the fifth century BCE (Kaptan 2003). An artefact such as the Polyxena sarcophagus from Gümüşçay (c. 500 BCE, featuring the first representation of Achilles' tomb and of a Trojan War myth in the Troad) reveals the extent to which Greek lore remained fixed in the area, despite Persian dominion (cf. Berlin 2002, 141; Boardman 2002, 54).
[89] See e.g. Ammianus Marcellinus 22.8.4 for a list of such sites (among which features Abydos as the place from which Xerxes crossed the Hellespont). For a general discussion of these sites, see Luce 1998, 37–44. See also §2.2.3 for a discussion of tumuli in the Troad as mnemotopes.

see it'. There, he sacrificed extravagantly to Athena and the heroes. Another notable feature in this region are Xerxes' ship bridges, marked by the bridgeheads of Abydos and Sestos.

In this chapter I argue that this episode may be a product of Greek imagination in the fifty years between the wars and the publication of the *Histories*, with the landscapes of the Troad and the Hellespont functioning as a catalyst. It will primarily do so by discussing the mentioned locations, tracing their Iliadic associations and exposing topographical problems. I will also argue that the mnemotopes of the region helped to frame Xerxes' invasion of Greece as a hubristic crossing of the boundary of Asia and Europe. While this chapter is not concerned with the historicity of the episode per se (which is, after all, beyond recovery), it will be argued that it is problematic to assume it. What follows is that we can be open to the idea that Xerxes' visited the Troad only in Greek imagination.

2.2.1 Mount Ida

The arrival of Xerxes' army in the Troad follows a seemingly prosaic recount of its route from Sardis (7.42):

> ἐποιέετο δὲ τὴν ὁδὸν ἐκ τῆς Λυδίης ὁ στρατὸς ἐπί τε ποταμὸν Κάικον καὶ γῆν τὴν Μυσίην, ἀπὸ δὲ Καΐκου ὁρμώμενος, Κάνης ὄρος ἔχων ἐν ἀριστερῇ, διὰ τοῦ Ἀταρνέος ἐς Καρήνην πόλιν· ἀπὸ δὲ ταύτης διὰ Θήβης πεδίου ἐπορεύετο, Ἀδραμύττειόν τε πόλιν καὶ Ἄντανδρον τὴν Πελασγίδα παραμειβόμενος. τὴν Ἴδην δὲ λαβών, ἐς ἀριστερὴν χεῖρα ἤιε ἐς τὴν Ἰλιάδα γῆν. καὶ πρῶτα μέν οἱ ὑπὸ τῇ Ἴδῃ νύκτα ἀναμείναντι βρονταί τε καὶ πρηστῆρες ἐπεσπίπτουσι καί τινα αὐτοῦ ταύτῃ συχνὸν ὅμιλον διέφθειραν.

> The army made its way from Lydia to the river Kaikos and the land of Mysia, advancing from the Kaikos, having Mount Kane on its left, through Atarneos to the city of Karene. From there it marched through the plain of Thebe, passing by the cities of Adramytteion and Pelasgian Antandros. And keeping the Ida on the left, it went to the land of Ilion. And for the first time thunder and electric storms befell them, as they stayed the night under the Ida, and these destroyed a relatively large number of men right there.

Until Antandros, the route seems plausible enough.[90] The account abruptly turns improbable with Herodotus' remark that Xerxes kept the Ida to his left:[91] Mount Ida

---

90 The topography in this chapter may be based on itineraries (Eckstein 1989, 324). Remarkably, the mentioned cities and geographical features are all situated on or near the sea, revealing once again the nautical perspective that went into formulating Xerxes' movements around the Aegean. On possible routes from Sardis to Abydos, see Macan 1908, II 133–134. The degree of detail from Sardis onwards is in marked contrast with the road in inner Anatolia (Macan 1908, II 127; Pohlenz 1961, 130).
91 Cook 1973, 392–393.

(modern Kaz Dağı) is only the highest peak of a substantial mountain range, and in the absence of a good road across this range from Antandros to the Scamander area (even today), it is unlikely that Xerxes had attempted to take his large force along it. From Antandros, it would have made much more sense to follow the coast past modern Ayvacık,[92] but along this route the Ida is always on the right.

Although it is possible that Herodotus had seen Mount Ida during his travels in or along the coast of western Asia Minor, there is no evidence for this. Also, the confused geography does not suggest autopsy; apparently Herodotus did not know much about the passibility of this part of Troy's hinterland. What, then, are we to make of Herodotus' seeming geographical error? The simplest solution is to assume that he was less than exact: he may have employed imprecise maps or itineraries, or simply have confused left and right.[93] Müller, who is convinced that the army crossed west of the peak, suggests a solution in which ἐς ἀριστερὴν χεῖρα qualifies ᾔε ἐς τὴν Ἰλιάδα γῆν in stead of τὴν Ἴδην δὲ λαβών, so that the sentence would read 'Taking the Ida, he went to his left hand to the land of Ilion', and the placement of the comma in Wilson's text edition suggests that he reads the passage in the same way.[94] However, the use of λαμβάνω in the sense of 'going by' is unattested; moreover, in Thucydides 7.1 we find a very similar construction to the normal reading (ἐν δεξιᾷ λαμβάνω). Other authors believe that Xerxes did, in fact, take the coastal route, and that Herodotus wrongly identified Mount Ida as the modern Çığrı Dağı, a mountain further west in the Troad which is on the left when one goes north to Troy.[95] Other scholars have suggested that the Ida itself was traversed, and have gone so far as to connect the rock-cut 'Porta' north of Zeytinli along this route to Xerxes' passing,[96] or that "[Xerxes'] purpose perhaps, like that of Zeus [...], was to see Troy and the Hellespont spread out below him from the ridge of Ida."[97] Some have even localised the exact spot where the storm struck the camp.[98]

---

[92] Müller 1994, 33–34.
[93] Grundy 1901, 217.
[94] Müller 1994, 33–34.
[95] Thus Schliemann 1881, 194–195 note 1; Leaf 1923, 264, who has the army pass the modern village of Zeytinli; Maurice 1930, 222, note 35a; Cook 1973, 393; cf. Macan 1908, I 62–63.
[96] Leaf 1912, 39–41 (with plate IV); Leaf 1916, 415; Virchow 1982, 978–982 (with photograph); Hammond 1988, 536. This Porta was allegedly also used by Xenophon (*Anabasis* 7.8.7).
[97] Hammond 1988, 536.
[98] This camp was located by Leaf (1923, 264) at the bed of an ancient lake with a modern saw-mill, while Müller (1994, 34 and 1997, 845–846) locates it at or just south of modern Ayvacık.

64 — 2 Topographical Case Studies

Fig. 8: The Gargaron peak of Mount Ida.

As the topographical problem remains, it seems more worthwhile to explore the significance of Mount Ida to fifth-century BCE Greeks. To Herodotus' ancient readership, the mention of the mountain would have conjured up images of a mountain towering above Troy, as far from the reality as this may be. We should not be surprised that Herodotus uses the definite article when referring to the mountain: after all this was the Ida. In Antiquity, the mountain was not only a backdrop for the Trojan War, it was also the location of various events during that war.[99] Most important, however, is Mount Ida's connection with Zeus; it was his place of worship for the Trojans (particularly its peak Gargaron), with a religious infrastructure.[100] Accordingly, it was the mountain from which Zeus watched the battle, and from where the sky god hurled down his lightning.[101] Herodotus' story about the Persians at the Ida should be understood in the light of these strong Iliadic associations.

---

99 For example, it is the place where the Greeks found wood for Patroclus' funeral pyre (23.115–122) and its thicket-clad slopes were a refuge for the Trojan warrior Agenor. It was also the place where Aeneas was conceived (2.820–821). From Strabo (13.1.51) we learn that it was the place where Paris' judgement took place. Zwingmann 2012, 75 gives the evidence for mnemotopes on Mount Ida.
100 For the association of Zeus with Ida, see *Iliad* 7.202; 14.158–159; 14.292; 15.152–153; for the idea that the Trojans performed sacrifices to Zeus at the mountain, see *Iliad* 8.47–48; 16.603–607; 22.169–171.
101 See especially *Iliad* 8.170; 8.75; 8.207; and de Jong (forthcoming).

The mountain's role as a mnemotope for the Trojan War could have led to its development as a mnemotope for Xerxes' invasion. That story has, in fact, elements which may be explained as commonplaces. One is the idea of the 'storm at the mountain', with such storms disrupting the progress of the Persians three more times in the *Histories*, at Mount Athos (6.44), Mount Pelion (§2.4.2) and Mount Parnassos (§2.6.3), and which for the Ida has a parallel in the *Iliad* (21.331-341). Even more significant is the death of a number of soldiers due to a thunder storm: as so often in the *Histories*, such deaths follow an act of hubris. Herodotus may have implied that by hubristically taking the direct route through Zeus' private territory, Xerxes ruthlessly exposed his men to the anger of the supreme god of the Greeks.[102] Relevant in this context is the warning given not much earlier to Xerxes by Artabanos that anything big is likely to arouse the anger of the god and risk being hit by lightning (7.10.ε). This council reverberates with established Herodotean themes such as the downfall of mighty empires.[103] Also note the possibility that Herodotus' assertion that the Ida remained on the left side contains the Iliadic and more widespread Greek notion that signs, such as thunder, on the left are inauspicious.[104]

Perhaps, then, we should not be surprised about the topographical problem described above. We will look in vain for the easiest route across the Ida until we realise that the Ida was a location likely to attract such stories in Greek imagination. Note that it was not necessarily Herodotus himself who 'fabricated' this route, but he may have been amenable to an idea that existed in other sources, or in local folklore.

2.2.2 The Scamander river

After the events at Mount Ida, more misery befalls Xerxes' army in 7.43:

> ἀπικομένου δὲ τοῦ στρατοῦ ἐπὶ τὸν Σκάμανδρον, ὃς πρῶτος ποταμῶν, ἐπείτε ἐκ Σαρδίων ὁρμηθέντες ἐπεχείρησαν τῇ ὁδῷ, ἐπέλιπε τὸ ῥέεθρον οὐδ' ἀπέχρησε τῇ στρατιῇ τε καὶ τοῖσι κτήνεσι πινόμενος [...]
>
> And when the army had arrived at the Scamander river, which was the first river since they had hit the road having set out from Sardis, it ran dry, and it was not enough for the army and the animals to be drunk from [...]

---

102 Hauvette 1894, 303–304; Bischoff 1932, 61; von Haehling 1993, 94–95 notes the literary flavour of the scene, including the setting at night and the later panic in the camp.
103 Accordingly, Flory (1987, 86) has described that Xerxes appears here in a sympathetic, tragic light. The Persians were portrayed by Xenophon (*Cyropaedia* 1.6.1; 7.13) as seeing lightning as positive, but this idea has also been challenged (de Jong 1997, 262–263, explaining the Xenophon passage as unlikely to derive from a Persian source).
104 The right appears as the favourable side for observing lightning (*Iliad* 2.353; 9.236–237) and birds (13.821–822). For an overview of thunderstorms used for divination in Greek war narratives, see Pritchett 1979a, 119–125.

The Scamander is unproblematically identified with the modern (Kara) Menderes of Çanakkale province: it corresponds perfectly with the geographical indications of Strabo (13.1.31; 13.1-33-34; 13.1.36), and the present river still matches Homer's description.[105] Although Strabo's account postdates that of Herodotus by several centuries, its proximity to the Hellespont and Troy-Hisarlık will have ensured its continuous identification.[106]

Fig. 9: The Scamander shortly before debouching into the Hellespont.

It is possible that a real visit by Xerxes' army underlies Herodotus account. If his reconstruction of the route until Antandros is sound, it is probable that the army crossed the Scamander before arriving at the Hellespont.[107] Nevertheless, like Mount Ida, the Scamander may also be seen as a location on which stories were projected. A reason for this view is Herodotus' assertion that the Scamander's water was not

---

[105] Luce 1998, 71–75.
[106] For the Scamander as a mnemotope, see Zwingmann 2012, 76.
[107] Hammond (1988, 536), who believes that the army crossed the Ida range, even supposes that the entire Scamander valley was followed. Müller (1997, 936) says that the army may have reached the Scamander at modern Ezine, and that the camp was on its banks close to Hisarlık.

sufficient for the army, and that it was the first river where the Persians encountered this problem. Some scholars have indicated that the Scamander really was not sufficient for the army, for example because it tends to become nearly dry in summer.[108] One scholar has even gone so far as to assume that the sheer size of the army would have damaged the local hydrology.[109] However, the Scamander is a substantial river (cf. the photograph and its Homeric epithet βαθυδίνης 'deep-whirling'), and the remark is more readily understandable as hyperbole which served to highlight the army's size, perhaps inspired in local folklore by the river's decreased waterlevels in summer.

While later in northern Greece, Xerxes' army would drink more rivers dry, the Scamander, as Herodotus stresses, was the first of them (πρῶτος ποταμῶν). But why should this be so? The answer is readily found in the river's prominence in the *Iliad*: the Scamander is the main river of the Trojan plain and the location of many battles. However, we should not forget that Homer's Scamander is not an ordinary river: it has both a human name (Scamander) and a divine one (Xanthos), as Homer alleges in *Iliad* 20.74. Sometimes, the Scamander itself appears as a divine force: it was begotten by Zeus (21.223) and as a god, it supported the Trojans (20.40). It also had a priest (Dolopion, 5.76-78) and received sacrifices (21.130-132). Finally, battles not only took place near the river, but also with the river (21.233-384). Herodotus' account could have conjured up images of this fight.[110] An even more important precedent can be found in 21.219, where the Scamander requests Achilles to remove from its bedding the bodies that obstruct the water flow. A Greek audience, familiar with the *Iliad*, would have regarded the Scamander as a divine force not to be trifled with, and we may agree with Bowie that Xerxes' hubris, like that of Achilles long before him, does not elicit a warm welcome from this numen of the Trojan plain.[111]

2.2.3 Troy: the temple of Athena Ilias and the tombs of the heroes

Xerxes then ascends the acropolis of Troy itself (7.43):

> [...] ἐπὶ τοῦτον δὴ τὸν ποταμὸν ὡς ἀπίκετο Ξέρξης, ἐς τὸ Πριάμου Πέργαμον ἀνέβη ἵμερον ἔχων θεήσασθαι. θεησάμενος δὲ καὶ πυθόμενος ἐκείνων ἕκαστα τῇ Ἀθηναίῃ τῇ Ἰλιάδι ἔθυσε βοῦς χιλίας, χοὰς δὲ οἱ Μάγοι τοῖσι ἥρωσι ἐχέαντο. ταῦτα δὲ ποιησαμένοισι νυκτὸς φόβος ἐς τὸ στρατόπεδον ἐνέπεσε. ἅμα ἡμέρῃ δὲ ἐπορεύετο ἐνθεῦτεν, ἐν ἀριστερῇ μὲν ἀπέργων Ῥοίτιον πόλιν καὶ Ὀφρύνειον καὶ Δάρδανον, ἥ περ δὴ Ἀβύδῳ ὅμουρός ἐστι, ἐν δεξιῇ δὲ Γέργιθας Τευκρούς.

---

108 E.g. Hauvette 1894, 304; Grundy 1901, 218; Meyer 1954, 353; Gnoli 1998, 62; Luce 1998, 72.
109 Hertel 2003, 224.
110 Elayi 1978, 137.
111 Bowie 2012, 275–276.

> [...] when Xerxes had arrived at this river, he went up to Priam's Pergamos, desiring to see it. And when he had seen and heard everything about it, he offered a thousand cattle to Athena of Ilion, and the Magi poured libations to the heroes. When they had done so, fear came over them in the camp at night. At daytime they marched from there, keeping the cities of Rhoition, Ophryneion and Dardanos, which shares a border with Abydos, on the left, and on the right the Teucrian Gergithes.

On the quest for Troy much has been written; few would now contest that it should be identified with Hisarlık.[112] While Herodotus' Troy is not necessarily the same as that of later authors such as Strabo, his association of Troy with the Scamander, as well as with Rhoiteion, Ophryneion and Dardanos, which have safe identifications,[113] automatically lead to Hisarlık.[114] The passage may even be regarded as the *terminus ante quem* for this identification.[115] When we consider that in Antiquity, Troy-Hisarlık was closer to the much-travelled Hellespont than presently, and that there was no discontinuity in habitation, it is conceivable that the city's name was never forgotten.[116] As such, Troy-Hisarlık, and the monuments in the surrounding countryside, must have been a visually remarkable feature in the landscape. Herodotus may have seen the city himself.[117]

Herodotus' claim that Xerxes offered a thousand cows to Athena presupposes some sort of religious infrastructure at Troy. We know that the latter-day Trojans

---

112 An overview can be found in Cook 1973, 92–103.
113 For the identification of Rhoiteion with Baba Kale near İn Tepe, see Leaf 1923, 155–158; Cook 1973, 81; Müller 1997, 914–917. For possible locations of Ophryneion around modern Erenköy, see Cook 1973, 72–77; Müller 1994, 889–892; against Leaf 1923, 153–155. For the identification of Dardanos with Şehitlik Batarya (Mal Tepe), immediately south of modern Çanakkale, see Leaf 1923, 151–152; Cook 1973, 57–60; Müller 1997, 807–808.
114 On the identification of Herodotus' Ilion with Hisarlık, see Schliemann 1881, 193–195. The alternative Troy in the Troad (originally proposed by Lechavelier) is Ballı Dağ, sometimes called the 'false Troy'. It is close to the Scamander, as well as near the much-discussed springs of Pınarbaşı. It has barrows immediately to its north and is visually more impressive than Hisarlık. It has not yielded Bronze Age remains, but only from the Classical and Hellenistic periods (cf. Cook 1973, 128–140). Still, the substantial remains at Hisarlık from the fifth century and its later (Hellenistic-Roman) identification as Ilion make it likely that Herodotus' Troy was Hisarlık. It is noteworthy that Strabo (13.1.27) doubted the claims of the locals of Ilion (Hisarlık) that their village was Homer's Troy; he believed it dated only to Lydian rule (13.1.42). Herodotus may have been less critical (cf. Leaf 1923, 198).
115 Rose 1998, 407.
116 There is archaeological evidence that Hisarlık was occupied during the Dark Ages, with a few buildings being repaired. However, this occupation was not necessarily continuous with that of the Bronze Age (Rose 2006, 189). From the second half of the eighth century, activities in the city were increasing (Cook 1973, 101), and we can be sure that there was a small town on the site in the fifth century BCE. The walls of Troy VI may still have been visible (Müller 1997, 966–967).
117 If Herodotus sailed up the Hellespont on his way to Scythia, he would have passed the Troad. Also note his remark that the land around Ilion was an alluvial plain (2.10; cf. Müller 1997, 965).

worshipped the Anatolian fertility goddess Cybele,[118] and there is secure evidence for a temple of Athena on the northern side of the city from the Hellenistic period onwards;[119] but we are not informed about the situation in the fifth century BCE. If there were any archaic or classical layers, they were destroyed for this temple's construction.[120] Nevertheless, there is little reason to doubt a continuity of cultic activity at Hisarlık, and there is now some evidence that the upper city of Hisarlık was in use as a ritual center in the late fifth century BCE.[121] Whether the temple existed or not, it is likely that Herodotus' account was directly inspired by the mention of the temple in *Iliad* 6.297-304 (νηὸν [...] Ἀθήνης ἐν πόλει ἄκρῃ 'temple of Athena in the highest part of the city').[122] The assertion that the Persians interpreted Athena as the Persian goddess Anahitā cannot be substantiated.[123]

Most scholars continue to see the visit of Xerxes to Troy as historically authentic.[124] But that idea is most unusual against the military background of the narrative in which it is embedded. How would Xerxes have benefited from this time-consuming act of propaganda at Troy at the time of his campaign?[125] Herodotus' focus on Troy

---

118 Rose 2006, 189–190: big predators, probably lions, were kept in her archaic sanctuary at the southwest side of the city.
119 For a reconstruction of the Hellenistic temple (begun in the later third century BCE) see Rose 2003.
120 See Goethert & Schleif 1962 for a discussion of the archaeological remains of the temple. Epigraphic evidence for the cult of Athena Ilias is found in *SEG* 53.1373.6; 55.1320. For a discussion of the lack of classical material see Schliemann 1881, 679–681; Schliemann 1884, 218–220; Rose 2006, 190.
121 Berlin (2002) discusses a ritual deposit of mostly fourth-century pottery (mostly table vessels) on the southern end of the upper citadel. She believes that the 'pale porous bassins' in these deposits are unquestionably Persian, as parallels are only known in Achaemenid centers such as Daskyleion and Persepolis. However, the rest of the deposited vessels undoubtedly display Greek influence. She explains the basins as a "ritual rapprochement" between Greek and Achaemenid rulers here.
122 See Hertel 2003, 94–96 for a discussion of the evidence. He assumes that Homer based his remark on an actual temple, which would show that there was a temple of Athena in the eighth century BCE. He refutes Dörpfeld's suggestion that there was no temple in the fifth century BCE, as Herodotus does not refer to an actual building.
123 This *interpretatio iranica* is advocated by Gnoli 1998, 62, mentioning Iranian sources showing that Anahitā sometimes received thousands of cows; he further argues that worship of Anahitā, who is a water goddess, was relevant here because the Scamander's water did not suffice. On Herodotus' representation of Anahitā, see de Jong 1997, 104–107; 269–270. For a different view see Hauvette 1894, 303–304.
124 For the view that the passage is essentially historical, see e.g. Instinsky 1949, 56–58; Boyce 1982, 166; Briquel & Desnier 1983, 27; Shahbazi 1985, 502; Müller 1994, 38; 1997, 964–965; Gnoli 1998, 60; Hertel 2003, 173; 178; 221–222; 226–227; Rosenberger 2003, 72; Brenza 2004, 101–102; Lenfant 2004, 78–82; Zwingmann 2012, 45 note 77; 90 with note 365; Dusinberre 2013, 53; Minchin 2016, 264–265; Kienast (1995, 119–120; 1996, 294) treats Xerxes' visit as evidence that the Persian-Trojan connection existed before Herodotus. Critical observations were made by Macan 1908, I 65: "Hdt. may have gone rather far in this item."; de Jong 1997, 302; 353.
125 Kienast (1995, 119–120; 1996, 294) saw the sacrifice of 1,000 cattle as a means to provide food to the army.

Fig. 10: The Hellenistic foundations of the temple of Athena at Hisarlık.

becomes all the more problematic given the complete omission in this account of the city of Daskyleion (modern Ergili), the most important Persian center of northwest Anatolia, where a palace has been found as well as many seals mentioning Xerxes.[126] While the seals may have been imported from Persia, it seems rather unlikely that Xerxes would have given the city a wide berth, as Herodotus' account suggests.

When the Magi pour libations to 'the heroes', this might have been pictured as a spontaneous ritual not linked to any particular place in the landscape of the Troad.[127] Still, Herodotus' remark could be based on some sort of real Trojan cult of the heroes who fought in the epic battle. There is no archaeological evidence for such worship at Hisarlık itself, but the surrounding landscape is dotted with twenty-nine burial mounds.[128]

---

[126] For an overview of historical and archaeological evidence for Persian settlement in this area see Sekunda 1988; Kaptan 2003; Dusinberre 2013, 56–59. For the seals mentioning Xerxes, see Balkan 1959; Kaptan 2002, 194–196; Dusinberre 2013, 65–69.

[127] Note that libations are performed in Troy itself in *Iliad* 6.259 and 7.478–482.

[128] Some of these are known to have been used or even constructed in the Classical or Hellenistic periods; in others, limited Bronze Age remains exist: Cook 1973, 91: "Tumuli have been excavated in the hope that they might prove to be heroic [...] but it seems clear now that nothing can be hoped for

Some of these were in historical times associated with Iliadic heroes: Paris' tomb is at Çoban Tepe (near Pınarbaşı);[129] Ajax's tomb is at modern İn Tepe near Rhoiteion;[130] Achilles, as well as his friend Patroclus, had two main sites associated with them: Sevri (or Sivri, or Beşik) Tepe,[131] as well as two tumuli at Sigeion (Kumtepe, close to modern Yenişehir).[132] Here was also the supposed grave of Antilochus (Kesik Tepe).[133]

---

from such operations." A good example of a 'modern' tumulus is the highest mound in Trojan plain, Üvecik Tepe. The tumulus, with foundations dating to the classical period, was enlarged by Caracalla for his friend Festus, whom he was said to have murdered to make his life conform to that of Achilles and Patroclus; cf. Cook 1973, 172–173. For an overview of Bronze Age *tepeler* in the Troad see Aslan & Bieg 2003.

129 Cook 1973, 129.

130 See Strabo 13.1.30–32, who mentions a cult for Ajax here (including a heroon and a statue); and Pliny the Elder (*Naturalis Historia* 5.33) who indicates that this was also the place where Ajax's men were stationed. For the archaeological identification, see Pococke 1745, II.2 104–105; Schliemann 1881, 725–727; Leaf 1923, 157–158; Cook 1973, 88–89; Hertel 2003, 176–178; Zwingmann 2012, 62. The present tumulus is a reconstruction by Hadrian, after the original one (with statue and bones) washed away in the water of the Hellespont (Philostratus, *Heroicus* 8.1). Pausanias (1.35.4–5) claims that a Mysian man had entered the tomb and seen the hero's larger-than-lifesize bones.

131 This is a Hellenistic tumulus, although the foundations contained Bronze Age remains; Cook 1973, 173–174; Luce 1998, 109; Boardman 2002, 54; Gabriel 2006, 357–359; Minchin 2016, 263. Heuck Allen (1999, 257–258) considers this the burial mound visited by Xerxes and Alexander. Against any association with Achilles is Hertel 2003, 161–165. By the sixth century BCE (as we know from Herodotus, who mentions a city of Achilles in 5.94), a small town founded by Mytileneans had grown around this tumulus at Yassı Tepe (Cook 1973, 185–186). We see here that the mythical geography of the landscape played a role in establishing rights of land ownership to the Greeks, corresponding to Herodotus' story in 5.94 that the Athenians did not agree with the Mytileneans as they had also played a part in the Trojan War (cf. Vandiver 1991, 61).

132 The identifications are again based on Strabo (13.1.32), who mentions that only these heroes, in addition to Ajax, were worshipped by the Ilians. Cf. Pococke 1745, II.2 105; Cook 1973, 181–185; Hertel 2003, 165–176 (adducing evidence for cults that well precede the fifth century BCE); Zwingmann 2012, 60–61; Minchin 2016, 262–263. Sigeion corresponds best to Homer's own description of Achilles' mound, when Hector fantasises about the grave of a Greek warrior killed by him (*Iliad* 7.84–91 and *Odyssey* 24.80–84; cf. Nagy 1979, 339–344). These mounds may also be the ones honoured with chariot races by Alexander and Hephaistion, as the sources say that they both went to a different one (cf. Cook 1973, 160). Note that there was still a bay between Sigeion and Rhoiteion, so that Achilles' tomb formed a pendant with Ajax's tomb at İn Tepe (Rhoiteion), as appears from the description by Pliny (*Naturalis Historia* 5.33). The larger of the two extant tombs, the tomb of Achilles was excavated by Schliemann (1881, 727–729; 1884, 271–282) and contained pottery from as early as Troy I to classical. See Cook 1973, 161–164 for an overview of the mound's excavation history. It was heavily battered in the World Wars and its original shape is now hard to make out. The smaller tomb of Patroclus (Kum Tepe), whose original shape is better preserved, had pottery of similar type (Schliemann 1884, 282–284; Cook 1973, 164). Although the tumulus dates from c. 500 BCE, excavations have also revealed a residential occupation going back to the fifth millennium BCE (Gabriel 2006, 355–357).

133 For Antilochus' cult, see Cook 1973, 165–166; the cult connotations of this mound survived into later times, as indicated by the chapels of Agios Dimitrios and Athanasios; note that the hill is not man-made.

It is possible that in the later fifth century BCE some of the tumuli functioned as mnemotopes not only for the burial of Iliadic heroes, but also for a real or imagined visit by Xerxes and the Magi.[134] After all, most of the mounds mentioned were easily visitable from the Aegean and the Hellespont. Moreover, there is evidence that they were in use as tourist sites (in addition to the various other mnemotopes along the Troad's coasts).[135] The littoral may therefore be regarded as a cultic hotspot with many epic mnemotopes that elicited the creation of new anecdotes about interaction with these places by historical persons.

Fig. 11: Sivri Tepe.

---

134 Hertel (2003, 173; 178) connects the worship specifically with Achilles' mound at Sigeion and with that of Ajax at İn Tepe; cf. Boedeker 1988, 47; Rose 1998, 407.
135 A general discussion of these tumuli as the aim of sightseeing is found in Zwingmann 2012, 59–73. Other mnemotopes include the beach at Yeniköy where Heracles saved Trojan princess Hesione from the sea monster sent by Poseidon (Strabo 13.1.32; Leaf 1923, 166–168.); the Sigeion ridge area was the conjectured naval station of the Greeks in the Trojan War (Strabo 13.1.31; Cook 1973, 171–172), and Hector had a sacred grove at Ophryneion (Strabo 13.1.29; for a discussion of the location, which remains unknown, and a potential tumulus see Hertel 2003, 179–180; Zwingmann 2012, 63).

Despite the existence of this elaborate memory landscape in the Troad, scholars have discussed the exact meaning of Herodotus' phrase 'the heroes', with some scholars believing that the Magi can only have meant to sacrifice to Trojan (i.e. Asiatic) heroes such as Hector, or even that they interpreted them as Zoroastrian *fravaši* (spirits).[136] However, there is no direct evidence for such assertions, and the fact that most extant tombs were associated with Greek heroes suggests otherwise.[137]

Supporters of the scene's historicity have explained it in various ways. One could assume that by giving a lavish royal display at Troy, Xerxes would have claimed Asian ownership of the city and avenge the actions of the Greeks at Troy.[138] This observation ties in well with Herodotus' remark that the Persians believed that their enmity with the Greeks started with their siege of Troy, which they claimed as an Asian city (1.5).[139] Another option is to see this offering as a conciliation with the Greeks of Asia, both those fighting in Xerxes' army and those who lived in the area, who may have been enraged about the destruction brought upon their country by the Athenian destruction of Sardis.[140] One scholar has advocated a third interpretation: Xerxes may have been attracted to the city merely because it was a famous place.[141] While these three explanations are, in principle, viable, there is little evidence to support them. Regarding the first explanation, we have no evidence that the concepts 'Europe' and 'Asia' had any relevance to the Persians.[142] Moreover, notwithstanding Herodotus' remarks in 1.3-1.5, it seems unlikely that the Trojan saga was of any interest to the Persians.[143]

Underlying all of these explanations for the historicity of the scene is the idea that the Persians were conscious of cults in conquered areas, and that they were usually

---

136 Gnoli 1998, 60–62. For more on *fravaši* in Greek texts see de Jong 1997, 301–302.
137 We are told that Alexander the Great sacrificed at the tombs of Achilles, Ajax and Patroclus (Diodorus Siculus 17.17.6–7; Justinian 11.5.12; Plutarchus, *Alexander* 15.4; Arrian, *Anabasis Alexandri* 1.11.7–8).
138 Georges 1994, 48, 61–62; Vermeule 1995, 467–468 (suggesting that Xerxes visited Troy "probably to honor King Priam for his celebrated resistance to a prolonged Greek assault."); Green 1996, 78; Kienast 1996, 294. Haubold 2007, 55; Hartmann 2010, 217; Saïd 2012, 96; Bridges 2015, 95 note 56. De Jong 1997, 353 argues that Persian interference with the Trojan War is a topos in the *Histories* (and perhaps the reason for writing it), but "extremely unlikely" in a historical sense.
139 Kienast 1996, 294–295; Haubold 2007; Saïd 2012, 95–96.
140 How & Wells 1912, II 147; so too Georges (1994, 60–62), who suspects the Peisistratids, who had a base at Sigeion, as the ones who inspired Xerxes to do this.
141 Erskine 2001, 85.
142 Lenfant 2004, 81. Cataudella (1998, 61) argues that the Persians did not lay claim to territory outside Asia; however, he bases this idea on Herodotus alone. For a discussion of Troy as a European city in Herodotus' view, see Cobet 2010, 42 and the passages 1.4, 7.33 and 7.174.
143 Gnoli (1998, 61) argues that Herodotus' mention of the Persian wise men in book 1 suggests that the Persians may have had access to the Trojan mythology. This cannot be excluded, but it remains unclear who these wise men were, where they lived and to what extent their knowledge was relevant to the king. The Trojan war seems to have been a Greek-only affair, and there is no evidence that it played a role further east than northwest Asia Minor.

tolerant of them.¹⁴⁴ It is accordingly pointed out that the Achaemenids were apt at appropriating 'foreign' cultural elements into their own culture (a notion embodied in the *apadana* at Persepolis, which contains elements from all corners of the empire).¹⁴⁵ It has also been suggested that there is evidence from the Persian heartland that the Persians were more polytheistic than they claimed to be in their inscriptions.¹⁴⁶ But more often, the *Histories* themselves are mined for material that endorses this view: for example, it has been pointed out that Herodotus mentions specialists of Greek religion as part of Xerxes' army.¹⁴⁷ Another legitimation of this view is found in the many examples of this tolerance 'recorded' by Herodotus: apart from the Troy episode, the Persians seem to respect or even participate in the worship of various Greek divinities and/or heroes, including Apollo at Delos (6.118); the Strymon at Ennea Hodoi (§2.3.4), Thetis and the Nereids at Sepias (§2.4.2), Athamas and/or Zeus Laphystios at Halos (§2.3.9), Athena at Athens (§2.7.4) and Protesilaos at Elaious (§2.10.4).

As an outsider in the field of Iranology, I lack the expertise to fully assess the discussion from that perspective. However, there is no solid basis to maintain the historicity of the stories about Persians historically worshipping Greek deities (see §3.2.3). But even more importantly, none of these stories is found outside the *Histories*. At the same time, these instances are inconsistent with Herodotus' own remarks about Persian religion: Herodotus describes the Persians as opposed to temples and Greek-style polytheism, revering only Zeus (Ahuramazda), Mithra-Aphrodite and the natural elements, and he also says that the Magi do not perform libations (1.131-132).¹⁴⁸ One could overcome this inconsistency by pointing out that the Persians may have interpreted Greek divinities as Iranian, but this is problematic in itself.¹⁴⁹

---

144 E.g. Bowie 2007, 143; Funke 2007, 26–27; Kuhrt 2007, 242; de Bakker 2010, 224–225.
145 Haubold 2007, 50–52.
146 The so-called Gadatas letter, allegedly sent from Darius to Gadatas, his satrap in Ionia, is occasionally taken as reflecting Achaemenid piety of Greek gods (e.g. Walser 1984, 51).
147 Briant 1996, 564–566: Onomakritos (7.6), Teisamenos, Hegesistratos, Hippomachos of Leukas (9.37-38).
148 On this problem see Georges 1994, 60; de Jong 1997, 111–112; 352–353. Murray 1987, 108 suggested that Herodotus only had a superficial understanding of Persian religion and the Magi, which means that he did not have contact with them. On the other hand, we should not underestimate the extent to which knowledge about Persian religion was available in classical Greece, as evidenced by the fifth-century BCE Derveni papyrus which gives details on Magi rituals (Tsantsanoglou 2008).
149 E.g Cook 1983, 148–149; on the *interpretatio graeca* of Iranian divinities, see de Jong 1997, 29–34, stressing that we must be cautious; Mikalson 2003, 159–161 points out that the stories about Persians worshipping Greek gods are problematic because we know that Herodotus hellenised the religious beliefs of the Persians. Herodotus' information about Persian religion is not necessarily accurate; for a reflection on Herodotus' sources in this matter see de Jong 1997, 88–89. On Greek knowledge of the Magi, see de Jong 1997, 387–402, who points out (page 392) that Herodotus presents the Magi as a known category, so that presumably knowledge about them was available; see also Tsantsanoglou 2008.

In addition, such examples seem extraordinary in the light of Xerxes' own words as laid down in the Daiva inscription from Persepolis (XPh). The king here literally proclaims that 'the pagan gods [daivas] may not be worshipped!', after saying that he burnt down a temple in one of the many lands that he controlled (which may or may not be a reference to the destruction of one or more temples on the Athenian Acropolis).[150] Scholars have recently argued against the idea that this text may reveal anything about Persian attitudes to Greek religion. A currently widespread idea is that this text should be seen as a ceremonial continuation of earlier inscriptions.[151] It has been also been suggested that the text reflects an inner-Iranian issue, as the opposition between Ahuramazda and the daivas is a well-known dogmatic issue in later Iranian thought.[152] But although it is true that the Daiva inscription as a whole connects to earlier inscriptions by using formulaic language, its contents are not necessarily ceremonial: the objections do not preclude that the inscription may give some insight into Xerxes' religious ideology, and at the very least it shows that Xerxes prided himself in eradicating the cult of foreign gods.[153] It remains a legitimate question whether it is possible that someone who had these words set in stone had really sacrificed 1,000 cows to Athena. It cannot be excluded, but in this case the hypocrisy projected on the historical Xerxes is unmatched.

The alleged tolerance of the Persians is also inconsistent with the more ample references to hostility towards Greek cults in Herodotus, including the destruction of temples in Phocis, Boeotia and Attica and the assault of Delphi.[154] The point is not

---

150 Although Xerxes may have referred to the Acropolis of Athens, the destruction of the temple may have taken place in any area of the empire (e.g. Babylon or Egypt). Sancisi-Weerdenburg 1980, 7–8 and Boyce 1982, 174 disconnected the reference from the Acropolis, as they took Herodotus' assertion that the Athenians were allowed to worship their own gods as historical (which it may not be); Sancisi-Weerdenburg (1980, 14; 29–31) Briant 1996, 569 stressed that the Daiva inscription is imprecise geographically and chronologically and that this may have been done on purpose, for example to make the inscription a timeless memorial. See also Sancisi-Weerdenburg 1999, 97.
151 Sancisi-Weerdenburg 1980, especially 15–16 and 34–36; she argues that Xerxes' use of the word 'daiva' does not mean that he was a Zoroastrian (pages 4–5; 19–21); see also Walser 1984, 51; Wiesehöfer 1993, 87–88; Sancisi-Weerdenburg 1994a, 207–209. Bridges 2015, 89–95 also argues against a historical reading of the Daiva inscription, stressing the inscription's imperialist message which paints Xerxes as an ideal king.
152 In der Smitten 1973, argueing that the word 'daiva' referred to non-Zoroastrian pagan gods; Cook 1983, 147–148; Ahn 1992, 120–122.
153 Harrison 2011, 80–82 rightly argues that we may have gone too far in abstracting the daiva inscription, and that actual destruction of sanctuaries took place, albeit perhaps not for religious reasons per se, but for political ones (e.g. the suppression of rebellions). For a discussion of the exact Zoroastrian beliefs (rather: which Zoroastrian beliefs) and the difficulties we have to reconstruct this, see Wiesehöfer 1993, 139–148; on the problems of reconstructing the history of Zoroastrianism, see de Jong 1997, 39–75.
154 Wecklein 1867, 260–261 suggested that Xerxes was tolerant of Greek religion and could only be attributed the destruction of the Acropolis. He also (pages 268–269) suggested that the Persians were

so much that these examples of hostility prove that the Persians were always hostile (destruction of whatever cause may have been projected by Greeks on 'sacrilegious' Persians); rather, they remind us how hard it is to reconstruct the religious attitudes of the Persians towards their own and foreign gods in this early period on the basis of Herodotus' writings.[155] Thomas Harrison, warning of the dangers in accepting the currently popular view of tolerant Acheaemenids and problematising the use of the term 'tolerance', rightly points out that "A positive narrative of Persian imperialism has arguably become so entrenched that contrary currents of evidence are now *understated*."[156]

Xerxes' visit is sometimes discussed in relation to that of later famous visitors who made offerings to Athena or the heroes. These include Mindarus,[157] Alexander the Great,[158] Antiochus III,[159] Scipio and Livius Salinator[160] and even Mehmet II.[161] The belief in the historicity of these later visits may have helped to give credence to Herodotus' story about Xerxes.[162] But it is possible that the authors in which these stories appear were inspired by Herodotus' story about Xerxes; many of them (such as Kritoboulos) are obviously inspired by the *Histories* on a stylistic level, and feature legendary elements.[163]

---

depicted as intolerant to increase Greek national hate against them, and to strengthen the belief that the Gods had acted in defence of Greece.
155 Scheer 2000, 204 rightfully argues: "Die Duldung einheimischer Kulte im unterworfenen Gebiet ist jedoch nicht zu verwechseln mit allgemeiner religiöser Scheu vor den Göttern der Unterworfenen oder der Kriegsgegner im Kriegsfall." Rocchi (1980, 426) points out that Xerxes consistently offends the main Greek gods, but has disproportional respect for marginal divinities (Thetis, Nereids, Athamas); however, she does not discuss the cult of Athena in Troy. Also, there may have been individual differences between the Achaemenids; an example of this variety is found in a comparison of Darius and Xerxes; in XPh, Xerxes appears decidedly more orthodox than his father in DB IV, where Darius claims that he was helped by Ahuramazda and 'the other gods'.
156 Harrison 2011, 73–90 (quote on page 75); see also Asheri et al. 2010, 233–234.
157 Xenophon, *Hellenica* 1.1.4.
158 Diodorus Siculus 17.17.2–3; Zahrnt 1996, 135 suggests that Alexander would have gone independent of whether Xerxes had gone here; cf. Georges 1994, 64; Erskine 2001, 226.
159 Livy 35.43; cf. Erskine 2001, 225–226; see Erskine 2001 232–233 for other evidence of Hellenistic rulers interacting with the temple.
160 Livy 37.37.2–3; cf. Georges 1994, 65; Erskine 2001, 234–235.
161 Cobet 2010, 47–48 suggests that this may be simply an allusion to Herodotus by the historian Kritoboulos.
162 Instinsky 1949, 54–67 believed that Alexander planned his actions to align them as retributions to what Xerxes had done, according to Herodotus. See also the reviews of this work by Walbank (1950) and Strasburger (1951), who did not believe that Alexander knew Herodotus' work personally. For the relationship between the Alexander and Xerxes figures, see Bridges 2015, 119–125; she also sees Alexander's alleged revisiting of 'Xerxes sites' such as the grave of Protesilaos and Troy as historical.
163 E.g. Diodorus Siculus (17.17.6) says that a statue of a Phrygian satrap had ominously collapsed on Alexander's visit.

If previous explanations of Herodotus' story about Xerxes' visit do not seem particularly convincing, how should we interpret it then? I propose that it should, first, be understood within the context of Xerxes' invasion at large: it adds a powerful touch of dramatic irony to the Persian invasion, because Xerxes offers to the same goddess whose Athenian sanctuary he is going to destroy, ultimately leading to the demise of the entire expedition. By sending panic to Xerxes and the Magi after the offerings, Athena and 'the heroes' show that they were hostile towards the Persian presence in the Troad and their subsequent plans.[164] The effect to Herodotus' audience must have been bordering on the comical. They may well have thought that Xerxes was foolish in trying to appease the territorial numina with such strong Greek associations, and ignore the powerful warnings that ensue.[165]

Secondly, I propose that the story can be thought of as interacting with Troy as an Iliadic mnemotope. It is obvious that Herodotus was familiar with the Trojan War saga and Homer's works in particular. There is a wealth of evidence that suggests Troy was the most important tourist site of Anatolia throughout the later centuries of Antiquity,[166] and there is no reason to assume it did not have a similar function in the fifth century BCE.[167] This observation corresponds remarkably well to the above passage, in which Xerxes is made a quasi-tourist who has a great desire to know everything about such an important historical place. However, this background does not in itself prove that Xerxes visited the city, but rather makes it plausible that such a thought could enter folklore about Xerxes' invasion in the immediate post-war period. Only few scholars have recognised this perspective.[168]

---

[164] This idea is found in Hauvette 1894, 303–304; Bischoff 1932, 61; Waters 1985, 85–86; 171; Vandiver 1991, 212–213 (making the interesting observation that if Herodotus regarded the heroes as Trojan, the message may have been that Xerxes did not learn from previous mistakes, as these heroes had during the Trojan War not prevented Greek victory); Mikalson 2003, 44. Bridges 2015, 63 believes that the episode is an example of how Herodotus makes Xerxes a more pious person. Some earlier authors saw the panic as historically authentic: Macan (1908, I 65) thought the panic was connected to the thunderstorm at the Ida; Pritchett (1974, 163) attributed it to another thunderstorm. Even Aly 1969 (first edition 1921), 173, who was on the lookout for folkloric elements in Herodotus' work, believed: "Das Volk hat für solche Zwischenfälle wie das Gewitter am Ida (42), die Panik bei Ilion (43) ein gutes Gedächtnis."
[165] Hauvette 1894, 303–304; cf. Flory 1987, 86–87, who points out that Herodotus places Xerxes in a tragic light.
[166] For a thorough discussion of all the evidence, see Zwingmann 2012, 31–106; see also Hertel 2003, 296–297; Patzek 2006.
[167] For the important symbolic role that Troy had for the Greeks and especially the Athenians, see Berlin 2002, 140–141; 145–147.
[168] Cobet (2010, 42) points out that the scene only testifies to the cultic status that Troy had attained by Herodotus' time. Grethlein (2009, 205) compared Xerxes' touristic interests here and elsewhere in the *Histories* to that of Herodotus himself.

To contemporaries of Herodotus, Xerxes' visit would be of deeply symbolic importance, as Xerxes treads in Priam's footsteps. Vandiver notes, "the mention of [the heroes] in this context serves as a type of metonymy for the whole rich mythology of the Trojan War, and would irresistibly remind Herodotus' Greek audience of the results when Greek and Asian met at Homer's Troy."[169] A specific element that ancient recipients would have recognised as having an Iliadic precedent is the offering of cattle to Athena. It brings to mind the scene of Trojan women offering cattle and a peplos to her (*Iliad* 6.86-95): and that sacrifice had been just as futile as Xerxes'.

2.2.4 Abydos: Xerxes' throne (I) and the Hellespont bridges

According to Herodotus, the bridging of the Hellespont took place some time before Xerxes came to Abydos and was directed from Sousa and Sardis. Contrary to popular belief (perhaps inspired by illustrations, or by the association of the scene at Salamis, see §2.8.3 and §2.8.6), Herodotus never mentions that Xerxes was personally present at the Hellespont to oversee construction of the bridges. The locations of the bridgeheads are given in 7.33-34:

> μετὰ δὲ ταῦτα παρεσκευάζετο ὡς ἐλῶν ἐς Ἄβυδον. οἱ δὲ ἐν τούτῳ τὸν Ἑλλήσποντον ἐζεύγνυσαν ἐκ τῆς Ἀσίης ἐς τὴν Εὐρώπην. ἔστι δὲ τῆς Χερσονήσου τῆς ἐν Ἑλλησπόντῳ, Σηστοῦ τε πόλιος μεταξὺ καὶ Μαδύτου, ἀκτὴ τρηχέα ἐς θάλασσαν κατήκουσα Ἀβύδῳ καταντίον. ἐς ταύτην ὦν τὴν ἀκτὴν ἐξ Ἀβύδου ὁρμώμενοι ἐγεφύρουν τοῖσι προσέκειτο, τὴν μὲν λευκολίνου Φοίνικες, τὴν δ' ἑτέρην τὴν βυβλίνην Αἰγύπτιοι. ἔστι δὲ ἑπτὰ στάδιοι ἐξ Ἀβύδου ἐς τὴν ἀπαντίον.

> After this, he prepared to march to Abydos. At that moment they were bridging the Hellespont from Asia to Europe. The peninsula which is in the Hellespont has a rough coast, between the city of Sestos and Madytos, which comes down to the sea opposite Abydos. So the men to whom it was assigned constructed a bridge to that coast, setting out from Abydos, the Phoenicians the one of flax, and the Egyptians the other one of papyrus. There are seven stades from Abydos to the other side.

Xerxes himself only reaches the Hellespont in 7.44, a few years after the construction of the bridges:

---

169 Vandiver 1991, 212; equally Heuck Allen 1999, 37: "those later chapters were written over the Homeric narrative like a palimpsest, inscribing the actions of other heroes pursuing their own fates and ends." Baragwanath (2008, 266) argues that the passage brings to mind Homer's equal treatment of Trojans and Greeks and therefore sets "the stage for a conflict of equals" in the following passage featuring Artabanos. However, there does not seem to be a compelling reason to see symbolic continuity between the passages. Baragwanath does not mention the panic in the camp which closes the anecdote.

ἐπεὶ δ' ἐγένετο ἐν Ἀβύδῳ μέσῃ, ἠθέλησε Ξέρξης ἰδέσθαι πάντα τὸν στρατόν. καὶ προεπεποίητο γὰρ ἐπὶ κολωνοῦ ἐπίτηδες αὐτῷ ταύτῃ προεξέδρη λίθου λευκοῦ, (ἐποίησαν δὲ Ἀβυδηνοὶ ἐντειλαμένου πρότερον βασιλέος), ἐνθαῦτα ὡς ἵζετο, κατορῶν ἐπὶ τῆς ἠιόνος ἐθηεῖτο καὶ τὸν πεζὸν καὶ τὰς νέας, θηεύμενος δὲ ἱμέρθη τῶν νεῶν ἅμιλλαν γινομένην ἰδέσθαι. ἐπεὶ δὲ ἐγένετό τε καὶ ἐνίκων Φοίνικες Σιδώνιοι, ἥσθη τε τῇ ἀμίλλῃ καὶ τῇ στρατιῇ.

When he came inside the city of Abydos, Xerxes wanted to see his entire army, because right there on a hill a throne of white stone had been conveniently constructed for him in advance; the people of Abydos had made it after the king had ordered it beforehand. As he sat there, looking down on the coast, he gazed at his infantry and ships, and as he saw them, he desired to see a competition between the ships. This then was done and the Sidonian Phoenicians won, and he was pleased with the competition and the army.

Abydos lay in the northern part of modern city of Çanakkale; here, a hill called Mal Tepe (Turkish for 'Treasure Hill') at Cape Nağara is usually taken as the starting point of the two bridges.[170] The area is currently inaccessible, due to its designation as a military zone (which may not be entirely coincidental). A nineteenth-century report talks about a "ridge of rocks, where Xerxes commenced the construction of his bridge",[171] and several objects from the site are known, among which a Persian lion-shaped bronze weight with Aramaic writing.[172] Although Herodotus does not give an exact localisation, Mal Tepe is usually also taken as the hill where Xerxes' throne stood and from where he looked over his army.[173] Early traveller Nassau William Senior reports that the Turks had excavated the hill to raise earthworks there, and had found the marble throne, as well as an inscription in which Xerxes grants rights to the city of Abydos.[174] This report cannot be verified, however, because according to Senior, the Turks had destroyed the throne and lost the inscription.

---

170 For the identification of Abydos, see Leake 1841, 229–230; Leaf 1923, 117; 121–125; Müller 1997, 757–760. Myres (1953, 220–221) and Hammond & Roseman (1996, 90) specifically mention the coast which runs east of the cape. Strabo (13.1.22) details that the Asian bridgehead was located at a point some distance north of Abydos. Cape Nağara has the best harbour in the Troad, and a vessel sailing up the Hellespont likely needed to spend some time waiting here (cf. Polybius 16.29.13; Müller 1997, 759).
171 Walsch 1836, 216.
172 Cook 1973, 56–57.
173 Leaf 1923, 117–119; Müller 1997, 760; this Mal Tepe is not to be confused with that on the Thracian Chersonesos, which was the grave of Hecuba (cf. Casson 1926, 221).
174 Senior 1859, 155.

Fig. 12: Mal Tepe.

Sestos was located on the hills northeast of the fortress Bigalı Kalesi (partially constructed from building material from Sestos), close to the village of Akbaş.[175] The name of Madytos is continued in the town of Maydos, the former name of Eceabat.[176] The ἀκτή was earlier taken as a promontory, but it now seems clear that this word in Herodotus means 'coast'.[177] Strabo (13.1.22) tells us that the European bridgehead was located at a point some distance south of Sestos, called Ἀποβάθρα ('place of disembarkation'). The bridgehead has therefore been identified with the plain today marked by the fort of Bigalı Kalesi.[178]

---

175 Isaac 1986, 195–196; Müller 1997, 927–931.
176 Müller 1997, 876–877.
177 Scholars assuming that ἀκτή means 'promontory' have identified this with the hill now called Poyraz Tepe, immediately west of Bigalı Kalesi (Leaf 1923, 123; Hammond 1988, 530–532; Müller 1994, 35). This confused Macan (1908, II 146) and Müller (1997, 839), who noted that the bridges must have ended upon nearby level country. Leake (1841, 230) makes the bridges end at the plain east of the hill of Sestos. For the idea that ἀκτή in Herodotus always means 'coast', see Bowen 1998, 353.
178 Scholars believe that this plain is an ideal place for the army to collect before marching on, especially in the presence of wheeled vehicles, and may be thought of as representing Strabo's Ἀποβάθρα; cf. Hauvette 1894, 295; Casson 1926, 211–212, 217; Maurice 1930, 216; Myres 1953, 220–221.

Fig. 13: The Hellespont from the European bridgehead (Bigalı Kalesi).

The bridges themselves, however, remain elusive. Two topographical problems can be identified. First, the distance crossed by the bridges, which is mostly given as seven stades (1,250 metres) by Herodotus (4.85) and others,[179] does not match the locations of Abydos and Sestos, which are two kilometres distant. The word ἑπταστάδιον may, of course, simply be a 'legendary' epithet.[180] At any rate, the location given by Herodotus and Strabo may be an 'educated guess', does not need to be historical and does not exclude that others had identified the bridgeheads differently. The best candidate for an alternative location of the bridges is between the landmark fortresses Çimenlik (at Çanakkale) and Kilitbahir (at Eceabat), where the Hellespont is at its narrowest at 1,400 meters, slightly over 7.4 stades.[181]

---

179 Strabo 2.5.22; 13.1.22; Pliny the Elder, *Naturalis Historia* 4.49; 5.141.
180 Leaf (1923, 122) suggested that the word ἑπταστάδιον was simply a fancy epithet owing to the bridges' fame, and should not be taken literally. Xenophon, *Hellenica* 4.8.5 has the distance as eight stades.
181 The location between these castles, which were formerly thought to mark the sites of Abydos and Sestos (cf. Pococke 1745, II.2 103) corresponds better to Polybius' description of the Abydos-Sestos stretch as a 'gate' (16.29.11), a statement which the size of the later fortresses attests to. Müller (1997, 839), who firmly advocates the historicity of the location given by Herodotus, explains the observation

The exact location is not the only problem: it may, more generally, be doubted whether the Hellespont was ever successfully bridged by ships. Although the technique was available,[182] and the historicity of the Hellespont bridges is usually taken for granted and has also received an elaborate defence,[183] there are no parallels, even in modern times, for ship bridges which spanned the distance which the Hellespont requires.[184] We can, therefore, remain open to the possibility that the bridges *at the Hellespont* existed only in the Greek imagination.

Herodotus' account gives a possible source that may have fuelled the fantasy: a painting of ship bridges in the temple of Hera at Samos, seen by Herodotus himself (4.87-88). Although Herodotus tells us that this painting depicted Darius at the Bosporus near Byzantium, it has been suggested that it may have formed the inspiration for more stories.[185] Within this context, it is relevant to note that, although the Hellespont and Bosporus refer to two different sea straits today, the names were used

---

that the bridges were not built between Çimenlik and Kilitbahir by pointing at the strong currents. He suggests that it was erroneously believed in antiquity that the ἑπταστάδιον (Çimenlik-Kilitbahir) applied to the line Abydos-Sestos, which was more marked, as shown by its later mnemotopical status for the myth of Hero and Leander (cf. below).

182 Herodotus detailed technical description (7.25; 7.36) is matched by modern examples in Asia, see Obst 1913, 48; Hammond & Roseman 1996, 91. Nevertheless, Hammond (1988, 527–530) discusses problems with Herodotus' description of the bridges. It has also been pointed out that the manner in which Herodotus describes the Bosporus bridge reveals that he had not actually seen such a bridge (Cawkwell 2005, 5).

183 A defence of the historicity of the bridges and a detailed reconstruction of what they might have looked like is found in Hammond & Roseman 1996, who claim that "Classical scholars have generally found these accounts inadequate and even inexplicable" (page 88), but that they were nevertheless "well within the capacity of the engineers of the day to design and build." (page 95).

184 An important consideration in this respect is that the water level has risen since 480 BCE, so that the distance to be bridged was considerably shorter (see the map in Hammond & Roseman 1996, 93). Nevertheless, the span of seven stades is probably beyond technical possibilities and was not reached until modern times. It remains possible that Xerxes or other Persian rulers had attempted to build them: the initial failure which Herodotus records (7.34), as well as the broken state in which the bridges were allegedly seen by Greeks who had made a special trip to Abydos for this purpose after the battle of Mykale (9.114) may simply reflect that Xerxes (or someone else) had begun the project, but later abandoned it.

185 As West (2013, 124) notes: "No doubt among those who frequented the Heraion were people happy to provide a commentary on the picture and explain who were depicted; it would not be surprising if their exposition owed something to their own speculation." She also discusses other material in Herodotus that may have been inspired by this picture (the description of Darius' and Xerxes' forces and the belief dat Darius campaigned in Europe); see also Tallis 2010. Note that the historicity of the Bosporus bridges is also uncertain, but that the sea strait there is narrower and therefore more 'bridgeable' than the Hellespont; moreover pontoon bridges were possible on the nearby Golden Horn, as the stories about the bridge built by Justinian the Great and the early nineteenth-century bridge built by Mahmud II, as well as the modern Galata Bridge suggest.

interchangeably by some authors. This may or may not have constituted an error.[186] A story about a historical ship bridge at the Bosporus (or Golden Horn?) may therefore have been erroneously reinterpreted as referring to the Hellespont. The story can alternatively or additionally have been catalysed by alleged relics of the bridges seen in situ after the battle of Mykale (9.114) or by purported cables or even ships which were later on display in the "sanctuaries of Athens" (9.121), which Herodotus himself may have seen.[187] As Proietti notes, these relics "costituiscono un elemento cruciale dell'immaginario immediatamente post-persiano".[188]

We do not know for certain whether the Hellespont bridges were ever begun or completed, or never existed at all, Nevertheless, it is clear that the story had become an important idea in the Greek conception of the Persian invasion of Europe in the period between the wars and Herodotus' research. The waters between Abydos and Sestos constituted a mnemotope where one could imagine the bridges before one's eyes.

On closer inspection it seems that the success of the idea of the bridges depended on their relevance in colouring the character of the Persian king as a 'great builder': Herodotus himself thought that Xerxes' project was a form of competition with his father Darius.[189] We have already seen that such infrastructural projects are a common type of mnemotopes in the *Histories* (§1.4.2). We will see that this theme appears at various additional mnemotopes connected to Xerxes' invasion (§3.1.3).

To the Greeks of the later fifth century BCE the construction of the Hellespont bridges was an act of transgression as well, because the Hellespont was at that time regarded as the inviolable boundary between Asia and Europe (a notion which was perhaps a result of the Persian Wars).[190] This is underlined by the story that Onomakritos had predicted the crossing (7.6) and that Artabanos had warned against it (7.10.β; 7.10.γ). Xerxes'

---

186 The name Bosporus was used for the Hellespont by Aeschylus (*Persae* 723; 746) and Sophocles (*Ajax* 884); and at least two modern scholars have done the same (Grethlein 2009; 2010; Tallis 2010).
187 Where the Athenians deposited the cables is not made explicit; presumably, at least some of them was taken to the Acropolis (Gauer 1968, 37). Despite the absence of concrete evidence, Amandry (1953, 111–121) makes a case for a dedication in the Athenian stoa at Delphi. See also Elayi 1979, 141; Gauer 1968, 101–102. Against this view, see Walsh 1986. In addition, Gauer (1968, 73) makes a case for the dedication of a ship from the Hellespont on the Acropolis.
188 Proietti 2015a, 164.
189 Kienast 1996, 295; see especially 7.8.α and 7.8.β for Herodotus' presentation of these ideas.
190 The opposition between Europe and Asia along the Hellespont is not yet found in the Iliad, which details that both Sestos and Abydos were on the Trojan side during the war and even led by a general called Asios (2.835–839). In Herodotus it is more clear, appearing for example in 6.33, where Herodotus says that in the years before Darius' invasion of Greece, the Ionians had captured the European side, and the Persians the Asian side. See also Herodotus' remarks about Asia (9.89). For the idea of the Hellespont as a symbolic space, see Rood 2012, 124–125. Haubold (2013, 114–117) suggests that the Greek portrayal of the Hellespont as a boundary reflects an Achaemenid (or even Mesopotamian) imperial mental map. For the crossing of rivers in the Near East as a symbolic act, see Desnier 1995.

aggression is apparent in the story about his anger upon the destruction of the bridges by a storm, prompting his whipping, fettering and even branding of the water (7.35), later followed by a libation and an offering to the sun or the Hellespont itself (7.54; Herodotus was not certain), which he did by throwing a cup, a golden mixing bowl and a Persian sword into the Hellespont.[191] Rather than evidence for Zoroastrian cults,[192] these anecdotes are more easily explained as originating in Greek imagination as an example of Xerxes' hubris.[193] The notion of transgression can also be seen in the stories about the Greek attempt to destroy the bridges (9.106): they found them already broken (9.114). This episode, found towards the end of Herodotus' work, probably carried symbolic weight by restoring the 'natural' boundary between Europe and Asia.[194] Herodotus does not say how this happened, but it is possible that he or other Greeks regarded the destruction

---

Abydos – Sestos was also regarded as the passage by which the Turks entered Europe in historiography of the early Ottoman empire (cf. Walsch 1836, 216–217).

191 Baragwanath (2008, 281–282) suggests that Herodotus, by leaving open the option whether Xerxes offered to the sun or to the Hellespont, tries to make his readers think about the two possibilities.

192 Rollinger (2013, 102–111) places Xerxes' cult at the Hellespont in a Near Eastern tradition, and suggests that this was Herodotus' source. For the idea that the Persians regarded salt water as evil, see also Hauvette 1894, 298–299; Burn 1962, 320–321; Boyce 1982, 166. Another way to regard the event as historical is to assume that Xerxes, in his position as Great King chosen by Ahuramazda himself, addressed with his punishment and offerings various Zoroastrian gods: Boyce 1982, 167 (Mithra and Varuna); Briquel & Desnier 1983 (the water god Apąm Napāt); Ahn 1992, 118–119; Balcer 1995, 235 (Angra Mainyu); Kienast 1996, 296 (an unspecified daiva). Briant (1996, 565) suggested that Xerxes consciously addressed a Greek divinity, but Boedeker (1988, 43) points out that Herodotus' audience would have noticed that no Greek divinities were worshipped. However, de Jong (1997, 227; 416–417) treats the passage with suspicion, arguing that the whipping is at odds with the respect for water in Zoroastrian religion. Alexander allegedly offered to Poseidon and the Nereids from a golden bowl at this exact spot, and also offered a bull (Arrian, *Anabasis Alexandri* 1.11.6). It is not possible to argue for the historicity of Herodotus' episode on the basis of that story, as it may itself have been inspired by Herodotus' story about Xerxes. In 1.11, Arrian, who was influenced by Herodotus (his *Indica* was even written in Herodotus' Ionic dialect) seems to have delivered Xerxes' invasion of Greece in reverse and projected it on Alexander. The influence of the Herodotean anecdote is evident, but whether it influenced the Macedonian prince himself (see Instinsky 1949, e.g. 41–53) or merely the literary tradition about him, remains an open question.

193 For the idea that the story highlights Xerxes' ruthlessness and hubris, see Obst 1913, 56; Rocchi 1980; Mikalson 2003, 45–47 (pointing out that the word ἀτάσθαλος 'reckless' is a word with strong Homeric connotations). The tradition is already found in Aeschylus (*Persae* 739–752) and has a Herodotean precedent in 1.189, where one of Cyrus' horses drowns in the river Gyndes prompting the king's anger and canalisation of the river: see Briquel & Desnier 1983, 25–26; Bridges 2015, 58–59. Bridges (2015, 57–58) argues that in addition to the tyrannical image, Herodotus also blends in an image of Xerxes as being able to learn from his mistakes. It may also be noted that the storm element is found elsewhere in the *Histories* as hindering the progress of the Persian king at Mount Athos (6.44); Sepias (§2.4.2); and at Mount Ida (§2.2.1, immediately before the Hellespont episode).

194 Immerwahr 1966, 43; Gauer 1968, 36–37; Bowie 2012, 274. Plutarch (*Aristides* 9.3) relates that Themistocles intended to destroy the bridges in order to λαβεῖν ἐν τῇ Εὐρώπῃ τὴν Ἀσίαν 'catch Asia in Europe'. However, if Herodotus is to be believed, it was by these bridges that Xerxes managed to

as caused by divine intervention; this would match Herodotus' report that the cables were brought to Athenian sanctuaries. It has also been suggested that the verb ζευγνύναι, whose basic meaning is 'to yoke', is revealing of the notion of transgression,[195] but this may have been a fairly general way to refer to bridges.

The idea of the inviolable water border is also found in Xerxes' own crossing of the Halys (§2.1.1) and the Strymon (§2.3.4). Moreover, scholars have pointed out that such stories often had disastrous outcomes for other eastern kings: the clearest parallel is Cyrus' crossing of the Araxes by the above-mentioned pontoon bridge, which ultimately led to his death at the hands of the queen of the Massagetai, Tomyris (1.205-214).[196] Other examples are Croesus' crossing of the Halys,[197] and Cyrus' crossing of the Gyndes (1.189). It remains an open question whether such crossings were as momentous for the Persian kings themselves, but we know that Darius (inscription DPg) and Xerxes (XPh) claimed the land across the 'bitter water'. This term is usually taken as referring to the Aegean sea, but it has also been suggested that it more specifically referred to the (salt water) Bosporus-Hellespont system.[198] If this is true, its appearance in the royal inscriptions might reveal that the Hellespont was regarded as holding special significance as far away as the Achaemenid heartland.

Associated to the Hellespont bridges was the nearby mnemotope of Xerxes' throne, from where he allegedly observed a contest between his ships. Herodotus describes an identical scene for an enthroned Darius at the Bosporus in Mandrokles' painting in the temple of Hera at Samos (4.88); if this painting did not directly inspire the idea that was Xerxes was seated on a throne at Abydos, the correspondence suggests that the throne scene was an obligatory complement to the bridge scene.[199] If the account of Nassau William Senior is to be believed it may also have been catalysed by the marble throne, if, indeed, it stood here in Herodotus' time (it could have been later addition in an attempt to make the mnemotope even more graphical).[200] Taken together with Xerxes' thrones at Thermopylae (§2.5.1) and Salamis (§2.8.3), the one at Abydos constitutes a common place which resonates forcefully with many other examples in Greek literature of monarchs and gods on lookout points (§3.3.6). In this case, the scene further highlights the king's

---

escape back to Asia (8.108–110; 8.117). Cf. Waters 2014, 125–126, who points out that it is difficult to assess the historicity of the stories about the broken bridges.
195 Boedeker 1988, 43–44; the theme is also found in Aeschylus (*Persae* 71; 130–131; 723). See also Bridges 2015, 15–16.
196 Flory 1987, 115.
197 Flory (1987, 54–62) believed that the story about Croesus at the Halys and Cambyses' disastrous traversing of the Egyptian desert, "unmistakably prefigure" (p. 58) Xerxes' crossing of the Hellespont and the Strymon.
198 On the notion of the bitter river in these inscriptions, see Haubold 2013, 107–113.
199 Baragwanath (2008, 267) also notes the resemblances between the scenes of Xerxes at the Hellespont and that of Darius at the Bosporus.
200 Senior 1859, 155.

megalomania,²⁰¹ but it was also the setting for the 'existentialist' conversations between Xerxes and his uncle Artabanos (7.45-7.53), including the dramatic scene of Xerxes' weeping. It is unclear how these episodes arose, but literary influence from Aeschylus' depiction of the king at Salamis in the *Persae* (465-467) has been surmised.²⁰²

The question remains why the bridges were imagined specifically between Abydos and Sestos. The answer seems to be that the narrowness of the strait at this point (it was imagined as a gate, cf. Polybius 16.29.11) was not only strategic, but also visually compelling, and therefore invited the establishment of the story. The bridgeheads of Abydos and Sestos already had landmark status in the *Iliad* (2.836), and from the Roman period onwards, the castles of the two cities would appear as the mnemotopes for the myth of Leander, who lived in Abydos and swam every night across the Hellespont to meet his lover Hero, who lived in Sestos, until one night he drowned, prompting Hero to jump from her tower into the sea and drown as well. While there is no evidence that this story already existed in Herodotus' time, it is illustrative of the way in which the castles of Abydos and Sestos could become mnemotopes based on their striking juxtaposition at the narrowest part of the Hellespont.²⁰³ The story about the bridges could well have arisen by a similar process.

2.2.5 Agore and Helle's grave

Before leaving the Thracian Chersonesos and entering Thrace proper, the army passed a significant landmark (7.58):

> ὁ δὲ κατ' ἤπειρον στρατὸς πρὸς ἠῶ τε καὶ ἡλίου ἀνατολὰς ἐποιέετο τὴν ὁδὸν διὰ τῆς Χερσονήσου, ἐν δεξιῇ μὲν ἔχων τὸν Ἕλλης τάφον τῆς Ἀθάμαντος, ἐν ἀριστερῇ δὲ Καρδίην πόλιν, διὰ μέσης δὲ πορευόμενος πόλιος τῇ οὔνομα τυγχάνει ἐὸν Ἀγορή.

The land army made its way to the sunrise and the east and across the Chersonesos, having the grave of Helle, daughter of Athamas, on its right, and on its left the city of Kardie, marching right through a city whose name happens to be Agore.

---

201 The scene is usually taken as historical, and sometimes a rationalisation is given that the ship race was a propaganda measure to impress the Greeks (Kelly 2003, 203). Nevertheless, there are doubts that Xerxes had really seen his entire army for organisational reasons (Macan 1908, II 135; Burn 1962, 329). The scene has also been interpreted as a reflection of Herodotus' own research, and a monumentalisation of the past, Grethlein 2009, 210. Kienast (1996, 295) suggests that the white colour of the throne symbolised the 'solar character' of Xerxes' rule. The account of the army's crossing (7.55-7.56) contains much hyperbole: it took no less than seven days and nights for the army to cross, and a local man likened the greatness of Xerxes to that of Zeus.
202 Pohlenz 1961, 132–133. For the idea that this episode is fictitious see Waters 1966, 165.
203 For mnemotopes of the Hero and Leander myth see Antipater's poem in *Anthologia Graeca* 7.666. Strabo (13.1.11) mentions a tower of Hero very close to Sestos, and another tower opposite Sestos on the Asian side, presumably that of Leander.

According to Müller, the harbour town Kardie was probably located at the Bakla Limanı, four kilometres north of Bolayır.[204] Agore occupied modern Bolayır itself, with the acropolis now used as a graveyard.[205] Herodotus seems to regard it as mildly funny that the army should have passed through the centre of a town whose name 'happens to be' (τυγχάνει) 'assembly place' (Ἀγορή). As in several other instances in Herodotus' account of the Persian Wars, a speaking toponym, i.e. a toponymical aetiology may have made the place into a mnemotope for the passing of Xerxes (§3.1.1), which may or may not reflect historical reality.

The location of Helle's grave has proven more elusive. No description of it exists. We may surmise that it amounted to a burial mound, like those found around Troy: Helle was, after all, a character of the heroic age, and the grave's use as a landmark by Herodotus suggests that it was a substantial element in the landscape and visible to sailors on the Hellespont, whose very name was (believed to have) derived from that of the mythical princess.[206] On the basis of Herodotus' topographical remark relating to Kardie and Agore, as well as on the basis of a reference in Herodotus' contemporary Hellanicus of Lesbos (*FGrH* 4 F127), we can surmise that Helle's grave was at or near the town of Paktye, three kilometres south of Bolayır. There is, however, no material evidence available at Paktye itself.[207] Some authors have speculated that Helle's grave is to be identified with a remarkable natural hill halfway between Gelibolu and Bolayır which is so symmetrical that, viewed from the Hellespont, it looks like a burial mound.[208] Another candidate may be a similar hill southeast of Koruköy (see picture).

---

204 Isaac 1986, 187–188; Müller 1997, 852–855; reporting black and red gloss ware in the fields around this harbour. Strabo mentions that Kardie was a little more than four hundred stades from Elaious. Maurice 1930, 219, however, located Kardie at Bolayir.
205 Müller 1997, 766–770. Maurice (1930, 219) located Agore between modern Kavakköy and Kızılcaterzi.
206 The association between the myth and the sea strait (if it did not arise by folk etymology) possibly antedates Homer, because the name Hellespont features already there (2.845; 12.30); cf. Danov 1976, 194. Aeschylus refers to the waterway as πορθμὸς Ἕλλης 'strait of Helle' (*Persae* 69–70; 722; 799). Another mnemotope related to Helle's death was Sigeion, believed to be the place where she fell into the sea (Pseudo-Apollodorus 1.9.1). Greek merchant ships plying the route between the Aegean and the Black Sea colonies had no other choice but to use the dangerously narrow waterway (Homer, in the mentioned passages, calls the Hellespont ἀγάρροος 'fast-flowing'), where one would often seek shelter on the coast to wait for the current and the winds to become more favourable (cf. Polybius 16.29.13).
207 Casson 1926, 215; Isaac 1986, 196–197; Müller 1997, 895–896 (mentioning that a fountain 800 meter east of Helle's grave may contain building blocks from the ancient city).
208 Maurice 1930, 219 (mentioning ancient remains); Kahrstedt 1954, 6, note 6; Müller 1994, 34; 1997, 827–828.

Fig. 14: A striking mound-like hill southeast of Koruköy (Helle's grave?).

Why does Herodotus refer to this mnemotope in relation to the march of Xerxes? It is possible that he copied the reference from one of the itineraries on which he was basing himself.[209] But Angus Bowie suggests that the location also carried a symbolic meaning, and draws a parallel with the tragic death of Helle and the future demise of Persian rule in Europe.[210] Long before Xerxes arrived at the 'bitter river', Helle had travelled across it by flying on the ram Chrysomallos, and she had hubristically ignored a warning by looking down to the sea, which led to her death. By mentioning the Persians as passing the grave in the above passage, Herodotus may be suggesting that the Persians ignored another important sign that their mission was doomed. This dovetails well with Herodotus' mention of omens, two of which are described immediately before the passage at hand: the birth of a hermaphrodite mule and that of a hare from a horse (7.57). To Bowie's suggestion may be added that it seems relevant that Helle's death took place on the border between Europe and Asia. In addition,

---

209 Eckstein 1989, 324.
210 Bowie 2012, 276. Referring to a grave as an orientation point is something that happens in the *Iliad*, where it may have carried a symbolic significance: cf. *Iliad* 11.166, where the grave of Ilos, ancestor of the Ilians, is passed by Agamemnon and Hector.

Herodotus specifically mentions Athamas, Helle's wicked father, when he points out that Xerxes passed the grave. He later discusses Xerxes' visit to and worship of Athamas' house in Halos in Thessaly, where he may hint at a hubristic correlation between Athamas and Xerxes (§2.3.9).

2.2.6 Summary

As Herodotus sailed towards the Black Sea, the banks of the 'Bitter River' must have appeared like a continuous theatre stage. The stories from the heroic age were prompted by Troy itself, then still close to the shore, as well as the numerous (purported) burial mounds on both coasts: Ajax, Achilles and Hector had seemingly all received majestic funeral mounds here. And further up the Hellespont, towards the Sea of Marmara, Helle was buried. Here, mirages of the Trojan War became connected Xerxes' invasion of Europe through the presence of mnemotopes where these stories accumulated.

On close inspection, these stories were meaningful for a contemporary Greek audience interested in the historical figure of Xerxes and the Persian Empire. Lightning struck on the Ida, the army emptied the Scamander, and an idle offering to Athena and the heroes at Troy itself only brought panic to the army. Clearly, Xerxes was not welcomed by the same divine forces which he tried to appease. They gave Herodotus' readership a religious answer to the question why Xerxes was to fail in his attempts to control Greece. Similarly, the grave of Helle, who was by her tragic death doomed to stay in Europe, was a reminder that the border between Europe and Asia was inviolable. Yet Xerxes ignored the advice that the landscape, and many omens, gave him: by constructing his Hellespont bridges, he connected two continents that should have remained separate.

The historical authenticity of these stories is impossible to prove; nevertheless, I have attempted to show that the military inconvenience or even impossibility of the route, the unlikeliness of Persian interest in the Trojan sagas and in participation in Greek cults, and the literary parallels with the *Iliad* are so pressing that the authenticity of the episode's topography cannot be taken for granted. In the end, this account only existed with the precedent of the Trojan War pressing so heavily on the landscape: in Herodotus' mind or in that of his sources, there was no way Xerxes' army could get around it.

2.3 The march through northern Greece

The northern part of the Greek mainland, consisting of the regions of Thrace, Macedonia and Thessaly was used by the land army as the corridor into Greece.[211]

---

[211] A selection of places mentioned in this chapter features on Map 1.

Unlike the southern part of the Greek mainland, these areas were already under Persian influence when Xerxes came, and Thracians, Macedonians and Thessalians formed part of the Persian army (7.75).[212] The degree of topographical detail in the descriptions of Thrace and eastern Macedonia is unparalleled in the account of the Persian invasion; by contrast, central Macedonia and Thessaly and more southern areas are hardly given any description at all.[213] It has been suggested that this information is based on Herodotean autopsy, or on pre-existing geographical works, such as that by Hecataeus.[214]

In the following I will discuss the places to which stories of Xerxes' march were connected. We will see that there are reasons to believe that these stories were shaped by processes of (folk) memory in the period between 480 BCE and the publication of the *Histories*, and that they may therefore be explained as mnemotopes. While the historicity of these stories is not our main concern, it has to be noted that topographical problems have been identified in them. For example, Herodotus tells us that Xerxes had split the army into three groups that followed three different routes; however, it has been pointed out that this puts a strain on the topography, and may reflect the existence of three roads which Herodotus incorrectly attributed to Xerxes' invasion.[215]

---

[212] Thrace in particular had come under Persian control during Darius' invasion, and remained so throughout the fifth century BCE; cf. Balcer 1988.

[213] Rood (2012, 128) pointed out that the level of geographical detail of the invasion drops after Thermopylae presumably because Herodotus assumed that the more southern areas were more familiar to his audience.

[214] Topographical descriptions are found in 7.58–59, 7.108–113, 7.115, 7.122–124 and 7.127; on these routes see Müller 1975, 1. Autopsy is assumed by Casson 1926, 265; Myres 1953, 225; Pohlenz 1961, 130. More critical evaluations of Herodotus' autopsy are found in Danov 1976, 283–284; Hammond 1988, 537–538 (positing a visit to Thasos and Eïon). Asheri (1990, 133–134) believed that Herodotus had good knowledge of the coast of Thrace, but may never have visited the hinterland. See Zahrnt 1971, 4–12 for the possibility that previous geographical treatises underlie Herodotus' account.

[215] See Tuplin 2003, 386–388; 402–403 for such errors, which he attributes to Herodotus' inconsistent use of various map-like sources for the area; he suggested that when Herodotus says that Xerxes passed a place, this may have been simply a logical deduction without much historical value. Boteva (2011, 750–751) believes that Herodotus reconstruction of Xerxes' route is impossible, and that some parts are based on a Greek-Thracian source, others on a Persian one. Decourt (1990, 82–83) believed that there was a division which was kept until Thessaly. Tuplin 2003, 389–390 points out that the fact that some stories about Xerxes in Thrace are told not in book 7, but in book 8, shows that Xerxes' real movements may be distinct from what Herodotus reports in gazetteer-style narrative in book 7. Fehling (1971, 27) suggests that Herodotus was prone to associate everything he knew about these lands with Xerxes' march, even when there was no reason to do so.

2.3.1 The 'Royal Road' through Thrace

We start with Xerxes' road through Thrace as a mnemotope in itself. While describing the route from Eïon to Akanthos, Herodotus recounts the following remarkable observation (7.115):

> τὴν δὲ ὁδὸν ταύτην, τῇ βασιλεὺς Ξέρξης τὸν στρατὸν ἤλασε, οὔτε συγχέουσι Θρήικες οὔτ' ἐπισπείρουσι, σέβονταί τε μεγάλως τὸ μέχρι ἐμεῦ.
>
> The Thracians do not obliterate the road along which king Xerxes drove his army, nor do they sow on it, and they respect it greatly until my time.

Apparently, an entire road had become a mnemotope for Xerxes' invasion. It is unclear whether Herodotus refers to a particular part of the road but it is possible that he simply means the route from Eïon to Akanthos which he has just described, or the entire road through Thrace. It has also been suggested that the road was a causeway across lake Bolbe (modern Volvi).[216] It is also possible that the road is identical to an old Thracian inland route which was remembered as the 'king's road' and mentioned in Livy (39.27).[217] But there are more questions: was the road built by Xerxes? What did the respect entail? And why would the Thracians do this?

We do not have ready answers. The road may have been an infrastructural tour de force and therefore revered.[218] It is impossible to say whether Herodotus wants us to believe that the road was built by the Persian authorities or not. However, comparable mnemotopical roads serve as a warning that traditions about them may easily be distorted. For example, Pausanias (10.31.7) mentions a road in Phrygia that locals pointed out as the one used by Ethiopian king Memnon on his way to Troy. We may also compare other traditions about the visits of foreign monarchs to Thrace: on the basis of purported stelai, Herodotus claims that Thrace had been conquered by Egyptian king Sesostris, and the Teucrians and Mysians (2.103; 2.106).[219] Also, the Thracians' respect for the road may be an exaggeration.[220] The reason for Herodotus to show interest in the road may be wholly different. It may have been an interesting

---

[216] Myres 1953, 323.
[217] Hammond (1988, 538) identified this with Xerxes' road; cf. Archibald 1998, 89: "Locally, the building of the road is likely to have been remembered and retold long after the exotic armies had gone."
[218] Danov 1976, 141.
[219] For a detailed discussion of these 'conquests', see Asheri 1990, 150–155.
[220] It is normal for the major route across a country not to be used for agriculture or to be obliterated. Cf. Casson 1926, 43: the road must have been old so it was not in the Thracians' own interest to stop using it. Tuplin (2003, 389) believes that the road was on former farmland, but is undecided whether it was constructed on purpose or simply created by the passing of the army. See also Visser 1982, 410 note 26.

point of sightseeing,[221] and a rather amazing one: it would strike an inhabitant of post-war Athens as abhorrent that one should worship the road of a conqueror like Xerxes.

2.3.2 The cape of Sarpedon and lake Stentoris

The first more detailed points of interest in the area appear after Xerxes' passing of the Hellespont (7.58):

> ὁ δὲ ναυτικὸς ἔξω τὸν Ἑλλήσποντον πλέων παρὰ γῆν ἐκομίζετο, τὰ ἔμπαλιν πρήσσων τοῦ πεζοῦ. ὃ μὲν γὰρ πρὸς ἑσπέρην ἔπλεε, ἐπὶ Σαρπηδονίης ἄκρης ποιεύμενος τὴν ἄπιξιν, ἐς τὴν αὐτῷ προείρητο ἀπικομένῳ περιμένειν: [...] ἐνθεῦτεν δὲ κάμπτων τὸν κόλπον τὸν Μέλανα καλεόμενον καὶ Μέλανα ποταμόν, οὐκ ἀντισχόντα τότε τῇ στρατιῇ τὸ ῥέεθρον ἀλλ' ἐπιλιπόντα, τοῦτον τὸν ποταμὸν διαβάς, ἐπ' οὗ καὶ ὁ κόλπος οὗτος τὴν ἐπωνυμίην ἔχει, ἤιε πρὸς ἑσπέρην, Αἶνόν τε πόλιν Αἰολίδα καὶ Στεντορίδα λίμνην παρεξιών, ἐς ὃ ἀπίκετο ἐς Δορίσκον.

> The naval army, sailing outside of the Hellespont, went along the coast, going the opposite way from the land army. They went west and arrived at the cape of Sarpedon, where it was ordered to wait after it had arrived. [...] From [Agore] the [land army] went around the bay called Melas and the river Melas, which then did not have sufficient water for the army and ran dry. Traversing this river, where the bay has the same name, it went west, passing the Aeolian city of Ainos and lake Stentoris, until it arrived at Doriskos.

The cape of Sarpedon is also mentioned by Strabo (7, fragment 52) where it is called a rock by the river Erginos (the modern Ergene). It can be identified with a modern headland called Gremea or Paxi, twelve kilometres south of the Turkish city of Enez.[222] The Stentoris lake has been identified with Gala Gölü, a lake in Turkish Thrace, close to the Greek border, north of Enez;[223] though given Herodotus' coastal perspective, the coastal lagoon Dalyan near Enez is another candidate. The Melas river is the modern Kavaksuyu.[224] The Melas bay is the Saros Körfezi.[225]

One wonders what Sarpedon, mythical king of Lydia or Lycia, was doing here, in this remote area of Thrace. Perhaps this was not the 'Iliadic' Sarpedon (Herodotus knew him too, cf. 1.173), but the son of Poseidon and a local king, who was killed here by Heracles (Pseudo-Apollodorus 2.5.9).[226] For Bowie, the interaction of the Persian army with cape Sarpedon was inspired by its mythical connotation of the death of a

---

[221] The mention of the road is seen as evidence for Herodotean autopsy of the area (Hauvette 1894, 315; Casson 1926, 265), but, of course, this is not necessary.
[222] Müller 1997, 925.
[223] Casson 1926, 12; Müller 1997, 941.
[224] Müller 1997, 878–879.
[225] Müller 1997, 880.
[226] Macan (1907, I 79) rightly asks: "But can we recognize more than one Sarpedon?".

hubristic tyrant, which would be a prefiguration for Xerxes' demise; likewise, Bowie argues that Stentor was killed when challenging Hermes, which again would give us a hubris precedent at a site visited by Xerxes.²²⁷ Although Herodotus here does not seem to stress Xerxes' passing of these places such symbolism may well have been present (as seems to have been the case at many other Trojan sites, see §2.2). It may be the reason why these places were connected to the invasion in the first place.

Cape Sarpedon was also the location where Boreas brought the nymph Oreïthyia after kidnapping her at the Ilissos river near Athens (Apollonius Rhodius, *Argonautica* 1.216). We know that Simonides wrote a poem about the battle of Artemision (Priscian, *De metris fabularum Terentii* 24; *Suda* s.v. Σιμωνίδης), which contained references to Oreïthyia's abduction to Thrace by Boreas.²²⁸ As we will see in the discussion of the battle of Artemision (§2.4.2), Oreïthyia was believed to have caused the storm in which many Persian ships were lost. Perhaps the place therefore deemed significant to Xerxes' invasion.

2.3.3 Doriskos

After passing these landmarks, Xerxes arrived at the fort of Doriskos where he reviewed his troops (7.59):

> ὁ δὲ Δορίσκος ἐστὶ τῆς Θρηίκης αἰγιαλός τε καὶ πεδίον μέγα, διὰ δὲ αὐτοῦ ῥέει ποταμὸς μέγας Ἕβρος· ἐν τῷ τεῖχός τε ἐδέδμητο βασιλήιον τοῦτο τὸ δὴ Δορίσκος κέκληται, καὶ Περσέων φρουρὴ ἐν αὐτῷ κατεστήκεε ὑπὸ Δαρείου ἐξ ἐκείνου τοῦ χρόνου ἐπείτε ἐπὶ Σκύθας ἐστρατεύετο. ἔδοξε ὦν τῷ Ξέρξῃ ὁ χῶρος εἶναι ἐπιτήδεος ἐνδιατάξαι τε καὶ ἐξαριθμῆσαι τὸν στρατόν, καὶ ἐποίεε ταῦτα. τὰς μὲν δὴ νέας τὰς πάσας ἀπικομένας ἐς Δορίσκον οἱ ναύαρχοι κελεύσαντος Ξέρξεω ἐς τὸν αἰγιαλὸν τὸν προσεχέα Δορίσκῳ ἐκόμισαν, ἐν τῷ Σάλη τε Σαμοθρηικίη πεπόλισται πόλις καὶ Ζώνη, τελευτᾷ δὲ αὐτοῦ Σέρρειον ἄκρη ὀνομαστή. ὁ δὲ χῶρος οὗτος τὸ παλαιὸν ἦν Κικόνων. ἐς τοῦτον τὸν αἰγιαλὸν κατασχόντες τὰς νέας ἀνέψυχον ἀνελκύσαντες. ὁ δὲ ἐν τῷ Δορίσκῳ τοῦτον τὸν χρόνον τῆς στρατιῆς ἀριθμὸν ἐποιέετο.

> Doriskos is a beach of Thrace and a great plain, and through it flows a great river, the Hebros. In it, a royal walled fort has been built which is also called Doriskos. And a guard of the Persians had been sent there under Darius from the time he marched against the Scythians. Xerxes thought this was a fit place to order and completely count his army, and so he did. After Xerxes had ordered to do so, the captains brought all the ships to the beach close to Doriskos. Here, Samothracian Sale and Zone have been founded, and at its end is the famous cape Serreion. This land used to be Ciconian territory. To this place they brought the ships and after dragging them up, they let them dry. And he counted the army that was in Doriskos at that time.

---

227 Bowie 2012, 276. For the general idea that places with a mythological connection in Herodotus' work may prompt such symbolic interpretations, see Rood 2012, 125–126.
228 Scholion on Apollonius Rhodius (s.v. Ζήτης καὶ Κάλαϊς). On the poem see Kowerski 2005, 22–33.

Next, Herodotus recounts how the counting was performed (7.60): ten thousand men were driven together to one spot; around them a circle was drawn on which a low wall (αἱμασιά) was built as high as a man's navel, allowing for fast counting of the rest.

The plain where this counting procedure was carried out is now identified with the Evros (Hebros) delta, a triangular plain between Alexandroupoli, Enez and Feres, which is approximately fifteen kilometres wide.[229] The location of the fort may be the Saraya ('Palace') hill at modern Doriskos (formerly known as Urumçik) which has remains of fortifications and a high concentration of ancient potsherds.[230] The place was already deserted by the time of Demosthenes (*Philippica* 4, 8).

Fig. 15: The Saraya hill, believed to be the location of ancient Doriskos.

The episode is an illustration of various ways in which the Greeks of Herodotus' time thought about Xerxes. First, it underlines Xerxes' hubristic megalomania and power

---

229 Casson 1926, 11–12; 264; Isaac 1986, 137–140;
230 Müller 1987, 52 with literature; Archibald 1998, 87 with note 42 and literature. This is probably the same hill described by Maurice 1930, 220. Doriskos seems to have been a regional political centre, because we hear that one Maskames was appointed as satrap of Doriskos, who was not dethroned by the Greeks after the invasion (7.105–106).

over his subjects.²³¹ Second, it has been pointed out that the hubris of the Doriskos scene is underlined by what comes next: Xerxes interviews former Spartan king Damaratos regarding the odds of a successful Greek resistance but dismisses him with a smile (7.101-105).²³² Third, as Christ points out, the Doriskos scene is an example of the commonplace of the 'researching king' and may have to do with Herodotus' own obsession with measurements.²³³ To this may be added that the description of the counting process, which is exactly the way in which cattle is counted, may underline both the enormous size of the army, and the tyrannical power Xerxes wielded over his soldiers.²³⁴ The counting episode has usually been accepted as historical.²³⁵ However, some scholars have expressed doubts.²³⁶ In any case, the scene brings to mind the manner of 'counting' 6,000 in the Athenian *ekklesia*, seemingly performed by bringing together as many people as fitted within a circle of red rope (Aristophanes, *Acharnenses* 20).

How did Doriskos become associated with this scene? It is possible that Herodotus or his sources, like Müller, identified this area with Xerxes' counting ground because of its sheer vastness coupled with the existence of the landmark castle, which was conceivable as Xerxes' lookout point.²³⁷ Perhaps, the circular wall described by Herodotus was visible on the spot. It is not impossible that there was some stone circle in the area that had inspired the story.

2.3.4 The Strymon river and Ennea Hodoi

Continuing the march through Thrace, the Persian army arrived at the Strymon river at the place Ennea Hodoi ('Nine Ways'), where a bridge had been constructed for the passing of the army. This was the location of a horrible sacrifice by the Persians (7.113-114):

> ἐς τὸν οἱ Μάγοι ἐκαλλιερέοντο σφάζοντες ἵππους λευκούς. φαρμακεύσαντες δὲ ταῦτα ἐς τὸν ποταμὸν καὶ ἄλλα πολλὰ πρὸς τούτοισι ἐν Ἐννέα ὁδοῖσι τῇσι Ἡδωνῶν ἐπορεύοντο κατὰ τὰς γεφύρας, τὸν Στρυμόνα εὑρόντες ἐζευγμένον. Ἐννέα δὲ ὁδοὺς πυνθανόμενοι τὸν χῶρον τοῦτον

---

231 Christ 1994, 174–175.
232 Rollinger 2003.
233 Christ 1994, 174–175. Grethlein (2009, 206–207) drew attention to the fact that Herodotus' narrative is embedded in Xerxes' perspective and that Xerxes plays an authorial role, especially in 7.100 when he 'researches' the army, and is even portrayed as compiling the army catalogue that Herodotus transmits; cf. Kuhrt 2007, 240.
234 Cawkwell 2005, 92.
235 Most scholars are silent, but Burn (1962, 329) and Flory (1987, 86) make more explicit remarks in defence of the historicity.
236 Grundy 1901, 218: "The method of numeration reported may or may not have been actually employed." Skeptical remarks are also found in Waters 1985, 61.
237 Müller 1975, 3: "Man kann sich gut vorstellen, daß Xerxes von hier aus sein Heer betrachtete."

καλέεσθαι, τοσούτους ἐν αὐτῷ παῖδάς τε καὶ παρθένους ἀνδρῶν τῶν ἐπιχωρίων ζώοντας κατώρυσσον. Περσικὸν δὲ τὸ ζώοντας κατορύσσειν, ἐπεὶ καὶ Ἄμηστριν τὴν Ξέρξεω γυναῖκα πυνθάνομαι γηράσασαν δὶς ἑπτὰ Περσέων παῖδας, ἐόντων ἐπιφανέων ἀνδρῶν ὑπὲρ ἑωυτῆς τῷ ὑπὸ γῆν λεγομένῳ εἶναι θεῷ ἀντιχαριζομένην κατορύσσουσαν.

The Magi sacrificed white horses [to the Strymon river], and tried to appease it. And after using this sorcery to the river and many additional actions in Nine Ways of Edonia, they marched across the bridges. And when they heard that the place was called Nine Ways, they buried alive as many boys and girls of the local people there. It is typically Persian to bury alive, because I hear that Amestris, Xerxes' wife, after she had reached old age, also buried twice seven children of famous men for herself to thank the god who is said to be under the earth.

The Strymon river is the modern Strymonas of Bulgaria and Greece; Ennea Hodoi was located at the only point in the coastal area where one could cross this river, i.e. between the Prasias (Kerkinitis) lake to the north and the marshes to the south, near modern Amphipoli.[238] Ennea Hodoi must therefore be approximately the precursor to this city, and this is what Thucydides (1.100; 4.102) explicitly states. The Strymon bridge, which Herodotus says was built by Xerxes in preparation for his march (7.24), is also archaeologically attested.[239]

Fig. 16: The hill of Amphipolis and the Strymon river. The site of the bridge is approximately where the bottom of the hill meets the river.

---

238 Müller 1975, 7.
239 The bridge appears to be part of the city territory (Thucydides 4.103.4–5; 4.108.1). For the archaeological remains, see the *Erga* by the Archaeological Society in Athens of 1976 (published 1977) 27–29; 1978 (published 1979), 14–15 (thirty-six wooden palissades).

Although we know its location, it is less clear how Ennea Hodoi became the mnemotope for this story, and there are many conundrums. Why do the Magi offer horses to the river? Is it really possible that they buried local children alive? Why did the Persians think of doing so at Ennea Hodoi? What is the relation of this story to that of Amestris? And who is the god under the earth?

It is important that, despite the assertions of a few scholars,[240] the tacit acceptance of the story's historicity by many others, and various additional stories about Persians engaging in live burial and horse sacrifice,[241] we have no non-Greek sources which tell us that the Persians actually engaged in these practices.[242] Moreover, as De Jong notes, "There is no such god in Zoroastrianism, as indeed the entire practice violates many Zoroastrian rules."[243] Instead, the stories can be explained as "atrocity propaganda" or simply as dramatic episodes that fitted the stereotype of the Persians as cruel savages.[244] The stereotype of human sacrifice has further relevance in Thrace, because the Thracians are known to practise human sacrifice. They would later offer the Persian Oiobazos to a local god (9.116) and Herodotus relates how the Thracians lament a person's birth and rejoice in someone's death, because they believe that a person's death is his deliverance from evil (5.4).[245] The question then rises why Ennea Hodoi developed in a mnemotope for the sacrifice, whether historically authentic or not.

---

240 Boyce (1982, 167) connected the horse offering to water divinities, and suggested that the human sacrifice must have been a pagan survival, "practiced thus at times of communal or individual stress." She compares the episode at the Strymon to Xerxes' visit to Halos (7.197), the sacrifice of the first Greek captured during the battle of Artemision (7.180), the Greek offering of three beautiful Persian youths to Dionysos (Plutarch, *Themistocles* 13.2-3), and the Thracian sacrifice of the Persian commander Oiobazos (9.119). See also Rawlinson 1880, 94; Hauvette 1894, 315; Briquel & Desnier 1983, 27. It may also be mentioned that Herodotus noted elsewhere that the Persians worshipped rivers (1.138).
241 In 3.35, Herodotus recounts that Cambyses had once ordered fifteen noble Persians to be buried alive until their necks. The offering of horses, seems to have been regarded as a typical eastern exploit, with the *Iliad* (21.132) mentioning a Trojan offering of horses to appease the Scamander, and Tacitus describes something similar for the Parthians (6.37).
242 De Jong 1997, 314–315.
243 De Jong 1997, 314–315.
244 Human sacrifice appears in Greek mythology as a cruel *ultimum remedium* to pacify a god or a hero, as in the cases of the Athenian children and the Minotaur, Iphigeneia and Polyxena. Green 1996, 88 used the phrase 'atrocity propaganda'; Isaac 2004, 474–475 placed it in a context of ancient racism; Parker 2004, 151–153 suggested that the story may well represent forms of Greek orientalism attributed to the barbarian 'other'. He also identifies the 'twice seven' element as potential Greek influence on the Amestris story; Bridges 2015, 58 note 36 compared the scene of the Strymon offerings to that of Xerxes at the Hellespont; Waters 1985, 171 noted that Herodotus may have regarded the offerings of the Magi as ridiculous.
245 Asheri 1990, 148–150 discusses Herodotus' report of Thracian notions of immortality as a mirror to normal Greek beliefs.

I would like to offer three answers that are not mutually exclusive. The first process relevant to the sacrifice of Ennea Hodoi is folk etymology. This is hinted at by Herodotus himself, when he explains that the Persians decided to bury nine children alive after learning that the place was called 'Nine Ways'. Part of Herodotus' message seems to be that the Persians are ruthless for deciding to perform the child burial at the whim of learning about the name of the locality. As elsewhere in the *Histories* the name of the place may have inspired the story directly (§3.1.1).

The second catalyst for the connection of the story to Ennea Hodoi may have been the importance of the Strymon in the 'mental map' of the Greeks. This is demonstrated by the river's frequent appearance in Herodotus' work, while other large Thracian rivers such as the Nestos are omitted.[246] The Strymon features in the various stories about Xerxes' return trip to Persia after the battle of Salamis. In Herodotus' first version (8.115-117, in which he finally arrives at the Hellespont), Xerxes discovers that Zeus' chariot, which he had lent to the Paeonians in the city of Siris, was taken by the Thracians who lived at the sources of the Strymon.[247] In the second version (8.118) Xerxes embarks on a boat in Eïon and is troubled by a dangerous 'Strymonian wind', a topos seen elsewhere in Greek literature.[248] In yet another version of Xerxes' flight found in Aeschylus' *Persae* (495-507), many Persians die while crossing the frozen

---

246 The Strymon is mentioned in e.g. 5.1; 5.13; 5.23; 7.24; 7.107, where it is recounted that Persian satrap Boges of Eïon committed suicide and threw all the city's gold and silver into the river (reminding Aly 1969, 176 of stories about Sardanapalus and the Rheingold). This focus at the cost of other main rivers has been explained by pointing at a difference in depth between the Strymon and the Nestos (Müller 1975, 6); or by saying that the Strymon had a more "threatening setting" than such rivers as the Nestos or Hebros (Tuplin 2003, 403, note 29). Also cf. Macan 1908, I 37–38.
247 This story about the chariot reaching Siris may well be historical (e.g. Kienast 1996, 306–307). Furthermore, this chariot was a fitting attribute for the Persian king: in Babylon and Assyria there were divine empty chariots with white horses (cf. Xenophon, *Cyropaedia* 8.3.12; Calmeyer 1974; Shahbazi 1985, 500–502; de Jong 1997, 262); Xerxes may have ordered such a chariot for himself after having seen it in Babylon; this way, he could be an "irdischer Stellvertreter" of Ahuramazda (Kienast 1996, 285–291; see also Tripodi 1986). Nevertheless, the story puts considerable strain on the map. Siris is probably the modern city of Serres, some fifty kilometres northwest of Amphipolis (cf. Müller 1987, 99). If Amphipolis and Akanthos were both visited as Herodotus seems to claim, a trip to Siris would be a strange detour. Tuplin (2003, 400) remedied this by suggesting that Xerxes did not go to Siris, but simply sent his chariot there. Moreover, Rhesus is described in the *Iliad* (10.438-41) and Euripides' *Rhesus* (301–302) as possessing a golden chariot unfit for mortals. Serris is therefore best regarded as a mnemotope for this story, possibly mediated by a real chariot, or depictions of a chariot, such as those on coins struck by the Thracian king of the Derrones (cf. Kienast 1996, 308–310).
248 Terrible Strymonian winds are also mentioned in Aeschylus' *Agamemnon* (192). This fits a wider pattern that the winds from Thrace caused problems (Morton 2001, 129): *Iliad* 9.4; Hesiod, *Opera et dies* 504 and further; 547; Theophrastus, fragment 6.35 (= *De signis*); Aeschylus' *Agamemnon* 653 and 1416. For a discussion of this version of Xerxes' return story, see Flory 1987, 56–61. The Thracian wind from the Strymon is also listed in Aristoteles' *De ventorum situ et nominibus* 2.17–18, and Boreas is said to be a son of the Strymon (Hereas, *FGrH* 486 F3).

river, when the ice suddenly melts.²⁴⁹ The Greek notion of the Strymon as an icy river that could wreak havoc makes it understandable that stories circulated according to which the Persians had somehow tried to appease it. It seems that the narratives about Xerxes in Thrace could simply not do without some engagement with this river. In addition, these stories highlighted the irony that the offerings did not help: not only did a Strymonian wind cause problems in the second version of Xerxes' return trip; storms would frustrate the Persians before and during the battle of Artemision (see §2.4.2 and §2.4.5). Given this background, it may well be that the Greeks regarded the offerings of horses and children not only as wrong in themselves, but also as futile (or even counterproductive) attempts at appeasing the gods. Similarly, like other infrastructural projects, the bridges that Xerxes built over the Strymon river (historical or not) may to Herodotus and his audience have symbolised the ruler's hubris.²⁵⁰

Another significant reason why this particular story appears at Ennea Hodoi is its link with the myth of Rhesus, a mythical king of Thrace. This king is chiefly known from the *Iliad* (10.431-479), which recounts how Diomedes and Odysseus kill Rhesus and twelve other Thracians, and steal his horses; (Pseudo-)Euripides devoted his play *Rhesus* to him, and Philostratus discusses him briefly in his *Heroicus* (17.3-6). Important elements of the myth are readily mirrored in the passage about Xerxes quoted above. First, both Xerxes' and Rhesus' horses are specifically white: it is said that Rhesus had beautiful horses whiter than snow (*Iliad* 10.436-437; *Rhesus* 304), and Philostratus calls him a breeder of horses. Second, both Xerxes and Rhesus sacrifice horses to a river (Rhesus is said to have sacrificed to the Scamander river: cf. the D-scholion on *Iliad* 10.435; Virgil, *Aeneis* 1.469-473); finally, Rhesus is made to live in an underground cave as a man-god Prophecy of Dionysus (Euripides, *Rhesus* 962-973), while Herodotus in the same passage talks about an unnamed god who lives under the earth while referring to Amestris' burial of fourteen children.²⁵¹

---

249 Aeschylus' account has been treated as essentially true (Dumortier 1963), or as having a kernel of truth (Green 1996, 216). Munro (1902, 332) has drawn the parallel with the famous 'ice episode' at the battle of Austerlitz, when the French shot the ice so that many Russians allegedly drowned.
250 That it is not easy to associate the bridge with the Persians is highlighted by the circumstance that scholars who have taken Herodotus' assertion that the bridge was a Persian structure seriously, have to explain the construction of the bridge as something that could be completed relatively fast: Burn (1962, 338) suggested that the bridges were probably pontoon bridges, while Hammond (1988, 527) suggests wooden piles in the river as was done here in 425 BCE. Kelly (2003, 194) asserts that the construction did not take very long.
251 Herodotus is probably employing one of his characteristic euphemisms when he says 'the god who lives under the earth'. It does not mean he had Rhesus in mind; it may also be Hades, or Poseidon. What is important to note, however, is that the tradition on which he relies may have originated with the Rhesus cult in Thrace. Interestingly, Herodotus knew about an oracle of Dionysos in Thrace (7.110). The localisation is unclear, but again this may be connected to the Rhesus cult as we understand it from Philostratos and Euripides' *Rhesus*.

If these correspondences were not enough to make a case that Herodotus' story is somehow modelled on the Rhesus myth, the various geographical correspondences between them are very suggestive. Not only was Rhesus the king of Thrace; he was specifically from Eïon: the *Iliad* already calls him a παῖς Ἠϊονῆος (10.435), and in the *Rhesus* (279 and elsewhere) his father is the Strymon river; in *De fluviis* 11 by Pseudo-Plutarch, it is recounted how the river was previously called Palaistinos (arguably related to παλαιστέω, 'to throw by hand') and acquired its name when Rhesus' father Strymon threw himself into it upon hearing that his son had been killed. Polyaenus (*Strategemata* 6.53) recounts that Amphipolis was founded on the very spot next to the Strymon river where Rhesus' bones were reburied in his native soil. The underground chamber was supposed to be on nearby Mount Pangaion (the modern Pangeo).[252] Thus, the rites which the Magi performed at Ennea Hodoi look like a re-enactment of the sacrifice in the Rhesus myth, and they take place at the very spot that Rhesus had called home and where his bones were believed to be buried.

We can only speculate about the ways in which this coincidence arose. First, there is evidence that Amphipolis had a Rhesus cult: Marsyas of Pella (according to the Vita-argumentum-scholion on Euripides' *Rhesus* 346) mentioned a temple of Kleio (Rhesus' mother) in Amphipolis on a hill opposite a memorial of Rhesus.[253] We may surmise that Herodotus' story has crystallised around existing cults and monuments at this spot. The area also had various remarkable funerary monuments that may have somehow played a role.[254]

Alternatively or additionally, the story may have been based on a depiction of the myth which was misinterpreted. The figure of Rhesus has been connected with the well-attested Thracian cult of a figure known in modern scholarship as Heros equitans.[255] Similarities between the figures include that they are both healing gods, hunters, and connected with horses (Rhesus is a horsebreeder, and the Heros equitans is normally if not always depicted riding a horse), and have connections to the underworld (Heros Equitans is often found in graves or as a part of funerary iconography).

---

[252] Archibald 1998, 101 with note 36 and rich literature; note that in Philostratos' *Heroicus*, Rhesus is connected with Rhodope, an area much more east in Thrace. Mount Pangaion was the place where local king Lykourgos was eaten by man-eating horses (Pseudo-Apollodorus 3.5.1).
[253] Cf. Isaac 1986, 55–58 with rich literature.
[254] The famous Kastas tomb is a remarkable burial site with various native Thracian tombs, pithoi graves and child burials; cf. Archibald 1998, 75 with rich literature; the *Ergon* of the Archaeological Society in Athens of 1976 (published 1977), 32–36; and the *Praktika* of the Archaeological Society in Athens of 1976 (published 1978), 88–98. In addition, horse sacrifices are commonly attested in Thrace (for example in most tombs of the Valley of the Thracian Rulers), and in 2015 news reports circulated that archaeologists had found child sacrifices in Mursalevo on the Strymon river in Bulgaria (cf. http://archaeologynewsnetwork.blogspot.nl/2015/04/thracian-child-sacrifices-found-in.html, last consulted on 12 July 2017).
[255] Liapis 2011; cf. *LIMC* s.v. 'Heros equitans' (VI.1 1019–1981).

Also, the name Rhesus, which probably meant something like 'King' in the Thracian language, matches the invocation of the Heros Equitans as κύριος or δεσπότης. Liapis notes that "even if Philostratus is merely confusing the Heros with Rhesus, this could be due at least partly to genuine cultic affinities between the two figures."[256]

The resemblances between what we know of the Rhesus cult and what Herodotus transmits about the Magi's offerings at Ennea Hodoi are suggestive. It is possible that Herodotus himself did not notice the parallel; but that does not mean that it had arisen somewhere in the traditions on which he relied. Although we should be careful to make recourse to symbolic interpretations when an episode of Xerxes' invasion is mirrored in mythology (see §3.1.2), the symbolism is particularly strong in this case: an oracle had presaged that the Trojans would be invincible if they drowned Rhesus' horses in the Scamander river. It is possible that the ultimate point of the tradition on which Herodotus was that Xerxes followed an epic example without understanding that the outcome in the myth was futile.

2.3.5 The canal through the Athos peninsula

Further west was one of the most famous locations associated with Xerxes' advance (7.23-24):[257]

> [...] ὤρυσσον δὲ ὧδε δασάμενοι τὸν χῶρον οἱ βάρβαροι κατὰ ἔθνεα· κατὰ Σάνην πόλιν σχοινοτενὲς ποιησάμενοι, ἐπείτε ἐγίνετο βαθέα ἡ διῶρυξ, οἱ μὲν κατώτατα ἑστεῶτες ὤρυσσον, ἕτεροι δὲ παρεδίδοσαν τὸν αἰεὶ ἐξορυσσόμενον χοῦν ἄλλοισι κατύπερθε ἑστεῶσι ἐπὶ βάθρων, οἱ δ' αὖ ἐκδεκόμενοι ἑτέροισι, ἕως ἀπίκοντο ἐς τοὺς ἀνωτάτω· οὗτοι δὲ ἐξεφόρεόν τε καὶ ἐξέβαλλον. τοῖσι μέν νυν ἄλλοισι πλὴν Φοινίκων καταρρηγνύμενοι οἱ κρημνοὶ τοῦ ὀρύγματος πόνον διπλήσιον παρεῖχον· ἅτε γὰρ τοῦ τε ἄνω στόματος καὶ τοῦ κάτω τὰ αὐτὰ μέτρα ποιευμένων ἔμελλέ σφι τοιοῦτο ἀποβήσεσθαι. οἱ δὲ Φοίνικες σοφίην ἔν τε τοῖσι ἄλλοισι ἔργοισι ἀποδείκνυνται καὶ δὴ καὶ ἐν ἐκείνῳ. ἀπολαχόντες γὰρ μόριον ὅσον αὐτοῖσι ἐπέβαλλε, ὤρυσσον τὸ μὲν ἄνω στόμα τῆς διώρυχος ποιεῦντες διπλήσιον ἢ ὅσον ἔδει αὐτὴν τὴν διώρυχα γενέσθαι, προβαίνοντος δὲ τοῦ ἔργου συνῆγον αἰεί· κάτω τε δὴ ἐγίνετο καὶ ἐξισοῦτο τοῖσι ἄλλοισι τὸ ἔργον. ὡς μὲν ἐμὲ συμβαλλόμενον εὑρίσκειν, μεγαλοφροσύνης εἵνεκεν αὐτὸ Ξέρξης ὀρύσσειν ἐκέλευε, ἐθέλων τε δύναμιν ἀποδείκνυσθαι καὶ μνημόσυνα λιπέσθαι· παρεὸν γὰρ μηδένα πόνον λαβόντας τὸν ἰσθμὸν τὰς νέας διειρύσαι, ὀρύσσειν ἐκέλευε διώρυχα τῇ θαλάσσῃ εὖρος ὡς δύο τριήρεας πλέειν ὁμοῦ ἐλαστρεομένας. τοῖσι δὲ αὐτοῖσι τούτοισι, τοῖσί περ καὶ τὸ ὄρυγμα, προσετέτακτο καὶ τὸν Στρυμόνα ποταμὸν ζεύξαντας γεφυρῶσαι.

> [...] After dividing the land by nation, the barbarians built the canal as follows. They made a straight line at the town of Sane, and when the canal had gotten deep, some were digging while standing at the very bottom, while others transferred the constantly excavated dirt to yet others, who were standing higher on the ladders. When these men received it, they transferred it to

---
256 Liapis 2011, 97.
257 The detail Herodotus gives has been described as "exaggerated" (Casson 1926, 265). Pohlenz (1961, 130) suggested that knowledge about the canal was deeply rooted in oral traditions.

others still, until they came to those that were highest. And these men carried it out of the trench and threw it away. The collapsing sides of the canal gave all double labour, except the Phoenicians: for as the upper and lower ends of the trench were made with the same measurements, this was bound to happen to them. But the Phoenicians show wisdom in other projects too, and also in this one: working on the part that happened to be given to them, they dug the top end of the trench in such a way that made it twice the width that the canal was supposed to be. While continuing the work they narrowed down the width, and at the bottom the work was equal to that of the others. I reckon that Xerxes ordered to dig the canal because of his megalomania, desiring both to show off his power and to leave behind a memorial. Even though there was no problem in pulling the ships across the isthmus, he ordered a sea canal with a width so that two triremes could at once sail through if they were being rowed. And these same men that had been ordered to make the canal were also ordered to build a bridge across the Strymon river.

The canal remained a well-known feature after the invasion (Thucydides calls it τὸ βασιλέως διόρυγμα 'the King's channel', 4.109). The canal has left archaeological remains, extensively studied by the Isserlin team.[258] The archaeological remains have been nearly unanimously accepted as evidence for Xerxes' canal project.[259] They have been called "the most impressive surviving monument of Persia's short-lived imperial presence in Europe".[260] From the eighteenth century, travellers to the area gave descriptions of the canal and identified traces of it on the surface.[261] On the most detailed map (by Spratt) remnants of the canal appear as swampy hollows and a small local stream indicates the south end of the canal.[262] In the more recent investigations by the Isserlin team the swampy parts had turned into more solid soil, albeit lower than the surrounding areas and with different vegetation; the pool at the south end was still there, and is visible on Google Earth satellite images.[263] When I visited the southern end of the canal in June 2017, this remnant of the waterway was still plainly visible (see the photograph below).

---

[258] Isserlin 1991; Isserlin et al. 2003 (adding the evidence of seismic tomography and bore holes).
[259] This reasoning is found in Macan 1908, I 36–37; 1908, II 147–148 (stressing, however, the technical faultiness of Herodotus' description); Obst 1913, 45–46; Instinsky 1956; Danov 1976, 274; Hammond 1988, 526; Pritchett 1993, 292; Kelly 2003, 194 (pointing out that work on the canal would not have taken very long, and surely not four years); Weiskopf 2008, 85; Haubold 2013, 112 (explaining the construction as one of Xerxes' attempts at conquest of the sea). The notion of Xerxes' canal was so strong that early modern cartographers depicted Athos as a more or less round island (della Dora 2009, 114–116).
[260] Isserlin 1991, 83.
[261] E.g. Leake 1835, III 144–146; Spratt 1847; Struck 1907 (with a description of the accounts of many previous visitors on pages 120–127). Notably, Pococke (1745, II.2 144) did not believe the canal existed and did not see any traces of it.
[262] Spratt 1847, 145: "[...] I offer a few observations to explain the accompanying plan which was then made of it, the more particularly as the few remaining traces of this canal may have totally disappeared in another century, when the absence of such evidence might perhaps again produce doubts upon the truth of this historical record, such as have been expressed with regard to the veracity of Herodotus on this point, both in ancient and modern times."
[263] Isserlin 1991, 89; he describes the grounds near the river pool as a series of terraces, which may be man-made.

Fig. 17: A remnant of the Athos canal at its southwestern end.

Darius' Suez inscription (DZc), commemorating the construction of the Suez canal (2.158, 4.39) and the opening up of a new trade route, leaves no doubt about the status-enhancing properties of canals for Achaemenid kings.[264] At the same time, it has been pointed out that the story about the Athos canal was one that could easily be imagined in the landscape: it is reported that locals of Chalkidike, at least in the early twentieth century, alleged that canals had once been built across the other 'fingers' of Chalkidike as well, even though archaeological evidence for those projects is lacking.[265] Veronica della Dora has argued that the striking landscape of Athos itself elicited legendary accounts and moral values such as Xerxes' hubris;[266] she accordingly describes the archaeological expeditions aimed at tracing the canal, as well as a modern sign indicating the presence of the canal, as endeavours to reconstruct an invisible structure which only existed as a landscape of myth, and seems to be agnostic about the existence of the canal.[267]

---

264 Kienast (1996, 295) calls the canal "ein Dependant zum Suezkanal des Dareios". On Darius' Suez canal (and a discussion of the sources), see Tuplin 1991 and Allen 2005b, 54–55 who argue that the benefits of this canal were limited and that it was a symbolic construct.
265 Struck 1907, 130.
266 Della Dora 2009.
267 Della Dora 2009, 122–125.

Even so, the canal's existence is hard to deny. As the seas around Athos are notoriously dangerous, a canal could make sense.[268] But it may indeed be the case that the evocative landscape exaggerated the canal's importance; and there is some reason for skepticism regarding the direct relevance of the canal for specifically Xerxes' invasion.[269] Although Herodotus claims that this was only a prestige project for Xerxes, earlier (7.22) he mentioned that the reason for Xerxes to construct this canal was to avoid sailing around the Athos peninsula, where the Persians had supposedly suffered losses during Darius' invasion (6.44). But the canal seems to have been of a little practical use to Xerxes' invasion: Herodotus already highlighted flaws in the construction, and Strabo (7, fragment 35) mentioned that (according to Demetrios of Skepsis) it was not possible to dig the canal all the way through the peninsula owing to the rocky soil, and that it was not dug deep enough. The borehole samples of the Isserlin team found that the canal had only a very short life, as no marine organisms were found in the bottom layers.[270] Moreover the canal's construction seems a rather strange decision: the shortcut for the one-off movement of the Persian armada does not seem to justify the effort required in the construction, as the circumnavigation of the Athos peninsula is not insurmountable despite the dangers.[271]

The futility of constructing a canal which was not even necessary may be one reason why the story was as successful as it was. Accordingly, the construction has been explained as an example of Xerxes' folly or hubris, because with it, Xerxes violated the land of Macedonia.[272] Earlier in the *Histories* (1.174), Herodotus tells the

---

268 Miles 2016, 165 stresses the real danger in travelling around the Athos, as the landmass of the mountain creates strong winds. Leake 1835, III 145, suggested that it would make sense to reconstruct the canal: "and there can be no doubt that it would be useful to the navigation of the *Aegean*, for such is the fear entertained by the Greek boatmen of the strength and uncertain direction of the currents around Mount Athos, and of the gales and high sea to which the vicinity of the mountain is subject during half the year, and which are rendered more formidable by the deficiency of harbours in the Gulf of Orfaná, that I could not, as long as I was on the peninsula, and though offering a high price, prevail upon any boat to carry me from the eastern side of the peninsula to the western, or even from Xiropotamí to Vatopédhi."
269 Wallinga 2005, 24–25 suggests that there may have been multiple concurrent stories about the date. Other evidence for Persian activity in the area has been seen in a hoard of some three hundred Darics, found at or near the Athos canal: it was at first dated to early fifth century BCE, but now seems to postdate the construction because it contained at least one fourth-century BCE coin (Burn 1962, 318; but see Nicolet-Pierre 1992 for an earlier date).
270 Isserlin et al. 2003, 375.
271 Hauvette 1894, 292–293 gave priority to this tradition. But cf. Waters 2014, 126, who says that "practicality and vanity are not necessarily mutually exclusive". There exist stories about pirates who use the isthmus to drag ships over it; see Casson 1926, 29, note 2 (with literature).
272 For the canal as an example of Xerxes' folly, see Hauvette 1894, 292–293; Macan 1908, II 148; Flory (1987, 42) argues that Herodotus thinks that Xerxes profanes nature by digging the Athos canal, but this is not the case: for Herodotus it is simply a magnificent project. On the contrary, Baragwanath (2008, 254–265) argues unconvincingly that Herodotus' message here is that the canal made sense ac-

story about the Knidians who wanted to make their land an island by digging a canal through the local isthmus. When the construction caused problems, the Delphic oracle told them: Ἰσθμὸν δὲ μὴ πυργοῦτε μηδ' ὀρύσσετε· Ζεὺς γάρ κ' ἔθηκε νῆσον, εἴ κ' ἐβούλετο. 'Do not build a wall or a canal on the isthmus, as Zeus would have made an island, if he had wanted to.' By recounting this oracle, Herodotus explicitly records the idea that the land should not be violated.[273] Xerxes' work at Athos is thus not only megalomaniac, vain or hubristic; it is also irreligious. In the same way that Herodotus later tells us that winds from the Hellespont wreaked havoc to the Persian ships in Magnesia (§2.4.2), underlining Xerxes' irreverence to the Hellespont, Herodotus or his sources may have perceived a causal connection between this violation of the land and the later problems that Xerxes encountered during the expedition.[274]

In the later fifth century BCE, the mnemotopical landscape at the Athos isthmus, which consisted of a (half-collapsed?) canal, a market place and a tumulus (see below, §2.3.6) fitted common notions about Xerxes' invasion which were highly relevant at the time. While the Athos canal may have been a Persian enterprise whose construction made sense within long-term Persian domination of this area, it is difficult to connect with the specific event of Xerxes' invasion as securely as Herodotus does: but when there were points about hubris to be made, synchronising the construction of these monuments with Xerxes' visit was an obvious step for whomever talked last to Herodotus.

2.3.6 The tomb of Artachaies

The memory landscape of the Athos canal was supplemented by another salient location (7.117-7.118):

> ἐν Ἀκάνθῳ δὲ ἐόντος Ξέρξεω συνήνεικε ὑπὸ νούσου ἀποθανεῖν τὸν ἐπεστεῶτα τῆς διώρυχος Ἀρταχαίην, δόκιμον ἐόντα παρὰ Ξέρξῃ καὶ γένος Ἀχαιμενίδην, μεγάθεΐ τε μέγιστον ἐόντα Περσέων (ἀπὸ γὰρ πέντε πηχέων βασιληίων ἀπέλειπε τέσσερας δακτύλους) φωνέοντά τε μέγιστον ἀνθρώπων, ὥστε Ξέρξην συμφορὴν ποιησάμενον μεγάλην ἐξενεῖκαί τε αὐτὸν κάλλιστα καὶ θάψαι· ἐτυμβοχόεε δὲ πᾶσα ἡ στρατιή. τούτῳ δὲ τῷ Ἀρταχαίῃ θύουσι Ἀκάνθιοι ἐκ θεοπροπίου ὡς ἥρωι, ἐπονομάζοντες τὸ οὔνομα. βασιλεὺς μὲν δὴ Ξέρξης ἀπολομένου Ἀρταχαίεω ἐποιέετο συμφορήν·

> When Xerxes was at Akanthos, it happened that Artachaies, who had overseen the construction of the canal, died of a disease. Because he was highly esteemed by Xerxes, of Achaemenid descent, the tallest of the Persians (five royal cubits minus four daktyloi), and could scream

---

cording to Persian customs, and that the hubris is only a Greek interpretation. Bridges 2015, 56–57 also sees the episode as separate from the notion of a hubristic Xerxes. However, these scholars disregard the Artachaies incident which may have been connected to the canal's construction and have put it in a more negative light (see §2.3.6).
273 E.g. Kirchberg 1965, 38–39; Lateiner 1985, 89; Pritchett 1993, 292–293, note 242; Miles 2014, 122.
274 This is hinted at by Montevecchi 1989, 25.

loudest of all men, Xerxes, regarding this as a great misfortune, splendidly paid him his last honour and buried him. The entire army helped to build the burial mound. The Akanthians sacrifice by oracular command to this Artachaies, as if to a hero, while they call out his name. King Xerxes regarded the death of Artachaies as a misfortune.

Although Herodotus does not offer precise indications about the location of Artachaies' tumulus, early travellers identified it with a small mound on top of a hill ridge, at the southern end of the canal on its east side near the modern village of Trypiti.[275] This spot was surveyed by the Isserlin team, but only sherds of Hellenistic date were discovered.[276] The mound has not been excavated, so this identification remains hypothetical.

Artachaies seems to be an authentic Persian name and it is not impossible that he received worship from local inhabitants, even if they were ethnically Greek.[277] The fact that this part of the Aegean coasts had long been (and would remain) part of the Achaemenid Empire and that the Akanthians were allegedly on good terms with Xerxes (7.116) makes this even more likely. Yet 'not impossible' is not the same as 'unremarkable', and remarkable the story is in many ways. Herodotus describes Artachaies' funeral in epic fashion: like the Homeric heroes, Artachaies was larger than life,[278] and Greeks of the fifth century BCE could have associated the construction of a tumulus with hero cult;[279] by contrast, there is no tumulus tradition for Achaemenid Persians. Perhaps the story reflects an old local tradition in which a tumulus or natural hill, which antedated the Persian invasion, was somehow reinterpreted as the grave of Artachaies, in the same way that tell mounds were interpreted as the graves of Homeric heroes (§2.2.3), and a natural hill was interpreted as the grave of

---

[275] Spratt 1847, 149–150 (mentioning five or six hewn blocks at the base of the mound); Struck 1908, 130; Rawlinson 1880, 96 pointed out that Herodotus' wording suggests that the tumulus was at Akanthos, i.e. at the northern end of the canal.

[276] Isserlin et al. 2003, 379.

[277] Macan 1908, I 148; Visser (1982) and Parker (2011, 117–118), while not questioning the historicity of the scene, mention it as part of a long list of examples in which an enemy hero receives worship, which is usually demanded by an oracle to lift a curse: in Herodotus, the Kairetans' sacrifices to the Phokaians (1.165–167), Philippos of Kroton (5.47) and the Amathusians' sacrifice to Onesilos (5.114–115). Cf. the story about Pyrrhus who was killed by Demeter but still received a burial in her temple at Argos (Pausanias 1.13.7–8 and Plutarch, *Pyrrhus* 34); the scene also bears resemblance to Antaeus in Tingis (seen by Quintus Sertorius); Visser suggests that the worship in this case was prompted "because he was amazing", and perhaps to honour his role as a canal builder (1982, 411 and note 27). Artachaies is thought to be referred to by Aristophanes in *Acharnenses* 709 (Borthwick 1970; Parker 2011, 117 note 31).

[278] Green 1996, 89; Petropoulou 2008, 15–18 suggests that worship of large men was not foreign to the Persians; see also Asheri 1990, 161: "*Ergo*, exceptional physical gifts and beauty prevail in some civilized societies—sometimes with the help of an oracle—over frontiers and hatred."

[279] Cf. Petropoulou 2008, 18, who connects the description of Artachaies' funeral to that of Patroclus in the *Iliad*.

Fig. 18: A tumulus near the Athos canal, believed to be that of Artachaies.

Helle (§2.2.5).[280] Whatever the historicity of the story of the death of the man who supervised the construction of the Athos canal, it showed that Persian violation of the land was subject to immediate divine retribution. Noteworthy in this respect is that Herodotus specifies that the death happened 'when Xerxes was in Akanthos', thereby directly connecting the death to the invasion.

2.3.7 The Tempe valley

After Potidaia, the Persian army arrived at the Macedonian town of Therme (near modern Thessaloniki), where the invasion of Thessaly and southern Greece was planned. The most direct way into Thessaly was by way of the narrow Tempe valley through which the Peneios river runs. In 7.128, Herodotus describes how Xerxes makes a special trip to the Tempe valley to contemplate what to do:

---

280 Macan 1908, I 147. Mayor 2000 (especially 104–156) discusses the ways in which fossil remains of large extinct animal species could have been reinterpreted as the bones of heroes.

Ξέρξης δὲ ὁρέων ἐκ τῆς Θέρμης ὄρεα τὰ Θεσσαλικά, τόν τε Ὄλυμπον καὶ τὴν Ὄσσαν, μεγάθεΐ ὑπερμήκεα ἐόντα, διὰ μέσου τε αὐτῶν αὐλῶνα στεινὸν πυνθανόμενος εἶναι, δι' οὗ ῥέει ὁ Πηνειός, ἀκούων τε ταύτῃ εἶναι ὁδὸν ἐς Θεσσαλίην φέρουσαν, ἐπεθύμησε πλώσας θεήσασθαι τὴν ἐκβολὴν τοῦ Πηνειοῦ, ὅτι τὴν ἄνω ὁδὸν ἔμελλε ἐλᾶν διὰ Μακεδόνων τῶν κατύπερθε οἰκημένων ἔστε Περραιβοὺς παρὰ Γόννον πόλιν· ταύτῃ γὰρ ἀσφαλέστατον ἐπυνθάνετο εἶναι. ὡς δὲ ἐπεθύμησε, καὶ ἐποίεε ταῦτα· ἐσβὰς ἐς Σιδωνίην νέα, ἐς τήν περ ἐσέβαινε αἰεὶ ὅκως τι ἐθέλοι τοιοῦτο ποιῆσαι, ἀνέδεξε σημήιον καὶ τοῖσι ἄλλοισι ἀνάγεσθαι, καταλιπὼν αὐτοῦ τὸν πεζὸν στρατόν. ἐπεὶ δὲ ἀπίκετο καὶ ἐθεήσατο Ξέρξης τὴν ἐκβολὴν τοῦ Πηνειοῦ, ἐν θώματι μεγάλῳ ἐνέσχετο, καλέσας δὲ τοὺς κατηγεμόνας τῆς ὁδοῦ εἴρετο εἰ τὸν ποταμὸν ἐστὶ παρατρέψαντα ἑτέρῃ ἐς θάλασσαν ἐξαγαγεῖν.

And when Xerxes saw from Therme how enormous the Thessalian mountains, the Olympus and the Ossa, were, and heard that a narrow passage runs between them through which the Peneios river flows, and that there is a road leading to Thessaly there, he wanted to sail there to observe the mouth of the Peneios. For he was going to take the high road through the land of the Macedonians who live in the highlands and that of the Perrhaibians along the city of Gonnos. He learned that this was the safest way. And he did as he planned: he embarked on a Sidonian ship, on which he always embarked whenever he wanted to do something like that. He hoisted a flag to notify the others to follow, and left the land army behind. When Xerxes arrived and saw the mouth of the Peneios river, he was struck with awe. He called his guides and asked whether the river could be diverted so as to be led into the sea by a different way.

Herodotus subsequently (7.129) digresses on the natural geography of Thessaly, theorising that the Thessalian plain used to be a lake, and that the Tempe valley was the result of an earthquake caused by Poseidon: the water then flowed through the exit that this earthquake created, causing the former Thessalian lake to dry up. The anecdote about Xerxes continues in 7.130:

οἱ δὲ κατηγεόμενοι εἰρομένου Ξέρξεω εἰ ἔστι ἄλλη ἔξοδος ἐς θάλασσαν τῷ Πηνειῷ, ἐξεπιστάμενοι ἀτρεκέως εἶπον· Βασιλεῦ, ποταμῷ τούτῳ οὐκ ἔστι ἄλλη ἐξήλυσις ἐς θάλασσαν κατήκουσα, ἀλλ' ἢ αὕτη· ὄρεσι γὰρ περιεστεφάνωται πᾶσα Θεσσαλίη. Ξέρξην δὲ λέγεται εἰπεῖν πρὸς ταῦτα· Σοφοὶ ἄνδρες εἰσὶ Θεσσαλοί. ταῦτ' ἄρα πρὸ πολλοῦ ἐφυλάξαντο γνωσιμαχέοντες καὶ τἆλλα καὶ ὅτι χώρην ἄρα εἶχον εὐαίρετόν τε καὶ ταχυάλωτον. τὸν γὰρ ποταμὸν πρῆγμα ἂν ἦν μοῦνον ἐπεῖναι σφέων ἐπὶ τὴν χώρην, χώματι ἐκ τοῦ αὐλῶνος ἐκβιβάσαντα καὶ παρατρέψαντα δι' ὧν νῦν ῥέει ῥεέθρων, ὥστε Θεσσαλίην πᾶσαν ἔξω τῶν ὀρέων ὑπόβρυχα γενέσθαι. ταῦτα δὲ ἔχοντα ἔλεγε ἐς τοὺς Ἀλεύεω παῖδας, ὅτι πρῶτοι Ἑλλήνων ἐόντες Θεσσαλοὶ ἔδοσαν ἑωυτοὺς βασιλέι, δοκέων ὁ Ξέρξης ἀπὸ παντός σφεας τοῦ ἔθνεος ἐπαγγέλλεσθαι φιλίην. εἴπας δὲ ταῦτα καὶ θεησάμενος ἀπέπλεε ἐς τὴν Θέρμην.

And when Xerxes asked whether the Peneios river has another outlet into the sea, the guides, who knew the area perfectly, said: "Sire, the river does not have another mouth as it comes down to the sea, except for this one, for all of Thessaly is surrounded by mountains." It is told that Xerxes gave the following answer: "The Thessalians are wise men. So long ago they were prudent enough to surrender, knowing that they have a land that can be conquered easily and quickly, because one can make the river flood the entire country by diverting it with a dam from the channel through which the current runs now, so that all Thessaly outside the mountains is flooded.'" Xerxes said this to the sons of Aleues because the Thessalians were the first of the Greeks who surrendered to the king, and he thought that they had announced him the friendship of the entire nation. Having said that and having looked at it he sailed back to Therme.

The valley, accentuated by the Olympus massif to the north ("the bastion of Greece"[281]), was a veritable landmark in the mental map of the ancients.[282] Herodotus notes it for three other reasons: he marks it as the southernmost point reached by the Teucrians and Mysians during their invasion of Greece (7.20); as an alternative defence location to Thermopylae where soldiers were in fact despatched (7.173),[283] and as the spot to which Phormos the Athenian was chased by the Persians, and where he washed ashore (7.182).

Fig. 19: The Tempe valley near its eastern end.

---

281 Hammond 1988, 539.
282 The Tempe valley was already known to Homer (*Iliad* 2.753); the fact that it is now used for the motorway testifies to the idea of Tempe as an easily defendable gateway into Greece. Livy (44.6) gives an especially vivid description.
283 The account is considered true by some, and it is a sensible plan because unlike at Thermopylae, it was impossible to perform a backstab action (Robertson 1976, 116).

A real visit could underlie the story, as some scholars believe.[284] At the same time, there are two ways in which the Tempe valley functioned as a mnemotope in the time of Herodotus.[285] First, it has been pointed out that the anecdote dovetails well with the well-established Herodotean theme of the 'gazing Persian'.[286] At other places, both Xerxes and his father Darius are reported to have had a similar sense of awe, such as Xerxes' reverence for the plane tree at Kallatebos and for the city of Troy, while his father Darius was impressed by the Black Sea (4.85).[287] Earlier in his work (3.136), Herodotus reported that the Persians had sailed along the coasts of Greece for sightseeing purposes. It may be that Herodotus projects his own experience as a researcher on Xerxes;[288] however, this kind of stereotyping may also have been more widespread in folkloric conceptions of the Persian kings.

Second, the scene may be connected with the notion of Achaemenid kings as great builders. Throughout the invasion (at the Hellespont, Athos and Salamis) Xerxes is represented as prone to exhibiting his hobby of building large infrastructural works (cf. §3.1.3). Perhaps the grandness of the idea of building a dam in the Peneios river was considered fit to connect with Xerxes as well.[289] Here, Xerxes' work rivalled that of the gods: Herodotus in 7.129 describes the Tempe valley as Poseidon's work: when Xerxes considers damming up the valley, he considers it possible to make this god's work undone.[290]

2.3.8 The Macedonian mountain

After Xerxes and his army finally set out from Therme to Athens, they found their way obstructed by the Pierian mountains, Mount Olympus, and Mount Ossa, which

---

[284] Burn 1962, 339; Hammond 1988, 546; Green 1996, 91–92; Grethlein 2009, 206.
[285] Macan 1908, II 189–190 suggested that the episode served as an apology of the Thessalians, who had taken sides with the Persians: Herodotus' explanation seems to be that the Thessalians had no other choice but to accept.
[286] Cf. Christ 1994, 179–180; Waters 2014, 126.
[287] For Obst (1913, 60) the parallel would reveal that Herodotus used a written source.
[288] Hence, some feel it highlights above all Herodotus' own visit of the area and his own impressions with it. Macan 1908, I 163 and II 189–190; Pohlenz (1961, 130): "Um den Eindruck, den noch heute der Reisende empfängt, wenn er plötzlich die weite, von einem Bergkranz umgebene Landschaft Thessaliens erblickt, dem Leser zu vermitteln, wendet Herodot denselben literarischen Kunstgriff wie bei der Beschreibung des Pontos an: er läßt Xerxes einen Abstecher dorthin machen und „die Mündung des Peneios betrachten.""; Hignett 1963, 108; indeed, the geographical detail gives reason to assume that Herodotus has seen the area himself (e.g. Westlake 1936, 19; Myres 1953, 4; Pritchett 1961, 370).
[289] Fehling 1971, 27: "vom Athosdurchstich her konnte er schon auf den Gedanken verfallen."; see also Christ 1994, 179–180; Weiskopf 2008, 85; Miles 2014, 122.
[290] The Peneios was prone to attracting such stories: in Callimachus' *In Delum* (106–152) meddling with the Peneios river seems to be the reserve of the gods: this poem contains a story about a fight between Ares and the Peneios, in which the river is threatened with disappearance. Note that at Potidaia, Poseidon was probably believed to be responsible for the disappearance of the Persian army (see §2.8.9).

together constitute the highest mountain range in Greece. The only easy way by which Thessaly could be reached was the Tempe valley, which runs between these mountains. But upon hearing that this route was unsafe, Xerxes is said to have decided to take an alternative 'high' route (ἄνω ὁδός) through Macedonia into Perrhaibia and the town of Gonnoi (7.128).[291] In 7.131, Herodotus says that Xerxes stayed in Pieria, while one third of his army was clearing the forest (ἔκειρε) of the 'Macedonian mountain' to cross into Perrhaibia. The Greeks initially decided to guard the Tempe valley, but fled, Herodotus theorises, because the Persians took the alternative route (7.172-173).

Gonnoi has been identified with a site immediately east of modern Gonni (formerly Dereli), and the approximate locations of Pieria (the most southern region of Macedonia, around modern Katerini) and Perrhaibia (northern Thessaly, around Elassona) are also known. However, it is not immediately clear what Herodotus means by the 'Macedonian mountain'. Depending on the exact extent of Pieria and Perrhaibia, it may refer to either the Pierian mountains or to the Olympus massif, which consists of the Olympus proper in the north and the Oktolophos or Kato Olympos mountains to its south. Vermio, known to Herodotus as Bermion, and Ossa are probably too far north and south.[292] It is, however, doubtful whether the Pierian massif was on Herodotus' radar as he does not mention it elsewhere. It seems more likely that the Macedonian mountain referred to the Olympus massif itself.[293] A look at the map reveals that this mountain range constitutes much of the border between Pieria (southern Macedonia) and Perrhaibia (northern Thessaly), as Herodotus explicitly says (7.129; 7.173).[294] Even more importantly, if Herodotus did not mean the Olympus, his story that the army passed Gonnoi would be difficult to understand, because Gonnoi lay in the foothills of the Olympus massif. Also note that Herodotus already connected this mountain with Xerxes by making the Persian king observe it from faraway Therme (7.128; cf. §2.3.7). A difficulty with the identification of the mountain with the Olympus is that there is no conceivable reason why Herodotus would have refrained from calling the mountain by its name.

Regardless of which of the mentioned mountains Herodotus regarded as the Macedonian mountain, the feasibility of crossing it with a large army is virtually nonexistent. Scholars who discuss the episode have tried to come up with 'explanations' for the impossibility of the topographical situation, by either supposing that Xerxes

---

291 It is probably this same route that Herodotus hints at in 9.89 regarding Artabazos' escape from Plataea; cf. Tuplin 2003, 401, note 26.
292 Bermion was the location of the Gardens of Midas (8.138). As Vandiver (1991, 79–80) notes, the Gardens of Midas are only mentioned as an incidental detail that is not connected to the main narrative about Xerxes' invasion.
293 This is done by Leake 1841, 240; Müller 1987, 269; (seemingly) Hauvette 1894, 343–345.
294 Later, Strabo (7, fragments 14 and 15; 10.3.17) also considered the Olympus to be a Macedonian mountain.

made use of one of the passes (Petra and/or Volustana), that the army never came by Gonnoi,[295] or that Herodotus was wrong, and that Xerxes did use the Tempe valley to reach Gonnoi.[296]

Fig. 20: Remains of Gonnoi, looking east towards the Tempe valley, with foothills of Mount Olympus to the left.

However, such discussions typically assume not only that Herodotus had a perfect topographical understanding of the region, but also that he is in principle historically accurate when localising events. But these assumptions are dangerous: we do not know what kind of sources or maps Herodotus was using, and his conception of the world

---

295 Macan 1908, II 251–252; Müller 1987, 242–250; Hammond 1988, 546; Tuplin (2003, 401, note 26) suggests that the army either crossed the Vermio first, or used the valley between higher and lower Olympus. Robertson (1976, 115–116) suggested that the 'error' arose because Herodotus connected the position of allies at Tempe to the Persian mountain route at Dion. Pritchett (1993, 32–34; 1961), who believed the factual accuracy of the entire episode suggested that the route to Gonnoi was possible if one assumes that ἄνω Μακεδωνία was around Katerini.
296 Hignett 1963, 109: "Herodotus seems to have been impressed by what he had heard, perhaps at Tempe, about the Gonnos route, and somehow picked up the mistaken idea that it was the route followed by Xerxes and his army."; see also Macan 1908, I 164–165; Cawkwell 2005, 93.

has been shown to be more schematic than factually correct in various instances (see §2.1.1 and §2.5.1). In addition, there are various circumstances that reveal the importance of the story in Herodotus' time, and that suggest that the Macedonian mountain should be understood primarily as a mnemotope for the passing of the army. The most important consideration is that the episode of the bypass of the Tempe valley is exemplary for what the Persians do in many instances throughout the *Histories*, in which they avoid the direct confrontation with the Greeks and take an alternative route that is implausible if not impossible (see §3.3.5).[297] Second, the episode is exemplary of the hyperbole with which Herodotus describes Xerxes' army; in this respect it is not unlike other episodes in which the army is pictured as a nearly monstrous machine, destroying everything in its path and drinking lakes and rivers dry. And in the same way that the stories about the lakes and rivers may be based on actual observations of drying up of these water bodies, the story about the deforestation may have offered an aetiology for the fact that large parts of the Olympus massif (or other mountains) are bare. If, indeed, the Macedonian mountain refers to the Olympus proper, Herodotus' topographical remarks bring Xerxes and his army directly to the abode of the gods: of course, especially Zeus was connected to the mountain (cf. e.g. *Iliad* 1.221; 4.276). We have already seen that Xerxes was not only likened to Zeus himself, but also that he was thought to have visited Zeus' other abode at Mount Ida in the Troad (§2.2.1).

2.3.9 The temple of Zeus Laphystios at Halos

When Xerxes' army had bypassed Tempe, the road was clear until the next bottleneck, the pass of Thermopylae. In Achaea Phthiotis, the southern part of Thessaly, we hear of another anecdote connected to the passing of the Persians (7.197):

ἐς Ἇλον δὲ τῆς Ἀχαιίης ἀπικομένῳ Ξέρξῃ οἱ κατηγεμόνες τῆς ὁδοῦ βουλόμενοι τὸ πᾶν ἐξηγέεσθαι ἔλεγον οἱ ἐπιχώριον λόγον, τὰ περὶ τὸ ἱρὸν τοῦ Λαφυστίου Διός, ὡς Ἀθάμας ὁ Αἰόλου ἐμηχανήσατο Φρίξῳ μόρον σὺν Ἰνοῖ βουλεύσας μετέπειτα δὲ ὡς ἐκ θεοπροπίου Ἀχαιοὶ προτιθεῖσι τοῖσι ἐκείνου ἀπογόνοισι ἀέθλους τοιούσδε: ὃς ἂν ᾖ τοῦ γένεος τούτου πρεσβύτατος, τούτῳ ἐπιτάξαντες ἔργεσθαι τοῦ ληίτου αὐτοὶ φυλακὰς ἔχουσι (λήιτον δὲ καλέουσι τὸ πρυτανήιον οἱ Ἀχαιοί): ἢν δὲ ἐσέλθῃ, οὐκ ἔστι ὅκως ἔξεισι πρὶν ἢ θύσεσθαι μέλλῃ: ὥς τ' ἔτι πρὸς τούτοισι πολλοὶ ἤδη τούτων τῶν μελλόντων θύσεσθαι δείσαντες οἴχοντο ἀποδράντες ἐς ἄλλην χώρην, χρόνου δὲ προϊόντος ὀπίσω κατελθόντες ἂν ἡλίσκοντο ἐσελθόντες ἐς τὸ πρυτανήιον, ὡς θύεταί τε ἐξηγέοντο στέμμασι πᾶς πυκασθεὶς καὶ ὡς σὺν πομπῇ ἐξαχθείς. ταῦτα δὲ πάσχουσι οἱ Κυτισσώρου τοῦ Φρίξου παιδὸς ἀπόγονοι, διότι καθαρμὸν τῆς χώρης ποιευμένων Ἀχαιῶν ἐκ θεοπροπίου Ἀθάμαντα τὸν Αἰόλου καὶ μελλόντων μιν θύειν ἀπικόμενος οὗτος ὁ Κυτίσσωρος ἐξ Αἴης τῆς Κολχίδος ἐρρύσατο, ποιήσας δὲ τοῦτο τοῖσι ἐπιγενομένοισι ἐξ ἑωυτοῦ μῆνιν τοῦ θεοῦ ἐνέβαλε. Ξέρξης δὲ ταῦτα ἀκούσας ὡς κατὰ

---

297 The similarity of the episode to the bypass of Thermopylae was noted by Westlake 1936, 19; he suggested that it was literary drama; this observation, however, has not reverberated.

τὸ ἄλσος ἐγίνετο, αὐτός τε ἔργετο αὐτοῦ καὶ τῇ στρατιῇ πάσῃ παρήγγειλε, τῶν τε Ἀθάμαντος ἀπογόνων τὴν οἰκίην ὁμοίως καὶ τὸ τέμενος ἐσέβετο.

After Xerxes arrived in Halos of Achaea, his guides, who wanted to explain him everything, told him a local story concerning the sanctuary of Zeus Laphystios. They told him that Athamas, son of Aiolos, together with Ino plotted and enacted the death of Phrixos, and that afterwards by oracular command the Achaeans gave the following tasks to his descendants: they commanded whoever happens to be the oldest of the family to stay out of the lēïton, and they watch the place themselves (the Achaeans call the prytaneion a lēïton). But if he goes in, it is not possible for him to go out without being sacrificed. They add to this that many of those who are going to be sacrificed escape in fear and go abroad. And if, after some time, they come back and are caught going into the prytaneion, this person is sacrificed and they lead him outside, covered entirely with garlands, and he is led away as if in a procession. This is the treatment that the descendants of Kytissoros, son of Phrixos, receive; for when by oracular command the Achaeans made Athamas, son of Aiolos, an exile of the country, and when they wanted to sacrifice him, this Kytissoros came from Aia in Colchis and saved him. And having done so, he brought the wrath of the god onto his descendants. And when Xerxes himself came to the sacred grove and heard all about this, he stayed clear of it and ordered the same to his entire army, and he paid respect to the house of the descendants of Athamas and the temenos alike.

Halos was a prominent settlement in Thessaly situated at the point where the Thessalian plain meets the sea.[298] The 'new town' of Halos, dating from Hellenistic times, has been extensively researched. Herodotus' story shows that this settlement had a predecessor, as does the mention of the city by Homer, who says that it was ruled by Achilles and was the provenance of the Myrmidons (*Iliad* 2.682). This 'pre-Hellenistic' Halos was situated on or close to the sea, as appears from Herodotus 7.173 and Demosthenes, *De falsa legatione* 163. It was destroyed in 346 BCE by the Macedonian general Parmenion, after which New Halos was founded (Strabo 9.5.8). The location of Pre-Hellenistic Halos has long been elusive and the Copenhagen Polis Center classifies its location as 'unknown'.[299] However, the archaeologist Vollgraff in the early twentieth century proposed the Plataniotiki Magoula, a hillock several kilometres northeast of Hellenistic Halos, as the site. He performed a small excavation here in 1906, unearthing classical Greek black-gloss ware and the foundations of a monumental building which were still visible at the time; he identified it with the temple of Zeus Laphystios.[300] Unfortunately, the publication of the results was only synoptic and the location of this building on the site is unknown. In 1925, a small bronze figurine of a bearded man, possibly depicting Zeus and dated to the seventh century

---

298 The city of Halos in Achaea Phthiotis features in 7.173 as the place of disembarkation for 10,000 hoplites on their way to the Tempe valley. The location of Halos is said to be influenced by its proximity to Itonos, where there was a temple of Athena, and because it is strategic point (Robertson 1976, 111).
299 Decourt, Nielsen & Helly 2004, 714.
300 Vollgraff 1907–1908; cf. Stählin 1924, 180. Zeus Laphystios was also worshipped in Orchomenos in Boeotia (Pausanias 1.24.2).

BCE, was found on the purported site of the temple in pre-Hellenistic Halos, but again, the indications are too scanty to verify the claim.³⁰¹ Subsequent surveys, most recently in 2013–2016, have shown that the magoula was indeed the location of a large settlement.³⁰² While the exact location of the temple remains unknown for the moment, the location of pre-Hellenistic Halos is now reasonably certain.

Fig. 21: Magoula Plataniotiki, the site of Pre-Hellenistic Halos.
Photo courtesy of Koen Blok.

Xerxes' visit to Halos has usually been treated as historically authentic.³⁰³ However, it is inconsistent with the statement that the army drank the Onochonos river (the modern Karoumbalis) dry, which flows much further west near modern Karditsa (7.196). Tuplin remedies this by suggesting that there were different columns

---

301 Giannopoulou 1925–1926.
302 It was revealed that the Plataniotiki Magoula was the centre of a settlement eleven hectares in size as evidenced by roof tiles, red-figured and black-glazed sherds, loomweights, amphora knobs, a few coins and limestone blocks. See Efstathiou et al. 1991; Reinders 1988, 159–164; Stissi et al. 2017; Dijkstra, van Rookhuijzen & Kamphorst 2017.
303 E.g. Wecklein 1876, 260–261 (who is otherwise skeptical); Walser 1984, 51.

marching through Thessaly.[304] But if one accepts that certain sites were later added to the list of sites which Xerxes and his army visited, then there is no need to reconcile all locations given by Herodotus; Obst, for instance, believed that the episode was inauthentic for this reason.[305] Given this background, there is even more scope to discuss the various reasons why the temple functioned as a mnemotope for the story.

At Halos, Xerxes finds himself in the heartland of the heroic age: this was Achaea Phthiotis, steeped in Trojan War lore, with Achilles, the Myrmidons and Protesilaos all hailing from here (cf. *Iliad* 2.681-685), but also the land of the Argonautic sagas: Halos was the home town of Phrixos and Helle. Herodotus makes Xerxes interact with a strand of the 'prehistory' of this latter body of myth.[306] Earlier, at Troy, he was also portrayed as interested in the heroic age of the Greeks. This has led to the assertion that the story is a mirror image of Herodotus' own aspirations.[307] In addition to this it seems fruitful to look at the story as a 'temple legend' told by local priests, like so many stories in the *Histories*.[308] After all, this sanctuary, and the lore about Phrixos and Helle attached to it, were Halos' claim to fame: Zeus and Phrixos or Helle appear on the city's coinage of the Classical and Hellenistic period. Herodotus was undoubtedly fascinated with this cult featuring human sacrifice.[309] The story about Xerxes interacting with these myths would have added to the sanctuary's prominence, which seems to have faced 'cultic competition' from Orchomenos, where the Athamas legend and Zeus Laphystios were alternatively connected to, if the testimonies of Apollonius Rhodius (*Argonautica* 2.1140-1156) and Pausanias (9.34.5) are to be believed.

The other curious detail is that Xerxes chooses to stay out of the sacred grove. This may directly be compared to stories which highlight that it is sacrilegious for Persians to enter temple grounds: from Pausanias (9.25.9) we learn that Xerxes' men who had stayed in Boeotia with Mardonios had jumped into the sea after entering the temple of the Kabeiroi in Thebes. In the *Histories*, a related story is that about

---

304 Macan 1908, I 292; Tuplin 2003, 401, note 26. For the identification of the Onochonos with the Karoumbalis see Müller 1987, 348.
305 Obst 1913, 100.
306 The enigmatic son of Phrixos, Kytissoros, is attested only once again in Greek literature, in Apollonius Rhodius' *Argonautica*, 2.1140–1156, where we learn that he was one of four brothers who travelled from Colchis to Orchomenos (not Halos) to claim the possessions of their grandfather Athamas. Note that Athamas was the central character of lost plays by Aeschylus and Sophocles. The agricultural plane near Halos, around modern Almyros, was called the Athamantian plane (Pausanias 9.24.1).
307 Grethlein 2009, 205 (wrongly identifying Halos as a river).
308 Obst 1913, 100 suggested that the story may have been be fabricated by local priests to give Xerxes a "nimbus".
309 It has been suggested that Herodotus recorded this story to digress about the cult of Zeus Laphystios: Macan 1908, I 292, cf. 296; Hignett 1963, 111; Vandiver 1991, 219.

the temple of Demeter at Plataea (§2.9.6), where the goddess herself was said to have warded off the barbarians from her temenos. Here in Halos Xerxes keeps clear of the temple, which has led to the assertion that the episode is an example of how Herodotus makes Xerxes a more pious person.[310] Nevertheless, the Persian king violates a religious rule: he respects the descendants of Athamas and Kytissoros despite the fact that he has just heard that the wrath of the god is upon them.[311] It is also relevant that by honouring Athamas and his offspring, Xerxes' aligns himself with the mad father of a mythical figure, Helle, whom he has disrespected at the Hellespont, not long before his arrival at Halos.[312] Xerxes had also passed the grave of Helle at Paktye (7.58; cf. §2.2.5); here, Herodotus was careful to point out that she was Athamas' daughter.

2.3.10 Summary

Xerxes' march along the northern shore of the Aegean left behind many mnemotopes where stories about the king's passing lived. They enlivened various stereotypes about Xerxes: the Persian king was pictured as a hubristic builder at Athos, where he constructed a canal, and at the Temple valley where he fantasised about building a dam to flood the Thessalian plain; as an onlooking monarch at Doriskos and Tempe; and as a respecter of local cults at the temple of Zeus Laphystios in Halos and at the Strymon river near Ennea Hodoi, where he buried alive nine children. In addition, I point out that Herodotus' audience would have been interested in the remarkable stories about the locals of this region, who, we are told, not only revered the grave of the Persian nobleman Artachaies, but also the king's road itself.

It has not been the aim of this chapter to establish how many of these mnemotopes commemorate historical events; instead, I have attempted to show that the places could have become mnemotopes for these stories by other processes than by the memory of actual historical events. Whether these mnemotopes accurately describe Xerxes' movements or not, they should foremost be understood as the stages of tales constructed around the king's advance into Greece.

---

310 Bridges 2015, 63.
311 Cf. Vandiver 1991, 222: "Xerxes here seems to choose to ally himself with a figure whose history is far from admirable and whose dependants suffered for his actions." Similarly Bowie (2012, 278) points out that for Herodotus, there may have been a deeply symbolic meaning to the visit: Xerxes does not destroy the temple, but pays respect to the god. This would signify that it is ultimately the cosmic will for him to fall.
312 Vandiver 1991, 221–222.

Map 4: Central Greece.

2.4 The advance of the armada and the battle of Artemision

The battle of Artemision, the nautical counterpart of the battle of Thermopylae (to be discussed in §2.5), enfolded in the seascapes of Magnesia and Euboea.[313] The battle itself was believed to have been fought in the waters near Artemision, while a detached contingent of two hundred Persian ships perished in a storm at the elusive 'Hollows' of Euboea. To the battle may be added its prelude, consisting of the problematic arrival of the Persian armada in the area. Stories about these events had mnemotopes on and off the coasts of Magnesia, the large peninsula comprising much of eastern Thessaly and dominated by Mount Pelion. Here, the Greeks believed, the Persians suffered important losses due to a violent storm.

---

[313] A selection of places mentioned in this chapter features on Map 4.

2.4 The advance of the armada and the battle of Artemision

The account of the battle of Artemision is highly dramatised,[314] and the battle gave rise to a small commemoration process and even mythology.[315] We know that Simonides wrote a poem about the battle of Artemision (Priscian, *De metris fabularum Terentii* 24; *Suda* s.v. Σιμωνίδης), and on the authority of a scholium on Apollonius Rhodius (s.v. Ζήτης καὶ Κάλαϊς), this poem contained references to Oreïthyia's abduction to Thrace by Boreas.[316]

Myth was intimately bound op with the stories about the battle that circulated in the late fifth century BCE. What follows is an argumentation that Herodotus' topography could have its origin in folk belief, rather than in coherent 'sources' that immediately take us back to the historical events of 480 BCE; a process which even continues today in this area.[317] Also, new identifications of several of the places which Herodotus mentions will be given, enabled by the realisation that they do not necessarily find their origin in a historically coherent story.

---

314 Cawkwell 2005, 93–94. Examples of anecdotes whose historicity has been questioned are the Greek retreat to Chalkis, which according to Herodotus was inspired by the first sighting of the size of the Persian fleet (Grundy 1897a, 217–218) and the story of the bribery of the Euboeans (Wallace 1974, 22–23). Most importantly, the various storm scenes are thought to have been invented or exaggerated (e.g. Hammond 1988, 548; Cawkwell 2005, 104). There are also several problems with the chronology (Grundy 1897a, 229; Hignett 1963, 379–385). Munro suggested that the account of the battle of Artemision was confused, and that Herodotus used three different eyewitnesses (Munro 1926a, 284). But see also Hart 1982, 95. "Here Herodotus gives us realism, for no mythology sprang up around these encounters".
315 Meyer (1954, 361, note 2) and Gauer (1968, 11, 120) stress the sparsity of commemorative efforts, but they did exist. Plutarch mentions Artemision as a source of pride for the Athenians, quoting Pindar (*De gloria Atheniensium* 7; cf. *De Herodoti malignitate* 867d-f, in which Plutarch criticises Herodotus for downplaying the glory of the Athenians), and it is also referred to by Aristophanes (*Lysistrata* 1251) and Isocrates (*Panegyricus* 90). Gauer (1968, 27–28) hypothesises that spoils were taken from this battle, although there is no concrete indication for this. That said, Herodotus does have surprisingly vivid descriptions of the Persians' armour (7.89–99). The Peparethians had got hold of two Carian battle ships (see Gauer 1968, 74, with literature), presumably from this episode. Gauer (1968, 40) advocates the alternative view that these ships were captured during the Persians' northward flight.
316 On the poem see Kowerski 2005, 22–33 (raising doubts about the connection of the new Simonides fragment 3 W^2 to the lost poem).
317 Even today, the battle of Artemision gives rise to new mnemotopes: in a striking example, the name of the village of Vasilika in the northwest corner of Euboea was named, according to several websites aimed at promoting tourism, by its identification as the place where Xerxes' ships had beached. See http://www.evia-guide.gr/town/βασιλικά.html (last consulted on 12 July 2017). Below we will encounter some other examples.

2.4.1 The Myrmex reef

The first specific site mentioned by Herodotus in this area appears in 7.183, in relation to an expedition of Persian scouts, sent ahead of Xerxes and his infantry and armada who were still at Therme (modern Thessaloniki) in Macedonia.

> τῶν δὲ δέκα νεῶν τῶν βαρβάρων τρεῖς ἐπήλασαν περὶ τὸ ἕρμα τὸ μεταξὺ ἐὸν Σκιάθου τε καὶ Μαγνησίης, καλεόμενον δὲ Μύρμηκα. ἐνθαῦτα οἱ βάρβαροι ἐπειδὴ στήλην λίθου ἐπέθηκαν κομίσαντες ἐπὶ τὸ ἕρμα, ὁρμηθέντες αὐτοὶ ἐκ Θέρμης, ὥς σφι τὸ ἐμποδὼν ἐγεγόνεε καθαρόν, ἔπλεον πάσῃσι τῇσι νηυσί, ἕνδεκα ἡμέρας παρέντες μετὰ τὴν βασιλέος ἐξέλασιν ἐκ Θέρμης. τὸ δὲ ἕρμα σφι κατηγήσατο ἐὸν ἐν πόρῳ μάλιστα Πάμμων Σκύριος.

> Of the ten ships of the Barbarians, three ran aground around the reef between Skiathos and Magnesia called 'Ant'. Thereupon, the Barbarians placed on the reef there a stone pillar which they had brought with them. On their way from Therme, as the obstacle had been cleared away for them, they sailed on all the ships, eleven days after the king's departure from Therme. It was Pammon of Skyros who indicated to them that the reef was certainly in their way.

Herodotus' precise indications allow for the identification of the Myrmex with what is now called the Lefteri or Lefkari reef.[318] Why the reef was called 'Ant' is not clear. Ants do appear a few times in Greek mythology, but the association of any of these myths with the reef cannot be substantiated.[319] A more plausible scenario is that the reef was named for its shape.[320] It is still dangerous today, as evidenced by several modern shipwrecks around it. Knowledge about the reef was probably widespread among sailors in antiquity.

There is, furthermore, archaeological evidence that there was indeed a stone pillar on the Myrmex: in 1928, Stylianos Lykoudis, founder of the Greek lighthouse service and member of the Academy of Athens, discovered six stone blocks, weighing 350 and 600-1100 kg each, at approximately 20 metres to the east of the lighthouse at a depth of 2-4 metres, at the edge of the reef's crag.[321] Lykoudis reported that the

---

[318] Lykoudis 1928; Köster 1934, 56–57, 60–61 (making a big point of the toil involved); Müller 1987, 345–346; Green 1996, 119 (interpreting the name Leftari as a corruption of Lithari, 'rock').
[319] Borgeaud (1995, 28) connects the Myrmex with the Myrmidons, Achilles' elite warrior troops who accompanied him to Troy. It could have been thought that the Myrmidons had passed the reef on their way to Troy from their homeland Phthia. Another speculation could be that the reef was considered the place where Zeus had intercourse with Eurymedousa, mythical princess of Phthia, after turning her into an ant (or perhaps the reef was a petrified Eurymedousa herself). However, there is a lack of evidence to support either mythical association.
[320] In the Roman period, a few other 'Ants' were known: there was an island called Myrmex in the province of Cyrenaica (Ptolemy, *Geographia* 4.4.15; *Stadiasmus Maris Magni* 10.3) and rocks called Myrmices in the Gulf of Smyrna (Pliny the Elder, *Naturalis Historia* 5.119).
[321] Lykoudis 1928. He mentions that a sample from one of these blocks was studied and identified as 'dolomite', whereas a sample from the reef turned out to be quartz.

blocks were half-worked and smoothened, and believed that they had belonged to the structure referred to by Herodotus. There were more such blocks, but these had fallen from the underwater cliff and were too deep to approach at the time. There has been no reference to these blocks ever since and the publication has seemingly gone unnoticed to modern scholarship.[322] The blocks are presumably still where they were found. Although Lykoudis' account is difficult to verify without field research, we may provisionally accept, for the moment at least, that this was the stone pillar of the Myrmex reef that Herodotus describes.

However, this does not necessarily mean that the story is entirely historical. There is, in fact, reason to believe that the pillar had not been, as Herodotus asserts, set up by the Persians. First, it is hardly plausible that the Persians would have bothered to bring the heavy blocks on their ships with the specific aim to mark the reef, which could also have been avoided by the large armada using a guiding ship for this single expedition. It is also difficult to believe that the Greeks themselves had not marked it long before to provide safer sailing for their many merchant ships. It is therefore not unthinkable that the pillar already existed before the invasion, and was later ascribed to the Persians in the tradition on which Herodotus relied, thereby creating another mnemotope where one could trace a specific episode of the Persian Wars.[323]

These speculations do not disprove the historicity of the story. We can only say that by Herodotus' time, the mnemotope consisting of the pillar and the reef were enveloped in the narratives about of the shipwreck and were pointed out as such. How did this come about? First, as we will see below in the discussions of Sepias and the 'Hollows of Euboea', it fits a theme that runs throughout the narrative of the battle of Artemision concerning Persian shipwrecks. The Myrmex, a well-known landmark in the sea, could easily have inspired one of those stories that the Persians had lost ships and tried to prevent further losses (much like at Athos): all their toil was in vain because the storms at Sepias and the Hollows destroyed many more of their ships, while the rest of the armada would be defeated in the battle of Salamis. Within this story, Pammon of Skyros appears as a traitor figure, like Ephialtes at Thermopylae. At the same time, the pillar was also an interesting vestige of the passing of the Persian armada, and the infrastructural project commissioned by the Persian king (§3.1.3).

---

322 An exception is a website about Greek lighthouses, where Lykoudis' findings are mentioned: http://www.faroi.com/gr/pontikonisi_gr.htm (last consulted 12 July 2017). This website also features some underwater video footage and photographs of the area.
323 Note that O'Sullivan (1977) emends ἐπήλασαν 'they ran aground' to ἐστήλασαν 'they were sent' for grammatical reasons. If this is correct, there was no Persian shipwreck at the Myrmex.

2.4.2 The beach where the Persian armada moored and Sepias[324]

Magnesia appears in Herodotus' account at the moment when the Persian fleet turns south from Therme (at modern Thessaloniki) on its way to Athens (7.183, 7.188; a ship catalogue intervenes). Here, the Persians were surprised by a vicious storm, which destroyed many ships.

> πανημερὸν δὲ πλέοντες οἱ βάρβαροι ἐξανύουσι τῆς Μαγνησίης χώρης ἐπὶ Σηπιάδα τε καὶ τὸν αἰγιαλὸν τὸν μεταξὺ Κασθαναίης τε πόλιος ἐόντα καὶ Σηπιάδος ἀκτῆς. [...] Ὁ δὲ δὴ ναυτικὸς στρατὸς ἐπείτε ὁρμηθεὶς ἔπλεε καὶ κατέσχε τῆς Μαγνησίης χώρης ἐς τὸν αἰγιαλὸν τὸν μεταξὺ Κασθαναίης τε πόλιος ἐόντα καὶ Σηπιάδος ἀκτῆς, αἱ μὲν δὴ πρῶται τῶν νεῶν ὅρμεον πρὸς γῇ, ἄλλαι δ' ἐπ' ἐκείνῃσι ἐπ' ἀγκυρέων· ἅτε γὰρ τοῦ αἰγιαλοῦ ἐόντος οὐ μεγάλου πρόκροσσαι ὅρμεον τὸ ἐς πόντον καὶ ἐπὶ ὀκτὼ νέας. ταύτην μὲν τὴν εὐφρόνην οὕτω, ἅμα δὲ ὄρθρῳ ἐξ αἰθρίης τε καὶ νηνεμίης τῆς θαλάσσης ζεσάσης ἐπέπεσέ σφι χειμών τε μέγας καὶ πολλὸς ἄνεμος ἀπηλιώτης, τὸν δὴ Ἑλλησποντίην καλέουσι οἱ περὶ ταῦτα τὰ χωρία οἰκημένοι. ὅσοι μέν νυν αὐτῶν αὐξόμενον ἔμαθον τὸν ἄνεμον καὶ τοῖσι οὕτω εἶχε αὐτῶν αὐξόμενον ἔμαθον τὸν ἄνεμον καὶ τοῖσι οὕτω εἶχε ὅρμου, οἱ δ' ἔφθησαν τὸν χειμῶνα ἀνασπάσαντες τὰς νέας· καὶ αὐτοί τε περιῆσαν καὶ αἱ νέες αὐτῶν· ὅσας δὲ τῶν νεῶν μεταρσίας ἔλαβε, τὰς μὲν ἐξέφερε πρὸς Ἴπνους καλεομένους τοὺς ἐν Πηλίωι, τὰς δὲ ἐς τὸν αἰγιαλόν· αἱ δὲ περὶ αὐτὴν τὴν Σηπιάδα περιέπιπτον, αἱ δὲ ἐς Μελίβοιαν πόλιν, αἱ δὲ ἐς Κασθαναίην ἐξεβράσσοντο. ἦν τε τοῦ χειμῶνος χρῆμα ἀφόρητον.

> And after sailing all day, the Barbarians reached the land of Magnesia at Sepias and the beach that is between the city of Kasthanaia and the coast of Sepias [...] So when the fleet, having set out, sailed and put into the land of Magnesia at the beach which is between the city of Kasthanaia and the coast of Sepias, the first ships moored next to the land, and the others after them at anchor. As the beach was not big, they anchored in rows into the sea at a depth of eight ships. That night was spent as such, but at dawn from the clear sky and windlessness, when the sea was boiling, a strong and mighty wind from the east surprised them, which the people who live there call 'Hellespontian'. The men who realised that the wind was coming and those that were moored in that manner, pulling their ships up the beach, remained ahead of the storm and they survived, as well as their ships. Those ships which [the wind] caught at sea, it carried off; some it brought to the so-called Ovens in Mount Pelion, others to the beach; some wrecked near Sepias itself, others at the city of Meliboia, yet others were cast to Kasthanaia. The force of the storm was unbearable.

The subsequent actions of the Persians are outlined in 7.191-192:

> σιταγωγῶν δὲ ὁλκάδων καὶ τῶν ἄλλων πλοίων διαφθειρομένων οὐκ ἐπῆν ἀριθμός, ὥστε δείσαντες οἱ στρατηγοὶ τοῦ ναυτικοῦ στρατοῦ μή σφι κεκακωμένοισι ἐπιθέωνται οἱ Θεσσαλοί, ἕρκος ὑψηλὸν ἐκ τῶν ναυηγίων περιεβάλοντο. ἡμέρας γὰρ δὴ ἐχείμαζε τρεῖς· τέλος δὲ ἔντομά τε ποιεῦντες καὶ καταείδοντες γόησι οἱ μάγοι τῷ ἀνέμῳ, πρὸς δὲ τούτοισι καὶ τῇ Θέτι καὶ τῇσι Νηρηίσι θύοντες ἔπαυσαν τετάρτῃ ἡμέρῃ, ἢ ἄλλως κως αὐτὸς ἐθέλων ἐκόπασε. τῇ δὲ Θέτι ἔθυον

---

[324] This subchapter has appeared, in modified form, as a separate article in *The Journal of Hellenic Studies* (van Rookhuijzen 2017e). The present text has been included with kind permission from the editors.

πυθόμενοι παρὰ τῶν Ἰώνων τὸν λόγον ὡς ἐκ τοῦ χώρου τούτου ἁρπασθείη ὑπὸ Πηλέος, εἴη τε ἅπασα ἡ ἀκτὴ ἡ Σηπιὰς ἐκείνης τε καὶ τῶν ἀλλέων Νηρηίδων.

The number of lost grain ships and of the other ships was beyond counting. As the generals of the armada feared that the Thessalians would attack them in their miserable state, they constructed around them a high fence from the wrecks. The storm lasted for three days, but finally the Magi, sacrificing to the wind and singing chants to appease it, and moreover offering to Thetis and the Nereids, stopped it on the fourth day, or perhaps it stopped because of its own will. They offered to Thetis after hearing from the Ionians the story that she was abducted from that place by Peleus, and that the entire coast of Sepias belonged to her and the other Nereids.

It is striking that Herodotus was able to give the exact places where the Persians had been stationed and where the shipwrecks had occurred. Meliboia and the 'Ovens' (Ἵπνοι) are easily identifiable. Meliboia (which appears in the ship catalogue, *Iliad* 2.717) was located at Skiti or at Kastro Velika.[325] The 'Ovens' have been identified with eighteen large sea caves near the modern village of Veneto, close to the modern church of Agios Nikolaos. Their semi-circular shape resembles a traditional Greek oven.[326] The location of Kasthanaia is less secure; the best guess seems to be that it has to be located in the area of the modern towns of Sklithro and Keramidi.[327]

Most discussion has surrounded the location of Sepias. One factor clouding its localisation is the uncertainty about what kind of place it was. Herodotus describes Sepias as an ἀκτή, as does Strabo (9.5.22). This word may either mean 'coast' or, more specifically, 'promontory, cape'. The latter option seems preferable, because Apollonius (1.582) and Athenaeus (*Deipnosophistae* 1.55) describe Sepias using the word ἄκρη, while Pliny the Elder (*Naturalis Historia* 4.32) has Sepias as a promontorium Sepias. But it has also been argued that Herodotus' ἀκτή should mean 'coast'.[328] At

---

[325] For Skiti (where tile stamps mentioning Δημ[οσ]ία Μελιβοιέων have been found), cf. Hignett 1963, 169; Pritchett 1963, 2; Müller 1987, 344–45 (with further literature). The coastal site of Polydendri may have functioned as a predecessor or port town of Skiti; the name may have applied to both the town and the port in Roman times, but the port seems to be oldest (fifth-century sherds and fourth-century masonry have been found here). For Kastro Velika as the identification (which had led to the modern renaming of the town of Athanatou to Melivia) see Hansen & Nielsen 2004, 720.
[326] Georgiadis 1894, 19; 142 (*non vidi*, as cited in Bowen 1998, 356, note 49); Pritchett 1963.
[327] Kasthanaia has been located at Zagora (Tarn 1908, 211; Hignett 1963, 169; Borgeaud 1995, 27; Green 1996, 119–20) or at modern Melivia (Bowen 1998, 357); but Zagora and Melivia do not have any substantial ancient remains. However, at the 'Kastro' of Keramidi there are ruins of an ancient town (Bursian 1862, 99; Pritchett 1963, 3; Müller 1987, 332–33). Moreover, it is recorded that the former Turkish name of the nearby village of Sklithro was Kestaneköy ('Chestnut Town'), perhaps echoing the ancient name. The area is today noted for its chestnut production. See also Hansen & Nielsen 2004, 719.
[328] See the discussion in Bowen 1998, 353 for reasons to see Sepias as a coast; he identifies it as the entire coast between the 'Ovens' and Kasthanaia. In fact, the interpretation as a coast was already made in Philipsson & Kirsten 1950, 161 n. 1 (*non vidi*, as cited in Bowen 1998, 353 n. 29), more specifically the entire coast between the capes of Agios Giorgios (the south-eastern point of the Magnesia

Fig. 22: Keramidi, in whose vicinity the town of Kasthanaia has been surmised.

the same time, Sepias seems to have been the name of a town, too (it appears as such in Strabo 9.5.15, and perhaps in the inscription mentioned below). But the different uses are not incompatible: it is, of course, possible that the name of the town was loosely applied to the surrounding coasts, which may or may not have featured a cape.

Scholars have tried to locate Sepias on the basis of Herodotus' chronological indications, assumptions about sailing speeds and the idea that the Greeks who were at Euboea could see the shipwrecks, as Herodotus seems to say in 7.192.[329] Accordingly, it was formerly identified with the cape of Agios Giorgios,[330] but the alternative, more

---

peninsula) and Pouri (further north); Borgeaud 1995 makes an unnecessary distinction between the actual Sepias (a cape) and Herodotus' Sepias; on this basis he discredits Cape Pouri, because this was only necessitated by the assumption that the Persians sailed for one day.

329 Lazenby 1993, 5 has argued that it is impossible that the Greeks on Euboea saw the shipwrecks at Sepias.

330 Mézières 1853, 62–64; Tarn 1908, 211; Macan 1908, I 271; Köster 1934, 61 note 1; Borgeaud 1995, 23–25 note 11; 28 (connecting it with ancient remains in Liri reported in Wace & Droop 1906–1907 as well as with the proximity of the Myrmex reef (§2.4.1), "qui attire les Barbares vers les lieux des catastrophes", not realising that Aphetai is already very close to the Myrmex); Green 1996, 120. One of the reasons for this identification has been a reference in Apollonius Rhodius (1.582), in which

northern cape Pouri (or Pori) is preferred in most recent literature.³³¹ The argument for this is that this cape is much more prominent than the cape of Agios Giorgios, and hence more likely to have been used as a landmark. In addition, it would be easier to understand that the Persians had waited here, because the cape of Agios Giorgios would have been rounded to find a more suitable, protected site. It is thought that the identification of Sepias with Pouri, as opposed to Agios Giorgios, may be further supported by a second-century CE tombstone found on the hill opposite the 'Kastro' of Keramidi, on which the word Σηπιάδι appears.³³² However, it will be explained below that the inscription is closer to an alternative location.

Herodotus tells us that the beach where the Persians were first anchored was situated between Kasthanaia and the Sepias coast (which was presumably further south).³³³ There are not many beaches on the inhospitable coasts of Magnesia large enough to qualify as this beach, but there is one just east of Keramidi called Kamari.³³⁴ This beach is some three hundred metres in length and cove-shaped, making it conceivable that a fleet anchored here, or rather was imagined to have done so. However, those who place credence in Herodotus' numbers point out that the inlet is too small to have accommodated an armada as large as Herodotus suggests.³³⁵ Instead, they suggest the beach of Agiokambos, north of Keramidi.³³⁶ But one of the most active topographers of Herodotus, Kendrick Pritchett, rightly points out that the length of the Agiokambos beach (six kilometres) would not have required the clumsy πρόκροσσαι (row) formation that Herodotus explicitly mentions.³³⁷ Nevertheless, Pritchett's trust in Herodotus' calculations of the size of the armada led him to doubt that the Kamari beach was the only place where the Persians were stationed: 'In suggesting that the beach of Keramidi was Herodotos' strand, we are once again reminded of a practice of his referring to a point on the map, so to speak, as the assembly place of a large body. In this case, he obviously has in mind only the fighting force which accompanied the high command.'

---

the Argonauts encounter Sepias just before Aphetai, which usually identified with Platania on the southernmost point of Magnesia (although it is my surmise, for reasons which cannot be explained here, that it was actually located at modern Afissos). The cape is now also called Sipiada, whence the historically incorrect name 'Sipiada' for the former municipality here. Moreover, Apollonius' account has a seriously garbled topography and should not be used to locate Herodotus' Sepias.

331 Wace 1906, 146–7; Wace and Droop 1906–1907, 311; Pritchett 1963, 3–4; Müller 1987, 361–3, Morton 2001, 73 n. 8; Barrington Atlas of the Greek and Roman World.
332 Woodward 1910, 158.
333 Discussion has focused on the meaning of the word αἰγιαλός, but see Pritchett 1963, 4–5 for convincing arguments to interpret it as 'beach'.
334 Pritchett 1963, 5; Müller 1987, 363–64.
335 Müller 1987, 344–5; 363; cf. Tarn 1908, 212: 'the burden of proof would be on anyone who should assert that the 'Sepiad strand' ever existed. The topography then lends no support to Herodotus' narrative'.
336 Bowen 1998, 352.
337 Pritchett 1963, 5.

In this traditional strand of scholarship, it is assumed to be a sound practice to judge locations solely on the basis of historical feasibility. But this may not work in all cases, as we are sometimes at the mercy of the traditions' (and historian's) imagination. Whatever happened in 480 BCE, a place such as the Kamari beach, whether it could really have accommodated the Persian armada or not, could easily 'acquire' the story because it stood out as a safe haven on the inhospitable Magnesian coast. Moreover, the mention of the πρόκροσσαι formation serves to explain that the fleet was far too large for the beach. The alternative beach, Agiokambos, is not only too big, but is also simply situated too far north to have been associated with Sepias. Thus the beach of Kamari remains the best match for Herodotus' story.

Fig. 23: The beach of Kamari.

The shipwreck at Sepias, as well as the ensuing battle of Artemision were important in later commemoration of the Persian Wars as these events were thought to have contributed to the Greek victory at Salamis by diminishing the size of the Persian fleet. Strabo relates (9.5.22): 'The Sepias coast was sung in tragedies and hymns after this because of the disappearance of the Persian fleet there.'[338] Unfortunately, most

---

[338] ἡ μέντοι Σηπιὰς ἀκτὴ καὶ τετραγῳδῆται μετὰ ταῦτα καὶ ἐξύμνηται διὰ τὸν ἐνταῦθα ἀφανισμὸν τοῦ Περσικοῦ στόλου.

of these plays and songs are now lost, but Strabo's words hint at the sort of information on which Herodotus may have based his account, which also shows signs of dramatisation.[339] As the Greeks attached so much importance to the storm, its occurrence was linked to the action of various deities (though, as we have seen, Herodotus himself hesitated to accept this).[340] In particular, the story formed part of lore surrounding two instances of Greek invocation of the winds. The first was the worship of Boreas (the North Wind) and Oreïthyia (the 'Lady of Mountain Storms') at Athens (7.189). The temple of Boreas at the Ilissos river in Athens was supposedly founded to thank this god for his help in decreasing the Persian forces at the very spot where he had kidnapped Oreïthyia. As the story about the storm was one of the aetiologies for the founding of this temple, it is possible that Herodotus received at least some of his information about the shipwrecks here.[341] The second instance of a Greek cult of the wind connected to the Sepias storm scene was the worship of an obscure nymph called Thyia at a place with the same name in or close to Delphi (7.178).[342] While the nymph had a local Delphic pedigree (Pausanias 10.6.4), we may surmise that she was simply the Delphic manifestation of the Lady of Mountain Storms (the name looks like an abbreviation of Oreïthyia). Apart from the wind gods, the sea gods were also thought to be responsible for the disaster: the Persian Magi are said to have tried

---

339 Cawkwell 2005, 93–94. Examples of questionable anecdotes are the Greek retreat to Chalkis, which Herodotus says happened after the Greek first observed the size of the Persian fleet (Grundy 1897a, 217–18) and the story of the bribery of the Euboeans (Wallace 1974, 22–23). Most importantly, the various storm scenes are thought to have been invented or exaggerated (e.g. Hammond 1988, 548; Cawkwell 2005, 104). There are also several problems with the chronology, see Grundy 1897, 229; Hignett 1963, 379–85). Munro 1926a, 284 suggested that the account of the battle of Artemision was confused, and that Herodotus used three different eyewitnesses.
340 It has been remarked that the storm at Sepias "is the best and most developed example of such divinely motivated phenomena that Herodotus offers for the Persian Wars and is a splendid example of Greek polytheism in practice" (Mikalson 2003, 61–62).
341 This cult was allegedly inspired by an oracle which had advised the Athenians to worship the 'brother-in-law', interpreted by the Athenians as a reference to Boreas (7.189). The location of the temple is still elusive. It may have stood just south of the Olympieion, see Müller 1987, 631; Plato (Phaedrus 229b-c) has an anecdote in which Socrates and Phaedrus are busy looking for the temple. The oracle, the storm at Sepias and the kidnapping were three different aetiologies for essentially the same cult, and the narrative transmitted by Herodotus seems designed to encompass all three. On the cult of Boreas, see Hölscher 2010, 136; Parker 2011, 273. The myth of Boreas and Oreïthyia was popular in fifth-century Athens, as attested by its use in Aeschylus and Sophocles and many other texts, its depiction on the sculpture of the temple of the Athenians at Delos, as well as its popularity in post-479 Athenian vase painting (Agard 1966, 241). For the different versions of the myth and the local Athenian perspectives, including that of the temple at the Ilissos, see Finkelberg 2014.
342 The location of this shrine (if we may call it that) has been hypothesised at Arachova, whose ancient name was Anemoreia, or near the monastery of Agios Ilias northwest of Delphi (Müller 1987, 590); but these suggestions cannot be substantiated.

to appease Thetis and the other Nereids in order to calm down the sea. [343] This cult reflects local Magnesian mythology: Herodotus notes that Sepias was 'of' Thetis and the Nereids, and describes Sepias as the site of a particular mythological narrative: allegedly, Thetis was abducted here by Peleus (7.191). [344] This leads to the question why Thetis and the Nereids, as well as Peleus were associated with this rather obscure locality.

Two answers to this question have been offered. First, folk etymology may have been at work. The resemblance between Πήλιον, the mountain range that dominates Magnesia, and Πηλεύς is striking, and Sepias itself may have been associated with the σηπία or 'cuttlefish': from Tzetzes (*Scholia in Lycophronem* 175b; 178) we learn that Thetis turned into a cuttlefish when Peleus attempted to carry her off. Scholars have used this cuttlefish imagery to explain why Thetis was associated with Sepias.[345]

---

343 Various rationalisations of the Persians' worship of the Greek Nereids have been offered. Burn 1962, 316 hypothesised that the Persians considered Thetis one of the Zoroastrian water-spirits who feature in the Avestan Yasna Haptanghaiti — a wild guess, given our limited understanding of Zoroastrian religion in the fifth century BCE (on Iranian wind and water gods, see de Jong 1997, 101–02). According to Haubold 2007, 56, however, the Persian Magi would have worshipped Greek divinities for the purpose of propaganda to the Greeks. This is only one of his examples of Persian propaganda, but it does not stand up to scrutiny. Even if we assume the Magi did in fact sacrifice to the gods, they did this from fear. See below for the idea that the story of the worship was a means of dramatisation. For the role of chanting in Zoroastrian religion, and examples of those in other Greek texts, see de Jong 1997, 362–67. Note that detailed knowledge of the Magi was available in fifth-century BCEGreece, as evidenced by the Derveni papyrus, in which a Greek mystery cult is compared to rituals performed by the Magi, including incantations (e.g. Tsantsanoglou 2008).

344 The Sepias coast has two additional, but much weaker mythical associations. As discussed above, Apollonius Rhodius mentioned it in relation to the journey of the Argonauts (1.582), but his reference to Sepias may well be a 'learned' one, based on Herodotus. In addition, Mount Pelion was particularly famous for its mythical connection to Cheiron, teacher of Achilles. A cave sacred to him was here: a scholion on *Iliad* 16.144 describes it as a west-pointing ἄκρα above the ἄκρα of Sepias; see Aston 2006 for an appraisal of these sites. The wedding of Peleus and Thetis took place in this cave according to Euripides (*Iphigenia Aulidensis* 705–07): he connects the rape and the wedding geographically (Borgeaud 1995, 25; earlier the wedding had been located at Pharsalos). Aston 2009, 89–94 also suggests that there is an opposition between Thetis as a 'mobile' sea goddess who does not need a specific cult site, with Cheiron, who was associated with a cave on Mount Pelion. However, whether such vague thematic dichotomies between Cheiron's and Thetis' cult truly existed in Greek thought is questionable; not only is the link between the two mythological figures rather indirect (the wedding of Peleus and Thetis takes place in Cheiron's cave, but this is only one of many myths in which Thetis features). More importantly, as we will see below, Thetis did have a fixed mnemotope.

345 Morton 2001, 73–74 note 8 explains the myth as a secondary aetiology, either for the name, or for a possible abundance of cuttlefish here (cf. Athenaeus, *Deipnosophistae* 1.55: ἐκαλεῖτο ... Σηπιὰς ἄκρα ἀπὸ τῶν περὶ αὐτὴν σηπιῶν 'Cape Sepias was named after the cuttlefish around it'); Nagy 1979, 344 asserts that Herodotus also says that Cape Sepias was named after the myth, but this is clearly not the case. He also connects Thetis with the concept of μῆτις 'wisdom' (1979, 345). Similar approaches are found in Borgeaud 1995, 23 and Aston 2009, 83; 103–06; these scholars maintain that the cuttlefish imagery fits the myth, in which Thetis tried to escape Peleus by turning into the animal that hides

However, this explanation does not stand up to scrutiny. There are no early references for the myth that Thetis turned into a cuttlefish, and the cuttlefish does not appear a single time in the various depictions of the myth in sixth- and fifth-century BCE vase painting. Here, Thetis is usually turned into a lion, snake or sea monster to escape Peleus.[346] In addition, Tzetzes cannot be used to substantiate the claim, as his testimony may easily involve a later 'learned' aetiology of the toponym Sepias. These considerations need to be accounted for by those who believe in a folk-etymological explanation for Thetis' association with Sepias. The second explanation for the myth's association with Sepias is the assumption of the existence of a real cult of Thetis at Sepias. Because there is no material or literary evidence for a temple of Thetis in the area (despite a claim in this direction),[347] it is maintained that Sepias was sacred to the nymph in a more general way.[348]

A different approach, which to my knowledge has not been attempted so far, is to look at natural landmarks. Easily the most striking natural feature of the area is the aforementioned concentration of sea caves at Veneto, known to Herodotus as the Ipnoi or 'Ovens'. It is possible that these were the anchor point for the Thetis myth, not only because caves often have stories attached to them,[349] but also because the association with Thetis is consistent with the picture painted of the sea nymphs elsewhere in ancient literature. In the *Iliad* Thetis resides in an ἀργύφεον σπέος 'shiny cave' (18.50) under the sea; it is also described as a σπέος γλαφυρόν 'hollow cave' (18.402; 24.82) περὶ δὲ ῥόος Ὠκεανοῖο ἀφρῷ μορμύρων ῥέεν ἄσπετος 'around which streamed

---

by ejecting a black liquid into the water. It is also felt that the cuttlefish's combination of white and black fits the benign and malevolent actions of Thetis. However, it is not certain whether there was any knowledge (let alone wide knowledge!) about the function of the ink for the cuttlefish in Ancient Greece.

346 Cf. *LIMC* s.v. 'Nereides' (VI.1 785–824) 'Peleus' (VII.1 251–269) and 'Thetis' (VIII.1 6–14) and Gantz 1996, 229 for discussions of the transformation in early versions of the myth.

347 There is hardly any evidence for cults of the goddess. Some sort of worship of Thetis is recorded in Laconia only at Sparta and Migonion (Pausanias 3.14.4; 3.22.2), and a Thetideion has been recorded in Pharsalos in central Thessaly (Strabo 3.5.6). This temple also appears in Euripides' *Andromache* (16–25); on the basis of that text, it seems that it was yet another site that claimed to be the location of the marriage of Peleus and Thetis. The slight remains of a Doric temple under a church of the Virgin in Theotokou, near Liri and the cape of Agios Giorgios (Wace & Droop 1906–1907 have also been interpreted as a 'Thetideion' (e.g. by Borgeaud 1995, 23–25 note 11), but this is speculative. Thetis does appear on coins from Larisa Kremaste (near modern Pelasgia), in the extreme southern part of Thessaly. However, these coins cannot be used as evidence for a cult of Thetis, because she is always pictured on the reverse with the armour that she delivered to Achilles at Troy, and is therefore invoked as his 'mythical companion'.

348 Aston 2006, 358; 2009 85–86.

349 On the importance of caves in Greek mythology, see Buxton 1994, 104–08. He comments upon the frequent role of caves as the site of myths that were outside the norm, and mentions several examples of caves as hiding places. Caves were often interpreted as prisons or refuges, cf. Boardman 2002, 104–06; Zwingmann 2012, 311–13.

roaringly the immeasurable stream of Okeanos' (18.402-403).³⁵⁰ In addition, Homer speaks of Thetis' κόλπος, with reference to the hiding place of Dionysos (6.136) and Hephaistos (18.398). This word could denote 'bosom' or 'womb', but was also metaphorically used for bosom-like hollows, including geographical features (cf. *LSJ* s.v.); in the Hephaistos passage the place where Hephaistos hides is both a κόλπος and a σπέος γλαφυρόν (18.398-402).³⁵¹ Another indication is that Homer (*Iliad* 18.40) calls one of the Nereids Σπειώ, a name obviously derived from the word σπέος 'cave.'³⁵² Finally, Pliny the Elder (*Naturalis Historia* 9.5) records a tantalising story about dead Nereids which had allegedly beached at a sea cave near Lisbon. Given the strong association of the Nereids with caves, any Greek could certainly have regarded the 'Ovens' of Veneto, some of the most impressive sea caves in the Aegean, as the place where they were hiding.

Fig. 24: Several of the 'Ovens' on the coast of Sepias.

---

350 This is also how her abode is described in later (Roman) literature: e.g. Ovidius, *Metamorphoses* 11.217–65; here it also refers to Peleus' rape.
351 *LSJ* (s.v.) rather enigmatically interprets Homer's use of the word κόλπος in these passages as 'any bosom-like hollow ... of the sea, first in a half-literal sense, of a sea-goddess ...'. Elsewhere in Homer, the word κόλπος may indicate a bay (*Iliad* 18.140; 21.125; *Odyssey* 4.435) or waves (*Odyssey* 5.52).
352 A Nereid called Speio is found in most enumerations of the Nereids, e.g. in Hesiod (*Theogonia* 245) and Pseudo-Apollodorus (1.2.7).

Even though Herodotus does not explicitly associate Sepias or Thetis with caves, Euripides did so in his *Andromache* (1263-9), a play which is more or less synchronous with the *Histories*. In this text, Thetis' abode is not only described as a hollow chamber, but it is specifically called 'the rock of Sepias'.[353]

ἀλλ' ἕρπε Δελφῶν ἐς θεόδμητον πόλιν νεκρὸν κομίζων τόνδε, καὶ κρύψας χθονὶ ἐλθὼν παλαιᾶς χοιράδος κοῖλον μυχὸν Σηπιάδος ἵζου· μίμνε δ' ἔστ' ἂν ἐξ ἁλὸς λαβοῦσα πεντήκοντα Νηρῄδων χορὸν ἔλθω κομιστήν σου· τὸ γὰρ πεπρωμένον δεῖ σ' ἐκκομίζειν, Ζηνὶ γὰρ δοκεῖ τάδε.

But come to the god-built city of Delphi, taking this corpse with you, and after hiding it in the earth, come to the hollow chamber of the old rock of Sepias and sit there. And wait, until from the sea, taking a chorus of fifty Nereids, I will come to accompany you, because what is predestined, you must carry out, for Zeus has decided this.

If the connection is not already obvious from Euripides' wording, it is also the reading that we have in a scholion on the word χοιράς in line 1265:

πέτραν οὖν φασί τινα σπήλαιον ἔχουσαν, ἐν ᾗ εἰώθει διατρίβειν ἐκ θαλάσσης ἀνιοῦσα ἡ Θέτις. Σηπιὰς δὲ τόπος περὶ τὸ σπήλαιον, ὅπου τὴν Θέτιν ἥρπασεν ὁ Πηλεὺς εἰς σηπίαν μεταβληθεῖσαν.

He therefore says that the rock had some sort of cave, in which Thetis used to dwell, coming up from the sea. And Sepias is the place around the cave, where Peleus abducted Thetis, who was turned into a cuttle-fish.

While the information contained in this scholion seems to have been ignored by previous scholars who commented on the location of Sepias, the idea has re-emerged in modern folklore: the Veneto caves are now even in use as a wedding location; the promotional text of the company mentions that ἐκεί παντρεύτηκαν οι γονείς του Αχιλλέα, 'Achilles' parents got married there'.[354] On the one hand, of course, the scholion and the Greek website are too late to prove that the association existed in Herodotus' time. On the other, however, they underline that the myth of Thetis and Peleus was easily located at undeniably impressive caves. The grottos allow us to understand why Thetis and the Nereids were thought to reside at this particular spot of Magnesia.[355]

---

353 Note that Mézières 1853, 62–64 localised this episode at sea caves near the cape of Agios Giorgios, further south.
354 See http://www.olympusadventure.com/aegean-weddings.html (last consulted on 12 July 2017). A search on the Internet will reveal more examples where the myth is mentioned in relation to the caves.
355 Aston states in her conclusion (2009, 107): "If we knew more about the cult of Thetis, in Thessaly and elsewhere, this complexity would surely only increase." However, rather the opposite is true.

It is unclear how this idea appeared in Euripides and in modern narratives about the caves, but it is certainly not taken from Herodotus, who located Thetis and Peleus only at the Sepias coast, a place that he seemingly distinguished from the 'Ovens', the obvious identification of the grottoes of Veneto. How can we explain this inconsistency? Might it be possible that the 'Ovens' coast is to be identified with, or at least seen as part of the Sepias coast? Not if we follow the traditional way in which the final part of 7.188 has been explained and translated. It mentions five places as the location of the Persian shipwreck: the beach, the Ovens, Sepias, Meliboia and Kasthanaia. Scholars and translators have always believed that Sepias was the third of the five places, and therefore, so to speak, a different 'point' on the map from the other four places. We could hypothesise that Herodotus' was simply misinformed here, but that should be an argument of last resort. Instead, there is scope to offer a slightly different translation of the passage, in which Herodotus used the toponym Sepias to summarise the two geographical entities in the immediately preceding sentence: the Ovens (as well as the beach, notwithstanding Herodotus' earlier remark that the beach was between the Sepias coast and Kasthanaia) can be regarded as forming part of the general area of Sepias. There are various arguments to support this view. First, there is a sentence break just before Sepias, Meliboia and Kasthanaia are introduced, and both the main verb and the grammatical case of the ships change. One might object that this is an example of Herodotus' stylistic variatio, and that the enumeration continues after this break because there is no second μέν in the new sentence. However, as enumerating strings of δέ can also occur without μέν, the new sentence may contain a separate enumeration; and even if the enumeration continues, the five items are not necessarily equivalent. This is shown by the second point: Sepias is accompanied by the demonstrative αὐτήν 'itself' or 'that'; an emphasis which would be strange if Sepias was simply the third of five equivalent places, but understandable if it marks 'Sepias' as a restatement of the places mentioned in the first sentence. Third, Strabo (9.5.22), who probably paraphrases Herodotus, does not mention Sepias among the places where the ships landed, but only the other four locations. This suggests that Strabo, at least, read the Herodotus passage in the way I propose here. Note that regardless of whether one presumes that Sepias was a cape, coast, town or any combination of these, the name could apply to the coast around Veneto, which has a cape called Koutsoumbou that could easily (and more so than Pouri) qualify as an ἄκρη.

We may further consider why the identification of Sepias with the coast on which the Ovens are located works much better than the other options. There were never compelling arguments for any of the previous identifications that have been put forward for the Sepias coast (the capes of Agios Giorgios and Pouri). As we have seen, these were simply guesses on the basis of, mainly, chronological indications, and they depended also on assumptions about the relation of Sepias to the other places in the text. Not only does the new identification allow us to understand why Herodotus claimed that the entire coast was 'of' Thetis and the Nereids; it also fits better with the topographical situation. First, the new identification makes it easier to understand that the Magi were thought to have performed their sacrifices and chants to Thetis and the Nereids at the Kamari beach (which, as we have seen above, was the best candidate for the beach where the Persians moored), as the Veneto caves, the abode of the Nereids, are relatively close to Kamari (the distance is eight kilometres); Cape Pouri is some eight kilometres further southeast, and the other alternatives are even further away. Second, Herodotus would hardly have described the beach as being 'between the Sepias coast and Kasthanaia', had Sepias not been as far north as the Ovens: in this scenario, Sepias and the Sklithro/Keramidi area (the approximate location of Kasthanaia) are roughly equidistant from the Kamari beach. Any of the more southern identifications of Sepias make Herodotus' reference less understandable. Third, it should be noted that the only epigraphic mention of Sepias was found at Keramidi itself. The toponym would have travelled a long way, if it were applied to what is now Cape Pouri, the cape of Agios Giorgios or a place even further south. Finally, the many 'Ovens' are truly impressive natural wonders. While sea caves exist elsewhere in the Greek world, the size and number of the 'Ovens' is remarkable. That this stretch of the Magnesian coast would have acquired a special name (as opposed to the hundreds of kilometres of 'nondescript' coast in Magnesia) is unsurprising. The name Sepias itself remains to be explained. Although a connection with σηπία 'cuttle-fish' is difficult to rule out completely, I suggest that we can now also look for a connection with words denoting geographical elements, for which there are several options.[356]

The new identification makes the maritime perspective of traditions about the area apparent: sailors who followed the east coast of Magnesia from the south would first have seen the impressive Sepias coast with its many caves; next, the Kamari beach served as one of the few safe anchor points in this inhospitable area; it was followed by the towns of Kasthanaia and Meliboia, which may also have had some function as orientation points. The mythical and historical stories connected to these sites provided an interesting and suggestive supplement to the 'sailor's map'.[357] In

---

[356] We may, perhaps, connect with the toponym Sepias the group of words of unclear (possibly Pre-Greek) etymology starting with σπ-, meaning 'cave' (e.g. σπέος, σπήλαιον, σπήλυγξ; on the etymology of these words cf. Beekes 2010 s.v.) Also note the existence of the word ἡ σπιλάς (gen. σπιλάδος), formally equivalent to the toponym ἡ Σηπιάς (gen. Σηπιάδος), cf. Beekes 2010 s.v. σπίλος. It normally means 'rock in the sea', and the association with caves is there as well; *LSJ* s.v. claim it means 'hollow rock, cave' in an epigram by Simonides (*Anthologia Graeca* 6.217). An example of its use reveals that the word is a fitting description of the Sepias area: κοῖλαι δὲ σπήλυγγες ὑπὸ σπιλάδας τρηχείας κλυζούσης ἁλὸς ἔνδον ἐβόμβεον ('the hollow caves under the sharp rock resounded with the sea washing inside', Apollonius Rhodius 2.568). Nevertheless, these suggestions about the etymology of Sepias remain only speculations from my side, as they cannot be formally substantiated (but note that Greek word groups of substrate origin sometimes show unexplained vowel elision, cf. Beekes 2010 xxxii).
[357] One may wonder whether there were other 'landmarks' in the area that have long disappeared but that provided additional anchor points for the stories in the fifth century BCE. There could have been actual shipwrecks at the beach or in the Ovens that were still visible. It is curious that the Kamari beach

this respect, note the existence of the nearby place Aphetai, which was regarded not only as the starting position of the Persians during the battle of Artemision, but also as the place from which the Argonauts had departed to Colchis (cf. Herodotus 7.193). We thus arrive at a 'memory space' which is consistent with an observation made already by Maurice Halbwachs mentioned in §1.3.5, i.e. that episodes of one story very often cluster together in the same general area.

Nevertheless, in the case of the storm scene at Sepias there is scope to regard the story in part or in its entirety as suspect. First, the idea of natural disasters destroying parts of the Persian land army or fleet is so common in the *Histories* that we may regard it as a topos that could easily arise in post-war folklore. Examples include the storms in the Egyptian desert (3.26), at Mount Athos (6.44), Mount Ida (§2.2.1), at the Hollows of Euboea (§2.4.5), as well as the tsunami at Potidaia (§2.8.9). The historicity of these stories is suspect given the sheer number of them. Taken together, one almost begins to feel compassion for the Persians as they suffer so many natural disasters. It seems further significant that the storm at Sepias is foreshadowed in an anecdote at the Hellespont (7.49), where the 'wise advisor' Artabanos warns Xerxes about the dangers of following the Greek coast where not many safe harbours are available.[358]

A second reason to regard the story as historically suspect is that some of the scenes and even words are reminiscent of the *Iliad*.[359] The similarities have been interpreted

---

has a huge rock that looks like a beached ship. In this respect, note the existence of 'petrified ship' mnemotopes elsewhere (Thucydides 1.25; Herodotus 8.107). Also note that Herodotus (7.190) relates the story about a local of Sepias, Ameinokles, who became rich of the gold and silver cups and many other Persian treasures that had beached here. Whether these treasures, and the wrecks that may have been still visible, were indeed Persian, or had another provenance, and were only later reinterpreted as Persian is an issue on which Herodotus could probably not reflect accurately. On cults that catered particularly if not exclusively to sailors, see Parker (2011) 244–46, particularly regarding the cult of Achilles in the Black Sea, which could have been facilitated by the fact that his mother was a sea nymph.
358 Cf. Morton 2001, 17.
359 This has been expounded by Harrison 2002, 561. It has, for example, been pointed out that good Iliadic antecedents are available for the storm blowing from Thrace and scattering the ships (*Iliad* 9.4–7; 15.26–27). A tradition that Greek warriors returning from Troy found their death during a storm off this coast of Thessaly is preserved in Lycophron, *Alexandra* 898–908; but this may be based on Herodotus' story. By mentioning the trivia that the locals of Magnesia called this kind of storm 'Hellespontine', Herodotus may subtly blend in the possibility that the storm is a retribution for Xerxes' earlier irreverence towards the Hellespont, where Troy was located. Borgeaud 1995, 28 sees the name rather as a reference to Achilles Pontarches, who had a stele on the Hellespont; however, this runs contrary to the reality of the importance of the Hellespont in the *Histories*, where it only features as a place connected to the passing of Xerxes' army. The wall from wreckage built around the ships resembles the wall around the Greek ships in *Iliad* 7.435–41 and 14.33. Tarn 1908, 214 remarked that this behaviour is strange, considering that the Thessalians had chosen the side of the Persians. Homeric epic may also resound in the word πρόκροσσαι which denotes the pyramidal formation of the ships in the sea (*Iliad* 14.34–36), see Tarn 1908, 214; Hignett 1963, 170–71; Bowen 1998, 354–55. The image itself is repeated in *Iliad* 18.68–69, where the ships of the Myrmidons are situated close to each

as subtle references by Herodotus or his sources to associate the Persian Wars with the Trojan War. This is advocated by Haubold, who argues that in this story, Xerxes seems to try to convince the Ionians that they were Asian,[360] as well as to 'rewrite Greek epic' by 'retracing the history of the Trojan War from the sack of Troy to the rape of Thetis'.[361] This may be an overstatement: I believe that we do not need to assume that Herodotus, the Persians or anyone else deliberately tried to link Xerxes' expedition with the myth. But a minimal conclusion can be that the account of the storm at Sepias was subconsciously (re)modelled to fit dramatic scenes also found in Homeric epic.

The final factor that strips the story of some of its credence is the degree to which it depended on belief in divine intervention. We have already seen that the story was connected to cults in Athens and Delphi, where it underlined the power of the wind divinities Boreas and 'the Lady of Mountain Storms' Oreïthyia in the creation of storms. At the 'Ovens', moreover, the story emphasises the role of Thetis and the Nereids as divinities capable of upsetting and calming down the sea. This may perhaps strike us as surprising, because Thetis is a fairly minor divinity; but she appears in the *Iliad* as a goddess whom one could summon for help.[362] Herodotus' story could well reflect a real Greek cult practice near the Ovens: the scarcity of mooring possibilities along these coasts may have created a demand among sailors to ask the water nymphs for protection. Given the strong ties of the shipwreck story to existing cult practises, it is possible that it arose, or became embellished, as a 'temple legend' that made one or more of the cult sites in question more memorable. Note that there may have been a connection between the Athenian and Magnesian traditions: it seems relevant that Oreïthyia, whom, the Athenians believed, helped create a storm at the place where the Nereids were supposed to reside, was herself known as a Nereid by Homer (*Iliad* 18.48).[363]

---

other around Achilles. The scene of the Magi sacrificing at or near the Sepias coast bears resemblance to Achilles going down to the beach and praying to his mother Thetis (*Iliad* 1.349–51), to his prayer to the winds to kindle Patroclus' funeral pyre (*Iliad* 23.192–225), and to the Greeks offering a libation to Zeus as he was thundering (*Iliad* 7.478–82). Perhaps the most striking 'coincidence' is the fact that the eastern opponents crash at the exact place where Thetis was abducted, one of the crucial events leading up to the Trojan War itself. Bowie 2012, 277 labels the divine intervention in the passage as Iliadic, but it is also more generally a Greek (and not only a Greek) way of thinking.
360 Haubold 2007, 58–59.
361 Haubold 2007, 58; a similar view is found in Hartmann 2010, 217.
362 In some of the stories surrounding Thetis, for example when she called upon Aigaion (one of the titan-like Hecatonchires) to save Zeus (*Iliad* 1.398), she appears to be a veritable cosmic power. Like any Greek divinity, Thetis could also be angered. Boedeker 2007 has shown that a normally peaceful goddess, Demeter, was an aggressive force in many Persian War battles. In the Magi scene, something similar may have been the case with Thetis: in the *Iliad* we encounter her as a mater dolorosa who is mainly concerned with the fate of her son Achilles; but at her abode in Magnesia, the Persians do not receive a warm welcome. See Slatkin 1986 for an overview of Thetis' thematic role in the *Iliad* and other texts.
363 Is it possible that the Athenian tradition about Oreïthyia's help is somehow related to, or perhaps even the ultimate source of, the story about the Persian shipwreck at Sepias? This must remain a

An element of irony may even be discerned. The Magi's effort to appease these essentially Greek divinities does not work, but only results in more devastation. During the battle itself, another storm was to follow, which inspired panic in the Persian base in Magnesia because the dead bodies and wrecks beached there (8.12), and caused the sinking of two hundred ships at the 'Hollows' of Euboea (8.13).[364] Implicit in the story may be that Thetis and the other gods were enraged at the Persian invasion. In fact, the scene is very reminiscent of Xerxes' earlier visit to Troy (§2.2.3), which was apparently also recommended by Greeks in the army; after Xerxes' and the Magi's sacrifice to Athena and the 'heroes', panic descends upon the army (§2.2.3). Here in Magnesia, the theme of divine retribution is further underlined by the anecdote about Ameinokles, a local man of Sepias (see above), who became rich from the Persian treasures after the wrecks, but subsequently suffered the tragedy of killing his own son. Stories featuring a theme of divine retribution are well-known in Herodotus' work, but the reason that he records so many of them may well have its basis in folklore about the Persian Wars.

2.4.3 Artemision

The confrontation of the Greek and Persian fleets took place in the waters off Artemision, where the Greeks had made their base. Herodotus gives a description of the place in 7.176:

> τοῦτο μὲν τὸ Ἀρτεμίσιον τὸ πέλαγος τὸ Θρηίκιον ἐξ εὐρέος συνάγεται ἐς στεινὸν ἔς τε τὸν πόρον τὸν μεταξὺ νήσου τε Σκιάθου καὶ ἠπείρου Μαγνησίης· ἐκ δὲ τοῦ στεινοῦ τῆς Εὐβοίης ἤδη τὸ Ἀρτεμίσιον δέκεται αἰγιαλός, ἐν δὲ Ἀρτέμιδος ἱρόν.

> This is Artemision: the Thracian Sea one is drawn from a wide part to a narrow part, which is the way between the island of Skiathos and the mainland Magnesia. And from this strait of Euboea one soon arrives at Artemision, a beach, and there is a temple of Artemis there.

Artemision was not only designated as the Greek base during the battle, it also became the location of various anecdotes and events during the fighting. For example, this place marked the end of Skyllias' dive (8.8; cf. below).

According to Plutarch (*Themistocles* 8.2-3), Artemision was a beach oriented to the north, opposite Olizon; the temple of Artemis, who had the epithet Proseoa ('to the sunrise'), would be surrounded by trees and surrounded by a circle of white stone stelai, which, when rubbed, gave off the colour and fragrance of saffron. It is

---

guess, and admittedly there is no indication that the Athenians regarded Oreïthyia as a Nereid in the strict sense (she was rather seen as Erechtheus' daughter).
364 Waters 1985, 171 noted that Herodotus makes the offerings of the Magi at Sepias ridiculous.

now often incorrectly thought that Artemision was a promontory or cape, an entire stretch of coast,[365] or even the sea passage between Euboea and Magnesia itself,[366] but both Herodotus and Plutarch assert that Artemision was a beach. Artemision seems to have been situated in the area of Histiaia (7.175) and Herodotus thought that from here it was possible to see fire signals from Skiathos (7.183). Despite other claims,[367] it is now virtually certain that the temple of Artemis was located on a small hill east of the modern town of Pefki. At the west foot of this hill, a second-century BCE inscription (*IG* XII,9 1189) was found listing private contributors to the restoration of a temple of Artemis Proseoa.[368] Architectural remains that could have belonged to this temple were seen around the church of Agios Giorgios on the hill. The nearby village has, accordingly, been renamed 'Artemisio'. Artemision was a strategic location from where both sides of the mountainous island of Euboea could be controlled, and close enough to Thermopylae to stay in touch with the troops there (7.175).[369] In addition, Artemision may be thought of as one of the few stopping places in the area where fresh drinking water could be found and shelter from the currents around Euboea was available.

The locality of Artemision became a memorial space for the battle at large, which was thought to have taken place in the nearby waters.[370] Herodotus' account reveals

---

365 E.g. Macan 1908, II 264; another example is provided by the famous statue of Poseidon or Zeus in the National Museum in Athens, whose provenance is traditionally listed as 'Cape Artemision'. The designation of Artemision as a cape is already apparent in the *Suda* (s.v. ἀρτεμίσιος), where it is called an ἀκρωτήριον; the scholion on Aristophanes' *Lysistrata* 1251 has it as ἄκρα. Stephanus Byzantinus (*Ethnica* s.v. Ἀρτεμίσιον) has it as a πόλις, and Pliny the Elder (*Naturalis Historia* 4.64) seems to list Artemisium as an urbs. For a correction, see Hignett 1963, 150–151.
366 Borgeaud 1995.
367 The most important alternative identification of Artemision is the northernmost tip of Euboea, the promontory 'pointing' at the sea channel between Skiathos and Magnesia. This is the more strategic alternative, and seems to match best with Herodotus' description, especially regarding the visibility from Skiathos. There are several beaches in the area, but there is no trace of a temple to Artemis. The location proposed by Grundy (1897a, 219–220; though his view changed to the northeast coast 1901, 322), a promontory near Oreoi, has been discarded because it does not match the criterion of visibility from Aphetai. Obst (1913, 117) implausibly suggested that Herodotus got it all wrong and that Artemision should be sought inside the Pagasetic Gulf. Köster (1934, 66) proposed the entire coast from Pefki to Orei.
368 For the inscription and a general topographical investigation of the area, see Lolling 1883 (pointing out that some of the extant marble fragments give off an orange colour when rubbed). This location was accepted by Hignett 1963, 150; Müller 1987, 313–315; Bowen 1998, 358. The temple is also mentioned in an epigram attributed to Simonides in *IG* VII 53, a commemorative inscription (fifth-century CE) from Megara. See Eibl 2007 for the most elaborate description and a catalogue of all the archaeological material connected with the temple.
369 Sidebotham (1982, 182–185), however, remarks that the conventional site of Artemision was not as safe as further in the channel at Oreoi, and that this place was closer to Thermopylae.
370 See Gauer 1968, 117–120 (with literature).

Fig. 25: Remains of the temple of Artemis at the hill of Agios Giorgios.

that this process had already started in the late fifth century BCE. He refers to an inscription carved by Themistocles in 'the rocks' (8.22; it is also referred to in 9.98, and retold by Plutarch, *Themistocles* 9.1-2, in which multiple sites are mentioned). In the text, Themistocles begs the Ionians and Carians, whom he expected to land there soon after, to desert from the Persian army. Herodotus does not indicate that he had seen this message himself, and as an anecdote it is so dramatic (it foreshadows the ramming of a Persian ship by Artemisia of Halicarnassus during the battle of Salamis) that we must be suspicious about its authenticity.[371] Whatever the historicity, the story was relevant for Herodotus: as a native of Caria, tensions between Asian and European Greeks were of interest to him.

---

[371] West 1985, 285–286 argues that this inscription is far from authentic, and only an "imaginative reconstruction largely based on subsequent events", much like Herodotus invents speeches for his characters. In this case, the inscription serves to illustrate Themistocles' military genius, and had the consequence that the Ionians became suspect to, for instance, the Phoenicians (8.90). See also Macan 1908, I 386, who stresses the 'oral' character of the inscription; Bowie 2007, 113–114, pointing out that the story may be connected to Themistocles' portrayal as a 'trickster'.

Further mnemotopes appear in Plutarch. He tells us (*Themistocles* 8.4) that one of the white stelai surrounding the temple of Artemis had the following inscription: 'here, the sons of the Athenians once overpowered the races of all kinds of men from Asia in a sea battle. When the army of Medes was destroyed, they placed these signs for the virgin Artemis.'[372] Plutarch also mentions a place on the beach where the wrecks and bodies were burnt, as black ash-like dust could be found there. Plutarch (*De Herodoti malignitate* 867f) also mentions a trophy for the battle. The precise locations of the black soil and the trophy are not specified and now beyond recovery.[373] It is impossible to say when these monuments were erected. They may be considerably later than Herodotus.

Finally, it has been argued that the temple of Artemis, which Herodotus already knew, itself was a victory monument for the battle, as the archaeological evidence indicates that it postdated the battle. Furthermore, the inscription connects Artemis Proseoa with the *pyrriche* (arms dances), which shows that she was worshipped here as a war goddess; and the epithet Proseoa 'Eastwards', is also reflected in the orientation of walls found near the temple, which point towards the Strait of Skiathos, the place of the battlefield.[374] Although Artemis' cult here was probably pre-existing and guaranteed the safe voyage along the dangerous coasts of Euboea,[375] there are many examples of divine intervention in other Persian War battles (see the typology) and Plutarch's account suggests that this was the case, as he mentions that Artemis was thanked for the Greek successes.[376]

---

[372] παντοδαπῶν ἀνδρῶν γενεὰς Ἀσίας ἀπὸ / χώρας παῖδες Ἀθηναίων τῷδέ ποτ᾽ ἐν πελάγει / ναυμαχίῃ δαμάσαντες, ἐπεὶ στρατὸς ὤλετο Μήδων, / σήματα ταῦτ᾽ ἔθεσαν παρθένῳ Ἀρτέμιδι. Plutarch gives the same inscription in *De Herodoti malignitate* 867f. White stelai, one of which had a gorgoneion, found by Lolling at the church of Agios Giorgios are possibly to be identified with them (Eibl 2007, 249). On the inscription as a commemorative monument, see Clairmont 1983, 117.

[373] Eibl 2007, 246 suggested that some of the burials near the temple of Artemis could be connected to the battle.

[374] Eibl 2007, 256–259: "Legt man also gemäß den aufgefundenen Mauern eine nordöstliche Ausrichtung des Tempels zugrunde, 'blickte' Artemis genau in Feindesrichtung und erhielt dadurch einen gleichsam apotropäischen Charakter."

[375] Artemis' sanctuaries appear to be often located near important and potentially dangerous passageways (Cole 2000, 474–475); the waters around Euboea constituted exactly such an environment. While there is no pre-existing mythological mnemotope in this part of Euboea that we know of one potential 'connection' can be found in the myth of Agamemnon's sacrifice of Iphigeneia at Aulis in Boeotia, opposite Euboea. Agamemnon's aim was to appease Artemis, who was wrathful because his men had killed a pregnant hare, and had therefore made a wind blow in the channel, impeding the king's voyage. This particular myth may be thought of as an aetiology for the occurrence of strong winds and currents in the channel. Perhaps it is for this reason that Artemis became an essential goddess for sailors to worship at Aulis, and around Euboea in general.

[376] See Gauer 1968, 118.

2.4.4 Aphetai

While the Greeks were based at Artemision, the Persians who had survived the storm at Sepias rounded the tip of Magnesia and anchored at Aphetai. Herodotus reports that this place was also known as a halting place of the Argonauts during their voyage to Colchis (7.193):

> οἱ δὲ βάρβαροι, ὡς ἐπαύσατό τε ὁ ἄνεμος καὶ τὸ κῦμα ἔστρωτο, κατασπάσαντες τὰς νέας ἔπλεον παρὰ τὴν ἤπειρον, κάμψαντες δὲ τὴν ἄκρην τῆς Μαγνησίης ἰθέαν ἔπλεον ἐς τὸν κόλπον τὸν ἐπὶ Παγασέων φέροντα. ἔστι δὲ χῶρος ἐν τῷ κόλπῳ τούτῳ τῆς Μαγνησίης, ἔνθα λέγεται τὸν Ἡρακλέα καταλειφθῆναι ὑπὸ Ἰήσονος τε καὶ τῶν συνεταίρων ἐκ τῆς Ἀργοῦς ἐπ' ὕδωρ πεμφθέντα, εὖτ' ἐπὶ τὸ κῶας ἔπλεον ἐς Αἶαν τὴν Κολχίδα: ἐνθεῦτεν γὰρ ἔμελλον ὑδρευσάμενοι ἐς τὸ πέλαγος ἀφήσειν. ἐπὶ τούτου δὲ τῷ χώρῳ οὔνομα γέγονε Ἀφέται. ἐν τούτῳ ὦν ὅρμον οἱ Ξέρξεω ἐποιεῦντο.

> But the barbarians, when the wind had stopped and the waves had calmed down, pulled their ships into the sea and sailed along the mainland. After turning around the tip of Magnesia they sailed straight into the bay that leads to Pagasai. In this gulf of Magnesia there is a spot where Heracles is said to have been left by Jason and his comrades from the Argo, sent to look for water, when they were sailing to Aia in Colchis for the Fleece. There they wanted to set sail after having found water. Therefore the place was called Aphetai. So in this place Xerxes' men anchored.

There is no agreement about the location of Aphetai. We do not know whether it was a settlement or something else,[377] but it can be distilled from Herodotus' account that the distance from Artemision was eighty stades or c. 14 kilometres (cf. 8.8; the indication is part of an anecdote according to which one Skyllias would have swum this distance under water from Aphetai to Artemision). Also, the place would be directly visible from Artemision (8.4 and 8.6). These criteria, if valid, limit the area where Aphetai may be sought to the north shore of the strait which leads up to the Pagasetic Gulf (the Gulf of Volos) and is now called the channel of Artemision. Here, several locations have been put forward;[378] the most accepted of these is the beach of modern Platania as it is directly visible from Artemision, matches the distance of eighty stades from there, and has a good harbour and a water source.[379]

---

377 Herodotus called Aphetai a χῶρος, which does not reveal much about its nature. Hammond 1998, 552 calls it an 'advanced naval station'.
378 Proposed locations here include the beach of Agia Kyriaki near Trikeri (Leake 1835, IV 397; Grundy 1897a, 219; 1901, 326), although there is no water here and it does not qualify as a good harbour, see Bowen 1998, 359); and Ormos Andriami (Wace 1906, 145). Prentice 1920, 7 believed that Aphetai was situated at or near the entrance of the Pagasetic Gulf, as did Wallace 1984, who suggested that the Persian fleet occupied multiple harbours near Trikeri, as well as that of Achillio. In his view, the entire mouth of the Pagasetic Gulf was called Aphetai, a rendering of the word ἀφετήριον which is used for outlets of bodies of water.
379 Wace 1906, 146; Fabricius 1926 (mentioning that a local water source, originally called Afilianes, was renamed Afetanes by local school teachers); Kromayer 1931, 582; Köster 1934, 63–65; Hignett 1963,

However, if Aphetai was a prominent mnemotope, Platania seems a strange place for it. It can hardly be considered a landmark, and there is no evidence that there was an ancient town here. In addition, a complete reliance on the mentioned criteria distilled from Herodotus' text can be deceiving. The visibility argument is in itself problematic, but in this particular instance, it seems to have been misused. Herodotus in 8.4 does not say that the Greeks at Artemision saw Aphetai from there, but only that the Persians were making their way (κατάχθεισαν) to Aphetai. Likewise the Persian observation of Artemision (8.6), expressed by the aorist participle ἰδόντες, is not to be taken synchronous with, but conform to the normal use of aorist participles, precedes the arrival in Aphetai, expressed by ἐπείτε ἀπίκατο. It also has to be considered that the distance of eighty stades between Artemision and Aphetai was found in the anecdote about Skyllias of Skione, which Herodotus found problematic himself.[380] Apart from this, numbers are easily corrupted. If such criteria are taken away, the area where Aphetai may be sought is much larger. Furthermore, the scholars who adhere to the identification of Aphetai with Platania have given an interpretation to two topographical remarks in the passage which are difficult to uphold. First, they believe that Herodotus' 'gulf of Magnesia that leads to Pagasai' referred to the Strait of Artemision, while it more likely refers to the Pagasetic Gulf. Second, they identify the ἄκρη of Magnesia (which, Herodotus tells us, the Persians rounded before arriving at Aphetai) with the cape of Agios Giorgios, instead of the much more ἄκρη-like tip of Magnesia at Trikeri.

Herodotus' account thus suggests that Aphetai was located inside the Pagasetic Gulf. That Aphetai is to be sought here is not a new suggestion. Strabo (9.5.15) and later Stephanus Byzantinus (*Ethnica* s.v. Ἀφέται) located the site close to Pagasai, near modern Volos. In addition, the modern scholar Georgiadis located it at the modern coastal town of Afissos (in Modern Greek spelled Ἀφυ(σ)σος or Ἀφησσος), 26 km southeast of Volos, where he saw a fountain with remarkably clear and abundant water.[381] This identification has firmly established itself locally. A village close to Afissos was renamed from Niaou to Ἀφέτες, and the entire municipality had this name before the administrative reforms of 2011. In addition, touristic descriptions of

---

177; Müller 1987, 307–308; Lazenby 1993, 128; Borgeaud 1995, 26, note 11; Green 1996, 119; Bowen 1998, 358–359; Thomas 2010 (with ample modern Greek literature).

380 Aly 1969 (first edition 1921), 186–187 regarded this story as a folktale, especially because the name Skyllias is that of a sea monster.

381 Georgiadis 1894, 114 ("Οὐδαμοῦ δὲ ἀλλαχοῦ τῆς Μαγνητικῆς παραλίας παρατηρεῖται πηγὴ ποσίμων ὑδάτων, ὅπως ἐνταῦθα"). A location near Volos was also proposed by Pococke 1745, II.2 153; Leake (1841, 243) placed Aphetai in the Pagasetic Gulf but in the district of Olizon; Obst (1913, 99) while locating Aphetai in de Strait of Orei, suggested that Herodotus was wrong and that the true station of the Persians was somewhere inside the Pagasetic Gulf.

Afissos often mention that the Argonauts used the fountain on the town square.[382] Afissos does accord with Strabo's and Stephanus' indications, and the continuity of the name, while not proving the case, is suggestive.[383] The only problem is that this Afissos does not adhere to the distance of eighty stades.[384]

Fig. 26: The central square of Afissos with the fountain water issueing into the Pagasetic Gulf.

---

382 E.g. http://www.discoverpelio.com/el/village/afissos (last consulted 16 February 2015; site no longer online as of 12 July 2017).
383 The modern name Ἄφυσσος may be a corruption of ancient Ἀφέται, as toponyms do not always adhere to sound laws .
384 There are other candidates inside the gulf that match the distance: an example is the modern town of Achillio, west of the narrow passage to the Pagasetic Gulf: this place, currently a port, is sheltered by Cape Pteleon (Prioni) and Poseideion (Stavros). This location, which matches the distance of eighty stades from Artemision, also offered easy access to the supposed route of the land army, which, we are told, passed nearby Halos. We should therefore not discredit this area as a possible site of Aphetai, originally proposed by Lolling 1883. It is also one of the locations for Aphetai proposed by Wallace 1984. Another possibility is the bay of Agios Andreas near the town of Mylina. Here, the distance between the Pagasetic Gulf and the Strait of Artemision is only two kilometres; this place is therefore consistent with Herodotus' indication that Aphetai was located inside the Pagasetic Gulf, and with the Skyllias episode who swam 'only' 14 kilometres to Artemision.

Wherever Aphetai was really located, it is unsurprising that it became enveloped in the Argonaut saga as a mnemotope (even though this particular story was also placed in Mysia).³⁸⁵ Iolkos, home of the Argonauts, was also situated in this part of Greece, as was Pagasai, the place where the Argo was sent from.³⁸⁶ In the case of Aphetai, it is apparent that its name had inspired the story by way of folk etymology: in 7.193 Herodotus himself connects the name Ἀφέται to ἀφήσειν 'to set sail'. Stephanus Byzantinus (*Ethnica* s.v. Ἀφέται) preserves a tradition according to which the name arose because the Argo made its second departure from there. But Aphetai's name went two ways: ἀφήσειν could also mean 'release (on the land)', as the Argonauts had done to Heracles.³⁸⁷ The belief that the starting position of the Persians during the battle of Artemision was located here was based on the same folk-etymological principle: whether the point of the mnemotope was that the Persians anchored here, departed from here, or both, it worked. Perhaps, then, Aphetai was a 'usual dock', the obvious answer to the question 'where was the Persian base during the battle?'. If the location of Aphetai inside the Pagasetic Gulf seems not compatible with the historical narrative, that should not concern us: historical feasibility did not stop the town of Vasilika in Euboea from claiming the same status in modern times. Alternatively or additionally, it is striking that Herodotus makes the Persians land on a spot connected with one of the first west-versus-east conflicts.³⁸⁸ It is hard to deny that Herodotus' audience would not have been sensitive to such parallels.

2.4.5 The Koila of Euboea

The final locality connected to the battle of Artemision appears in an anecdote about a special Persian contingent of two hundred ships, which was sent around Euboea to prevent the Greeks from fleeing into the Euripos. What happened to this contingent is related in 8.13: the Persians who were sent to bypass the Greeks and attack them from behind, died in a shipwreck near the 'Koila of Euboea'.

> καὶ τούτοισι μὲν τοιαύτη νὺξ ἐγίνετο, τοῖσι δὲ ταχθεῖσι αὐτῶν περιπλώειν Εὔβοιαν ἡ αὐτή περ ἐοῦσα νὺξ πολλὸν ἦν ἔτι ἀγριωτέρη, τοσούτῳ ὅσῳ ἐν πελάγεϊ φερομένοισι ἐπέπιπτε, καὶ τὸ τέλος σφι ἐγίνετο ἄχαρι· ὡς γὰρ δὴ πλώουσι αὐτοῖσι χειμών τε καὶ τὸ ὕδωρ ἐπεγίνετο ἐοῦσι κατὰ τὰ

---

385 Interestingly, this particular story of Heracles (and Hylas) was regularly placed in Mysia at the south shore of Sea of Marmara (cf. Pseudo-Apollodorus 1.9.19), but this may be considerably later; on this see Dewing 1924, 477.
386 Another strange association appears in Apollonius Rhodius (*Argonautica* 1.580–591), who mentions a tomb of one Dolops at the place. We cannot be sure which of the several mythological figures called Dolops this might have been, despite a scholiast's comment that it was Dolops, son of Hermes.
387 Macan 1908, I 287: Herodotus could have used te Ionic ἀπήσειν, but that would have "spoilt the point". On the etymology of Aphetai see also Thomas 2010, 4.
388 Obst (1913, 99) noted that Herodotus located the Persian base at Aphetai because of the Argonautic connection.

Κοῖλα τῆς Εὐβοίης, φερόμενοι τῷ πνεύματι καὶ οὐκ εἰδότες τῇ ἐφέροντο ἐξέπιπτον πρὸς τὰς πέτρας. ἐποιέετό τε πᾶν ὑπὸ τοῦ θεοῦ ὅκως ἂν ἐξισωθείη τῷ Ἑλληνικῷ τὸ Περσικὸν μηδὲ πολλῷ πλέον εἴη.

For [the Persians at Aphetai] the night turned out as such, but for the ones who were appointed to sail around Euboea, that very same night was much more hostile, because it surprised them when they were on the sea, and their end turned out to be unpleasant. When the storm and the rain came upon them when they were along the Koila of Euboea, they were carried by the wind; not knowing where they were being carried, they crashed onto the rocks. And this was all done by the god, so that the Persian army was balanced against the Greek army, and not much greater.

Herodotus' sparse indications of the location of the shipwreck imply that the Koila were a well-known locality in his time.[389] The location is elusive. The adjective κοῖλος primarily means 'hollow' and is used for cavities (as we have seen above) but it may also be used to describe valleys or depressions (see, for example *Odyssey* 4.1), or bays (*Odyssey* 22.385). Several ancient and modern researchers have located the Koila on the southwest coast of Euboea, where the coastline consists of several adjacent bays.[390] This is also consistent with Euripides, who refers in several of his plays to one or more κοῖλοι μυχοί 'hollow recesses' of Euboea. Although he connects them to Aulis in one instance, it is not certain whether these are to be equated with Herodotus' Koila.[391] Others have identified the Hollows with the concave northeast coastline of southern Euboea, west of Cape Doro, which would be more consistent with the wind direction (northeast) and with Herodotus' statement that the Persians were on open sea.[392] Both options are viable. A problem remains: the interpretation of Koila as referring to one or more bays seems little specific, as the Euboean coast is indented everywhere, meaning that practically any place on the coast could be said to be part of such a 'hollow'. Moreover, it is suspicious that a plural is used; it does not seem to apply easily to what is essentially a very large bay.

---

389 Hignett 1963, 387.
390 Strabo 10.1.2 (between Chalkis and Geraistos); Valerius Maximus 1.8.10 (between Rhamnous and Karystos); Leake 1841, 247; Grundy 1901, 335; Munro 1926a, 290; Hignett 1963, 387. Livy (31.47) calls the area *sinus Euboicus*.
391 In *Troades* 84 he makes Athena, angry with the returning Greeks, tell Poseidon: 'and fill Euboea's hollow recess with dead bodies'; Poseidon agrees and says, among other things: 'the Kaphereian capes, too, will have the bodies of many dead' (90). In the discussion of the Sepias coast above, Euripides' *Andromache* was quoted, in which he also refers to a κοῖλος μυχός (1265). In *Iphigenia Aulidensis* (1600) Euripides uses the same word in the speech of Kalchas to the Greeks to refer to the harbour area of Aulis from where the Aegean was to be crossed.
392 Ptolemy, *Geographia* 3.14.22; Prentice 1920, 12, note 11; Mason & Wallace 1972, 139; Müller 1987, 420–422; Hammond 1988, 555. Macan (1908, I 376) leaves open the possibility that the term designated both sides of the southern part of Euboea. Köster (1934, 69–71 with note 3) identified the Koila with the entire east coast of Euboea. Richards (1930) suggested that the Hollows may have denoted the low-lying area around Dystos. For the problem of the wind direction, see Grundy (1897, 221–222). See also Asheri et al. 2010, 215.

I would like to point out that the available evidence allows for a third alternative, namely the inhospitable rocky coast west of modern Kymi, in the middle of the Aegean coast of Euboea. It is possible that the Koila referred to sea caves, which are concentrated in this area. Dio Chrysostom (first century CE) in his seventh oration recounts the personal anecdote of his landing during a storm on the Hollows of Euboea on a trip from Chios. This suggests that the Hollows were on the northeast coast of the island: from there it is a straight line to Chios.[393] While the rough Aegean coast of Euboea has many sea caves, they are found in a big concentration at Chiliadou beach, thirteen kilometres north of the village of Stropones, west of Kymi. This area is mountainous (the highest mountain of Euboea, Dirphys, towers above it) and remote from towns of any size. An alternative is the rocky coast east of Chiliadou. Both locations are oriented towards Troy and Chios, and immediately at the coast the sea drops steeply to a depth of a hundred metres, a situation conducive to high waves. Another argument in favour of this identification is a seeming continuity of the name: various small islands near Kymi are still today called Kili (Κοίλη).[394] The name of the nearby coastal town of Chili is another manifestation of this word, and the name Chiliadou could be a derivation of an (unattested) name *Κοιλιάς.

If the situation of the Koila in this area is correct, Cape Kaphereus, which ancient sources mention in relation to the Koila,[395] may be identified with the much more prominent cape near Kymi (known today as Cape Kymi). There seems to be no scholarly discussion regarding the identification of Cape Kaphereus. It is tacitly assumed to be the modern Cape Doro.[396] However, there is no ancient source which necessitates this identification. On the other hand, the potential identification of the Hollows with the Chiliadou area invites us to look at alternatives. A scholion on Euripides, *Troiades* 89 claims that Cape Kaphereus is an ἀκρωτήριον Εὐβοίας, μεταξὺ Σκύρου 'a cape of Euboea, between [i.e. pointing at] Skyros', the *Vita-argumentum*-scholion on the same passage uses the preposition καταντικρύ 'right opposite'. This can only refer to the cape in the middle of the Aegean coast of Euboea, on which Kymi lies. More evidence for this identification appears in Philostratus' *Vita Apollonii* (1.24): τὸ γὰρ πολὺ

---

393 As Dio is walking on the beach, he meets a local hunter, who tells him that many ships are wrecked on the coast, where no harbour is found. The landscape is described as having a beach (3), with towering mountains (6), with many rocks that posed a danger for ships (7), there was no city nearby as the hunter had been only twice in 'the city' (21), and there were no harbours (22–23). In sum, the whole point of the Κοῖλα is that they are in a harbourless coastal area, which travellers from the Northeast (Troy, Chios) easily hit upon. It is further stated that the hunter lives above Cape Kaphereus, which is very remote from any city (31, 38).
394 For the Kymi area as the location of the Koila, see Labarbe 1952, 401–402, note 4; Lazenby 1993, 122–123; Bowie 2007, 106.
395 Euripides, *Troades* 84–90; Tzetzes, *Scholia in Lycophronem* 386; 1095.
396 E.g. Leake 1841, 247; Müller 1987, 415; *Barrington Atlas of the Greek and Roman World*; Miles 2016, 167.

τῆς Ἐρετρίας τὸν Καφηρέα ἀνέφυγε καὶ ὅ τι ἀκρότατον τῆς Εὐβοίας 'because most people of Eretria fled to Kaphereus and the highest parts of Euboea'. The highest part of Euboea is the Dirphys, with Cape Kaphereus behind it. This area is part of Eretria's hinterland, unlike the southeastern extremities of Euboea. Herodotus himself also throws some light on the problem (8.7): ἔξωθεν Σκιάθου [...] περιπλώουσαι Εὔβοιαν κατά τε Καφηρέα καὶ περὶ Γεραιστὸν ἐς τὸν Εὔριπον, 'outside Skiathos, sailing around Euboea past/along Kaphereus and around Geraistos to the Euripos.' It may be inferred that Kaphereus was a landmark one simply passed, while Geraistos was one to be rounded. Therefore, Cape Doro is disqualified: if Kaphereus was Cape Doro, Herodotus would probably not have used the preposition κατά. Also indicative for this 'new' identification is that Herodotus' description of the Euboean Periplous is much more 'symmetrical': from Skiathos, Geraistos is the far end of Euboea, while Euripos and Kaphereus are the middle points of both coasts. However, this alternative identification must remain tentative.

Fig. 27: The environs of Cape Kymi (Cape Kaphereus?).

The expedition as described by Herodotus is absurd from a strategical perspective: a circumnavigation of Euboea amounts to at least 450 km. The plan would therefore have taken the investment of over sixty hours of non-stop sailing when the battle was imminent.³⁹⁷ Therefore, some scholars have sensibly suggested that the entire Euboean expedition arose to 'explain' the altogether balanced numbers of Greek and Persian ships during the battle of Salamis, and it also allowed one to see the helping hand of the gods; as is clear from Herodotus' words, the story had this meaning to him.³⁹⁸ Against viewing the story as historical, I would like to propose the additional argument that the episode is one of several in the *Histories* in which the Persians try to bypass the Greeks to perform a surprise attack (see §3.3.5). In this case, the tradition on which Herodotus relied made the Persian contingent travel hundreds of kilometres to make them service this topos. In this context, I would like to remind that scholars have pointed out that the manoever resembles the Anopaia episode at Thermopylae (§2.5.3).³⁹⁹ In addition, the shipwreck at the Koila is only one of the many disasters befalling the Persians in the *Histories*: Cambyses' army disappeared during a sandstorm in the Libyan desert (3.26) and other storms killed Persians at Athos (6.44), Mount Ida (§2.2.1), and Sepias (§2.4.2).

If the historicity of the event is problematic, the question becomes more urgent: why was it believed to have happened at the Koila? The answer is readily found in the ancient perception of this place as a 'usual shipwreck mnemotope', a Greek Bermuda triangle. There are several references in which this idea finds support: we already encountered the story about Dio Chrysostom above; the reference in Euripides may also point in this direction. In Philostratus' *Vita Apollonii* (1.24) the Koila are said to be filled with dangerous reefs and that many ship wrecks protruded from the sea. Furthermore, nearby Cape Kaphereus had similar associations: many authors testify that it was here that the Greeks who returned from Troy wrecked. They were attracted by beacons lit by king Nauplios, who was furious about his son Palamedes' death at the hands of other Greeks.⁴⁰⁰ Accordingly, Pseudo-Apollodorus (Epitomae 6.11) calls the region ξυλοφάγος 'wood-eating'.⁴⁰¹ Another tragic death in the area may have been that of Ajax the Lesser, who on his nostos from Troy perished on the so-called Gyrai rocks (*Odyssey* 4.500), which may be sought near Cape Kaphereus, if the localisation

---

397 For this idea see Bowie 2007, 97–98.
398 Hignett 1963, 386–392; Cawkwell 2005, 93. It is not clear which god Herodotus had in mind; both wind gods (7.178) and Poseidon (7.192) are good candidates, as is a more general notion of divinity (although see Harrison 2000, 158–181 and Mikalson 2003, 131–133, who point out that when Herodotus credits the 'divine', this is because he does not know which god or hero it is, or it is used in a collective sense). However, if he meant Poseidon, we may perhaps see in this passage a reference to *Odyssey* 3.176–179.
399 Hauvette 1894, 370–371; Bowie 2007, 12 (both listing more points of overlap between the battles).
400 This is a true commonplace: Euripides, *Helena* 766; 1129; Pseudo-Apollodorus, *Epitomae* 6.7a-7b; 6.11; 6.15a-b; Dio Chrysostom, *Orationes* 7.32; Pausanias 2.23.1, 4.36.6; Strabo 8.6.2; Neanthes of Cyzicus *FGrH* 84 F38 (interestingly claiming that the name of the cape was first Καθαρεύς, 'Cleanser', cf. Stephanus Byzantinus, *Ethnica* s.v.).
401 Cf. Morton 2001, 73–74.

by Roman author Hyginus (*Fabulae* 116) has any worth. To these references may be added that the seas around Euboea were generally known to be dangerous.⁴⁰² Whether the story about the disappearance of the Persian contingent reflects reality or not, when one needed a location for it, the Koila was the obvious candidate.

2.4.6 Summary

The battle of Artemision and its prelude enfolded in the mythical seascape off Magnesia and around Euboea where Peleus had courted Thetis. Storms and rough waters had frustrated Greek warriors at the time of the voyage of the Argonauts and the Trojan war. We have discussed the mnemotopes that Herodotus gives for these events. Some of these appear to have had pre-existing stories attached to them because of their physical form. For example, it has been suggested above that the 'Ovens' at the Sepias coast inspired the area's connection with Thetis and the Nereids (in the process allowing for the identification of the Sepias coast with the Ovens themselves). Likewise, folk etymology played a role, for example in the events pictured at Aphetai, by its name a 'usual dock'. This coincidence of myth and history can be variously explained. A certain symbolism can only be argued for at Sepias and the Koila of Euboea: it is here that the Trojan War association may have worked as an antecedent to those during Xerxes' invasion. However, symbolic explanations are difficult to verify. The coincidences may, additionally or alternatively, also be inspired by the salience of the sites themselves. The stories helped to supply landmarks (most of these are only visible from the sea) on the 'sailor's map' of the area.

2.5 The battle of Thermopylae

The pass of Thermopylae has become an almost obligatory stop for tourists en route between northern and southern Greece.⁴⁰³ Helped by mental images from Hollywood films and an enormous modern monument, the historical sensation that right where one stands, the most famous military encounter of Antiquity took place, as well as its most heroic example of self-sacrifice, assails even the most indifferent passer-by. When Leonidas and his 300 Spartans fought the invading Persians at Thermopylae,

---

402 See Miles 2016, 167–168. At Geraistos, on the south tip of the island, Nestor had offered to Poseidon (*Odyssey* 3.176–179), and we have seen above that Artemis controlled the winds Euripos strait, obstructing Agamemnon's journey when he had killed a pregnant hare.
403 A selection of places mentioned in this chapter features on Map 4.

they also fought their way into the historical consciousness of the West.[404] As such, Thermopylae is today the best-known memory landscape of Xerxes' invasion.[405]

The historical sensation which one has at Thermopylae is not limited to the modern period. Already in the fifth century BCE the site seems to have been visited by tourists who wished to see the famous battlefield. Among them was Herodotus, who in his reconstruction of the battle gives a vivid description of its topography.[406] As will be discussed in this chapter, his account, the oldest that we have, already shows that the site had become a place of commemoration. Accordingly, local landmarks in the pass were pointed out as mnemotopes for specific elements of the battle. Among these are featured the base of the Persians, the Phocian wall, the Anopaia path, and the 'hill of the last stance'. Herodotus supplements these with various mnemotopes related to Heraclean mythology. As will be explained, there is reason to believe that the sacred landscape of Heracles came to be associated with that of Leonidas.

The realisation that Herodotus' topography is a collection of mnemotopes and therefore reflects the post-war period in which (folk) memory had attached stories to prominent landmarks does not in itself prove or disprove the historicity of the events that Herodotus believed took place at these sites. However, this realisation does make it increasingly problematic to use the topography in Herodotus' account as a means to get a fuller understanding of the historical topography of the battle, as has often been done.[407] A critical assessment of Herodotus' account congrues with the existence of old, alternative traditions about the battle that differed in key aspects from that of Herodotus;[408] with accumulating research that suggests that Herodotus' account

---

[404] The legacy of the battle in later centuries is a popular avenue of study in itself: e.g. Cartledge 2006, 177–211; Albertz 2006; Moggi 2007 (on the development of ideas about the battle in the post-war period); Christien & Le Tallec 2013, 143–346.
[405] See Albertz 2006, 42–44 for the engagement of early modern travellers with Thermopylae as a memory landscape.
[406] Cf. Cherf 2001, 362–363, who suggested that Herodotus "visits as a tourist the area, two generations after the fact. What would he see? He comes down south from Thessaly, comes walking in, probably stopped at the hot baths – it was a tough trip – got out of the hot baths, wandered over to the lion monument, the Polyandrion, and saw Simonides' poetry – what would he think? Even before he started asking questions to locals, he has already been impressed."
[407] Such literal readings are e.g. found in Marinatos 1951, 43: "Herodotus was an admirable topographer, quite especially for Thermopylae, which he studied on the spot, apparently with great care"; Myres 1953, 4; Burn 1962, 380; Sacks 1979; Hart 1982, 92; 95: "Finally Herodotus gives us as full a picture of the ground as could be imagined, full of an actual map. The topography of Thermopylae does raise some problems, but all solutions are squarely founded on the numerous details in his text"; Müller 1987, 375; Ray 2009, 71–83. See Morris 2000; 2007 for the impact of the landscape on various English travellers, and how Thermopylae played an important role in the Greek war of independence.
[408] One alternative is known from Diodorus Siculus (11.5–11.10) and Plutarch (*De Herodoti malignitate* 866a), both of which are believed to be based on an account by Ephorus (fourth century BCE). Another tradition may have been present in Simonides' poem on Thermopylae (*PMG* fragment 26); unfortunately, too little of his work has been preserved to be certain. Plutarch knew about Simonides'

of Thermopylae is already mythicised and features common narrative motives and invented traditions;[409] and the problem that the Spartan expedition is difficult to explain as a serious attempt to stop the Persian invasion.[410]

2.5.1 The pass, the Persian base at Trachis and Xerxes' throne (II)

Before the account of the battle, Herodotus describes the topography of the pass of Thermopylae in two long passages (7.176 and 7.198-201):

> ἡ δὲ αὖ διὰ Τρηχῖνος ἔσοδος ἐς τὴν Ἑλλάδα ἐστὶ τῇ στεινοτάτῃ ἡμίπλεθρον. οὐ μέντοι κατὰ τοῦτό γε ἐστὶ τὸ στεινότατον τῆς χώρης τῆς παραλίης, ἀλλ' ἔμπροσθέ τε Θερμοπυλέων καὶ ὄπισθε, κατά τε Ἀλπηνοὺς, ὄπισθε ἐόντας, ἐοῦσα ἁμαξιτὸς μούνη, καὶ ἔμπροσθε κατὰ Φοίνικα ποταμὸν ἀγχοῦ Ἀνθήλης πόλιος, ἄλλη ἁμαξιτὸς μούνη. τῶν δὲ Θερμοπυλέων τὸ μὲν πρὸς ἑσπέρης ὄρος ἄβατόν τε καὶ ἀπόκρημνον, ὑψηλόν, ἀνατεῖνον ἐς τὴν Οἴτην· τὸ δὲ πρὸς τὴν ἠῶ τῆς ὁδοῦ θάλασσα ὑποδέκεται καὶ τενάγεα. ἔστι δὲ ἐν τῇ ἐσόδῳ ταύτῃ θερμὰ λουτρά, τὰ Χύτρους καλέουσι οἱ ἐπιχώριοι, καὶ βωμὸς ἵδρυται Ἡρακλέος ἐπ' αὐτοῖσι. [...] κώμη δὲ ἐστὶ ἀγχοτάτω τῆς ὁδοῦ, Ἀλπηνοὶ οὔνομα· ἐκ ταύτης δὲ ἐπισιτιεῖσθαι ἐλογίζοντο οἱ Ἕλληνες.

The entry into Greece through Trachis, then, is fifty feet (fifteen meters) at its narrowest. However, the narrowest part of the coast is not around there, but before Thermopylae and behind it, around Alpenoi, which lies behind it, where the land is only a cart's breadth. The mountain to the west of Thermopylae is impassable and like a cliff, high, and stretches towards Mount Oita. To the east

---

poem (Plutarch used the rare verb ἀμαυρόω 'to obscure', which we also find in Simonides, in a seemingly ironic way: Herodotus would have obscured the Spartans' true heroic deeds by giving a wrong account of them) but he was probably influenced by Ephorus, too (Flower 1998, 370–371). Scholarship on the Persian Wars has occasionally been hostile to Ephorus: for example, Hignett (1963, 19) thought that he had "fatally corrupted" the historical tradition of the Persian Wars. On Simonides' poems also see Molyneux 1992, 175–187.

409 Burn 1962, 407, noting that it "lies, in point of literary form, somewhere between sober history and the *Chanson de Roland*"; Hölkeskamp 2001, 335, describing Thermopylae as a place of memory; Sánchez-Moreno 2010, 1417: "[s]in duda un paisaje complejo, articulado y sacralizado, muy lejos de la generalizada idea de las Termópilas como mero desfiladero." Cherf (2001, 356) points out that Herodotus' story about Thermopylae may be dramatised to show a heroic tragedy because it was needed as a counterpoint to the victory of Salamis ("How much different is this revisionist Hollywood review of ancient history, when compared to the selective tale told to us by Herodotus?"). Flower (1998, 374) and Meier (2010, 101) point out that the dark is consistently the time when the Persians act, while the Greeks only move in the light, and important themes (such as the hubris of the Persian king, the clash of continents) feature prominently. Flower (1998, 375) and Marincola (2007, 117) argue that the struggle for Leonidas' body has Iliadic resonances. A foreshadowing takes place in 7.180, where Herodotus conjectures that the Troezian Leon had his name to thank for his death by the hands of the Persians; he does not explain why, but it is tempting to associate the name Leon 'Lion' with Leonidas 'Son of a Lion': both men lost their lives as a result of their excellence (for the connotations of reference to lions in Herodotus, see Brock 2004, 170–171).
410 See Albertz 2006, 36–37 on the struggle of scholarship to explain the Spartan expedition in historical terms.

Fig. 28: The pass of Thermopylae.

of the road there is a sea and shallow waters. In that entry there are hot baths, which the locals call the 'Pots', and an altar has been founded for Heracles near them. [...] There is a village at the narrowest part of the road called Alpenoi. The Greeks planned to get their provisions from here.

περὶ δὲ τὸν κόλπον τοῦτον ἐστὶ χῶρος πεδινός, τῇ μὲν εὐρύς, τῇ δὲ καὶ κάρτα στεινός: περὶ δὲ τὸν χῶρον ὄρεα ὑψηλὰ καὶ ἄβατα περικληίει πᾶσαν τὴν Μηλίδα γῆν, Τρηχίνιαι πέτραι καλεόμεναι. πρώτη μέν νυν πόλις ἐστὶ ἐν τῷ κόλπῳ ἰόντι ἀπὸ Ἀχαιίης Ἀντικύρη, παρ' ἣν Σπερχειὸς ποταμὸς ῥέων ἐξ Ἐνιήνων ἐς θάλασσαν ἐκδιδοῖ. ἀπὸ δὲ τούτου διὰ εἴκοσί κου σταδίων ἄλλος ποταμὸς τῷ οὔνομα κεῖται Δύρας, τὸν βοηθέοντα τῷ Ἡρακλέι καιομένῳ λόγος ἐστὶ ἀναφανῆναι. ἀπὸ δὲ τούτου δι' ἄλλων εἴκοσι σταδίων ἄλλος ποταμός ἐστι ὃς καλέεται Μέλας. Τρηχὶς δὲ πόλις ἀπὸ τοῦ Μέλανος τούτου ποταμοῦ πέντε στάδια ἀπέχει. ταύτῃ δὲ καὶ εὐρύτατον ἐστὶ πάσης τῆς χώρης ταύτης ἐκ τῶν ὀρέων ἐς θάλασσαν, κατ' ἃ Τρηχὶς πεπόλισται: δισχίλιά τε γὰρ καὶ δισμύρια πλέθρα τοῦ πεδίου ἐστί. τοῦ δὲ ὄρεος τὸ περικληίει τὴν γῆν τὴν Τρηχινίην ἐστὶ διασφὰξ πρὸς μεσαμβρίην Τρηχῖνος, διὰ δὲ τῆς διασφάγος Ἀσωπὸς ποταμὸς ῥέει παρὰ τὴν ὑπωρείαν τοῦ ὄρεος. ἔστι δὲ ἄλλος Φοῖνιξ ποταμὸς οὐ μέγας πρὸς μεσαμβρίην τοῦ Ἀσωποῦ, ὃς ἐκ τῶν ὀρέων τούτων ῥέων ἐς τὸν Ἀσωπὸν ἐκδιδοῖ. κατὰ δὲ τὸν Φοίνικα ποταμὸν στεινότατον ἐστί: ἁμαξιτὸς γὰρ μούνη δέδμηται. ἀπὸ δὲ τοῦ Φοίνικος ποταμοῦ πεντεκαίδεκα στάδιά ἐστι ἐς Θερμοπύλας. ἐν δὲ τῷ μεταξὺ Φοίνικος ποταμοῦ καὶ Θερμοπυλέων κώμη τε ἐστὶ τῇ οὔνομα Ἀνθήλη κεῖται, παρ' ἣν δὴ παραρρέων ὁ Ἀσωπὸς ἐς θάλασσαν ἐκδιδοῖ, καὶ χῶρος περὶ αὐτὴν εὐρύς, ἐν τῷ Δήμητρός τε ἱρόν Ἀμφικτυονίδος ἵδρυται καὶ ἕδραι εἰσὶ Ἀμφικτύοσι καὶ αὐτοῦ τοῦ Ἀμφικτύονος ἱρόν. ἔστι δὲ ἄλλος Φοῖνιξ ποταμὸς οὐ μέγας πρὸς μεσαμβρίην τοῦ Ἀσωποῦ, ὃς ἐκ τῶν ὀρέων τούτων ῥέων ἐς τὸν Ἀσωπὸν ἐκδιδοῖ. κατὰ δὲ τὸν Φοίνικα ποταμὸν στεινότατον ἐστί: ἁμαξιτὸς γὰρ μούνη δέδμηται. ἀπὸ δὲ τοῦ Φοίνικος ποταμοῦ πεντεκαίδεκα στάδιά ἐστι ἐς Θερμοπύλας. ἐν δὲ τῷ μεταξὺ Φοίνικος ποταμοῦ καὶ Θερμοπυλέων κώμη τε ἐστὶ τῇ οὔνομα Ἀνθήλη κεῖται, παρ' ἥν δὴ παραρρέων ὁ Ἀσωπὸς ἐς θάλασσαν ἐκδιδοῖ, καὶ χῶρος περὶ αὐτὴν εὐρύς, ἐν τῷ Δήμητρός τε ἱρὸν Ἀμφικτυονίδος ἵδρυται καὶ ἕδραι εἰσὶ Ἀμφικτύοσι καὶ αὐτοῦ τοῦ Ἀμφικτύονος ἱρόν. Βασιλεὺς μὲν δὴ Ξέρξης ἐστρατοπεδεύετο τῆς Μηλίδος ἐν τῇ Τρηχινίῃ, οἱ δὲ Ἕλληνες ἐν τῇ διόδῳ· καλέεται δὲ ὁ χῶρος οὗτος ὑπὸ μὲν τῶν πλεόνων Ἑλλήνων Θερμοπύλαι, ὑπὸ δὲ τῶν ἐπιχωρίων καὶ περιοίκων Πύλαι. ἐστρατοπεδεύοντο μέν νυν ἑκάτεροι ἐν τούτοισι τοῖσι χωρίοισι, ἐπεκράτεε δὲ ὃ μὲν τῶν πρὸς βορέην ἄνεμον ἐχόντων πάντων μέχρι Τρηχῖνος, οἱ δὲ τῶν πρὸς νότον καὶ μεσαμβρίην φερόντων τὸ ἐπὶ ταύτης τῆς ἠπείρου.

Around [the Malian Gulf] there is a field-like land, which is broad in some places and very narrow in others. Around that place high and impassable mountains, called the Trachinian Rocks, enclose the entire land of Malis. Now for someone coming from Achaia, the first city in the bay is Antikyre, along which the Spercheios river runs from Enienia, issueing into the sea. From there, after some four kilometres, there is another river with the name Dyras, which, the story goes, sprang up as it helped the burning Heracles. Another four kilometres from there is another river which is called Melas. The city of Trachis lies five stades [one kilometre] from that river Melas. At that point, where Trachis has been founded, is also the widest part from mountain to sea of all this land, as the field is 22,000 plethra [c. 20 km²]. There is a ravine in the mountain which encloses the Trachinian land, to the south of Trachis. Through the ravine runs the river Asopos through the foothills of the mountain. There is another river called Phoinix, which is not large, south of the Asopos, which runs through those mountains and then flows into the Asopos. At the Phoinix river is the narrowest part, because a road of only one cart's width has been constructed there. From the Phoinix river it is fifteen stades to Thermopylae. In the area between the Phoinix river and Thermopylae is a village called Anthele. The Asopos runs along it and issues into the sea and the land around it is wide. Here a temple of Demeter Amphiktyonis has been founded, and there are the seats of the Amphiktyons and a temple of Amphiktyon himself. King Xerxes camped in this part of Melis, Trachinia, while the Greeks did so in the passage. That place is called by most Greeks Thermopylae, but by the local and nearby residents it is called Pylai. Both parties camped in these places; the one had everything which lay north towards Trachis, the others what was towards the south and southwest on the mainland.

Many of the places which Herodotus mentions are still traceable today. Trachis has usually been located near the modern towns of Ano Vardates and Delfino.[411] The site of Anthele has been identified with a level piece of land inside the west 'gate' of the pass, close to modern Loutra.[412] The sites of the temple of Demeter, the seats of the Amphiktyons (a council of a dozen central Greek cities) and the temple of Amphik-

---

411 On the location of Trachis, see Grundy 1901, 282–283 (at Konvelo); Kromayer 1924, 23–24; Hignett 1963, 356–360; Kontorlis 1972, 8; Pritchett 1985a, 199–204; 1993, 312–317 (identifying it with the later Herakleia); Müller 1987, 390–392; Szemler, Cherf & Kraft 1996, 33–40 with extensive literature, identify it with a plateau called Rachitam, northwest of the Asopos gorge, approximately at modern Delfino.
412 Grundy 1901, 284; Béquignon 1934, 26–33; Pritchett 1993, 308–309; Szemler, Cherf & Kraft 1996, 40–42. Although Herodotus' account can be interpreted either way, Müller (1987, 303) argues that Anthele was situated to the west of the western gate, and not inside, as this is consistent with the assertion that the χῶρος surrounding the village was εὐρύς. There are remains of a stoa and a stadium in this area; the temples, however, have not been found.

tyon may also be located here, but have not been retrieved.⁴¹³ The hot springs can still be found here today;⁴¹⁴ the altar of Heracles must be sought nearby.⁴¹⁵

Fig. 29: The hot spring at Thermopylae.

Following Herodotus, topographers have placed the Persian camp between Trachis and Anthele.⁴¹⁶ From a strategical perspective it seems logical that the Persians were garrisoned in the fields surrounding Trachis, while the Greeks guarded the pass. Here, the Persians could stay in touch with their war ships, and prevent a sudden attack by

---

413 The temple of Demeter (Strabo 9.3.7; 9.4.17) has been hypothesised at the north slope of the hill of Anthele (Thalmann 1980), but no remains have been identified here. The seats of the Amphiktyons may have been anything; Stählin (1936, 2406) speculated that they were "wohl einfache Steine im Halbrund um einen Altar unter freiem Himmel und das heroön des Amphiktion"; see also Marinatos 1951, 52. Thermopylae was a natural meeting point for people from the north and the south; it gave Anthele a supraregional and strategical significance (Sánchez-Moreno 2010, 1421; 2013b, 341).
414 See Marinatos 1951, 53. Even today, the unnaturally blue (cf. Pausanias 4.35.9), sulphureous water is believed to be beneficial for those suffering from rheumatoid arthritis.
415 Müller 1987, 379; the altar has not been retrieved, but may, according to Stählin (1936, 2410) have been located on a platform immediately west of the springs, high enough not to be sintered over.
416 Kromayer 1924, 57; Hignett 1963, 142; Pritchett 1982, 179–181; Green 1996, 126.

the Greeks. However, there are various reasons why we may also view the field of Trachis as a mnemotope for the Persian camp. Fifty years after the war, a visitor to the area would have placed the army automatically at the broadest part of the pass. In the above passage, it is notable that Herodotus is preoccupied with the wideness of this part.

A particular mnemotope within this topographical passage is an instance of Xerxes' throne, which Herodotus elsewhere describes as being present near the Persian camp (7.212):

> ἐν ταύτῃσι τῇσι προσόδοισι τῆς μάχης λέγεται βασιλέα θηεύμενον τρὶς ἀναδραμεῖν ἐκ τοῦ θρόνου, δείσαντα περὶ τῇ στρατιῇ.
>
> The story goes that, during those attacks, the king, who was watching, jumped up three times from his throne, out of fear for his army.

The 'vision' of Xerxes seated on a throne is also encountered at the Hellespont (§2.2.4) and Salamis (§2.8.3), where the idea was probably connected to or inspired by prominent mountain tops (for the significance of this idea, see also §3.3.6). In the case of Thermopylae, Herodotus does not say where Xerxes' throne exactly stood, so it remains uncertain whether his account relied on any real mnemotope in the landscape. The vagueness did not stop modern scholars from identifying the place of the throne with a hill near Anthele.[417]

We may also consider the pass as a whole to be a mnemotope. Thermopylae was considered to mark the northern gate of Greece.[418] In fact, the pass appears as the location of at least ten additional invasions: Herodotus himself relates of earlier confrontations of Thessalians and Phocians (7.176), and the site was later associated with the invasions or passings of: Philip II of Macedon in 339 BCE (Diodorus Siculus 16.38.1); the Celts in 279 BCE (Pausanias 10.20-21); Philip V of Macedon versus the Aetolians in 207 BCE (Livy 32.4); Antiochus of Syria versus the Romans in 191 BCE (Livy 36.15), Alaric in 395 CE (Zosimus 5.5); Justinian (Procopius, *De aedificiis* 4.2); Boniface of Monferrat in 1204 CE (Nicetas Choniates, *Historia* 604-609); Athanasios Diakos in the Greek War of Independence (1821); and the Germans during the Second World War (1941).[419] In addition, at least one mythical battle took place in the pass at Trachis: namely the battle between Heracles and Cycnus, as most famously recounted in the *Scutum* (a work sometimes attributed to Hesiod). Although only a few of these historical and mythical encounters antedate Herodotus, they testify that

---

[417] Kraft et al. (1987, 185) assert that the hill west of Anthele would be the only possible place for Xerxes to have watched over the battle, which Herodotus asserts he did in 7.212. Macan 1908, I 315 notes literary parallels with Darius (3.155) and with Aidoneus in the *Iliad* (20.62).
[418] See 7.176 and "Thermopylae" in *Der Neue Pauly*, with literature.
[419] For these invasions and further literature see Kraft et al. 1987, 183, note 2. Strabo (9.4.13 and 9.4.16) names several forts in or near Thermopylae. See also Stählin 1936, 2419–2423; Pritchett 1985a, 191–193.

the dramatic landscape of Thermopylae was liable to be associated with confrontations between invaders from the north and defenders from the south, whether this had a basis in historical truth or not. This location fits the topos of the 'usual battle site' (§3.3.1).

Seeing the pass as a mnemotope offers a way out of a particularly vexed topographical problem concerning the movements of Xerxes' army. Herodotus says that, after Thermopylae, the army ravaged the land of Phocis via Doris, a small region immediately southeast of Mount Oita (8.31), which it would largely bypass if it had taken the route through Thermopylae. This comment has puzzled scholars, because it would mean that the army, after the battle, did not enter Greece via the coastal route along Thermopylae: if it were true that the Persians could enter southern Greece through Doris, the fight at Thermopylae as described by Herodotus would not have been necessary, because the Persians could, in that scenario, have by-passed Thermopylae. Scholars have therefore come up with various theories why the coastal route was taken after all.[420] Another group of scholars, however, believed that the army did, in fact, take the Doris route through the so-called 'Dhema Gap' between the Oita and the Kallidromos. They argue that there was no pass of Thermopylae in the fifth century BCE, as the shoreline would have reached until the present *kolonos*, the 'hill of the last stance' (see §2.5.4), which would thus have blocked the road and made the passage by the Persians difficult.[421] This view would show that Herodotus himself had already received invented traditions about the battle.

This view has not found wide acceptance. It is pointed out more convincingly that the geographical data are deceptive; that it would not have made sense for Herodotus to localise a battle here when there was no usable road; and that the traditions about military confrontations at Hyampolis in Phocis (see §2.6.1) would make no sense if Thermopylae was not regarded as the main bottleneck that gave access to the south.[422] I would additionally like to point out that inherent in the perspective of mnemotopes is the methodological viewpoint that it is not necessary that places

---

420 E.g. Hauvette 1894, 353–355 and Müller 1987, 439–440 supposed that only a part of Xerxes' army used the Doris route, and that the main part had used the coastal route. Müller argues that Herodotus never says that the entire army had used the Doris route, and that Abai and Hyampolis were easily reachable from the coast. However, the first argument is ex silentio, and Abai and Hyampolis are within easy reach from the Kephisos, too. McInerney 1999, 336–337 suggests that the Persians took the Doris route because this allowed the medising Thessalians to burn every town in Phocis. Tuplin 2003, 401, note 26 reasons that the Persians still went along Thermopylae.
421 Kase & Szemler 1982; Szemler 1986; Chase 2001. They accordingly stress the degree to which Herodotus may have mythicised his battle narrative of Thermopylae. The argument sparked a fierce debate with a proponent of the traditional theory, Pritchett, who vehemently attacked the team's conclusions (Pritchett 1982, 211–233; 1985; responses in Kraft et al. 1987, 187; Szemler 1989; Pritchett 1993, 317–328; Szemler, Cherf & Kraft 1996). See Albertz 2006, 37–39 for a discussion of the debate.
422 McInerney 1999, 334–336; Sánchez-Moreno 2010, 1428.

fit in the rest of the narrative about the Persian advance, as historical feasibility is not a determining factor in the establishment of mnemotopes (§1.3.6). The passing through Doris may have served to explain the destruction of Phocis, of which, we will see, the historicity is problematic (§2.6.1). Whatever the historicity of the events which Herodotus transmits about Thermopylae, surely the pass was in the course of the fifth century BCE regarded as the place 'where it all happened'. We will see below (§2.5.4) that pre-existing traditions also played a role in this process.

2.5.2 The Phocian wall

The next location in Herodotus' account is the so-called Phocian wall, the most important defensive structure of the pass (7.176):

> ἐδέδμητο δὲ τεῖχος κατὰ ταύτας τὰς ἐσβολάς, καὶ τό γε παλαιὸν πύλαι ἐπῆσαν. ἔδειμαν δὲ Φωκέες τὸ τεῖχος δείσαντες, ἐπεὶ Θεσσαλοὶ ἦλθον ἐκ Θεσπρωτῶν οἰκήσοντες γῆν τὴν Αἰολίδα τὴν νῦν ἐκτέαται. ἅτε δὴ πειρωμένων τῶν Θεσσαλῶν καταστρέφεσθαι σφέας, τοῦτο προεφυλάξαντο οἱ Φωκέες, καὶ τὸ ὕδωρ τὸ θερμὸν τότε ἐπῆκαν ἐπὶ τὴν ἔσοδον, ὡς ἂν χαραδρωθείη ὁ χῶρος, πᾶν μηχανώμενοι ὅκως μή σφι ἐσβάλοιεν οἱ Θεσσαλοὶ ἐπὶ τὴν χώρην. τὸ μέν νυν τεῖχος τὸ ἀρχαῖον ἐκ παλαιοῦ τε ἐδέδμητο καὶ τὸ πλέον αὐτοῦ ἤδη ὑπὸ χρόνου ἔκειτο· τοῖσι δὲ αὖτις ὀρθώσασι ἔδοξε ταύτῃ ἀπαμύνειν ἀπὸ τῆς Ἑλλάδος τὸν βάρβαρον.

> In that pass a wall has been built, and in the past there were gates at them. The wall was built by the Phocians out of fear, because the Thessalians came from Thesprotia to live in the land of Aiolis, which they now possess. As the Thessalians were trying to subject them, the Phocians took precautions against this, and they then diverted the hot water to the entrance, so that the land was divided by the mountain stream; they did everything so that the Thessalians could not invade their country. Now the old wall had been built long ago and most of it lay in ruins. By re-erecting it, [the Spartans] thought to keep the Barbarians at bay from Greece.

During his excavations in 1939, Spyridon Marinatos identified the Phocian wall as a zigzagging stretch of wall of 200 metres with stones of irregular shape.[423] Surprisingly, it did not block the pass, but was oriented west-east, parallel to the pass, so as to protect a higher area. He also claimed that the surviving structures which do block the pass, earlier identified as the Phocian wall, are of Byzantine date.[424] The existence of a tower-like structure, whose entrance originally was to the north, indicated

---

[423] Marinatos 1940, 336–337; 1951, 56–59, mentioning at least one gate in this wall, which was later blocked up; Meyer 1956. Marinatos believed that these gates, and not the pass itself, was the source of the name 'Thermopylae' or 'Pylae'. The blocking-up of one of the gates can hardly be regarded as evidence for the Spartan reconstruction of the wall, as Marinatos suggested. Müller (1997, 383) places the Greek camp in the depression to the east of the hill with the Phocian Wall (Hill I), and south of Hill II (the kolonos, see below).
[424] Marinatos 1951, 56–57; Kromayer 1924, 38 identified the blocking wall with the Phocian Wall.

that the wall was defending the area to the north from invaders from the south.[425] Pritchett remedied this unwelcome observation by suggesting that the wall was originally Phocian but had soon after the battle of Thermopylae been reconstructed by the Trachinians so as to face south.[426]

Fig. 30: Part of the defensive structure usually identified as the Phocian wall.

However, we should be careful in accepting Marinatos' identification. It is possible that he identified the west-east wall as the Phocian wall, because he believed in the historicity of the wall's construction by the Phocians. Furthermore, the irregularity of the stonework would prove that its construction happened in the archaic period. However, the irregular stonework is not a guarantee that this wall is of archaic date, because this kind of wall is simply undateable; similarly, the north-south wall cannot be dated securely to the Byzantine period. Moreover, from Herodotus' account it is quite clear

---

425 Marinatos 1940, 336; 1951, 58–59 (reporting that the tower contained the bones of children, which dated to the nineteenth century; they were probably interred there because the local people interpreted the structure as an old church); Pritchett 1958, 212–213; Müller 1987, 381–382, and the map on page 379; Domínguez Monedero 2013, 448.
426 Pritchett 1958, 212–213.

that the wall which he had in mind blocked the pass: he says that the Persians needed to partly demolish it to get to the hill where the last stance happened (7.225).

The perspective of mnemotopes invites us to think that when Herodotus visited the area, remains of recent structures had been projected on a more distant past which was relevant to the current rivalry between Phocians and Thessalians.[427] Accordingly, Adolfo Domínguez Monedero points out that Herodotus could not reflect accurately on the wall's date and may have associated it with the Phocians because of this rivalry; he instead suggests that it may have been built by Thessalians or Locrians, as it defends the area toward the north.[428]

Whatever the exact role of the defensive structure during the battle of Thermopylae, and whatever its age, for later visitors and locals interested in reconstructing the battle, the wall was liable to appear as a mnemotope in the narratives about it. This is shown by its inclusion in three different stories: it is mentioned again in 7.208 in relation to an anecdote according to which a Persian horseman, set out to spy on the Greeks, was perplexed at the sight of Spartans performing gymnastic exercises in front of the wall, which was too high to reveal the extent and nature of the Greek army installed behind it; in 7.215 it appears in relation to the Anopaia path, which was supposedly 'discovered' by the Malians when the Phocians had built their wall; and in 7.225 in relation to a story according to which the Persians had demolished the wall to get access to the 'hill of the last stance' (§2.5.4). Perhaps this incident helped to explain why the wall lay in ruins.

2.5.3 The Anopaia path

Anopaia, the secret path on the mountains believed to allow enemies at Thermopylae to bypass a blocking army, marks one of the most famed episodes in Greek history, and is crucial to the 'idea' of Thermopylae. Herodotus describes what he knew of the topography of the path in 7.216:

> ἔχει δὲ ὧδε ἡ ἀτραπὸς αὕτη: ἄρχεται μὲν ἀπὸ τοῦ Ἀσωποῦ ποταμοῦ τοῦ διὰ τῆς διασφάγος ῥέοντος, οὔνομα δὲ τῷ ὄρεϊ τούτῳ καὶ τῇ ἀτραπῷ τὠυτὸ κεῖται, Ἀνόπαια: τείνει δὲ ἡ Ἀνόπαια αὕτη κατὰ ῥάχιν τοῦ ὄρεος, λήγει δὲ κατά τε Ἀλπηνὸν πόλιν, πρώτην ἐοῦσαν τῶν Λοκρίδων πρὸς τῶν Μηλιέων, καὶ κατὰ Μελαμπύγου τε καλεόμενον λίθον καὶ Κερκώπων ἕδρας, τῇ καὶ τὸ στεινότατόν ἐστί.

> This path is as follows: it starts from the river Asopos which runs through the ravine, and the name of the mountain and the path is the same: Anopaia. This Anopaia stretches along the top of the mountain, and it ends at the city of Alpenos, which is the first city of Locris towards Malis, and at the rock called Melampygos and the seats of the Kerkopes, at the narrowest part [of the pass].

---

427 McInerney 1999, 174–175 connects the construction of the wall to a Phocian revolt not long before the Persian Wars.
428 Domínguez Monedero 2013, 448–451.

The starting point of the path was at the impressive ravine formed by the river Asopos, described by Herodotus in some detail in 7.199.[429] It was later known as the Karvounaria and today again as the Asopos.

Fig. 31: The gorge of the Asopos river.

The end of the path, as it joined the main road towards Boeotia and Attica, was marked by a rock called Melampygos or 'Black-buttocks'. It has been identified with a huge boulder, known as the Bastion rock, located on the north side of the hill on which Alpenoi once stood.[430]

---

429 E.g. Stählin 1936, 2416–2417; Pritchett 1982, 181–182; Müller 1987, 300–301 (photographs); Hignett (1963, 362) notes that it features in the narrative because Herodotus was "impressed by the sight", but that it cannot have been the true starting point.
430 For a discussion of the sites see e.g. Pritchett 1958, 211; 1982, 194–198; Müller 1987, 342–343; Pasqual 2013a, 77–78 with note 25 (suggesting, however, that Herodotus' account points to a more southern location). The hill is about four kilometres east of the springs, in an olive grove between the old road and the motorway. Leake 1835, II 52 identified the Melampygos with a hill just east of the kolonos. For Alpenos, see Pritchett 1993, 301–302 (with literature); Pasqual 2013a, 74–88.

Fig. 32: The Bastion rock, identified with the Melampygos rock.

The Melampygos rock was another mnemotope connected to Heraclean lore.[431] The word μελάμπυγος was an epithet of Heracles in his dealings with the Kerkopes. Because these mischievous gnome-like creatures had stolen his weapons, Heracles bound them by their feet to a carrying pole; hanging down, they started to giggle at the hero's black bottom. In an alternative myth, the Kerkopes were petrified for deceiving Zeus.[432] Both versions could be imagined at the Melampygos rock. It is uncertain whether the 'Seats of the Kerkopes' refer to this rock as well, or to one or more different features in the landscape nearby.[433]

---

431 Marinatos (1951, 54–55) supposed that the legend arose at Thermopylae because of the strong Heraclean traditions here; he speculates that the name Kerkopes may refer to "a forgotten people who once inhabited this region" and compares the ethnonyms Almopes, Dryopes, Dolopes. The Kerkopes were also localised elsewhere in the Greek world, and there were other mythical 'brigands' in the Thermopylae area, such as the Kylikranes and the Dryopes (Malkin 1994, 231). As an extraordinary example of the depiction of a humorous story on Greek sacral architecture, the scene features on metopes of temple C at Selinous and on the Heraion of Foce del Sele near Paestum. For more examples of conspicuous rocks as mnemotopes see Hartmann 2010, 91.
432 Suda s.v. Κέρκωπες; scholion on Lucian, *Alexander* 4.
433 Müller 1987, 343; Stählin 1936, 2414 asserted that the seats refer to the lower parts of the main rock.

It is unclear whether Herodotus' mention of the myth of the Kerkopes had more than merely a 'touristic' quality. Vandiver supposed that "the effect is to keep Heracles present in the reader's mind as the story of Thermopylae unfolds."[434] That may well be the case, but it also shows that the Anopaia path had crystallised around local landmarks which had pre-existing associations.

The beginning and end points of the Anopaia path are easily identifiable, but the exact route of the path between them has been subject to an intense debate and has spawned a huge literature.[435] Central to the debate is a location along the path that Herodotus mentions (7.212; 7.217-7.218): the area where the local Phocian people were keeping watch, and the hill to which they retreated as the Persians came close, identified with a pyramid-shaped hill.[436] In *Cato Maior* 13, Plutarch vividly describes how in 191 BCE Cato directed his army over the Anopaia path, but struggled to find the right way. This story shows that the path was not obvious.

The uncertainty about the route prompts a skeptical question: was Herodotus right in assuming the existence of a path that could be guarded? It now seems that there was not a single path, but rather a network of mountain paths, and that the exact route of the Persians can simply not be established.[437] This might show that the tradition in Herodotus, in suggesting that there was only one path which the Phocians guarded, is a dramatical one that does not fit the actual topography of Kallidromos. Herodotus' description of the topography is consistent with the perspective of someone who visited the Thermopylae pass, and stayed near the coast. It is evident that the Asopos gorge and the Melampygos rock sufficiently 'marked' the path, even though they only related to its beginning and end points. For someone visiting the pass, the towering mountains may easily have been connected to a story that was inspired by the defeat of the Spartans.

It thus remains an open question whether the mountains were ever successfully used to bypass defenders of Thermopylae. In this context, it is worth noting that the toponym Anopaia could mean 'unseen',[438] and that the name of the local who led the Persians onto the path, Ephialtes, means 'nightmare'.[439] These speaking names

---

434 Vandiver 1991, 185–186.
435 Studies include Leake 1835, II 53–55; Grundy 1901, 301–303; Macan 1908, II 270–271 (suggesting there was more than one possible route); Kromayer 1924, 43–57; Munro 1926a, 292; Stählin 1936, 2415; Burn 1962, 380; Pritchett 1982, 183–194; Müller 1987, 296–302; Pritchett 1993, 309–311; Green 1996, 115–116; Sánchez-Moreno 2013a, 313–320; Waters 2014, 127.
436 The 'Pyramid hill' has been identified with a rubble wall immediately northeast of Nevropolis (Pritchett 1958, 210; Müller 1987, 301–302). Another possible location is the Sastano 'saddle' near Old Drakospilia (Kromayer 1924, 53; Hignett 1963, 133).
437 Albertz 2006, 42; Sánchez-Moreno 2013a, 317–318.
438 The word Ἀνόπαια is also encountered in *Odyssey* 1.320 with reference to a bird that flies away; it meant 'unseen' here according to Aelius Herodianus (*Περὶ Ὀδυσσειακῆς προσῳδίας* 133).
439 The word is derived from the verb ἐφιάλλομαι 'to leap upon'.

underline the legend-like qualities of the narrative, and as it turns out, Herodotus had access to an alternative to the Ephialtes story, according to which the path was shown by Onetes and Korydallos (7.214), but nevertheless he preferred the Ephialtes version because, he reasons, the delegates to the Amphiktyonic council at Thermopylae had allegedly put a price on his head. But the historicity of the Anopaia path does not concern us here, and is probably beyond recovery. On the other hand, Herodotus' account at least shows that in his time, it was *believed* that there was a path which the Persian army had used to bypass the Greeks.

The 'idea' of the path may be thought of as a topos which was welcomed (if not originating) in local folk memory, as it offered a dramatisation of the battle story.[440] The story also provided an answer to the question why the Greeks had lost, even though their strategical position was good and their courage high: the Persians had to resort to treachery to trap them.[441] It is important to realise that 'the enemy's bypass' is a well-established topos both in the *Histories* and in battle narratives generally (§3.3.5). The fact that Polyaenus (*Strategemata* 7.15.5) lists it as such in his discussion of the barbarians makes it clear that the Anopaia episode could be considered an example of a typically Persian stratagem. The story also features in other traditions about invading armies in Thermopylae. Herodotus mentions the invasion of the Thessalians (7.215) and from later sources we can add the invasion of the Celts (279 BCE; Pausanias 10.19.4-23.9; cf. the convergence of the Persian and Celtic assaults of Delphi in §2.6.3) and a battle between the Romans and the Seleucids of 191 BCE (Appian, *Syriaca* 75-77; Livy 36.16-19).

2.5.4 The hill of the last stance of the three hundred Spartans

Herodotus' topography remains detailed in the final episodes of his account. The remaining Greeks spread into the area where the pass was a little broader, and started to fight the Persians, some of whom fell into the sea (7.223). As they perceived that they were attacked in the back by the Persians who had taken the Anopaia path, they returned to the narrow part of the pass, behind the Phocian wall (7.225). There, the final location appears: the hill of the last stance.

> ὡς δὲ τούτους ἥκειν ἐπύθοντο οἱ Ἕλληνες, ἐνθεῦτεν ἤδη ἑτεροιοῦτο τὸ νεῖκος· ἔς τε γὰρ τὸ στεινὸν τῆς ὁδοῦ ἀνεχώρεον ὀπίσω καὶ παραμειψάμενοι τὸ τεῖχος ἐλθόντες ἵζοντο ἐπὶ τὸν κολωνὸν πάντες ἁλέες οἱ ἄλλοι πλὴν Θηβαίων. ὁ δὲ κολωνός ἐστι ἐν τῇ ἐσόδῳ, ὅκου νῦν ὁ λίθινος λέων ἕστηκε ἐπὶ Λεωνίδῃ. ἐν τούτῳ σφέας τῷ χώρῳ ἀλεξομένους μαχαίρῃσι, τοῖσι

---

[440] The dramatisation of the episode is furthermore clear because of several elements: the movement of the Persians during the night (7.217) and the rustling of leaves under their feet (7.218). These details were taken as historical facts as recently as Hammond 1988, 557.
[441] Albertz 2006, 52 points out that Herodotus' account is intentionally structured in order to give an answer to such questions as 'Why did the Spartans lose the battle?'.

αὐτῶν ἐτύγχανον ἔτι περιεοῦσαι, καὶ χερσὶ καὶ στόμασι κατέχωσαν οἱ βάρβαροι βάλλοντες, οἳ μὲν ἐξ ἐναντίης ἐπισπόμενοι καὶ τὸ ἔρυμα τοῦ τείχεος συγχώσαντες, οἳ δὲ περιελθόντες πάντοθεν περισταδόν.

When the Greeks realised that [Ephialtes and the Persians] were coming, they quickly changed the location of the battle: they went back to the narrowest part of the road, passed by the wall and retreated onto the hill, all of them thronged together except the Thebans. The hill is in the entry, where now the stone lion in honour of Leonidas stands. In this place they defended themselves with their swords, which they happened to still have, and with their hands and mouths. The Barbarians covered them in arrows, some facing them from the front after demolishing the defence of the wall, others by going around and standing around them on all sides.

Herodotus relates that the Greek dead were buried where they fell, i.e. inside or close to the hill (7.228).[442] Marinatos' identification of this kolonos with a hill opposite the modern Leonidas memorial has found widespread acceptance.[443] Marinatos hoped to find archaeological confirmation for the battle here: "Signs of the battle should appear, at least, the numerous arrowheads under which Persians «buried» the heroes."[444] He did find what he was looking for: a lance head, a sauroter, a lead lamp, many bronze artefacts including bells (which he believed belonged to armour) and, most importantly many bronze and iron arrowheads of, he claimed, oriental (Egyptian, Assyrian and Persian) type.[445] He concluded that "[t]here is thus no doubt possible [...] that we today can take in our hands the arrowheads under the blows of which the last survivors of Leonidas died."[446] The identification of the arrowheads as those fired by the Persians was commonly accepted at the time and they are still displayed as such in the National Archaeological Museum in Athens.[447]

---

442 Herodotus tells us about the special treatment (i.e. impaling) of Leonidas' head by the Persians (7.238; 9.78–79); this makes the *Histories* a more dramatic narrative in the light of an earlier account (6.58), which highlights the great social significance of royal burials at Sparta. See also Xenophon, *De republica Lacedaemoniorum* 15.9. Another quasi-prefiguration in the *Histories* is the Spartan quest for Orestes' bones (1.67–68). However, Herodotus does not give any indication of the place where the body was deposited; he may have assumed that it was lumped together with the others in the kolonos. Jung 2011b, 98 speculates that even in absence of the body, some ceremony must have been carried out for Leonidas at Sparta, perhaps with an eidolon. From Pausanias (3.14.1) we know that Leonidas' bones were indeed relocated to Sparta forty years 'later' (ὕστερον), which would give us a date of 440 BCE. Jung 2011b, 99 points out that this date should be taken approximately. If Herodotus had really seen the bones in Sparta, he would have made this explicit in his work. The relocation can therefore be assumed to postdate the *Histories*. According to Meier (2010, 108–109), this act of 're-appropriation' is understandable at this moment because testimonies of the Persian Wars were dying out, and a new way of remembering had to be invented.
443 Marinatos 1940, 337; 1951, 61–63; Meyer 1956; Hignett 1963, 131–132; Müller 1987, 383–384.
444 Marinatos 1951, 64.
445 Marinatos 1940, 337–339.
446 Marinatos 1951, 64.
447 Blegen 1939, 600–700; Meyer 1956, 103; Grant 1961; Albertz 2006, 87.

Fig. 33: The hill of the last stance of the Greeks with the modern epigram of Simonides.

We should, however, be cautious: the arrowheads found in the hill are not necessarily a direct testimony to an actual battle. As Michael Flower points out, they may also constitute a commemorative offering (for which there is a parallel at Marathon), or simply as an 'ingredient' of filling material.[448] As we have seen above (§2.5.1), criticism of the location of the kolonos itself was given by scholars who believed that Xerxes' army in the end did not pass through Thermopylae. Pritchett, however, in his monumental work *The liar school of Herodotus* in turn defended Marinatos' hill as the true site of the last stance.[449] More recently several scholars have pointed out that the 'kamikaze' version of the death of the Spartans (preserved by Diodorus Siculus 11.9.3-4 and 11.10 and attributed to Ephorus), according to which Leonidas would have performed a nightly assault on the Persian camp and died there, competed with the 'last stance' version and is perhaps more likely from a historical point

---

[448] Flower 1998, 378, mentioning that identical arrowheads have been found in a later (possibly Hellenistic) bastion in the filling material.
[449] Pritchett 1993, 303: "I know of no one who has questioned the Kolonos hill as the site of the final battle, with the exception of the Doris team."

of view.⁴⁵⁰ It has also been pointed out that the number of three hundred Spartans is a feature of other battles, too.⁴⁵¹

The scholarly debate about the kolonos has been framed within the question of the historical location of 'the last stance', but its historicity is probably beyond recovery. From Herodotus' account, we can only deduce that in his time the hill was regarded as such. The quest for a mnemotope of the last stance was relevant to those who were remembering the battle of Thermopylae in the post-war period: the location showcased the heroism of the Greeks vis-a-vis their eastern enemies, and highlighted the military prowess of Sparta, an idea with much relevance in the Peloponnessian wars, which developed at the time Herodotus was writing. Consistent with the idea that the hill was a mnemotope are the monumentalisation efforts, which included epitaphs and a lion sculpture (7.228). These show that the hill had by the late fifth century BCE developed into what we may call a tourist attraction.⁴⁵² It has even been suggested that these commemoration practises themselves gave rise to the designation of the hill as a mnemotope of the 'last stance'.⁴⁵³

Another observation consistent with the idea that the hill was a mnemotope is that archaeological investigation could not confirm the burial of the Spartans, which

---

450 Flower 1998, 366; 373 points out that it is not unlikely that Herodotus knew about the tradition of the nightly assault, but chose to omit it. Ray 2009, 80–81 argues that this version is more likely historical than the Anopaia version, because Xerxes was at the rear of the battlefield and therefore relatively close to Leonidas. However, Albertz 2006, 86–87 labels the kamikaze version as post-Herodotean because he believes it is not compatible with the archaeological find of the arrowheads in the kolonos.
451 Dillery 1996, 220 points out that this is the case in the battle of Thyrea between Argos and Sparta (perhaps in the mid-sixth century BCE; 1.82): in this conflict there also was only single survivor. He also remarks that Pausanias (10.1.5) mentions a war between three hundred Phocians and Thessalians. See also Albertz 2006, 45–46; Cartledge 2006, 129.
452 The epitaphs mentioned by Herodotus were still seen by Strabo (9.4.16), but he does not mention the lion. None of the objects have been retrieved. Marinatos 1940, 338–340 suggests that their loss may be due to a later building activity on the hill. More epigrams (possibly epitaphs) of the battle of Thermopylae were transmitted by Philiades (fragment 1) and Simonides (*FGE* 7, 13 and 83a-b). Interestingly, it was not the Spartans, but the local Greeks who were responsible for the on-site commemoration: Herodotus reveals that it was the Pylagorai, the representatives of the Amphiktyony members at Thermopylae, who had commissioned the grave stelai at Thermopylae, except the one for the seer Megistias, which would have been ordered by Simonides himself (7.228). That Thermopylae was something of a 'tourist site in Antiquity is hinted at by the descriptions of the area by Philostratus (*Vita Apollonii* 4.23) and Strabo (9.4.16).
453 Flower 1998, 377: "it is also possible that the placing of a lion on that hill in honour of Leonidas (Hdt. 7.225.2) and the burial of the dead there (Hdt. 7.228.1) gave rise to a post-Simonidean tradition that the Spartans had made their last stand there as well." Other authors who have expressed doubt about the historicity of the last stance include Hignett 1963, 371–378; Lendering 2011. On the mythicisation of the idea of the last stance in the fifth century BCE and through Herodotus' work, see Albertz 2006, 50–66. Because Thermopylae was not won by the Greeks, a trophy was not relevant here (Gauer 1968, 11). However, perhaps there was a Persian trophy, as Isocrates (*Philippus* 148) suggests; but this may be a rhetorical device, too (Jacquemin 2000, 64).

appears in Herodotus and in Simonides *PMG* fragment 26.[454] The hill seems to have been a cenotaph.[455] Apparently, the hill was so important that after the battle, it was also seen as the site of the burial. It has been suggested that the monuments bore no exact relation to the graves, and that they simply marked the general area as their location.[456] We will see a similar phenomenon at the battle of Plataea (§2.9.7). The purported 20,000 Persian dead have also vanished without a trace. Herodotus says that Xerxes hid most of them in order to make the number of casualties seem lower (8.24-8.25). In 1939 Marinatos dug a trench on the widest part of the plain, at a place where he supposed the Persians to have been buried. However, he did not find any pre-Byzantine material.[457] Thus, the Persian graves remain enigmatic. It has also been pointed out that this story probably functioned as a means of stereotyping Xerxes.[458]

From a mnemotopical perspective it is also relevant that Leonidas died at approximately the same location as his forefather Heracles.[459] Although the kolonos itself

---

454 This fragment comes from Diodorus Siculus (11.11.6). The tomb mentioned in line 6 ("ἀνδρῶν ἀγαθῶν ὅδε σηκός") could refer to a sacred enclosure in Sparta, or in Thermopylae itself. Bowra 1933 believes that the poem was used in a cult for Maron and Alpheios at a shrine in Sparta (mentioned by Pausanias in 3.12.9), two of the best fighters in the battle (Herodotus 7.227); the reasoning is that Leonidas seems to be a mere stander-by in the poem. Steiner 1999 believes that Simonides refers to an imaginary structure. The emphatic ἐν Θερμοπύλαις would not have been necessary, if the poem was really used at Thermopylae. The easiest solution is to associate this poem with the yearly Leonidaia festival mentioned by Pausanias (3.14.1), if this did not start as late as the Roman period, as is sometimes suggested.
455 The burials discovered in the kolonos dated only from Roman and Byzantine times: Marinatos 1940, 337, 340; 1951, 65–68; Flower 1998, 378. Marinatos asserted that the south-east bastion of the kolonos fortifications were used as a monument to Thermopylae in later times; but this is only based on the presence of lime plaster. Wade-Gery 1933, 72–73 suggested that the epigrams mentioned by Herodotus did not mark graves, as he thinks it is unlikely that the Greek dead could have been buried given that Xerxes possessed the area, but were commissioned later. Marinatos (1951, 68–69) believed that the remains of the dead were transported to Sparta. For the view that the epigraphs were part of inscriptions erected on tombs, see Clairmont 1983, 223–224.
456 Clairmont 1983, 114–115.
457 Marinatos 1951, 69. The episode is sometimes explained as historically authentic: e.g. Caspari 1911, 106–107 believes that "the fact that innumerable lighters were seen plying between the positions of the navy and the army can hardly be an invention", and connected this to a Persian strategy to victual the army.
458 Macan 1908, I 388 regarded this episode as a "comic Nemesis which Greek anecdote-mongers inflicted upon Xerxes"; Grethlein 2009, 213 argues that Xerxes is portrayed here as reshaping history, like Herodotus himself. At the same time the episode shows the Persian king as a megalomaniac ruler prone to deceiving even his own men with propaganda measures (Xerxes' night-time burial was considered a stratagem in Polyaenus' *Strategemata* 7.15). Furthermore, not giving the dead a proper funeral was considered blasphemous (Mikalson 2003, 31). Interestingly, in the tradition of the Celtic attack at Thermopylae in 279 BCE, the dead were initially also left unburied (Pausanias 10.21.6). This may be a reprisal of the same theme (despite the claim by Churchin 1995 that this was considered honourable in the Celtic tradition). On this episode see also Bowie 2007, 116; Asheri et al. 2010, 224.
459 Leonidas' Heraclean ancestry is made explicit by Herodotus in 7.204 and again mentioned in 7.208 (in passing) and 7.220 (in an oracle to the Spartans); see Vandiver 1991, 184–185; Meier 2010,

does not seem to have been associated with Heracles, there was, as we have seen, no shortage of nearby mnemotopes connected to the hero's death, such as the Dyras river, which had helped to extinguish the fire that endangered Heracles,[460] and the altar at the hot springs. It was believed that Athena had placed the sulphurous hot springs here for Heracles. The water had acquired its specific qualities because Heracles had poisoned them with his toxic tunic, which had caught fire. This story is already found in the sixth-century BCE poet Pisander of Camiros (*Heraclea* fragment 7).[461] The site of Heracles' death itself was Mount Oita immediately west of the pass.[462] The pass was also associated with a fight between the hero and the Thessalian brigand Cycnus, son of Ares. Diodorus Siculus (4.36.5-37.4) specifically mentions Trachis, and therefore the pass of Thermopylae, as the site of their confrontation. There also existed a tradition according to which the Heraclids had been given asylum by another mythical figure of the area, king Keyx of Trachis. The story was already known to Hecataeus of Miletus (*FGrH* 1 F30) and therefore antedates Herodotus and the Persian invasion.[463]

How can we explain the mnemotopical coincidence between Heraclean lore and that of his descendant Leonidas? As Albertz rightly points out: "Dieses Landschaftsbild wird [...] zu einer ‚heroischen' Landschaft, in die Taten aus mythischer Vorzeit bereits eingelagert sind."[464] But did this picture originate with Herodotus or his informants? The mythical stories about Heracles at Thermopylae all seem to antedate the *Histories* and the battle. This suggests that as early as the sixth century BCE a mythical topography of Heraclean lore existed in the pass, which by the time of Herodotus had been supplemented with that of the Persians. One line of reasoning is that the overlap was created by the Spartans themselves, as they would have been attracted to the location because of its mythical prehistory.[465] It has also been suggested that the overlap can be attributed to Herodotus' archaic conception of the world,[466] but it seems more

---

104. On Leonidas' descent from Heracles, see Vandiver 1991, 52–54, arguing that both Heracles and Leonidas figure as protectors of Greece.
460 The Dyras river is the modern Gorgopotamos (Kromayer 1924, 25). Macan 1908, I 298 suggested that this river may have been confused with the Tyras of Scythia (the modern Dniester in Moldova), where Herodotus reported a footprint of Heracles (4.82). Marinatos 1951, 50 localised Heracles' funeral pyre in the ravine of the Gorgopotamos. See also Strabo 9.4.14.
461 See also Strabo 9.4.13; Tzetzes, *Scholia in Lycophronem* 50–51.
462 Sophocles' *Trachiniae* (especially 684–704) and Seneca's *Hercules Oetaeus* are the most important literary testimonies of this myth. There is archaeological evidence of a sixth-century BCE cult here to the hero (Malkin 1994, 228 with literature). Pausanias related that Deaneira died in Trachis: her grave was near that of Heracles (Pausanias 2.23.5).
463 See also Pseudo-Apollodorus 2.7.6-7; 2.8.1; Diodorus Siculus 4.57.1.
464 Albertz 2006, 40.
465 Cartledge 2006, 126–127. The appearance of Heraclean mnemotopes is observed everywhere in the Greek world (Huttner 1997, 11–12).
466 Vandiver 1991, 187–188: "Here we see Herodotus' literary style at its most archaic, working within the framework of mythic allusions to counterpoint and enhance his historical narrative".

likely that he relied on stories about Leonidas which had arisen in the immediate postwar period, and fitted patterns already known in myth (on this process see §2.7.1 and §3.1.2). The two traditions reshaped each other in conjunction. The stories about Leonidas were most pertinent at Sparta, where the battle was commemorated.[467] But we also know that Spartans were interested in the area: we hear from Thucydides (3.92; 5.52) that the Spartans had colonised the area of Trachis to consolidate their allies in the area, the Dorians and Trachinians, and to make sure Spartans could extend its influence in Northern Greece. They renamed the town Herakleia Trachinia. The date of this event is unclear, but may certainly date to the fifth century BCE, i.e. from the time that the traditions which Herodotus tells us about, arose.[468]

Perhaps the story of the battle at Thermopylae arose in part to support the founding of Herakleia, which dates right from around the time of Herodotus' research. Although one could say that pre-Herodotean Simonides epigrams mention the battle, Herodotus was the first to present it as a sacrifice.[469] More importantly, the alleged testimonies of Simonides all date from later sources and may have been corrupted: Diodorus Siculus 11.11.16 (Simonides, *PMG* fragment 26), and Herodotus 7.228 (attributing only the Megistias poem to Simonides).

---

[467] See Gauer 1968, 102–103; Förtsch 2001, 48–49; 56–60; Low 2011, 1–13 (speaking of "Spartan disengagement from the physical site of the battle"). Pausanias saw a stele at Sparta with the names of the 300 Spartans (3.14.1). He also mentions a monument for Leonidas next to that of 'the other Pausanias', the Spartan commander at Plataea. Jung (2011b, 96) stresses the significance of this juxtaposition. Sparta also had a 'Persian stoa' which connected the agora to the acropolis (Pausanias 3.11.3). According to Vitruvius (1.1.6), this stoa was built after the battle of Plataea and featured Persian 'caryatids'. A statue was found here that has been identified with Leonidas.
[468] Malkin 1994, 219–235: "Herakleia Trachinia was already [...] 'French' before the 'French' arrived. Herakles was Trachinian, and Mt Oita was the scene of his cult long before any Spartan aspired to take it over. Thus the myth of Herakles could have articulated both the challenge of colonization and control over the natives and that of decolonization and autonomy." (quote on page 221). But the strategic location was perhaps the most important factor in Spartan involvement here: Thucydides states in the same passage that dockyards were built in the pass for easy protection (cf. Strabo 9.4.17). In addition, Herakleia was also to have a convenient base from which to send troops to Euboea and Thrace. While the Heracles saga is very old and even predates the Persian Wars, 426 BCE as the date of the founding of Herakleia is merely a guess in the scholarly tradition, and Spartan involvement in the area may be much older. Macan (1908, I 298) already suggested that the city was already founded by Herodotus' time, but that Herodotus simply forgot to mention it. If the harbour mentioned in Thucydides' story is identified with the bay to the west of the kolonos, it marked the exact place where the Greeks had put up their camps in 480 BCE. On the basis of about eighty coins, Marinatos 1940, 340 concluded that the kolonos was the site of this port; this was accepted by Müller 1987, 384; Stählin (1936, 2409) asserted that the harbour already existed in 480 BCE. See also Pasqual 2013b, 378.
[469] Moggi 2007, 16.

2.5.5 Summary

When Herodotus visited the pass of Thermopylae some fifty years after the events, he found himself in the position to reflect on an old battle between Persians and Greeks. We have seen that the topography present in his account is a reflection of local mnemotopes relevant to visitors in the later fifth century BCE. At Trachis, the Persian camp was imagined, and there may have been a hill where Xerxes' throne was believed to have once stood. The Ephialtes episode was imagined as a path through the mountains towering above the pass. In the pass itself, the starting and ending point of the path were indicated as the Asopos gorge and the Melampygos rock. A small hill became the place where Leonidas and the three hundred Spartans had fought their last stance, and were subsequently buried.

Why does it matter that we can interpret Herodotus' topography of the battle as such? Rather than offering an answer to the question around which landmarks the battle 'happened', it brings us closer to the beliefs of later Greek visitors to the pass. In their minds, the Persians could not have won but by treachery, and the Spartans could not have lost but by a heroic last stance. They topographically connected the death of Leonidas with that of his mythical forefather Heracles. Whether such beliefs were grounded in a historical truth is irrelevant to this conclusion: as the real battle of Thermopylae slips away into the mists of time, its mnemotopes continue to tell its famous story to anyone who passes by.

2.6 The march through Phocis

When Xerxes had defeated the Greeks at Thermopylae, the road to southern Greece was open.[470] The first land on the way was Phocis, where the memory of the Persian invasion was shaped by terror: Herodotus tells us that the army destroyed everything in its path. The most notable target was Delphi, which was the only place that escaped Persian violence.

In this chapter, the topography of Phocis concerning Xerxes' invasion as transmitted to us by Herodotus will be discussed. I will argue that particular places within this topography can successfully be explained as mnemotopes which, rather than offering a window onto the events of 480 BCE, are a reflection of the post-war period in which (folk) memory had attached stories to prominent landmarks.

---

[470] A selection of places mentioned in this chapter features on Map 4.

2.6.1 The destruction of Phocis; Abai

Following the battle of Thermopylae, the Persians entered Phocis. Their destructive path is detailed in 8.32-33:

ὡς δὲ ἐκ τῆς Δωρίδος ἐς τὴν Φωκίδα ἐσέβαλον, αὐτοὺς μὲν τοὺς Φωκέας οὐκ αἱρέουσι. οἱ μὲν γὰρ τῶν Φωκέων ἐς τὰ ἄκρα τοῦ Παρνησοῦ ἀνέβησαν (ἔστι δὲ καὶ ἐπιτηδέη δέξασθαι ὅμιλον τοῦ Παρνησοῦ ἡ κορυφή κατὰ Νέωνα πόλιν κειμένη ἐπ' ἑωυτῆς, Τιθορέα οὔνομα αὐτῇ: ἐς τὴν δὴ ἀνηνείκαντο καὶ αὐτοὶ ἀνέβησαν): οἱ δὲ πλεῦνες αὐτῶν ἐς τοὺς Ὀζόλας Λοκροὺς ἐξεκομίσαντο, ἐς Ἄμφισσαν πόλιν τὴν ὑπὲρ τοῦ Κρισαίου πεδίου οἰκημένην. οἱ δὲ βάρβαροι τὴν χώρην πᾶσαν ἐπέδραμον τὴν Φωκίδα: Θεσσαλοί γὰρ οὕτω ἦγον τὸν στρατόν: ὁκόσα δὲ ἐπέσχον, πάντα ἐπέφλεγον καὶ ἔκειρον, καὶ ἐς τὰς πόλις ἐνιέντες πῦρ καὶ ἐς τὰ ἱρά. πορευόμενοι γὰρ ταύτῃ παρὰ τὸν Κηφισὸν ποταμὸν ἐδηίουν πάντα, καὶ κατὰ μὲν ἔκαυσαν Δρυμὸν πόλιν κατὰ δὲ Χαράδραν καὶ Ἔρωχον καὶ Τεθρώνιον καὶ Ἀμφίκαιαν καὶ Νέωνα καὶ Πεδιέας καὶ Τριτέας καὶ Ἐλάτειαν καὶ Ὑάμπολιν καὶ Παραποταμίους καὶ Ἄβας, ἔνθα ἦν ἱρὸν Ἀπόλλωνος πλούσιον, θησαυροῖς τε καὶ ἀναθήμασι πολλοῖσι κατεσκευασμένον: ἦν δὲ καὶ τότε καὶ νῦν ἔτι χρηστήριον αὐτόθι: καὶ τοῦτο τὸ ἱρὸν συλήσαντες ἐνέπρησαν. καί τινας διώκοντες εἷλον τῶν Φωκέων πρὸς τοῖσι ὄρεσι, καὶ γυναῖκας τινὰς διέφθειραν μισγόμενοι ὑπὸ πλήθεος.

When they rushed into Phocis from Doris, they did not take the Phocians themselves, as some of the Phocians went up to the tops of Mount Parnassos (the peak of Parnassos at the city of Neon, which lies on it, is sufficiently large to accommodate a large group of people. It is called Tithorea; they brought their stuff to this peak, and went up themselves). Most of them arrived at the Ozolian Locrians, at the city of Amphissa which lies over the Krisaian field. The barbarians overran the entire field of Phocis, as the Thessalians led the army that way. They put fire to and destroyed whatever they acquired, and they set fire to the cities and the temples. Marching that way along the river Kephisos, they ravaged everything, and they burnt down the cities of Drymos, Charadra, Erochos, Tethronion, Amphikaia, Neon, Pedieai, Triteai, Elateia, Hyampolis, Parapotamioi and Abai, where there was a rich temple of Apollo with many treasures and votive offerings. There was both then and still now is an oracle there. They also plundered and set fire to this temple. And they chased and caught some Phocians near the mountains, and they killed some women after gang raping them.

Subsequently Herodotus explains that Xerxes reorganised and divided his army in a place called Panopeai, with a small part being diverted to Delphi (8.34; see §2.6.3). He then recounts that Panopeai, Daulis and Aiolidai were also ravaged by the second contingent (8.35).

It has usually been assumed that historical events underlie Herodotus' assertions,[471] and Margaret Miles calls the list of towns a "geographical roll call of those places that resisted".[472] However, we know that destruction can often be exaggerated or completely invented (see §3.2.1). In the case of Phocis, we possess only faint

---

[471] I have not encountered doubts about the historicity other than the studies cited below. Explicit belief in the historicity is found in Boyce 1982, 169.
[472] Miles 2014, 118.

Fig. 34: Remains of Drymos, a Phocian city destroyed by Xerxes' army.

archaeological evidence that the towns mentioned in this passage were destroyed.[473] Most of them are little more than names to us. Their identifications are not always certain, and archaeological exploration of these sites is minimal.[474] The extent of real

---

473 Munro 1902, 319–320; Ferrari 2002, 26–27, note 95.
474 Drymos was located on a spur of the Kallidromos, 1.5 kilometres southwest of modern Drymea (Müller 1987, 485; McInerney 1999, 272); Charadra has been identified with the Paleokastro of Mariolata (Müller 1987, 460; McInerney 1999, 265–266); Erochos was southwest of Polydrosos, with inscriptional evidence (Müller 1987, 489–490; McInerney 1999, 269–270); Tethronion was five kilometres south of modern Tithronio (Müller 1987, 582–583; McInerney 1999, 273–274); Amphikaia was at the cemetery of modern Amfiklia (Müller 1987, 452–453; McInerney 1999, 275–277); Neon was probably at modern Tithorea (Müller 1987, 527–528; McInerney 1999, 278–280); Pedieai was perhaps on the Kephisos, three kilometres northwest of Kato Tithorea (Müller 1987, 541; McInerney 1999, 282); Triteai is probably to be identified with the Paleokastro of Modi (Müller 1987, 591; McInerney 1999, 282–283); Elateia was four kilometres north of modern Elatia (Müller 1987, 486; McInerney 1999, 287); Hyampolis was 3.5 kilometres west of Exarchos, guarding a mountain pass which was probably the pass described by Herodotus (Müller 1987, 495–497); Hyampolis (also known as Hya, cf. Diodorus Siculus 16.56.1, Strabo 9.2.42; 9.3.15) was situated near modern Kalapodi (Yorke 1896, 303–304; Ellinger 1993, 24; McInerney 1999, 290–292). Parapotamioi was on a hill on the Kephisos river, west of Anthochori

destruction underlying Herodotus' account remains therefore uncertain. The main exception is the relatively strong archaeological evidence for destruction at the site of Kalapodi, believed by some to be the site of Abai (cf. below). However, historicity aside, we know that by Herodotus' time, the above list of Phocian towns was regarded as having been destroyed. I would like to propose various ways that may have contributed to this idea.

The first way in which the topic may be approached is that Phocis, and the Phocians, may have been stereotyped by other Greeks. Although Herodotus records more stories about Persian destruction as part of Xerxes' invasion (see particularly §2.7.3; §2.7.5; §2.10.4; §3.2.1), it is notable that only Phocis, and not Attica (except for Athens and Eleusis) or Boeotia suffered this fate. It has been suggested that the story of the Persian destruction of Phocis originated with the Phocians themselves to repair their damaged name in the rest of Greece for their alleged medism (similar to what happened in Delphi, see §2.6.3).[475] However, there is no evidence that Phocis medised.

Instead, the stories about Phocis are more successfully explained from an outsider's perspective. McInerney notes that in these traditions, the Phocians appear as a single people, even though in reality, the region was quite fragmented.[476] Although he suggests that Thessalian hegemony in the region may have required the people of Phocis to unify, I would like to point out that the fact that the Phocians appear in the sources as one people might also suggest that these stories reflect the ideas of outsiders.

Why would anyone have singled out Phocis as victimised in the first place? Whatever its historic worth, a tradition of Persian destruction which was so strongly focused on Phocis should be understood within the lore about Phocis that went around simultaneously. There did, in fact, exist a strong tradition in Greece according to which Phocis, like an ancient Belgium or Poland, was seen as prone to being invaded. The Phocians in particular appear in perpetual enmity with their northern neighbours, the Thessalians.[477] They tried to win their battles by using stratagems. During the battle of the white chalk (8.27-28) four thousand Thessalians were massacred at the hands of

---

(Müller 1987, 534–536; McInerney 1999, 293–294); Pausanias did not see any ruins here, 10.33.8. Panopeai was on the hill south of Agios Vlasios (Müller 1987, 531–532; McInerney 1999, 295–296); it is probably the same place known to Thucydides (4.76) as Phanotis and to Stephanus Byzantinus (*Ethnica* s.v.) as Phanoteus (Pausanias in 10.4.1 does curiously have it as Panopeus, describing it as unworthy of the name 'city'); it was a natural road junction where those coming from Athens and Delphi could meet (Pausanias 10.4.2-3). Daulis was situated on a hill 800 meters south of modern Davlia (Müller 1987, 461; McInerney 1999, 297–299). Aiolidai was possibly east of Arachova (Macan 1908, I 407; Müller 1987, 449; McInerney 1999, 303–306). For Abai, see below.
475 E.g. Hauvette 1894, 383–384; Munro 1902, 314.
476 McInerney 1999, 176–177.
477 Ellinger 1993, 13–17 speaks of the Phocis vs. Thessaly conflict as the national Phocian legend.

six hundred white-chalked Phocians.[478] In another battle, the Phocians broke the legs of Thessalian horses by burying pots at Hyampolis (8.28; Pausanias 10.1.3-6).[479] Pausanias (10.1.6-7) while describing an incident of mass suicide of the Phocians during, again, a war with Thessaly, points out that the Greeks gave the name 'Phocian despair' to such ruthless behaviour.[480] There also existed Phocian mnemotopes elsewhere, such as the wall at Thermopylae (§2.5.2) and the cave of Tithorea (§2.6.2).

In accordance with the view that the Phocians were 'usual victims' of enemies from the north, a possible source for the story about the Persian destruction is pre-existing lore about the wars with the Thessalians (who, perhaps not coincidentally, formed an important part of the Persian army), as has been pointed out by several scholars.[481] Herodotus' account may reflect a confusion of Thessalian attacks with Xerxes' invasion, or the projection of this stereotype onto the Persians and a 'gazetteer' list of towns. Perhaps not coincidentally, Herodotus' list of cities is nearly identical to the list of cities destroyed in the Sacred (Phocian) War of 348 BCE according to Pausanias (10.3.1-2).

Among the Phocian towns mentioned, the case of Abai is especially problematic.[482] If other stories in Herodotus are to be believed, the oracle of Apollo at Abai was not destroyed, but remained functioning during the Persian Wars because it was consulted by Xerxes' general Mardonios (8.27; 8.134).[483] Pausanias' account shows that it was believed in his time that the oracle was not completely destroyed: he says the Phocians used it as a refuge and oracle during the Sacred War (347 BCE; 4.32.5), and

---

478 Ellinger 1993, 35 locates the site of this legendary battle in the pass of Hyampolis. For a (perhaps too far ranging) contextualisation of the gypsum in this legend, see Ellinger 1993, 47–195. See also McInerney 1999, 175–176.
479 Ellinger 1993, 35; 204–222 locates the site of that legendary battle in the pass of Hyampolis. He describes the event as a Phocian stratagem and compares it to the episodes of the blocking of Anopaia during the Persian and Celtic invasions, and with the episode of the Phocian wall at Thermopylae. See also McInerney 1999, 175–176.
480 Ellinger 1993, 35 locates this battle on the plain of Kalapodi. For the theme of the Phocian despair see Ellinger 1993, 233–246; 269–310. He compares the story of the Phocian despair with various similar stories, both outside the *Histories* and inside it, including the Persian siege of Xanthos (1.176) and the story about Boges of Eïon (7.107).
481 For the idea that the Thessalians were the culprits of the destruction, see Wecklein 1867, 260–261; 267–268; McInerney 1999, 50; 336–337. The confusion of enemies in memory about a battle is also seen in the battle of Roncesvalles (778 CE), which was fought between Charlemagne and Basque brigands, who were in later tellings of the battle substituted by Saracens (muslims); cf. Brall-Tuchel 2003, 36–37.
482 The temple of Abai has been identified with a hill west of Exarchos, northwest of the polis site; there is evidence of later reconstruction: Yorke 1896, 294–302; Müller 1987, 446–449; but see Ellinger 1993, 25 for the view that that site was too small for the famous oracle; instead, he proposed that the oracle was within the walls of Abai itself. Later excavations suggest that the oracle may perhaps be identified with the big temple near Kalapodi, although this may also be a temple of Artemis Elaphebolos: Felsch, Kienast & Schuler 1980; Felsch et al. 1987; Ellinger 1993, 25–37 (argueing that this is a temple of Artemis); Felsch 1996; McInerney 1999, 288–289 with further literature; Felsch 2007.
483 Munro 1902, 319.

Fig. 35: The site of Kalapodi, believed by some to be the oracle of Abai.

that it was only destroyed by the Thebans, after which it remained standing as a monumental ruin (10.35.3).[484] He even claims to have seen ancient statues here (8.27.5).[485] Some scholars have noted the inconsistency, and have tried to explain Herodotus' assertion that the temple was destroyed.[486]

Perserschutt and traces of burning in the clay and in some architectural elements, including even melted roof tiles, show that the archaic temple at Kalapodi, the most likely candidate for the temple of Apollo (and if not, an important temple of Hyampolis), may have been destroyed by fire in the early fifth century BCE.[487] The excavators showed that immediately after the fire, there was a makeshift cult place while construction of the new temple was ongoing (which could explain the continued

---

[484] Ferrari 2002, 26–27, note 95.
[485] Hignett 1963, 197 suggested that the statues may have been replicas.
[486] Macan 1908, I 404 suggested that the devastation actually happened only much later after the battle of Plataea. Hauvette (1894, 382–383) and Hignett (1963, 197) pointed out that the account of the consultation of the oracle by Mardonios does not refute the historicity of the devastation, because the oracle might simply have been rebuilt.
[487] Felsch, Kienast & Schuler 1980, 84–85; Felsch et al. 1987, 24; Ellinger 2003, 29; Miles 2014, 124.

consultation of the oracle as reported by Herodotus) and that for that new temple, architectural elements of the destroyed temple were reused.[488] As at the Athenian Acropolis (see §2.7.3 and §2.7.4) conspicuous traces of destruction may have fuelled memories about the invasion later in the fifth century BCE.

As strong as the archaeological case may be, the site's uncertain identification with the oracle of Abai does not allow us to ascertain that the oracle, and not another site was destroyed.[489] At the same time, the story certainly existed in the later fifth century BCE, and we may ask why it was told. Part of the answer may be that Herodotus recounts his version of the Persian siege of Delphi immediately afterwards (see §2.6.3). As with the temples of Demeter at Eleusis (§2.7.5) and Plataea (§2.9.6), it seems that Herodotus tries to say, albeit implicitly, that the Persian hubris at Abai has a direct consequence in Delphi: the failure of the Persian expedition to plunder the oracle. Note that a reverse instance of divine vengeance is apparent in Diodorus Siculus' account of the destruction of the temple of Apollo at Abai (16.58.4): here, the temple is burnt down with Phocians, who had just robbed the temple of Apollo at Delphi, inside.

2.6.2 Tithorea

Apart from the destroyed cities, in the passage quoted above Herodotus singles out the location to which the Phocians fled: the mountain Tithorea. Ulrichs identified Tithorea with the remains at the village formerly known as Velitsa (and now as Tithorea), basing himself on inscriptions.[490] He placed Herodotus' Neon at the ruins called Palea Thiva in his time.[491] By contrast, others identified Neon with Velitsa because Pausanias (10.32.8) remarked that the Neon of his time was Herodotus' Tithorea. But Herodotus' Tithorea is a mountain (as its name 'Breast Mountain' suggests), so there is little room for confusion: the name originally applied to the mountain, and was later transferred to the village called Neon.[492]

---

488 Felsch, Kienast & Schuler 1980, 85–99; Felsch et al. 1987, 25.
489 Scheer 2000, 211 (pointing out that there is no evidence that this temple had been destroyed by the Persians); Hartmann 2010, 182. The view that the destruction was historical is also still found, e.g. Kousser 2009, 269.
490 Ulrichs 1843, 544.
491 Ulrichs 1843, 548–549.
492 On this issue see McInerney 1999, 278–280. Stephanus Byzantinus (*Ethnica* s.v. Τιθοραία) says that it was on top of the Parnassos, and that Zethos and Amphion were buried here. Leake (1835, II 79) identified Tithorea with the great summit of Parnassos above Velitsa, and not the peak near Velitsa itself, believing that that peak was too small to host the entire group of Phocians who took refuge here. Pausanias derived the name of the mountain from a nymph Tithorea, and said that there was a theatre, agora and temple of Athena (10.32.8).

Fig. 36: Mavri Troupa, the 'Cave of Odysseas Androutsos' near Tithorea.

As Tithorea is essentially a sheer cliff, one wonders how the Phocians made their way up the Parnassos as Herodotus says and many scholars believe.[493] While the historicity is not our concern, it possible to see Tithorea as a mnemotope onto which such stories could be projected. Like the Korykian cave at Delphi (see §2.6.4), Tithorea appears elsewhere, too, as a 'usual hiding place': the Phocian leader Philemelos fled here during the Third Sacred War (Diodorus Siculus 16.31.3-5); Plutarch (*Sulla* 15) says that the Phocians retreated to Tithorea, and that Hortensius camped here during the Mithradaic war, as a strong fortress surrounded by cliffs.

Within the rockface there is a large cave, today called Mavri Troupa, 'black hole', clearly visible from afar. It is currently believed that the cave was the hiding place of Odysseas Androutsos, a hero of the Greek war of independence, whence the alternative name Σπηλιά του Οδυσσέα, 'Cave of Odysseus', and there also exists a story that around this time, Edward John Trelawny, a friend of Lord Byron, lived in the cave.[494]

---

493 For photographs, see Papachatzi 1981, 4419–422; Hignett 1963, 197; Müller 1987, 540.
494 McInerney 1999, 46–47.

It has also been suggested that both Hortensius' and the Phocian retreat took place here.⁴⁹⁵ The Mavri Troupa was a convenient mnemotope for such stories, and it may be the origin for Herodotus' story about the retreat of the Phocians.

2.6.3 The sanctuary of Athena Pronaia at Delphi⁴⁹⁶

The oracle of Delphi, a major repository of Persian War monuments,⁴⁹⁷ played a special role in Herodotus' reconstruction of the Persian Wars. He visited the sanctuary himself,⁴⁹⁸ and he probably sourced the oracles concerning the Persian Wars here. This was also the place where he heard a story according to which Delphi had been the scene of an event during Xerxes' invasion. During that invasion, Delphi itself had been besieged by Persian troops. But the siege was not successful. Herodotus tells us that Apollo and two local heroes miraculously appeared to defend the sanctuary (8.38). He next describes the place where this happened (8.39):

> τούτους δὲ τοὺς δύο Δελφοὶ λέγουσι εἶναι ἐπιχωρίους ἥρωας, Φύλακόν τε καὶ Αὐτόνοον, τῶν τὰ τεμένεα ἐστὶ περὶ τὸ ἱρόν, Φυλάκου μὲν παρ' αὐτὴν τὴν ὁδὸν κατύπερθε τοῦ ἱροῦ τῆς Προνηίης, Αὐτονόου δὲ πέλας τῆς Κασταλίης ὑπὸ τῇ Ὑαμπείῃ κορυφῇ. οἱ δὲ πεσόντες ἀπὸ τοῦ Παρνησοῦ λίθοι ἔτι καὶ ἐς ἡμέας ἦσαν σόοι, ἐν τῷ τεμένεϊ τῆς Προναίης Ἀθηναίης κείμενοι, ἐς τὸ ἐνέσκηψαν διὰ τῶν βαρβάρων φερόμενοι. τούτων μέν νυν τῶν ἀνδρῶν αὕτη ἀπὸ τοῦ ἱροῦ ἀπαλλαγή γίνεται.

> The Delphians say that these two [who appeared to be fighting the Persians] are local heroes, Phylakos and Autonoös. Their sanctuaries are near the temple, that of Phylakos by the road itself, above the temple of Pronaia, and that of Autonoös close to the Kastalian spring, under the mountain Hyampeia. The rocks which fell from the Parnassos were still preserved in my day, lying in the temenos of Athena Pronaia, into which they fell after dashing through the barbarians. These men then withdrew from the sanctuary.

---

495 Ulrichs 1843, 547–548. Caves were often and interpreted as prisons or refuges (Boardman 2002, 104–106; Zwingmann 2012, 311–313 with many examples in Asia Minor).
496 This subchapter was the basis for an article in *Distant Worlds Journal* (van Rookhuijzen 2017b). The present text (deviating from the text in the article on various points) has been included with kind permission from the editors.
497 E.g. the Serpent Column, the Athenian Treasury and the Stoa of the Athenians; this structure may have been specifically built to house artefacts from Persian Wars (Maass 2010, 72; see however Walsh 1986 for the view that the building was associated with the Peloponnesian Wars). Herodotus' account of the war is also influenced by stories told at Delphi that revolved around such objects (Boedeker 2007, 66).
498 Herodotus is likely to have heard this story during one or more personal visits (Jacoby 1913, 250; Myres 1953, 4; Waters 1985, 80; 106–108) during which he heard various stories from the Delphians themselves, as evidenced by his repeated use of the phrase οἱ Δελφοί λέγουσι 'the Delphians say'. Throughout the *Histories*, Herodotus displays a good knowledge of Delphi and its monuments. Cf. Jacoby 1913, 478; Elayi 1978 and 1979; Flower 2013.

Uniquely among episodes of the Persian Wars, most scholars believe that the siege, which is also recounted by Ctesias,[499] was not historical, but an invented tradition.[500] Why is that the case? It has been felt that Herodotus tries to 'apologise' the Delphians for their alleged role during the Persian wars, as many people believe, on the basis of various oracles found in Herodotus, that Delphi had chosen the side of the Persians. According to these scholars, Herodotus' work may have served to restore the reputation of the oracle. They say that the story was "la plus magnifique apologie d'Apollon Pythien".[501] However, it should be noted that there is no good evidence for this alleged medism, because the oracular texts in Herodotus are not explicitly pro-Persian. In addition, the reputation of Delphi was never damaged. It seems that the idea of Delphi's medism is a modern scholarly myth. This insight has come to the fore in most recent research on this topic.[502]

Another reason why scholars have seen the story as an invented tradition, is the claim that it was policy of the Achaemenid kings to respect foreign sanctuaries, as appears in other instances in the *Histories* (see §3.2.3). This argument is, however, part of longstanding and unresolved discussion; nevertheless, it seems significant that all examples of Persian piety in Greece come from Herodotus and have a clear narrative function; they become even less likely if we remember Xerxes' own maxim, set in stone in the much-discussed and problematic Daiva inscription from Persepolis (XPh): "The pagan gods may not be worshipped!" We can then ask ourselves how the story arose. It is my surmise that the story stems from traditions which circulated around local landmarks, or mnemotopes, in Delphi in the years after 480 BCE. Herodotus himself heard these from a local guide, possibly a priest.[503] I would like to propose that certain places of the topography can be explained a such. Herodotus' account thus does not

---

499 Ctesias (in Photius, *Bibliotheca* 72.39b) relates that Mardonios was sent to plunder the temple of Apollo, but died in a hailstorm; he also preserves a tradition (72.40a) according to which Delphi was plundered by the eunuch Matakas, but only after the war.
500 Notable exceptions are Hauvette 1894, 384–389; Munro 1902, 320, who had the opinion that the story could not be a complete invention and that the Phocians had come to protect the shrine against other plunderers; he even suggested that the Persians were attacked by religious zealots.
501 Casson 1914, 145–146; Hignett 1963, 445–446; Elayi 1978; 1979 (especially 116–151; quote on page 126); Scheer 2000, 206–207; Asheri et al. 2010, 235–236; Hartmann 2010, 541. Defradas 1954 has treated Delphi's attempts at propaganda at book-length.
502 The idea that Delphi medised is a popular misconception based on the oracles 'recorded' in 7.140, 7.148 and 7.169, which hardly suggest anything (cf. Maurizio 1997 who suggests that all oracles had been reshaped in the years between 480 BCE and Herodotus' research). A strong argument against the medism is that there is a complete lack of evidence for the idea that the reputation of Delphi had been damaged after the war: Price 1985, 152–153; Green 1996, 67; Scott 2014, 81, note 30.
503 The idea that Herodotus encountered this story as a temple legend is found in e.g. Wecklein 1867, 265; Hauvette 1894, 384–385; Fairbanks 1906, 42; Macan 1908, II 234–235; Munro 1926a, 301; Meyer 1954, 362; Pohlenz 1961, 97; Hignett 1963, 196, 445–446; Walser 1984, 51; von Haehling 1993, 96, especially note 66; Green 1996, 165; Rosenberger 2003, 66; Rösler 2013.

tell us much about what happened in 480 BCE, but rather about what was in folklore believed to have happened in the sacred landscape of Delphi.

Herodotus refers primarily to the smaller sanctuary of Athena Pronaia, rather than to the main sanctuary of Apollo. The small hero shrines of Phylakos and Autonoös are certainly not to be equated, as on modern tourist maps, with the two small (reportedly sixth-century BCE) structures on the eastern terrace of the sanctuary of Athena Pronaia.[504] This location does not match Herodotus' directions. Instead, Autonoös' shrine is described as being close to the Kastalian spring, i.e. further up the road to the sanctuary of Apollo. Architectural remains here have been associated with this temple,[505] but the identification remains uncertain.

Herodotus describes the shrine of Phylakos as by the road, above (κατύπερθε, presumably further towards the temple of Apollo) the temple of Athena Pronaia. Some scholars have identified it with one of the treasury-like buildings in the northeast part of the temenos.[506] The hero is probably mentioned as Φυλακ[...] in a third-century BCE funerary or dedicatory inscription (*BCH* 83 (1959) 472,6) which was reportedly found in Delphi's east necropolis, not far from the temenos of Athena Pronaia. One idea was that the shrine was immediately northwest of the Athena Pronaia terrain.[507] Another possibility is that Phylakos is to be associated with the so-called *bothros*, a circular structure of small stones (4 meter in diameter), north of the famous tholos inside the sacred precinct, and antedating both the tholos and the temple of Athena.[508] It is likely that the tholos, which was a famous structure in Antiquity (a lost treatise was written about it by Theodoros of Phocaea, cf. Vitruvius, 7.praef.12), was meant to replace this circular structure.

---

504 This identification was originally proposed by Homolle 1904. Robert 1909, 281 accepted this identification because it would be the only possible explanation for Herodotus' remark that the shrine was πρὸς τῷ ἱερῷ τῆς Προναίας. See also Karo 1910, 220–221, who stresses that Herodotus' description necessitates a location outside the temenos, but allows that the two structures were not part of the temenos. He also suggests that their status as the most eastern edifices at Delphi would fit a hero whose function is to protect the temple, much like Athena Pronaia herself. See also Keramopoullos 1935, 92–93; Bommelaer 1991, 52. Poulsen 1908, 369–370 said that these structures do not look like heroons or even treasuries, and Demangel 1926a, 74 argued that "rien n'autorise à attribuer à ces petits bâtiments un autre rôle que celui des diverses constructions — trésors ou bases d'ex-voto." For an architectural description of these edifices see Demangel 1926a, 74–77.
505 Papachatzi 1981, 306; this may be the 'temenos wall' seen by Bursian (1862, 172).
506 Bousquet 1963, 191–192; Daux 1959, 472 pointed out that the inscription, which is a list of names, is not specific enough to prove that it concerns the hero Phylakos. On the meaning of κατύπερθε see Widdra 1963, 39; Settis 1967–1968, 365–366.
507 Frickenhaus 1910, 244–245 note 2.
508 Poulsen 1908, 362; 372–376; Demangel 1926a, 101–107; Karo 1910, 218–220 interprets these remains as the base of an undefined monument, while he suggests that the bothros was made by later treasure hunters.

Fig. 37: The tholos in the sanctuary of Athena Pronaia.

Although there are many competing theories about the function of the tholos,[509] there are several good arguments for identifying it with the shrine of Phylakos.[510] First, it fits the description of the area by Pausanias: before describing the gymnasium (whose location is secured further west), he mentions the temenos of Phylakos as

---

[509] For an overview of interpretations of the tholos, see Kyriakidis 2010. The association with Athena (Charbonneaux 1925, 30–31) is nothing more than a guess that seems not to work well with the fact that there was already a temple of Athena, but see Hoepfner 2000, 107 for the suggestion that the tholos was an annex of the actual temple for special cult statues. See Pomtow 1912 for the speculative hypothesis that the tholos was a prytaneion (contra Charbonneaux 1925, 28–29). Robert 1939, 410–422 hypothesised that the building served a chthonic cult, but thought it had to do with a feminine (pre-Athena) cult because he believed that the topographical indications of Pausanias and Herodotus did not allow for the identification with Phylakos. Bousquet 1960 identified the tholos with a temple of Artemis, which he presumed to have been present in the area because of the legend of the white maidens who had protected the shrine during the purported Celtic attack of 279 BCE described by Diodorus Siculus (22.9.5).
[510] Proponents of the view that the tholos is the shrine of Phylakos include Graef 1902; Demangel 1926a, 106–107; Widdra 1963, 41 (see his note 29 for more literature); Settis 1967–1968 (with rich literature at 355–363). Charbonneaux 1925, 28 unconvincingly argued that the identification with the shrine of Phylakos is difficult because of the structure's rich decoration, late date and southern orientation.

situated close to the temple of Athena.[511] Second, the temenos of Athena Pronaia in its classical form seems to have been divided into two parts by a wall, an observation that matches the use of the term temenos by both Herodotus and Pausanias, and Pausanias' identification of only two of the temples he saw in this area with a particular deity: those of Athena and Phylakos, which suggests that these were the most significant.[512] Third, the identification with Phylakos fits the notion that the architectural form of the tholos should be connected to hero worship, because similar structures seem to have had this function at Epidaurus (Asklepios?) and Olympia (Philip's family);[513] rather suggestively, at Pella there was even a tholos dedicated to Heracles Phylakos.[514] Fourth, the theme of the tholos' sculptural programme, which consists of an Amazonomachy and a Centauromachy,[515] is elsewhere (such as at the Parthenon and the Stoa Poikile) believed to have been associated with the Persian Wars,[516] and

---

511 Pausanias mentions four temples (ναοί) in this area (10.8.6–7): the first was in ruins, the second did not have any statues, the third had statues of Roman emperors, and the fourth was the temple of Athena. The identification of these temples is not certain, because at least five structures have been excavated: from east to west the big poros temple, two treasuries, the tholos, and the limestone temple. Scholars differ in their views on which of the extant structure was not mentioned by Pausanias. For the idea that the unmentioned structure was the tholos see Robert 1909, 277–286; Daux 1936, 61; 66–67; Widdra 1963, 40; Settis 1967–1968, 362. Pausanias' term ναός would have been reserved for rectangular buildings, including treasuries; Daux suggested that Pausanias did not refer to the tholos at all as he was preoccupied with the temple of Apollo. He believed (page 68–70) that the tholos could not be the shrine of Phylakos because it was inside the temenos of Athena, and that it should instead be sought in the unexcavated area between the Marmaria and the gymnasion (this is approximating what Frickenhaus 1910, 244–245 note 2 had already suggested). Widdra 1963, 40, however, convincingly argued that Pausanias simply saved the description of the tholos until after his discussion of the four ναοί. This also fits his remark that the shrine of Phylakos was πρὸς δὲ τῷ ἱερῷ τῆς Προνοίας, 'hard by the temple of Pronoia'. Fingarette 1970 and Le Roy 1977, however, assumed that the first ('Doric') treasury was not mentioned; accordingly, the temple with the statues of Roman emperors may have been the tholos. It is usually assumed that Pausanias' ruined temple is the old (poros) temple of Athena; what he calls the temple of Athena is probably the newer temple of Athena (the west-most temple of the precinct), as it cannot be the tholos because Pausanias mentions a pronaos; see also Widdra 1963, 39–40; Papachatzi 1981, 299–305. The suggestion by Maass (1993, 221) that only the big poros temple may have been Pausanias' temple of Athena because it is close to the big altar is not convincing. The likely scenario is that the old poros temple was the temple of Athena Pronaia in Herodotus' time; after this temple collapsed, a new one was constructed to the west (Poulsen 1908, 371–373; Widdra 1963, 40). For the structures between the old poros temple and the tholos, see Poulsen 1908, 378–388.
512 Settis 1967–1968, 368–370. Le Roy 1977, 251, however, explains the wall as a supporting wall.
513 Poulsen 1908, 376–377. See Robert 1939 for a book-length study on tholoi; he thought these buildings were generally conceived as buildings for chthonic cults.
514 Hadzisteliou Price 1973.
515 For photographs and a discussion of the sculptures, see École française d'Athènes 1991, 66–76; Maass 1993, 225–226.
516 For a concise discussion of the meaning(s) of the Centauromachy and Amazonomachy, see duBois 1982, 49–77.

would be a fitting iconography to the alleged Persian siege that took place on this spot. In conclusion, if the tholos is not part of the temenos of Phylakos, we are confronted with the situation that there are two authorities (Herodotus and Pausanias) who mention his shrine in relation to the temple of Athena Pronaia, while at the same time, a remarkable building survives whose function cannot be identified.[517]

Poulsen specified that the building with a vestibule and two rooms, at the west side of the sanctuary, and partly underneath the new temple of Athena, was the original hero-shrine of Phylakos. The bothros underneath the tholos would be the tomb of the hero; the tholos, replacing the bothros, would then be a thank offering for Phylakos' assistance during the Persian invasion.[518] He said it was possible that the tholos existed in tandem with the hero-shrine, until the latter had to disappear when the new temple of Athena Pronaia was constructed.

The exact location of the rocks that fell from the Parnassos is now unclear, but that they were there, should not be doubted: landslides are frequent here, and dangerous (as the modern Greeks also warn you when you go here!).[519] And not without reason: a natural rock can currently be seen inside the old temple of Athena Pronaia itself, which fell down from Parnassos in 1905 in bad weather and destroyed the restoration efforts of the French excavators.[520] It provides a dramatic illustration of what Herodotus may have encountered. Although the rocks were used by Herodotus as proof that the Delphian story was true,[521] they may in fact have formed the very inspiration for the story.[522] Supporters of the historicity of Herodotus' account of Xerxes' invasion have argued that the story was essentially true once stripped of its supernatural element: Grundy stated that "doubtless the refugees on their summit rained a shower of rocks on the advancing Persian band, who fled in disorder", and Hammond in 1988 still remarked "[c]omplete sceptics have to account for the arrival of the great rocks".[523] However, it is questionable if the rocks which Herodotus saw rolled down the mountain during a Persian attack.[524] Such remarkable features of the sanctuary landscape could easily attract anecdotes to them, especially when they

---

[517] Or, as Settis (1967–1968, 362) put it: "un'ipotesi « conciliativa », chè allora sapremmo d'un colpo la destinazione della tholos e la collocazione del Phylakeion, e non dovremmo più chieder ragione a Pausania di un « irritante » silenzio."
[518] Poulsen 1908, 377.
[519] Elayi 1979, 127.
[520] Keramopoullos 1935, 92. However, it is probably this rock which Poulsen 1908, 335 describes as being partly under the soil level, which could mean that it is much older.
[521] Elayi 1979, 127.
[522] Macan 1908 I 414: "the phrase has the note of Hdt.'s 'autopsy,' and the argument the stamp, alas ! of Hdt.'s logic." For more examples of conspicuous rocks as mnemotopes see Hartmann 2010, 91.
[523] Grundy 1901, 350; Hammond 1988, 565, note 84. Müller 1987, 481 and Pritchett 1993, 10–11 are seemingly also confident that the Persian siege could really have been crushed by such rocks.
[524] Lazenby 1993, 152; Jacquemin 2011, 23.

could subsequently function as evidence that the Persian army had reached Delphi. The rocks helped pilgrims to the sanctuary to visualise the dramatic and religiously significant event which could have functioned as a warning against sacrilege, and may also have helped to identify the point until where the Persians had invaded the sanctuary.[525]

Fig. 38: A rock in the temenos of Athena Pronaia.

Diodorus Siculus (11.14) also makes mention of an elegiac inscription which the Delphians set up next to the temple of Athena Pronaia with the goal of commemorating the Persian siege:

> μνᾶμά τ' ἀλεξάνδρου πολέμου καὶ μάρτυρα νίκας Δελφοί με στᾶσαν, Ζανὶ χαριζόμενοι σὺν Φοίβῳ, πτολίπορθον ἀπωσαμένοις στίχα Μήδων καὶ χαλκοστέφανον ῥυσαμένοις τέμενος.

> As a monument of the man-defending war and a witness of the victory, the Delphians put me up, thanking Zeus and Phoebus, who pushed back the city-sacking rank of Medes and saving the bronze-crowned sanctuary.

---

525 Macan 1908 I, 414.

Remains of this inscription (*SEG* 28.495.2) were seen near the Kastalian spring by Francis Vernon in the seventeenth century,[526] and the base for this monument (or trophy?) has been identified with a base south of the small temples between the tholos and the big poros temple;[527] or with a structure in front of the 'thesauroi' next to the tholos.[528] The monument is thought to date from the fourth century BCE if not later.[529]

The tholos, the inscription and the rock show the extent to which this particular area of Delphi was a mnemotope for the siege episode. It was a fitting one: here, Athena, a protector deity par excellence, was not without reason called Pronaia 'Before-the-temple', because at this point, invaders were on the threshold of the treasure-rich sanctuary of Apollo.[530] It was a logical religious practise to worship 'guardian' deities, such as Phylakos ('Guardian') and Autonoös ('Self-thinking'), precisely here. It was a logical consequence that, sooner or later, stories would arise which showed that such worship could be reciprocated.[531] Rocks, which occasionally fell down from the Parnassos into the sacred temple precinct, could be inserted into the narratives that crystallised here.

The story is therefore understandable as a temple legend which explained natural phenomena and played a role in the religious experience of the sanctuary. The episode may be seen as an ex posto invention which 'proved' an oracle recounted later in the *Histories* (9.42) by Mardonios, according to which the Persians in Greece would only perish if they plundered the temple of Delphi.[532] It is unclear what Herodotus tries to tell us here, as we know that the temple was not plundered. He may play with the fact that the oracle did not exclude the outcome that the Persians would be thoroughly beaten, and that Mardonios does not understand him. It may also show that there was an alternative tradition that explained the immunity of Delphi during the invasion.

A further argument against the historicity of the scene is that its constituent elements also feature in other accounts. The story elements of the weapons that appear outside the temple finds a parallel in an anecdote recorded by Pausanias (10.14.5-6), in which the Pythia did not grant permission to Themistocles to deposit Persian weapons in the temple of Apollo. The episode is also marked by the interference of Apollo, Phylakos and Autonoös. Although it goes too far to call the involvement of these deities

---

[526] See Meritt 1947 for a scan of Vernon's journal and a transcription.
[527] Poulsen 1908, 363.
[528] Papachatzi 1981, 304.
[529] Poulsen 1908, 363; Meritt 1947, 60 mentions the fact that ου is written as ο; Hammond 1988, 565, note 84.
[530] Macan 1908, I 411 even named Athena "chief witness for the [Persian] defence".
[531] On the names of heroes as denoting special functions, see Foucart 1918, 53–54
[532] Kirchberg 1965, 110–111; Bowie 2007, 125.

specifically 'Iliadic',[533] the scene can be compared to other examples of divine intervention in the *Histories* (§3.2.2). Herodotus did not doubt this.[534]

I would finally like to contextualise the episode with three "common places" which often appear in Delphi. First, the episode fits the Herodotean story of the eastern king who has a desire to interact with Delphi, a stereotype which is also applied to the Lydian king Croesus.[535] Herodotus also speculates that Xerxes knew more about the treasures of Delphi than about those in his own palace (8.35). Although we cannot prove or disprove the historicity of such claims, we should also recognise that it makes sense from a Delphic perspective to claim that foreign kings from the east were interested in the sanctuary.

A second topos to which this story adheres is that of the siege itself. Pausanias (10.7.1) records no less than seven attacks on Delphi, by Euboean brigands, the Phlegyans, Pyrrhos (Achilles' son), the Persians, the Phocians, the Celts and the emperor Nero (who stole 500 statues); furthermore, in Berlin Papyrus 11517 (second century AD) there is a story of an attack by the brigand Daulis.[536] The most famous siege was that of the Celts (279-278 BCE). Interestingly, that siege was remembered along similar lines as that of the Persians. In Pausanias' account of this siege (1.4.4), thunder and rocks help to push back the Celts, as do ghostly appearances of hoplites, which the Delphians this time explained as the Hyperborean heroes Hyperochos and Amadokos, as well as Achilles' son Pyrrhos. In the second account (10.23), we find Laodokos instead of Amadokos and, indeed, Phylakos, an ἐπιχώριος ἥρως ('local hero').[537] Divine involvement also appears in Diodorus Siculus (22.9.5) and Cicero (*De divinatione* 1.37); both preserve an anecdote that Athena Pronaia and Artemis ('the White Virgins') were fated, according to a Pythian oracle, to defend the sanctuary from the Celts; in the passage in Diodorus temples of both Athena and Artemis are mentioned, suggesting, again, a mnemotopical anchoring of the story. An inscription

---

533 For the interpretation of the scene as Iliadic, see Bowie 2012, 277. Note that the names of the heroes also exist in Homeric epic: Phylakos was the founder of the polis of Phylake in Thessaly (*Odyssey* 15.231); the name also appears in the *Iliad* as the name of a Trojan warrior (16.181). The name Autonoös is applied to two minor Iliadic characters, one on the Greek side, the other on the Trojan (11.301; 16.694). Whether there was some relationship between the Homeric characters and the Delphic ones is difficult to say. There may not have been any, as the names are fairly generic.
534 Kirchberg 1965, 102–103 suggested that Herodotus may have been prone to believe the story because he believed in divine powers working in divine places.
535 On eastern kings visiting Delphi, see Maass 2010, 64.
536 For a discussion of this attack see Fontenrose 1969, 109–111.
537 See also Callimachus, *In Delum* 171–191. Fontenrose (1969, 117) equated Pyrrhos with Phylakos. See Bearzot 1989 for the idea that the Celtic siege was not a copy of the Herodotean tale, but a story in its own right which had a real siege at its core, during which there was snow. Priestley 2014, 158–161 notes that the Persian and Celtic invasions were assimilated, but that it is uncertain what the role of Herodotus' account is in this.

from far-away Kos (*IG* XII,4,1 68) is a decree for the sacrifice of a bull with gold-plated horns to thank Apollo for his involvement in routing the Celts.

The Celtic siege was remembered in the Delphic Soteria 'Rescue' festival.[538] While this siege appears prominently in our source material, we may believe with Robert Parker that "there is no reason to doubt that the underlying thought pattern is older".[539] When the Celts came, the idea that this most holy of places on earth had been under attack, and withstood it, was much older and the root of various narratives, such as of the foundation myth of the Delphic sanctuary, in which the site was occupied by the serpent Python who was slain by Apollo. Sophocles (*Odysseus Tyrannus* 897) even uses the word ἄθικτον 'untouched' to describe Delphi. Note that Apollo had a reputation as a successful temple defender elsewhere: at Delos, the immunity of the sanctuary during the Persian Wars was explained by the Datis legends.[540] The imagined Persian siege of 480 BCE fitted neatly in this pattern.

Finally, the rock anecdote may be compared to three additional Delphian 'rolling stone' stories. The first story concerns the famous ὀμφαλός or 'navel stone', a large boulder allegedly dropped by Zeus from the sky to locate the center of the earth, when he saw that two eagles or crows crossed paths here. This object, adorned with fillets and the two birds, was kept as a sacred relic in the temple of Apollo (Strabo 9.3.6) and featured on Delphi's coins. A copy of this stone can now be seen in the Delphi Museum. The second story is as old as Hesiod's *Theogonia* (497-499) and concerns a large boulder allegedly swallowed and vomited by Kronos. It was on display in Delphi as a θαῦμα θνητοῖσι βροτοῖσιν, a 'wonder for mortal men'. When Pausanias (10.24.6) visited Delphi some eight hundred years later, there was still a large boulder near the temple of Apollo which was said to be that rock. The Delphians venerated it by ritually pouring oil over it. Perhaps Pausanias saw the large conical stone currently on display near the Athenian treasury. The third story appears in Livy (42.15), who tells us that two huge boulders once crashed down onto the king of Pergamon, Eumenes II, in an assault by associates of Perseus of Macedon. This episode may just as well have been connected to or even inspired by actual rocks that were visible along the road. Apparently, the Delphians always found a good story to attach to boulders rolling down from the Parnassos.

2.6.4 The Korykian cave

Delphi's other specific location connected to the Persian Wars is the Korykian cave, mentioned as the refuge of the Delphians in 8.36:

---

[538] See Champion 1995 for an overview of our knowledge of this festival, including the many epigraphical sources.
[539] Parker 2011, 219 (in referring to the Soteria festival).
[540] Scheer 2000, 206–207.

[...] αὐτῶν δὲ οἱ μὲν πλεῖστοι ἀνέβησαν ἐς τοῦ Παρνησοῦ τὰς κορυφὰς καὶ ἐς τὸ Κωρύκιον ἄντρον ἀνηνείκαντο [...]

[...] and most of them went up to the tops of Mount Parnassos and brought their belongings to the Korykian cave [...]

The Korykian cave was a fixture of Delphi's sacred landscape (cf. Aeschylus, *Eumenides* 21; Euripides, *Bacchae* 559). It was also visited by Pausanias (10.32.2-7), who admiringly described it as sacred to the Korykian nymphs and Pan, and it was mentioned by Strabo (9.3.1) as the most famous and beautiful cave of Parnassos. It has been identified with a cave north of Delphi by inscriptions near the entrance. It is accessible by a hiking trail from the sanctuary, which presumably follows the ancient path. Excavations of the cave revealed an abundance of votive offerings and identified the cave as an important cult site for the nymphs.[541]

Fig. 39: The Korykian cave on Mount Parnassos.

Although the cave is accessible, it is a long trek from Delphi, hardly a comfortable place to hide, and probably too small to have housed a significant number

---

541 Amandry 1972.

of people. We may question therefore whether 'most' of the Delphians went here, as Herodotus claims. The cave fits the idea of the Parnassos area as a usual area of retreat, a topos which appears in many ancient sources: Livy (42.15) mentions the Parnassos as the refuge area for the assailants of Eumenes II, and Pausanias preserves a tradition in which the Delphians had fled to the tops of the Parnassos because their city was destroyed by Deucalion's flood (10.6.2).[542] We have also seen that the Parnassos was a safe haven for the Tithoreans as they were attacked by the Persians (8.32). Again, a cave near Tithorea may have been the reason why this story arose. The notion of a cave to which people retreat is a topos which appears in many other contexts (§3.3.4). Thus, in local Delphian lore, the cave, an important landmark, may have acquired the dramatic story of the evacuation. Additionally, much like the rocks, it may have served as 'proof' that the siege of Delphi really happened.

2.6.5 Summary

The invasion of Xerxes' army in Phocis on its way to Athens left its marks in popular stories told one to two generations after the war. These stories highlighted the Greek conception of the Persian army as a pillaging machine, destroying everything in its path. These stories were spatially motivated by landmarks or mnemotopes in the landscape of Phocis. The temples of Phocis, in ruins or not, were monuments for Persian sacrilege, whether committed or not. The cave of Tithorea and the Korykian cave were typical refuges. At Delphi itself, the shrine of its main guard Phylakos was pointed out as the location of a miraculous stance of local numina against the Persians. I have shown that there is reason to believe that the tholos of Delphi was a monument commemorating this alleged attack. Rocks, widely available underneath the Parnassos, were sure proof that the gods had acted. This essentially fitted a pattern central to the sanctuary's mythology.

In all of these examples, the landscape is not simply a context for the stories; rather, there is a complex interaction between the landscape and the story. In some instances, it can be argued that the landscape even inspired the story in the first place. Importantly, it was such stories that shaped Herodotus' account of these invasions.

---

[542] Bowie 2007, 128 calls this event a mythical precedent to the flight during the Persian attack. For other mythical associations of the Parnassos massif see McInerney 1999, 44–45.

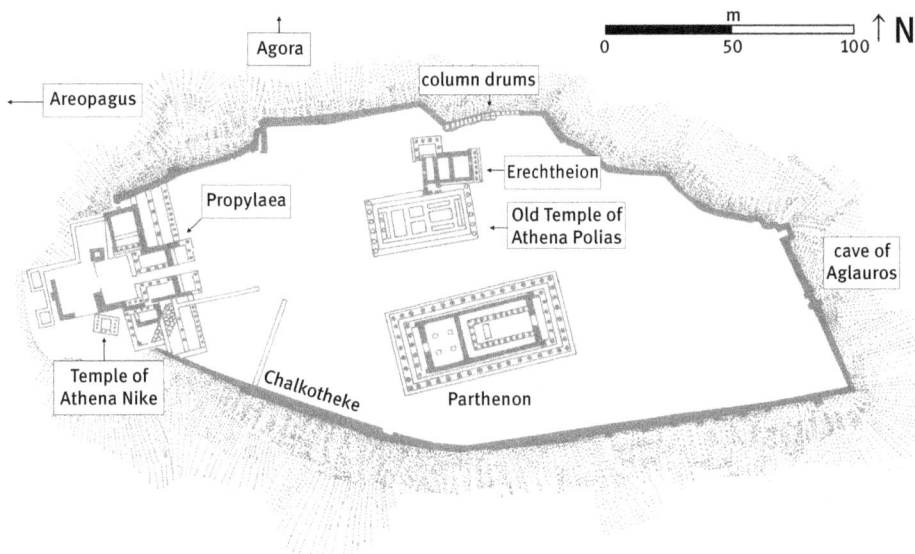

Map 5: Plan of Acropolis.
Note: This map shows a simplified and anachronistic plan of the Acropolis. It only serves as an illustration to §2.7.

2.7 The destructions of Athens and Eleusis

Athens, the 'big city' of the Greek world in the fifth century BCE, was a place where much was remember.[543] The city was dotted with monuments and mnemotopes for mythical and historical events.[544] The Persian Wars, too, could be experienced here, because the Acropolis and the Agora, soon after the departure of Xerxes developed into a memorial space of the wars where architecture and objects told the story of that conflict.[545] For example, Pausanias (1.27.1) and Demosthenes (*Adversus Androtionem* 13)

---

[543] This chapter was the basis for an article in the volume *Conflict in Communities. Memories of the past and expectations for the future in archaic and classical Greece* edited by Elena Franchi and Giorgia Proietti (van Rookhuijzen 2017f). The present text (deviating from the text in the article on various points) has been included with kind permission from the editors. A selection of places mentioned in this chapter features on Map 5.
[544] See Hölscher 2010 for an overview of Athens as a memorial space. He points out that remembering in Athens most often took the place of monuments (Hölscher 2010, 137–140); these could be placed anywhere, but often their physical situation was determined by the spectator: not very surprisingly, countless monuments dotted the Agora and the Kerameikos (Hölscher 2010, 140–145).
[545] On monumentalisation efforts see Gauer 1968, 128 ("Mit kaum einem Ort in Griechenland war die Erinnerung an die Perserkriege so unmittelbar verknüpft, wie mit der Akropolis.") and Monaco 2015. The colossal bronze statue of Athena Promachos was allegedly made in the 460s from Persian bronze

mention that the armour of Masistios and Mardonios, Persian men killed in the battle of Plataea, was kept in the Old Temple of Athena Polias (1.27.1), and Demosthenes (*In Timocratem* 129) even reports that Xerxes' silver-footed throne from the battle of Salamis (§2.8.3) was kept in the Parthenon; all of these may have been 'invented objects'.[546] Athens was therefore an unmissable stop on Herodotus' tours, and it is, in fact, generally believed that Herodotus spent considerable time in Athens, or that he was at least well-acquainted with the city.[547] On the basis of the prominent role of the Athenians in the *Histories* it has been argued that Herodotus had a special relation to Athens; some authors even discern an Athenian bias in his work.[548]

In this chapter we focus on the event during the wars for which the Acropolis itself had been the scene: the Persian siege of 480 BCE.[549] When Herodotus, our only

---

spoils after the battle of Marathon (cf. Ferrari 2002, 25–26). It also possible that Pericles' odeon, at the foot of the Acropolis, was based on a Persian tent seen at Plataea (Pausanias 1.20.4, Plutarch, *Pericles* 13.5, Vitruvius 5.9.1; see Broneer 1944; Miller 1999, 218–242). In addition, the nearby Agora was a suitable public space where memories of the Persian Wars could be pointed out. Examples include the Metroon and the temple of Apollos Patroos, which were not rebuilt after their destruction, and the sculptures of Harmodios and Aristogeiton, symbols of the battle against tyranny, acquired a new anecdote because they were allegedly stolen by Xerxes (and later returned by Antiochus: Arrian, *Anabasis Alexandri* 3.16.7–8; 7.19.2; Pausanias 1.8.5).

[546] Harris 1995, 204–205 and 217; Miller 1999, 53–55; Proietti 2015a, 163. For the view that these objects were historically accurate see Thompson 1954. Pausanias did not believe that the Spartans would have given away the sword of a man who was killed by a Spartan. Epigraphically, several akinakai, an aulos-case, a phiale, shekels and darics, and bridles appear as Persian booty displayed in Athenian temples (Harris 1995, 109–110).

[547] It is often thought Herodotus was around forty years of age when he came to Athens in 445 BCE, after his travels; Jacoby 1913, 237, 251; Myres 1953, 4; Podlecki 1977. Apart from the sites which will be discussed in this chapter, Herodotus knew about various other places in Athens, including the Pan cult surrounding one of the Acropolis caves (6.105) and the temple of Boreas on the Ilissos river (7.189). Perhaps the best testimony of Herodotus' autopsy is his description of a bronze quadriga and its inscription in the northwest corner of the Acropolis: the inscription on the base of the quadriga was still present in Pausanias' time (1.28.2) and seems to have been partly retrieved (*IG* I² 394; see West 1985, 283–285; Hurwit 1999, 146).

[548] Herodotus singles out the Athenians as the saviours of Greece in 7.139. On the issue of the existence of pro-Athenian sentiments in the account, see How & Wells 1912, I 39, 41–42; Jacoby 1913, 359; de Sélincourt 1967, 39–43; Strasburger 1955; Walser 1984, 40; Waters 1985, 121–125. For potential criticism of the Athenian empire, see Moles 2002, 51; Dewald & Marincola 2006, 3–4. Athens has also been described as a "paradigm of universal processes" for the *Histories* (Moles 2002, 52).

[549] Unsurprisingly, stories of sieges of the Acropolis abound: Some of these stories already feature in Herodotus and are set in the pre-Persian period: Peisistratos' retaking of the Acropolis on a chariot alongside the woman Phya who was dressed up as Athena (1.60), and that of Kylon, a victor in the Olympic games who took the Acropolis with a mob and took position at the cult statue of Athena as a suppliant (5.71; Thucydides 1.126), others are found in later sources, such as the sieges by Sulla (Appian, *Mithridatica* 149–152) and the Heruli (Dexippus, *FGrH* 100 F28a). Connelly 2014, 62 points out that such siege stories "illustrate the dominance of the Acropolis plateau as an ever-visible landmark and target for takeover".

extensive source for the Persian invasion of Attica, visited the Acropolis around 430 BCE, some fifty years after the event, his perspective was not wholly different from that of a modern visitor. He, too, interacted with the very places on and near the Acropolis where the Persians had violently assaulted the Athenians and their buildings. He endeavoured to substantiate his claims about the siege by pointing at those spots in his text.

But can we unproblematically take this 'topography' as historically accurate? In this chapter I argue that the perspective of mnemotopes is beneficial in understanding the topography in Herodotus' account of the Persian invasion of Attica, and that folklore and local oral traditions play an important role in the establishment of this topography.[550] I will explain how memories of Xerxes' invasion came to be connected to four mnemotopes on or near the Acropolis: the Areopagus, the sanctuary of Aglauros, the μέγαρον, and the olive tree at the Erechtheion. All of these sites were not only famous landmarks, but some of them also had pre-existing mythological associations that helped to associate the Persian invasion with them. This chapter also includes a discussion of the Anaktoron of Eleusis and its problematic archaeology.

2.7.1 The Areopagus

Herodotus tells us that the Persians were stationed on the Areopagus during their siege of the Athenian citadel (8.52):

> οἱ δὲ Πέρσαι, ἱζόμενοι ἐπὶ τὸν καταντίον τῆς ἀκροπόλιος ὄχθον, τὸν Ἀθηναῖοι καλέουσι Ἀρήιον πάγον, ἐπολιόρκεον τρόπον τοιόνδε· ὅκως στυππεῖον περὶ τοὺς ὀϊστοὺς περιθέντες ἄψειαν, ἐτόξευον ἐς τὸ φράγμα. ἐνθαῦτα Ἀθηναίων οἱ πολιορκεόμενοι ὅμως ἠμύνοντο, καίπερ ἐς τὸ ἔσχατον κακοῦ ἀπιγμένοι καὶ τοῦ φράγματος προδεδωκότος· οὐδὲ λόγους τῶν Πεισιστρατιδέων προσφερόντων περὶ ὁμολογίης ἐνεδέκοντο, ἀμυνόμενοι δὲ ἄλλα τε ἀντεμηχανῶντο καὶ δὴ καὶ προσιόντων τῶν βαρβάρων πρὸς τὰς πύλας ὀλοιτρόχους ἀπίεσαν, ὥστε Ξέρξην ἐπὶ χρόνον συχνὸν ἀπορίῃσι ἐνέχεσθαι, οὐ δυνάμενόν σφεας ἑλεῖν.

> The Persians occupied the rock opposite the Acropolis which the Athenians call the Hill of Ares, and tried to besiege it in the following manner: they put hemp around their arrows, lighted them, and fired them towards the fence. There, those of the Athenians who were being besieged, were still defending themselves, although they had arrived to the worst of evil and the fence had given in. Nor, when the Peisistratids were offering them words about a truce, did they accept these, and they devised other things while defending themselves, and when the Barbarians came close to the gates they rolled down disc-shaped stones, so that Xerxes for a long time did not know what to do, as he could not capture them.

---

550 See e.g. Luraghi 2001, 149–150 for the idea that the information which Herodotus' local informants would have conveyed should be understood in terms of memory. Especially notable is the work of Giorgia Proietti (e.g. 2012c), whose work highlights that the perspective of memory is a crucial instrument for understanding the account of the Persian Wars as recounted by Herodotus.

The Areopagus is the rocky outcropping directly in front of the Propylaea of the Acropolis.[551] We need not doubt that there was a Persian siege of the Acropolis. However, Herodotus focuses on the Areopagus when describing the Persian position. Even if only a fraction of Herodotus' numbers of the Persian troops is correct, the Persian 'base' surely extended much beyond the hill itself, which would fit perhaps only a few hundred men. Moreover, the rocky hill can hardly be regarded a very convenient base. But when, fifty years after the battle, a visitor to Athens would ask around 'where the Persians had been', the Areopagus was what the answer would have amounted to. Apparently, the Areopagus, a convenient landmark, had become a mnemotope of the siege. There may have been more mnemotopes for this part of the account. There is in particular reason to believe that rocks which lay in the valley between the Acropolis and the Areopagus were believed to have been thrown down from the Acropolis by defending Athenians. At the north slope of the Acropolis there is today a large column drum, perhaps a leftover from the Parthenon.[552] I propose that it may be one of the very 'disc-shaped stones' (ὀλοίτροχοι) which inspired the story that Herodotus records.[553] A similar process was at work in Delphi, where boulders in the temenos of Athena Pronaia were 'evidence' for the intervention of Apollo himself during the Persian siege (§2.6.3). Fifty years later, such rocks may have acquired a role in local touristic lore, which subsequently reached visitors including Herodotus.[554]

Because the Areopagus was such a recognisable landmark in the topography of Athens, its mnemotopical potential was enormous. The stories recorded as taking place here often feature a theme of death and vengeance, which is perhaps not surprising given the (folk-?)etymological connection of the hill's name with the word

---

[551] See already Leake 1821, 36–38 for the identification. See Longo & Tofi 2010 for a topographical investigation of the Areopagus.

[552] This and another column drum were excavated by Broneer (1935, 120–121) on the north slope, northeast of the Erechtheion. He assigned them, like the other column drums in the Acropolis north wall, to the Older Parthenon. The two drums excavated by Broneer perhaps never arrived at the top of the Acropolis to be thrown down during the siege, but were simply left at the slope. Broneer himself notes, regarding the better preserved one, that "It remains a mystery how it rolled down the rocky, precipitous hill without breaking to pieces [...]" p. 120).

[553] The obscure word ὀλοίτροχος is given by LSJ as 'large stone, boulder', but its etymology with ὀλοί- related to εἰλέω 'to roll' or 'to compress' (cf. Bowie 2007, 139) or ὄλλυμι 'destroy', and τροχός, which denotes various circular objects such as wheels, as well as the word's alternative definition as τὸ κυλινδρικὸν σχῆμα (Democritus 162) suggest that a translation 'disc-shaped stone', or perhaps 'millstone' is to be preferred. See Wesenberg 2004 for an elaborate discussion of the word and the ancient and modern traditions in which it was translated or explained as meaning 'round stone' with a steam-roller like effect when rolled down from above. His suggestion that the word instead referred to normal stones does not convince, because it is mostly based on arguments of Sachkritik which not only takes Herodotus' depiction of the siege at face value, but also fails to include the perspective of memory studies.

[554] For the belief that the Athenians really hurled down rocks from the Acropolis (taken from the Mycenaean fortification), see Mylonas Shear 1999, 119–120; Bowie 2007, 139.

Fig. 40: The Areopagus (right) in relation to the Acropolis.

ἀρή 'bane', or with the numina derived from that word: the Arai (also known as the Erinyes), the goddesses of vengeance, and Ares, the god of warfare.⁵⁵⁵ As such, the Areopagus was considered the high criminal court of Athens in mythical times: Ares himself was put on a trial here for killing Poseidon's son Halirrothios, as was Orestes for killing his mother Klytaimnestra.⁵⁵⁶ Such stories offered a prefiguration of the court that historically existed here. In addition, a grave of Oedipus was pointed out on the rock, and there existed a tradition that Oreïthyia was abducted from it by Boreas.⁵⁵⁷

But there had once been other occupants of the Areopagus, who may have played a role in the placement of the Persians on the Areopagus: the Amazons. This had

---

555 For the worship of the Arai see Pausanias 1.28.6. On the connection with Ares see Blok 1995, 182–183.
556 Ares' trial: Hellanicus *FGrH* 4 F169a; Pausanias 1.28.5. Orestes' trial: Aeschylus' *Eumenides*; Pausanias 1.28.5. This myth was also present at other mnemotopes in Herodotus' account (see §2.3.2 and §2.4.2).
557 Oedipus' grave: Valerius Maximus 5.3.ext.3f; Pausanias 1.28.7. The abduction of Oreïthyia: Plato, *Phaedrus* 229d. Furthermore, it was here that Paul the Apostle is believed to have delivered his sermon to the Athenians, asking them to abandon the pagan gods (*Acta apostolorum* 17.19–34).

happened during the so-called Attic War, when the famous warrior women had attempted to free their queen Antiope, whom Theseus had taken to Athens.[558] Like the Persians, the Amazons were thought to have made their basecamp on the Areopagus. As such, it appears already in Aeschylus' *Eumenides* (681-695). The passage is worth quoting in full as it gives an impression of how the notion of the Areopagus as a place of 'crime' was a suitable one to connect to the Amazon and Persian sieges; Athena proclaims:

> κλύοιτ' ἂν ἤδη θεσμόν, Ἀττικὸς λεώς, πρώτας δίκας κρίνοντες αἵματος χυτοῦ. ἔσται δὲ καὶ τὸ λοιπὸν Αἰγέως στρατῷ αἰεὶ δικαστῶν τοῦτο βουλευτήριον. πάγον δ' Ἄρειον τόνδ', Ἀμαζόνων ἕδραν σκηνάς θ', ὅτ' ἦλθον Θησέως κατὰ φθόνον στρατηλατοῦσαι, καὶ πόλη νεόπτολιν τήνδ' ὑψίπυργον ἀντεπύργωσαν τότε, Ἄρει δ' ἔθυον, ἔνθεν ἔστ' ἐπώνυμος πέτρα πάγος τ' Ἄρειος· ἐν δὲ τῷ σέβας ἀστῶν φόβος τε ξυγγενὴς τὸ μὴ ἀδικεῖν σχήσει τόδ', ἦμαρ καὶ κατ' εὐφρόνην ὁμῶς, αὐτῶν πολιτῶν μὴ 'πικαινόντων νόμους κακαῖς ἐπιρροῆσι· βορβόρῳ δ' ὕδωρ λαμπρὸν μιαίνων οὔποθ' εὑρήσεις ποτόν.

> Hear my institution, people of Attica, judging the first trial for the pouring of blood. This council of judges will always be there in the future for the people of Aigeus. This hill of Ares, the seat of the Amazons and their camps, when they marched in hate of Theseus, they made a fortification opposite against this citadel, just-founded and high-towered, and they offered to Ares; hence this rock is nicknamed Ares' hill. On this rock, the Piety of citizens and its relative Fear will guard against illegal activities, both by day and night, when they do not innovate the laws of those same citizens. By defiling clear water with bad currents and filth, you will never find a drink.

Around the conspicuous rock various other places had an alleged Amazon pedigree, including graves[559] and a mysterious Amazoneion, which may have amounted to fortifications believed to have left behind by the Amazons, to their graves, or to something else.[560] Plutarch also mentions a place called the Horkomosion close to

---

558 Cf. Pseudo-Apollodorus, *Epitomae* 1.16.
559 Plutarch (*Theseus* 27.2–5) specifies that Amazons were buried at the Amazoneion, and on both sides of the street which led to the gate of Piraeus. Furthermore, Molpadia had a stele close to the temple of Olympian Ge (at the Olympieion). Graves of Antiope and Molpadia were also seen by Pausanias (1.2.1). Mayor (2014, 275–277) surmises that ancient Mycenaean and Dark Age burials were reinterpreted by later Greeks as hero or Amazon graves.
560 Diodorus Siculus (4.28.1–4) and Plutarch (*Theseus* 27, basing himself on Clidemus of Athens = FGrH 323 F 1) preserve a tradition according to which the left wing of the Amazons took position at the Amazoneion (while the right wing was oriented towards the Pnyx near Chrysa). This place was close to the Mouseion, because the Athenians were stationed there. Aelius Herodianus (*Ἡ καθ' ὅλου προσῳδία* 374) and Stephanus Byzantinus (*Ethnica* s.v. Ἀμαζόνειον) simply state that the Amazoneion was the place where Theseus had beaten the Amazons. If this 'place of the Amazons' was at the Areopagus, as has been proposed (Judeich 1931, 300) we may carefully posit that the Areopagus contained architectural structures amounting to a πύργος which were thought to date to the Amazonian invasion of Athens (in the fragment quoted above, Aeschylus notes that

the temple of Theseus, named after the oath sworn at the end of the war.[561] Such mnemotopes constituted proof for the idea that the Amazons had based themselves in this part of the city, as Plutarch states explicitly (*Theseus* 27.2): 'that [the Amazons] encamped in the city itself is evidenced also by the names of the places and the graves of those that fell.' In addition, the Areopagus was not too far from the Theseion and the Stoa Poikile, both of which had paintings of the Amazonomachy,[562] and it seems significant that the west metopes of the Parthenon, which depict the Amazonomachy, directly faced the Areopagus.[563] As such, in the later fifth century BCE, the Areopagus was the centrepiece of what we may call a memory landscape of the Amazonomachy.

But that memory landscape existed in tandem with that of the Persian siege. The topographical parallel of the Amazons and the Persians at the Areopagus fits their comparison in other media. It may be true that Amazons in Greek art do not directly represent Persians,[564] but the popularity of the myth can be connected to its function as a mythical precedent to the Persian invasion. In literature, the two enemies are occasionally correlated,[565] and this connection may also explain the rise in popularity of the Amazonomachy in Athenian vase painting during the fifth century BCE.[566] But most evidence can be found in depictions of Amazons in public buildings in Athens and elsewhere: the parallelism may be argued for the Amazonomachies of the Parthenon (the west metopes), the Pergamene monuments on the Acropolis, the Stoa Poikile, the temple of Hephaistos on the Agora, the Athenian treasury at Delphi, and perhaps the Delphian tholos (see §2.6.3).[567] The most crucial example is the shield of Pheidias' cult statue of Athena Parthenos which stood inside the Parthenon and seems to have

---

the Amazons 'fortified' (ἀντεπύργωσαν) the hill 'against' the Acropolis). Robertson (1992, 137) thought that the Amazoneion amounted to nothing more than a grave stele, and put the Amazoneion southwest of the Olympieion.

561 The Horkomosion may be sought in the area of the archaic Agora, on the east side of the Acropolis (Robertson 1998, 284; 295–298).

562 For the Theseion, see Pausanias 1.17.4. For the Stoa Poikile, see Aristophanes, *Lysistrata* 677–679; Pausanias 1.15. Tyrrell (1984, 12) has suggested that the Theseion and the Stoa Poikile were the disseminators of the myth.

563 Cf. duBois 1982, 61–64; Tyrrell 1984, 19–21.

564 Arafat 2013, 215; Mayor 2014, 280–283.

565 E.g. Isocrates (*Panathenaicus* 193–195), where both Amazons and Persians feature in a long list of armies that invaded Attica. On the role of the Amazons in Athenian oratory, see Tyrrell 1984, 13–19; 114–116. Pausanias also generalises the Amazonomachy as the first battle against eastern foes in 5.11.8 and 1.17.2 (on these passages cf. Arafat 2013, 13). On the role of the Amazons in Greek literature from the fifth century BCE onwards, see Tyrrell 1984, 21–22.

566 Bovon (1963, 600) discusses the prominence of Amazons in Greek vase painting, attributing a rise in the popularity in the fifth century BCE to mythicisation of the Persian invasion.

567 West metopes of the Parthenon: Harrison 1966; 1981, 301. Pergamene monuments: Pausanias 1.25.2. Stoa Poikile: Aristophanes, *Lysistrata* 677–679; Pausanias 1.15; Tyrrell 1984, 12–13; Kousser 2009, 273. Temple of Hephaestus: e.g. Kousser 2009, 273. Athenian treasury: e.g. duBois 1982, 57–61

included a depiction of the Areopagus, as well as people throwing rocks.[568] I propose that one or more rocks or column drums in the valley between the Acropolis and the Areopagus which, I suggested above, may have inspired the story that the Athenians had defended themselves by hurling down 'millstones', could have simultaneously had a similar function for the Amazonomachy.[569]

The myth of the Amazonomachy of Athens already existed before Herodotus' work: he mentions it as part of the speech of the Athenians before the battle of Plataea (9.27). It also seems that it existed before the historical Persian invasion in 480 BCE, because it was in use as a subject for vase painting in the late sixth century BCE, and it probably appears at the same time in the sculpture of the temple at Eretria. The myth was the subject of a work by Pherecydes of Athens (Plutarch, *Theseus* 26.1 = *FGrH* 3 F 151) and of an epic poem called the *Theseid* (Plutarch, *Theseus* 28.1). There may even have been an archaic 'mystery building' on the Acropolis or its south slope, hypothesised on the basis of a high-relief metope of an Amazon found south of the Acropolis that could have belonged to a building destroyed by the Persians.[570]

Because Aeschylus' *Eumenides* antedates Herodotus' *Histories*, we know that the specific tradition according to which the Amazons had been based on the Areopagus also antedates Herodotus' work. But we do not know whether this tradition already existed when the Persians historically came to Athens, in 480 BCE. It therefore remains unclear whether the Amazons or the Persians came first to the Areopagus in the Athenian imagination. The common opinion holds that the version of the tale featuring the Areopagus arose only after the Persian siege, as a mythical precedent.[571] But it is also possible that the myth, including the Areopagus, already existed before the Persian invasion and helped to reshape popular conceptions of the attack. One scholar has, in fact, suggested that the story about the Persian

---

who suggests that the treasury predates the Persian Wars, and that it "enacts the transformation of the Amazonomachy from Herakles to Theseus." (quote on page 58).

568 Harrison 1966, 128–129; she elaborated her thesis in an article from 1981, where she argued (p. 295–310) that the shield depicted a schematic topography of Athens amidst the battle of Marathon in the lower half, and the Athenian Amazonomachy in the upper half, including depictions of the temple of Athena (p. 303), the Areopagus (301; 303–304), perhaps the olive tree (p. 303; 310) and other holy places, while the Greeks are to be interpreted as figures from Athens' legendary past, including Kekrops and Erechtheus (p. 300–301). The imaginary siege of the Acropolis in Lucian's *Revivescentes sive piscator* (42) involves ladders at the Anakeion (the temple of the Dioscuri), which was probably located on the east side of the Acropolis (cf. Robertson 1992, 45). See also Kousser 2009, 277.

569 On the shield, see Kousser 2009, 277; Mayor 2014, 274. Harrison (1966, 129) suggested that the stone-throwing heroes on the Athena Parthenos shield were inspired by the rocks thrown at the Persians in 480 BCE. However, it is also possible that the inspiration worked vice versa.

570 Hurwit 1999, 136; 169; Korres 1994b, 175–176.

571 E.g. Harrison 1966, 128–129; duBois 1982, 63–64; Tyrrell 1984, 9–21; Francis & Vickers 1988, 150; Hurwit 1999, 232; Asheri et al. 2010, 254.

siege should be interpreted within the framework of the Amazon myth.[572] The relationship may have been even more complex: a tradition of the Athenian Amazonomachy, even if invented after the Persian siege of the Acropolis as a precedent to them, may then in turn have reshaped popular conception of this event before Herodotus wrote his *Histories*. Most likely, the two traditions arose in conjunction. During that process, the mnemotopes for the Amazon siege could easily have been reused for the Persian siege.

2.7.2 The sanctuary of Aglauros

The Persians were initially unsuccessful in their attempt to take the Acropolis, but the tide turned after they made an important discovery (8.53):

> χρόνῳ δ' ἐκ τῶν ἀπόρων ἐφάνη δή τις ἔσοδος τοῖσι βαρβάροισι· ἔδεε γὰρ κατὰ τὸ θεοπρόπιον πᾶσαν τὴν Ἀττικὴν τὴν ἐν τῇ ἠπείρῳ γενέσθαι ὑπὸ Πέρσῃσι. ἔμπροσθε ὦν τῆς ἀκροπόλιος, ὄπισθε δὲ τῶν πυλέων καὶ τῆς ἀνόδου, τῇ δὴ οὔτε τις ἐφύλασσε οὔτ' ἂν ἤλπισε μή κοτέ τις κατὰ τοῦτο ἀναβαίη ἀνθρώπων, ταύτῃ ἀνέβησάν τινες κατὰ τὸ ἱρὸν τῆς Κέκροπος θυγατρὸς Ἀγλαύρου, καίπερ ἀποκρήμνου ἐόντος τοῦ χώρου. ὡς δὲ εἶδον αὐτοὺς ἀναβεβηκότας οἱ Ἀθηναῖοι ἐπὶ τὴν ἀκρόπολιν, οἱ μὲν ἐρρίπτεον ἑωυτοὺς κατὰ τοῦ τείχεος κάτω καὶ διεφθείροντο [...]

> But after a while, there appeared a way out from the difficulty for the Barbarians, for according to the oracle, all of Attica on the mainland needed to come under control of the Persians. In front of the Acropolis, behind the gates and the ascent, where nobody was guarding and nobody had expected that anybody could ever go up, a few went up at the sanctuary of Aglauros, daughter of Kekrops, even though the place is a cliff. When the Athenians on the Acropolis saw that they had gone up, some threw themselves down from the wall and died [...]

As appears from this passage, the story about the Persian success during the siege of the Acropolis found its mnemotope in the sanctuary (ἱρόν) of Aglauros, a mythical Athenian princess who was most famous for discovering the snake Erichthonios and then jumping down the Acropolis. The location of her shrine was long unclear, because Herodotus' indication ἔμπροσθε 'in front' can be understood in different ways.[573] Early topographers have therefore turned to common sense to locate the shrine. Unsurpris-

---

[572] Blok 1995, 138–139.
[573] Herodotus' reference to this location as ἔμπροσθε ὦν πρὸ τῆς ἀκροπόλιος, ὄπισθε δὲ τῶν πυλέων has been explained by arguing that the point of reference for ἔμπροσθε is the area around the Prytaneion, where the old agora may have been located and which could have been regarded as the centre of Athens (cf. Dontas 1983, 59–61; Hurwit 1999, 136). Alternatively, the terms ἔμπροσθε and ὄπισθε are relative and malleable. The only reason for their use may have been to underline the circumstance that this part was unguarded. For a reconstruction of the old agora on the east side of the Acropolis, and more references to Aglauros, see Robertson 1992, 43–48; 1998. Cf. Pausanias 1.18.2, who mentions

ingly, they came up with a localisation where the Persians could physically have been able to climb the Acropolis, i.e. the western part of its north slope, where there are still the remains of a staircase.[574] There is even some archaeological material from this area which has been associated with the battle, consisting of arrowheads and a skeleton.[575] However, the discovery of a third-century BCE marble stele (*IG* II² 663) in 1980 in the large cave on the east side of the Acropolis showed that this view was incorrect. This stele has an inscription which mentions that it was meant to be set up inside the sanctuary of Aglauros. Because the inscription was found in situ, it secures the cave, in which evidence for cult practice has been found, as the identification of or as tied up with the sanctuary of Aglauros.[576]

The new location of the sanctuary of Aglauros leads to the conclusion that, in the tradition recorded by Herodotus, the Persians climbed a steep slope of the citadel, which was also a location for various stories of people jumping down (see below). Climbing this place is in reality nearly (though perhaps not completely) impossible. But this is precisely the point that Herodotus wants to make, as underlined by his καίτοι περ 'even though'. Faced with the reality of the temple's location, scholars have on the whole been tacit about the problem. Those who do comment on the episode, still assume its historicity: if the facts do not fit the Persian Wars, the Persian Wars fit the facts.[577] There are scholars who see the discovery of the sanctuary's location as a confirmation of the historicity of Herodotus' account, because they found it hard to believe that a Persian ascent at the north side could have gone unnoticed.[578] However,

---

a prytaneion and the temple of the Dioscuri here. Jeppesen (1987, 40) simply thought Herodotus or the textual transmission was wrong, and that the old agora theory is too complicated.

574 E.g. Leake 1821, 126–131; Macan 1908, I 440; Judeich 1931, 303; Papachatzi 1974, 267; Travlos 1981, 72–73; For more references see Dontas 1983, 58, note 32–33.

575 For the arrowheads, see Broneer 1933, 342 and 1935 114–115. However, the find context of the first group contained much later material, and the second group of arrows were all of types common in Greece (which did not stop Broneer from associating them with the Persians, as "their original supplies would have been exhausted"). For the skeleton, see Broneer 1935, 117.

576 See Dontas 1983 for a full text of the inscription and an analysis. The new identification has found wide acceptance, e.g. Hurwit 1999, 135–136; Saporiti 2010, 159. Leake (1821, 126–131) already reported that scholars before him had surmised that the sanctuary was at the eastern end, but he himself believed that that view was incorrect. For an exploration of the cave, which yielded scant evidence for ritual practises, see Broneer & Pease 1936. On the cult of Aglauros see Parker 2005, 434.

577 Müller (1987, 614) for example, admitted that the new location made it understandable that the Persians went 'unseen'. Dontas (1983, 59) even found it necessary to point out that "it is obvious that [Herodotus] does not mean by this a detachment of regular soldiers but rather those especially trained in mountain warfare." Although it is perhaps possible that Xerxes had taken such soldiers with him to Greece, this is idea is ad hoc explanation.

578 Wesenberg 2004, 160; Kousser 2009, 279, note 25.

Fig. 41: The cave on the east side of the Acropolis: the shrine of Aglauros.

if the ascent is all but impossible at the sanctuary of Aglauros, we have to be open to the view that it never happened, or at least not at this particular place.

The drama of the story becomes apparent when it is compared to the many stories in the *Histories* (and elsewhere) that follow the pattern of what we may call the topos of 'the enemy's bypass'. As part of Xerxes' invasion, such bypass stories are also encountered at many other places (see §3.3.5).[579] Whatever the historicity of these stories, they were not only effective narrative topics, but also a means of stereotyping the Persian as weak, prone to try to win by stealth, and unheroic. Another example from Herodotus may be added which resonates perfectly with the siege of the Athenian Acropolis: the sixth-century BCE Persian siege of the Acropolis of Sardis in Asia Minor (1.84; cf. §2.1.5).[580] In that case, the Persians want to take the citadel, but

---

[579] As part of Xerxes' invasion, such bypass stories are also encountered at the 'Macedonian mountain' (7.131), during the battles of Thermopylae (7.216–218) and Artemision (8.13), and during the sieges of Potidaia (8.129) and Sestos (9.118). There are many examples elsewhere in Herodotus' work and in Greek literature. The similarity of the Athens episode to Thermopylae is noted by Bowie 2007, 137–138.
[580] It has, as far as I know, been acknowledged only once that both sieges follow the same pattern: Hart 1982, 97: "the citadel was taken in a manner recalling the fall of Sardis." Hart did not question the story's historicity.

initially fail because it is well-fortified and guarded at the entrance. However, there is an unguarded spot at the steepest side. The defenders mistakenly believe that it is not possible to reach the citadel along this way. Then, a helmet rolls down the slope. A Persian sees this and gets the idea that this is possible. The Persians climb up and finally, the citadel is taken. While the Persian destruction of Sardis has reportedly left traces in the archaeological record,[581] a few scholars have pointed out that the story of the bypass adheres to a well-established topos.[582] For the Athenian story, the point has not been made yet. It may be, however, that the traditions on which Herodotus relied had recast the story to fit the by-pass pattern, and that it was served or even prompted by the local topography, i.e. the shrine of Aglauros.

Why, then, was the story of the bypass told at the sanctuary of Aglauros? Its location at the 'hidden' backside of the Acropolis could, by itself, have made the shrine the location par excellence of the climbing episode. Additionally, there may have been two mythical 'catalysts' at this spot. First, our sources say that the sanctuary was founded after the princess had jumped down from the Acropolis to end the war between Athens and Eleusis.[583] Although Aglauros' role as a city-saving priestess was just one version of her myth, it was the version which was probably most strongly connected to her cult.[584] Therefore, in Herodotus' story, the Persians climb the Acropolis at a place which marked the heroic death of an important person in Athens' mythical history. If the symbolism was not already obvious, Herodotus additionally details that some Athenians jumped down from the Acropolis when they saw that their death was near.[585] It seems that it was believed that the myth had repeated itself on the same spot.

The second catalyst for the story about the Persian ascent may, as in the case of the Areopagus, have been the Athenian Amazonomachy. We have seen above that the Amazons who besiege the Athenian Acropolis on the shield of Pheidias' statue Athena

---

581 Evidence includes a wide array of armour, skeletal remains and traces of fire, as mudbrick from the upper old fortification wall was dumped on the lower parts (Cahill 2010, 344–357).
582 It has been recognised that the anecdote of the Sardis siege is a variety of the universal folk-tale of the Achilles' heel (Hansen 2002, 481–489); Cahill (2010, 341) suggests that the story had become embellished by the time it reached Herodotus. Nevertheless, other commentators have connected burnt levels in the stratigraphy of various points in the lower city, and arrowheads found on the south slopes with the invasion (Mierse 1983a, 101; Müller 1997, 709). Another siege story about Sardis in the *Histories* on the hands of the Ionians and Athenians as part of the Ionian revolt in 498 BCE (5.100–102). The city was burnt completely, safe for the acropolis, which was controlled by the Persian general Artaphrenes. Trapped by the fire, the Persians and Lydians fled to the Paktolos river in the agora. As this happened, the Ionians were frightened and fled.
583 Philochorus *FGrH* 328 F105–106.
584 For an elaborate discussion on all aspects of the Aglauros myth, see Sourvinou-Inwood & Parker 2011, 24–50. On the temple as a mnemotope for the myth, see Hölscher 2010, 133.
585 This seems to be usually taken as a historical fact, cf. (seemingly) Bowie 2007, 140 ("one wonders if some [of the Athenians who jumped down] thought of the myth when they realised that they, like the daughters of Cecrops, had made a bad mistake"); Kousser 2009, 265.

Parthenos are believed to be a mythical reflection upon the historical siege of the Persians. Elements in the plot of the Persian siege 'projected' upon the Amazon siege in the shield included scaling by ladders, the shooting of arrows and the moment before the discovery of the secret path, and the moment of setting fire to the Acropolis. Here, too, figures are depicted who fall down from the Acropolis.

As we have seen in the case of the Areopagus, it is difficult to secure whether it was the myth or the history that was reshaped. I suggest that history may have been reinterpreted against the storylines that already existed in the myths of Aglauros and the Amazons, and, more generally, that the steep citadel itself was liable to attract such stories. There are, after all, more stories of figures jumping down from the Acropolis to their death: Aegeus was sometimes thought to have found his death by throwing himself down from the Acropolis in the false belief that his son Theseus had been killed by the Minotaur (Pseudo-Apollodorus, *Epitomae* 1.10), and Konstantinos Koukidis, one of the euzonoi on guard on the Acropolis on the day that the Germans took the city in the Second World War, is supposed to have jumped down from the east side of the Acropolis after wrapping himself in the Greek flag, so that the Germans could not capture it.[586] That last story, still widely believed in modern Greece, has recently lost much of its credibility as an investigation could not ascertain the very existence of Koukidis.[587]

2.7.3 The μέγαρον

When the Persians were finally in possession of the Acropolis, the sanctuary (ἱρόν) on it was plundered and the whole Acropolis was set on fire (8.53):

> [...] οἱ δὲ ἐς τὸ μέγαρον κατέφευγον. τῶν δὲ Περσέων οἱ ἀναβεβηκότες πρῶτον μὲν ἐτράποντο πρὸς τὰς πύλας, ταύτας δὲ ἀνοίξαντες τοὺς ἱκέτας ἐφόνευον· ἐπεὶ δέ σφι πάντες κατέστρωντο, τὸ ἱρὸν συλήσαντες ἐνέπρησαν πᾶσαν τὴν ἀκρόπολιν. [...]

> [...] other [defendants of the Acropolis] fled into the hall. Those of the Persians who had gone up went to the gates first, and having opened them they killed the suppliants. And when all had been killed, they plundered the temple and set the entire Acropolis on fire. [...]

---

586 Stories of heroes throwing themselves down from citadels or towers also occur in other contexts. In the battle of Chapultepec citadel in Mexico City during an invasion by American forces in 1847, a defender of the citadel, Juan Escutia, is said to have thrown himself down the Acropolis wrapped in the Mexican flag, so that it could not be captured by the Americans (I am thankful to Thomas Figueira for pointing out this parallel). In another story from the Dutch town of Barneveld taking place during the Hook and Cod Wars in 1482, commander Jan van Schaffelaar jumped down from the church tower to save his besieged troops (the story first appears in a source from 1698).
587 See http://www.iospress.gr/ios2000/ios20001022a.htm (last consulted on 12 July 2017).

The identification of this μέγαρον or 'hall' has proven difficult for various reasons. First, Herodotus' terminology in these passages is rather confusing. While the use of the word ἱκέται as a description of the people who fled into the μέγαρον demonstrates that this 'hall' was a religious building, in conformity with other instances of Herodotus' use of the word,[588] its relation to the ἱρόν (presumably 'sanctuary') is unclear. They may or may not refer to the same structure. Even so, the very lack of any elucidation given by Herodotus suggests that there was only one structure worthy to be called τὸ μέγαρον or *'the* hall'.[589] This mirrors his description of 'the' sanctuary (ἱρόν) in the story about Kleomenes, who sought refuge there when he was being besieged by the Athenians (5.72), as well as in the famous story about the disappearance of the temple snake (8.41).

Second, the archaeology of the archaic and classical Acropolis is notoriously complex. In Herodotus' time, the Acropolis was probably a building site with a mix of partly ruined, older buildings and several new ones, allegedly begun by Pericles, in various states of completion.[590]

While some scholars have in passing assumed that Herodotus' μέγαρον refers to a Parthenon (anachronistically) or its purported predecessor, the Older Parthenon,[591] less casual commentators have instead proposed the Old Temple of Athena Polias as its identification.[592] The foundations of that temple, discovered by Wilhelm Dörpfeld in 1885, can still be seen between the Parthenon and the Erechtheion.[593] It has been argued that architectural material of poros stone consisting of architraves, triglyphs and geisa in the Acropolis north wall (some of which preserves its original painting), Doric capitals and column drums found during nearby excavations, and other material, also belonged to this temple.[594] Despite earlier suggestions that the Old Temple

---

588 See *LSJ* s.v. μέγαρον, where it is claimed that Herodotus uses this word only for temples or shrines, as in 1.47; 1.65; 2.143; and 6.134.
589 Penrose 1891, 275–276.
590 The Erechtheion (dated to 406 BCE) and the temple of Athena Nike (dated to 427–410 BCE) almost certainly postdate the publication of the *Histories*, if we tentatively set this at 430 BCE. Herodotus may still have taken notice of the construction of the Parthenon (begin of construction dated after 447 BCE) and the *Propylaea* (begin of construction dated after 432 BCE).
591 For the Parthenon or one of its earlier stages as the identification of the hall, see Penrose 1891, 295–296 (the Bluebeard temple; believing that the Old Temple of Athena Polias was to a large extent already dismantled); Jeppesen 1987, 39; Robertson 1996, 42; Asheri et al. 2010, 256.
592 E.g. Dörpfeld & Petersen 1887, 27; Furtwängler 1893, 157; Preißhofen 1977, 82–84; Müller 1987, 614; Ferrari 2002, 15. For the identification of the temple in the story of Kleomenes with the temple of Athena Polias see e.g. Preißhofen 1977, 82.
593 Dörpfeld 1885; 1886; 1887; Wiegand 1904, 115–126. For an overview of research on the temple of Athena Polias, see Monaco 2010.
594 Dörpfeld 1885, 1886, 341–342; Wiegand 1904, 118–119. Penrose 1891, 27–276, however, connected this material in the Acropolis north wall to the hypothetical predecessor of the Parthenon, the

Fig. 42: The fundament of the Old Temple of Athena Polias.

had been razed to the ground by the Persians,[595] it has been suggested on the basis of literary and inscriptional evidence a case has been made that parts of it remained in use as one or more shrines throughout Antiquity.[596] When Herodotus visited the Acropolis, the temple, however scarred, was therefore still there for him to see.

A further complication is that Herodotus in his own work mentions another μέγαρον on the Acropolis. He refers to it in passing in order to locate the fetters by which the Athenians had once taken Boeotians and Chalcidians captive (5.77):

Hekatompedon. Kissas 2008 assigned to this building fragments of geisa (pages 56–86) and acroterium bases (87–98).
595 This idea started with Dörpfeld 1885, who (at that time, before his redating of the Parthenon substructure to 490–480 BCE) believed that there was no other major temple on the Athenian Acropolis.
596 Ferrari 2002. The Old Temple was a "point of relay to which the other buildings responded" (page 14). Not only did the south wall of Erechtheion partially coincide with the north wall foundation, and the east wall of the Erechtheion's cella align with the east peristyle of the temple of Athena; the Caryatids were precisely visible through the gap between cella and opisthodomos (pages 21–24). Accordingly, a picture emerges of a Periclean Erechtheion whose strange shape was partly inspired by the remains of the adjacent temple of Athena, and formed a marked contrast with it, much like the Kaiser Wilhelm Memorial Church in Berlin (page 28).

αἵ περ ἔτι καὶ ἐς ἐμὲ ἦσαν περιεοῦσαι, κρεμάμεναι ἐκ τειχέων περιπεφλευσμένων πυρὶ ὑπὸ τοῦ Μήδου, ἀντίον δὲ τοῦ μεγάρου τοῦ πρὸς ἑσπέρην τετραμμένου.

These were still present in my time, hanging from walls scorched by fire by the Mede, and opposite the hall which faces the west.

While this west-facing μέγαρον was apparently extant in Herodotus' time, it has been unclear whether Herodotus envisaged it to have been coexistent with (or even identical to) the 'hideout' μέγαρον of the siege in 480 BCE. Scholars who recognised the west-facing μέγαρον in a room of the Old Temple of Athena Polias have given various identifications for the walls on which the fetters were hung.[597] But a more obvious candidate of this hall seems to be the great opisthodomos of the 'Periclean' Parthenon, (near-)finished in Herodotus' time, and which was only accessible from the west.[598] This identification makes the likely candidate for the scorched walls the western part of the Acropolis south retaining wall which faces the opisthodomos of the Parthenon, and which would be part of, or later be incorporated into, the Chalkotheke or 'metal store'. Now, the puzzle seems to fall into place: if one were to identify the place of the fetters, and Herodotus had not given any clues, the first guess would have been the Chalkotheke, which is known to have contained military spoils.[599] This indicates that the 'west-facing μέγαρον' was not necessarily the same as or even contemporary with the 'hide-out' μέγαρον, and its existence has no bearing on the question of the identification of that other hall.

The ground for the view that Herodotus' μέγαρον should be identified with the Old Temple of Athena Polias is the conventional reconstruction of the Acropolis on the eve of the arrival the Persians. According to this reconstruction, only that temple was finished, for the place where the Parthenon would later stand was at this time the construction site of its precursor, the so-called Older Parthenon.[600] It is now commonly believed that the Older Parthenon was conceived as a thank offer to Athena

---

[597] E.g. Preißhofen 1977, 82; Bundgaard 1976, 118; Dinsmoor 1980, 5. The walls may then have belonged to any structure in this area, including the Acropolis' fortifications or the Propylaea (Jeppesen 1987, 38; Müller 1987, 614–615; Hurwit 1999, 144); or the inner hall of the Pandroseion (Bundgaard 1976, 118). Robertson (1996, 42) maintained that the west-facing μέγαρον was in fact a building in the southeast corner of the Acropolis, which he also identifies with the temple of Erechtheus (it is usually identified as a workshop or as the shrine of Pandion). According to this view, the walls on which the fetters hung were part of the precinct of Zeus Polieus.
[598] Jeppesen 1987, 39.
[599] The existence of this building is known from various inscriptions mentioning military spoils (cf. Hurwit 2004, 198–200; Camia 2010).
[600] The theory of the Older Parthenon was first proposed by Dörpfeld (1892), and its main reconstruction, still unchallenged today, is that of Hill (1912), who showed that the foundation consisted of two poros steps, one kara step and two marble steps and the temple as a peristyle of 6 by 16 columns. This building is supposed to have been equal to the 'Periclean' Parthenon in all of its features except

for the victory in the battle of Marathon (490 BCE), and should hence be dated to the 'peaceful' decade between the battle of Marathon (490 BCE) and Xerxes' invasion (480 BCE).[601] For this temple, the pre-existing Bluebeard temple would have been willingly dismantled. The Older Parthenon would have been far from complete when the Persians destroyed it: work had only progressed to its foundation and the columns.

However, there are serious problems with this theory. The conventional dating of the Older Parthenon to the period between Darius' and Xerxes' invasions has been challenged numerous times.[602] Moreover, it is possible to doubt the very existence of this building, as the material evidence for it can be more comfortably assigned to the 'Periclean' Parthenon and the Bluebeard temple.[603] If there is some argumentative room for the assertion that the Older Parthenon did not exist, or at least that it was not begun until after 480 BCE, we also have to be open to the idea that the Bluebeard temple was still standing in tandem with the Old Temple when the Persians arrived in Athens.

If there were possibly at least two major temples on the Acropolis in 480 BCE, why does Herodotus make us guess about the identification of the hide-out of the Athenians on the Acropolis, τὸ μέγαρον? The Older Parthenon theory seemed to solve this problem, for it dictated that there was only one major finished temple on the Acropolis in 480 BCE, the Old Temple. But even in this scenario, various explanations for Herodotus' use of the definite article are available.

As elsewhere on the Acropolis, the perspective of memory has to be acknowledged. When the Father of History climbed the Acropolis around 430 BCE, what did he observe, and what stories would locals have told him? Could he accurately

---

for the older building's narrower dimensions that suited an earlier stage of the Parthenon fundament (Bundgaard 1976, 61–62; Korres 2003, 10–12).

601 The interwar dating is followed by most textbooks and overview works, but also by e.g. Tölle-Kastenbein 1983, 582; Steskal 2004, 151–154 (believing that Athens could simply not afford to build the Older Parthenon after the wars). Korres 1994a, 41–42; 1997, 239–240 (specifically connecting the decision to stop building the Older Parthenon with Xerxes' enthronement in 485 BCE); Connelly 2014, 71. See also di Cesare 2010.
602 E.g. Kolbe 1936, 23–27; Tschira 1940, 260; Schefold 1953–1954, 141–142; Carpenter 1970, 44; Kalpaxis 1986, 112.
603 For the conventional idea that the wall is a memorial, conspicuously reusing material from the Older Parthenon see e.g. Dörpfeld 1885, 27; Dörpfeld 1902, 412; Korres 1994a, 41–42; 1994c, 58; Rhodes 1995, 32–34; Hurwit 1999, 142; Ferrari 2002, 25; Connelly 2014, 74; Miles 2014, 111; 123–124. For the idea that the lapis primus (*IG* I³ 259) was an architrave block from the Older Parthenon, see Miles 2011. For the view that the drums in the north wall are not necessarily a memorial, see Kalpaxis 1986, 113 with note 859; Steskal 2004, 210–211. As I intend to argue at full force in a future article, I also hypothesise that this material may potentially be seen as rejected building material of the 'Periclean' Parthenon. This matches the idea of Tschira (1940, 247–251) that the column drums that still had bosses had belonged the Periclean Parthenon. The first (smaller) phase of the Parthenon fundament, on which the Older Parthenon would have stood, is in fact of uncertain date and can instead be assigned to the Bluebeard temple.

reflect on the state of the Acropolis building ensemble in 480 BCE? Perhaps Herodotus could, and knew that there had been two temples at the time. In that scenario, one can maintain that the main chamber of the Bluebeard temple was Herodotus' μέγαρον. Further evidence for the view that the Bluebeard temple was simply 'the' temple is furnished by the so-called Hekatompedon inscription (*IG* I³ 3 and 4) which may be seen to employ the terms τὸ Ἑκατόμπεδον and ὁ νηός interchangeably.⁶⁰⁴ This dovetails with the references to its successor, the Parthenon, in the epigraphic record, in which it is often simply called 'the temple', even though others existed simultaneously.

Herodotean scholars at last recognise that the *Histories* often do not offer a direct window onto the events that they describe. It is possible that Herodotus, or the sources on which he relied, had assumed that the buildings standing in his time, albeit new, were exemplary for the old situation. After all, he does not mark any of the temples as 'former' or 'still-existing', perhaps because the new buildings were regarded as continuations of the former ones, so that a distinction was not made. It is possible that the enormous 'Periclean' Parthenon (under construction or just finished) was then the obvious focal point of the Acropolis, and worthy to be called τὸ μέγαρον. But perhaps more likely, Herodotus may not have been aware that the Acropolis once housed the Bluebeard temple which at the time of his visit had long been torn down to make space for its successor and to furnish material for the Acropolis walls and fills. He would have projected his stories on the clearly older, mutilated, but still extant Old Temple of Athena Polias.

We may imagine this venerable ruin not just to have been a magnet of attention from tourists desiring to see a relic of the invasion; it may, in that process, have prompted various stories by its very existence. For example, it may have been responsible for the tradition about the oath of Plataea, according to which the Greeks would have vowed to keep the ruined temples standing, as eternal reminders of the Persian havoc. Similarly, the temple may also have elicited the dramatic story of the hideout in its μέγαρον. The drama was especially poignant because the story invited the idea that the horror committed by Xerxes would eventually meet divine retribution at Salamis.⁶⁰⁵ The Old Temple was thereby enveloped in the narrative constructed about the siege within folk memory and transmitted as such by Herodotus, just like the Areopagus and the sanctuary of Aglauros. This does not in itself disprove the historicity of the story. But we should be weary of accepting it at face value.⁶⁰⁶ The idea that we may, before anything else, see the temple as a mnemotope, is in agreement with the

---

604 In favour of two temples: Preißhofen 1977, 77–78; Connelly 2014, 58. In favour of one temple: e.g. Kissas 2008, 45.
605 Mikalson 2003, 73–74 points out that the killing of the Athenian suppliants was a hubristic breach of *nomos*, which would always lead to punishment.
606 See e.g. Kousser 2009, 265 for the idea that the hiding episode is historical.

observation that 'refuge' mnemotopes are a common occurrence elsewhere in Herodotus' account of the Persian Wars (§3.3.4). Moreover, the story is understandable as a 'temple legend' which made the sanctuary more interesting, like other temples in the stories about the Persian invasions (§3.2).

We have also seen that the Old Temple probably was the locality for the story about the snake. The stories about the hide-out and the disappearance of the snake are, after all, connected. The disappearance of the snake was a satisfying clarification given to any visitor of the Acropolis in Herodotus' time, who was wondering why the city's patron goddess had not come to the rescue of the defendants in her temple. The answer was that she herself had abandoned the Acropolis.

2.7.4 The temple of Erechtheus and Athena's olive tree

An inferno allegedly swept over the Acropolis. Herodotus recounts that Xerxes afterwards commanded the Greeks in his army to go up the Acropolis and to sacrifice to the goddess. They then saw that Athena's sacred olive tree had miraculously survived the fire (8.54-55):

> σχὼν δὲ παντελέως τὰς Ἀθήνας Ξέρξης ἀπέπεμψε ἐς Σοῦσα ἄγγελον ἱππέα Ἀρταβάνῳ ἀγγελέοντα τὴν παρεοῦσάν σφι εὐπρηξίην. ἀπὸ δὲ τῆς πέμψιος τοῦ κήρυκος δευτέρῃ ἡμέρῃ συγκαλέσας Ἀθηναίων τοὺς φυγάδας, ἑωυτῷ δὲ ἑπομένους, ἐκέλευε τρόπῳ τῷ σφετέρῳ θῦσαι τὰ ἱρὰ ἀναβάντας ἐς τὴν ἀκρόπολιν, εἴτε δὴ ὦν ὄψιν τινὰ ἰδὼν ἐνυπνίου ἐνετέλλετο ταῦτα, εἴτε καὶ ἐνθύμιόν οἱ ἐγένετο ἐμπρήσαντι τὸ ἱρόν. οἱ δὲ φυγάδες τῶν Ἀθηναίων ἐποίησαν τὰ ἐντεταλμένα. τοῦ δὲ εἵνεκεν τούτων ἐπεμνήσθην, φράσω. ἔστι ἐν τῇ ἀκροπόλι ταύτῃ Ἐρεχθέος τοῦ γηγενέος λεγομένου εἶναι νηός, ἐν τῷ ἐλαίη τε καὶ θάλασσα ἔνι, τὰ λόγος παρὰ Ἀθηναίων Ποσειδέωνά τε καὶ Ἀθηναίην ἐρίσαντας περὶ τῆς χώρης μαρτύρια θέσθαι. ταύτην ὦν τὴν ἐλαίην ἅμα τῷ ἄλλῳ ἱρῷ κατέλαβε ἐμπρησθῆναι ὑπὸ τῶν βαρβάρων· δευτέρῃ δὲ ἡμέρῃ ἀπὸ τῆς ἐμπρήσιος Ἀθηναίων οἱ θύειν ὑπὸ βασιλέος κελευόμενοι ὡς ἀνέβησαν ἐς τὸ ἱρόν, ὥρων βλαστὸν ἐκ τοῦ στελέχεος ὅσον τε πηχυαῖον ἀναδεδραμηκότα. οὗτοι μέν νυν ταῦτα ἔφρασαν.

> Now possessing Athens entirely, Xerxes sent a messenger to Sousa to tell Artabanos about their success. On the second day after they had sent the messenger, and had called together the exiles of the Athenians, he ordered them to go up the Acropolis and to sacrifice in their own manner. He ordered this either because he had seen the vision of a dream or because he regretted having set the temple on fire. The exiles of the Athenians did what had been ordered. I will say why I mentioned this. On this Acropolis there is a temple of Erechtheus, who is said to be 'earthborn', inside of which there is an olive tree and a salt-water pond, which (according to the story of the Athenians) Poseidon and Athena, who had quarrelled about the land, put there as testimonies. That olive tree happened to be put to fire by the barbarians, together with the rest of the temple. On the second day after the fire, when the Athenians who were ordered by the king to sacrifice went up to the temple, they saw a shoot from the trunk, which had grown to a cubit in length. Immediately they started spreading the news.

Herodotus refers to the shrine of Erechtheus both by the words νηός ('temple') and ἱρόν ('sanctuary'). Because Herodotus' story is situated in 480 BCE, one could surmise that there once was an Older Erechtheion.⁶⁰⁷ But as we have seen in the quest for τὸ μέγαρον, it is possible that Herodotus projected the situation of the Acropolis in his own time onto events fifty years earlier. In the light of this, and the sparsity of archaeological evidence for an Older Erechtheion, we cannot ascertain the existence of that building. However, a minimal conclusion is that we may take Herodotus to refer to the area where today stands the 'Periclean' Erechtheion, because the mnemotopes of the olive tree and the saltwater pond are widely believed to have been present in or near that temple in earlier times, and not likely to have moved around, as the unconventional shape of the 'Periclean' Erechtheion partly serves to accommodate them.⁶⁰⁸ The third-century BCE historian Philochorus (*FGrH* 328 F67) describes the olive tree in close relation to the Old Temple of Athena Polias, the Pandroseion and the altar of Zeus Herkeios, in the approximate location of the modern olive tree. Remains of bosses on the Erechtheion's west facade and on the roof of the Caryatid porch, which apparently could not be polished away, have been supposed to mark the place where the olive tree touched the building and show that the Erechtheion was partially conceived as a support for the already full grown olive tree.⁶⁰⁹ A tree was still present in Pausanias' time (1.27.2).

When Herodotus visited the Acropolis several decades after the war, the olive tree apparently had become a mnemotope for the story which he describes. It may well be that a new tree was visible on top of a burnt (or more generally dead?) trunk, as is not uncommon in olive trees. It is, in itself, not strange that trees develop into mnemotopes (in the context of Xerxes' invasion, we may compare the story about a beautiful plane tree near Kallatebos in Lydia which Xerxes would have adorned with gold; §2.1.4). Here we witness a process of 'accumulation' of mnemotopes: the story about the siege added to the tree's prominence, which was already in place, because it supposedly was the tree which Athena herself had given to the city, as Herodotus emphasises. The miracle story appealed to any ancient visitor of the Acropolis, who had just seen the Areopagus and the Old Temple, and thus re-experienced the story of the Persian siege before his eyes. After all, one question was not answered yet: 'How was Athens finally rescued?' The olive tree responded to this question by telling

---

607 Bundgaard 1976, 103–111 believed that the surviving building largely corresponds to its predecessor. Müller 1987, 616 suggested that Herodotus' ἱρόν of Erechtheus referred to part of the temple of Athena Polias. Jeppesen 1987, 38–44 and Robertson 1996, 37–42 locate the Erechtheion elsewhere on the Acropolis. Robertson specifically identified it with a building in the southeast corner of the Acropolis. He also supposes that there were two sacred olive trees on the Acropolis, the other being in the Pandroseion (pages 42–43). See also Hurwit 1999, 144–145.
608 Ferrari (2002, 16 note 30) believes that it is not possible to see the Erechtheion in another location because of the cultic continuity and the Philochorus fragment (*FGrH* 328 F67). For the Erechtheion as a collection of different mnemotopes, see e.g. Boardman 2002, 109–110; Hölscher 2010, 132–134.
609 Bundgaard 1976, 87–100 with figures 50, 58 and 66.

Fig. 43: The 'Periclean' Erechtheion and the olive tree.

a story of hope in times of utter despair, because the shoot from which it had grown signalled that Athens would rise from its ashes.[610]

Herodotus details that it was Xerxes, the destroyer of its citadel, who had made that possible, by making the Greeks in his army worship according to their custom. This story is still often explained as a historical event and as evidence for the popular idea that the Achaemenids were not Zoroastrian zealots, but actually tolerant towards other religions.[611] Instead, however, it is also possible that it arose in touristic lore in response to the olive tree's miraculous 'revival'. The story, and thereby the shoot, then highlights Xerxes' temperament. The act appears in stark contrast with his earlier blasphemy of temple-burning, the gravest offence to the gods one can think of. Moreover, by using the word κελεύω, Herodotus does not present Xerxes' act as an instance

---

610 On the symbolism of the event, see Vandiver 1991, 99–102; Hollmann 2011, 71. On the olive trees of the Acropolis, see Demandt 2002, 78–82. See Demandt 2002, 208–209 for more modern parallels of trees as symbol of the resurrection of a city. Note that Herodotus elsewhere (6.37) refers to pine trees as the only trees that cannot grow new shoots after they have been burnt (the parallel is noted by Ferrari 2002, 30).
611 E.g. Macan 1908, I 441; Boyce 1982, 169–170; Georges 1994, 57 (suggesting that the fire was meant to cleanse the Acropolis of the demons in order to institute a cult of Ahuramazda there); Briant 1996, 566 (suggesting that Xerxes may have felt a real need to appease the territorial gods); Rosenberger 2003, 72; Allen 2005a, 55; Kousser 2009, 269. Hauvette 1894, 399 noted that Herodotus himself had a slight reserve about the story's historicity.

of religious tolerance, but rather as a command that used the Greeks in his army to appease the goddess for the havoc caused by his own men. The remedy was too little, too late, as Xerxes would lose the battle of Salamis not much later.[612] The story can be compared to other futile Persian attempts to appease Greek divinities, to Athena and the heroes at Troy (§2.2.3) or to Thetis and the Nereids at Sepias in Thessaly (§2.4.2).[613]

2.7.5 The Anaktoron of Demeter in Eleusis

The final locality in Attica where Herodotus records an event during Xerxes' invasion is the sanctuary of Demeter and Persephone at Eleusis.[614] This event is only known from a passage in which Herodotus claims that the Persians had not entered the temenos of Demeter in Plataea (cf. §2.9.6) because the goddess was angry about the fact that the Persians had set fire to the ἀνάκτορον or 'palace' at Eleusis (9.65):

> θῶμα δέ μοι ὅκως παρὰ τῆς Δήμητρος τὸ ἄλσος μαχομένων οὐδὲ εἷς ἐφάνη τῶν Περσέων οὔτε ἐσελθὼν ἐς τὸ τέμενος οὔτε ἐναποθανών, περί τε τὸ ἱρὸν οἱ πλεῖστοι ἐν τῷ βεβήλῳ ἔπεσον. δοκέω δέ, εἴ τι περὶ τῶν θείων πρηγμάτων δοκέειν δεῖ, ἡ θεὸς αὐτή σφεας οὐκ ἐδέκετο ἐμπρήσαντας τὸ ἱρὸν τὸ ἐν Ἐλευσῖνι ἀνάκτορον.

> It is a marvel to me that no-one of the Persians who fought near the sacred grove of Demeter, appeared to have entered the sanctuary or died within it; most fell round the temple on profane ground. But I think, if one may think anything about divine affairs, that the goddess herself did not allow inside those who had put fire to her holy palace in Eleusis.

Apart from this short reference, we do not possess ancient testimonies about the activities of the Persians at Eleusis.[615] The ἀνάκτορον is probably identical to the palace of Keleos, which is also mentioned in the *Homeric hymn to Demeter* (line 96). It presumably refers to a section of the Telesterion, a large hall in the precinct where the Eleusinian mysteries were performed and of which large parts have been preserved.[616]

---

612 It has been suggested that the mention of Poseidon's 'sea' and Athena's olive tree evoke the imminent victories of the Greeks at Salamis and Plataea: Xerxes' burning of the temples on the Acropolis triggered the vengeance of the gods (Bowie 2012, 277).
613 Scheer (2000, 207) supposes that Xerxes' reconciliation at Athens is unlikely and connects the worship to the return of Athenian exiles. That Herodotus thought in terms of divine vengeance is shown by his story of another eastern king, Alyattes (1.19): he had accidentally burnt the temple of Athena at Assesos. The Lydian ruler suffered ill health until the temple was rebuilt. For the correspondence between these events see Baragwanath 2008, 285–286, suggesting that Herodotus gives his readers a conscious choice: did Xerxes sacrifice here because of repentance or divine cogency?
614 The location of Eleusis is indicated on Map 6.
615 Boedeker 2007, 69–70. Isocrates (*Panegyricus* 157) relates that Barbarians were excluded from the Eleusinian mysteries because of the permanent hatred against them; there is no reference to the burning of the palace.
616 Mylonas 1961, 83–88.

Herodotus' account is usually taken as reflecting a historical truth by historians and archaeologists. As a result, the Persian destruction of the Telesterion has become a watershed date in archaeological study of the site.[617] The main excavator, Mylonas, identified the structure destroyed by the Persians with a sixth-century BCE square temple built in the time of Peisistratos.[618] Mylonas suggested that this building was set to fire in 480 along with the Athenians Acropolis, or in 479 when Mardonios went to Megara.[619] After the wars the Telesterion had to be rebuilt, because the temple could not be moved from the fixed mnemotopes of Demeter's story; also, it would have been in order to thank Demeter for her help during the battle of Plataea (9.65).[620] There is evidence for various constructions activities, including the restoration of a wall.[621] An important corroboration of Herodotus' story was found in the so-called Rheitos bridge decree from Eleusis (*IG* I³ 79, c. 422 BCE), which suggests that several walls of an 'ancient temple' (the 'Peisistratean' structure?) were left standing after the wars and became part of the new structure, so that the destruction of the building's precursor remained visible.[622] In addition, *IG* I³ 386 and 387 (407/6 BCE) are sometimes believed to mention materials from this structure.

However, other scholars have pointed out that the archaeological picture is not so clear. Shear, for example, maintained that the Telesterion cannot have been the building described by Herodotus, because it was just being constructed when the Persians attacked.[623] It has also been pointed out that the damage to the roof tiles was not such that the roof was deliberately destroyed.[624] Recently, Boedeker proposed that the Telesterion was never set to fire:[625] she doubts the authenticity of Herodotus' text, suggesting that τὸ ἐν Ἐλευσῖνι ἀνάκτορον was a learned but wrong

---

617 For example, the sculpture of the 'fleeing maiden', believed to have adorned the front of the temple of Demeter and now in the archaeological museum of Eleusis, was stylistically dated to the immediate post-Persian period (Noack 1927, 218–219).
618 Mylonas 1961, 78–87.
619 Mylonas 1961, 90.
620 Mylonas 1961, 106–108: "The importance of the cult depended upon the fact that the initiates found themselves in the same spot visited by the Goddess and could see the sacred landmarks sanctified by her sojourn. This of course would have tended to keep fresh and exact the memory of the past." Mylonas believed that Kimon was responsible for the reconstruction programme, and that Pericles had continued the work after Kimon's ostracism in 461 BCE.
621 Mylonas 1961, 107–113.
622 Ferrari 2002, 26.
623 Shear 1982; he suggested that large parts of the archaic Telesterion were not destroyed and that the building was repaired, with many wooden construction elements apparently having survived the destruction (if the materials summed up in *IG* I³ 386 and 387 can really be attributed to the Peisistran Telesterion).
624 Noack 1927, 93 (note that this scholar believed that the temple was destroyed by the Persians on the basis of various broken archaic sculptures).
625 Boedeker 2007, 70–72; Bowie 2012, 277, note 29.

Fig. 44: Remains of the Telesterion at Eleusis.

interpolation, and underlines that there is an absence of other textual sources. She also stresses that the material record cannot be used to offer a corroboration, and that the inscription of building material from the archaic Telesterion (*IG* I³ 386, lines 103-20) mentions wooden doors, which would not have survived a fire. Boedeker suggests that Herodotus instead referred to the temple of Demeter on the north slope of the Athenian Acropolis, which is more likely to have been destroyed along with the other buildings here. This Eleusinion was the building where the objects were kept which were taken from Eleusis each year during the Panathenaia.[626] Note that there was another Eleusinion on the Athenian Agora, which also seems to have been destroyed because debris deposits were found nearby; its destruction has also been attributed to the Persians.[627] It is certainly possible that Herodotus referred to a different temple where Demeter was worshipped. However, Boedeker's idea that Herodotus never indicated that the building was in Eleusis

---

[626] The most thorough study on this complex is Miles 1998; on the localisation of the site and the ancient testimonia see pages 1–3. See also Malacrino 2010.
[627] Miles 1998, 41.

remains conjectural, as no textual problems are reported for this passage, and the grammar is not faulty.

I believe that it is also possible that the text is correct, and that Herodotus really believed that the Telesterion at Eleusis was set to fire, despite the fact that there is a lack of textual, archaeological and inscriptionary evidence. Popular traditions in the post-war period may have attributed Persian destruction to the structure in Eleusis, as part of the stereotype of the Persians as a destructive force, regardless of the historical truth. This is not to say that the building was not 'impaired' in Herodotus' day, but the impairment may have been caused by an earthquake or by the fact that the building was being reconstructed, and then abandoned until the late fifth century BCE, as Shear suggests. As discussed in the introduction, the phenomenon of wrong attribution of damage is known from other contexts (see §3.2.1).

Regardless of what really happened in 480 or 479 BCE, it is not surprising that a story about the burning of the Telesterion at Eleusis arose, given the fact that other stories circulated in which Demeter appears as a furious goddess at Eleusis. This starts with the founding myth of the sanctuary itself: Demeter was angry when she originally came to Eleusis on her search for Persephone.[628] Even more telling are the legends which Herodotus records surrounding the suicide of Kleomenes, king of Sparta in the sixth century BCE: the Argive version of this myth explained that Kleomenes had done this after executing fugitives in the temple of Argos, while other Greeks said he had bribed the Pythian oracle. However, the Athenians recounted a version according to which this was the result of cutting down the trees in the temenos of Demeter at Eleusis (6.75).[629] If such a story about an enemy's sacrilege and Demeter's vengeance at Eleusis could arise in Athenian folklore about a Spartan king, we should not be surprised that a similar anecdote could attach itself to new enemies, the Persians. Also note Herodotus' story about the dust cloud which arose near Eleusis and descended on the Greeks at Salamis, who understood that they were going to win, because a *iakchos* cry was heard which was readily associated with Demeter and Persephone (8.65).[630] At Eleusis, Demeter had no patience with intruders and Athenian folk tradition knew about this.

---

628 The foundation myth of Demeter's temple at Eleusis is told in the *Homeric hymn to Demeter*; see also Mylonas 1961, 3–6.
629 On this story, see Boedeker 1988, 46. The common hubris element in the stories about Kleomenes and the Persians at Eleusis is noted by Bowden 2010, 39.
630 See Cartledge 2002 (first published 1993), 184 for the idea that Demeter, Persephone and Dionysos came to the defence of their sanctuary at Eleusis. This story (which is also told by Plutarch in *Themistocles* 15.1, where a flashing light from Eleusis is mentioned) is seen by some scholars as having a historical kernel: Green (1996, 205) suggests that the cloud was caused by the army that went to the isthmus. Mylonas (1961, 255) suggested that the *iakchos* cry became a more important part of the processions after Xerxes' invasion.

2.7.6 Summary

I have argued that during the course of the fifth century BCE, after the Persian invasion of Athens, the Acropolis developed into a memorial space where the Persian siege could be re-experienced by mnemotopes where the stories about the siege were told. This localisation of the account in important landmarks within Athenian topography enhanced its plausibility: no-one seems to have doubted the tourist stories which Herodotus had encountered during his visit. Thus, the siege of the Acropolis, through its landmarks, was made to adhere to the dramatic and common 'bypass story', to resonate with the Athenian Amazonomachy and the myth of Aglauros, and to tell the story of Athena's return when all hope was lost. Meanwhile, the archaeological corroboration of the stories of the destructions of the Acropolis and Demeter's sanctuary in Eleusis remains problematic.

That such processes are at the basis of Herodotus' account of the Persian siege of Athens' holy citadel is a new perspective. Perhaps, the delay in its appearance can be sought in the overall staunch belief in the story's exact historicity. That belief can be misleading, as the case of the quest for the location of the temple of Aglauros demonstrates. However, the perspective of memory in itself does not touch upon the historical events, but only seeks to explain why we find the story in our sources and in this shape. In the end, trying to find the real place where the Persians once climbed up the Acropolis, may be no different from trying to find the real place where a mythical princess once fell down.

2.8 The battle of Salamis and Xerxes' escape

After the devastation inflicted upon Athens and other places in Greece, the battle of Salamis was a turning point in the war.[631] As the first victory for the Greeks, it was naturally subject to elaborate commemorative traditions. Dedications commemorating the battle are reported for various places in Greece,[632] and Simonides is said to

---

[631] A selection of places mentioned in this chapter features on Map 6.
[632] On commemoration practises see especially Gauer 1968, 32–33; 36; 71–74; 122–124; Alcock 2002, 78–79 (for the Roman period). In Delphi, first-fruits, and a statue of Apollo and the mast pole of the Aiginetans were offered (Herodotus 8.121–122; Pausanias 10.14.5). The statue of Zeus at Olympia had a depiction of a personification of Salamis (Pausanias 5.11.5). On the Acropolis monuments were erected by Phayllos (an athlete), Ekphantos and Hegelochos. At Corinth, a cult of Leto was installed. At Phlya, a parasemon of a Persian battle ship was offered to Apollo Daphnephoros by Lykomedes (Plutarch, *Themistocles* 15.3). The Athenian Agora had a statue of Athenian women and children (Pausanias 2.31.7). Other spoils and inscriptions (Simonides *FGE* 12) were placed at the Isthmus, Sounion and Salamis. Gauer suggests that such locations were chosen because Salamis, after all, was associated with Poseidon, Athena and Ajax. The temple of Athena Nike on the Athenian Acropolis, seemingly

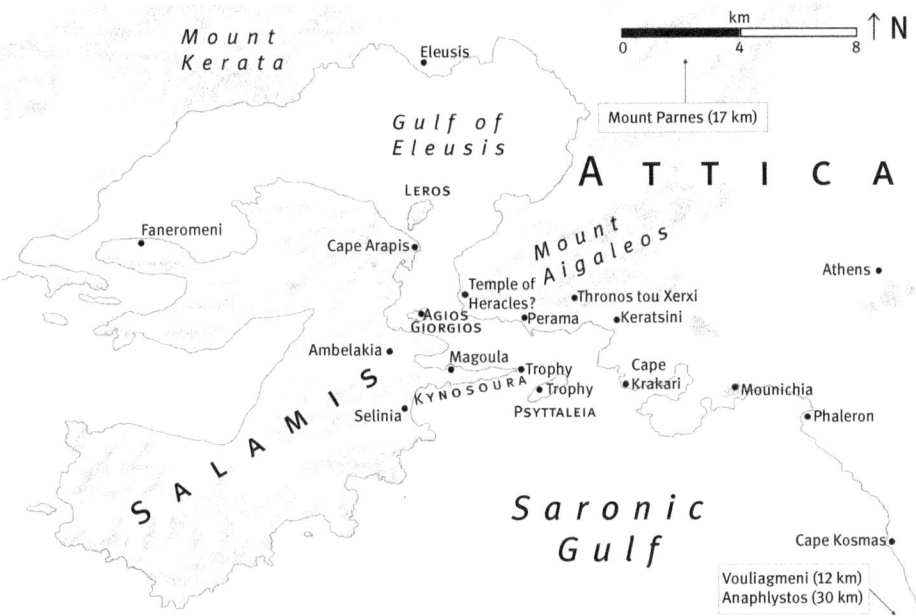

Map 6: Salamis and a part of Attica.

have written a lost poem celebrating the victory.[633] As we will see below, commemorative engagement with the actual battlefield itself occurred too: trophies were erected on conspicuous points near the waters where the battle was believed to have been fought, and the Aianteia festival included boat races in which the youth of Athens interacted with the battlefield.

This chapter concerns the topography of the battle as it appears in Herodotus' account, as well as various stories connected to Xerxes' escape after the battle (an event already briefly discussed in §2.3.4). It argues that the perspective of mnemotopes can be used to understand the topography in this account, as the places given by Herodotus do not allow us to reconstruct the topography of the battle, but only to localise the places where various anecdotes were believed to have taken place.[634]

---

oriented towards the battlefield, may have been the most elaborate commemoration effort; but that temple may also have referred to the Persian Wars or other conflicts in a more general sense.

633 *Vita Pindari* 2.21; Suda s.v. Σιμωνίδης; Kowerski 2005, 33–39 points out that the new Simonides fragments 6 and 7 W^2 cannot be connected to this poem with certainty.

634 Many scholars 'complain' that Herodotus gives mainly incidents of the battle, not a full strategical appraisal, nor an explanation of why the Persians lost: Grundy 1897b, 230; Hignett 1963, 231; Hammond 1988, 579; Cawkwell 2005, 99 ("Herodotus' report of the battle of Salamis is in essence a rag-bag of stories [...]"). Examples of anecdotal material include the messages from Themistocles to Xerxes: this account is also found in *Persae* 335, with some minor discrepancies (Hignett 1963, 403–408);

This fits the observation by many scholars that some parts of the account are dramatised.[635] In addition, it will become clear that this framework helps us in explaining why Herodotus made recourse to a few landmarks on the coasts of Attica and Salamis, as well as to various islands in the channel.[636]

Uniquely among episodes of Xerxes' invasion, we can in the following analysis supplement Herodotus' account of the battle of Salamis with a preceding source, Aeschylus' *Persae*, thought to be written relatively soon after 479 BCE. Aeschylus is usually believed to have been an eye-witness of the battle,[637] this is only based on a scholion on *Persae* 429.[638] However, the two cannot be regarded as independent sources: it is probable that Herodotus knew Aeschylus' tragedy and used it for his own account.[639]

2.8.1 Psyttaleia

As Herodotus informs the reader about the Persian preparations for the battle, the attention shifts to the island of Psyttaleia (8.76):

> τοῖσι δὲ ὡς πιστὰ ἐγίνετο τὰ ἀγγελθέντα, τοῦτο μὲν ἐς τὴν νησῖδα τὴν Ψυττάλειαν μεταξὺ Σαλαμῖνός τε κειμένην καὶ τῆς ἠπείρου πολλοὺς τῶν Περσέων ἀπεβίβασαν: [...] ἐς δὲ τὴν νησῖδα τὴν Ψυττάλειαν καλεομένην ἀπεβίβαζον τῶν Περσέων τῶνδε εἵνεκα, ὡς ἐπεὰν γίνηται ναυμαχίη, ἐνθαῦτα μάλιστα ἐξοισομένων τῶν τε ἀνδρῶν καὶ τῶν ναυηγίων (ἐν γὰρ δὴ πόρῳ τῆς ναυμαχίης τῆς μελλούσης ἔσεσθαι ἔκειτο ἡ νῆσος), ἵνα τοὺς μὲν περιποιέωσι τοὺς δὲ διαφθείρωσι. ἐποίευν δὲ σιγῇ ταῦτα, ὡς μὴ πυνθανοίατο οἱ ἐναντίοι. οἱ μὲν δὴ ταῦτα τῆς νυκτὸς οὐδὲν ἀποκοιμηθέντες παραρτέοντο.

Aristides' report of sneaking past the Persians (8.95; Hignett 1963, 408–411); the Mnesiphilos scene (Waters 1966, 167); and the speeches of queen Artemisia (Waters 1966, 167). For a general appraisal of the battle narrative's structure see Immerwahr 1966, 267–287; de Jong 1999, 217–275; 262–271.

635 The movement at night by the Persians is to be regarded as a literary device (Grundy 1897b, 231; Goodwin 1906). It has been recognised that the Greek movement back and forth to their ships is reminiscent of book two of the *Iliad* (Pohlenz 1961, 212–213) and that the episode in which the (images of) the Aeacids arrive from Aegina (8.83) gives the battle an Iliadic quality (Bowie 2012, 277; cf. Erskine 2001, 62–63). De Bakker (2010, 223–225, 228) points out that the fire beacons have a parallel in the opening scene of Aeschylus' *Agamemnon* and that they may be ironic: when the Greek heroes used such signals at Troy, there was negative news to report. Here, Mardonios is still ignorant of his impending death at Plataea. Nevertheless, the beacons may still be regarded as historical depending on one's assessment of their historicity during the battle of Artemision.

636 Wallinga 2005, 58–60.

637 E.g. Green 1996, 196–197: "Aeschylus gave a reasonably trustworthy account of the battle itself – eight years after the event he could scarcely do otherwise [...]."

638 See Wallinga 2005, 117 for the idea that Aeschylus did not fight in he battle, but was simply familiar with it, is more plausible.

639 Aeschylus is mentioned once in the *Histories* (2.156).

And when [the Persian generals] believed the messages, they first brought many Persians to the islet of Psyttaleia, which lies between Salamis and the mainland [...] And they brought the Persian troops to the islet called Psyttaleia, for when the battle would break out, the men and wrecks would mostly wash up there (for the island lay in the way of the sea-battle that was going to take place), so that they could save some, and kill others. They did this in silence, so that their adversaries would not find out. They prepared their plan at night, not having slept.

Later in his account, Herodotus tells us that the Persians at Psyttaleia were killed, an event which ended the battle (8.95):

Ἀριστείδης δὲ ὁ Λυσιμάχου ἀνὴρ Ἀθηναῖος, τοῦ καὶ ὀλίγῳ τι πρότερον τούτων ἐπεμνήσθην ὡς ἀνδρὸς ἀρίστου, οὗτος ἐν τῷ θορύβῳ τούτῳ τῷ περὶ Σαλαμῖνα γενομένῳ τάδε ἐποίεε: παραλαβὼν πολλοὺς τῶν ὁπλιτέων οἳ παρατετάχατο παρὰ τὴν ἀκτὴν τῆς Σαλαμινίης χώρης, γένος ἐόντες Ἀθηναῖοι, ἐς τὴν Ψυττάλειαν νῆσον ἀπέβησε ἄγων, οἳ τοὺς Πέρσας τοὺς ἐν τῇ νησῖδι ταύτῃ κατεφόνευσαν πάντας.

Aristides, son of Lysimachos, an Athenian, whom I mentioned a little while before these events as a good man, did the following in the chaos that had arisen around Salamis. He took many of the hoplites that had been arranged along the coast of the land of Salamis, Athenians by origin, and landed on the island of Psyttaleia while he led them, and they slaughtered all the Persians who were on that island.

In other accounts of the battle, Psyttaleia is even more prominent: Aeschylus (*Persae* 447-471) has a vivid description of the island.[640] In Plutarch (*Aristides* 9.2), too, the island appears as the centre of the fight: 'most of the crashing of the ships and the worst part of the battle seems to have happened around that place: that is why a trophy stands on Psyttaleia'. Pausanias (4.36.6) likewise presents it as well-known because 'the Persians died on it'. On the basis of the available literary and epigraphic evidence, Giorgia Proietti convincingly argues that the confrontation that took place on Psyttaleia was directly after the war seen as a very important battle and perhaps even as separate of (and equivalent to) the battle of Salamis proper, and that its importance had been watered down by the time Herodotus wrote.[641] She also suggests, like some earlier scholars, that the phrase πεζοί τε [καὶ ὠκυπόρων ἐπὶ νηῶ]ν on Lapis A of the Persian War inscriptions (*IG* I³ 503-504), which refers to a terrestrial and a naval encounter, is in fact a juxtaposition of Psyttaleia and Salamis as two equal battles.

Given its prominence in the extant accounts, Psyttaleia has dominated topographical discussions of the battle of Salamis. While earlier authors have tried to identify the island with Agios Giorgios,[642] there are no compelling arguments for that

---

640 The island is not named by Aeschylus; see Wallace 1969, 298 for the easy identification with Psyttaleia. Georges 1994, 84 explains that Aeschylus portrays Psyttaleia as the "richest and most concentrated slaughter of the real enemy".
641 Proietti 2015b.
642 This was first proposed by Beloch 1908, 477–482 and again advocated at greater length by Hammond 1956; 1973. The argument (neatly summarised in Wallace 1969, 294–299) runs first that Pausani-

claim; instead, I surmise that Agios Giorgios may have been the 'island of Ajax' known to Aeschylus (*Persae* 307; 368).[643] It is now commonly accepted that Psyttaleia referred to the island later called Leipsokoutali, before it was renamed Psyttaleia again.[644] Perhaps the most compelling of the many arguments is that the name Leipsokoutali may reflect a French or Italian rendering of the ancient name (something like 'La Psittalia') during the Frankish occupation.[645] Another important point is that the modern name Leipsokoutali, which contains the word κουτάλι 'spoon', may reflect that of its old name Psyttaleia, which contains the word ψύττα, also meaning 'spoon'.[646] According to this theory, Agios Giorgios is to be identified as one of the two Pharmakoussai islands (the other is a reef, today submerged, between Perama and Agios Giorgios).

In the middle of nineteenth century, Ludwig Ross identified some traces of the trophy which Plutarch (*Aristides* 9.2) mentions on the small peninsula on the northwest

---

as was referring to the town of Salamis when saying that Psyttaleia was 'before' it; but this inference is not substantiated. Second, Stephanus Byzantinus records the existence of inhabitants of Atalante (*Ethnica* s.v. Ἀταλάντη), which would mean that it is to be identified with Leipsokoutali; however, Stephanus referred to Atalante near Euboea. Third, Strabo speaks of 'another island' in addition to Psyttaleia and Atalante when describing the strait from north to south, implying that Psyttaleia should be sought further north than Leipsokoutali. However, the phrase 'another island' may plausibly refer to Atalante. Fourth, it is described as a competitor to Piraeus by Strabo, but Psyttaleia has inhospitable shores; however, Strabo merely uses the word λήμη 'rheum in the eye', which does not allow the inference that it was a harbour. Finally Xerxes is supposed to have seen Psyttaleia from Mount Aigaleos, but it is not possible to see Leipsokoutali from there; however, this arguments runs too heavily on Aeschylus' and Herodotus' testimonies, which do not allow such inferences.

643 Aeschylus mentions the island of Ajax as a topographical marker of the battle of Salamis: the ships were positioned around it. This is usually interpreted as a poetic reference to the whole island of Salamis (cf. Simonides *FGE* 11). However, it is rather inconceivable that the Persian ships would be arranged in a circular fashion around the entire island of Salamis, and Aeschylus' words seem to refer to a relatively small island. Some scholars therefore found it necessary to limit Aeschylus' island of Ajax to only a part of Salamis (Kromayer 1924, 86; Munro 1902, 327). However, a better identification is Agios Giorgios: this island is not otherwise known to have had an ancient name. Wilhelm 1929, 16 identified it with Psyttaleia or Strabo's 'other island'. The temple of Ajax that we know from an inscription (*IG* II² 1035) has not yet been located; although it has been surmised on the Kynosoura peninsula (Culley 1977, 295–296), there is no compelling reason to place it there.

644 E.g. Leake 1841, 267; Milchhoefer 1895, 29; Grundy 1901, 375; Judeich 1912; Obst 1913, 145–149 (maintaining that the island referred to by Aeschylus was the modern Agios Giorgios, and that Herodotus really meant Psyttaleia but had misunderstood his text); Munro 1926a, 308; Wilhelm 1929, 16; Kromayer 1924, 87–89; Burn 1962, 454; Hignett 1963, 402; Pritchett 1959, 256–262; Pritchett 1965, 100–103; Bayer 1969 (who adduces an unconvincing argument based on Alciphron 2.3.10); Wallace 1969, 297–302; Taylor 1997, 119 note 39; Wallinga 2005, 62–63; ; Bowie 2007, 165.

645 Burn 1962, 473–474; followed by Wallace 1969, 297–298. The case is especially strong considering the similarity of the names Talandonisi and Atalante. Hammond (1956, 38 note 23), however, was adamant in his view that ancient names are hardly ever represented in modern Greek toponymy. Note that the name Psyttaleia was already deformed into Συπταλ[ία] in a fourth-century BCE inscription from the island (*IG* II² 1590a; cf. Taylor 1997, 119)

646 The word ψύττα is defined as σκαφίον or πρόχυμα by Hesychius (s.v.); cf. Wallace 1969, 298.

Fig. 45: Psyttaleia.

side of the island. They were seen again in 1967, but were then beyond description.[647] It would be very interesting to know more about this monument and a new investigation of the site is a desideratum, if the trophy has not been lost forever after the construction of Europe's biggest sewage treatment plant on the island in the 1990s. If there indeed was a trophy, it shows that at some point in antiquity the locality was awarded this significance. As with the other trophies of the Persian Wars, it may have been erected after Herodotus' time (§3.3.3).

The historicity of the massacre has been taken for granted by most scholars, with only few exceptions.[648] But would a Persian general really station his troops on a small

---

647 Wallace 1969, 302 (reporting that Ludwig Ross had described a rectangular base at the north side of the island). It is possible that this trophy is hinted at by Pausanias (1.36.1), Plato (*Menexenus* 245a), Xenophon (*Anabasis* 3.2.13) and Lycurgus (*Oratio in Leocratem* 73). Beschi 2002, 70–71 and Proietti 2015a, 159–160 point out that the archaeological evidence is minimal. Plutarch's account may be a counter-narrative to that of Herodotus, who arguably downplays the importance of the battle on Psyttaleia. See also Proietti 2015b.
648 It has been suggested that Psyttaleia was perhaps only occupied to protect Persian ships and men at a later point in the battle (Macan 1908, II 307; Wallinga 2005, 91). Fornara 1966 stressed the

island without any water, in order to kill any Greeks that might wash up there? While it is clear that something happened on Psyttaleia, the exact event is beyond recovery. At any rate, Psyttaleia was an important mnemotope in Aeschylus' and Herodotus' time, and we can try to answer the question why and how Psyttaleia had received that status.

We can, first, observe that while much of the scholarly debate on Salamis has focused on the location of the 'actual' battle; its topography is, in fact, impossible to ascertain using the accounts of Herodotus and Aeschylus, which offer only some terrestrial landmarks. In the fifth century BCE, Psyttaleia amounted to the best possible answer to the question 'Where was the battle of Salamis fought?' After all, it was impossible to point out the exact areas of the seas near Salamis where individual ships had sailed.[649] Psyttaleia was also the answer to the question 'What happened to the Persians?' The importance awarded to Psyttaleia by Herodotus, Aeschylus and Pausanias may be a direct result of its prominence in the strait.

Several parallels may be given for the indication of a small island as the location for an event during a battle. During the Trojan War, the Greeks hid their fleet at Tenedos,[650] and the battle for Miletus between Persians and Greeks (494 BCE) was fought near Lade (Herodotus 6.7-8). The Psyttaleia massacre is very similar to the battle of Sphacteria during the Peloponnesian War (425 BCE, Thucydides 4.8-4.38), in which 148 Spartans were killed by an Athenian force; the similarity between the Sphacteria and Psyttaleia episodes was already noted by Pausanias (4.36.6). The parallels between Psyttaleia and a fourth island, Asteris, where Penelope's suitors awaited Telemachos in ambush, are also striking. The scene is described by Homer (*Odyssey* 4.844-847): 'there is a rocky island in the middle of the sea between Ithaka and rugged Samos, Asteris, not big, and there are two ship-sheltering havens in it. There the Achaeans awaited him, lying in ambush.'[651] The idea of enemies lying in ambush on a small, rocky island in a sea strait is common to both texts. Aeschylus structures his verses in a similar way to Homer's: 'there is an island before the places of Salamis, small, difficult to anchor for ships, where Pan, lover of choral dance, treads on the shores of the sea. There [...]'.[652] Both passages start with 'There is an island', and are followed by a short ekphrasis, after which the presence of the enemies is introduced.

---

fact that the episode is independent from the main battle narrative, and questioned the historicity Herodotus' version of the story. Wallace (1969, 293) described the events here as "mopping-up" after the real battle.
649 For the idea that the entire battlefield was visible from Psyttaleia, and that this was the justification for its recording, see Hammond 1988, 581; Ray 2009, 84. Wallinga (2005, 87) points out that Psyttaleia was the only part of the original Persian plan that was remembered.
650 This story first appears in Virgil, *Aeneis* 2.21–24.
651 "ἔστι δέ τις νῆσος μέσση ἁλὶ πετρήεσσα // μεσσηγὺς Ἰθάκης τε Σάμοιό τε παιπαλοέσσης, // Ἀστερίς, οὐ μεγάλη· λιμένες δ' ἔνι ναύλοχοι αὐτῇ // ἀμφίδυμοι· τῇ τόν γε μένον λοχόωντες Ἀχαιοί".
652 "νῆσος τίς ἐστι πρόσθε Σαλαμῖνος τόπων, // βαιά, δύσορμος ναυσίν, ἣν ὁ φιλόχορος // Πὰν ἐμβατεύει ποντίας ἀκτῆς ἔπι // ἐνταῦθα [...]".

The Psyttaleia scene in Aeschylus may have been embellished in the tradition by this reference to a scene from the *Odyssey*. Even if the description of Psyttaleia in Aeschylus' *Persae* is independent of Homer's *Odyssey* and the parallel only coincidental, it shows us a more general point: in narratives of conflicts in a seascape setting, islands can be singled out as the central mnemotope, in particular showcasing the place where the enemies retreated, and where they were subsequently (and deservedly) slaughtered. Terrestrial versions of that scene were encountered at the forts of Skolos at Plataea (§2.9.1) and Skolopoeis at Mykale (§2.10.2).

Cahen has pointed out that Aeschylus' insistence on Psyttaleia as an important place was mostly inspired by the scene's illustration of Persian hubris: the plan to kill off any surviving Greeks, floating helplessly around the island, was evil.[653] This brings us to the final mnemotopical point about Psyttaleia: its connection to the god Pan, which was noted by Aeschylus (in the passage quoted above) and Pausanias (1.36.2, referring to many wooden statues). It seems strange to imagine a god normally associated with forested mountain valleys on an island which (at least today) is not much more than a barren rock. However, the island's association with Pan may have started with a purely poetic reference in Aeschylus. To say that the island, where Persians were stationed to kill beached Greeks, and where Greeks finally killed the Persians, is sacred to the god of terror and panic is a remarkably accurate poetic device for this particular narrative.[654] This may also be the reason why Sophocles calls Pan ἁλίπλαγκτος 'sea-roaming' (*Ajax* 695; cf. *Suda* s.v. ἁλίπλαγκτος).

It is also possible that a real cult of Pan arose on the island after the battle. We know that that happened after the battle of Marathon: Herodotus himself (6.105) recounts that a sanctuary of Pan was established on the slopes of the Acropolis after Philippides had encountered Pan on Mount Parthenion close to Tegea, where Pan claimed to have helped the Athenians at Marathon.[655] The worship of Pan there surely predates Herodotus as we have a reference to a statue set up by Miltiades in Simonides *FGE* 5.[656] Thus, the battle could have inspired the worship of Pan on Psyttaleia; the *Persae* may have acted as a catalyst for this worship, or Aeschylus may record an already existing tradition in which the god who helped the Athenians at Marathon was associated with the divinity responsible for the victory at Salamis. This worship will have further contributed to the designation of Psyttaleia as one of the foremost mnemotopes of the battle of Salamis.

---

653 Cahen 1924, 309.
654 Cahen 1924, 313.
655 Nonnus, *Dionysiaca* 27.290; *Suda* s.v. Ἱππίας. Pausanias 8.54.6 mentions that a shrine had been built on the spot in Arcadia itself.
656 "τὸν τραγόπουν ἐμὲ Πᾶνα, τὸν Ἀρκάδα, τὸν κατὰ Μήδων, // τὸν μετ' Ἀθηναίων στήσατο Μιλτιάδης": 'Miltiades set up me, goat-footed Pan, the Arcadian, the one against the Persians, the one supporting the Athenians.'

2.8.2 Artemis' coast and Mounichia: the trophy and the tomb

After stationing some of his men at Psyttaleia, Xerxes directed part of his armada so as to line up between Kynosoura and Mounichia (8.76):

[...] τοῦτο δέ, ἐπειδὴ ἐγίνοντο μέσαι νύκτες, ἀνῆγον μὲν τὸ ἀπ' ἑσπέρης κέρας κυκλούμενοι πρὸς τὴν Ἐλευσῖνα, ἀνῆγον δὲ οἱ ἀμφὶ τὴν Κέον τε καὶ τὴν Κυνόσουραν τεταγμένοι, κατεῖχόν τε μέχρι Μουνυχίης πάντα τὸν πορθμὸν τῇσι νηυσί. τῶνδε δὲ εἵνεκα ἀνῆγον τὰς νέας, ἵνα δὴ τοῖσι Ἕλλησι μὴ διαφυγεῖν ἐξῇ, ἀλλ' ἀπολαμφθέντες ἐν τῇ Σαλαμῖνι δοῖεν τίσιν τῶν ἐπ' Ἀρτεμισίῳ ἀγωνισμάτων.

[...] and second, when it had become midnight, they led the western wing in a circle to Eleusis, and those posted around Keos and Kynosoura, and they occupied until Mounichia the entire strait with their ships. And they directed their ships so that it was impossible for the Greeks to flee; being trapped in Salamis, they would give recompense for the sufferings at Artemision.

This was in an apparent fulfilment of an oracle which Herodotus quotes directly afterwards (8.77):[657]

"ἀλλ' ὅταν Ἀρτέμιδος χρυσαόρου ἱερὸν ἀκτὴν νηυσὶ γεφυρώσωσι καὶ εἰναλίην Κυνόσουραν, ἐλπίδι μαινομένῃ λιπαρὰς πέρσαντες Ἀθήνας δῖα δίκη σβέσσει κρατερὸν Κόρον, Ὕβριος υἱόν, δεινὸν μαιμώοντα, δοκεῦντ' ἀνὰ πάντα πίεσθαι [...]"

"But when, with mad hope, they bridge the holy coast of Artemis with the golden sword and the Dog's Tail in the sea, after having sacked splendid Athens, divine Justice will smother strong Arrogance, the son of Hubris, eager and threatening, planning to engulf everything [...]"

The coast of Artemis with the golden sword refers to the temple of the goddess at Mounichia, which is currently the Kastello hill in the eastern part of Piraeus.[658] It seems that 'Artemis' coast' in the oracles refers to the entire peninsula on which Piraeus was located: after all, Artemis' temple was the port city's central shrine. After the war, Artemis Mounichia was regarded to have played a role during the battle, because she

---

657 Some scholars believe that the Kynosoura mentioned here refers to the Kynosoura peninsula of Marathon, while the coast of Artemis would refer to Euboea (Munro 1902, 306–307; 1926b, 309; Myres 1953, 265; Wallace 1969, 300). However, Herodotus seems to have believed that the indications referred to the Salamis area; after all, he mentions it in the Salamis narrative (see also Macan 1908, II 293–294). For an analysis of the oracle, see Kirchberg 1965, 103–105. On the ambiguity of the text see Maurizio 1997, 326–327.
658 The temple is mentioned by Pausanias 1.1.4. For all possibilities for the location of this temple see Macan 1908, I 480–481; Hammond 1969, 53; 1988, 574 (suggesting that it referred to the temple of Artemis in Salamis); Papachatzi 1974, 119–122; Müller 1987, 706–707; Papadopoulou 2014, 111; 118 (mentioning that this location overlooks the battlefield).

had shone onto the battlefield with a full moon (Plutarch, *De gloria Atheniensium* 7): a temple to the goddess, with the epithet Aristoboule, was erected by Themistocles near his house in Melite, a district of Athens (Plutarch, *Themistocles* 22.1-2), and the Mounichia festival was at some point before the second century BCE reorganised so as to thank Artemis for her assistance in the battle of Salamis.[659]

For Keos several candidates exist.[660] Kynosoura ('Dog's Tail') is a long, narrow peninsula of the island of Salamis, pointing towards Piraeus. While Herodotus does not explicitly localise any anecdotes at Kynosoura, it nevertheless became a mnemotope for the battle. This is shown by the fact that two monuments were erected on the peninsula. The first of these monuments was a trophy mentioned in various literary and epigraphical sources.[661] Archaeology suggests that the trophy was set up at the very tip of the Kynosoura peninsula, which is, perhaps not coincidentally, known as cape Varvari (Βάρβαρι): here, marble blocks were seen by early modern travellers and interpreted as the trophy.[662] One of them, Giambattista Casti, reported in 1788 that the Venetian ambassador in the Ottoman Empire, Girolamo Zulian, had taken three blocks from that site to Venice.[663] These have now disappeared, although an accompanying text for the blocks is currently used as a support for the statue of a sea nymph in the Archaeological Museum of Venice.[664] The trophy's connection to

---

659 See Parker 2005, 231 note 59; Papadopoulou 2014, 119–120 for the evidence regarding the festival.
660 Among them are Leros (Lolling 1884, 4–5, emending Κέον to Λέρον); Obst 1913, 147; Keramos, the Attic headland east of Kynosoura and Psyttaleia (Wilhelm 1929, 30–31, emending Κέον to Κέραμόν); the Zea harbour of Piraeus (Burn 1962, 472, pointing out that Zea may be a corruption of Keos); Talandonisi (Hammond 1988, 574); between the bay of Keratsini and Kleftolimeno (Kromayer 1931, 582–583); or Poros Megaron (Wallinga 2005, 50).
661 Ancient sources which may mention this trophy are Timotheus, *Persae* 196; Plato, *Menexenus* 245a; Xenophon *Anabasis* 3.2.13; Athenaeus *Deipnosophistae* 1.37 (mentioning that Sophocles used to dance around the trophy); Lycurgus, *Oratio in Leocratem* 73; Pausanias 1.36.1; *IG* I³ 255; *IG* II², 1035. There is discussion about the identification of the site of the trophy. Wallace 1969, 301 points out that it cannot have been at Salamis town, because an inscription shows that participants had to visit the trophy by sailing from Salamis town. However, Hammond 1956, 34 note 3 maintained, on the basis of Pausanias, that it was situated at Salamis town, localised in the vicinity of modern Ambelakia (Pritchett 1959, 352) and that cape Tropaia referred to the peninsula north of Ambelakia bay. A scholion on Aristophanes, *Equites* 785 mentions a rock called Eiresia 'rowing' or Eiresione 'crowning', supposedly 'because of the name it was a trophy of the victory against the Persians.'
662 Wallace 1969, 299–302. One block was still at this location when I visited the peninsula in January 2015. Culley 1977, 296–297 followed Wallace and reconstructed the trophy as a "column of white marble on a circular base in a square limestone foundation. It may have been surmounted originally by an Ionic capital and a Nike, as the Marathon trophy probably was, or (since it commemorated a naval victory) by a model of a trireme." See also Clairmont 1983, 118; Beschi 2002, 68–69.
663 *Relazione d'un mio viaggio fatto da Venezia a Costantinopoli* (1802), 467–468 (*non vidi*) in Stefanini 1977, 162.
664 Beschi 2002, 69–70.

the commemoration of the battle remains speculative,[665] but clearly the peninsula would be a suitable point to erect such a trophy because this was the part of Salamis closest to Athens. It was here that a monument of the battle could be observed best by the Athenians on the mainland.[666] Even more importantly, as a trophy was meant to mark the place where the climax of the battle had taken place, this was the best possible site to put it, close to Psyttaleia. It therefore helped to mark the peninsula as a mnemotope for the battle.[667] There also exists archaeological and inscriptionary evidence for the erection of trophies in Piraeus, on the so-called tomb of Themistocles (where the column had been reconstructed) and on Cape Krakari.[668] The date of these trophies is uncertain, but they show that Piraeus was at some point included in the memorialisation of the battlefield. The trophies marked the endpoints of the ships mentioned by the oracle, and therefore may have had a function of helping visitors to visualise that line of ships before their eyes.

In the second and first centuries BCE we hear of the Aianteia festival in inscriptions.[669] This festival included boat races, as well as sacrifices to Ajax, Artemis Mounichia and Zeus Tropaios at one or more of the trophies. It testifies to the importance of the landscape around Kynosoura as a place of mnemotopes and seems to have been specifically designed to allow the Athenian youth to engage with the battlefield.[670]

The second monument related to the battle on the Kynosoura peninsula is a hill in the middle of the peninsula's north shore, which currently is also the place of a modern sculpture which commemorates the battle. It has sometimes been suggested that this *magoula* was a tumulus containing the victims of the battle, because we hear about a *polyandreion* in a first-century BCE inscription (*IG* II² 1035).[671] Although similar burial mounds existed near Plataea (§2.9.7) and one still exists near Marathon, there is no further evidence to substantiate this suggestion; we only hear about an inscription mentioning Corinthian graves near Salamis town (retrieved at

---

[665] Proietti 2015a, 158–159, arguing that the sources do not allow us to assume that the trophy was a monument, and underlines its role in the re-memoralisation of the battle.
[666] Hammond 1988, 581; Ray 2009, 84.
[667] The effect has been described by Wallace 1969, 302 as follows: "It is surely more than a coincidence that foundations of a size to suggest a trophy existed both on the Cynosoura and on Leipsokoutali, and at the point where the peninsula and the island are closest to each other. The Greeks realized how important the narrowness of the straits had been for their victory (Hdt. 8.60), and the area between the Cynosoura and the peninsula of Psyttaleia is the narrowest part of the straits. These two land projections did much to win the battle, for doubtless many Persian ships were driven ashore here. The Greeks would probably have thought it fitting to erect the memorials of the battle on the two peninsulas." Also see Clairmont 1983, 118.
[668] Beschi 2002, 71–90 (with photographs); Proietti 2015a.
[669] *IG* II² 1006; 1008; 1009; 1011; 1028; 1029; *IG* V,1 657.
[670] Deubner 1932, 179–180; Culley 1977, 294–295; Taylor 1997, 187; Parker 2005, 456; Proietti 2015a, 158.
[671] Milchhoefer 1895, 29; Pritchett 1965, 95–96; Culley 1977; Jacquemin 2000, 67–68.

Fig. 46: The block on the tip of the Kynosoura peninsula.

Ambelakia, *IG* I³ 1143), and about a separate epitaph for the Corinthian leader Adeimantos (Plutarch, *De Herodoti malignitate* 870e = Simonides *FGE* 10-11). Regardless, it has also been pointed out that only late fifth-century BCE graves have been found in the magoula, and that the mass grave was, instead, near the trophy at the tip of Kynosoura, underneath currently abandoned buildings of the Greek navy.[672] This is also suggested by the inscription, which seems to mention the grave in relation to the trophy.

If the hill was not the mass grave of the Greeks who fell in the battle of Salamis, what was it then? There are various reasons to associate the magoula with the mythical king of Salamis Kychreus, who was the son of Poseidon and Salamis and known to have either killed or raised a snake or being a snake himself.[673] The association of Kychreus with Salamis was so strong, that Strabo (9.1.9) even mentioned Kychreia

---

[672] Tsirivakos 1967; Culley 1977, 293–298 (placing the grave on the south-shore of the peninsula).
[673] Killed: Pseudo-Apollodorus 3.12.7; Diodorus Siculus 4.72.4. Raised: Strabo 9.1.9. A snake himself: Stephanus Byzantinus, *Ethnica* s.v. Κυχρεῖος. See Wallace 1969, 300–301 for an overview of all references to this hero.

Fig. 47: The alleged burial mound of the Greeks who fell during the battle of Salamis.

as an alternative name for Salamis.[674] We read in Pausanias (1.36.1) and the above-mentioned inscription (*IG* II² 1035) that the island accommodated a shrine to this hero, and there also existed a cave sacred to him (Lycophron, *Alexandra* 451). Other sources suggest that the shrine amounted to a hill on the coast.[675] Therefore, perhaps, the hill and shrine of Kychreus are to be identified with the magoula. Excavations of the hill have brought to light walls and possibly an altar.[676]

Even though a case can be made for the identification of the magoula with the shrine of Kychreus, it is, in line with the accumulation of stories at mnemotopes described in the introduction (§1.3.5), possible that the mnemotope had acquired

---

674 The passage in Strabo and the above-mentioned inscription (*IG* II² 1035), in which also Kychreia appears, have prompted speculation about an older and a younger city on the Kynosoura peninsula (Culley 1977, 291–292). But see the discussions in Milchhoefer 1895, 28–29 and Langdon 2007, 112–116 for the more common view that the city was in the south of the island.
675 Euphorion fragment 30: ἐνὶ ψαφαρῇ Σαλαμῖνι 'on the beach of Salamis'; Stephanus Byzantinus *Ethnica* s.v., mentioning Sophocles' *Teukros* as a source.
676 Lolling 1884, 8–10; Wallace 1969, 301; Culley 1977, 292–294. One of the arguments is that there are sea caves on the west side of the hill, which could be the cave mentioned by Lycophron.

a new meaning as the imagined grave of those who had fallen in the battle. From an Athenian perspective in the post-war period, Salamis was synonymous with the battle. Existing monuments and their cults could then easily have been enveloped in commemoration practises and have become designated as mnemotopes. It has been observed that the cult for Kychreus had become more important after the Persian Wars.[677] Perhaps this reflected a (renewed?) engagement with this landscape. Similarly, the burials dating to the later fifth century BCE on the magoula could, perhaps, suggest that in this period, the hill was perceived as the last resting place of the Greek soldiers. The modern monument for the battle on the hill, erected in 2006, is an illustration of the same process that the hill underwent inour own period. Even though the real status of the hill is unclear, it has become an mnemotope for the battle.

There are some other idiosyncratic stories connected to Kynosoura that are not found in Herodotus, but nevertheless show how easily anecdotes of the battle could be associated with the peninsula. Aeschylus (*Persae* 302-303) mentions the rocky beach of Seliniai where the body of Artembares, a Persian general had washed up. It is identified with the beach at the south base of Kynosoura, now called Ormos Selinion, or alternatively with Psyttaleia.[678] Plutarch (*Themistocles* 10.6) preserves a story according to which Xanthippos' dog had followed his master to Salamis by swimming across the sea, after which he died, and that there was a spot called Kynossema ('Dog's Grave'); more specifically, it may have been an aetiology for the magoula at Kynosoura, which may have acquired the name Kynossema.[679] Finally, Pausanias (1.36.1) remarks that Kychreus appeared in the battle of Salamis as a snake. The hero's association with snakes is readily understandable: the Kynosoura peninsula was as much a dog's tail as an enormous snake. This has lead to the following suggestion by Wallace:[680] "Perhaps the part this promontory played in destroying the Persian fleet, coupled with the name and sanctuary of the serpent god, gave birth to the story that a serpent appeared in the fleet, which was the hero Cychreus [...] it certainly fought for the Greeks when it appeared between the two fleets." But the tradition could also be the reason why the hill became a mnemotope connected with the battle. It seems that a tradition had arisen by which Kynosoura was imagined as a giant petrified snake; and if that is true, it may help to explain why the cult of Kychreus was bound up with the commemoration of the battle at large.

---

[677] Culley 1977, 295.
[678] Ormos Selinion: Milchhoefer 1895, 5; Wilhelm 1929, 30; Wallace 1969, 301. The reference to the Silens could also point to Psyttaleia, which, we have seen above, was sacred to Pan; cf. Hammond 1988, 54. Papachatzi 1974, 461 leaves open the possibility that both Psyttaleia's and Kynosoura's coasts were the Silenian beaches.
[679] For the story about the dog as a later fabrication, see e.g. Wecklein 1867, 287; Hignett 1963, 199.
[680] Wallace 1969, 301.

2.8.3 Xerxes' throne (III)

Topographical and historical investigations of the battle of Salamis almost traditionally start with the quest of the place from which Xerxes is said to have watched the activities of his armada. The scene is described by Herodotus in 8.90:

> ὅκως γάρ τινα ἴδοι Ξέρξης τῶν ἑωυτοῦ ἔργον τι ἀποδεικνύμενον ἐν τῇ ναυμαχίῃ, κατήμενος ὑπὸ τῷ ὄρεϊ τῷ ἀντίον Σαλαμῖνος τὸ καλέεται Αἰγάλεως, ἀνεπυνθάνετο τὸν ποιήσαντα, καὶ οἱ γραμματισταὶ ἀνέγραφον πατρόθεν τὸν τριήραρχον καὶ τὴν πόλιν.

> For whenever Xerxes, as he sat under the mountain called Aigaleos opposite Salamis, saw one of his men demonstrating a certain achievement in the sea-battle, he inquired about the person who did it, and the scribes wrote down the name of the trierarch, his father's name, and his city.

The scene appears in most other accounts of the battle of Salamis, and also, before Herodotus, in Aeschylus' *Persae* (465-467).[681] Rather surprisingly, neither Aeschylus nor Herodotus mention a throne, but in later sources, the scene is embellished to include one: in Demosthenes (*In Timocratem* 129) we read that Xerxes' silver-footed δίφρος could be seen in the Parthenon![682] By the time of Plutarch (*Themistocles* 13.1), the throne on Mount Aigaleos has become golden. The vision of an enraged Xerxes overlooking the fighting has become a quintessential scene of the battle of Salamis: in modern popular illustrations, Xerxes is always pictured as overlooking the battle seated on a throne, and it is usually marked on maps of the battlefield.

Accordingly, considerable discussion has concerned the exact spot where Xerxes' throne once stood. This localisation is, however, hardly possible from the accounts of Aeschylus and Herodotus. These texts only allow us to locate the throne under Mount Aigaleos, in modern Perama. Mount Aigaleos is, in fact, a small massif with several different peaks, and there is considerable confusion in scholarship which peak it was; and although Herodotus says ὑπὸ τῷ ὄρεϊ 'under the mountain', this seems to be usually disregarded. Later authors offer more specific sites: according to one Phanodemos (on the authority of Plutarch, *Themistocles* 13.1), the throne stood above a temple of Heracles, where the strait was at its narrowest and where Xerxes was thought to have built his mole and pontoon bridge. The narrowest part is at the western end of the Aigaleos ridge, where a considerable hill exists which may be described as lying 'under' the Aigaleos. But the temple of Heracles has also been surmised further east towards or in Piraeus.[683] Another ancient scholar, Acestodorus (on the authority of

---

681 For the image of Xerxes on the throne in Aeschylus see Bridges 2015, 24.
682 See Frost 1973; Harris 1995, 205 ("there is some confusion or conflation in the sources about this."); Proietti 2015a, 163–164 underlines that this monument would have reminded visitors of the Aigaleos scene.
683 Leake 1841, 33–34 identified the temple with the Tetrakomon Herakleion near Echelidai (cf. Stephanus Byzantinus, *Ethnica* s.v. Ἐχελίδαι); cf. Bigwood 1978, 41. For the identification with the

Fig. 48: The Aigaleos ridge.

Plutarch, *Themistocles* 13.1) placed the throne at Mount Kerata at the border of Attica and Megara, west of modern Eleusis. Even more bizarre is Aristodemus' (*FGrH* 104 F1) localisation of Xerxes' throne on the Parnes (modern Parnitha) mountain, twenty-five kilometres northeast of Mount Aigaleos. Most authors have followed Phanodemus' identification, the crucial attraction being that from here the entire strait of Salamis is in view.[684] The search for the throne continues today in Perama, with locals still calling yet another peak of Aigaleos, between Keratsini and Perama, the Θρόνος του Ξέρξη, and one website even reports plans of local authorities to reconstruct the

---

headland between the mouth of harbour of Piraeus and the bay of Keratsini, see Goodwin 1906, 96; Munro 1926a, 312; Myres 1953, 267. cf. Caspari 1911, 103; note 12.

684 We find this location also in Ctesias' *Persica* (on the authority of Photius, *Bibliotheca* 72.39b); Grundy 1897b, 234–235; 1901, 398; Goodwin 1906, 95–96; Beloch 1908, 482–483; Obst 1913, 17; 148; Myres 1953, 276 (who, remarkably, sees the hill southeast of Grigoriou Lampraki street as the traditional location). Leake (1841, 271–272) and Hauvette (1894, 418) offered a location in the middle of the range.

throne here as a tourist site.[685] One scholar identified it with a mysterious structure of white stones northeast of the church of Agios Giorgios of Keratsini.[686]

Thus not one, but many mountains were believed to be the site of Xerxes' throne. There is no reason to assign particular value to any of these identifications. Apparently, there is a great demand to localise the throne, as much today as in Antiquity. But why? One 'justification' for the quest for the throne has been and still is its perceived importance in determining the locations of other landmarks of the battle of Salamis: the assumption runs that they need to have been visible from Xerxes' throne.[687] But this particular information is hardly relevant for our understanding of the battle itself.[688]

It is my surmise that the quest for this mnemotope depends on the dramatic picture which it paints of the battle: it increases its epic quality. We have already seen that Herodotus himself is as much concerned with Xerxes' reaction to the fighting as with the fighting itself; the Persians fought better because Xerxes could see them (8.86).[689] And of course, Salamis was not the only site where Xerxes had a throne: they also appear at the Hellespont (§2.2.4) and Thermopylae (§2.5.1), while a similar scene is painted at Doriskos (§2.3.3). Moreover, as we will come to discuss (§3.3.6), comparable scenes abound in the *Iliad*, where Priam, as well as the gods, view the war from Troy's walls and prominent hills in the area, respectively. We may also compare the attention paid to the throne to television shots of important people (trainers, state leaders etc.) during sport matches. The scene of the onlooking monarch may be regarded as a topos, as shown by Irene de Jong.[690]

While the scene is usually regarded as authentic,[691] it may just as well only have existed in the minds of later Greeks. Although it remains a valid question to try to locate the historical question of Xerxes' throne, we also need to acknowledge that it may be enough to see the various sites of Xerxes' throne as mnemotopes.

---

685 When visiting the area in January 2015, local school children pointed me to this hill. At the time of writing, this modern local viewpoint is explained at http://www.koutouzis.gr/peramiotika.htm (last consulted on 12 July 2017) and http://www.dperama.gr/Gr/files/kserksis.html, mentioning that the older residents of Perama claimed that a marble throne was visible on the top of the hill until the 1960s (last consulted on 12 July 2017).
686 Rediadis 1906, 239–244.
687 For the idea that Herodotus is preoccupied with this, see Pritchett 1965, 101–102. Frost 1973 suggested that Xerxes himself did not determine where the battle took place, but rather must have followed the ships which tried to enclose the Greeks in the strait. Hammond (1956, 38 with note 24) seems to have had an interest in saving the narrative of Xerxes' watching over the entire battlefield, as he states that the passages in Herodotus must be taken at face value.
688 Macan 1908, II 294.
689 Grethlein 2009, 207–208, pointing out that Xerxes is not always accurate, such as about Artemisia (8.88), which "throws into relief the accuracy of Herodotus' account."
690 De Jong (forthcoming).
691 E.g. Sancisi-Weerdenburg 1980, 75 (describing the scene as "historisch onbetwistbaar"); Green 1996, 189–190.

2.8.4 The temple of Athena Skiras

Herodotus' account of the fighting during the battle of Salamis consists mainly of anecdotes without clear topographical indications. An exception is the story of the flight of the Corinthians (8.94):

> Ἀδείμαντον δὲ τὸν Κορίνθιον στρατηγὸν λέγουσι Ἀθηναῖοι αὐτίκα κατ' ἀρχάς, ὡς συνέμισγον αἱ νέες, ἐκπλαγέντα τε καὶ ὑπερδείσαντα, τὰ ἱστία ἀειράμενον οἴχεσθαι φεύγοντα, ἰδόντας δὲ τοὺς Κορινθίους τὴν στρατηγίδα φεύγουσαν ὡσαύτως οἴχεσθαι. ὡς δὲ ἄρα φεύγοντας γίνεσθαι τῆς Σαλαμινίης κατὰ ἱρὸν Ἀθηναίης Σκιράδος, περιπίπτειν σφι κέλητα θείῃ πομπῇ, τὸν οὔτε πέμψαντα φανῆναι οὐδένα, οὔτε τι τῶν ἀπὸ τῆς στρατιῆς εἰδόσι προσφέρεσθαι τοῖσι Κορινθίοισι. τῇδε δὲ συμβάλλονται εἶναι θεῖον τὸ πρῆγμα· ὡς γὰρ ἀγχοῦ γενέσθαι τῶν νεῶν, τοὺς ἀπὸ τοῦ κέλητος λέγειν τάδε· Ἀδείμαντε, σὺ μὲν ἀποστρέψας τὰς νέας ἐς φυγὴν ὅρμησαι καταπροδοὺς τοὺς Ἕλληνας· οἱ δὲ καὶ δὴ νικῶσι ὅσον αὐτοὶ ἠρῶντο ἐπικρατῆσαι τῶν ἐχθρῶν. ταῦτα λεγόντων ἀπιστέειν γὰρ τὸν Ἀδείμαντον, αὖτις τάδε λέγειν, ὡς αὐτοὶ ἕτοιμοι εἶεν ἀγόμενοι ὅμηροι ἀποθνήσκειν, ἢν μὴ νικῶντες φαίνωνται οἱ Ἕλληνες. οὕτω δὴ ἀποστρέψαντα τὴν νέα αὐτόν τε καὶ τοὺς ἄλλους ἐπ' ἐξεργασμένοισι ἐλθεῖν ἐς τὸ στρατόπεδον. τούτους μὲν τοιαύτη φάτις ἔχει ὑπὸ Ἀθηναίων, οὐ μέντοι αὐτοί γε Κορίνθιοι ὁμολογέουσι, ἀλλ' ἐν πρώτοισι σφέας αὐτοὺς τῆς ναυμαχίης νομίζουσι γενέσθαι· μαρτυρέει δέ σφι καὶ ἡ ἄλλη Ἑλλάς.

> The Athenians say that Adeimantos, the Corinthian general, immediately at the start, when the ships clashed together, got startled and extremely scared, hoisted the sails, and went away in flight. They also say that the Corinthians also fled as they saw the general's ship escaping; and that, when they were thus fleeing and came upon a temple of Salaminian Athena Skiras, a boat came to them under divine guidance, that did not seem to have been sent by anyone, and that it arrived at the Corinthians, who did not know anything about the affairs of the army. They concur that the episode was divine, because the people on the boat said the following, as it came near the ships: "Adeimantos, you have turned away the ships to take flight while betraying the Greeks; but they are winning anyway as they have asked to defeat their enemies." They also say that Adeimantos did not believe what they had said, and that they said that they were ready to be taken hostage and die if the Greeks did not seem to be winning, and also that he himself and the others turned the ships around to the battlefield to see what had happened. Such an anecdote is told about them by the Athenians, but the Corinthians themselves do not concur, but hold the opinion that they were among the most prominent in the battle. The rest of Greece also testifies to them.

There is considerable confusion about the location of the temple of Athena Skiras in our ancient sources and in modern scholarship. Locations for the temple have been suggested on Salamis itself,[692] but also at the mainland, where suggestions include

---

[692] It has been suggested that the temple had to be far enough from the battle site for the battle to have been over by the time the Corinthians returned; a proposed location in this context is the Faneromeni monastery on a northwestern peninsula of the island (Leake 1841, 171–173; Milchhoefer 1895, 35–37; Munro 1902, 329; Hignett 1963, 411–414). However, a Skiradion is mentioned by Plutarch (*Solon* 9.4) in relation to a commemoration practice for Solon's conquest of Salamis town, as well as a temple of Enyalios (Ares), founded by Solon. This shows that the temple of Athena cannot have been

Phaleron on the authority of Pausanias (1.1.4; 1.36.4), or in the town of Skiron between Athens and Eleusis, which was also the location of the Skironian plain.[693] Perhaps there was more than one. Cults at Skiron involved both Demeter and Athena, and the field was a mnemotope for a legendary battle between Athens and Eleusis.[694] A temple of Athena is also mentioned in various inscriptions related to the genos of Salaminioi.[695] It has been suggested that the temple in these inscriptions refers to the temple of Athena Skiras in Phaleron.[696] Both the temples at Phaleron and at Skiron may be considered mnemotopes for another myth, Theseus' creation of a gypsum statue of Athena Skiras (an etiological myth for the toponym, as there were various words starting with σκιρ- that meant 'gypsum').[697]

Herodotus himself regarded the story, which seems to have functioned as an instrument to strengthen one polis' pride to the detriment of another, as incredible, as do many modern scholars.[698] Evans pointed out that this tradition "fitted an interpretation of the battle that gratified the Athenians in the latter half of the fifth century, when Corinth had become bitterly hostile."[699] Poems by Simonides (*FGE* 10-16), one of which (11) has been retrieved at Ambelaki (*IG* I³ 1143), honouring, among other things, the fallen Corinthians and their leader Adeimantos, shows that the Corinthians did, in fact, claim to have participated actively in the battle.[700]

---

too far from Salamis town at Ambelakia. A better option than Faneromeni is cape Arapis, on Salamis at the northern end of the strait, where a rock-cut inscription mentioning an unnamed female goddess was discovered (Hammond 1956, 49; Wallinga 2005, 126; Langdon 1997, 117–120). For the connection between Athena Skiras and Salamis see also Kledt 2004, 180–181.

693 Strabo (9.1.9) and Pausanias (1.36.4) say that there was a place called Skiron on a headland between Athens and Eleusis. The toponym was connected to Skiros, a seer from Eleusis, and this was also the site of the Skira harvest festival. There was a temple here where Demeter, Kore, Athena and Poseidon were worshipped (Pausanias 1.37.2), which may have furnished the traditions of Athena Skiras (Kledt 2004, 179–180). For a discussion of the cultic connections of Skiros, see Sourvinou-Inwood & Parker 2011, 35–36 with literature. Robertson (1992, 127–128) observes that the toponym σαλαμίς meant 'salt flat', which could refer to the landscape around Phaleron. The grave of Aristides was also here (Plutarch, *Aristides* 27.1). On the location and festivities at Skiron, see Deubner 1932, 46–47; Kledt 2004, 155–157. On the Skira festival, see Parker 2005, 173–177.
694 Kledt 2004, 157–163.
695 *IG* II² 1232; *Agora XIX, Leases L* 4a; *SEG* 21.527. On the Salaminioi, see Lambert 1997; Taylor 1997; Parker 2005, 214–215.
696 Sourvinou-Inwood & Parker 2011, 163–164.
697 Ellinger 1993, 76–88; Kledt 2004, 181–184 (with rich ancient literature).
698 The typical, skeptical view is found in e.g. Hignett 1963, 411–414. Views of the episode as historical: Hart 1982, 99: "The sailing off can hardly have been invented, it was seen by too many"; Wallinga 2005, 126–128.
699 Evans 1991, 128–129.
700 For the inscription see Clairmont 1983, 225–227.

Wherever the temple of Athena Skiras was, it seems to have become a mnemotope for the story.⁷⁰¹ There may have been an element of divine intervention: everyone knew that Athena's main sanctuary on the Acropolis had been assaulted; it was then all too likely that a story would arise in which she would help the Athenians in some way. This is a common function of temples in the stories about Xerxes' invasion (§3.2). Finally, the shrine may have been enveloped in commemoration practises for the battle of Salamis.

2.8.5 The beach of Kolias

Herodotus describes the beach of Kolias as the place where the shipwrecks stranded after the battle (8.96):

τῶν δὲ ναυηγίων πολλὰ ὑπολαβὼν ἄνεμος ζέφυρος ἔφερε τῆς Ἀττικῆς ἐπὶ τὴν ἠιόνα τὴν καλεομένην Κωλιάδα, ὥστε ἀποπλησθῆναι τὸν χρησμὸν τόν τε ἄλλον πάντα τὸν περὶ τῆς ναυμαχίης ταύτης εἰρημένοι Βάκιδι καὶ Μουσαίῳ, καὶ δὴ καὶ κατὰ τὰ ναυήγια τὰ ταύτῃ ἐξενειχθέντα τὸ εἰρημένον πολλοῖσι ἔτεσι πρότερον τούτων ἐν χρησμῷ Λυσιστράτῳ Ἀθηναίῳ ἀνδρὶ χρησμολόγῳ, τὸ ἐλελήθεε πάντας τοὺς Ἕλληνας, "Κωλιάδες δὲ γυναῖκες ἐρετμοῖσι φρύξουσι." τοῦτο δὲ ἔμελλε ἀπελάσαντος βασιλέος ἔσεσθαι.

A western wind captured many of the shipwrecks and it brought them to the beach of Attica called Kolias. And so was fulfilled all the rest of the oracle about that sea battle, which was given by Bakis and Mousaios, but also what was said many years earlier than these events about the shipwrecks that beached there in the oracle of Lysistratos, an Athenian prophet, that had escaped all the Greeks, "the women of Kolias will cook with oars". But this was supposed to happen after the flight of the king.

From Pausanias (1.1.5) we learn that this beach was twenty stadia (approximately 3.7 km) from Phaleron, which allows us to identify it with Cape Kosmas in the modern Athenian suburb of Elliniko.⁷⁰² On the basis of Strabo (9.1.21), however, one is led to believe that the beach was much further southeast, at Anaphlystos (modern Anavyssos).⁷⁰³ The Anaphlystos beach seems to be the better of the alternatives, because Strabo says that there was a temple of Artemis Kolias here.⁷⁰⁴

---

701 Wecklein (1867, 252–253) already seems to have interpreted the temple of Athena Skiras as the origin of the story.
702 E.g. Leake 1841, 269; Papachatzi 1974, 131; Müller 1987, 648–649; Asheri et al. 2010, 297.
703 Hammond 1956, 48 note 65.
704 The religious infrastructure of the Kolias beach appears confused in our sources. Herodotus does not mention any temple here; besides the temple of Artemis Kolias, Strabo mentions 'the' temple of Pan at Anaphlystos. Plutarch (*Solon* 8.4), on the other hand, records a temple of Demeter. For the cult of Aphrodite Kolias, see Parker 2005, 432.

Herodotus' story indicates that Kolias was regarded as 'the' place where all of the ship wrecks had washed ashore. But was this truly the case? The accounts of both Aeschylus (*Persae* 272-273) and Herodotus (8.96) suggest that there were other places besides Kolias.[705] We see that a particular element of the battle (the stranding of ship-wrecks) is concentrated and located at a single beach. Why should this be the case at Kolias? There may not be a specific reason, but it seems that Kolias was singled out as a 'bridgehead' on the Attic coast: Kolias also appears as such in an anecdote about the conquest of Salamis by the Athenians (Plutarch, *Solon* 8.4).[706]

2.8.6 Xerxes' causeway and ship bridge

The story goes that, when Xerxes realised that he had lost the battle, he ordered the construction of an earthen causeway and a pontoon bridge (8.97):

> Ξέρξης δὲ ὡς ἔμαθε τὸ γεγονὸς πάθος, δείσας μή τις τῶν Ἰώνων ὑποθῆται τοῖσι Ἕλλησι ἢ αὐτοὶ νοήσωσι πλέειν ἐς τὸν Ἑλλήσποντον λύσοντες τὰς γεφύρας καὶ ἀπολαμφθεὶς ἐν τῇ Εὐρώπῃ κινδυνεύσῃ ἀπολέσθαι, δρησμὸν ἐβούλευε· θέλων δὲ μὴ ἐπίδηλος εἶναι μήτε τοῖσι Ἕλλησι μήτε τοῖσι ἑωυτοῦ ἐς τὴν Σαλαμῖνα χῶμα ἐπειρᾶτο διαχοῦν, γαύλους τε Φοινικηίους συνέδεε, ἵνα ἀντί τε σχεδίης ἔωσι καὶ τείχεος, ἀρτέετό τε ἐς πόλεμον ὡς ναυμαχίην ἄλλην ποιησόμενος. ὁρῶντες δέ μιν πάντες οἱ ἄλλοι ταῦτα πρήσσοντα εὖ ἠπιστέατο ὡς ἐκ παντὸς νόου παρεσκεύασται μένων πολεμήσειν· Μαρδόνιον δ' οὐδὲν τούτων ἐλάνθανε ὡς μάλιστα ἔμπειρον ἐόντα τῆς ἐκείνου διανοίης.

> Xerxs decided to flee when he heard about the sufferance that had happened, fearing that one of the Ionians would advise the Greeks, or that they would conceive it themselves, to sail to the Hellespont to untie the bridges, and that he would risk death being left behind in Europe. Because he did not want this to be evident to the Greeks, nor to his own men, he tried to construct a causeway across to Salamis, and tied Phoenician ships together, to serve as a pontoon bridge and a wall. Thus he pretended for the enemy as if he was going to deliver another sea battle. And as all the others saw him doing this, they were convinced that he prepared by all means to stay and wage war. But nothing of this deceived Mardonios, as he was the one who had the most experience with his character.

Both ancient and modern commentators have tried to locate Xerxes' dam and bridge. Ctesias' Persica (on the authority of Photius, *Bibliotheca* 72.39b) informs us that the point where the dam started was at the temple of Heracles, which is one of the locations of Xerxes' throne (see §2.8.3). Strabo (9.1.13) positioned the starting point of the causeway at the quarries of Cape Amphiale. These quarries, and the cape, may have

---

[705] Hignett 1963, 238–239 believed that Kolias was merely one of the many places where the wrecks ended up. For the oracle see Kirchberg 1965, 106; Maurizio 1997, 327–328 (suggesting that there is no way of knowing whether this oracle originally referred to the battle of Salamis).
[706] For the idea that Kolias was the Attic bridgehead, see Müller 1987, 706–707.

been at the western end of Mount Aigaleos, north of the Perama-Salamis ferry line.[707] On this basis it has been surmised that the causeway and bridge went from this point to a small submerged island (which may have been one of the Pharmakoussai), from there to Agios Giorgios, and finally to Salamis at modern Kamatero.[708] It has also been proposed that it was Xerxes' aim to reach Psyttaleia as some of his men were stationed there.[709] Some scholars who comment on the passage believe that a trace of the causeway might still be visible.[710]

The location of the dam remains problematic; but it is also not entirely clear what Herodotus means, nor why there should have been both a causeway and a pontoon bridge. It is possible that Herodotus used the words χῶμα and διαχοῦν metaphorically and that his subsequent remarks about the ships explained what the χῶμα consisted of.[711] Furthermore, there exists an alternative tradition about the structure(s), preserved in the Ctesias excerpt and Strabo (9.1.13). According to this story, Xerxes would have begun the construction before the battle, an admittedly more credible story than the one Herodotus tells.[712] A few scholars have tried to vindicate Herodotus,[713] or twisted the strategy behind the event by assuming that the plan was conceived as a serious undertaking to gain access to the island, and would confine the Greek army to the bay of Eleusis.[714] Many other scholars take a more skeptical view, pointing out that

---

[707] Pritchett 1959, 255; Wallace 1969, 295; the quarries were perhaps around the modern church of Agios Nikolaos.
[708] Lolling 1884, 5–7; Macan 1908, II 320; Obst 1913, 15; Myres 1953, 266 (suggesting that the strait may not have been very deep, and that the construction was facilitated by the use of the islets); Hammond 1956, 34 (citing a local sailor as evidence); 1988, 569–570; Lazenby 1993, 163; Green 1996, 172–173. Plutarch (*Themistocles* 16.1), who also records the story of the causeway, makes explicit that it was Xerxes' aim to reach the Greeks on Salamis.
[709] Caspari 2011, 108.
[710] Macan 1908, I 510–511; II 320 believed that the structure was only a pier, meant as a point of embarkation and that it was hardly begun, or that it had disappeared. Wallinga 2005, 65 asserts that it only stretched to the eastern Pharmakoussa island, and not to Salamis itself. Ray 2009, 83 suggests that remnants might still be visible. In accordance with the localisation of the dam, the temple of Heracles is also placed at modern Perama (Macan 1908, II 320: "a little to the east of Cape Amphiale"; Hammond 1956, 34; 1988, 569).
[711] Caspari 2011, 108 note 39.
[712] Ctesias' account is preferred on his point by Wecklein 1867, 293–294; Macan 1908, I 510–511; II 319; Hart 1982, 100.
[713] Leake 1841, 269; Macan 1908, II 319; Burn 1984, 467; Lazenby 1993, 163–165; Green 1996, 172 (noting that nothing was "inherently improbable about such an undertaking" and that Xerxes was "probably influenced by his earlier bridging of the Dardanelles [...]") ; Holland 2005, 328; Wallinga 2005, 65–66 (suggesting that there probably was some activity, but that the exact purpose and moment of the construction was confused in the oral tradition); Haubold 2013, 112 with note 135 (finding plausibility in Herodotus' idea that Xerxes feigned a new engagement).
[714] Munro 1926a, 305; Hammond 1956, 42; 1988, 569–570; 583.

the construction that Herodotus describes must have been extremely strenuous.[715] The struggle of both ancient and modern scholarship to understand Xerxes' dam raises a question of historicity: did it really exist? Notably, Herodotus himself does not give the location for the causeway, and may have been relying on a vague story himself.

Even though the structure is problematic from a historical point of view, it apparently existed in the imagination of Greeks of Herodotus' time as a mnemotope. For them, the idea of the causeway may have, again, served as an example of Xerxes' ruthlessness, especially with regard to building projects, which Herodotus draws attention to elsewhere, such as at the Hellespont (§2.2.4), the Athos canal (§2.3.5) and the Tempe valley (§2.3.7); see in general §3.1.3.[716] It is remarkable that the Hellespont bridges are referred to in the same passage: Xerxes was afraid that they would be destroyed. It was a good story that here in Attica, he would quickly build another bridge to deceive both the Greeks and his own soldiers by feigning that the battle was not over. This is reminiscent of the deceit of his own men in Thermopylae, where Xerxes hides most of the fallen Persians in order to make his losses seem less serious (8.24-25; cf. §2.5.4).

Why was the dam believed to have existed in the strait of Salamis? There may, perhaps, have been a real geographical structure, such as a small spit or projecting headland (close to a place believed to be the throne of Xerxes?), that gave rise to, or was later 'explained' as Xerxes' causeway.[717] Whatever people may have seen in the strait of Salamis, it is clear that they could be impressed by such structures, and they could be given a mythical or quasi-historical aetiology.[718] Second, I would suggest that, alternatively or additionally to the physical background, the idea of the causeway may have been inspired by two texts. First, the oracle quoted above (8.77)

---

[715] Obst 1913, 153–154; Hignett 1963, 415–417; Cawkwell 2005, 92; Weiskopf 2008, 85.
[716] E.g. Munro 1902, 332; Asheri et al. 2010: "Non va escluso in Erodoto un collegamento simbolico tra i timori persiani perla sorte dei ponti sull'Ellesponto e il nuovo progetto di Serse mosso da *hybris*."
[717] A potential source of this story is the shallow part between Agios Giorgios and the mainland, which was dangerous for sea traffic. However, satellite images of the area shows that many possibilities exist. Munro 1902, 332 conjectured that Xerxes threw a boom across one of the channels, which then gave rise to the causeway tradition. I would like to propose that Kynosoura itself, the most strangely shaped peninsula of the area, may in local folklore have been considered a dam; its tip, as it appears today, consists of large boulders and looks man-made.
[718] The causeway between Old Tyre and the island of Heracles was said to be built by Alexander the Great during his siege of the city (Diodorus Siculus 17.40.5–43.2); Herodotus himself listed a χῶμα in the harbour of Samos as one of the three greatest engineering feats of the Greeks (3.60; cf. Tölle-Kastenbein 1976, 72–89), and there is at least one instance where such a structure was accounted for mythically: Pausanias (2.29.10) records a χῶμα in the 'hidden harbour' of Aegina, allegedly constructed by Telamon to defend himself from charges by Aiakos, who would not let him set foot on the island. Remains of this 'dam' still exist (Papachatzi 1976, 235). We may also compare the Ἀχιλλήιος δρόμος ('Achilles' racecourse, Herodotus 4.45), currently known as the Tenderovskaya Kosa in southern Ukraine, a remarkably long (65 km) spit in the Black Sea, whose construction was associated with Achilles.

talks about the spanning of the strait by ships.[719] The wording is ambiguous: νηυσὶ γεφυρώσωσι translates as 'they will bridge with ships', but a γέφυρα normally refers to a dam or causeway. While this part of the oracle may have been meant as a poetic allusion to the multitude of ships in the strait of Salamis, and understood as such by Herodotus, this does not preclude that it may also have given rise to a tradition in which there was a real γέφυρα. The ship bridge mentioned by Herodotus also seems to correspond well to the νηυσί part of the oracle.[720]

The second possible source of Herodotus' story about Xerxes' dam is the tradition preserved in Timotheus, *Persae* 72-78, where a Persian speaks to the water of the strait of Salamis: 'You, in your arrogance, already had your turbulent neck confined in a flax-bound fetter in the past, and now my lord will stir up your mud with mountain-born pines, and he will confine your navigable plains with wandering sailors.' Even though the exact meaning of the passage is unclear (it may have been, again, a poetic reference to the multitude of ships), it could have been reinterpreted as a reference to a causeway and/or a ship bridge. Note that if the oracle really was the inspiration for the story, the topographical indications contained within the oracle could give further clues as to where these structures were originally imagined: between the Kynosoura peninsula and the coast of Artemis, the identification of which was discussed above.

2.8.7 Cape Zoster

Xerxes lost the battle and he and a large part of his army fled. Stories about their escape circulated at various places in Greece. The first of these concerns a moment of panic experienced by several Persian generals on their way back to Asia along the coast of Attica (8.107):

> ἐπεὶ δὲ ἀγχοῦ ἦσαν Ζωστῆρος πλώοντες οἱ βάρβαροι, ἀνατείνουσι γὰρ ἄκραι λεπταὶ τῆς ἠπείρου ταύτης, ἔδοξάν τε νέας εἶναι καὶ ἔφευγον ἐπὶ πολλόν. χρόνῳ δὲ μαθόντες ὅτι οὐ νέες εἶεν ἀλλ' ἄκραι, συλλεχθέντες ἐκομίζοντο.

> When the Barbarians sailed close to Zoster, they believed that small headlands here, which stretch out from the mainland, were ships and they fled far away. Learning after some time that these were not ships but promontories, they came together and departed.

---

719 The connection between the story of the dam and the oracle was noted by Milchhoefer 1895, 31, but this was not picked up in later scholarship. Rocchi 1980, 417 seemed to believe that an actual structure that inspired the oracle: "La vittoria di Salamina era indicata dall'oracolo come punizione divina per Serse che aveva devastato Atene e unito l'isola alla terraferma mediante un ponte." On the ambiguity of this oracle and the idea that it may have been used as a confirmation of more than one story, see Maurizio 1997, 326–327.
720 Aristodemus (fragment 1.1–2) asserts that there was a ship bridge. Macan 1908, II 320 believed that the ship bridge was an absurdity.

Fig. 49: The cape of Vouliagmeni, which has been identified with cape Zoster.

The Zoster promontory is easily equated with modern Vouliagmeni, where a temple of Apollo has been excavated, and Athena, Artemis and Leto had altars here.[721] At Vouliagmeni, several promontories and reefs exist which may have been the inspiration for the story. As Aly has argued, this story is a folktale that can be compared to other 'petrification stories'.[722] More specifically, this is an explicit version of the 'petrified ship' mnemotope, which we have discussed above in relation to Kerkyra (§1.3.6); I have also suggested that a rock which looks like a beached ship on the beach of Kamari near Sepias may have inspired the story that the Persians had moored here (§2.4.2).

Pausanias (1.31.1) also mentions Zoster and records the etiological story according to which the place was named 'Zoster' because Leto had unfastened her girdle here on her way to Delos, where she would give birth to Apollo and Artemis (cf. the case of Zone in Thrace, §2.8.8, and in general the phenomenon of 'speaking toponyms', §3.1.1).

---

721 Papachatzi 1974, 397; Müller 1987, 724–725; Green 1996, 201; Parker 2005, 69–70; cf. Strabo 9.1.21.
722 Aly 1969 (first edition 1921), 187, comparing this story to Grimm's story type 32 about petrified dwarfs.

2.8.8 Xerxes' flight to Abdera

About Xerxes' return trip multiple stories existed. According to one of these, he went back to Persia through Thrace, where he visited the city of Abdera (8.120):

> μέγα δὲ καὶ τόδε μαρτύριον· φαίνεται γὰρ Ξέρξης ἐν τῇ ὀπίσω κομιδῇ ἀπικόμενος ἐς Ἄβδηρα καὶ ξεινίην τέ σφι συνθέμενος καὶ δωρησάμενος αὐτοὺς ἀκινάκῃ τε χρυσέῳ καὶ τιήρῃ χρυσοπάστῳ. καὶ ὡς αὐτοὶ λέγουσι Ἀβδηρῖται, λέγοντες ἔμοιγε οὐδαμῶς πιστά, πρῶτον ἐλύσατο τὴν ζώνην φεύγων ἐξ Ἀθηνέων ὀπίσω, ὡς ἐν ἀδείῃ ἐών. τὰ δὲ Ἄβδηρα ἵδρυται πρὸς τοῦ Ἑλλησπόντου μᾶλλον τοῦ Στρυμόνος καὶ τῆς Ἠιόνος, ὅθεν δή μιν φασὶ ἐπιβῆναι ἐπὶ τὴν νέα.

> This piece of evidence [for the theory that Xerxes took an overland route back to Persia] is also important: it seems that Xerxes during his return flight came to Abdera and engaged with them in guest friendship and gave them a golden dagger and a tiara embroidered with gold. And as the Abderites themselves say (and I think what they say is not convincing at all), he first unfastened his belt as he fled back from Athens, because he was safe there. Abdera is situated closer to the Hellespont than to the Strymon and Eïon, from where they say he embarked on his ship.

Abdera has been identified with remains on a coastal hill south of the modern village of Lefkippos.[723] Abdera appears several (additional) times in the *Histories*, and Herodotus was knowledgeable about the city's foundation myths (1.168). It is also mentioned as one of the many cities passed by the army when it invaded Greece (7.109). Herodotus adds an anecdote (7.120), according to which the Abderites were lucky that Xerxes' many soldiers only ate once a day; if they had eaten twice, that would have depleted the city's resources.[724]

Scholars, including Herodotus himself, have suggested that Xerxes' panic-driven flight through Thrace never took place.[725] But as the locals of Abdera claimed that their town was visited by Xerxes, the town was a mnemotope of the invasion. Apparently, various pieces of 'evidence' were available that Xerxes had visited the town. In this respect it is noteworthy that according to a tradition recorded much later by Philostratus,

---

[723] Müller 1975, 6; 1987, 37–41. For an overview of the site and a history of the city, see Isaac 1986, 73–78.
[724] The story about the Persian meals has been seen as historical and connected to self-discipline of Zoroastrians (Boyce 1982, 168–169). However, it is also understandable as a folk story that was a part of the lore about the presence of the Persian king in Abdera.
[725] This point is elaborated by Kuhrt (2007, 240 273, note 1), who stresses that this dramatic return trip was not true because northern Greece remained loyal to the Persians; see also Waters 2014, 130. Hammond (1988, 583) hypothesised that Xerxes may simply have left after the destruction of Athens to plunder other places; likewise, Cawkwell 2005, 108: "Xerxes never intended to spend more time in Greece than the time he actually did spend". Macan (1908, II 323–324) suggested that the subsequent events show that there was a plan behind Xerxes' return. The return through Thrace also features in Aeschylus' *Persae* (483–495). On the uncertainties about Xerxes' withdrawal see Harrison 2011, 47.

Xerxes and the Magi had visited the house of Protagoras' father (*Vitae sophistarum* 1.494).[726]

It is tempting to relate the stories about Xerxes in Abdera to the reputation of the locals as simpletons.[727] There is, however, no evidence that this stereotype already existed in Herodotus' time. Nevertheless, the anecdote about the loosening of the belt strikes a comical note.[728] It has been explained as referring to Abdera as the first point where Xerxes could rest, or as a symbolic gesture underlining his friendship to the city.[729] However, the expression could also be a euphemism for something more obscene.[730]

I would like to offer a particular origin for the story: the area east of Abdera, the Doriskos beach, was the location of a Samothracian fort called Zone (Ζώνη, 'Belt'; 7.59). It has been identified by some with the area's most important archaeological site west of modern Mesimvria; but other scholars have situated it at Makri.[731] It is not at all unlikely that locals of the area, fifty years after the Persian Wars, came up with a folk-etymological association that explained the name of the fort; this is a well-established mnemotope-forming process (cf. §3.1.1). A near-identical parallel is the folk-etymology of the place Zoster in Attica, where Leto was believed to have unfastened her girdle (§2.8.7).[732]

2.8.9 The siege of Potidaia

Another story connected to the departure of the Persians is the siege of the city of Potidaia by Persian general Artabazos, which happened as a response to a revolt of Potidaia after Xerxes left Greece (8.129):

---

726 Isaac 1986, 90 note 97: "it could be true".
727 E.g. Demosthenes, Περὶ τῶν πρὸς Ἀλέξανδρον συνθηκῶν 23; Galenus, *Quod animi mores corporis temperamenta sequantur* 822.
728 Cawkwell (2005, 8–9) stresses the humour which these and the two previous captions contain. It has been noted that the episode resembles Histiaos' promise to Darius not to take off his chiton until he brought Sardinia under Persian command (5.106; cf. Bowie 2007, 212). Aly 1969 (first edition 1921), 187 labeled the story as "durch Kritik beeinträchtigt".
729 Rest: Macan 1908, I 547; Asheri et al. 2010, 320. Friendship: Lenfant 2002.
730 This would not be out of place in this rather humorous part of the account of Xerxes' invasion (cf. in this respect Aristophanes, *Acharnenses* 80–82). Moreover, the unloosening of the girdle was a normal euphemistic expression referring to sex or the start of giving birth (cf. *LSJ* s.v. with various examples; and note the expression τὸ στρόφιον ἤδη λύομαι in Aristophanes' *Lysistrata* 931, when Myrrhine is about to have sex with Kinesias).
731 On the location of this fort see Müller 1975, 3; Green 1996, 79. Zone was also noted for its association with Orpheus (Apollonius Rhodius, *Argonautica* 1.28–30).
732 A similar toponymical folk anecdote is known in the Netherlands with regard to the siege of the town Brielle (also known as Den Briel) by the Watergeuzen rebels during the Dutch War of Independence. The anecdote takes place at the time when the Netherlands were ruled by the 'Iron' Duke of Alva. This event was remembered in collective memory with the comical sentence: "Op 1 april verloor Alva zijn bril" 'On April 1st, Alva lost his glasses', playing on the similarity of the words 'bril' and Den Briel.

Fig. 50: Remains of the fortress city of Zone near modern Mesimvria.

Ἀρταβάζῳ δὲ ἐπειδὴ πολιορκέοντι ἐγεγόνεσαν τρεῖς μῆνες, γίνεται ἄμπωτις τῆς θαλάσσης μεγάλη καὶ χρόνον ἐπὶ πολλόν. ἰδόντες δὲ οἱ βάρβαροι τέναγος γενόμενον παρήισαν ἐς τὴν Παλλήνην. ὡς δὲ τὰς δύο μὲν μοίρας διοδοιπορήκεσαν, ἔτι δὲ τρεῖς ὑπόλοιποι ἦσαν, τὰς διελθόντας χρῆν εἶναι ἔσω ἐν τῇ Παλλήνῃ, ἐπῆλθε πλημυρὶς τῆς θαλάσσης μεγάλη, ὅση οὐδαμά κω, ὡς οἱ ἐπιχώριοι λέγουσι, πολλάκις γινομένη. οἱ μὲν δὴ νέειν αὐτῶν οὐκ ἐπιστάμενοι διεφθείροντο, τοὺς δὲ ἐπισταμένους οἱ Ποτιδαιῆται ἐπιπλώσαντες πλοίοισι ἀπώλεσαν. αἴτιον δὲ λέγουσι Ποτιδαιῆται τῆς τε ῥηχίης καὶ τῆς πλημυρίδος καὶ τοῦ Περσικοῦ πάθεος γενέσθαι τόδε, ὅτι τοῦ Ποσειδέωνος ἐς τὸν νηὸν καὶ τὸ ἄγαλμα τὸ ἐν τῷ προαστίῳ ἠσέβησαν οὗτοι τῶν Περσέων οἵ περ καὶ διεφθάρησαν ὑπὸ τῆς θαλάσσης· αἴτιον δὲ τοῦτο λέγοντες εὖ λέγειν ἔμοιγε δοκέουσι. τοὺς δὲ περιγενομένους ἀπῆγε Ἀρτάβαζος ἐς Θεσσαλίην παρὰ Μαρδόνιον.

When three months had passed during which Artabazos was besieging [Potidaia], there occurred a big and long-lasting ebb of the sea. When the barbarians saw that the sea had become shallow they crossed over to Pallene. When two parts of them had crossed, and still three parts were left that needed to cross to Pallene, there came a big flood of the sea, as big as never had been during the many times it happened before, as the locals say. Those who did not know how to swim died, and those that knew were killed by the Potidaians who had embarked on their ships. The Potidaians say that the cause of the flood and the tidal wave and the Persian tragedy is that the Persians who were killed by the sea had desecrated the temple of Poseidon and the statue that is in the area before the city. In telling such a cause, they seem to me to be telling the truth. Artabazos led the survivors away to Thessaly, to Mardonios.

Potidaia guarded the entrance to the Pallene peninsula (the modern Kassandria peninsula) at the point where the land narrows to a width of only 500 metres. The ancient city was probably located south of the modern town of Nea Potidaia.[733] The temple of Poseidon, the source of the town's name, was probably situated at the site of the (today partly submerged) Roman temple southwest of the city.[734] Worship of Poseidon was appropriate at this isthmus (the isthmus of Corinth had a similar association). It is likely that the image of Poseidon on horseback, which appears on coins struck at Potidaia, is a depiction of this statue.[735]

How was this mnemotope created? The crossing of the Persians is usually accepted as a historical fact; the divine element of the story is taken away by scaling down the tragedy to a simple 'ebb-flood' situation or to volcanic activity.[736] This idea has recently been supported by research which shows that the area is, indeed, prone to tsunamis.[737] However, even though it may be proven that tsunamis here are possible, this does in and by itself not prove that the Persians were killed in one. This may or may not be true. What is clear, however, is that in the late fifth century BCE, stories such as these made sense because it ascribed the demise of the Persians to divine intervention. Not only does it look like one of the 'lost army' legends in the *Histories* and elsewhere that are independent of the main narrative;[738] it is also exemplary for the idea of the Persians as by-passing their enemies (§3.3.5). The story worked perfectly at specifically Potidaia, because at this isthmus the sea prevents the passing of an army. In addition, the story may have arisen here in response to the damaged sculpture and temple of Poseidon, which may or may not have been the work of the Persians; Herodotus seems to suggest that Poseidon himself acted as the avenger.[739]

---

733 Müller 1987, 198. For remains of the walls, see Alexander 1963, 2–3.
734 Herbig 1929, 603 (after communication with the excavator, St. Pelikidis, who opted for the association with Poseidon because of its location and on the basis of a headless statuette); Alexander 1963, 4; 8 (for several column capitals possibly to be associated with the temple); Müller 1987, 198.
735 For the coins see Kraay 1976, 134 with plates 471 and 474. These coins are all thought to directly antedate 480 BCE because of Herodotus' story; however, because it is possible that the sculpture was restored, Herodotus' account cannot be automatically used for dating purposes.
736 Grundy 1901, 430; Munro 1926a, 316; Pohlenz 1961, 105–106; Alexander 1963, 33–34; Müller 1987, 197–200.
737 Reicherter et al. 2010.
738 The notion of a tidal wave swallowing an army is also found in Athenaeus' *Deipnosophistae* (8.7). We may also compare, in Herodotus, the disappearance of Cambyses' army during a sandstorm in the Libyan desert (3.26) and the storms that destroyed Persians at Athos (6.44), Mount Ida (§2.2.1), Sepias (§2.4.2) and the Hollows of Euboea (§2.4.5). For a discussion of two other examples of tsunamis in Greek literature, see Smid 1970. Outside of the Greek tradition, a good parallel is the biblical tale of the disappearance the Egyptian army in the Red Sea (*Exodus* 13.17–14.29).
739 Flower & Marincola 2002, 221–222.

Fig. 51: Remains of fortifications near Potidaia. The ancient city was located on the coast visible in the background.

2.8.10 Summary

Herodotus' topography of the battle of Salamis can be seen as a collection of mnemotopes that together form a historical 'seascape' on the coasts of Salamis and Attica. The island of Psyttaleia became the climactical mnemotope of the battle, as it was thought that the Persians had been finally defeated here. The Kynosoura peninsula sported a trophy for the battle and had a hill, possibly sacred to Kychreus, which was interpreted as the grave of the Greeks who had fallen in the battle. The temple of Athena Skiras had given rise to a tradition according to which the Corinthians had tried to escape from the battle, but were turned back by the goddess. The Kolias beach was where the wrecks had beached, as an oracle had predicted. And various mountain tops were designated as the site of Xerxes' throne. It was imagined that Xerxes had begun constructing a causeway and/or ship bridge, a story which may have been inspired by an actual feature in the landscape and/or by poetic references to the many ships that filled up the strait during the battle. At cape Zoster, where rocks in the sea looked like ships, a story sprung up that the Persians did not dare to pass. Finally, anecdotes in Abdera and Potidaia showed that the army had retreated along the Thracian route which they had also taken to invade Greece.

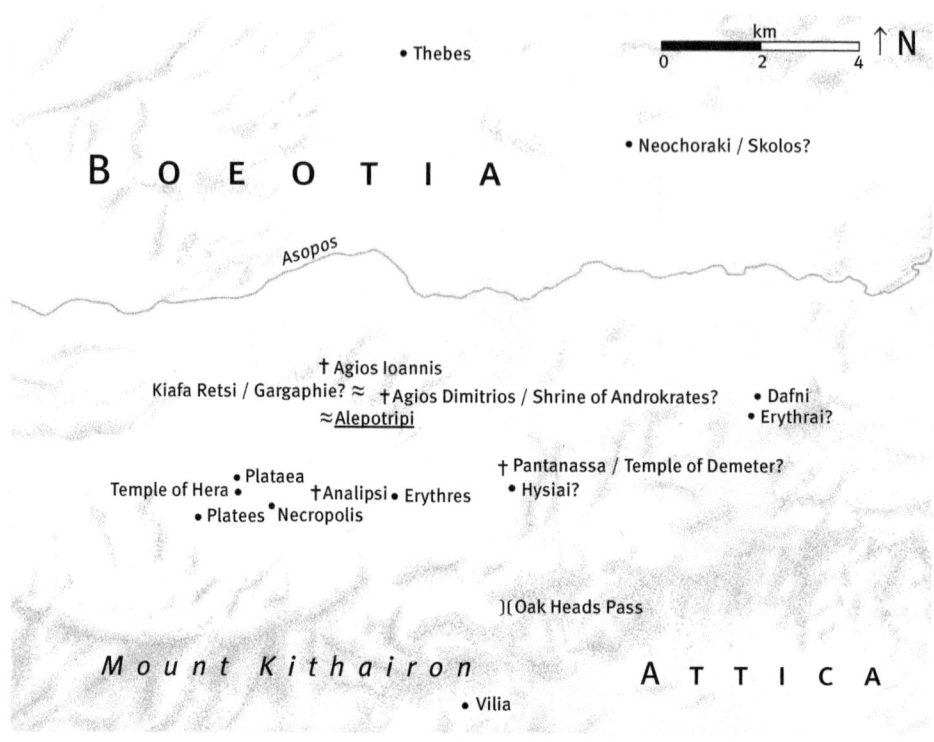

Map 7: The battlefield of Plataea.

Why does it matter that we can interpret Herodotus' topography of the battle as such? Rather than offering an answer to the question where the battle 'happened', it brings us closer to the beliefs of later visitors to the strait east of Salamis. They projected the battle onto coastal sites, and found that the Persians had lain in ambush, that local gods had interfered and that Xerxes once sat on a mountain, dramatically watching the battle enfold under his eyes.

2.9 The battle of Plataea

The battle of Plataea took place in 479 BCE in the plains between Thebes and Mount Kithairon.[740] Xerxes himself had already fled to Persia in the wake of the battle of Salamis, leaving behind in Boeotia Mardonios and a large number of troops. Although the battle is arguably less famous than some of the other confrontations during the

---

[740] A selection of places mentioned in this chapter features on Map 7.

Persian Wars and has been described as the 'Cinderella' of the Persian War battles,[741] it was an important historical event because it ended Persian influence in central Greece. Accordingly, the Greeks themselves held the battle in high regard. Monuments commemorating the battle were set up in many places in the Greek world.[742] Individual cities stressed their own role in it, and contested that of others;[743] but at the same time, this battle was also most suited to be commemorated in a Panhellenic manner. We find this idea already in Simonides' Plataean elegy (partly construed on the basis of the new fragments, 8-18 W^2), where the battle was compared to the 'Panhellenic' Trojan expedition,[744] and in the inscription of the Serpent Column.[745]

Engagement with the battle also took place on the battlefield itself, and the fields around Plataea thereby developed into a memory landscape.[746] This process is already apparent in Herodotus' account of the battle, written some fifty years after

---

[741] Cartledge 2013, xi.
[742] These monuments include Mardonios' feeding trough at Tegea (9.70); at Delphi, the Serpent Column (9.81; Gauer 1968, 75–96; Jung 2006, 244–246), a bull (Pausanias 10.15.1; Gauer 1968, 100–101), as well as golden shields donated later by the Athenians (Aeschines, *In Ctesiphontem* 116); at Olympia, the colossal Zeus statue by Anaxagoras (9.81; Pausanias 5.23.1–3; Gauer 1968, 96–97; Jung 2006, 256); and finally another large statue of Poseidon at the Isthmus (9.81). For the spoils in Athens, see below. Pausanias the general also dedicated a tripod at Delphi, inscription quoted by Thucydides 1.132 (Förtsch 2001, 53–55). See Gauer 1968, 28 on Herodotus' autopsy of such monuments.
[743] If Herodotus (9.17) is to be believed, more Greeks were fighting on the Persian side than on the Greek side (Cartledge 2013, 61). For the use of the battle of Plataea in later identity-building, see Jung 2006, 298–383. On the commemoration of the battle, see Jung 2006, 259–262. Places with cults included Megara (*IG* VII 53), and Athens where a 'Plataea Day' was celebrated according to Plutarch (*De gloria Atheniensium* 7). For Sparta, we have evidence for a cult of Pausanias, whose bones were relocated to Sparta, where he was venerated alongside Leonidas (*IG* V,1 18; 660; see also Thucydides 1.134; Pausanias 3.17.7–9). As Low 2011, 9–11 points out, the cultic juxtaposition of Pausanias and Leonidas is not surprising because Plataea was a 'retribution' for Thermopylae (8.114; 9.79; on the theme of retribution see also Asheri 1998). Jung 2011b, 104 has questioned whether this relocation of Pausanias' bones, commissioned by Delphi, can be seen as a political act. Sparta also had the fifth-century BCE 'Persian stoa', in which the Spartans put emphasis on their own efforts at Plataea (Jung 2006, 257).
[744] Kowerski 2005, 63–107; Jung 2006, 229–230. Even though the poem seems to place more emphasis on the Spartans, several other cities are mentioned (Flower 1998, 371; Sbardella 2000, making a case for an essentially Spartan context; Jung 2006, 235–238). See Boedeker 2001a, 121–124 and 2001b for evidence of heroisation of the Plataiomachoi in this poem, which Herodotus probably knew; however, there are also several important differences, as Herodotus may have wanted to leave his own mark on the story (Boedeker 2001a, 131–134). On possible identifications of the location of Simonides' poems at Plataea mentioned by Pausanias, see Molyneux 1992, 197–202. See Kowerski 2005, 39–58 for doubts about the connection of some of the new fragments to the battle of Plataea and the difficulty in positing the existence of a separate Plataea poem.
[745] See Steinhart 1997, 53–69 for a different view.
[746] For a general overview of the development of this memory landscape, see Hölkeskamp 2001, 335; Hartmann 2010, 318–327.

the event. It is highly probable that he visited the battlefield himself.⁷⁴⁷ But it has also been observed that the actual battlefield of Plataea is more complex than Herodotus' schematic depiction of it suggests.⁷⁴⁸ This is in line with observations that certain events during the battle are dramatised,⁷⁴⁹ and that Herodotus lacked the information to comment accurately on the battle's military dimensions.⁷⁵⁰

This chapter expands on this view and argues that the topography within Herodotus' account, fiercely debated,⁷⁵¹ and still often taken at face value,⁷⁵² can instead be successfully explained as a collection of mnemotopes. It will be shown that this topography, more than any other episode of the Persian Wars, can be understood as a 'concatenation' of these mnemotopes, which placed the narrative in the landscape (see §1.3.5).

2.9.1 The Persian fort

The battle took place near the Persian fort at Thebes, built by Xerxes' general Mardonios. The fort's location is described in 9.15:

ἐν Τανάγρῃ δὲ νύκτα ἐναυλισάμενος, καὶ τραπόμενος τῇ ὑστεραίῃ ἐς Σκῶλον ἐν γῇ τῇ Θηβαίων ἦν. ἐνθαῦτα δὲ τῶν Θηβαίων καίπερ μηδιζόντων ἔκειρε τοὺς χώρους, οὔτι κατὰ ἔχθος αὐτῶν ἀλλ' ὑπ' ἀναγκαίης μεγάλης ἐχόμενος, βουλόμενος ἔρυμά τε τῷ στρατῷ ποιήσασθαι, καὶ ἢν

---

747 It is generally agreed upon that Herodotus visited the site of the battle (Myres 1953, 4; Pritchett 1957, 9; Müller 1987, 552; Barron 1988, 599); more hesitant is Macan 1908, II 359–360. Herodotus mentions locals from Orchomenos (9.16), who allegedly dined with the Persians before the battle, where he was told that the Greeks were predestined to win (on the doubtful historicity of this story see Flower & Marincola 2002, 126), and Plataea itself (9.51).
748 Flower & Marincola 2002, 23. Pritchett 1985a, 126–127 pointed out that Herodotus' topographical references are essentially "terminal checkpoints", giving only rough estimates of the whereabouts of individual events. However, he did not realise that the locations could also be completely invented, meaning that for him, the estimate locations were reason enough to embark on a topographical reconstruction of the battle.
749 Woodhouse 1898, 33 noted that Herodotus' account is "moulded by the epic cast of the writer's genius." Dramatised elements include the quarrel between the Athenians and the Tegeans (9.26–28), the nocturnal visit of Alexander (9.46–47), and Mardonios' offer to make the combat between the Spartans and the Persians decide the battle (9.48). See also Woodhouse 1898, 41–45; Hignett 1963, 316–317; Barron 1988, 606. As elsewhere in Herodotus' work, the speeches, employed to display his interpretation of events (Solmsen 1944) are to be regarded as fictitious. Furthermore, it has been noted that there are difficulties with reconciling the number of troops on both the Greek and the Persian sides with the topography of the plain (Hignett 1963, 306).
750 E.g. Woodhouse 1898, 45–53; Cawkwell 2005, 113–115; Sabin 2007, 95–99; for the opposite view see Ferrill 1966, 112–113.
751 Pritchett 1957, 9; Barron 1988, 599: "the campaign at Plataea has been almost as bitterly contested by modern topographers as it was by the original belligerents". See Clark 1917, 35 for remarks on the confusing nature of Herodotus' topographical remarks.
752 E.g. Olsen 2003; Ray 2009, 90–103; Konijnendijk 2012.

συμβαλόντι οἱ μὴ ἐκβαίνῃ ὁκοῖόν τι ἐθέλοι, κρησφύγετον τοῦτο ἐποιέετο. παρῆκε δὲ αὐτοῦ τὸ στρατόπεδον ἀρξάμενον ἀπὸ Ἐρυθρέων παρὰ Ὑσιάς, κατέτεινε δὲ ἐς τὴν Πλαταιΐδα γῆν, παρὰ τὸν Ἀσωπὸν ποταμὸν τεταγμένον. οὐ μέντοι τό γε τεῖχος τοσοῦτο ἐποιέετο, ἀλλ' ὡς ἐπὶ δέκα σταδίους μάλιστά κῃ μέτωπον ἕκαστον.

[Mardonius], having bivouacked the night in Tanagra and turned to Skolos the following day, was in Theban territory. Although the Thebans were siding with the Persians, he cleared the land of trees, not because he was furious with them, but because he sorely needed to provide a means of defence for his army. And if, as he put his men to battle, things would not turn out for him how he wanted, he made this as a place of retreat. His camp extended from Erythrai via Hysiai, and it stretched towards the land of Plataea, arrayed along the Asopos river. He did not, however, make the fort of this size, but each side was approximately ten stades.

The fort is mentioned again in 9.65 and 9.70 as the place where the Persians finally retreated and where they were successfully besieged by the Spartans, Athenians and Tegeans. Nearly all Persians were killed.[753] It was also known to Diodorus Siculus (11.30.1), as well as to Xenophon (*Hellenica* 5.4.49), who refers to the site as τὸ κατὰ Σκῶλον σταύρωμα ('the palisade at Skolos') in his description of the Boeotian War. Plutarch mentions the fort and the encampment (*Aristides* 11.2), but his account is clearly based on that of Herodotus and it does not necessarily imply autopsy.[754] When Pausanias (9.2.1; 9.4.4) visited, the towns of the battlefield, including Skolos, were in ruins although he could discern a half-finished temple of Demeter and Kore there (see §2.9.6).[755]

Herodotus himself does not tell us exactly where the camp was. It has even been suggested that "[t]he one clear fact about this fortification is that Herodotus has no clear ideas about it".[756] On the basis of 9.31, 9.40 and 9.59 it seems evident that the Persians were stationed immediately north of the Asopos river.[757] Herodotus' indication that the

---

[753] Herodotus implausibly tells us that out of 300,000 Persians, only 3,000 survived, while only 159 Greeks fell (9.70). The anecdotes about the anchor-wielding Athenian Sophanes (9.74) may be connected to this part of the battle, as it marks the only episode when the Athenians were actively combatting the Persians. Although Herodotus does not say so explicitly, the fort may have been associated with the anecdote about the concubine from Kos (9.76); the rage of the Matineans and Eleans, disappointed with their leaders for having missed the battle (9.77); the story about Lampon the Aeginetan who suggested Pausanias to impale the body of Mardonios, much to the Spartan general's anger (9.78–79); the collection and division of the spoils (9.80–81); and Pausanias' Persian-style dinner (9.82).
[754] See Hignett 1963, 418–421 for an unfavourable review of Plutarch's account. Munro (1926b, 326), basing himself on it, assumed that there were four palisade walls at the other side of the Asopos, but not a square with towers (as Herodotus seems to suggest); he adds that Herodotus may have confused this fort with that of Mykale.
[755] See Schachter 1981, 160–161. At Hysiai, there was also a half-finished temple of Apollo and an oracular well.
[756] Munro 1926b, 325.
[757] Winter 1909, 19–22; Pritchett 1957, 24; Müller 1987, 554–556. However, Grundy 1894, 14–15 believed that it lay on both sides of the Asopos, and that the road from Athens to Thebes went right

fort was at Skolos, a town appearing in the *Iliad* (2.497), is not very helpful, because the location of this place, nor of those of the other towns of the Plataean battlefield is completely secure.[758] Locations offered for the camp include inside the bend of the Asopos south of Thebes,[759] or near the modern town of Neochoraki.[760] But we should not doubt that around 430 BCE, one could point out the former location of the fort in the landscape.

The creation of the mnemotope may be based on reliable, factual memories. But there may also have been some other catalysts. A curious consideration is that the name Skolos seems to be related to the word σκόλοψ 'pale', suggesting that the relation between the fort and the town may be folk-etymological (as will be explained in §2.10.2, a similar case can be made for the Persian palisade at Skolopoeis during the battle of Mykale, which resonates with the battle of Plataea in various aspects). Perhaps Skolos became the mnemotope of the Persian fort because of its name, in accordance with various other toponyms that inspired episodes of Xerxes' invasion (see §3.1.1 on the phenomenon of 'speaking toponyms'). Another story associated with the fort is that Mardonios cleared (ἔκειρε) a large area of trees for its construction (again, as at Mykale). Was there a particularly large open field where the fort was believed to have stood? We do not know; but I have suggested in §2.3.8 that empty areas on the Macedonian mountain triggered the story that Xerxes' army had cut down the forest while passing through here.

It seems further relevant that in Herodotus' account the Persians were initially stationed north of the Asopos river. This is understandable from a strategic perspective, but we also know that rivers can be regarded as important symbolical boundaries.[761] This makes it possible that, whatever the real historical situation in 479 BCE,

---

through it. Hignett (1963, 292–293) seems to prefer a location south of the Asopos (refuted by Barron 1988, 598, note 15).

758 Skolos is usually located near the town of Dafni, cf. Leake 1835, II 330–331; Pritchett located Skolos near the Metochi of Agios Meletios (Pritchett 1957, 22–23; 1985a, 99–103); for an alternative site see Burn 1962, 518 and Green 1996, 244; or near Kortsa (Kromayer 1924, 120). Hysiai is usually located on the hill of the Pantanassa chapel, cf. Leake 1835, II 328–329; Kromayer 1924, 115–120; Pritchett 1957, 22–23; 1982, 89–92; 1985a, 99–103. Grundy 1894, 15–16 and 1901, 464–465 instead believed that it was south of modern Erythres, and Zikos 1905, 23–24 placed it at Vergoutiani. Erythrai is usually located on the Agia Triada ridge: Leake 1835, II 328–329; Grundy 1894, 9–12; Winter 1909, 19; Hignett 1963, 425–427. Kromayer 1924, 120–121 and Pritchett 1982, 89–92; suggested the Metochi of Agios Meletios near Darimari. Zikos 1905, 22–24 located the town at the Pantanassa ridge (where others place Hysiai) and reported that the place was formerly called Rodoslavi. Papachatzi 1981, 47 placed it close to Dafni.
759 Leake 1835, II 339–340; Boucher 1915; Green 1996, 236.
760 Pritchett 1957, 24; 1982, 97–101; Schachter 1981, 160–161; Müller 1987, 577–578; Asheri et al. 2006, 192–193.
761 The Asopos (already mentioned in *Iliad* 4.383 and 10.287) constituted an important (both natural and symbolic) boundary, and was used by the Athenians to demarcate the territories of the Thebans and the Plataeans, their allies (6.108; Pausanias 9.4.4; Kirsten 1950, 2258–2259). Pausanias (9.1.1–2) preserves a local tradition in which Plataea was a daughter of the Asopos river, or alternatively, of a mythical king with the same name; she even had a hero-shrine in the city (9.2.7). Note that Strabo (9.2.31) seems to refer to the general area of the Asopos as the place where the battle happened.

the north side of the Asopos was by default demarcated as Persian territory, and that the fort was consequently also imagined here. In this respect, note that Herodotus' account implies that the Persians lost the battle once they crossed the river.[762]

2.9.2 Erythrai; the pass of the 'Oak Heads'

A subsequent string of mnemotopes marked a sequence of positions taken by the Greeks. Their initial position is described in 9.19 as mirroring the Persian position, at the foothills of Mount Kithairon at Erythrai; while the position is not detailed any further, the Greeks effectively controlled the passes over the mountains.[763] It was here that they were attacked by the Persian cavalry, commanded by the Persian 'hero' Masistios, who was eventually killed (9.20-24).[764]

Later in the account (9.39), the pass which the Greeks had guarded was the site of a lethal raid on the Greek supply lines by the Persian cavalry, during which five hundred beasts of burden and their owners, who had come from the Peloponnese to bring provisions to the Greeks, were killed:

> ἡμέραι δέ σφι ἀντικατημένοισι ἤδη ἐγεγόνεσαν ὀκτώ, ὅτε ταῦτα ἐκεῖνος συνεβούλευε Μαρδονίῳ. ὁ δὲ μαθὼν τὴν παραίνεσιν εὖ ἔχουσαν, ὡς εὐφρόνη ἐγένετο, πέμπει τὴν ἵππον ἐς τὰς ἐκβολὰς τὰς Κιθαιρωνίδας αἳ ἐπὶ Πλαταιέων φέρουσι, τὰς Βοιωτοὶ μὲν Τρεῖς κεφαλὰς καλέουσι, Ἀθηναῖοι δὲ Δρυὸς κεφαλάς.

> They had already sitting opposed to each other for eight days when [Timagenides] advised Mardonius [to block the pass at Kithairon]. When he understood that this was good advice, he sent, as the opportunity arose, his cavalry to the pass of the Kithairon that leads to Plataea, and which the Boeotians call 'Three Heads', and the Athenians 'Oak Heads'.

We can identify this pass with the route taken by the modern road from Athens to the modern town of Erythres; from the plain below, three hills are visible, possibly inspiring the name.[765] The same pass is also mentioned in Thucydides 3.24 as the route to Athens guarded by the Spartans in 428 BCE. The story about the blockage may

---

762 Lateiner 1985, 91. Masaracchia (1976, 173) treated Mardonios' crossing of the Asopos as "l'ultimo esempio della sua ἀγνωμοσύνη."
763 Pritchett 1957, 24–25; Müller 1987, 556–557; this location is also given by Diodorus Siculus (11.29.4).
764 For a thorough analysis of the Masistios episode see Petropoulou 2008, who suggests that his name may have meant 'Tallest' in Persian and have been so understood by the Greeks. The parading of the body may have been commemorated in the frieze of the temple to Athena Nike on the Acropolis (Gauer 1968, 17; Cartledge 2013, 150; but see Petropoulou 2008, 15 for a refutation). The episode is believed to contain various Homeric resonances (Obst 1913, 183; Barron 1988, 601; Petropoulou 2008, 15; 17–18).
765 Grundy 1894, 5–7; Kromayer 1924, 110–115; Pritchett 1957, 20–21; Müller 1987, 509. Hignett (1963, 289; 424) however, identified it with the Gyphtokastro pass (referred to by Xenophon in *Hellenica* 5.4.14) to the east of the route used by the modern road.

250 — 2 Topographical Case Studies

Fig. 52: The three hills marking the pass of the 'Oak Heads'.

be thought of as part of the various stories in Herodotus' account of the Persian Wars (and elsewhere in his account) which concern 'pass lore' (cf. §3.3.5).

2.9.3 The shrine of Androkrates and the Gargaphie spring

The Greeks then thought it fit to move their camp to a new position, closer to Plataea. This position was according to Herodotus marked by two landmarks: the so-called Gargaphie fountain and the shrine of the hero Androkrates (9.25):

> μετὰ δὲ ἔδοξέ σφι ἐπικαταβῆναι ἐς Πλαταιάς· ὁ γὰρ χῶρος ἐφαίνετο πολλῷ ἐὼν ἐπιτηδεότερός σφι ἐνστρατοπεδεύεσθαι ὁ Πλαταιικὸς τοῦ Ἐρυθραίου τά τε ἄλλα καὶ εὐυδρότερος. ἐς τοῦτον δὴ τὸν χῶρον καὶ ἐπὶ τὴν κρήνην τὴν Γαργαφίην τὴν ἐν τῷ χώρῳ τούτῳ ἐοῦσαν ἔδοξέ σφι χρεὸν εἶναι ἀπικέσθαι καὶ διαταχθέντας στρατοπεδεύεσθαι. ἀναλαβόντες δὲ τὰ ὅπλα ἤισαν διὰ τῆς ὑπωρείης τοῦ Κιθαιρῶνος παρὰ Ὑσιὰς ἐς τὴν Πλαταιίδα γῆν, ἀπικόμενοι δὲ ἐτάσσοντο κατὰ ἔθνεα πλησίον τῆς τε κρήνης τῆς Γαργαφίης καὶ τοῦ τεμένεος τοῦ Ἀνδροκράτεος τοῦ ἥρωος διὰ ὄχθων τε οὐκ ὑψηλῶν καὶ ἀπέδου χώρου.

> They then decided to go down to Plataea, as the land of Plataea appeared much better suited for establishing a camp than that of Erythrai, and, moreover, also better watered. So they thought it

best to go to this place and to the Gargaphie spring and to camp there according to their battle-order. Having taken up the arms, they went through the areas under Mount Kithairon, passing Hysiai, to the land of Plataea, and when they had arrived, they positioned themselves by tribe, close to the Gargaphie fountain and the sanctuary of the hero Androkrates, across low hills and flat land.

The location has been sought primarily on the basis of the Gargaphie fountain, for which Herodotus gives distances from other landmarks (9.51: ten stades from the 'Island'; 9.52: twenty stades from the temple of Hera near Plataea) and which has to reflect a water source in the landscape.[766] Unfortunately, the situation is unclear because the local hydrology may have changed considerably. Nevertheless, today there seems to be a consensus that the best identification is the Kiafa Retsi spring, described by Leake as "incased [...] in an artificial basin covered with squared stones of ancient fabric". The location of this spring matches the distance from the purported location of the temple of Hera at Plataea (see §2.9.5).[767] Other locations, have, however, also been suggested.[768] In addition, there are various other monumentalised fountains near Plataea, such as the Megali Vrisi and Vergoutiani (cf. below).[769]

---

[766] For example, we know that a canal was dug in the plain in 1981, disturbing some of the springs in the area (Pritchett 1985a, 95–96).

[767] Leake 1835, II 332–333; Hunt 1890, 466; Grundy 1894, 16–17; 1901, 466; Munro 1904, 159; Zikos 1905, 25 (reporting a 'Slavic' etymology, with *rietschka* meaning little river); Winter 1909, 41–43; Obst 1913, 188–189; Boucher 1915, 278; Pritchett 1957, 21–22; Burn 1962, 522; Papachatzi 1981, 47; Wallace 1982, 185–186; 1985, 97; Müller 1987, 557; Barron 1988, 602; Green 1996, 247. See Lazenby 1993, 225 for a photograph, with the amusing remark "note how easy it would have been to choke it up."

[768] The nearby Apotripi (or Alepotripi) spring was favoured by Woodhouse 1898, 37–38; for a description see Grundy 1894, 16. In his later work, Pritchett (1965, 113–115; 1985a, 103–105; 1993, 295) located Gargaphie at a hypothetical place, "100 yards SSE of two wells where in the 1950's there were three to four inch pipes", at the meeting point of the "road of the Towers" and the road from Plataea to Thebes. This location would match Herodotus' assertion that the fountain was twenty stades from the temple of Hera at Plataea. See also Hignett 1963, 428.

[769] See the map of the surroundings of Plataea in Leake 1835, II. Kromayer 1924, 130–133 identified Gargaphie with one of the sources 800 m northeast of the modern village of Plataies, where a marble cylinder and other ancient remains were found. This is the monumental Μεγάλη Βρύση ('Big Source') which lays immediately west of the ancient city of Plataea. See Papachatzi 1981, 44–45 for pictures (note that he does not identify this spring with Gargaphie). While this fountain does not fit the twenty stades from the commonly accepted location of the temple of Hera, it is not impossible that it was regarded as Gargaphie by Herodotus or later (visiting or local) Greeks; Pausanias mentions Gargaphie immediately after discussing the city of Plataea, while Plutarch mentions that the participants in the Eleutheria festival which commemorated the battle of Plataea drew water from Gargaphie. These observations might indicate that the fountain was not far from the city; also note that Pausanias' summoning of Hera indicates the that temple was visible from Gargaphie. Konecny, Aravantinos & Marchese 2013, 54–56 connect the spring to the worship of Hera and the Nymphs. Zikos (1905, 23–24) asserted that the Vergoutiani spring, which he reports was furnished with ancient stones, was erroneously identified as Gargaphie by Herodotus. He also reports ancient objects near the spring belonging to a temple, and spoils (inscribed stones and columns) in the nearby church of Agia Anna (pages 24–25).

Fig. 53: The spring Kiafa Retsi (Gargaphie?).

The location of Androkrates' shrine depends on the location of Gargaphie and on the interpretations of a passage in Thucydides (3.24), who describes the shrine as a landmark used by the Plataeans, who kept it to their right as they fled from the city on the Plataea-Thebes road. It is also mentioned in Plutarch (*Aristides* 11.7-8), who describes it as enveloped in a thick grove near the temple of Demeter of Hysiai. Plutarch's location does not seem to match that of Herodotus and Thucydides and is therefore often discredited.[770] If we take Kiafa Retsi as Gargaphie, the nearby hill of Agios Dimitrios seems the best option for the location of the shrine; but this place has also been identified with the temple of Demeter (see §2.9.6), and various alternatives exist.[771]

---

[770] Mele 1955, 9–10; Pritchett 1985, 106; Müller 1987, 558; we will return to the passage below.
[771] The Agios Dimitrios hill was proposed by Kromayer 1924, 135–138; Wallace 1982, 186–187; 1985, 97. The identification with the Agios Ioannis hill (slightly more distant from Kiafa Retsi) is advocated by Woodhouse 1898, 38–40; Munro 1904, 158; Macan 1908, I 640; Obst 1913, 187–188; Myres 1953, 285; Müller 1987, 558; it also appears approximately in this position on Leake's map (1835, II). Other scholars, however, maintain that the site was in the plain, not on a hill: see Winter 1909, 446 (agnostic; and explaining Plutarch's location as resulting from a distortion in the later tradition, in which the temple of Demeter became the focal point for battle reconstructions); Burn 1962, 522; Hignett 1963, 429–431. Pritchett 1965, 111–113 offered a location 100 metres southwest of the Apotripi fountain,

Fig. 54: The church of Agios Dimitrios, which may occupy the site of the shrine of Androkrates.

Some early scholars believed that Herodotus' insistence on Gargaphie was exaggerated.[772] But we can understand this exaggeration when we consider that springs can easily become mnemotopes,[773] and that Gargaphie was developed into one for visitors to the battlefield of Plataea (compare the appearance of the Makaria spring as a mnemotope of the battle of Marathon in Pausanias 1.32.6). The relevance of Gargaphie

---

where the ruins of small Byzantine church contained ancient artefacts which had been hidden there by the locals. The map in Zikos 1905 locates the shrine slightly northeast of ancient Plataea. See e.g. Olsen 1903, 4 and Masaracchia 1976, 148 for the idea that the shrine of Androkrates and Gargaphie formed the terminal points of the extension of the Greek army; however, from Herodotus' text it is quite clear that he positioned these landmarks near each other. Pritchett 1957, 25 (followed by Green 1996, 248–249) detailed that the army was stretched out from the hill of Agios Dimitrios to the Pyrgos hill northeast of Pantanassa (Hysiai).

772 Macan 1908, II 359 and Hignett 1963, 324 noted that it may have been too small to quench the thirst of an entire army. Wright 1904, 63 suggested that an Athenian source may have invented the story about the movement to the fountain to emphasise the responsibility of the Spartans in the loss of the spring.

773 On the importance of springs in Greek mythology, see Buxton 1994, 109–113. For springs as mnemotopes, see Hartmann 2010, 87.

lay in its demarcation of the beginning of the battle, as evidenced by Herodotus' decision to describe the original posts of the Greeks and the opposing Persians (9.28-9.32).

Gargaphie may also have been the mnemotope for various other events that added to the salience of the Gargaphie area to visitors in the years after the war.[774] Two of these are notable from a mnemotopical perspective. The first relevant story is the discussion between Pausanias the general and another Spartan captain, Amompharetos, who initially refused to move away from the camp (9.53); as a result, the Athenians halted as well. In 9.55, Amompharetos makes his point clear by placing a rock near Pausanias, playing on the custom of voting with pebbles.[775] Munro conjectured that "[...] the monument shown to Pausanias the Periegetes on the right of his road into Plataea as the tomb of Mardonius represented a warrior uplifting a rock in front of an august person, and was alternatively represented as Aeimnestus braining Mardonius, who was killed according to Plutarch by a stone, or Amompharetus recording his vote."[776] There is no evidence to support this conjecture, but it is not unthinkable that there was a rock near the Gargaphie spring which functioned as a mnemotope for this story to locals.

The second relevant story is explicitly localised at Gargaphie: the blocking of the source by the Persians (9.49). It may have been known to Aeschylus (*Persae* 482-484: στρατὸς δ' ὁ λοιπὸς ἔν τε Βοιωτῶν χθονί // διώλλυθ', οἳ μὲν ἀμφὶ κρηναῖον γάνος // δίψῃ πονοῦντες 'and the rest of the army was destroyed in the land of the Boeotians, some suffering from thirst around the refreshment of a fountain'). Plutarch (*Aristides* 16.5), too, mentions that springs close to Plataea were tampered with by the Persian cavalry. Pausanias mentions the spring (9.4.3) after a temple of Demeter (§2.9.6) and the memorial of Leïtos. He repeats the Herodotean account that it was obstructed by the Persians, and adds that it had been restored by the Plataeans afterwards. The historicity of this narrative (which could be a tourist story told to visitors of the battle site) is today unprovable, but it may or may not have been inspired by a drying up of the source.[777] Similarly, Pausanias' assertion that

---

774 E.g. the quarrel between the Athenians and the Tegeans about their positions in the battle formation (9.26–28); the ominous sacrifices by the Spartan diviner Teisamenos (9.33); the killing of Kallikrates (9.72); pinpricks from the side of the Persians (9.40); the arrival of Alexandros of Macedon, who served in the Persian army, to announce Mardonios' decision to attack at dawn (9.44–45); the Athenians' and Spartans' failed attempt to swap positions (9.46–47) and Mardonios' offer to make the combat between the Spartans and the Persians decide the battle (9.48).
775 Obst 1913, 197 explains this episode as an Athenian fantasy, assuming that the practice of voting with pebbles did not exist in Sparta.
776 Munro 1926b, 335, note 1. For the epic practise of picking up giant rocks as a weapon, see *Iliad* 7.264–266; 8.321–322; 12.380–381; 12.445–456.
777 Green (1996, 261) guesses that the Persians defiled the fountain by defecation. See Shear 1993, 417 for possible archaeological evidence for Persian well-blocking in the Athenian Agora using objects.

the spring had been repaired by the locals may simply reflect that the spring was functional at the time of his visit. The story also seems to reflect the notion of the enemy's unseen behaviour that was topographically motivated many times in Herodotus' account of Xerxes' invasion (§ 3.3.5).

It is possible that Gargaphie (whom scholars sometimes believe to be a water nymph on the basis of vase paintings)[778] and Androkrates were believed to have helped to fight against the Persians. We should not underestimate the influence which local cults may have had on the reconstruction of the Persian Wars by the ancients themselves. We will explore the ways by which such associations may have influenced Herodotus' account below, when discussing the temple of Demeter (§2.9.6). There is, indeed, an indication in Plutarch that the Plataeans regarded Androkrates as a protecting hero,[779] and as such, his shrine may have become associated with the battle in local folklore. But we do not get the impression from Herodotus' account that this was the case, let alone that Gargaphie or Androkrates helped the Greeks.

In an interesting example of mnemotopical accumulation (§1.3.5), the Gargaphie spring, in addition to its role in the battle of Plataea, was the mnemotope for a version of the myth of Aktaion and Artemis. Aktaion saw the goddess while she was bathing in this spring, and was then turned into a deer and devoured by his own dogs. We only have explicit references for the localisation of this story at Gargaphie from the Roman period. In authors who probably never travelled to the battlefield, the spring received additional associations with Hecate, the Graces, an otherwise-unknown Gergaphos, and the name Gargaphie was also applied to a valley.[780] Different versions of the Aktaion myth existed, but the element of Artemis'

---

[778] Kossatz-Deissmann 1978, 152; Lacy 1990, 36–42 (see further below). Etymologically, the toponym Gargaphie seems to refer to the region's hydrology or vegetation: it could perhaps, be connected either to γόργυρα 'underground drain' or to γάργα 'poplar' (Hesychius, s.v.), but this must remain speculative.

[779] Vandiver 1991, 81: "these references to heroes' shrines near the fields of battle may serve a symbolic as well as a topographical function. However, this must remain uncertain." In Plutarch (*Aristides* 11.3) we read that, during the battle, the Athenians were advised by the Delphic oracle to pay homage to various local heroes: Androkrates, Leukon, Peisandros, Damokrates, Hypsion, Aktaion, and Polyidos, ἀρχηγέται Πλαταιέων 'protecting heroes of the Plataeans'. It is possible that all of these heroes possessed cult sites (as we know Androkrates had one), but the list may also be the result of a learned tradition that connected all kinds of names that had a relation with Boeotia (Schachter 1986, 56; Vandiver 1991, 80–81).

[780] Pliny the Elder (*Naturalis Historia* 4.25) mentions Gargaphie in a list of Boeotian fountains, but does not mention the Aktaion myth. Ovid mentions Gargaphie in the *Metamorphoses* (3.155–156): "vallis erat piceis et acuta densa cupressu / nomine Gargaphie, succinctae sacra Dianae" ('There was a valley, thickly wooded with pine trees and the high cypress, with the name Gargaphie, sacred to the girded Diana'). Further on, Ovid continues the idyllic setting and describes how the fountain flowed next to a grotto. Hyginus (*Fabulae* 180 and 181) has a similar treatment: "Diana cum in valle opacissima cui nomen est Gargaphia aestivo tempore fatigata ex assidua venatione se ad fontem cui nomen est Parthenius perlueret [...]" ('When Diana, tired of the constant hunting,

bathing does not seem to be very old, first appearing in the third century BCE.⁷⁸¹ While it has been argued that several fourth-century BCE vase paintings show that a spring also featured in the older 'Semele' version of the myth (in which Aktaion was killed by Artemis after trying to court Semele), this does not bring us back to the fifth century BCE.⁷⁸² It seems, then, that the Aktaion myth was only localised at Gargaphie in the Hellenistic and Roman periods; this may have happened because the Aktaion myth was invariably placed in the general region of the Kithairon,

---

bathed in summertime at the spring called Parthenius in the very shady valley called Gargaphia [...]'). Spano (1928, 34–35) hypothesised that in the tradition represented by Ovid and Hyginus, the name of Gargaphie, a relatively well-known spring, was erroneously transferred to the valley around the spring of Artemis. In Vibius Sequester 172 we find "Gargaphie, Boeotiae, ubi Actaeon laceratus" and in Statius, *Thebais* 7.273–274 "Hecataeaque gurgite nutrit / Gargaphie." The reference to Hecate in this passage could well indicate a location at a crossroads (Wallace 1982, 186) but may also refer to Artemis (Schachter 1981, 231). One of Alciphron's letters (1.11.3), of unsure date, contains a literary fiction involving the fountain: εἴποις ἂν τὰς Χάριτας τὸν Ὀρχομενὸν ἀπολιπούσας καὶ τῆς Ἀργαφίας κρήνης ἀπονιψαμένας [...] 'you could say that the Graces, having left Orchomenos, and bathed themselves in the fountain Argaphia [...]'. Finally, Aelius Herodianus (*Περὶ παθῶν* 187) mentions Ἀργαφίη, from «νιψάμεναι κρήνης ἔδραμον Ἀργαφίης». τινὲς δὲ διὰ τοῦ ε ἀπὸ Γεργάφου τοῦ Ποσειδῶνος· τὸ δὲ ἐντελὲς ἐν τῷ Ἑρμῇ «κρήνης Γαργαφίης» ('they ran, after washing themselves in the fountain Argaphie. Some write an ε, based on Gergaphos, the son of Poseidon. But the best is in the Hermes: «κρήνης Γαργαφίης»').

781 See Lacy 1990, 26–27; 32–36 for an overview of the ancient (including Archaic) literature which contains the Aktaion myth. In yet another version known preserved in Diodorus Siculus (4.81.4) Aktaion tried to marry Artemis in her own temple after offering the first-fruits of his hunt. The bath version first appears in the third century BCE in Callimachus' *In lavacrum Palladis* (113–114), which is thought to draw on a similar story about Teiresias and Athena (Lacy 1990, 29). Nevertheless, as Lacy points out, this only gives us a *terminus ante quem*, with Callimachus (56) claiming that "μῦθος δ'οὐκ ἐμός, ἀλλ' ἑτέρων" and Pseudo-Apollodorus (3.4.4), who is thought to draw mainly on pre-Hellenistic material, mentioning that most sources have the bath version. Finally, Lacy argues, our archaic attestations, despite all mentioning the Semele version, are only extant because they offered something unusual to a Roman audience. Still, while these points are interesting, they cannot firmly establish the myth before the third century BCE.

782 The vases which depict the myth are a volute crater in Naples (SA 31), an Apulian bell-crater in Gothenburg (RKM 13–71) and a nestoris in Harvard University (60.367); see Lacy 1990, 36–42; all can be found in the *LIMC* s.v. 'Aktaion' (I.1 454–469). Kossatz-Deissmann 1978, 152 and Lacy 1990, 36–42 interpret the right woman on the Harvard nestoris, the Gothenburg bell crater, and an Apulian stamnos from Paris as the nymph Gargaphie (154–156). However, although these women may represent nymphs, this is not necessarily the case. According to Kossatz-Deissmann 1978, 152 the volute crater from Naples points at the inclusion of a spring in versions of the myth which are not primarily concerned with the bathing scene, in this case the 'Semele' version. She argues that the bath version was inspired by the inclusion of a spring in the older versions. Kossatz-Deissmann further (page 165) places the connection of the myth with the Plataean spring in the classical period, and more specifically with Aeschylus' lost work *Toxotides*: she argues that the tragedian had fought in Plataea, and that he may well have been inspired to write his play by cultic practices at the battle site.

where there were several mnemotopes connected with Aktaion and Artemis.[783] Lacy thought that the confusion of the spring of Aktaion with Gargaphie arose "because of the role both Aktaion and Gargaphia played in the conflict which culminated in the battle of Plataiai".[784] Although the mythical association most likely postdates the battle of Plataea by several centuries, it shows how easily stories could be attached to landmark springs.

2.9.4 The 'island'

Because the Greeks were now cut off from supplies and water, they contemplated retreating to the so-called 'island', a piece of land between two streams of the Oeroe river (9.50-51):

> βουλευομένοισι δὲ τοῖσι στρατηγοῖσι ἔδοξε, ἢν ὑπερβάλωνται ἐκείνην τὴν ἡμέρην οἱ Πέρσαι συμβολὴν μὴ ποιεύμενοι, ἐς τὴν νῆσον ἰέναι. ἡ δὲ ἐστὶ ἀπὸ τοῦ Ἀσωποῦ καὶ τῆς κρήνης τῆς Γαργαφίης, ἐπ' ᾗ ἐστρατοπεδεύοντο τότε, δέκα σταδίους ἀπέχουσα, πρὸ τῆς Πλαταιέων πόλιος. νῆσος δὲ οὕτω ἂν εἴη ἐν ἠπείρῳ: σχιζόμενος ὁ ποταμὸς ἄνωθεν ἐκ τοῦ Κιθαιρῶνος ῥέει κάτω ἐς τὸ πεδίον, διέχων ἀπ' ἀλλήλων τὰ ῥέεθρα ὅσον περ τρία στάδια, καὶ ἔπειτα συμμίσγει ἐς τὠυτό. οὔνομα δέ οἱ Ὠερόη. θυγατέρα δὲ ταύτην λέγουσι εἶναι Ἀσωποῦ οἱ ἐπιχώριοι.

> The deliberating generals resolved, if the Persians would postpone making an attack that day, to go to the island. This is situated at a distance of ten stades from the Asopos and the Gargaphie fountain, where they camped then, before the city of the Plataeans. It is an island, as it were, on the mainland: the river runs down from the Kithairon down to the plain and divides there, and the streams are as much as three stades apart; and then they unite again. Its name is Oeroe. The locals say that it is the daughter of the Asopos.

The Greeks, however, never reached the island. Its exact location is debated, as there is currently no stream in the area which splits in two and unites again to form an island. As noted above, the hydrology of the area has changed considerably. Herodotus' indications of distance and the phrase πρὸ τῆς Πλαταιέων πόλιος are too vague

---

783 Aktaion was among the local Plataian heroes listed in the oracle in Plutarch, *Aristides* 11.3, mentioned above. Artemis, as the goddess Eukleia, worshipped especially by couples before their weddings, had a widespread cult in Boeotia, and also a temple at Plataea (Plutarch, *Aristides* 20.6). Pausanias (9.2.3) mentions a spring of Artemis on the road from Megara to Plataea (passing the Kithairon at another point west from the main road) and a little further on a rock called Ἀκταίωνος κοίτη ('bed of Aktaion'). For this bed, several locations have been offered: early it was identified it with a rock near the Vergoutiani spring southeast of the site of Plataea (Leake 1835, II 333–334; Hunt 1890, 475 note 57; Grundy 1894, 7; Zikos 1905, 23–24 (asserting that this spring was erroneously identified as the Gargaphie spring by Herodotus); Pritchett 1957, 19). Edmonson 1964 however, has located these landmarks at circa 1.5 km west of modern Vilia, at the βρύση βασιλική, on the south slope of Mount Kithairon; see also Papachatzi 1981, 23 with photograph 31.
784 Lacy 1984, 83; 1990, 32, note 40.

Fig. 55: The hill of the Analipsi chapel, believed to be Herodotus' island.

to allow for any definitive conclusions. The area most often connected with this story in the literature is the hill marked by the Analipsi chapel.[785] Papachatzi identified the Oeroe with the modern Anapodo river.[786]

Wallace pointed out that the 'non-role' of the island in the battle of Plataea is suspect. He conjectured that Herodotus' story originated with locals and that it should not be considered historically accurate.[787] It is not possible for us to judge

---

785 Grundy 1894, 26–31; 1901, 480–487 already proposed this location. A problem seems to be Herodotus' indication that the island was ten stadia from both Gargaphie and the Asopos. Woodhouse 1898, 57 proposed that κ' (the number 20) had been dropped between Ἀσωποῦ and καὶ in the manuscripts; if this is restored, the Analipsi hill would be a perfect candidate. This solution is widely accepted, see Pritchett 1957, 60–61; Obst 1913, 194–195; Hignett 1963, 428–429; Pritchett 1965, 115–119; Pritchett 1985a, 117–120. Müller 1987, 560–562, however, remedied by simply assuming that different points on the island may have been used for this calculation. Flower & Marincola 2002, 198–199 also reject Woodhouse's suggestion, pointing out that Herodotus simply writes loosely. See also Zikos 1905, 27–28 for a location west of the Analipsi hill called Levetiza; Winter 1909, 70–72 for an identification with the area north of the Vergoutiani spring; and Boucher 2015, 278 for a location north of Plataea.
786 Papachatzi 1981, 47.
787 Wallace 1982, 185.

the historical reality of this story (or rather: an element of strategy which was never executed), but it is easy to see how a conspicuous hill-island in the river could have become drawn into stories about the battle. Moreover, from a narrative point of view, the inclusion of the story about the island makes perfect sense: the non-attainment of a 'safe haven' is a useful dramatic device (cf. §3.3.4).

2.9.5 The temple of Hera

As the raids from the Persian cavalry continued all day, many Greeks (or at least the Athenians; the account is not clear) did not reach the 'island' but instead retreated to the temple of Hera in front of the city of Plataea (9.52):[788]

> ταῦτα βουλευσάμενοι κείνην μὲν τὴν ἡμέρην πᾶσαν προσκειμένης τῆς ἵππου εἶχον πόνον ἄτρυτον· ὡς δὲ ἥ τε ἡμέρη ἔληγε καὶ οἱ ἱππέες ἐπέπαυντο, νυκτὸς δὴ γινομένης καὶ ἐούσης τῆς ὥρης ἐς τὴν συνέκειτό σφι ἀπαλλάσσεσθαι, ἐνθαῦτα ἀερθέντες οἱ πολλοὶ ἀπαλλάσσοντο, ἐς μὲν τὸν χῶρον ἐς τὸν συνέκειτο οὐκ ἐν νόῳ ἔχοντες, οἳ δὲ ὡς ἐκινήθησαν ἔφευγον ἄσμενοι τὴν ἵππον πρὸς τὴν Πλαταιέων πόλιν, φεύγοντες δὲ ἀπικνέονται ἐπὶ τὸ Ἥραιον. τὸ δὲ πρὸ τῆς πόλιος ἐστι τῆς Πλαταιέων, εἴκοσι σταδίους ἀπὸ τῆς κρήνης τῆς Γαργαφίης ἀπέχον· ἀπικόμενοι δὲ ἔθεντο πρὸ τοῦ ἱροῦ τὰ ὅπλα.

> Having decided [to retreat to the island], they were bothered continuously that whole day, as the cavalry remained close. But as the day ended, and the riders had stopped, and when night had come and the hour when they had agreed to change their position, most got up and changed positions, but not to the place they had in mind: when they were moving, they readily fled from the cavalry to the city of the Plataeans, and as they fled they arrived at the temple of Hera. This is in front of the city of the Plataeans, twenty stades from the fountain of Gargaphie. And when they had arrived, they placed their arms in front of the temple.

The temple of Hera also plays a role later in the battle (9.61), when heavy fighting was taking place around the temple of Demeter (§2.9.6):

> καὶ οὐ γάρ σφι ἐγίνετο τὰ σφάγια χρηστά, ἔπιπτόν τε αὐτῶν ἐν τούτῳ τῷ χρόνῳ πολλοὶ καὶ πολλῷ πλεῦνες ἐτρωματίζοντο· φράξαντες γὰρ τὰ γέρρα οἱ Πέρσαι ἀπίεσαν τῶν τοξευμάτων πολλὰ ἀφειδέως, οὕτω ὥστε πιεζομένων τῶν Σπαρτιητέων καὶ τῶν σφαγίων οὐ γινομένων ἀποβλέψαντα τὸν Παυσανίην πρὸς τὸ Ἥραιον τὸ Πλαταιέων ἐπικαλέσασθαι τὴν θεόν, χρηίζοντα μηδαμῶς σφέας ψευσθῆναι τῆς ἐλπίδος.

> And their sacrifices did not turn out favourable for [the Spartans], and at that time, there fell many of them and many more where wounded, because the Persians, having put up their wicker shields, shot their arrows without mercy. And so, as the Spartans were cornered and the sacrifices did not work, Pausanias looked towards the Heraion of the Plataeans and called upon the goddess, praying that they would not in any way be let down in their hope.

---

[788] Pritchett 1957, 27 suggests that this would imply that the 'island' was reached after all.

The temple is also mentioned by Pausanias (9.2.7) who calls it θέας ἄξιος ('worth seeing') because of its size and its beautiful sculptures of Rhea, Hera Teleia (both by Praxiteles) and Bridal Hera (by Kallimachos). It appears to have stood inside the city in Pausanias' time, as he mentions it immediately after the shrine for the goddess Plataia.

The site of ancient Plataea itself is clear. Extensive ruins are located northeast of modern Platees.[789] The location of the temple of Hera has a commonly accepted site, but is still not entirely secure. It has been identified with an archaic temple immediately southeast of the old part of the city. The observation that pre-classical Plataea was limited to the northern part of the later town, makes it possible that the temple of Hera is within the current borders of the ancient site, as Pausanias' account suggests.[790] Although the association with Hera is not certain, a terracotta figurine of a veiled, seated woman was found there, and the building's size (larger, for example, than the enormous temple of Apollo Epicurius at Bassae) matches well with the importance given to the temple of Hera in the texts.[791] However, the identification remains uncertain; we also know of a prominent temple of Athena Areia ('Warlike Athena') in Plataea, which was a place where votive offerings were deposited after the battle of Plataea.[792]

---

[789] Kirsten 1950, 2256–2257; IG VII 1688 seems to confirm the location. Curiously, the etymology of the town's former name Kokla may be Modern Greek κόκκαλα 'bones' (Kirsten 1950, 2256). The present site of Plataea is much bigger than in Herodotus' time; the oldest part may have been in the south, where the oldest walls are attested, or in the north on a plateau-like hill, which would better match the name, and is corroborated by Mycenaean and Archaic finds. The city of Plataea itself may also be regarded as a mnemotope, because it had allegedly been burned by the Persians a year before the battle (8.50). It may still have been in ruins in Herodotus' time (Macan 1908, I 706–707).

[790] Winter 1909, 74–75; Müller 1987, 548, 564. For an elaborate description of what is known of this temple, see Konecny, Aravantinos & Marchese 2013, 141–144, who also identify it as the Heraion; see also Schachter 1981, 242–245. Hunt 1890, 469–471 and Kromayer 1924, 130 note 3 (preferring the temple of Agios Dimitrios because Herodotus describes Pausanias as looking up) were skeptical of the identification. The temple's original location outside the city walls in the pre-Classical period has been corroborated by a recent pottery survey (Konecny et al. 2008, 49). Leake 1835, II placed the temple of Hera immediately east of the old part of the city.

[791] Washington 1891. Hera may be identified with a goddess appearing on Plataean coins, cf. Schachter 1981, 245.

[792] The temple was allegedly originally donated by the Athenians with spoils from the battle of Marathon (Pausanias 9.4.1–2; Gauer 1968, 98, arguing that the temple was new, because Herodotus would have mentioned it, had it existed in his time; a dangerous assertion). It had a lavish, partly gilded cult statue of the goddess by Pheidias, and two paintings by Polygnotus in the pronaos depicting Odysseus after killing Penelope's suitors and the first campaign of Adrastos, a mythical king of Argos, against Thebes. Arguably, these instances from the mythical past stressed the contemporary opposition between Plataea and Thebes (Jung 2006, 258). It may be an allusion to the defeat of the Persians by the Plataeans in their local area: we know that a portrait of Arimnestos (cf. 9.63) was placed at the cult statue, and the fact that the rebuilding was paid for from the spoils gathered after the battle (Plutarch, *Aristides* 20.3). See also Gauer 1968, 98–100 (with literature).

Fig. 56: The old fortification walls of Plataea as seen from the approximate location of the temple of Hera.

It has been pointed out that there are practical problems with the episode. It is, for example, not feasible that all of the Athenians were stationed here, as Herodotus suggests.[793] However, the story seems to be better understandable if we look at the temple of Hera as a mnemotope around which stories crystallised in the post-war period. It appears that the temple was regarded as the next 'station' of the Greeks during the battle. In this case, the mnemotope also inspired stories about divine intervention. It seems that the temple of Hera represented the idea of a refuge (see §3.3.4 for other refuge mnemotopes), and Herodotus' remark that the Athenians put their weapons in front of the temple suggests that Hera herself had protected them.[794] The power of the goddess becomes apparent later in the narrative, when Herodotus suggests (9.62)

---

793 Obst 1913, 196–197.
794 The effect is aptly summarised by Washington 1891, 402: "The sanctity of the spot would appeal to them as a protection, and on the plateau just below the site of our temple they would naturally halt, under the shadow of the sanctuary of the great goddess of the Platæans."

that Hera answered Pausanias' prayers, as the omens started to be favourable.[795] Such stories may have been told by locals (priests?) as an 'explanation' for the Greek victory (in which the Athenian part was underlined). A further point of relevance is the battle of Mykale, allegedly fought on the same day as the battle of Plataea: as discussed in §2.10.1, in that battle a temple of Hera also features as a meeting point of the Greeks.[796]

2.9.6 Argiopion and the temple of Demeter

The Spartans and Tegeans went in the opposite direction of the Athenians in order to follow a route closer to the Kithairon. They halted at a place called Argiopion. Here, Pausanias and Amompharetos reunited at the moment when the Persian cavalry catch up with them (9.57):[797]

> τὸ δὲ ἀπελθὸν ὅσον τε δέκα στάδια ἀνέμενε τὸν Ἀμομφαρέτου λόχον, περὶ ποταμὸν Μολόεντα ἱδρυμένον Ἀργιόπιόν τε χῶρον καλεόμενον, τῇ καὶ Δήμητρος Ἐλευσινίης ἱρὸν ἧσται·

> [The Spartan army], having gone a distance of ten stadia, waited for the troops of Amompharetos as they stood by the Moloeis river and a place called Argiopion, where there is a temple of Eleusinian Demeter.

---

[795] Plutarch refers to the temple when relating how Pausanias looked towards it and invoked the goddess (*Aristides* 18.1), but this is rather an elaborate rendering of Herodotus' 9.61. We may believe with Cartledge 2013, 115 that the Spartan general's supplication of the Plataean goddess is a case of "playing politics". Indeed, politics was a recurring theme in the sanctuaries of Plataea. Later involvement with the temple of Hera by the Thebans (Thucydides 3.68) was politically inspired: here, it is related that, after destroying the city, the Thebans built a pilgrim hotel (καταγώγιον) next to the sanctuary from de debris of the houses; they also dedicated beds, made from material in the city walls, as well as a stone chapel to Hera. Although Thucydides does not specify so, it is hard not to take this statement as symbolic: the Thebans seem to have embellished the very temple of the goddess who helped to cause their demise in 479 BCE (9.61).
[796] Bowie 2007, 13.
[797] Although Herodotus' story revolved around the Spartan relocation to the temple, there also existed lore according to which the Athenians had been willing to go here (this time seemingly politically motivated). Plutarch (*Aristides* 11.3–8) relates how the oracle of Delphi had advised the Athenians to retreat to the temple of Demeter and Kore ἐν γᾷ ἰδίᾳ, 'in their own land'. The Athenians prepared to move to Eleusis, until Arimnestos, leader of the Plataeans, pointed out that there was also such a temple near Plataea. To comply with the message from Delphi the Plataeans decided to cede their land to Athens. Alexander the Great is said to have rewarded the Plataeans for this (11.9). Hignett (1963, 419–420) saw this information as inauthentic, and indeed it may reflect an attempt by Plutarch or his sources to explain the role of this site in the battle. The idea that Alexander himself visited a temple of Kore near Plataea is encountered in the *Historia Alexandri Magni* (2.1).

This location marks the climax of the battle of Plataea. Here, as they were being besieged by the Persian army, the Spartans and Tegeans performed sacrifices.[798] Then, in a dramatic turn, Pausanias evoked Hera, as discussed above, after which positive omens started to appear. The temple of Demeter is specifically mentioned (9.62):

> ἐγίνετο δὲ πρῶτον περὶ τὰ γέρρα μάχη. ὡς δὲ ταῦτα ἐπεπτώκεε, ἤδη ἐγίνετο ἡ μάχη ἰσχυρὴ παρ' αὐτὸ τὸ Δημήτριον καὶ χρόνον ἐπὶ πολλόν, ἐς ὃ ἀπίκοντο ἐς ὠθισμόν· τὰ γὰρ δόρατα ἐπιλαμβανόμενοι κατέκλων οἱ βάρβαροι.

> First there was battle over the wicker shields. When these had fallen, the battle became fierce next to that temple of Demeter and for a long time, in which they started to push, because the Persians grabbed the spears and broke them.

In an almost magical account, Herodotus further specifies that wherever Mardonios went, mounted on a white horse, the Persians were able to resist (9.63). During this episode, Mardonios was killed by Aeimnestos,[799] and the battle was decided in favour of the Greeks. As soon as the Greeks (Athenians) who were stationed around the temple of Hera heard about the victory, they made their way to the temple of Demeter (9.69). Although this final stage of the fight had taken place near the temple, no Persian had allegedly ventured inside the temenos (9.65; the passage is cited in §2.7.5).

The location of the final battle also happens to be the most contested. It is unclear what place was referred to as Argiopion (or Argiopios),[800] nor can the name Moloeis be connected with certainty to one of the many streams in the area.[801] If Herodotus' account is followed, the temple was situated at ten stades from the Gargaphie fountain and in or close to the northern spurs of Kithairon. In establishing the location of the temple of Demeter, two much later discussions of the battlefield have to be taken into account. In Plutarch (*Aristides* 14.1), the temple is close to the town of Hysiai and at

---

798 According to Plutarch (*Aristides* 17.8), Pausanias' attendants, when the offerings were robbed by the Lydians, chased them and beat them with divining-rods and whips; this had become an aetiology for a ritual in Sparta which involved beating ephebes, as well as a Lydian procession.
799 De Bakker 2010, 230 argues that this is done in a manner reminiscent of heroes in the Trojan War; Hude 1927 has Ἀριμνήστου, but the manuscript tradition points to Ἀειμνήστου; see Huxley 1963, 5–6. Plutarch (*Aristides* 19.1) has him as a Spartan, but Herodotus merely says he was ἀνδρὸς ἐν Σπάρτῃ λογίμου. He is probably the same man mentioned in 9.72 and by Pausanias (9.4.1). See also Huxley 1963.
800 Leake's map (1835, II) identified Argiopion with an area between the Analipsi hill and Plataea. Zikos (1905, 28) identified it with a hill east of the Analipsi hill, locally called 'Ira' (Hera) or 'Gour-i-chtougout' (page 33). Kromayer 1924, 139 and Mele 1955, 13 identified Argiopion with a large field south of the Moloeis (A6). The etymology of the word may be 'white rock', cf. Hunt 1890, 468; Grundy 1901, 495 (reporting that there was a patch of white rock on the north side of Kithairon). Alternatively, the name may denote a cult site for a figure called Argiope; note that Pausanias (4.33.4) mentions a nymph of Parnassos with this name.
801 Winter 1909, 86–88; Kromayer 1924, 138–139; Mele 1955, 13; Müller 1987, 564. However, Grundy 1894, 33, identified it with A5.

the foot of Mount Kithairon, in an area unfit for cavalry ('in secure and rocky terrain'). Pausanias' account reveals, however, that the situation is complicated, as he noted two temples of Demeter in the area: one of Demeter of Eleusis (9.4.3) in the area of the city of Plataea, which was also close to a memorial (μνῆμα) of Leïtos, the only Boeotian warrior who had returned safely from Troy (cf. *Iliad* 2.494); and a second one of Demeter and Kore (9.4.4) in Skolos on the road to Thebes. Herodotus speaks of a temple of Demeter of Eleusis, so it probably has to be identified with Pausanias' first temple, although there is no guarantee that the identifications had not changed in the intervening centuries.

There is little reason to doubt that the temple of Demeter has to be identified with a site to the west of the Pantanassa ridge, near a well,[802] where temple remains were reported (a stylobate and an antefix) and two inscriptions mentioning Demeter were found.[803] Both refer to votive offerings to Demeter, one of which was a statue set up by a certain Kudadas.[804] They have been dated to the first quarter of the fifth century BCE, although the reasons for this are unclear; the lettering seems archaic. Although it has been pointed out that the inscriptions may have been moved about,[805] the fact that not one, but two inscriptions were found here makes it difficult to argue against the identification of the locality as at least a temple of Demeter; moreover the find spot matches well with Herodotus' and Plutarch's account that the temple was at the foot of the Kithairon. Nevertheless, the identification of the temple with this site has been challenged by Wallace, who, basing himself on a literal reading of Herodotus' text, instead proposed a site to the north of modern Erythres.[806] Various other options exist, the most important of which is the hill of Agios Dimitrios, which we have encountered above as a possible location of the shrine of Androkrates (§2.9.3).[807]

---

802 According to Pritchett 1985a, 105–110; 1993 296–297 this was probably the sacred well described by Pausanias. Wallace 1985, 98–99 reports that the well (if it is the one the locals called Xeropigado) was no longer extant upon his visits in 1981 and 1982, and he found no ancient remains.
803 Inscriptions: *IG* VII 1670 and 1671 ('ἀνέθειαν τᾶε Δάματρι'); Foucart 1879, 134–139; Munro 1904, 163; Winter 1909, 87–90; Kromayer 1924, 139–142; Pritchett 1979b; Papachatzi 1981, 47; Pritchett 1985a, 105–107; 113–115; plates 48 and 49 feature the site, which is now destroyed. Accepted by Mele 1955, 13; Schachter 1981, 154–155; Lazenby 1993, 239; Flower & Marincola 2002, 207; Boedeker 2007, 68. The site cannot be connected with Pausanias' second temple to Demeter and Kore at Skolos, because this town was further north.
804 Haussollier 1878; Pritchett 1979b; 1993, 297 restored]εισάμενος to Τεισάμενος, the Spartan diviner mentioned repeatedly by Herodotus (9.33; 9.35–36). However, the restoration as a form of ἵζω 'to found, to set up' is more plausible considering the fact that a sponsor named Kudadas (otherwise unknown) is already mentioned.
805 According to the locals consulted by Wallace (1985, 98), the inscriptions were moved, but their original spot was not known.
806 Wallace 1982, 187–189; refuted by Pritchett 1985a, 107–109; reprise in Wallace 1985, 98–99.
807 Hunt (1890, 468 with note 17), taking into account' Plutarch's indications, opted for a point southeast of Plataea, where there were the foundations of a large Byzantine church; apparently, steles, inscriptions, mosaic and marble were found here; "No doubt the temple became popular after this battle, and continued so down to Roman times." The hill with the modern church of Agios Dimitrios

Fig. 57: The approximate location of the temple of Demeter.

In Herodotus' account, the temple of Demeter appears as a prominent site for the battle at large. Although fighting had taken place 'at' other mnemotopes as well, it was here that the final and climactic battle took place. By necessity, this has to be

---

has also been proposed, but for this the text needs to be emended to have four stadia between Gargaphie and the temple. Proponents include Grundy 1894, 32–38 (employing the fact that Agios Dimitrios is on a hill, because it would offer an explanation why no Persians had died there); 1901, 494–498; Woodhouse 1898, 37; Myres 1953, 286; Hignett 1963, 433; Gilula 2003, 75–76. A seeming continuity in name may not strictly be used as an argument in this discussion (notwithstanding Grundy 1894, 33). For a refutation of the identification with the Agios Dimitrios hill, see Macan 1908, I 717–718; Wallace 1982, 189; Müller 1987, 565–567; the latter's assertion that the ἄλσος of the temple of Demeter could not have been at a hilltop as it needed water, is unfounded. A final option is to assume that Herodotus had two different temples in mind. Thus Obst 1913, 188, 198–199, 203; he points out that Herodotus omits the definite article for the temple, but has καί, which suggests that Herodotus may have also been aware of the existence of two temples. He also argues that the two Demeter temples were both sites of the final fight (the Tegeans at the church of Agios Dimitrios, the Spartans at Plutarch's temple). This is, however, not obvious from Herodotus' text; although he may have made the two mnemotopes coincide (cf. Macan 1908, II 359). See also Macan 1908, I 717, who identifies no less than five Demetria in this area. Zikos (1905, 28) placed the temple on a hill east of the Analipsi hill and reports that the local name of that hill was Tzefka, which he took to mean 'Girl' in 'Slavic'. See also Green 1996, 244.

a simplification: the fighting with even a fraction of the figures given by Herodotus can only have taken place in a much larger area. Nevertheless, the battle was condensed into a single spot, which had become the answer to visitors of the Plataea area who wanted to know 'where the main battle had happened'. One or more trophies for the battle, mentioned by among others Plato (*Menexenus* 245a) and Pausanias (9.2.6), seems to have been set up at approximately fifteen stades from the city. Given the silence of both Herodotus and Thucydides on this monument, it probably reflects a later re-memoralisation effort,[808] perhaps connected to rivalry between Athens and Sparta.[809] The location is unknown; Hignett suggested that it was situated at the temple of Demeter, which could match the distance of fifteen stades between that temple and the city.[810] If this is true, it shows that the temple of Demeter retained its status as the climax site of the battle, because trophies were usually set up there. However, there are some other conceivable locations for the monument.[811]

Despite attempts at rational explanations,[812] Herodotus' story about Demeter's anger in 9.65 clearly shows that a mythification process had enveloped the temple in the post-war period. The divine intervention of Demeter is found in three other sources, confirming the story's pervasiveness; but none of these is securely independent from Herodotus' account. The oldest reference to the goddess or her temple is in Simonides' Plataea elegy (fragment 17 W^2, line 1). Demeter is not the typical goddess to mention in this context, suggesting that this part of the poem probably addressed the details of the battle that we also find in Herodotus' story.[813] Perhaps this poem was one of Herodotus' sources; we know that Herodotus was familiar with Simonides'

---

[808] Schachter 1994, 131; Proietti 2015a, 160–161.
[809] Schachter 1994, 142–143. Isocrates (*Plataicus* 59), Plutarch (*Aristides* 20.3) and other sources mention more than one trophy, Plutarch (*De Herodoti malignitate* 873a-b) reveals that there existed rivalry between Athens and Sparta about the setting up of the trophies, and inscriptions mention the διάλογος, an event in which Athens and Sparta competed for leading the procession during the Eleutheria festival (Schachter 1994, 137).
[810] Hignett 1963, 432.
[811] The trophy has been surmised east of Plataea, on the road to the old highway near the temple of Hera (cf. Leake 1835, II 365–366); in the modern village of Erythres (Winter 1909, 91–92); or in the area of the Gargaphie fountain (Papachatzi 1981, 34). Interestingly, part of the commemoration ritual performed by the city chief was drawing water ἀπὸ τῆς κρήνης 'from the fountain' at the tombs to wash them (*Aristides* 20.5). Gargaphie was not the only fountain near Plataea, but its alleged role in the battle (see §2.9.3) would have made it the fountain par excellence to employ in a commemoration ritual. If true, it would imply that the tombs, trophy and fountain were all in the same general area. However, the fact that Gargaphie is mentioned later in Pausanias' account casts serious doubt over this possibility. According to Plutarch (*Aristides* 20.3) there were two trophies, one for the Spartans and one for the Athenians, further complicating the search.
[812] Grundy 1894, 32–38 thought that no Persian had died in the temenos because it was on the top of the Agios Dimitrios hill; Myres 1953, 295: "it was too obvious a death-trap".
[813] Boedeker 2001a, 129–130.

work (5.102; 7.228).⁸¹⁴ On the other hand, Herodotus' seeming familiarity with the terrain makes it possible that he alternatively or additionally heard the story from a local source. Whether or not the inscription commemorating the votive offering by Kudadas quoted above is an offering to Demeter for her help in the battle, as Boedeker suggests,⁸¹⁵ the story may have been mediated by such inscriptions.

The local perspective of the divine forces of Plataea (not only Demeter, but also Hera and possibly Androkrates) is also apparent in Thucydides (2.71), where the Plataeans in a speech to the Spartans in 429 dwell upon the importance of (unnamed) local gods and heroes as protectors of justice, and therefore of the outcome of local battles and of Plataea's independence. As a response the Spartans even directly invoke them (2.74): "All gods and heroes who govern the land of Plataea, please be witnesses that we have not come unjustly, with [the Plataeans] having first broken the common oath, to this land in which our ancestors conquered the Persians after having prayed to you, and which you made fit for the Greeks to fight in, nor now will we act unjustly in whatever we may do: we have made many reasonable proposals, but we have had no success. Please agree to punish those who first showed injustice, and that those who rightfully enact this are avenged." The temples feature again in the Plataeans' appeal to the Spartans (3.58.5). Such stories reveal that Plataea's temples and shrines were not merely places where historical events had allegedly occurred, but also the abodes of ancient forces in the landscape, mnemotopes of what had happened there in the past.⁸¹⁶

Herodotus believed that the Persian massacre at Plataea happened because the Persians had burnt down the Telesterion in Eleusis; but Athena, for instance, had also suffered destruction of her house on the Acropolis. Why was Demeter deemed so important? Deborah Boedeker recognises that narrative traditions surrounding this goddess appear in all major Greek victories during the Persian Wars.⁸¹⁷ To Boedeker's analysis may be added Herodotus' story (8.65) that before the battle of Salamis a giant dust cloud was seen rising near Eleusis, and from which the iakchos sound was heard even though all people in the area had been evacuated. The cloud crossed the water and descended upon the Greeks at Salamis.⁸¹⁸ The Pythian oracle in 7.141 also connected Demeter in an ambiguous way to Xerxes' invasion: the last line of this oracle reads ἤ που σκιδναμένης Δημήτερος ἤ συνιούσης 'when perhaps Demeter is scattered or collected'. The word Δημήτηρ in this sentence is usually taken as a metaphor of corn. The whole sentence would simply refer to the harvest

---

814 Boedeker 2001a, 129–130; Rutherford 2001, 49; Boedeker 2007, 67 connects the reference with the rare words δηρόν 'long' and ῥύσιον 'retribution' in subsequent lines of the poem (5 and 7).
815 Boedeker 2007, 68.
816 See also Mikalson 2003, 96–97.
817 Boedeker 2007, 66.
818 Cf. Cartledge 2002 (first published 1993), 184 for the idea that Demeter, Persephone and Dionysos came to the defence of their sanctuary at Eleusis.

time. However, it is also an explicit mention of the name of the goddess and given the multi-interpretability of Pythian oracles as they appear in Herodotus, it is possible that the line was taken to refer to Eleusis or even Plataea and thereby cemented the role of Demeter in Xerxes' invasion. This coincides with a mention of the goddess in Aeschylus (*Persae* 792-794), who suggests that she was responsible for a lack of grain for the Persians (cf. 7.49, where Artabanos warns Xerxes for famine).

Therefore, Boedeker has suggested, Demeter "was one important answer to the question, 'Why did the Greeks (or the Athenians) win the war?'"[819] But why specifically this goddess? Boedeker proposes two mutually non-exclusive reasons. First, the Athenians may have tried to promote 'their' Eleusinian Demeter as a Panhellenic goddess, in order to legitimate Athenian rule over Greece.[820] In this line of thinking, the fact that at Plataea, as we have seen, the temple of Demeter of Eleusis was the place where the Spartans fought, may then be explained by an Athenian attempt to make the Spartans win by the power of an 'Attic' goddess. In this context it is relevant to note that Plutarch (*Aristides* 11.3-8) preserves a tradition according to which the land around the temple was ceded to the Athenians.

A second explanation adduced by Boedeker for Demeter's apparent association with battle sites concerns her primary qualities as a goddess.[821] First, Demeter is commonly seen as a wrathful force, of which there are many examples (one of which is related by Herodotus in 6.91). Second, in line with a plausible etymology of her name as 'Mother Earth', the goddess often functions as a guardian of land.[822] This is evident from the location of her temples (on the land or, when intramural, not oriented towards inhabited ares) and anecdotes in Herodotus and elsewhere that suggest that the boundaries of Demeter's sanctuaries were not to be transgressed.[823]

---

[819] Boedeker 2007, 73.
[820] Boedeker 2007, 74–76.
[821] Boedeker 2007, 76–79. Normally, Demeter worship was connected to vegetation cults; for an overview of Demeter's temples as such, see Cole 1994.
[822] On Demeter as a the goddess of the earth, see Kledt 2004, 16–20. See Beekes 2010, s.v. for the etymology.
[823] According to a story told by the Athenians, Kleomenes had committed suicide as a result of cutting down the trees in the temenos of Demeter at Eleusis (6.75; Boedeker 1988, 46). In 6.134 we find the story of Miltiades, who trespassed into a temenos of Demeter on Paros, but was driven into a frenzy by the goddess and was wounded during his escape; Hartmann 2010, 543 stresses the ἄρρητα ἱρά to which this tradition was connected: relics which were valued by the Parians as protecting the city. In Pausanias (1.44.4; 2.21.4) we find the story that Pyrrhos was killed in Argos by a woman, believed to be Demeter, throwing a tile; subsequently, a sanctuary of Demeter was founded on the spot; and in 9.25.9 we learn that Xerxes' men who had stayed in Boeotia with Mardonios had jumped into the sea after entering the temple of the Kabeiroi in Thebes (cf. Dillon 1997, 179–180).

2.9.7 The necropolis

As the Greeks were now winning, the Persians retreated to their camp; what happened there has been discussed above (§2.9.1). The corpses were collected by the locals, and many treasures were found (9.83): gold and silver chests and a skull which appeared as one piece, belonging to a five-cubit tall man (9.83).[824] The Greek dead were buried in tombs (9.85):

> [...] οἱ δὲ Ἕλληνες ὡς ἐν Πλαταιῇσι τὴν ληίην διείλοντο, ἔθαπτον τοὺς ἑωυτῶν χωρὶς ἕκαστοι. Λακεδαιμόνιοι μὲν τριξὰς ἐποιήσαντο θήκας· ἔνθα μὲν τοὺς ἰρένας [Wilson: ἰρέας] ἔθαψαν, τῶν καὶ Ποσειδώνιος καὶ Ἀμομφάρετος ἦσαν καὶ Φιλοκύων τε καὶ Καλλικράτης. ἐν μὲν δὴ ἑνὶ τῶν τάφων ἐτάφησαν οἱ ἰρένες [Wilson: ἰρέες], ἐν δὲ τῷ ἑτέρῳ οἱ ἄλλοι Σπαρτιῆται, ἐν δὲ τῷ τρίτῳ οἱ εἵλωτες. οὗτοι μὲν οὕτω ἔθαπτον, Τεγεῆται δὲ χωρὶς πάντας ἔθαψαν ἁλέας, καὶ Ἀθηναῖοι τοὺς ἑωυτῶν ὁμοῦ, καὶ Μεγαρέες τε καὶ Φλειάσιοι τοὺς ὑπὸ τῆς ἵππου διαφθαρέντας. τούτων μὲν δὴ πάντων πλήρεες ἐγένοντο οἱ τάφοι· τῶν δὲ ἄλλων ὅσοι καὶ φαίνονται ἐν Πλαταιῇσι ἐόντες τάφοι, τούτους δέ, ὡς ἐγὼ πυνθάνομαι, ἐπαισχυνομένους τῇ ἀπεστοῖ τῆς μάχης ἑκάστους χώματα χῶσαι κεινὰ τῶν ἐπιγινομένων εἵνεκεν ἀνθρώπων, ἐπεὶ καὶ Αἰγινητέων ἐστὶ αὐτόθι καλεόμενος τάφος, τὸν ἐγὼ ἀκούω καὶ δέκα ἔτεσι ὕστερον μετὰ ταῦτα δεηθέντων τῶν Αἰγινητέων χῶσαι Κλεάδην τὸν Αὐτοδίκου ἄνδρα Πλαταιέα, πρόξεινον ἐόντα αὐτῶν.

> [...] and each group of the Greeks, when they had divided the booty at Plataea, buried their own men separately. The Spartans made three graves where they buried the young warriors, among which were also Poseidonios, Amompharetos, Philokyon and Kallikrates. In the first grave were the young warriors, in the second the other Spartans and in the third the helots. That is how these men performed the burials; the Tegeans, however, buried all their men together in a different place, and the Athenians their men at yet another place, and the Megareans and the Phleiasians those who had died on the hand of the cavalry. Of all of these, the graves were actually filled, but I have heard that each of the others, whose graves are at Plataea, embarrassed at their absence during the battle, constructed empty burial mounds for future generations, as there is also at that place a so-called grave of the Aeginetans, which, I have heard, Kleades of Autodikos, a Plataean and representative of the Aeginetans, constructed ten years after the events at their request.

The Plataean necropolis soon became a point of reference in rhetorical texts: in Thucydides' speech of the Plataeans to the Spartans (3.58.4-5, 3.59.2, quoted below) and in the Theban's reaction (3.67.2), the tombs are used to rhetorical effect. This theme is reprised in Isocrates' fourth-century BCE *Plataicus* (58), in which the Plataean land and the tombs of the battle are used to implore the aid of the Athenians. Isocrates makes reference to these monuments' Panhellenic flavour, and their shamefulness for the Thebans, who had medised (59). In 60 and 61, the Athenians are asked to pay obedience to the fallen heroes and the gods of the land, as they had a decisive role in the battle.

---

[824] Jung 2006, 241 suggests that it is not unlikely that Herodotus had personally seen these items.

Herodotus' account already shows that the battlefield of Plataea had by his time developed into a kind of tourist attraction, and that the absence of a grave of men from a certain polis was considered shameful.[825] The tombs are mentioned by various later authors.[826] Pausanias' account (9.2.5) is the most detailed: he mentions only three graves: one for the Athenians, one for the Spartans (both having epigrams by Simonides), and one for all of the other Greeks. They were close to the road leading up to Plataea from Megara. As Schachter points out, the variations show that clear ideas about the nature of the tombs and their number did not exist.[827]

There is evidence from the Roman period which shows that by that time the necropolis had turned into an even more elaborate memory landscape. On the basis of ample literary and epigraphical references, we know that a quadrennial 'Freedom Festival', the Eleutheria, which included a running competition and processions, was celebrated at Plataea.[828] These revolved around an altar of Zeus Eleutherios, where a commemorative inscription of Simonides was set up.[829] Plutarch and Diodorus Siculus (11.29.1) maintain that the festival was ordained immediately after the battle. Nevertheless, various modern authors assert that the Eleutheria postdated the fifth century BCE (the first references to commemoration are found in the third century BCE inscription,

---

825 Cf. Schachter 1994, 127.
826 Strabo could still point at ταφὴ δημοσία 'public graves' (9.2.31). Diodorus Siculus mentions that the Athenians embellished the tombs (11.33.3), but does not give any specific location for them. Plutarch mentions πολυάνδρια καὶ θῆκαι τοσαῦται καὶ μνήματα νεκρῶν 'so many common burials and graves and memorials of the dead' (*De Herodoti malignitate* 872f). As to the first grave of the Spartans (9.85), the textually transmitted ἱρέας would point to priests being buried. This seemed so strange to various editors, that it was emended to ἰρένας or ἰρένες, a word which refers to young warriors. Gilula 2003, 84–85 argues that this emendation was not justifiable.
827 Schachter 1994, 141–142.
828 Pausanias 9.2.6; Strabo 9.2.31; Plutarch, *Aristides* 21.1. The first inscription is *BCH* 99 (1975) 51–75. Plutarch details that the Hellenic Council and the Plataeans sacrificed every year on the alleged day of the battle at the altar of Zeus (*Aristides* 19.7). The ritual was a sacred procession to the graves detailed in *Aristides* 21.3–5, involving, among other things, trumpeting, myrtle-wreath-filled wagons, libation-pouring youths, and a purple-clad leader offering a black bull near the tombs. For a full discussion of the sources see Schachter 1994, 125–141. Alcock 2002, 79 points out that there is no evidence for new monumentalisation in the Roman Period.
829 Simonides *FGE* 15 = Plutarch, *Aristides* 19.6: τόνδε ποθ' Ἕλληνες νίκας κράτει, ἔργῳ Ἄρηος, Πέρσας ἐξελάσαντες ἐλευθέρᾳ Ἑλλάδι κοινὸν ἱδρύσαντο Διὸς βωμὸν ἐλευθερίου 'The Greeks, having once repelled the Persians with the strength of victory, Ares' work, constructed this as a common altar of Zeus Eleutherios, for a free Greece.' Strabo calls the altar a ἱερόν (9.2.31). Plutarch says that it was commissioned by the oracle of Delphi in *Aristides* 20.4; this was subject to the condition that the land was purified from the defilement of the Persians, using sacred fire from Delphi. Thucydides, in the speech of the Plataeans to the Spartans (2.71), says that Pausanias the general had offered to Zeus after the battle.

BCH 99 (1975 51-75)) and should be regarded as an invented tradition.[830] It has even been suggested that the Plataeans did this in an effort to increase tourism to their town.[831]

Two monuments of individuals are mentioned in these late sources. We hear of a 'tomb said to be that of Mardonius' north of the road from the highway to Hysiai (Pausanias 9.2.2), perhaps at the Alaphi peak, just south of modern Erythres.[832] And Plutarch (*Aristides* 20) recounts an epitaph for Euchidas, who had run nearly two hundred kilometres to Delphi and back, in order to obtain the sacred fire for the purification of the land after the battle.[833]

The Plataean memory landscape which appears in these sources may reflect many centuries of elaboration after Herodotus' time. We may expect him to have mentioned the altar and the inscription if he had seen them. Although Herodotus discusses the fate of Mardonios' body, he does not connect it to any location.[834]

The necropolis seems to have an archaeological correlate. With the help of Pausanias' account, the necropolis may be sought immediately east of Plataea:[835] Grundy mentions tombs hewn into the rock bed.[836] Many graves with skeletons were found here, too, and interpreted as one of the tombs of the Greeks who fought at Plataea.[837] The altar of Zeus Eleutherios may be identified with a platform (15 by 4 meters) two hundred metres north of the modern road and east of the east wall of Plataea.[838] Another piece of evidence are the inscriptions found in this area which concern the Eleutheria (*IG* VII 1667; 1672; 1675). A local stele mentions that it was to be set up next to the altar.[839]

From a mnemotopical perspective, it is relevant that Herodotus records the existence of cenotaphs in the necropolis, built by cities to feign participation in the battle.

---

[830] An important argument for this is the lack of a mention of the festival in earlier sources, such as Thucydides; see Prandi 1988, 161–179; Schachter 1994, 127–129; Jacquemin 2000, 78–79; Jung 2006, 281; Cartledge 2013, 89; 128; 159–160, attributing this 'renaissance' of commemoration at Plataea to the reign of emperor Augustus.
[831] Cartledge 2013, 120; 129; see also Jung 2006, 265.
[832] Pritchett 1957, 19, note 60. He also reported (14–15) how the overbuilding of potential foundation walls near the church of Agioi Anargyri, halfway between Platees and Erythres, was halted by local seniors, as they were thought to mark the tomb of Mardonios. On Leake's map (1835, II) the tomb of Mardonios is localised at the Analipsi hill. Winter 1909, 91–92 located the tomb (which he believed represented an apocryphal tradition) in the area of the village of Erythres.
[833] Cartledge 2013, 130 points out that this story probably postdates the similar anecdote from Marathon.
[834] Herodotus relates that many people claimed to have buried the corpse (9.84), including one Dionysophanes of Ephesus. The alleged locations are not revealed.
[835] Yet west of the city sarcophagi were found (Müller 1987, 567–569).
[836] Grundy 1894, 8.
[837] Spyropoulos 1972, 318–319; 1973 (with photographs).
[838] Leake 1835, II 365–367, mentioning a ruined church here; Spyropoulos 1973, 377–378 (with sketch); Papachatzi 1981, 32–33; Clairmont 1983, 121; Müller 1987, 567–569.
[839] Spyropoulos 1972, 318; 1973, 375–377.

Whether this anecdote was true, or an interesting 'tourist story' simply picked up by him, are questions which we cannot answer.[840] And at the same time, we can ask ourselves whether Herodotus' had rightfully accredited some tombs as 'real'. The account shows not only that it was possible that some of the mnemotopes were created ex post facto, but, more importantly, also that their (in)authenticity was a topic that fascinated visitors of the battlefield.

2.9.8 Summary

The above exploration shows that the topography of Herodotus' account of the battle of Plataea was densified into a series of mnemotopes around which stories crystallised. This case study shows many of the ways in which mnemotopes work. The different positions of the Greeks are 'concatenated' into a series of 'points' on the map. As we have seen (§1.3.5) this is a common process in the remembrance of battle sites. We have also seen the process of accumulation at work with the Gargaphie fountain, which was one of the stations in the battlefield, but later also the location of Artemis' bath in the Aktaion myth. Here, as in the pass of the Oak Heads, stories of 'cheating Persians' sprang up (see §3.3.5). Like many other rivers elsewhere, the Asopos became the mental dividing line between Persians and Greeks, and it is possible that the toponym Skolos and/or a treeless landscape was the place par excellence to imagine the Persian fort. Other places, such as the island and various temples were convenient landmarks. Herodotus' remark about the cenotaphs shows that some of these stories were fabricated on purpose, or fanciful interpretations by later visitors. Finally, and most dramatically, the belief that local divinities had influenced the battle is not only explicit in Herodotus' narrative, but it may also be the reason why events were localised at the corresponding temples around the sanctuaries.

The mnemotopes may also have played a role in contemporary politics. The tombs (and cenotaphs) at Plataea highlighted the role of individual cities in a positive or negative way. The Plataeans themselves, a likely source for Herodotus, may have exaggerated or embellished the mnemotopes of their land for territorial reasons: by stressing that these places 'helped' the Greeks in the battle they promoted their independence from Thebes. The battle may have functioned as a raison d'être, or a 'selling point', for Plataea. Finding an answer to the question 'where did it all happen?' was a question relevant for tourists, citizens of towns that participated in the battle, and locals alike.

---

840 Herodotus' claims about the cenotaphs are attacked by Plutarch in *De Herodoti malignitate* 873a. Hartmann 2010, 317–318 describes the phenomenon as an "Ausdruck gewollter Kommemoration der Vergangenheit."

2.10 The battle of Mykale and the fall of Sestos

This chapter concerns the final episodes of the Persian Wars which Herodotus records: the battle of Mykale and the fall of Sestos.[841] The battle of Mykale has received little treatment in both ancient and modern scholarship.[842] There are also only faint hints of commemoration in antiquity.[843] Nevertheless, within Herodotus' work, it seems that the battle served as an illustration of two notions.

The first 'point' of the battle of Mykale is that it was thought to have taken place on the same day as the battle of Plataea. Herodotus informs us that good news from Plataea reached the Greeks on the other side of the Aegean on the same day by divine intervention (9.100-101): the Athenians discovered a *kerykeion*, a herald's staff, on the beach, while a 'rumour' (φήμη) 'flew into' (ἐσέπτατο) the army.[844] Both battles, moreover, were characterised by the growing rivalry between Athens and Sparta.[845] Scholars are divided about the question how historical the chronological correspondence between the battles is.[846]

The second notion embodied by the battle of Mykale is Greek retribution: the Milesians' successful betrayal of the Persians is described as a second Ionian revolt

---

[841] A selection of places mentioned in §2.10.1-4 features on Map 2; a selection of places mentioned in §2.10.4-5 features on Map 3.
[842] While Plutarch mentions Mykale as a source of pride for the Athenians (*De gloria Atheniensium* 7), not all ancients included it among the 'canonical' battles of the Persian Wars (cf. Thucydides 1.23). Only Ephorus gives some prominence to it. Some scholars have asserted that even Herodotus himself was not very interested in this battle (Hignett 1963, 247; Cawkwell 2005, 99–100). Scholars tend to believe this is justifiable, as, in their eyes, the battle was only of minor historical importance. Lazenby (1993, 247), for instance, found that Mykale was not part of the defence of Greece.
[843] Herodotus mentions spoils, but nothing more is known (cf. Gauer 1968, 36). Pausanias saw a statue of Xanthippos on the Athenian Acropolis (Pausanias 1.25.1). Schefold 1953–1954, 142–144 proposed that a sculpture of a torso from the theatre in Miletus should be interpreted as a votive offering for the battle of Mykale.
[844] In addition to the goddess Pheme, it is also possible that Herodotus envisaged that Hermes, Iris or Nike had brought the encouraging news. These deities are depicted on fifth-century BCE Greek vases carrying a kerykeion.
[845] On these and other correspondences see Munro 1926b, 344; van Wees 1997, note 54.
[846] Bengtson (1965, 63) called it a Gleichzeitigkeitsfabel. See also Macan 1908, II 338 (still supposing a strategic connection between the two battles; cf. II 343); Immerwahr 1966, 287–303; Aly 1969 (first edition 1921), 193 (attributing the connection to folklore); Flower & Marincola 2002, 276–277 (pointing at a similar synchrony for the battles of Himera and Salamis found in Herodotus 7.166). For the view that the correspondence is historical, see Barron 1988, 614; Green 1996, 281. The news of the Plataean victory arriving in Mykale on the same day is then seen as genuine because a system of beacons may have been put into place. In reality the battle of Mykale may have been a detached battle that revolved around Persian control of the Hellespont and the islands (as Herodotus seems to hint at in 9.101). See also Diodorus Siculus 11.35.3, who maintained that the fable arose with Leotychides as a means to motivate his men.

(9.104), the event that had started the conflict, and symbolises the triumph of freedom over tyranny. The location of Mykale reinforced this idea: the battle took place close to the Panionion, where the Ionian Revolt was crushed. With the battle of Mykale, the narrative returns to where the conflict between Greece and Persia began.[847] The fall of Sestos, a city in the Thracian Chersonesos, too, was considered a retribution, in this case for the sacrilege of the tomb of Protesilaos at Elaious; but it also marked the end of the Persian domination of Europe.

These consideration give us a new agenda with which to analyse the topography featuring in Herodotus' account of these events: the muster point of the Greek forces at Samos, the Skolopoeis area of Mykale where the battle was fought; the secret route across Mount Mykale; the tomb of Protesilaos and the city of Sestos. In this chapter, we will concern ourselves with the questions where these places can be located in the landscape and how these came to be regarded as the locations of the events.

2.10.1 Kalamoi and the temple of Hera at Samos

Samos was the chosen destination of the three hundred Persian ships that had survived the battle of Salamis (8.130). In 9.96, it is recounted how the wrathful Greeks sailed from Delos to Samos, where they anchored in an area called Kalamoi ('Reeds').[848]

> τοῖσι δὲ Ἕλλησι ὡς ἐκαλλιέρησε, ἀνῆγον τὰς νέας ἐκ τῆς Δήλου πρὸς τὴν Σάμον. ἐπεὶ δὲ ἐγένοντο τῆς Σαμίης πρὸς Καλάμοισι, οἱ μὲν αὐτοῦ ὁρμισάμενοι κατὰ τὸ Ἥραιον τὸ ταύτῃ παρεσκευάζοντο ἐς ναυμαχίην [...]

> When favourable omens appeared for the Greeks, they sailed their ships from Delos to Samos. And when they came to Kalamoi of the Samian land, they anchored at the Heraion that was there, and prepared for a sea-battle. [...]

Kalamoi has been identified as the area around the mouth of the Imbrasos river, between the Heraion and the modern airport, which is still an area of wetlands with reeds.[849] The temple of Hera did not play a role as such during the war.[850] Why, then,

---

847 Shrimpton 1997, 208. The Panionion does not play a role during the battle of Mykale, but situated between Miletus and Ephesus, it was very close (cf. Müller 1997, 660). Remains of the Panionion have been found on a hill in the outskirts of the modern village of Güzelçamlı. A terrace with worked stone and foundation blocks, as well as remains of the altar to Poseidon Helikonios (Wiegand & Schrader 1904, 25–26; Müller 1997, 655–661).
848 After Herodotus, Kalamoi appears only in a quote of Alexis of Samos by Athenaeus (*FGrH* 539 F1 = *Deipnosophistae* 13.31) with reference to a statue of Aphrodite.
849 Myres 1953, 295; Tölle-Kastenbein 1976, 91 (pointing out that some manuscripts specify the place as κατὰ τὸ Ἥραιον); Müller 1987, 1030–1031.
850 Herodotus does not record Persian activity here, and contrary to Green 1996, 278–288, there is no evidence that the Persians had destroyed the temple.

does Herodotus mention this location at all? First, one may suppose that he does so because of his Herodotus' strong relation to Samos (he may even have lived there).[851] The temple of Hera was a formidable landmark, the largest Greek temple that Herodotus knew (3.60) and special reason to pay more attention to Samos. It seems that Herodotus knew the sanctuary well, as evidenced by his mention of several dedications here: a Spartan bowl (1.70), wooden statues of Amasis (2.182), Polykrates' dining set (3.123), Mandrokles' inscribed painting of Darius' crossing of the Bosporus (4.88), and a bowl from the local community (4.152).[852]

These objects not only show that Herodotus visited the temple himself; they showcase the extent to which it functioned as a storeroom of memories. Perhaps the story that the Greek navy had assembled at the temple, whatever its historicity, may have originated at the site itself. The rest of the battle narrative may have been 'stored' here as well: with Mount Mykale as the backdrop, the battlefield was visible from the temple. This is also apparent from the divine elements of the appearance of the kerykeion on the beach; which may have been attributed to the goddess. It has been suggested that Hera's name was used as a password during the battle (9.98), although the manuscripts have ἥβη.[853] The temple is also the likely source for the parallelism with the battle of Plataea, where the Greeks also assembled at the temple of Hera (9.52). Pausanias the general later in the account invokes her as he turns his gaze towards the temple (9.61; cf. §3.2.2).[854] Hera's hotline across the Aegean was a wonderful addition to the religious lore surrounding the temple.

2.10.2 Skolopoeis and the temple of Demeter

Meanwhile, the Persians decided that they wanted to fight on the land, not on the sea. This determined the location of the battle of Mykale on the south shore of the Mykale peninsula (9.96), where the Persians built a palisaded 'fort'. Herodotus gives details about its location in 9.97:

---

851 On this see Jacoby 1913, 208, 222; Tölle-Kastenbein 1976, 9–12. It is possible that Herodotus obtained his information about the Hellespont bridges here, too (Hammond & Roseman 1996, 93; for the bridges see §2.2.4). According to Waters (1966, 162), Samos features so much in Herodotus' account because it was the only big power of Greece near the Persian empire. Further evidence for the autopsy of Samos is Herodotus' mention of an inscription which commemorated the battle of Lade and stood in the agora (6.14).
852 West 1985, 283.
853 On this point see Immerwahr 1966, 288.
854 The occurrence of temples of Hera in both battles is noted by Immerwahr 1966, 288; Bowie 2007, 13.

ταῦτα βουλευσάμενοι ἀνήγοντο. ἀπικόμενοι δὲ παρὰ τὸ τῶν Ποτνιέων ἱρὸν τῆς Μυκάλης ἐς Γαίσωνά τε καὶ Σκολοπόεντα, τῇ Δήμητρος Ἐλευσινίης ἔστι ἱρόν, τὸ Φίλιστος ὁ Πασικλέος ἱδρύσατο Νείλεῳ τῷ Κόδρου ἐπισπόμενος ἐπὶ Μιλήτου κτιστύν, ἐνθαῦτα τάς τε νέας ἀνείρυσαν καὶ περιεβάλοντο ἕρκος καὶ λίθων καὶ ξύλων, δένδρεα ἐκκόψαντες ἥμερα, καὶ σκόλοπας περὶ τὸ ἕρκος κατέπηξαν. καὶ παρεσκευάδατο ὡς πολιορκησόμενοι καὶ ὡς νικήσοντες, ἐπ' ἀμφότερα ἐπιλεγόμενοι γὰρ παρεσκευάζοντο.

Having thus decided, they put out to sea. And after arriving, near the temple of the Potniai of Mykale, at Gaison and Skolopoeis, where there is a temple of Demeter of Eleusis, founded by Philistos, son of Pasikles, who accompanied Neileos, son of Kodros, to the founding of Miletus, they pulled their ships on the shore there and surrounded it with a fence of stone and wood after cutting down the fruit-bearing trees, and they fixed a palisade around the fence in the ground. They were ready to be besieged and to win, as they had prepared themselves while considering both possibilities.

The Persian army was stationed along the beach (9.98), a circumstance used by Leotychidas, who sailed close to the shore and addressed the Ionians in the Persian army in Greek to persuade them to join the other party or to make them distrusted by the Persians. The Persian fort also appears as the site of the actual fight (9.102), and was finally destroyed by the Greeks (9.106).

Fig. 58: New Priene and its acropolis.

Herodotus' wording suggests that the localities of Gaison and Skolopoeis and the temples of the Potniai and of Demeter were all approximately in the same area.[855] However, none of them has so far been securely identified. The only recent attempt at studying the topography of the battle of Mykale is by Müller (1997). However, his conclusions hinge upon the unwarranted assumption that Old Priene occupied the same site where New Priene (refounded in the fourth century BCE) now lies, contrary to the scholarly consensus and the fact that no material dating from before the fourth century was found here; Müller explains this last fact away by assuming the Persians destroyed the site so throughly, that no traces of the old city remained; a highly improbable suggestion.[856] In his reasoning, the lack of a mention of Priene in Herodotus' narrative proves that the battle occurred at a considerable distance west of the city. However, Old Priene was more likely located further east than the well-known remains of 'New' Priene; plausibly, the old city was abandoned in the fourth century and ultimately disappeared under the sediments of the Maeander river. Müller's conclusions are therefore unwarranted, and we may enlarge the area where candidates for Herodotus' battlefield can be found to include the area of New Priene, around modern Güllübahçe.

In fact, the hill on which New Priene was built matches the description of Herodotus' battlefield. First, this site offers the best possible defence on the entire south slope of Mount Mykale, with the acropolis of Priene steeply rising some three hundred metres above it: the optimal strategical location was one of the reasons why New Priene was founded here. Second, and more importantly, there is secure evidence for a temple of Demeter here, located in the upper reaches of the city near the steep rise of the Acropolis.[857] Although the temple is within the city walls of New Priene, its orientation is irregular within the fourth-century BCE Hippodamean city plan, which suggests that the new temple occupied a spot that had been considered sacred for a long time before the city was founded. Other suggestions for the temple have been put forward, but these cannot be substantiated with material correlates.[858]

---

855 The preposition παρά is vague, and may mean both 'near' or 'past' in the quoted passage. However, because there is no hint of any distance, we may presume that the temple of the Potniai was reasonably close to the other places.
856 Müller 1997, 674–680.
857 For the temple, see Wiegand & Schrader 1904, 147–183.
858 Rayet & Thomas 1877–1880, I 26 localised the camp and temple of Demeter at a small plain made by the Gaison river (which they believed to flow east of New Priene); Müller 1997, 632–634 suggests that it stood on the small, isolated hill on the west of was the small bay of Yuvacık, where he saw blocks and potsherds. Accordingly, he localises the battlefield in this area, between Atburgazı and Yuvaca, precisely around the temple.

Similarly, the temple of the Potniai, usually identified with Demeter and Kore,[859] may have its material correlate in other structures which formed part of New Priene, for example in one of the small temples in the southwestern reaches of the city, close to the ancient shoreline. Like the temple of Demeter, these structures do not correspond to the Hippodamean plan of the new city and were therefore likely pre-existing. The western temple is usually associated with Cybele, but without good grounds. Herodotus' use of the preposition παρά instead of ἐς is now easily understandable: these small temples were situated on the coast, while the temple of Demeter was at a height of 125 metres. Παρά thus signifies the place where the Persians went ashore, while their fort was built at a safe height. Müller, by contrast, places the temple of the Potniai immediately west of Atburgazı, because this would fit the order in which Herodotus describes the landmarks.[860] However, his suggestion remains speculative and depends on the unwarranted assumption about the location of Old Priene.

Skolopoeis itself is referred to in a fourth-century BCE inscription found in modern Doğanbey. From this attestation, we know that it must have been a town, because the word is Σκολοπούσιοι, inhabitants of Skolopoeis.[861] The inscription shows that Skolopoeis was situated between (Old) Priene and a town nearby named Thebes, leading some to identify Skolopoeis with the area around Doğanbey, the starting point of a path over mount Mykale.[862] Müller prefers the area around modern Atburgazı because there is a good route across the mountain from here (§2.10.3) assuming that Skolopoeis cannot have been situated close to Priene, because Herodotus would surely

---

859 Macan 1908, I 793. A fourth-century BCE inscription from Priene (*IPri* 196) also mentions the Potniai, which may be presumed to refer to Demeter and Persephone (Kore) here because of the epithets θεσμοφόροι and ἁγναί: ὑπνωθεὶς Φίλιος Κύπριος γένος ἐξαλαμῖνος // vacat υἱὸς Ἀρίστωνος Ναόλοχον εἶδεν ὄναρ // θεσμοφόρους τε //ἁγνὰς ποτνίας ἐμ φάρεσι λεοκοῖς· // vacat ὄψεσι δ' ἐν τρισσαῖς ἥρωα τόνδε σέβειν // ἤνωγον πόλεως φύλακογ χῶρόν τ'ἀπέδειξαν· //vacat ὦν ἕνεκα ἵδρυσεν τόνδε θεῖον Φίλιος. 'Sleeping, Philios, Cyprian by birth, from Salamis, a son of Ariston saw in a dream law-giving, chaste Mistresses in white cloaks. And in three visions, they commanded to respect this hero as protector of the city and they appointed the land; because of this, Philios erected this brimstone.' However, this equation is not necessary: the term 'Potnia' could be applied to any goddess. The use of the article in τὸ τῶν Ποτνιέων ἱρὸν τῆς Μυκάλης may be explained by the circumstance that Herodotus refers to it as a (considerably important?) landmark in passing.
860 Müller 1997, 632.
861 *IPri* 361: [..c.7..] Ἀριστομένεος αἱρεθεὶς ὑπὸ τõ // [δήμο] ἀποκατέστησε τοὺς ὅρους // [ἐκ τῶν] λευκωμάτων. ὅροι τῆς χώρας //[ἣν ἐνέμ]οντο Θηβαῖοι. ἀπὸ τõ Ἑρμέω // [τõ παρὰ τ]ὸ παλαιὸν τεῖχος εἰς τὰς πέτρας // [τὰς .c.2.]τι Κόρνο κῆπον· ἀπὸ δὲ τῷ[ν] // [πετρῶν] ἴλλει ἡ στεφάνη εἰς τὸν λό- // [φον τὸν] Σκολοπουσίων, ἀπὸ [δὲ τõ] // [λόφο πρ]ὸς ῥοδιὴ[ν] τὴν πο[–] // [.c.6..]το[–] '[...] of Aristomenes, chosen by the city, reinstalled the boundaries from the white slabs. The boundaries of the land that the Thebans controlled. From the herm by the old wall to the rocks [...] the garden of Kornos [...] from the rocks the cliff-edge fences off towards the hill of the people of Skolopoeis, and from the hill to the rose garden that [...].
862 Wiegand & Schrader 1904, 17; Myres 1953, 297, figure 25. According to this interpretation, the Gaison is a local stream in this area.

have mentioned this city at this point, nor near the end of the peninsula, because this area is too steep.[863] However, both attempts are unconvincing, because Herodotus' text simply does not necessitate a position of this path immediately at the battlefield, and as we have seen, the location of Old Priene is still unknown. Kromayer, by contrast, believed that the border between Thebes and Priene, and hence Skolopoeis, was further east.[864] This location better fits the available evidence: the inscription mentions a στεφάνη, a broad rock-cliff, in relation to the people of Skolopoeis, which may well refer to what later would become the acropolis of Priene and is an impressive natural landmark. Most strikingly, the ῥοδίη 'rose garden' mentioned in the inscription coincides with the name of the village just east of New Priene: Güllübahçe is Turkish for 'rose garden'. Moreover, the town's previous name, Kelebes, even sounds surprisingly like Skolopoeis.[865] The coincidence can perhaps not be proven, but is nonetheless suggestive.

Finally, a passage in Athenaeus (*Deipnosophistae* 7.87),[866] who quotes Neanthes of Cyzicus (*FGrH* 84 F3) and Ephorus (*FGrH* 70 F48), sheds some more light on Herodotus' Gaison. This river emptied in a lake called Gaisonis, between Priene and Miletus. It has been identified with a stream west of Atburgazı or with the Sadak Dere which flows through Doğanbey into the Karina lagoon.[867] However, given the silting processes, we may also identify the Gaison river with the stream east of the acropolis of Priene.[868] This is consistent with the Athenaeus passage, in which the river itself flowed περί Priene, which here presumably refers to New Priene.

The few things we can distill from our sources about the temples, Gaison and Skolopoeis draw us to the site that would later be occupied by New Priene. Interestingly, this is very much like the early suggestion by Rayet and Thomas that Skolopoeis is to be identified with the modern town of Güllübahçe (Kelebes), located southeast of New Priene.

---

[863] Müller 1997, 627–631; he discredits the identification with the Maeander (Menderes) river, put forward by Munro 1926b, 342. The river is presumably to be identified with the Gessus river mentioned by Pliny the Elder (*Naturalis Historia* 5.31), which was in Trogilion, the tip of the Mykale Peninsula (modern Dip Burun).
[864] Kromayer 1926, 12; he identified the stream of Atburgazı with the Gaison (173–174).
[865] Rayet & Thomas 1877–1880 I, 26. Note that Turkish-speakers cannot pronounce word-initial consonant clusters starting with s-.
[866] ὁ δὲ Γαίσων, οὗ Ἀρχέστρατος μνημονεύει, ἡ Γαισωνὶς λίμνη ἐστὶ μεταξὺ Πριήνης καὶ Μιλήτου ἡνωμένη τῆι θαλάσσηι, ὡς Νεάνθης ὁ Κυζικηνὸς ἱστορεῖ ἐν τῆι τῶν Ἑλληνικῶν. Ἔφορος δ' ἐν τῆι πέμπτηι ποταμὸν εἶναί φησι τὸν Γαίσωνα περὶ Πριήνην, ὃν εἰσρεῖν εἰς λίμνην. 'The Gaison, which Archestratos refers to, the Gaisonis lake is between Priene and Miletus, unified with the sea, as Neanthes of Cyzicus mentions in his *Hellenica*. And Ephoros in his fifth book says that the Gaison is a river around Priene, and that it flows into a lake.'
[867] Stream west of Atburgazı: Kromayer 1926, 173–174; Müller 1997, 628–631. Sadak Dere: Thonemann 2011, 325 with note 70.
[868] Rayet & Thomas 1877–1880 I, 26,

The military 'Sachkritik' employed by Müller to locate the battle is doubtful, as the account of the battle of Mykale was moulded to fit that of Plataea. This similarity applies to the topography as well: in addition to the chronological coincidence with the battle of Plataea, Herodotus reports the curious topographical coincidence that both Plataea and Mykale had a temple of Demeter of Eleusis (§2.9.6). Like the synchrony, some authors doubt the historicity 'syntopy' to such an extent that they discredit the entire existence of the temple at Mykale as an invention that merely serves Herodotus' (or the Greeks') love of parallelism.[869] However, to use the lack of an archaeological certification is dangerously *ex silentio*, and would be inconsistent with the fact that Herodotus' topographical knowledge mostly reflects the real world. A comparable coincidence exists with the two Heracles shrines at Marathon and Kynosarges, which both play a role during Darius' invasion (6.116):[870] although these temples have not been identified with material remains, no-one doubts their existence. Moreover, Herodotus relates another anecdote about this temple: the founder of the temple, Philistos, would have accompanied Neilos, the founder of Miletus.[871] It is hardly possible that such an anecdote was told for an otherwise non-existing shrine. Moreover, as stated above, a temple of Demeter is attested in New Priene.

The topographical parallelism does not rule out the existence of the temple. It is possible that the localisation of the battle was 'drawn' to the temple in post-war traditions, to facilitate notions about divine intervention and vengeance. We have seen that Herodotus does so at Plataea, and like there, Herodotus is careful to point out that divine intervention was not a force to be trifled with (9.100). Along these lines it is conceivable that a battle fought 'somewhere at Mykale' could easily be given a more precise localisation 'at the temple of Demeter'. If this makes sense, the putative location of the temple cannot be used for reconstructing the precise topography of the battle.

Apart from the parallels between the battles of Plataea and Mykale mentioned by Herodotus, we may add another one: the existence of a fort made of palisades.[872] Again, the parallelism should not compel us to dismiss the existence of the fort at Mykale, as Munro does, but it remains otherwise elusive. The name Skolopoeis echoes that of Skolos, the site of the Persian fort near Plataea (§2.9.1). There may have been a Persian fort at Skolopoeis, or even an older fort that the Persians reused, and which furnished the name Skolopoeis because of its palissades (σκόλοπες are explicitly mentioned by Herodotus in the above passage).[873] It has also been suggested that the town was founded after the fort had been built.[874] It is, however, also possible that

---

[869] Munro 1926b, 322, 344.
[870] Boedeker 2007, 68–69.
[871] Müller 1997, 632 note 34. Neilos' grave was pointed out in Miletus (Pausanias 7.2.6).
[872] Munro 1926b, 344; Immerwahr 1966, 288–289.
[873] Barron 1988, 613; Müller 1997, 627 (with literature).
[874] Flower & Marincola 2002, 272.

Fig. 59: The temple of Demeter and Kore at New Priene.

the name played a role in 'imagining' the Persian fort at this place. It would not be the first time that toponyms attract invented stories (§3.1.1). As at Plataea, the story was accompanied by the idea that the Persians had cleared local trees, in this case an orchard (see also the story of the wood felling for the army's passing at the Macedonian Mountain, §2.3.8).

2.10.3 The landing place of the Athenians and the route of the Spartans

Herodotus tells us that the Athenians and the Spartans sailed past Skolopoeis and landed at some distance from it along the shore (9.99). The Athenians marched along the beach (9.102), where they discovered the *kerykeion*, a herald's scepter, signalling for them the simultaneous victory at Plataea (9.100).[875] The Spartans, meanwhile, used a ravine and hills on Mount Mykale to escape attention initially (9.102), and arrived somewhat later to finish the battle (9.103). The Μυκάλης αἰπεινὰ κάρηνα

---

875 Could this be a reference to the Kerykes, a family controlling the Eleusinian mysteries?

('lofty mountaintops of Mykale' in *Iliad* 2.869) were a good place to hide: the Chians had done so during the battle of Lade (6.15), and the Persians made the Milesians guard the route across the mountain so that they would have a safe retreat there, because the Persians distrusted them rather than for strategic reasons (9.99; 9.104). Indeed, the Milesians defected by misguiding the Persians who fled into the mountains into the hands of their enemies (9.104); some stayed there and finally escaped to Sardis (9.107).

The locations of these events depend on the location of Skolopoeis. Accordingly, Müller hypothesises that the Athenians and Spartans came from the area east of Atburgazı.[876] However, if Skolopoeis was at modern Güllübahçe, the landing place must have been imagined east of that town. The exact route of the Spartans is difficult to reconstruct, as there is no mountain route that runs parallel to the coast; Müller makes them march through the valley of the brook that runs west of New Priene, and then two kilometres on the mountain slope. Although this would make for a difficult march, it made "ihr verspätetes Eintreffen bei der Schlacht ... verständlich."[877] Perhaps so, but the anecdote about the Spartans who stealthily approach the Persian fort to deliver the final blow to the Persian army is recognisable as a retribution for the fate of Leonidas and the 300 Spartans at Thermopylae, whose destiny was determined by the Persians who took the Anopaia path (§2.5.3); even Leonidas' name is mirrored in that of the Spartan leader at Mykale, Leotychidas. An important 'point' about the battle of Mykale in stories that circulated and which Herodotus heard, was that it functioned as a retribution for Thermopylae, much like the related battle of Plataea, as Herodotus himself pointed out (9.64).[878]

2.10.4 Protesilaos' grave

At the end of the *Histories*, Herodotus' gaze once again turns to the Hellespont, where Xerxes' had once transgressed the boundary between Asia and Europe (§2.2.4). The Thracian Chersonesos was home to the story of the last Persian general in Europe, Artaÿktes. He had desecrated the grave of Protesilaos, the Greek hero noted for being the first to die during the Trojan War after being hit by arrows, just before he could set foot on Asian soil.[879] The story of Artaÿktes was already hinted at in 7.33, but it is told

---

[876] Müller 1997, 634. His reasoning that it must be here, because the Persians did not flee into the Meander valley and that it must have been far enough from the fort to allow the Spartans to go unseen, is unconvincing.
[877] Müller 1997, 634.
[878] I believe that, in contrast to the battle of Plataea (Asheri 1998; Flower & Marincola 2002, 36; Low 2011, 9–11), it has never been remarked that Mykale was also perceived as a retribution for Thermopylae.
[879] *Iliad* 2.695–702; Anaxandrides devoted a play to the hero; cf. Pausanias 3.4.6.

in more detail in 9.116 (the sacrilege) and 9.120 (Protesilaos' revenge). The location itself is referred to in 9.116:

> ἐν γὰρ Ἐλαιοῦντι τῆς Χερσονήσου ἐστὶ Πρωτεσίλεω τάφος τε καὶ τέμενος περὶ αὐτόν, ἔνθα ἦν χρήματα πολλὰ καὶ φιάλαι χρύσεαι καὶ ἀργύρεαι καὶ χαλκὸς καὶ ἐσθὴς καὶ ἄλλα ἀναθήματα, τὰ Ἀρταΰκτης ἐσύλησε βασιλέος δόντος.
>
> For in Elaious on the Chersonesos there is a grave of Protesilaos, and a sacred enclosure around it, where there were many expensive objects, bowls of gold and silver, bronze, clothing, and other dedications which Artaÿktes carried off with the king's permission.

The city of Elaious was situated near the southern extremity of the Thracian Chersonesos, at the modern Çanakkale Martyrs' Memorial, east of Seddülbahir. It is commonly believed that the 'Protesilaion' is to be identified with a large tumulus near Elaious, called Karaağaç Tepe ('Elm Hill'), a settlement mound some two kilometres north of Seddülbahir.[880] Hertel, however, argues that the Karaağaç Tepe was not the mound associated with Protesilaos, as it was too large, too far from Sigeion (which he believes must have been visible) and did not yield much post-archaic pottery; instead he identifies Protesilaos' shrine with an unexcavated tumulus at the castle of Seddülbahir, prominently located at the cape of the peninsula.[881] Whichever it was, both mounds may predate any tradition about Protesilaos, and it is seems likely that the association with Protesilaos, whose name and story seem to be fictional, is of a late date.[882] Elaious was a fitting place for the memory of Protesilaos: just across was the place where the Greeks were believed to have first come ashore during the Trojan expedition, as well as the burial mounds identified with those of Achilles and Patroclus.[883] While it seems logical that Protesilaos would be buried on the continent which he never left, in some later traditions the tomb seems to be located on the Asian side, near Troy.[884]

---

[880] The tumulus was subjected to a brief and clandestine excavation by Schliemann in 1882, who discovered some black gloss ware, which he dated to Troy I (Schliemann 1884, 286–295; cf. Leaf 1923, 163; Casson 1926, 119, 218). Further investigation of the site in the 1920s resulted in more pottery finds, which can now be seen in the Archaeological Museum of Istanbul (for the report see Demangel 1926b). See also Aslan & Bieg 2003, 187–189; Minchin 2016, 261.
[881] Hertel 2003, 182; this identification works better with the coastal location implicit in Thucydides 8.102 and Strabo 13.1.31; 7, fragment 52. Demangel (1926b, 4–5) dismissed this location because it was too far from Elaious; however, the modern name for the cape, İlyas, is likely a continuation of the Greek name, suggesting that although the city itself was located further east, its name also applied to the cape. Müller (1997, 821) notes several tumuli at Seddülbahir but describes them as unimportant.
[882] Hertel 2003, 180–181; Minchin 2016, 261.
[883] Boedeker 1988, 36–37 says that Protesilaos' grave was in symbolic opposition to that of Achilles (Sigeion) and describes Protesilaos as an 'Achilles manqué', listing several interesting correspondences between the two heroes.
[884] See Boedeker 1988, 35–36 with literature.

Fig. 60: Karaağaç Tepe (Protesilaos' grave?). Photo courtesy of Raphael Hunsucker.

It remains unclear how much credence should be given to Herodotus' story. It has been assumed that Artaÿktes' sacrilegious act was symbolic for the Persians: they would have 'punished' Protesilaos for being the first to try to attack Asian soil.[885] However, it is doubtful whether the Persians would have been preoccupied with this 'minor' character from the *Iliad*, let alone his symbolic value.[886] Herodotus seems to imply that Xerxes would have prevented the sacrilege, had Artaÿktes not deceived Xerxes by calling the tomb a house.[887] It seems more plausible to explain the story, if it was historical, as a grave robbery.[888]

---

[885] Haubold 2007, 56; Hartmann 2010, 217; Boedeker 1988, 43: "An alleged wrong against Asia in the Trojan War is to be righted by Artayktes' plunder of the Protesilaion during the Persian War." Cf. Briant 1996, 565: "il paraît plus probable que la dévastation d'un temenos voué à un héros grec répond à l'exaltation du souvenir de Priam."
[886] Lenfant (2004, 81 with note 22), however, believes that this was not a case of Persian propaganda, because Xerxes, according to Herodotus, did not know about the legend.
[887] For the play on the word οἶκος as meaning both 'house' and 'heroon', see Hollmann 2011, 226–227.
[888] Lenfant 2004, 82.

Whether a real sacrilege underlies Herodotus' discussion of Protesilaos' grave or not, a minimal conclusion is that the grave had turned into a mnemotope around which stories had crystallised in local memory in the years following Xerxes' invasion. It is clear that Protesilaos' tomb was something of a tourist attraction in the Roman period,[889] and there is no reason to assume that the situation was different in Herodotus' time. Around such a landmark cult site, locals would have told Herodotus the kind of stories he was looking for, as Herodotus' himself suggests by mentioning the Chersonesians as his source (9.120). The stories added to the monument's touristic value: here one could make contact with both the heroic past and the recent past. Perhaps, the pillaging had left some visible marks in the Protesilaion.

There is, in fact, reason to believe that the story arose in the local communities because it adheres so much to the powerful Greek common place of oriental vandalism which, as will be discussed more fully in §3.2.1, was widespread in Greece in the fifth century BCE and even today is responsible for stories about temple destruction whose historicity is sometimes doubtful.[890] The story about Artaÿktes, more specifically, may have arisen with the power change in the area after the siege of Sestos (§2.10.5): when the Chersonesos was reclaimed by the Athenians, Artaÿktes, who was apparently executed, may have been locally remembered as a barbarian ruler, whatever the realities of his historical rule.

In addition, it has been suggested that the story may have carried a symbolic meaning to a Greek audience because the tomb of a Greek who could not set foot on Trojan soil was a marker of the 'natural' opposition between Europe and Asia, which was made undone by Persian rule of the Chersonesos and ridiculed by the tomb's desecration.[891] Some scholars suggest that the symbolism is reinforced by Herodotus' story about the first Greek to die at the hands of the Persians (Leon, 7.180), who,

---

[889] Protesilaos' cult statue was often depicted on Roman-period coins from Elaious. Pliny the Elder (*Naturalis Historia* 16.88) and Antiphilos of Byzantium (*Anthologia Graeca* 7.141) preserve a tradition according to which trees planted on the grave would grow until they could see Troy, and then wither. Pteleos, Protesilaos' Thessalian home, means 'elm'. Pausanias (1.34.2) mentions Protesilaos as a hero who received divine worship and to whom an entire city (Elaious) was sacred, underscoring the great pride the city must have received from this attraction. What may be the most elaborate description of the site in later times is found in Philostratus' *Heroicus*. In addition to a burial mound, the ruins of a temple and a cult statue on a prow are mentioned. Jones 2001, 144–145 stresses the real-life setting of the dialogue.
[890] For the idea that the Greeks considered sexual encounters in temples as barbarian see Vandiver 1991, 224–225. Aly 1969 (first edition 1921), 200 saw this element of the story (as well as the ensuing portent, but not the rest of the story) as originating in folklore, and adduced various other examples of the 'sex in the temple' motive.
[891] Boedeker (1988, 37) suggests that the people of the Thracian Chersonesos may have been enraged with the desecration by Asians of the tomb of a hero whose death marked the boundary between the two continents; cf. Vandiver 1991, 223–229. Boedeker (1988, 37–40) also stresses the hero's vegetal qualities, a background against which Artaÿktes' agricultural use of the sanctuary become

like Protesilaos, happens to be 'special' in that he is the most handsome man; also, both the names 'Leon' and 'Protesilaos' would point to being the first to be killed.[892] However, the assertion that the etymology of the names came into play is doubtful: Leon merely means 'Lion' and several explanations are possible for Protesilaos. The associations leading to a symbolic interpretation of the story of remain rather farfetched, and the episode may also be regarded, more simply, as an example of hubris which was preceded by a strange omen and led to punishment, like so many other stories in the *Histories*.

2.10.5 Sestos and the place of Artaÿktes' crucifixion

Later in the *Histories*, Sestos, whose location was discussed above (§2.2.4) because it was regarded as the bridgehead of the Hellespont bridges, appears as the last stronghold of the Persians in Europe (9.117-118):

> οἱ δὲ ἐν τῷ τείχεϊ ἐς πᾶν ἤδη κακοῦ ἀπιγμένοι ἦσαν, οὕτως ὥστε τοὺς τόνους ἕψοντες τῶν κλινέων ἐσιτέοντο. ἐπείτε δὲ οὐδὲ ταῦτα ἔτι εἶχον, οὕτω δὴ ὑπὸ νύκτα οἴχοντο ἀποδράντες οἵ τε Πέρσαι καὶ ὁ Ἀρταΰκτης καὶ ὁ Οἰόβαζος, ὄπισθε τοῦ τείχεος καταβάντες, τῇ ἦν ἐρημότατον τῶν πολεμίων. ὡς δὲ ἡμέρη ἐγένετο, οἱ Χερσονησῖται ἀπὸ τῶν πύργων ἐσήμηναν τοῖσι Ἀθηναίοισι τὸ γεγονὸς καὶ τὰς πύλας ἄνοιξαν. τῶν δὲ οἱ μὲν πλεῦνες ἐδίωκον, οἱ δὲ τὴν πόλιν εἶχον.

> Those within the fortress were in great distress, so that they cooked and ate the straps of their beds. And when they even ran out of those, the Persians and Artaÿktes and Oiobazos ran off and escaped at night, after going down at the backside of the wall, where there was the least number of enemies. After sunrise, the people of the Chersonesos signalled from the towers what had happened to the Athenians, and they opened the gates. Most Athenians went after the Persians, others occupied the city.

The story reads like the sieges of the citadels of Sardis and Athens (§2.7.2) in reverse. This time, not the Athenians, but the Persians are in great distress. They descend from the citadel of Sestos on the deserted backside, while in Athens, they had climbed the Acropolis on a similar spot. The story made Sestos, like the Acropolis, a mnemotope that highlighted Persian stealth (see §3.3.5).[893] The capture of Sestos may thereby also have symbolised the end of the Persian occupation of Europe, making it a fitting end

---

more serious as well as the offensiveness of sexually violating the tomb of a hero who was so soon separated from his wife.

892 Bowie 2012, 273–274; Vignolo Munson 2012, 200; Saïd 2012, 96, 99–100.
893 Hignett 1963, 262 was disappointed that Herodotus was "more interested in the fate of Artaÿktes than in the fate of Sestos." We may, in fact, go even further by saying that the whole point of the story about Sestos is the fate of Artaÿktes. Boedeker (1988, 34) mentions various stylistic parallels between the story about the siege of Sestos and the *Iliad*, which in her opinion would have been highlighted by the juxtaposition of the Protesilaos story.

to the *Histories*.⁸⁹⁴ It is, however, unclear whether the traditions were grounded in the physical reality of the city.

The Persian escape did not go unpunished, because Oiobazos and Artaÿktes both suffered terrible deaths. Oiobazos was killed by Thracians (9.119), but the Athenians caught Artaÿktes, and they crucified him because of his disrespect of the tomb of Protesilaos (which was discussed in §2.10.4). Herodotus locates the place of the crucifixion at a very special spot (7.33):

> [...] ἔνθα μετὰ ταῦτα, χρόνῳ ὕστερον οὐ πολλῷ, ἐπὶ Ξανθίππου τοῦ Ἀρίφρονος στρατηγοῦ Ἀθηναῖοι, Ἀρταΰκτην ἄνδρα Πέρσην λαβόντες Σηστοῦ ὕπαρχον ζῶντα πρὸς σανίδα διεπασσάλευσαν, ὃς καὶ ἐς τοῦ Πρωτεσίλεω τὸ ἱρὸν ἐς Ἐλαιοῦντα ἀγινεόμενος γυναῖκας ἀθέμιστα ἔρδεσκε.

> [...] there [on the coast between Sestos and Madytos], afterwards, not much later, when Xanthipposson of Ariphron was general, the Athenians took Artaÿktes, a Persian man and governor of Sestos, nailed alive to a wooden plank, as he used to illegally bring women into the sanctuary of Protesilaos in Elaious.

However, at the end of his work (9.120), Herodotus reveals that an alternative location featured in the lore about the event:

> ἀπαγαγόντες δὲ αὐτὸν ἐς τὴν ἀκτήν ἐς τὴν Ξέρξης ἔζευξε τὸν πόρον, οἱ δὲ λέγουσι ἐπὶ τὸν κολωνὸν τὸν ὑπὲρ Μαδύτου πόλιος, σανίδι προσπασσαλεύσαντες ἀνεκρέμασαν, τὸν δὲ παῖδα ἐν ὀφθαλμοῖσι τοῦ Ἀρταΰκτεω κατέλευσαν.

> They took him away to the coast where Xerxes bridged the strait. Others however say that they took him to the hill above the city of Madytos, and that they nailed him to wooden planks and hanged him. They stoned Artaÿktes' son to death before his eyes.

The location of the bridgehead has been discussed above (§2.2.4). The hill above Madytos has been identified with Kakma Dağı north and west of Eceabat,⁸⁹⁵ but this long ridge does not qualify as a κολωνός which usually refers to more modest hills. Instead, this word may have referred to the hill called Kilisetepe ('Church Hill') in modern Eceabat.⁸⁹⁶ Apparently, there was no agreement about the exact location, revealing something of the importance of the event to Greeks (both locals and

---

894 E.g. Macan 1908, I xl-xlv; Hignett 1963, 262–263; Immerwahr 1966, 8–9; Vandiver 1991, 227–228; Thomas 2000, 1–2; cf. Diodorus Siculus 11.37.6. Notably, Jacoby (1913, 232; 378) maintained that Herodotus died before he could finish his work; the perfect ending would have been the founding of the Athenian Empire.
895 Müller 1997, 876.
896 Müller (1997, 876) sees this hill as the acropolis of Madytos, mentioning pottery fragments as evidence. However, these do not prove that the hill was extensively inhabited in the fifth century BCE, making it possible that it was imagined as the site of Artaÿktes' crucifixion. See also Aslan & Bieg 2003, 187.

Athenians). It is also a good example of the phenomenon of alternative mnemotopes described in the introduction (§1.3.6).

The hill in Madytos may be compared to the other hills appearing as mnemotopes in the narratives about the Persian Wars, including the kolonos at Thermopylae (§2.5.4) and the Areopagus (§2.7.1). The alternative, the coast between Madytos and Sestos, was a more marked mnemotope for the very reason that it was also designated as the European landing point of the Hellespont bridges. In this case, the 'coincidence' may have been catalysed by the fact that both the Hellespont bridges and the crime of Artaÿktes were acts of transgression.[897] Moreover, the image of the Persian satrap dying while overseeing the place where Xerxes' hubristic bridges once lay, is a powerful one. Scholars believe that by referring to the story about Artaÿktes' death and that of his son, Herodotus made his *Histories* thematically come full circle, because Artaÿktes descended from the man who inspired Cyrus to conquer the world (9.121).[898] The 'accumulation' of the two transgressive acts was perhaps already relevant in the folk traditions on which Herodotus relied.[899] But Herodotus seems to have believed that the European bridgehead at Sestos was the true location of the crucifixion, which suggests that he was prone to localise stories on the basis of their thematic significance.[900]

2.10.6 Summary

The final mnemotopes of the *Histories* resonate strongly with tales in its earlier parts. The battle of Mykale was not only chronologically linked to the battle of Plataea, but also topographically. Herodotus noted this himself for the temples of Demeter around which the main battles were fought, but in both battles there are also temples of Hera that function as meeting points for the Greeks. Likewise, in both battles there is a 'Palisade Town' that became the default position of the Persian fort in the Greek

---

[897] The symbolic coincidence has been pointed out by Bischoff 1932, 82–83; Boedeker 1988, 41–43; Vandiver 1991, 226–227; Flower & Marincola 2002, 302; and Bowie 2012, 274, pointing out that the location now marked the site where Athens made an end to Persian hubris and so became the 'next Persia'. Bridges 2015, 68–69 sees the Artaÿktes episode as a reminder that Greeks could be barbarians, too; however, there is no evidence that a Greek audience would have seen this punishment as anything less than fitting.
[898] Bischoff 1932, 83; Myres 1953, 300; Heinrichs 1987, 531–533; Boedeker 1988, 35–48; Flower & Marincola 2002, 36–37; 302–303; Hollmann 2011, 237–239.
[899] Boedeker 1988, 33–34 argues that the two different locations reflect different needs by Athenians (interested in the fate of Sestos) and the Chersonesians (preoccupied with the desecration of Protesilaos' grave), which are partly (but not completely) intertwined by Herodotus. She also suggests (page 42) that the Athenians may be responsible for relocating the site of execution to Sestos.
[900] Boedeker 1988, 44–45.

imagination. I have argued that the battlefield at Skolopoeis as it appears from Herodotus is at modern Güllübahçe and therefore in the area of New Priene, where the temple of Demeter which predated the refoundation of the city may well be the one Herodotus referred to. I have also suggested that the narrative element of the Spartans who take a secret path on Mount Mykale may well be echo the Anopaia episode during the battle of Thermopylae. Even though the places which Herodotus refers to probably existed, and had developed into mnemotopes, caution is needed when attempts are made to reconstruct the battle on the basis of them. They cannot be used as 'checkmarks' to prove or to disprove Herodotus' account: as in other battle accounts, these landmarks together formed a chain of narratives (§3.3.2).

The *Histories* end with the Athenian capture of Sestos. This city was not only regarded as the European bridgehead of Xerxes' Hellespont bridges, but also as the site of the crucifixion of Artaÿktes, the city's Persian general. The crucifixion had alternative mnemotopes. One of them, at the European end of the Hellespont bridges, resounded powerfully with the idea that Xerxes' crossing of the natural boundary between Asia and Europe was an act of transgression. The fall of Sestos, which was remembered as a reversal of the typical siege story encountered most notably at the Acropolis of Athens, marked the end of Persian domination of Europe.

3 A Typology of Mnemotopes

In the above investigation of mnemotopes in Herodotus' account of Xerxes' invasion, we have repeatedly encountered mnemotopes that seem to have arisen by identical processes. By listing these patterns and contextualising them I arrive at a 'typology' of mnemotopes. Because this typology is based on one historical work, it is necessarily non-exhaustive, but it is transferable to other historical contexts, and may be seen as a supplement to the general investigation of mnemotopes in the introduction of this book (§1.3.1-6). The typology is divided into three broad categories: general processes by which mnemotopes come into existence, mnemotopes of religion and mythology, and military mnemotopes. These categories are not mutually exclusive.

3.1 General mnemotopical processes

3.1.1 Speaking toponyms

We have encountered eight mnemotopes for which it may be argued that the toponym itself prompted, as an aetiology, the story which allegedly took place there. Herodotus makes several explicit connections between the name of the place and the event that was supposed to have taken place there. The strongest is the name of the Persian base (and port of the Argonauts) Aphetai, which Herodotus derives from the verb ἀφίημι (§2.4.4). Herodotus elsewhere tells us that Xerxes' army went through the middle of a town which happened (τυγχάνει) to be called Agore (§2.2.5). He uses the same word to announce the peculiar name of the Katarrektes waterfall at Kelainai, which spelled out military failure to an ignorant Xerxes (§2.1.2). It has also been suggested that the name Kelainai ('Gloomy') itself had a similar connotation, but this is not explicit. It is perhaps no coincidence that Persian forts were imagined at places that mean 'Palisade': Skolos near Plataea (§2.9.1) and Skolopoeis at Mykale (§2.10.2). The name of the fort Zone near Abdera probably inspired the story that Xerxes had 'unfastened his girdle' there (§2.8.8), and the name Nine Ways (Ennea Hodoi) was connected to a story that the Persians had buried alive nine local children here (§2.3.4). Personal names were often considered ominous in antiquity, and this idea is reflected in Herodotus as well.[1]

---

[1] See Pritchett 1979a, 135. Some examples: Cicero, *De divinatione* 1.46; Plutarch, *Nicias* 1.3; Xenophon, *Anabasis* 1.8.16. On the symbolism of names in Herodotus, see Hollmann 2011, 143–162. Examples include Hegesistratos 'Army-Leader' (9.91), Onomakritos 'Name-Judger' (7.6), and a Leon who was destined to be the only one to die because of his name (7.180). Immerwahr (1966, 294) notes that Teisamenos means 'Avenger'. The name of the famous traitor at Thermopylae, Ephialtes, means 'Nightmare'. The similarity of the name of the Thracian Paionians and the word

But the mnemotope-inspiring quality of toponyms is not exceptional either, and even continues to this day.[2]

3.1.2 Accumulation

Herodotus' account features many events of the Persian Wars which are localised at places with a pre-existing mythological association that somehow seems relevant to the historical event: the death of Marsyas at Kelainai (§2.1.2), the epic memories in the Troad (§2.2.1–3), the exile of Phrixos' descendants at Halos (§2.3.9), the grave of Protesilaos at Elaious (§2.10.4), the grave of Helle at Paktye (§2.2.5), the death of Heracles at Thermopylae (§2.5.1; §2.5.4), the departure of the Argonauts at Aphetai (§2.4.4), the rape of Thetis at Sepias (§2.4.2), the lost ships at the Koila (§2.4.5), the mythical sieges of Delphi (§2.6.3), and the Amazonomachy and the death of Aglauros at Athens (§2.7.1–2). In some cases, we only know about the mythical association of a place from other sources (Troy); in others, Herodotus draws the parallel himself (Aphetai). Sometimes the event which Herodotus records at a site is only the first of a succession of similar events (Thermopylae, Delphi).

It is in itself unsurprising that Herodotus records mythological mnemotopes in his *Histories*. The mythical past was an important point of reference for the ancient Greeks.[3] Although some authors have argued that Herodotus regarded the mythical

---

παιωνίζω 'sing a victory song' gave rise to a story that the Paionians had attacked the Perinthians after these had performed such a song (5.1; cf. Asheri 1990, 155–156, who points out that although Perinthos and the Strymon are 300 km apart, "the joke was too good to be wasted"). There are certainly more such examples, and more research into this would surely increase our understanding. Ominous qualities could also adhere to toponyms: Pausanias (1.34.2) relates that in Harma ('Chariot') on the road from Thebes to Chalkis Amphiaraos vanished in the earth on his chariot.

2 We have seen the example of the Euboean village of Vasilika (§2.4) where it is claimed that Xerxes' docked his armada, because the name means 'royal'.

3 On the role of myth in social memory in Ancient Greece, see Buxton 1994; Steinbock 2013, 26–28. See Boardman 2002 for many examples. Complex genealogies were forged to establish a clear, almost measurable link with this age (Boardman 2002, 9–10; 74–75). A chronological link between the mythological and the historical age appears also from such documents as the Lindos Chronicles (see e.g. Price 2012, 16–19). The mythical past was exploited by the Greeks to explain cultural practises, justify claims to ownership and rule, and even to wage war: Boardman 2002, 18–19; Gehrke 2001, 304.

and the historical pasts as distinct time frames,⁴ he nevertheless saw the mythical past as 'real' and relevant to the present.⁵

How can we explain these coincidences, and their great number? A first line of explanation could be that Herodotus or his sources regarded the events of Xerxes' invasion as a sequel, continuation or contrast to events of the mythical past.⁶ The explanation also matches the finding that Herodotus was influenced by Homeric epic.⁷ Herodotus sometimes compares the Trojan War with the Persian Wars and sees both as examples of the continuing struggle between the West and the East.⁸

---

4 Assmann 1992, 48–56 draws an anthropologically warranted distinction between the distant and the recent past, separated by a floating gap: the distant past, the subject of cultural memory, can reach back hundreds of years and is enshrined in religion, mythology, festivals and song; by contrast, the recent past, the subject of communicative memory, can only reach back eighty to one hundred years, because all potential witnesses of a certain event are dead after this period; it is typically one commemorated by historians. According to Assmann (page 49), the *Histories* are firmly established in the recent past, and hence a form of communicative memory. Other scholars have argued for the existence of a 'floating gap' in Herodotus: Evans 1991, 120; Thomas 2001; Cobet 2002, 409–411. Herodotus sometimes distances himself from the use of mythological narratives as explanations for the world and its history (e.g. 1.5; 2.116).

5 Assessments of the role of the mythical past in the *Histories* can be found in Evans 1991, 106–107; Scheer 1993, 37–42; Boedeker 2002, 110 (with literature); Cobet 2002, 390; Osborne 2002; Saïd 2012, 88–90. Various scholars points out that a clear distinction between myth and factual history is not present in Herodotus (Flory 1987, 27; Vandiver 1991, 14–15; Osborne 2002, 497–498; Harrison 2003, 239). Several ancient sources credit or criticise Herodotus for his interest in myth (see Boedeker 2002, 109 for examples). De Sélincourt 1967, 58–59 argued that the Greeks, including Herodotus, generally regarded myth as history, but also questioned it sometimes (e.g. 2.143; 6.53; cf. Osborne 2002, 497).

6 This idea features most notably in the work of Bowie 2012 and Rood 2012, 125–126.

7 Herodotus was already paralleled to Homer in antiquity itself (many examples in Boedeker 2002, 97–98; but cf. Aristoteles, *Poetica* 9, 1451a-b; 23, 1459a). Marincola 2006 argues that the *Histories* would still, with one leg, be in Homer's world of oral poetry. Boedeker 2002, 99–100, 105 suggests that the *Histories* and Homeric epic share the broad aims of recounting a war and bestowing fame on various people, while at the same time being impartial in their discussions of Greeks and barbarians. There are also many stylistic parallels (Pohlenz 1961, 212–213; Grethlein 2010, 393–394). De Bakker (2010, 221–222) and Boedeker (2010, 101–104) point out that the 'court stories' contain much Homeric material. For a general overview of the ways in which early Greek historiography was close to Homeric epic, see Strasburger 1972.

8 For example, the catalogue of Xerxes' forces is very much like Homeric catalogue of ships and lists of Trojan allies (Vandiver 1991, 46–51) and the story of Artaÿktes reveals that there was some equation of Asians or Trojans and Persians, because the Persians are imagined here as resenting Greek actions (Protesilaos) in Asia (Erskine 2001, 85–86). See also Cuyler Young Jr. 1980, 213–216; Walser 1984, 45; Boardman 2002, 18; Bowie 2012, 271. For the Persian Wars as a continuation of the Trojan War, see e.g. 1.4; 7.150; 10.27. Within the scholarship that sees these references as historical, this has been explained as Persian appropriation of Greek epic as a means of political propaganda: Georges 1994, 66–71; Green 1996, 68; Gnoli 1998; Hartmann 2010, 216–217 (explaining the portrayal of Trojans in fifth-century Homeric reception as a reaction on the Persian actions). Lenfant (2004) believes that the parallelism

This comparison of the wars is already found in the poetry of Simonides,[9] and is also present in other literature and art of the fifth and fourth centuries BCE.[10] As we have seen in various case studies, we know that historical material could be recast so as to fit mythological mentalities,[11] and mnemotopes may catalyse this process (cf. §1.3.5).

A second way in which we may explain some correspondences between myth and history is that they may have served to highlight Xerxes' hubris. It has, for example, been suggested that the places visited by the Persians are given a mythological context to make the Greek land seem possessed by the gods, and whenever the Persians interact with the gods, something bad happens to them.[12] This fits with the observation that the themes of 'rise and fall' and 'retribution' are central to the *Histories*.[13]

---

in the *Histories* between the two enemies was limited. Gehrke (2010, 24–25) has suggested that Herodotus also parodies the equation.

9 Simonides' Plataea elegy shows that Herodotus was not the first to make the Trojan-Persian parallel. As fragments of this poem were discovered in 1992, it came as a surprise to many that the battle of Plataea was specifically connected with the Trojan War (e.g. Shaw 2001, 165: "[B]efore 1992 no one would have connected Achilles specifically with the battle of Plataea or with the Plataiomachoi"). Despite attempts to give a complex meaning to Simonides' metaphor (Shaw 2001, 178–181), the comparison between Troy and Plataea does not need to have a hidden message. It rather heroises the achievements of Greeks at Plataea (Jung 2006, 227–228; 239–240). In contrast to Simonides, Herodotus does not explicitly use the Trojan War to reflect on the Persian Wars from a Panhellenic perspective (Bowie 2012, 285–286).
10 Patzek 2006, 69–79 argues that the Troy myth became a part of historical memory in the fifth century BCE because of the role the Persian Wars had as a Panhellenic undertaking. Other instances of the parallel are the fact that the Trojans are presented as Persians in three tragedians (Lenfant 2004, 84–86) and in vase painting, Trojans are made to look like Persians (Lenfant 2004, 83–84); moreover the Stoa Poikile featured a juxtaposition of the battle of Marathon and the Trojan War; finally, the iconography of the Trojan War in fifth-century BCE temple sculpture may be seen as a reference to the Persian Wars. Temples in which the Trojan War appears as part of the sculptural programme are the north metopes of the Parthenon and the pediments of the temple of Aphaia at Aegina; more doubtful are the Hephaistion on the Athenian Agora, the Athene Nike temple, and the temple of Poseidon at Sounion. It gained momentum in the fourth century BCE (Lenfant 2004, 86–87, stressing the role of the analogy in legitimising aggression towards the Persians). Explicit parallels are found in Isocrates, *Panegyricus* 158–159; *Panathenaicus* 42.
11 Gehrke 2001, 301; Sourvinou-Inwood 1988, argueing that stories which are usually seen as legendary saga are structurally like myths on the basis of Herodotus' story about Periander and Lykophron (3.48; 3.50–53).
12 Harrison 2002, 560–561 (e.g. 1.189; 3.117; 4.91; 7.27; 7.35; 7.43; 8.54–55). According to de Bakker 2010, 227–228, Herodotus' attention paid to mythological-heroic references in the Xerxes' campaign is an explanation for its failure and an example of his hubris. Likewise, Bowie 2012, 272–276 suggests that "The fact that Herodotus mentions relatively few mythological figures and that these seem in almost every case to have a significance for the expedition perhaps suggests that we do have a mythological geography here that is not random [...]".
13 For the theme of 'rise and fall', see e.g. Raaflaub 2010, 199–203. For the theme of retribution, see e.g. Pohlenz 1961, 4–5.

However impressive the list of topographical correspondences between history and myth is, caution is needed, as has become clear in the individual examples of mnemotopes: to find symbolism is easily done, and sometimes justifiable (as with the siege of the Acropolis in §2.7), but in other cases difficult to warrant (as I argue for Xerxes' visit to Kelainai in §2.1.2). It also remains difficult to establish whether it was Herodotus himself who drew the parallels, or whether they had arisen already in the traditions on which he relied.[14] The safest general conclusion about such correspondences seems to be that mnemotopes which already were relevant for one story could easily acquire additional associations because these locations stood out within the Greek landscape, physically or otherwise (for example, by a 'speaking toponym' as suggested above). This is essentially a manifestation of the process labeled 'accumulation' in the introduction (§1.3.5).

3.1.3 Infrastructural mnemotopes

As mentioned in the introduction (§1.4.2), great man-made structures were especially likely to attract stories about the kings who were thought to have commissioned them. The *Histories* feature many of such works. Infrastructural mnemotopes which are part of Xerxes' invasion include the bridges across the Hellespont (§2.2.4) and the Strymon river (§2.3.4), the king's road in Thrace (§2.3.1), the Athos canal (§2.3.5), as well as Xerxes' imaginary dams in the Tempe valley (§2.3.7) and across the Salamis strait (§2.8.6).

Like many ancient and modern monarchs, the historical Xerxes endeavoured to be a great constructor; we know, for example, that he completed the enormous palace at Persepolis and built a new one at Sousa.[15] Likewise, there is inscriptionary evidence that his father Darius prided himself on having built the precursor to the Suez Canal. But even though the Achaemenid kings wished to be seen as great builders, that does not mean that the stereotype could not have been exaggerated in the minds of the Greeks. As the example of the Tempe valley shows, imaginary 'projections' onto the landscape are not unthinkable. The same may apply to other infrastructural feats, such as the dam at Salamis (often dismissed as one of Herodotus' fantasies), and, I have argued, the Hellespont bridges. Archaeological evidence for such a work exists only for the Athos canal; but even here, there is doubt whether this project had Xerxes as its instigator.

---

14 As Vandiver 1991, 13 remarks: "The extent to which Herodotus himself was conscious of precisely *how* he achieved this effect is not, in the final analysis, relevant to the demonstration of that achievement." Lane Fox 2008, 375 stresses the extent to which Herodotus had to rely on local sources for aetiologies.
15 Briant 1996, 571; Allen 2005b, 54.

If the historicity of Xerxes' construction programme in Greece is difficult to ascertain, a more fruitful question is why these stories were relevant to Herodotus' and his audience. The examples in the *Histories* of such infrastructural projects are in the first place an illustration of the power and organisational skills that, to Herodotus at least, only foreigners possessed (Herodotus deems three relatively minor works in Samos the greatest achievements of the Greeks, 3.60).[16] During the Persian invasions, however, examples of infrastructural works also serve other stereotypes: that of the ruthless, hubristic tyranny of the Persians. It has also been suggested that Herodotus has tried to exposit a theme of Persian domination of nature.[17] To that idea may be connected the examples of the felling of trees to make space for the army or fortifications (§2.3.8; §2.9.1; §2.10.2). However, it is not clear whether we can rely on such examples to reconstruct Herodotus' beliefs.[18]

3.2 Temple mnemotopes

Many of the mnemotopes that we have encountered in Herodotus' account of Xerxes' invasion are temples. Although discussion surrounds the identification of practically all of these, there is no reason to doubt that they were present at the places where Herodotus mentions them, even where no archaeological confirmation is possible. Note, however, that the tombs of the anonymous heroes of Troy (not mentioned directly, but still the most likely point of reference for their worship by the Magi, cf. §2.2.3), those of Protesilaos (§2.10.4) and Helle (§2.2.5) and probably others were reinterpretations of burial mounds or natural hills.

Temples were usually prominent features of Greek landscapes, and for that reason alone liable to become mnemotopes.[19] We have seen that they often feature in Herodotus' account as orientation points for movements. However, in accordance with the observation that Herodotus sourced much of his material at the temples

---

16 See Weiskopf 2008, 85 for Herodotus' views of technology.
17 See e.g. Harrison 2000, 238–239; the idea is that Herodotus adhered to the moral that the natural world should not be interfered with, and that not do so would prompt divine retribution; this is particularly clear in the example of the canal at Knidos (1.174).
18 Romm 2006, 189 states: "Competing in Herodotus' mind with a sense of the inviolability of nature [...] is an esteem for human technological progress, especially when it achieves monumental changes in the landscape or in the quality of civilised life." The best example of this is the monumentalised bridge across the Bosporus (cf. 7.36 and 9.121). In light of this, it goes too far to claim, as Romm (2006, 186–190) does, that Herodotus' focus on the natural world was triggered by concerns that the natural world as it was known was coming to an end with the advancing Persian army.
19 On seascapes see Churchill Semple 1927; Miles 2016, 161–170.

themselves,[20] there also exists room for the idea that the stories connected to the temples arose as 'temple legends' that added to the temple's prestige and sometimes served to explain visible properties, such as objects within a temenos, or structural damage. We may divide the stories told at temple mnemotopes into three types that are not always mutually exclusive: (1) Persian vandalism; (2) divine intervention; and (3) Persian involvement in Greek cult.

3.2.1 Persian vandalism

Herodotus reports Persian vandalism for many buildings, including temples in Phocis (§2.6.1), of Demeter's Anaktoron in Eleusis (§2.7.5), of the entire Athenian Acropolis (§2.7.3–4), as well as the desecration of grave or temple of Protesilaos at Elaious (§2.10.4).[21] Beyond the scope of this study, Herodotus' stories about the Ionian revolt feature temples that were destroyed by the Persians in all revolting cities except Samos (cf. 6.9; 6.13; 6.19; 6.25; 6.32); and there are many other examples in his work.[22]

The idea that Persians were vandals is explicitly voiced in the Athenian speech during the battle of Plataea (8.144) and was often repeated in later centuries.[23] As time went on more and more temples were claimed to have been destroyed by Persian fire. The most striking example is the temple of Haliartos in Boeotia, where Pausanias (9.32.5 and 10.35.2; cf. Strabo 9.2.30) saw the ruins of a temple that had allegedly been burnt down by the Persians. However, this is probably the same temple that Livy (42.63) mentions as burnt down in 181 BCE by the Macedonian king Perseus. The association with the Persians arose perhaps because the name of the Macedonian king was confused with that of the Persians.[24] At Phaleron, Pausanias (1.1.4 and 10.35.2) saw a ruined temple of Demeter, and on the road to Phaleron there was also a temple of Hera that no longer had a roof or doors and was allegedly destroyed by Mardonios; in this case Pausanias did not believe the story because the temple had a statue that,

---

[20] The dedications and monuments embedded within temples (mediated through explanations of temple staff) have been recognised as an important source for him: Evans 1991, 123–124.
[21] This paragraph was the basis for a Dutch-language article in *Tijdschrift voor Mediterrane Archeologie* (van Rookhuijzen 2017a). The present text has been included by kind permission from the editors.
[22] For an overview of the theme of burnt temples in Herodotus, see Miles 2014, 113–120.
[23] Isocrates, *Panegyricus* 155; Cicero, *De natura deorum* 1.115; Strabo (16.1.5) says that the grave of Belus in Babylon was destroyed by Xerxes. See Rosenberger 2003, 72–73 for the later characterisation of the Achaemenid kings as temple destroyers. Funke 2007 points out that the religious sacrilege of the Persians was an idea that arose among the Greeks only in the period after the Persian Wars. On the stereotype of the destructing barbarian see also Lindenlauf 1997, 82–83; Boardman 2002, 77; Kousser 2009, 274.
[24] Macan 1908, II 99; Papachatzi 1981, 437; Scheer 2000, 211 (stressing that there is no evidence that this temple had been destroyed by the Persians); Rosenberger 2003, 77; Hartmann 2010, 182.

he thought, pre-dated the Persian Wars (1.1.5).[25] The temple of Apollo at Phlya was supposedly destroyed by the Persians but later renovated by Themistocles (Plutarch, *Themistocles* 1.3).[26] In Phokaia, a temple of Athena was destroyed by the Persian Harpagos (cf. Pausanias 2.31.6; 7.5.4; Xenophon, *Hellenica* 1.3.1 mentions lightning as the source of the destruction). Pausanias (7.5.4) also alleged that the temple of Hera in Samos was burnt down by the Persians.

As has been discussed in the individual case studies, the exact historicity of such stories is often difficult to assess. That temples had been under attack is not unexpected, given their status as treasuries and points of retreat, and they may also simply have been burnt down with the cities in which they are located.[27] However, I have argued that such stories of destruction cannot be taken at face value. The armies under Xerxes' command had by the time of Herodotus become associated with all kinds of atrocities.[28] Ruined buildings, especially religious buildings, hold a powerful grip on the imagination cross-culturally.[29] Therefore, ruined buildings could acquire unhistorical stories in folk memory: their destruction can be attributed to a more 'likely' party, or even invented completely (when their collapse happened in an earthquake or fire or by negligence). A case in point is a temple near Corinth seen by Pausanias (2.5.4), devoted to either Apollo or Zeus, destroyed either by Pyrrhos or by lightning. Such traditions easily arise and stick, because they are difficult to verify: the ruin itself may look like sufficient evidence for the ruthlessness of an enemy. The ethnonym of the Persians also did not help: there is some evidence for a folk etymological derivation of the word Πέρσης from πέρθω 'to plunder'.[30]

Unfortunately the degree to which archaeology can offer an answer is rather limited because deliberate fire destruction is difficult to recognise in the archaeological record; the identification of specific actors is virtually impossible. Nevertheless, the idea of a great wave of destruction in Greece during the Persian Wars is the common assumption in much of archaeological scholarship and it has greatly impacted our understanding of individual sites (as we have seen most strikingly in

---

25 Scheer 2000, 211 stresses that there is no evidence that the temple of Demeter had been destroyed by the Persians. On the temple of Hera see Arafat 2013, 203.
26 Scheer 2000, 210–211 sees this as an example against the oath of Plataea (cf. §2.7.3).
27 Walser (1984, 52) and Scheer (2000, 204) suggest that Greek temples may not have been the aim of destruction, but were still destroyed because of the riches they contained and as a result of the burning of towns.
28 The confusion of enemies in memory is most famously known in the battle of Roncesvalles (778 CE), which was fought between Charlemagne and Basque brigands, who were in later tellings of the battle substituted by Saracens (Brall-Tuchel 2003, 36–37).
29 In modern Greece, ruined churches retain their sanctity; the Kaiser-Wilhelm-Gedächtniskirche in Berlin and the cathedral of Coventry, among many, have become memorials of the Second World War (Ferrari 2002; Arafat 2013, 201).
30 Kuhrt & Sherwin-White 1987; Rollinger 1998; cf. the word πέρσαντες in the oracle quoted in 8.77.

the cases of the Acropolis and Eleusis). This assumption even extends to cases where Persian destruction is not documented in the historical sources; here archaeologists occasionally advocate the Persian destruction of precursors of a classical temple (e.g. the communis opinio about the temple of Poseidon at Sounion is that it was destroyed by the Persians). The idea that not all stories about Persian vandalism are necessarily historical, but reflect a Greek stereotype, is also recognised by Iranologists.[31]

A related story type encountered in literature of the Roman period is that of 'Xerxes the thief': the sources tell us that he stole the cult statue of Artemis from Brauron (Pausanias 8.46.3); that of Apollo from Didyma (Pausanias 1.16.3; 8.46.3); and those of the Tyrannicides from Athens (Arrian, *Anabasis Alexandri* 3.16.7–8; 7.19.2; Pliny the Elder, *Naturalis Historia* 34.69–70; Pausanias 1.8.5; Valerius Maximus 2.10. ext.1); the statue of Artemis Kelkaia (Arrian, *Anabasis Alexandri* 7.19.2); and the books from the library of Peisistratos (Gellius 7.17.1–3; Isidore of Seville, *Etymologiae* 6.3.3). These stories often include the restoration of the statue by a Greek 'hero' such as Alexander the Great. There is, indeed, one example of booty taken to Sousa: a large bronze astragal-shaped weight with an inscription, which was a dedication to Apollo at Didyma. It was found in Sousa and is now in the Louvre. But probably none of the stories holds much historical value. Nevertheless, they show how easily this type of anecdote could have spring up around impressive artefacts, extant or not.[32]

3.2.2 Divine intervention

Another type of stories connected to temples mentioned in Herodotus' account of the Persian Wars is that of divine intervention. There are many explicit examples of gods or other divine forces helping the Greeks or counteracting the Persians: Zeus at the Ida (§2.2.1); Athena Ilias in Troy (§2.2.3); Protesilaos in Elaious (§2.10.4); Boreas and Oreïthyia, the winds and possibly Thetis and the Nereids in Sepias (§2.4.2); Apollo, Phylakos, Autonoös and Athena Pronaia in Delphi (§2.6.3); Athena at Athens (§2.7.4); Athena Skiras at Salamis (§2.8.4); Demeter at Plataea (§2.9.6) and possibly Mykale

---

31 Kuhrt & Sherwin-White 1987.
32 On these stories as historical fictions see Moggi 1973; Rosenberger 2003; Scheer 2003; Hartmann 2010, 182 ("Es zeigt sich also eine deutliche Tendenz, nicht mehr verstandene historische Monumente bedingt durch die Fokussierung des griechischen Geschichtsbewusstseins auf die Zeit der Perserkriege mit neuer Bedeutung zu füllen."); Arafat 2013, especially 203. Rosenberger 2003, 60–65 leaves open the possibility that the temple of Brauron was destroyed by Xerxes, but admits that, like the Apollo cult statue at Didyma, the Artemis statue was not yet famous during the Persian Wars. This would explain that the anecdote is probably a local story which dovetailed well with the myth that the statue could only be touched by the priestess as described in Euripides' *Iphigenia Taurica*. The view that the robbery and destructions of these temples was historical is also still found: Lindenlauf 1997, 85; Kousser 2009, 268–269; Greco 2010, 36 (on the case of the Tyrannicides).

(§2.10.2); Hera at Plataea (§2.9.5) and possibly Mykale (§2.10.1). Some of these gods were believed to have appeared on the battlefield, a common occurrence in historical narratives of this period.[33] In some cases the divine involvement is less explicit, but, as argued in individual cases, we do have to take into consideration that such beliefs were part of the narrative told at the mnemotope.

These examples suggest that, soon after the events, traditions had arisen that showed that the gods had favoured the Greeks and had played a crucial role in the Greek victory over their eastern invaders. The spatial motivation of this idea is clear: sanctuaries and other religiously charged places developed into crystallisation points for those stories.[34] Underlying such narratives is the idea that gods are especially powerful within their own sacred precincts.[35] Another reason for the large role of temples is that as religious buildings they are repositories of social memory.[36] Herodotus' own hand in the selection and reshaping of the material at his disposal is unclear. Herodotus seems to have been a religious man,[37] and he was also open to the belief that the

---

[33] Pritchett 1979, 11–46 counted forty-nine instances of divine epiphanies in Greek historical narratives, and mentions ample inscriptionary testimonies; they are noticeably absent in Thucydides. On epiphanies in the classical period see also Jacquemin 2000, 37; Rawlings 2007, 179–180, mentioning the later parallels of Saint George during the siege of Antioch and the Angel of Mons during the Great War.

[34] Wecklein 1867, 251 already suggested that the role of Pan in the battle of Marathon (6.105) should be attributed to the presence of the Pan cave (Pausanias 1.32.7). Pritchett 1979, 12–14 noted in his study of divine epiphanies that such divine appearances were commonly associated with sanctuaries. See also Mikalson 2003, 133–134: "The participation of [Athena, Demeter, Artemis, Hera and Aphrodite] was largely a geographical happenstance: because the cities or lands they protected became the sites of battle or were immediately threatened, they were acting from parochial motives."; see also Parker 2005, 397–403.

[35] As Malkin 2011, 131 notes (in a different context): "Gods and heroes were perceived as "holding the land" [...], regardless of which polis had control over it. [...] when arriving in a new land, reverence for the "local gods," particularly if these were somehow perceived as *archêgetai*, was expected." Funke 2004, 165 points out, with reference to the Panhellenic temples: "Herodotus' *Histories* reflect a sacred landscape that existed as a mental map in the minds of the Greeks and oriented their thoughts and actions." See also Foucart 1918, 76–77.

[36] Jung 2011a, 10. A good example of these processes is a series of wonders reported in relation to the battle of Leuktra (Xenophon, *Hellenica* 6.4.7): according to an oracle the Spartans were to be defeated at a monument for virgins who had been raped by Spartans, temples had magically opened and weapons had disappeared from a temple of Heracles. In many religions, sanctuaries are mnemotopes for stories connected to a particular myth, ex posto invented or not (Halbwachs 1941, 22 noted this process for the Holy Land).

[37] See Harrison 2000 and Mikalson 2003, 136–165 for a thorough overview of Herodotus' religious beliefs; cf. also Pohlenz 1961, 96–108. The clearest example is that Herodotus explained miraculous events theologically: Harrison 2000, 64–101; 2003, 239. However, to maintain that "one of [Herodotus'] primary aims in writing was an evangelising motive" (Harrison 2003, 252), or that he saw all events as a "Verwirklichung von Göttlichem" (von Haehling 1993) may go too far. Although Herodotus knew

gods (or rather a manifestation of divine power) had actively influenced events during the Persian invasion.³⁸

Some gods are credited more important role than others. Most notably Demeter appears as a wrathful defender of Greece in the battle of Plataea (§2.9.6), and there were temples to her on the battlefields of Thermopylae (§2.5.1) and Mykale (§2.10.2). It appears that the Greeks believed that the Persians had burnt down the Telesterion at Eleusis (§2.7.5), but otherwise it remains rather mysterious why Demeter was assigned such a large role; several ideas were advanced in §2.9.6 and §2.7.5. Athena was naturally involved as the patron deity of the Athenians. We hear of stories that Xerxes worshipped her in Troy, and then insulted her by destroying her main sanctuary and city. She is probably the divine force responsible for the panic in the camp at Troy (§2.2.3), the epiphany at Salamis (perhaps connected with the temple of Athena Skiras; §2.8.4), and the regrowth of the olive tree in the Erechtheion (§2.7.4). We have also seen that Zeus, as the supreme god of the Greeks, was believed to hinder the Persian advance.³⁹ Gods of the wind and the sea were believed to be involved in the conflict: in Magnesia two storms were attributed to Boreas and Oreïthyia, and perhaps to Thetis and the Nereids (§2.4.2).⁴⁰ In addition to the gods, heroes regularly rose up from their shrine or grave to help the Greeks, most explicitly at Delphi (§2.6.3) and Elaious (§2.10.4).⁴¹

---

that oracles could be misused for political purposes, he mostly respected them (Pohlenz 1961, 97; Harrison 2000, 122–157; Rosenberger 2003, 30).

38 Wecklein 1867, 250–255; Pagel 1927, 35–37 (with emphasis on τίσις); Pohlenz 1961, 96–97 (observing that Herodotus did not always believe that the gods participated); von Haehling 1993 (pointing out that when Herodotus tells stories of scared Greeks, this usually means that they did not have a good plan, while in the case of Persians it is a sign of divine intervention); Gould 1994, 94–96 (describing Herodotus' occasional hesitation towards the working of divine forces to the 'uncertainty principle' inherent in Greek religion, according to which it is believed that such inferences are never certain); Harrison 2000, 102–121; 2003, 239 (pointing out that the fact that Herodotus is at times sceptical about divine interventions in the real world shows that he truly believed that this was a possibility to take serious); Scheer 2000, 208–209; Flower & Marincola 2002, 39–44; Mikalson 2003, 8; 70–71 (observing that Herodotus' belief in divine intervention is sometimes in contrast with the information we have in inscriptions, in which human actions are central); Gehrke 2010, 25.

39 The Persian army is strangely rerouted through Zeus' private domains at Mount Ida (§2.2.1) and the Macedonian Mountain (§2.3.8). There are also many thunderstorms impeding the Persians (and never the Greeks), for example at the Ida, Pelion (§2.4.2) and Euboea (§2.4.5), as earlier at Athos. This inclement weather type was strongly associated with Zeus, and as discussed, we can assume that the god's influence is implied by Herodotus. After the battle of Plataea, Zeus (Eleutherios) was thanked for his role in the Persian Wars. For Herodotus' treatment of Zeus see Mora 1985, 81–84.

40 For a discussion of the characterisation of Thetis in Greek literature, see Slatkin 1986. For later battles in which Boreas played a role, see Jacquemin 2000, 38. For Herodotus' treatment of the elements as gods, see Mora 1985, 96–98.

41 Foucart 1918, 75–77 stressed the large perceived role of heroes during the Persian Wars. See Jung 2011a, 105 for a discussion of the territorial force of heroes. Parker 2011, 116–117 suggests that heroes were not necessarily territorial, but had more generally "a power genuinely effective for good or ill".

In contrast to the gods, heroes could only come to aid in the direct vicinity of their cult sites.⁴² On the whole, the traditions about divine intervention seem to have been quite random, and can be seen as 'mnemotopic' responses to whatever cult sites were present at the purported battlefields.⁴³

3.2.3 Persian participation in Greek cult

There existed several temple mnemotopes which commemorated stories that the Persians, most notably Xerxes and the Magi, tolerated, or even participated in cults for Greek gods: these include the cults for the Strymon river (§2.3.4); for Zeus and Athamas at Halos (§2.3.9); Athena Ilias and the heroes at Troy (§2.2.3); Boreas, Thetis and the Nereids at Sepias (§2.4.2), Athena and Erechtheus at the Acropolis (§2.7.4). To this list may be added the various narratives about Persians and Greek temples found elsewhere, such as the story of Miltiades, who trespassed into a temenos of Demeter on Paros, but was driven into a frenzy by the goddess and was wounded during his escape (6.134).⁴⁴ Similarly, Pausanias relates of the death of Pyrrhus in 2.21.4 and of the frenzy of the Persians at the temple of the Kabeiroi at Thebes (9.25.9). The notion of the 'worshipping conquerer' has parallels in other texts.⁴⁵

In the chapter about Troy (§2.2.3) it has been explained that these narratives are part of a longstanding discussion about the Achaemenid policies toward non-Persian religions. Even though I lack the expertise to fully assess that discussion from the Persian perspective, it is safe to say that it is uncertain whether narratives about interactions between Persians and Greek religion reflect historical events. If that is the case, how are they to be assessed? We have seen that these stories are all connected to well-known sightseeing spots or cult places. They may, for example, have helped to explain why a particular temple had survived the war unscathed. When a war had allegedly raged around the land, but specific temples remained unscathed, the obvious question was how this was possible. One answer was that the divinity

---

For the extent to which Herodotus used mythological heroes in symbolic ways, see Vandiver 1991. Mikalson (2003, 133) notes that heroes participated in person, unlike the gods.
42 Cf. Mikalson 2003, 129–131.
43 See Mikalson 2003 for the role of individual gods during the Persian Wars; 125–126 (Demeter); 111–113 (Zeus); 127–128 (Hera); 123–125 (Athena); 114–122 (Apollo); 127 (Artemis); 113–114 (Poseidon). The absence of Ares is remarkable; see Jacquemin 2000, 15–19 for an overview of cults for this god.
44 Hartmann 2010, 543 stresses the ἄρρητα ἱρά to which this tradition was connected: relics which were valued by the Parians as protecting the city.
45 E.g. Persian general Datis (Pausanias 10.28.6); Alexander the Great (Quintus Curtius 3.8.22). See also Briant 1996, 566.

itself had helped keeping the temenos free from enemies.[46] This may have had a religious meaning: it has been suggested that such stories existed to warn pilgrims not to trespass into temple buildings.[47] But the stories may also have served to underline the idea that the Persians did not understand Greek religion,[48] and were a variation from the more common theme of destroyed temples.[49]

3.3 Military mnemotopes

3.3.1 Usual battle sites

On a macro level, we may think about the battles of the Persian Wars as taking place at 'usual battle sites': mnemotopes (or entire memory landscapes) which are repeatedly singled out for their role in wars. Such coincidences may be grounded in reality, as a battle site's geography may make it prone to be a place of confrontation. We have seen some indications of this in Herodotus' account of Xerxes' invasion: the list of conflicts that happened at the pass of Thermopylae is long (§2.5.1); at Delphi, multiple invading forces were stopped near the temple of Athena Pronaia, with or without the help of Apollo, Phylakos and other supernatural forces (§2.6.3); the iconic Areopagus in Athens was repeatedly singled out as the 'base camp' of an invading force in Athens (§2.7.1); and the Asopos river between Plataea and Thebes was more than once the dividing line between opposing forces (§2.9.1). The phenomenon is wider than the Persian Wars: A good example of a 'usual battle site' can be found in Plutarch (*Agesilaus* 19.2), who relates that the battle of Coronea (394 BCE) took place around the temple of Athena Itonia, where an ancient trophy commemorated an earlier fight between the Boeotians and the Athenians. The phenomenon may be regarded as related to, and sometimes indistinct from, the accumulation of mythical and historical events noted above (§3.1.2).

---

[46] Halbwachs 1941, 83–84 mentioned the example of the Cenacle in Jerusalem, which survived destruction because the apostles who allegedly lived here after Jesus' ascension had founded the first Christian church in this building. Interestingly, there is evidence that this story was first localised at the other side of the city in the Cedron valley.
[47] Dillon 1997, 179–180.
[48] This stereotype is also found in Aeschylus' *Persae* (362; 373; 725).
[49] Miles 2014, 119.

3.3.2 Concatenation; vantage points

As has been noted in the individual case studies, in the accounts that we have, the chaotic reality of military confrontations was transformed into a much simplified narrative with a large focus on anecdotes.[50] They were topographically narrated by a chain of landmarks that loosely indicate the position of armies. The most elaborate example of this is Herodotus' treatment of the battle of Plataea (§2.9), but it is also present in the battles of Thermopylae (§2.5) and Mykale (§2.10), as well as in the sieges of Delphi (§2.6.3) and the Athenian Acropolis (§2.7). This phenomenon is comparable to category 3 in the analysis of Azaryahu & Foote 2008, discussed in the introduction (§1.3.5).

This effect is even more pronounced in the accounts of the sea battles of Artemision (§2.4) and Salamis (§2.8), where the featureless surface of the water required landmarks of nearby coastal areas to identify the place of the battle. This accords with observations elsewhere that stories which take place on the water are commonly told from nearby vantage points.[51] The 'coastal perspective' may have distorted the account of Xerxes' invasion: what we see is that events which must have taken place on the sea, are instead connected to the land.

Scholars sometimes note these biases in Herodotus' topography, but usually explain them as unproblematic and continue to use the topography to reconstruct the battles.[52] However, the observation that the narratives are fundamentally schematised makes it increasingly difficult to use them for the exact historicity of this topography. It is not only problematic whether the movements between the points are correct, but the landmarks themselves may be overly simplified or incorrect identifications of events, as they are with so many other mnemotopes.

We can only guess about the exact processes by which these stories arose, but it is consistent with the idea that Herodotus, whose mnemotopes always reflect existing landmarks, visited some of the battlefields, or had access to detailed accounts of other visitors.[53] Another part of his method consisted of interviewing persons, whether eyewitnesses or not, who claimed to 'know' details about the locations of the

---

[50] Ferrill 1966, 102; Meyer 1954, 230, noting that it is "völlig außerstande, ein reales Bild von einer Operation oder einer Schlacht zu entwerfen"; Whatley 1964 (discussed in §1.4.3) pointed out that the exact events of ancient battles are retrievable only to a very limited degree.
[51] Azaryahu & Foote 2008, 184, mentioning the modern example of the sinking of the Empress of Ireland in the St. Lawrence river in 1914, which is marked at Pointe-au-Père in Canada.
[52] Hignett 1963, 38 optimistically noted that "If he says that an army moved from point A to point B he is probably right, but when he tries to give a reason for the movement he may easily be wrong." Pritchett 1985a, 94 remarked that "(...) Herodotus has singled out prominent checkpoints in the landscape of his day (...) like flags stuck in with pins at a war map"; and 1993, 298: "One must always note that large armies, which must have taken up considerable space, are moved by Herodotus from a spring to a temple, as if they were individuals, but this feature is characteristic of all Greek historians."
[53] On Herodotus' visit to battlefields see Jacoby 1913, 270–272.

battle. Finally, literary and pictorial representations may have been a source, as we know existed for the battle of Marathon.[54]

3.3.3 Monumentalisation and tombs

Herodotus wrote at a point in time when the battles of Xerxes' invasion were fading out of living memory, but commemoration practises were going on and took various forms. Monuments had been erected in the public areas of participating cities such as Sparta or Athens, or in Panhellenic centres such as Delphi and Olympia, which were obvious sources of information for Herodotus.[55] In other cases there was also a demand to remember battles at the sites themselves. Alcock underlines that memorials on the spot of battle sites, albeit perhaps less frequented than 'urban' monuments, were more emotionally charged and gave a more intense experience.[56]

A particular type of monument that demarcated mnemotopes is the τροπαῖον or trophy, which marked the spot where the commemorators believed that the defeat of the enemies had become evident.[57] Herodotus, surprisingly, does not mention any, but the literary sources tell us about several examples in relation to the Persian War battles, some of which are archaeologically attested: Delphi (§2.6.3), Kynosoura (§2.8.2) and perhaps Psyttaleia (§2.8.1). The best-preserved trophy, but outside the scope of this study, is that of Marathon. It is unclear whether Herodotus' omission of these monuments means that their installation postdated his work.[58] Giorgia Proietti has argued that these trophies reflect re-memorialisation practises of sometimes very late dates.[59]

---

[54] The depiction of the battle of Marathon in the Stoa Poikile featured three paintings with three different settings: the temple of Heracles, the marshes and the coast where the Persians landed (Pausanias 1.15.3).
[55] On public memorials see Alcock 2002, 82 (emphasising the politicisation of Persian War commemoration); Rawlings 2007, 199–200. On such monuments as a source for Herodotus see How & Wells 1912, I 30.
[56] Alcock 2002, 76, 81.
[57] On trophies see Janssen 1957; West 1969, 13; Pritchett 1974, 252–253, with ample ancient literature where the word is associated with τροπή; Jacquemin 2000, 62–64; Rawlings 2007, 192; Bettalli 2009. Early attestations for the practice include Thucydides 2.92; 6.70; 7.54; Aeschylus, *Septem contra Thebem* 277; 954; *Batrachomyomachia* 159. For an overview of other literature, see Pritchett 1974, 246–275.
[58] Van Wees 2004, 138 suggests that the practice of erecting trophies postdates the Persian Wars. It is also possible that the trophies were placed at a later date, as commemoration of the Persian Wars became more important. Likewise, Pritchett 1974, 270 seems to suggest that trophies of the Persian Wars did exist in Herodotus' time, even though Herodotus did not care to tell us about them. A potential mention of a trophy which antedates Herodotus is found in fifth-century BCE poet Timotheus (*Persae* 196), who mentions them in relation to the battle of Salamis. See also Proietti 2015a, 150 with note 12, for some further references.
[59] Proietti 2015a.

Another form of commemoration is the burial of the fallen in tombs on the battlefield. These could also help to mark the location of the battle.⁶⁰ Herodotus mentions the kolonos at Thermopylae (§2.5.4), an entire necropolis at Plataea (§2.9.7), and the 'tomb' at Kynosoura at Salamis (§2.8.2). An important observation from a mnemotopical perspective is that the authenticity of the graves or tombs mentioned in relation to Xerxes' invasion has never been ascertained by archaeology. Interestingly, Herodotus realised that tombs could be 'fake', and mentions the cenotaph of the Aiginetans at Plataea, claiming that the Aiginetans constructed it to prove their participation in the battle.⁶¹ Similar identifications occur in modern scholarship: the kolonos at Thermopylae was readily interpreted as the grave of the 300 Spartans; likewise, the hill on the north side of the Kynosoura peninsular has been interpreted as the tumulus of those who fell during the battle of Salamis; however, both hills have not yielded the expected remains of the dead. By the Roman period even more 'fake' graves were pointed out, such as the tomb of Mardonios at Plataea. The existence of such cenotaphs is a clear indication that mnemotopes need not reflect historical events, but are indicative of the way in which communities want to remember these events.

3.3.4 Places of refuge

Another frequently occurring type of mnemotopes on or near sites of battle and siege are places of refuge. In the pass of Thermopylae a hill of refuge was pointed out as the place of the Spartans' heroic last stance (§2.5.4); the Phocians were thought to have fled into a cave at Tithorea (§2.6.2), and the Delphians into the Korykian cave (§2.6.4); on the Athenian Acropolis, the last defenders of the city fled into a μέγαρον (probably of the Old Temple of Athena Polias) where they were killed by the Persians (§2.7.3). At the battle of Plataea, the temples of Hera and Demeter appear as places of refuge, although we are not told that the Greeks actually hid in them (§2.9.5; §2.9.6).⁶²

While the Greeks took refuge in temples or caves, the Persian hideouts were their palisaded forts at Plataea (§2.9.1) and Mykale (§2.10.2). These Persian refuges also marked the end of the battles, when the Greeks managed to kill everyone inside. The island of Psyttaleia was regarded both as a Greek refuge and as a Persian 'fort' during the battle of Salamis: Greeks floating on the sea after their ships had been destroyed could find a safe haven here, had the Persians not decided to ambush on the island (§2.8.1). Here too, the final slaughter of the Persians ends the battle.

---

60 Hartmann 2010, 310–311. On the practice of erecting polyandreia on battlefields in the classical period see Pritchett 1985b, 249–251; Jacquemin 2000, 66–68; Rawlings 2007, 196–198.
61 Vansina (1985, 46) mentions a nearly exact parallel in which a king of the Shilluk of Suan built a fake tomb as evidence for a traditional history.
62 For more examples of temples in classical Greece as refuges see Jacquemin 2000, 129–134.

Again, the historicity of these escapes is beyond recovery. But we can observe that the idea of the 'place of retreat' was an important dramatic point in the stories about battles and sieges that showcased Greek despair before the final victory, or (at Thermopylae) heroism, and in the case of the Persians, a failed attempt to hide from the Greeks. In particular, the mnemotopisation of caves as hideouts appears in many other contexts.[63]

3.3.5 Pass lore: The enemy's bypass and blockades

We have seen various examples of anecdotes that feature Persians who, during a battle or siege, find a path around the main frontline to attack the Greeks at a weak point: this type of story is found in the bypass of Thermopylae by way of the Anopaia path (§2.5.3); the bypass of the Tempe valley by way of the 'Macedonian mountain' (§2.3.8); the bypass of Artemision by a re-routing of the armada along the 'Hollows' (§2.4.5); the bypass of the isthmus of Potidaia when the sea receded (§2.8.9); and the bypass of the Propylaea of the Acropolis by a few Persians who climbed up the citadel at the unguarded backside, paralleled by the siege of Sardis (§2.7.2); and during the Athenian siege of Sestos, a reversed situation takes places: here the Persians manage to leave the besieged the city by the hidden backside (§2.10.5).

A partial explanation why the Persian bypass was such a popular story in the postwar period, is that it may in some cases have characterised the Persians as unable to win in close combat. Avoiding the direct confrontation is, of course, an effective means to win a battle; but that does not mean that that idea could not have been exaggerated in the minds of the Greeks of Herodotus' time. In fact, the idea that enemies typically win by stealth is well attested in Greek literature.[64] Although it is

---

[63] Zwingmann 2012, 311–313 with many examples in Asia Minor. For caves as prisons, see Boardman 2002, 104–106. A more recent parallel are the caves which feature in local traditions in the Cévennes mountains of France as Camisard hideouts (Fentress & Wickham 1992, 93).

[64] In the *Iliad* (7.242–243), Hector proclaims to Ajax: οὐ γάρ σ' ἐθέλω βαλέειν τοιοῦτον ἐόντα λάθρῃ ὀπιπεύσας, ἀλλ' ἀμφαδόν, αἴ κε τύχωμι 'I do not want to hit you like you do, secretly spying, but openly, if I happen to do so.' Another example in the *Histories* is the Persian siege of Soloi in Cyprus, which was successful after a tunnel was dug (5.115). In Polybius (4.8.11) we find a clear vocalisation of this notion when the Cretans are described as 'irresistible for their ambushes, raids, theft from enemies and nightly assaults and all their use of deceitful and successive actions, but for charging openly and within sight in phalanx formation, they are too low-born and treacherous in their souls. The Achaeans and Macedonians are the opposite of this.' Polybius elsewhere (13.3.2–7; 36.9.9) stresses that the Greeks and Romans as civilised people normally do not employ these battle techniques. Pritchett (1974, 171; 174–177) mentions many similar examples, both ancient and modern. A negative valuation of such techniques was possibly widespread. For a study of ambushes in Greek literature, see Pritchett 1974, 178–189.

recognised that Herodotus sometimes mentions that the individual Persians had been brave, such as in the battle of Plataea,[65] it is reasonable to suspect that the traditions on which he relied more often portrayed the Persians as dangerous in some aspects, such as their great number, but morally defective and therefore prone to using stealth techniques.[66] In addition, the secret siege stories are known from many other cultural contexts.[67]

Given its very widespread occurrence, I propose that the type of anecdote featuring the bypass movement may be seen as a common place. This does not mean that every instance of it is unhistorical: this is a tried and proven method of capturing city or defeating a superior army. However, the study of the topography in the individual cases has shown that the bypass was practically impossible (such as the bypasses at Thermopylae and at the Acropolis), and many of these stories feature other legendary elements and were connected to a theme of divine retribution (such as the bypasses of Artemision and Potidaia). In these cases, it becomes increasingly difficult to use Herodotus' account as a means of establishing a historical topography of the battle.

The function of mnemotopes of this type in the local traditions in which they existed was providing an answer to the question 'how did the Persians manage to win the battle from our heroic forefathers?' The answer was: only by stealth. The validity of this point is shown by stories about wise advisors who suggest that Xerxes and Mardonios avoid a frontal confrontation with the Greeks[68]: Demaratus, Spartan exile king, and Artemisia, governor of Halicarnassus, both urge Xerxes to avoid meeting the Greeks in the waters near Salamis, and instead aim for the Peloponnese (7.235 and 8.68). Before the battle of Plataea, Artabazos advises Mardonios to use diplomacy instead of war, but Mardonios refuses, ironically remarking that attacking would be νόμῳ τῷ Περσέων 'according to Persian custom' (9.41).

There was no better way of 'proving' that the bypass happened than by pointing at landmarks in the local landscape. It made the story of the treacherous assault graphical, and thus credible.

---

65 Briant 1999, 110; Flower & Marincola 2002, 38; Isaac 2004, 263–264.
66 On Greek stereotyping of Persian soldiers as weak and decadent, see Briant 1989. In book 7 of his Strategemata, Polyaenus suggests that barbarian peoples (among who he counts the Medes, Lydians and Persians) were especially dependents on their use of 'stratagems' instead of military prowess, listing many examples. And indeed, in the examples of nightly surprise attacks in Greek historiography listed by Pritchett (1974, 164–169) the aggressors are usually Persians.
67 In an interesting parallel, Livy (5.47) describes how the Gauls took the Roman capitol in a manner immediately reminiscent of the Thermopylae episode. A similar story occurs during the battle of Traigh Ghruinneart in the United Kingdom (1598). We also read that during the siege of Carthago Nova (209 BCE), parts of the Roman army wade through the water to get access to the city (Livy 26.45).
68 I take these stories from Romm 1998, 196–197.

3.3.6 Thrones

The idea that the Persian king sat on a throne to look at his troops appears no less than three times in the account of Xerxes' invasion: at Abydos on the Hellespont (§2.2.4), at Trachis near Thermopylae (§2.5.1) and, most famously, on Mount Aigaleos overlooking the battle of Salamis (§2.8.3). Later, Xerxes was associated with a 'throne' sighted at Sardis (Strabo 13.4.5). The vision may be compared to other instances of the king overlooking his troops at Doriskos (§2.3.3) and his observation of the Tempe valley (§2.3.7).[69] Thrones were equally part of lore about his father Darius, who was imagined as sitting on a throne to look at his armies crossing the Bosporus (4.88). It has been suggested above that these 'visions' were mnemotopically motivated by prominent hilltops. In addition, the idea was related to a real silver-footed throne which was kept on the Acropolis and pointed out as that of Xerxes (Demosthenes, *In Timocratem* 129; the alleged throne of king Midas in Delphi may be compared with this relic, cf. 1.14) as well as to a painting of the Bosporus scene in the Heraion of Samos (4.88).

The idea of the monarch on the throne can safely be thought of as a common place, as various scholars have noted[70]; and it is part of a more general topos in which prominent characters watch something from mountains, called oroskopia by Irene de Jong.[71] The notion can, for example, be compared to the scenes portraying Priam or Apollo looking out over the Trojan troops in the plains around Ilion (e.g. *Iliad* 4.508; 21.526), and in that of Zeus watching battles from Mount Ida (8.75; 8.207).[72] In this text we also encounter Hera and other gods as χρυσόθρονος (1.611; 14.154; cf. 15.149–150); Hades leaps from his throne in fear (20.61–62); and Poseidon sits on the mountain peak of Samothrace to watch over the Troad (13.10–25). More generally, the designation of mountains as the locations of historical or mythical events is common.[73]

The historicity of these scenes is beyond recovery. But even when the Persian king did climb a steep hill to watch over a battle, the idea also appealed to the collective memory. Accordingly, the places where Xerxes' throne once stood were pointed out again and again.

---

69 Christ 1994 argues that the king showed his passion for research and counting, closely mimicking that of Herodotus himself.
70 On the topos of Xerxes' throne in Herodotus, see Immerwahr 1966, 182; Grethlein 2009, 209; Bridges 2015, 54–56; 59 (noting that Darius was pictured in similar fashion). See Allen 2005b on the image of the enthroned Achaemenid king in audience scenes that featured widely in imperial propaganda.
71 De Jong (forthcoming).
72 Grethlein 2009, 209–210.
73 On the importance of mountains in Greek mythology, see Buxton 1994, 81–96; he stresses the frequent association of mountains with Zeus.

4 Conclusion

The hypothesis of this book has been that the framework of mnemotopes is a useful heuristic tool for understanding the topography of Xerxes' invasion as recounted in Herodotus' *Histories* (§1.2). After a theoretical framework in which I gave the concept of mnemotope a clearer basis than has hitherto been done, I applied it to ten topographically arranged case studies which together cover the entirety of the topography in Herodotus' account of Xerxes' invasion.

As I endeavoured to show in these case studies, the heuristic concept of mnemotopes opened the door for new perspectives on most of the discussed sites. The workings of mnemotopes, I believe, are idiosyncratic, and depend on local traditions encountered and mostly transmitted as such by Herodotus. I find it important to remain conscious of the limitations of my approach. In many ways, the reflections that I offered on mnemotopes in the case studies must remain speculative, as hard evidence is often not available. Nevertheless, I suggest that we ask our texts a different question; not: 'Where did it happen?' but rather: 'Why did they think it happened right there?' An important conclusion of this study is that locations are intimately tied up with narratives, and are sometimes even the basis of the narrative itself. Mnemotopes do not just occasionally occur; they are ubiquitous and pervasive, and key to understanding the world of Herodotus.

Although I have sometimes explored explanations for the topography that move away from questions of historical nature, I have explicitly distanced myself from commenting on the historicity of the events and their topography. After all, the designation of a site as a mnemotope does not in itself disprove the historicity of the localisation or of the event (cf. §1.3.6). But there often exist multiple pathways by which mnemotopes of events arose in the minds of the Greeks. Nevertheless, I do have doubts as to the level of detail with which we can reconstruct the Persian Wars and their topography, for which Herodotus' work has all too often been taken at face value. In using it as a historical source we should be careful from the outset.

An added value of this study has been that several repeatedly occurring mnemotopical processes could be identified in the material, allowing the creation of a non-exhaustive typology of mnemotopes. By way of outlook, I hope that the model created in this book may be fruitful for future research, not only on other parts of Herodotus' work, but also on other works of history, inside and outside of the field of Classics.

In the text quoted as the motto of this book, Robert Wood talks about the "particular pleasure [of an] imagination warmed on the spot". This is the essence of the mnemotope. That pleasure has been very important to me while doing the research for this book in Greece and Turkey, and I that hope this book will invite some readers to experience the same.

Bibliography

Literature and scholia

Acta Sanctorum Octobris Tomus IV
　　Societas Bollandistarum (1780), *Acta Sanctorum Octobris Tomus IV*. Brussels: Koninklijke Bibliotheek.
Aelian
　　Varia historia: Rudolf Hercher (1866), *Claudii Aeliani de natura animalium libri xvii, varia historia, epistolae, fragmenta*. Leipzig: Teubner.
Aeschines
　　In Ctesiphontem: Guy de Budé & Victor Martin (1928), *Eschine*. Paris: Les Belles Lettres.
Aeschylus
　　Agamemnon, Eumenides, Persae & *Septem contra Thebem*: Martin L. West (1990), *Aeschyli Tragoediae cum incerti poetae Prometheo*. Stuttgart: Teubner.
　　Scholia on *Persae*: Wilhelm Dindorf (1851), *Aeschyli tragoediae superstites et deperditarum fragmenta*. Oxford: Oxford University Press.
Alciphron
　　Epistulae: M.A. Schepers (1905), *Alciphronis rhetoris epistularum libri iv*. Leipzig: Teubner.
Alexis of Samos = *FGrH* 539.
Ammianus Marcellinus
　　Res gestae: Wolfgang Seyfarth (1978), *Ammiani Marcellini Rerum gestarum libri qui supersunt*. Leipzig: Teubner.
Ad Avircium Marcellum contra Cataphrygas
　　Martin Joseph Routh (1846), *Reliquiae sacrae*. Oxford: Oxford University Press.
Anthologia Graeca
　　Herman Beckby (1965), *Anthologia Graeca*. Munich: Heimeran.
Antipater: see *Anthologia Graeca*.
Apollonius Rhodius
　　Argonautica: Hermann Fraenkel (1961), *Apollonii Rhodii Argonautica*. Oxford: Clarendon Press.
　　Scholia: Karl Wendel (1935), *Scholia in Apollonium Rhodium vetera*. Berlin: Weidmann.
Appian
　　Historia Romana: Anton Gerard Roos & Paul Viereck (1939), *Appiani historia Romana*. Leipzig: Teubner.
Aristodemus = *FGrH* 104.
Aristophanes
　　Acharnenses, Equites & *Lysistrata*: Nigel Wilson (2007), *Aristophanis Fabulae*. Oxford: Oxford University Press.
　　Scholia: Mervyn D. Jones & Nigel Wilson (1969), *Prolegomena de comoedia. Scholia in Acharnenses, Equites, Nubes*. Groningen: Wolters-Noordhoff.
Aristoteles
　　De ventorum situ et nominibus & *Poetica*: Immanuel Bekker (1831), *Aristotelis opera*. Berlin: Reimer.
Arrian
　　Anabasis Alexandri & *Indica*: Anton Gerard Roos & Gerhard Wirth (1967), *Flavii Arriani quae exstant omnia*. Leipzig: Teubner.
Athenaeus
　　Deipnosophistae: S. Douglas Olson (2006–2012), *The learned banqueters / Athenaeus*. Cambridge, Massachusetts: Harvard University Press.

Batrachomyomachia
    Thomas William Allen (1912), *Homeri opera*, vol. 5. Oxford: Clarendon Press.
Callimachus
    In Delum & *In lavacrum Palladis*: Rudolf Pfeiffer (1953), *Callimachus, vol. 2*. Oxford: Clarendon Press.
Cicero
    De divinatione: William Armistead Falconer (1923), *Cicero: De Senectute De Amicitia De Divinatione. With An English Translation*. Cambridge, Massachusetts: Harvard University Press.
    De natura deorum: Otto Plasberg (1917), *De Natura Deorum. M. Tullius Cicero*. Leipzig: Teubner.
    De oratore: Augustus Samuel Wilkins (1902), *M. Tvlli Ciceronis Rhetorica*. Oxford: Clarendon Press.
Claudian
    In Eutropium: Maurice Platnaeur (1922), *Claudian, Vol 1. Claudianus, Claudius*. London: William Heinemann.
Clidemus of Athens = *FGrH* 323.
Democritus
    Fragments: Hermann Diels & Walther Kranz (1952), *Die Fragmente der Vorsokratiker*. Berlin: Weidmann.
Demosthenes
    Adversus Androtionem & *In Timocratem*: S.H. Butcher (1907), *Demosthenis orationes*, vol. 2.1. Oxford: Clarendon Press.
    Philippica 4 & Περὶ τῶν πρὸς Ἀλέξανδρον συνθηκῶν: S.H. Butcher (1903), *Demosthenis orationes*, vol. 1. Oxford: Clarendon Press.
Dexippus = *FGrH* 100.
Dio Chrysostom
    Orationes: Hans Friedrich August von Arnim (1896), *Dionis Prusaensis quem vocant Chrysostomum quae exstant omnia*. Berlin: Weidmann.
Diodorus Siculus
    Bibliotheca historica: Kurt Theodor Fischer & Friedrich Vogel (1888–1906), *Diodori bibliotheca historica*. Leipzig: Teubner.
Ephorus = *FGrH* 70.
Euphorion
    Fragments: John U. Powell (1925), *Collectanea Alexandrina*. Oxford: Clarendon Press.
Euripides
    Andromache: James Diggle (1984), *Euripidis fabulae, vol. 1*. Oxford: Clarendon Press.
    Iphigenia Taurica & *Troades*: James Diggle (1981), *Euripidis fabulae, vol. 2*. Oxford: Clarendon Press.
    Bacchae, Helena, Iphigenia Aulidensis & *Rhesus*: James Diggle (1994), *Euripidis fabulae, vol. 3*. Oxford: Clarendon Press.
    Vita-argumentum-scholia: Eduard Schwartz (1887–1891), *Scholia in Euripidem*. Berlin: Reimer.
    Other scholia: Wilhelm Dindorf (1863), *Scholia Graeca in Euripidis tragoedias*. Oxford: Oxford University Press.
Eustathius
    Commentarii ad Homeri Odysseam: J. G. Stallbaum (1825–1826), *Eustathii archiepiscopi Thessalonicensis commentarii ad Homeri Odysseam*. Leipzig: Weigel.
Galen
    Quod animi mores corporis temperamenta sequantur: Georg Helmreich, Ioannes Marquardt & Iwan Philipp Eduard Müller (1884–1893), *Claudii Galeni Pergameni scripta minora, vol. 2*. Leipzig: Teubner.

Gellius
    Noctae Atticae: John C. Rolfe (1927), *The Attic Nights of Aulus Gellius. With An English Translation*. Cambridge, Massachusetts: Harvard University Press.
Hecataeus of Miletus = *FGrH* 1.
Hellanicus of Lesbos = *FGrH* 4.
Hereas = *FGrH* 486.
Herodianus (Aelius)
    Ἡ καθ' ὅλου προσῳδία: Augustus Lentz (1867), *Grammatici Graeci*, vol. 3.1. Leipzig: Teubner.
    Περὶ Ὀδυσσειακῆς προσῳδίας & Περὶ παθῶν: Augustus Lentz (1870), *Grammatici Graeci*, vol. 3.2. Leipzig: Teubner.
Herodotus
    Histories: Nigel Guy Wilson (2015), *Herodoti Historiae*. Oxford: Oxford University Press.-
Hesiod
    Opera et dies & *Theogonia*: Glen W. Most (2006), *Theogony ; Works and Days ; Testimonia*. Cambridge, Massachusetts: Harvard University Press.
    Scutum: Glen W. Most (2007), *The shield ; Catalogue of women ; other fragments*. Cambridge, Massachusetts: Harvard University Press.
Hesychius
    Lexicon Α—Ο: Kurt Latte (1953 & 1966), *Hesychii Alexandrini lexicon*. Copenhagen: Munksgaard.
    Lexicon Π—Ω: Moritz Schmidt (1861–1862), *Hesychii Alexandrini lexicon*. Jena: F. Maukii.
Historia Alexandri Magni
    Richard Stoneman (2012), *Il Romanzo di Alessandro*. Milan: Arnoldo Mondadori editore.
Homer
    Iliad: Martin L. West (1998–2000), *Homeri Ilias*. Stuttgart: Teubner & München: Saur.
    Odyssey: Peter von der Mühll (1962), *Homeri Odyssea*. Basel: Helbing & Lichtenhahn.
    D-scholia on the *Iliad*: Christian Gottlob Heyne (1834), *Homeri Ilias*. Oxford: Oxford University Press.
Homeric Hymn to Demeter
    Thomas W. Allen, William R. Halliday & Edward E. Sikes (1936), *The Homeric hymns*. Oxford: Clarendon Press.
Hyginus
    Fabulae: Albertus Werth (1901), *De Hygini Fabularum Indole*. Leipzig: Teubner.
Isocrates
    Panathenaicus & *Philippus*: Émile Brémond & Georges Mathieu (1962), *Isocrate. Discours*, vol. 4. Paris: Les Belles Lettres.
    Panegyricus & *Plataicus*: Émile Brémond & Georges Mathieu (1938), *Isocrate. Discours*, vol. 2. Paris: Les Belles Lettres.
Isidore of Seville
    Etymologiae: Wallace Lindsay (1911), *Isidori Hispalensis Episcopi Etymologiarum Sive Originum Libri XX*. Oxford: Clarendon Press.
Livy
    Ab urbe condita: Robertus Seymour Conway & Carolus Flamstead Walters (1914), *Titi Livi. Ab Urbe Condita*. Oxford: Clarendon Press.
Lucanus
    Pharsalia: Edward Ridley (1905): *M. Annaeus Lucanus*. London: Longmans, Green, and Co.
Lucian
    Alexander: A.M. Harmon (1925), *Lucian*, vol. 4. Cambridge, Massachusetts: Harvard University Press.

Revivescentes sive piscator: A.M. Harmon (1921), *Lucian*, vol. 3. Cambridge, Massachusetts: Harvard University Press.
Scholia: Hugo Rabe (1906), *Scholia in Lucianum*. Leipzig: Teubner.
Lycophron
Alexandra: Lorenzo Mascialino (1964), *Lycophronis Alexandra*. Leipzig: Teubner.
Scholia: E. Scheer (1958), *Lycophronis Alexandra, vol. 2*. Berlin: Weidmann.
Lycurgus
Oratio in Leocratem: N.C. Conomis (1970), *Lycurgi oratio in Leocratem*. Leipzig: Teubner.
Maximus
Dissertationes: Michael B. Trapp (1994), *Maximus Tyrius: Dissertationes*. Leipzig: Teubner.
Neanthes of Cyzicus = *FGrH* 84.
New Testament
Kurt Aland, Matthew Black, Carlo M. Martini, Bruce Metzger & Allen Wikgren (1968), *The Greek New Testament*. Stuttgart: Württemberg Bible Society (second edition).
Nicetas Choniates
Historia: Jan Louis van Dieten (1975), *Nicetae Choniatae historia, pars prior*. Berlin: De Gruyter.
Nonnus
Dionysiaca: Rudolf Keydell (1959), *Nonni Panopolitani Dionysiaca*. Berlin: Weidmann.
Ovid
Metamorphoses:
Book 3: Alessandro Barchiesi & Gianpiero Rosati (2009), *Ovidio: Metamorfosi. Volume II (Libri III-IV)*. Milan: Arnoldo Mondadori Editore (second edition, first published 2007).
Book 6: Gianpiero Rosati (2013), *Ovidio: Metamorfosi. Volume III (Libri V-VI)*. Milan: Arnoldo Mondadori Editore (second edition, first published 2009).
Book 11: Joseph D. Reed (2013), *Ovidio: Metamorfosi. Volume V (Libri X-XII)*. Milan: Arnoldo Mondadori Editore.
Pausanias
Periegesis: Friedrich Spiro (1903), *Pausaniae Graeciae descriptio*. Leipzig: Teubner.
Pisander of Camiros
Heraclea: Albertus Bernabé (1987), *Poetarum epicorum Graecorum testimonia et fragmenta*. Leipzig: Teubner.
Pherecydes of Athens = *FGrH* 3.
Philiades
Ernst Diehl (1949), *Anthologia lyrica Graeca*. Leipzig: Teubner (third edition).
Philochorus = *FGrH* 328.
Philostratus
Heroicus & *Vitae sophistarum*: L. de Lannoy (1977), *Flavii Philostrati Heroicus*. Leipzig: Teubner.
Vita Apollonii: Carl Ludwig Kayser (1870), *Flavii Philostrati opera*. Leipzig: Teubner.
Photius
Bibliotheca: René Henry (1959–1977), *Photius. Bibliothèque*. Paris: Les Belles Lettres.
Pindar
Vita Pindari: A.B. Drachmann (1903), *Scholia vetera in Pindari carmina*, vol. 1. Leipzig: Teubner.
Plato
Leges: John Burnet (1907), *Platonis opera*, vol. 5. Oxford: Clarendon Press.
Menexenus: John Burnet (1903), *Platonis opera*, vol. 3. Oxford: Clarendon Press.
Phaedrus: John Burnet (1901), *Platonis opera*, vol. 2. Oxford: Clarendon Press.

Pliny the Elder
   Naturalis Historia: Karl Mayhoff (1875–1906), *C. Plini Secundi Naturalis historiae libri XXXVII.* 5 vol. Leipzig: Teubner.
Plutarch
   Agesilaus, Alexander, Aristides, Cato Maior, Eumenes, Nicias, Pericles, Pyrrhus, Solon, Sulla, Themistocles & *Theseus*: Claes Lindskog & Konrat Ziegler (1964), *Plutarchi Vitae parallelae*. Leipzig: Teubner.
   De gloria Atheniensium, De Herodoti malignitate & *Mulierum virtutes*: Curt Hubert (1959–1967), *Plutarchi Moralia*. Leipzig: Teubner.
Polyaenus
   Strategemata: Johann Melber & Eduard von Woelfflin (1887), *Polyaeni strategematon libri viii*. Leipzig: Teubner.
Polybius
   Historiae: Theodor Büttner-Wobst (1893; 1904–1905), *Polybii historiae*. Leipzig: Teubner.
Priscian
   De metris fabularum Terentii: August Krehl (1819–1920), *Prisciani Caesariensis grammatici opera*. Leipzig: Weidmann.
Procopius
   De aedificiis: Gerhard Wirth (post Jacobus Haury) (1964), *Procopii Caesariensis opera omnia*, vol. 4. Leipzig: Teubner.
Pseudo-Apollodorus
   Bibliotheca & *Epitomae*: Richard Wagner (1894), *Apollodori bibliotheca. Pediasimi libellus de duodecim Herculis laboribus*. Leipzig: Teubner.
Pseudo-Plutarch
   De fluviis: Karl Müller (1861), *Geographi Graeci minores*, vol. 2, Paris: Didot.
Ptolemy
   Geographia: Gerd Grasshoff & Alfred Stückelberger (2006), *Klaudios Ptolemaios Handbuch der Geographie*. Basel: Schwabe.
Quintus Curtius
   Historiae Alexandri Magni: Edmund Hedicke (1908), *Q. Curti Rufi Historiarum Alexandri Magni Macedonis libri qui supersunt*. Leipzig: Teubner.
Seneca
   Hercules Oetaeus: John G. Fitch (2004), *Seneca: Oedipus, Agamemnon, Thyestes. [Seneca]: Hercules on Oeta, Octavia*. Cambridge, Massachusetts: Harvard University Press.
Simonides
   PMG: Denys Lionel Page (1962), *Poetae melici Graeci*. Oxford: Clarendon Press.
   FGE: Denys Lionel Page (1981), *Further Greek Epigrams: Epigrams before AD 50 from the Greek Anthology and other sources, not included in 'Hellenistic Epigrams' or 'The Garland of Philip'*. Cambridge: Cambridge University Press.
   W²: M.L. West (1992), *Iambi et Elegi Graeci ante Alexandrum cantati vol. II. editio altera*. Oxford: Oxford University Press.
Sophocles
   Ajax, Odysseus Tyrannus & *Trachiniae*: Hugh Lloyd-Jones & Nigel Guy Wilson (1990), *Sophoclis fabulae*. Oxford: Clarendon Press.
Stadiasmus Maris Magnis
   Karl Müller (1855), *Geographi Graeci minores, vol. 1*. Paris: Didot.
Statius
   Thebais: Alfredus Klotz (1973), *P. Papini Stati Thebais*. Leipzig: Teubner.
Stephanus Byzantinus
   Ethnica: August Meineke (1849), *Stephan von Byzanz. Ethnika*. Berlin: Reimer.

Strabo
   Geographica: Stefan Radt (2002–2011), *Strabons Geographika*. Göttingen: Vandenhoeck & Ruprecht.
Suda
   Ada Adler (1928–1935), *Suidae lexicon*. Leipzig: Teubner.
Theophrastus
   Historia plantarum: Arthur Hort (1916), *Theophrastus. Enquiry into plants*. Cambridge, Massachusetts: Harvard University Press.
   Fragments: Friedrich Wimmer (1866), *Theophrasti Eresii opera, quae supersunt, omnia*. Paris: Didot.
Thucydides
   Historiae: Henry Stuart Jones & J. Enoch Powell (1942), *Thucydidis historiae*. Oxford: Clarendon Press (second edition).
Timotheus
   Persae: Denys Lionel Page (1962), *Poetae melici Graeci*. Oxford: Clarendon Press.
Tzetzes
   Scholia in Lycophronem: Eduard Scheer (1958), *Lycophronis Alexandra*, vol. 2, Berlin: Weidmann.
Valerius Maximus
   Facta et Dicta Memorabilia: D.R. Shackleton Bailey (2000), *Valerius Maximus: Memorable Doings and Sayings*. Cambridge, Massachusetts: Harvard University Press.
Vibius Sequester
   De fluminibus, fontibus, lacubus, nemoribus, gentibus: Remus Gelsomino (1967), *De fluminibus, fontibus, lacubus, nemoribus, gentibus quorum apud poëtas mentio fit: Vibius Sequester*. Leipzig: Teubner.
Virgil
   Aeneis: Gian Biagio Conte (2009), *Aeneis, P. Vergilius Maro*. Berlin: Walter de Gruyter.
Vitruvius
   De Architectura: Morris Hicky Morgan (1914), *Vitruvius: The Ten Books on Architecture*. Vitruvius. Cambridge, Massachusetts: Harvard University Press.
Xenophon
   Anabasis: Edgar Cardew Marchant (1904), *Xenophontis opera omnia*, vol. 3. Oxford: Clarendon Press.
   Cyropaedia: Edgar Cardew Marchant (1910), *Xenophontis opera omnia*, vol. 4. Oxford: Clarendon Press.
   De republica Lacedaemoniorum: Edgar Cardew Marchant (1920), *Xenophontis opera omnia*, vol. 5. Oxford: Clarendon Press.
   Hellenica: Edgar Cardew Marchant (1900), *Xenophontis opera omnia*, vol. 1. Oxford: Clarendon Press.
   Oeconomicus: Edgar Cardew Marchant (1921), *Xenophontis opera omnia*, vol. 2. Oxford: Clarendon Press (second edition).
Zosimus
   Historia Nova: François Paschoud (1986), *Zosime. Histoire nouvelle*. Paris: Les Belles Lettres.

Inscriptions

Achaemenid Royal Inscriptions: *DPg, DZc, XPh*
   Roland G. Kent (1950), *Old Persian: Grammar, Texts, Lexicon*. New Haven: American Oriental Society.

Agora XIX, Leases L: 4a
   Michael B. Walbank, "Leases of Public Lands". In: Gerald V. Lalonde, Merle K. Langdon & Michael B. Walbank (1991), *The Athenian Agora XIX. Inscriptions. Horoi, Poletai, Leases of Public Lands*. Princeton: American School of Classical Studies at Athens.
BCH 15 (1891) 373–380
   Radet, Georges Albert (1891), "Notes de géographie ancienne (1)". *Bulletin de correspondance hellénique* (15), 373–380.
BCH 83 (1959) 472,6
   Daux, Georges (1959), "Inscriptions de Delphes". *Bulletin de correspondence hellénique* 83 (2), 466–495.
BCH 99 (1975) 51–75
   Piérart Marcel & Étienne Roland (1975), "Un décret du koinon des Hellènes à Platées en l'honneur de Glaucon, fils d'Étéoclès, d'Athènes". *Bulletin de correspondance hellénique* 99 (1), 51–75.
IG I^2: 394
   Fridericus Hiller de Gaertringen (ed.) (1924), *Inscriptiones Graecae. Vol. I (ed. altera): Inscriptiones Atticae Euclidis anno anteriores*. Berlin: Reimer.
IG I^3: 3–4; 79; 255; 259; 386–387; 503–504; 1143
   David Malcolm Lewis (ed.) (1981–1998), *Inscriptiones Graecae. Vol. I (ed. tertia): Inscriptiones Atticae Euclidis anno anteriores*. Berlin & New York: De Gruyter.
IG II^2: 663; 1006; 1008; 1009; 1011; 1028; 1029; 1035; 1232; 1590a
   Johannes Kirchner (ed.) (1913–1940), *Inscriptiones Graecae. Vol. II (ed. altera): Inscriptiones Atticae Euclidis anno posteriores*. Berlin: Reimer.
IG V,1: 18; 657; 660
   Walter Kolbe (ed.) (1913), *Inscriptiones Graecae. Vol. V,1: Inscriptiones Laconiae et Messeniae*. Berlin: Reimer.
IG VII: 53; 1667; 1670–1672; 1675; 1688
   Wilhelm Dittenberger (ed.) (1892), *Inscriptiones Graecae. Vol. VII: Inscriptiones Megaridis, Oropiae, Boeotiae*. Berlin: Reimer.
IG XII,4,1: 68
   Dimitris Bosnakis, Klaus Hallof & Kent Rigsby (ed.) (2010), *Inscriptiones Graecae. Vol. XII,4: Inscriptiones Coi, Calymnae, insularum Milesiarum. Pars I: Inscriptionum Coi insulae: Decreta, epistulae, edicta, tituli sacri*. Berlin: De Gruyter.
IG XII,9: 1189
   Erich Ziebarth (ed.) (1915), *Inscriptiones Graecae. Vol. XII,9: Inscriptiones Euboeae insulae*. Berlin: Reimer.
IPri: 196; 361
   Fridericus Hiller von Gaertringen (ed.) (1906), *Inschriften von Priene*. Berlin: Reimer.
Karabel A
   Hawkins, John David (1998), "Tarkasnawa King of Mira', 'Tarkondemos', 'Boğazköy sealings and Karabel'". *Anatolian Studies* 48, 1–31.
Papazarkadas 2014, 233–247
   Papazarkadas, Nikolaos (2014), "Two new epigrams from Thebes". In: Nikolaos Papazarkadas (ed.), *The Epigraphy and History of Boeotia: New Finds, New Prospects*. Leiden: Brill, 223–251.
SEG: 21.527; 22.274; 28.495.2; 53.1373.6; 55.1320
   A. Chaniotis, T. Corsten, N. Papazarkadas, & R.A. Tybout (current ed.), *Supplementum Epigraphicum Graecum*. Last consulted on 26 May 2017.

Secondary sources

A'lam, Hūšang (1990), "Čenār". *Encyclopædia Iranica* Vol. 5 (2), 129–133.
A'lam, Hūšang (1994), "Derakt". *Encyclopædia Iranica* Vol. 7 (3), 316–319.
Agard, Walter R. (1966), "Boreas at Athens". *The Classical Journal* 61 (6), 241–246.
Ahn, Gregor (1992), *Religiöse Herrscherlegitimation im Achämenidischen Iran. Die Voraussetzungen und die Struktur ihrer Argumentation (Acta Iranica* 31). Leiden: Brill.
Albertz, Anuschka (2006), *Exemplarisches Heldentum. Die Rezeptionsgeschiche der Schlacht an den Thermopylen von der Antike bis zur Gegenwart*. Munich: R. Oldenbourg Verlag.
Alcock, Susan E. (1994), "Landscapes of Memory and the Authority of Pausanias". In: Jean Bingen (ed.), *Pausanias Historien*. Vandœuvres-Geneva: Fondation Hardt, 241–276.
Alcock, Susan E. (2002), *Archaeologies of the Greek Past: Landscape, Monuments and Memories*. Cambridge: Cambridge University Press.
Alexander, John. A. (1963), *Potidaea: Its History and Remains*. Athens: University of Georgia Press.
Allen, Lindsay (2005a), "Le roi imaginaire: An Audience with the Achaemenid King". In: Olivier Hekster & Richard Fowler (eds.), *Imaginary Kings: Royal Images in the Ancient Near East, Greece and Rome*. Stuttgart: Franz Steiner Verlag, 39–62.
Allen, Lindsay (2005b), *The Persian Empire*. Chicago: The University of Chicago Press.
Alónso-Núñez, José-Miguel (2003), "Herodotus' Concept of Historical Space and the Beginnings of Universal History". In: Peter Derow & Robert Parker (eds.), *Herodotus and his World: Essays from a Conference in Memory of George Forrest*. Oxford: Oxford University Press, 145–152.
Aly, Wolf (1969), *Volksmärchen, Sage und Novelle bei Herodot und seinen Zeitgenossen. Eine Untersuchung über die volkstümlichen Elemente der altgriechischen Prosaerzählung*. Göttingen: Vandenhoeck & Ruprecht (second edition, first published 1921).
Amandry, Pierre (1953), *La Colonne des Naxiens et le Portique des Athéniens (École française d'Athènes: Fouilles de Delphes. Tome II: Topographie et Architecture)*. Paris: Éditions de Boccard.
Amandry, Pierre (1972), "Les fouilles de l'antre corycien près de Delphes". *Comptes rendus des séances de l'Académie des Inscriptions et Belles-Lettres* 116 (2), 255–267.
Ambühl, Annemarie (2016), "Thessaly as an Intertextual Landscape of Civil War in Latin Poetry". In: Jeremy McInerney & Ineke Sluiter (eds.), *Valueing Landscape in Classical Antiquity: Natural Environment and Cultural Imagination*. Leiden: Brill, 297–322.
Ankersmit, Frank Rudolf (1994), *History and tropology: the rise and fall of metaphor*. Berkeley: University of California Press.
Antonaccio, Carla M. (1995), *An archeology of ancestors: tomb cult and hero cult in early Greece*. Lanham: Rowman & Littlefield Publishers.
Arafat, Karim (2013), ""Records of Hate": Pausanias and the Persians". In: Kostas Buraselis & Elias Koulakiotis (eds.), *Marathon: the Day After. Symposium Proceedings, Delphi 2–4 July 2010*. Delphi: European Cultural Centre of Delphi, 201–216.
Archaeological Society in Athens (1977), *Τὸ Ἔργον τῆς ἀρχαιολογικῆς Ἑταιρείας κατὰ τὸ 1976*. Athens.
Archaeological Society in Athens (1978), *Πρακτικὰ τῆς ἐν Ἀθήναις Ἀρχαιολογικῆς Ἑταιρείας κατὰ τοῦ ἔτους 1976: τεῦχος Α'*. Athens.
Archaeological Society in Athens (1979), *Τὸ Ἔργον τῆς ἀρχαιολογικῆς Ἑταιρείας κατὰ τὸ 1978*. Athens.
Archibald, Z.H. (1998), *The Odrysian Kingdom of Thrace: Orpheus Unmasked*. Oxford: Oxford University Pres.
Armayor, O. Kimball (1980), "Sesostris and Herodotus' Autopsy of Thrace, Colchis, Inland Asia Minor, and the Levant". *Harvard Studies in Classical Archaeology* 84, 51–74.
Asheri, David (1990), "Herodotus on Thracian Society and History". In: Giuseppe Nenci (ed.), *Hérodote et les peuples non Grecs*. Vandœuvres-Geneva: Fondation Hardt, 131–169.

Asheri, David (1998), "Platea vendetta delle Termopili: alle origini di un motivo teologico erodoteo". In: Marta Sordi (ed.), *Responsabilità perdono e vendetta nel mondo antico* (Contributi dell'Istituto di storia antica 24). Milan: Vita e Pensiero, 65–86.

Asheri, David, Vannicelli, Pietro, Corcella, Aldo & Fraschetti, Augusto (2006), *Erodoto, Le Storie. Volume IX. Libro IX, La battaglia di Platea*. Milan: Fondazione Lorenzo Valla & Arnoldo Mondadori Editore.

Asheri, David, Vannicelli, Pietro, Corcella, Aldo & Fraschetti, Augusto (2010), *Erodoto, Le Storie. Volume VIII. Libro VIII, La vittoria di Temistocle*. Milan: Fondazione Lorenzo Valla & Arnoldo Mondadori Editore (second edition, first published 2003).

Aslan, Rüstem & Bieg, Gerhard (2003), "Die mittel- bis spätbronzezeitliche Besiedlung (Troia VI und Troia VIIA) der Troas und der Gelibolu-Halbinsel. Ein Überblick". *Studia Troica* 13, 165–213.

Assmann, Jan (1988), "Kollektives Gedächtnis und kulturelle Identität". In: Jan Assmann & Tonio Hölscher (eds.), *Kultur und Gedächtnis*. Frankfurt am Main: Suhrkamp, 9–19.

Assmann, Jan (1992), *Das Kulturelle Gedächtnis. Schrift, Erinnerung und Politische Identität in frühen Hochkulturen*. Munich: C.H. Beck.

Assmann, Jan (1997), *Moses the Egyptian: The Memory of Egypt in Western Monotheism*. Cambridge, Massachusetts: Harvard University Press.

Aston, Emma (2006), "The Absence of Chiron". *The Classical Quarterly* 56 (2), 349–362.

Aston, Emma (2009), "Thetis and Cheiron in Thessaly". *Kernos* 22, 83–107.

Azaryahu, Maoz & Foote, Kenneth E. (2008), "Historical space as narrative medium: on the configuration of spatial narratives of time at historical sites". *GeoJournal* 73, 179–194.

Balcer, Jack Martin (1988), "Persian Occupied Thrace (Skudra)". *Historia: Zeitschrift für Alte Geschichte* 37 (1), 1–21.

Balcer, Jack Martin (1995), *The Persian conquest of the Greeks 545–450 BC*. Konstanz: Universitätsverlag Konstanz.

Balkan, Kemal (1959), "Inscribed Bullae from Daskyleion-Ergili". *Anatolia* 4, 123–128.

Baragwanath, Emily (2008), *Motivation and Narrative in Herodotus*. Oxford: Oxford University Press.

Barrington Atlas of the Greek and Roman World (2000), ed. by Richard Talbert. Princeton: Princeton University Press.

Barron, J.P. (1988), "The Liberation of Greece". In: John Boardman, N.G.L. Hammond, D.M. Lewis, M. Ostwald (eds.), *The Cambridge Ancient History, Volume IV: Persia, Greece and the Western Mediterranean c. 525 to 479 B.C.* Cambridge: Cambridge University Press, 592–622.

Barth, Hannelore (1968), "Zur Bewertung und Auswahl des Stoffes durch Herodot (Die Begriffe θῶμα, θωμάζω, θωμάσιος und θωμαστός)". *Klio* 50, 93–110.

Barthes, Roland (1984), *Essais critiques IV. Le bruissement de la langue*. Paris: Éditions du Seuil.

Bassi, Karen (2014), "Croesus' Offerings and the Value of the Past in Herodotus' *Histories*". In: James Ker & Cristoph Pieper (eds.), *Valuing the past in the Greco-Roman world: proceedings from the Penn-Leiden Colloquia on Ancient Values VII*. Leiden: Brill, 174–196.

Bayer, Erich (1969), "Psyttaleia". *Historia: Zeitschrift für Alte Geschichte* 18 (5), 640.

Bearzot, Cinzia (1989), "Fenomeni naturali e prodigi nell'attacco celtico a Delfi (279 a.C.)". In: Marta Sordi (ed.), *Fenomeni naturali e avvenimenti storici nell'antichità*. Milan: Vita e Pensiero, 71–86.

Beekes, Robert S.P. (2010), *Etymological Dictionary of Greek*. Leiden: Brill.

Beloch, Karl Julius (1908), "Die Schlacht bei Salamis". *Klio* 8, 477–486.

Bengtson, Hermann (1965), *Griechen und Perser, Die Mittelmeerwelt im Altertum I*. Frankfurt am Main: Fischer Bücherei.

Béquignon, Y. (1934), "Recherches archéologiques dans la vallée du Spercheios". *Revue Archéologique* 6 (4), 14–33.

Berlin, Andrea M. (2002), "Ilion before Alexander: a Fourth-Century B.C. Ritual Deposit". *Studia Troica* 12, 131–166.

Bernabé, Albert (1987), *Poetarum epicorum Graecorum testimonia et fragmenta*. Leipzig: Teubner.
Beschi, L. (2002), "I trofei di Maratona e Salamina e le colonne del Pireo". *Rendiconti dell'Accademia nazionale dei Lincei. Classe di Scienze morali, storiche e filologiche* 9.13 (1), 51–94.
Bettalli, Marco (2009), "I trofei sui campi di battaglia nel mondo greco". *Mélanges de l'École française de Rome : antiquité* 121 (2), 363–371.
Beyer, Immo (1977), "Die Datierung der grossen Reliefgiebel des alten Athentempels der Akropolis". *Archäologischer Anzeiger* 1977 (1), 44–74.
Bieg, Gebhard (2006), "Archäologie und Geschichte einer Landschaft – Die Troas von der griechischen Kolonisation bis in die byzantinische Zeit". In: Manfred Osman Korfmann (ed.), *Troia: Archäologie eines Siedlungshügels und seiner Landschaft*. Mainz am Rhein: Verlag Philipp von Zabern, 361–372.
Bigwood, J.M. (1978), "Ctesias as Historian of the Persian Wars". *Phoenix* 32 (1), 19–41.
Birge, Darice (1994), "Trees in the landscape of Pausanias' *Periegesis*". In: Susan E. Alcock & Robin Osborne (eds.), *Placing the Gods: Sanctuaries and Sacred Space in Ancient Greece*. Oxford: Clarendon Press, 231–245.
Bischoff, Heinrich (1932), *Der Warner bei Herodot*. Borna-Leipzig: Universitätsverlag von Robert Noske.
Bleckmann, Bruno (2007), "Ktesias von Knidos und die Perserkriege: Historische Varianten zu Herodot". In: Bruno Bleckmann (ed.), *Herodot und die Epoche der Perserkriege: Realitäten und Fiktionen. Kolloquium zum 80. Geburtstag von Dietmar Kienast*. Cologne: Böhlau Verlag, 138–150.
Blegen, Elizabeth Pierce (1939), "News Items from Athens". *American Journal of Archaeology* 43 (4), 696–700.
Blok, Josine (1995), *The Early Amazons: Modern and Ancient Perspectives on a Persistent Myth*. Leiden: Brill.
Boardman, John (2002), *The Archaeology of Nostalgia: How the Greeks re-created their mythical past*. London: Thames & Hudson.
Boedeker, Deborah (1988), "Protesilaos and the End of Herodotus' "Histories"". *Classical Antiquity* 7 (1), 30–48.
Boedeker, Deborah (2001a), "Heroic Historiography: Simonides and Herodotus on Plataea". In: Deborah Boedeker & David Sider (eds.), *The New Simonides: Contexts of Praise and Desire*. Oxford: Oxford University Press, 120–134.
Boedeker, Deborah (2001b), "Paths to Heroization at Plataea". In: Deborah Boedeker & David Sider (eds.), *The New Simonides: Contexts of Praise and Desire*. Oxford: Oxford University Press, 148–163.
Boedeker, Deborah (2002), "Epic Heritage and Mythical Patterns in Herodotus". In: Egbert J. Bakker, Irene J.F. de Jong & Hans van Wees (eds.), *Brill's Companion to Herodotus*. Leiden: Brill, 97–116.
Boedeker, Deborah (2007), "The View from Eleusis: Demeter in the Persian Wars". In: Emma Bridges, Edith Hall & P. J. Rhodes (eds.) *Cultural Responses to the Persian Wars: Antiquity to the Third Millennium*. Oxford: Oxford University Press, 65–82.
Bommelaer, Jean-François (1991), *Guide de Delphes : le site*. Paris: Éditions de Boccard.
Borgeaud, Philippe (1995), "Note sur le Sépias. Mythe et histoire". *Kernos* 8, 23–29.
Borthwick, E.K (1970), "Aristophanes, *Acharnians* 709: An old Crux, and a New Solution". *Bulletin of the Institute of Classical Studies* 17, 107–110.
Boter, Gerard (2007), "Utopia". *Lampas* 40 (4), 343–352.
Boteva, Dilyana (2011), "Re-reading Herodotus on the Persian Campaigns in Thrace". In: Robert Rollinger, Brigitte Truschnegg & Reinhold Bichler (eds.), *Herodot und das Persische Weltreich. Akten des 3. Internationalen Kolloquiums zum Thema Vorderasien im Spannungsfeld klassischer und altorientalischer Überlieferungen, Innsbruck, 24.-28. November 2008*. Wiesbaden: Harrassowitz Verlag, 735–759.

Boucher, Colonel Arthur (1915), "La bataille de Platées d'après Hérodote". *Revue Archéologique* 5 (2), 257–320.
Bousquet, Jean (1960), "La destination de la Tholos de Delphes". *Revue Historique* 223 (2), 287–298.
Bousquet, Jean (1963), "Inscriptions de Delphes". *Bulletin de correspondance hellénique* 87 (1), 188–208.
Bovon, Anne (1963), "La représentation des guerriers perses et la notion de Barbare dans la première moitié du Ve siècle". *Bulletin de correspondance hellénique* 87 (2), 579–602.
Bowen, Anthony (1998), "The Place That Beached a Thousand Ships". *The Classical Quarterly* 48 (2), 345–364.
Bowden, Hugh (2010), *Mystery Cults in the Ancient World*. London: Thames & Hudson.
Bowie, A.M. (2007), *Herodotus: Histories Book VIII*. Cambridge: Cambridge University Press.
Bowie, A.M. (2012), "Mythology and the Expedition of Xerxes". In: Emily Baragwanath & Mathieu de Bakker (eds.), *Myth, Truth, and Narrative in Herodotus*. Oxford: Oxford University Press, 269–287.
Bowra, C.M. (1933), "Simonides on the Fallen of Thermopylae". *Classical Philology* 28 (4), 277–281
Boyce, Mary (1982), *A History of Zoroastrianism. Volume II: Under the Achaemenians*. Leiden & Cologne: Brill.
Brall-Tuchel, Helmut (2003), "Das Herz des Königs: Karl der Große, Roland und die Schlacht". In: Gerd Krumeich & Susanne Brandt (eds.), *Schlachtenmythen: Ereignis – Erzählung – Erinnerung*. Cologne: Böhlau Verlag, 33–62.
Brenza, Fabrizio (2004), "Trümmerromantik als Touristenziel? Kaiserliche Troia-Besuche in Antike und Neuzeit". In: Heinz Hofmann (ed.), *Troia: Von Homer bis heute*. Tübingen: Attempto Verlag, 101–117.
Briant, Pierre (1989), "Histoire et idéologie. Les Grecs et la "décadence perse"". In: Marie-Madeleine Mactoux & Evelyne Geny (eds.), *Mélanges Pierre Lévêque 2: Anthropologie et société*. Paris: Belles Lettres, 33–47.
Briant, Pierre (1996), *Histoire de l'empire perse de Cyrus à Alexandre*. Paris: Fayard.
Briant, Pierre (1999), "The Achaemenid Empire". In: Kurt Raaflaub & Nathan Rosenstein (eds.), *War and Society in the Ancient and Medieval Worlds: Asia, The Mediterranean, Europe, and Mesoamerica*. Washington, D.C.: Center for Hellenic Studies Trustees for Harvard University.
Briant, Pierre (2003), "À propos du roi-jardinier : remarques sur l'histoire d'un dossier documentaire". In: Wouter Henkelman & Amélie Kuhrt (eds.), *Achaemenid History XIII: A Persian Perspective: Essays in Memory of Heleen Sancisi-Weerdenburg*. Leiden: Nederlands Instituut voor het Nabije Oosten, 33–49.
Bridges, Emma (2015), *Imagining Xerxes: Ancient Perspectives on a Persian King*. London: Bloomsbury.
Briquel, D. & Desnier, J.-L. (1983), "Le passage de l'Hellespont par Xerxès". *Bulletin de l'Association Guillaume Budé* 1983, 22–30.
Brock, Roger (2003), "Authorial Voice and Narrative Management in Herodotus". In: Peter Derow & Robert Parker (eds.), *Herodotus and his World: Essays from a Conference in Memory of George Forrest*. Oxford: Oxford University Press, 3–16.
Brock, Roger (2004), "Political Imagery in Herodotus". In: Vassos Karageorghis & Ioannis Taifacos (eds.), *The World of Herodotus: Proceedings of an International Conference held at the Foundation Anastasios G. Leventis, Nicosia, September 18–21, 2003 and organized by the Foundation Anastasios G. Leventis and the Faculty of Letters, University of Cyprus*. Nicosia: Foundation Anastasios G. Leventis, 169–177.
Broneer, Oscar (1933), "Excavations on the North Slope of the Acropolis in Athens, 1931–1932". *Hesperia* 2 (3), 329–417.

Broneer, Oscar (1935), "Excavations on the North Slope of the Acropolis in Athens, 1933–1934". *Hesperia* 4 (2), 109–188.
Broneer, Oscar & Pease, M.Z. (1936), "The Cave on the East Slope of the Acropolis". *Hesperia* 5 (2), 247–272.
Broneer, Oscar (1944), "The Tent of Xerxes and the Greek Theater". *University of California Publications in Classical Archaeology* 1 (12), 305–312.
Bundgaard, J. A. (1976), *Parthenon and the Mycenaean City on the Heights*. Copenhagen: The National Museum of Denmark.
Buresch, Karl (1898), *Aus Lydien: epigraphisch-geographische Reisefrüchte*. Leipzig: Teubner.
Burn, Anthony R. (1962), *Persia and the Greeks: the Defence of the West, c. 546–478 B.C.* London: Edward Arnold.
Bursian, Conrad (1862), *Geographie von Griechenland. Erster Band: das nördliche Griechenland*. Leipzig: B.G. Teubner.
Bury, J.B. (1897), "The European Expedition of Darius". *The Classical Review* 11 (6), 277–282.
Butler, Howard Crosby (1925), *Sardis: Publications of the American Society for the Excavation of Sardis, Volume II: Architecture, Part I: the Temple of Artemis*. Leiden: Brill.
Buxton, Richard (1994), *Imaginary Greece: The contexts of mythology*. Cambridge: Cambridge University Press.
Cahen, Émile (1924), "Sur quelques traits du récit de «Salamine» dans les «Perses» d'Eschyle". *Revue des Études Anciennes* 26 (4), 297–313.
Cahill, Nicholas (2010), "Sardeis'te Pers Tahribi / The Persian Sack of Sardis". In: Nicholas Cahill (ed.), *Lidyalılar ve Dünyaları / The Lydians and Their World*. Istanbul: Yapi Kredi Kültür Merkezi, 339–361.
Calder, W.M. (1925), "The Royal Road in Herodotus". *The Classical Review* 39 (1 and 2), 7–11.
Calmeyer, Peter (1974), "Zur Genese altiranischer Motive II. Der leere Wagen". *Archäologische Mitteilungen aus Iran* (new series) 7, 49–77.
Camia, Francesco (2010), "La Calcoteca". In: Emanuele Greco (ed.), *Topografia di Atene: Sviluppo urbano e monumenti dalle origini al III secolo d.C. Tomo 1: Acropoli - Areopago - Tra Acropoli e Pnice*. Athens & Paestum: Pandemos, 94–95.
Carpenter, Rhys (1970), *The Architects of the Parthenon*. Middlesex: Penguin Books.
Cartledge, Paul (2002), *The Greeks: A Portrait of Self & Others*. Oxford: Oxford University Press (second edition, first published 1993).
Cartledge, Paul (2006), *Thermopylae: The Battle that Changed the World*. Woodstock & New York: The Overlook Press.
Cartledge, Paul (2013), *After Thermopylae: The Oath of Plataea and the End of the Graeco-Persian Wars*. Oxford: Oxford University Press.
Caspari, M.O.B. (1911), "Stray Notes on the Persian Wars". *The Journal of Hellenic Studies* 31, 100–109.
Casson, Stanley (1914), "The Persian Expedition to Delphi". *The Classical Review* 28 (5), 145–151.
Casson, Stanley (1926), *Macedonia, Thrace and Illyria: Their relations to Greece from the earliest times down to the time of Philip son of Amyntas*. Oxford: Oxford University Press.
Cataudella, Michele (1998), "Vendetta e imperialismo nella monarchia achemenide". In: Marta Sordi (ed.), *Responsabilità perdono e vendetta nel mondo antico* (*Contributi dell'Istituto di storia antica* 24). Milan: Vita e Pensiero, 47–63.
Cawkwell, George (2005), *The Greek Wars: The Failure of Persia*. Oxford: Oxford University Press.
Champion, Craige (1995), "The Soteria at Delphi: Aetolian Propaganda in the Epigraphical Record". *The American Journal of Philology* 116 (2), 213–220.
Charbonneaux, J. (1925), *La Tholos* (*École française d'Athènes : Fouilles de Delphes: Topographie et Architecture : Le Sanctuaire d'Athèna Pronaia*). Paris: Éditions de Boccard.

Cherf, William J. (2001), "Thermopylai. Myth and Reality in 480 BC". In: Dietrich Papenfuß & Volker Michael Strocka (eds.), *Gab es das Griechische Wunder? Griechenland zwischen dem Ende des 6. und der Mitte des 5. Jahrhunderts v. Chr.* Mainz: Verlag Philipp von Zabern, 355–363.
Christ, Matthew R. (1994), "Herodotean Kings and Historical Inquiry". *Classical Antiquity* 13 (2), 167–202.
Christien, Jacqueline & Le Tallec, Yohann (2013), *Léonidas. Histoire et mémoire d'un sacrifice*. Paris: Ellipses.
Churchill Semple, Ellen (1927), "The Templed Promontories of the Ancient Mediterranean". *Geographical Review* 17 (3), 353–386.
Churchin, Leonard A. (1995), "The Unburied Dead at Thermopylae (279 B.C.)". *The Ancient History Bulletin* 9 (2), 68–71.
Clairmont, Cristopher W. (1983), *Patrios Nomos: Public Burial in Athens during the Fifth and fourth Centuries B.C.* Oxford: B.A.R.
Clark, R.T. (1917), "The Campaign of Plataiai". *Classical Philology* 12 (1), 30–48.
Cobet, Justus (2002), "The Organization of Time in the *Histories*". In: Egbert J. Bakker, Irene J.F. de Jong & Hans van Wees (eds.), *Brill's Companion to Herodotus*. Leiden: Brill, 387–412.
Cobet, Justus (2010), "Troia – die Suche nach der 'Stadt des Priamos'". In: Elke Stein-Hölkeskamp & Karl-Joachim Hölkeskamp (eds.), *Erinnerungsorte der Antike: die griechische Welt*. Munich: C.H. Beck, 39–60.
Cole, Susan Guettel (1994), "Demeter in the Ancient Greek City and its Countryside". In: Susan E. Alcock & Robin Osborne (eds.), *Placing the Gods: Sanctuaries and Sacred Space in Ancient Greece*. Oxford: Clarendon Press, 199–216.
Cole, Sousan Guettel (2000), "Landscapes of Artemis". *The Classical World* 93 (5), 471–481.
Connelly, Joan Breton (2014), *The Parthenon Enigma*. New York: Alfred A. Knopf.
Cook, John Manuel (1973), *The Troad: An Achaeological and Topographical Study*. Oxford: Oxford University Press.
Cook, John Manuel (1983), *The Persian Empire*. London: J.M. Dent & Sons.
Crang, Mike & Travlou, Penny C. (2001), "The city and topologies of memory". *Environment and Planning D: Society and Space* 19, 161–177.
Culley, Gerald R. (1977), "The Restoration of Sanctuaries in Attica, II". *Hesperia* 46 (3), 282–298.
Cuyler Young Jr., T. (1980), "480/479 B.C. – A Persian Perspective". *Iranica Antiqua* 15, 213–239.
Dalley, Stephanie (2003), "Why did Herodotus not Mention the Hanging Gardens of Babylon?". In: Peter Derow & Robert Parker (eds.), *Herodotus and his World: Essays from a Conference in Memory of George Forrest*. Oxford: Oxford University Press, 171–189.
Dandamaev, M.A. (1989), *A Political History of the Achaemenid Empire*. Leiden: E.J. Brill. Translated by W.J. Vogelsang.
Danov, Christo M. (1976), *Altthrakien*. Berlin: Walter de Gruyter. Translated by Gerda Minkova.
Daux, Georges (1936), *Pausanias à Delphes*. Paris: Éditions A. Picard.
Daux, Georges (1959), "Inscriptions de Delphes". *Bulletin de Correspondence Hellénique* 83 (2), 466–495.
de Bakker, Mathieu (2010), "Oosterse helden in Herodotus' *Historiën*". *Lampas* 43, 219–234.
de Haan, Nathalie (2007), "Forum Romanum". *Lampas* 40 (4), 371–380.
de Jong, Albert (1997), *Traditions of the Magi: Zoroastrianism in Greek and Latin Literature*. Leiden: Brill.
de Jong, Irene J.F. (1999), "Aspects narratologique des Histories d'Hérodote". *Lalies* 19, 219–277.
de Jong, Irene J.F. (2001), "The Anachronical Structure of Herodotus' *Histories*". In: S.J. Harrison (ed.), *Texts, Ideas, and the Classics: Scholarship, Theory, and Classical Literature*. Oxford: Oxford University Press, 93–116.

de Jong, Irene J.F. (2012), "Introduction. Narratological Theory on Space". In: Irene J.F. de Jong (ed.), *Space in Ancient Greek Literature: Studies in Ancient Greek Narrative*. Leiden: Brill, 1–18.

de Jong, Irene J.F. (forthcoming), "The View from the Mountain (oroskopia) in Greek and Latin Literature". *Cambridge Classical Journal*.

de Sélincourt, Aubrey (1967), *Die Welt Herodots*. Wiesbaden: F.A. Brockhaus. Translated from the English original *The World of Herodotus* (1962) by Helmuth Eggert.

Decourt, Jean-Claude (1990), *La Vallée de l'Énipeus en Thessalie. Études de Topographie et de Géographie antique* (Bulletin de Correspondance Hellénique Supplément 21). Athens: École française d'Athènes.

Decourt, Jean-Claude, Nielsen, T.H. & Helly, B. (2004), "Thessalia and Adjacent Regions". In: M.H. Hansen, & T.H. Nielsen (eds.), *An Inventory of Archaic and Classical Poleis: an Investigation Conducted by the Copenhagen Polis Centre for the Danish National Research Foundation*. Oxford: Oxford University Press, 676–731.

Defradas, Jean (1954), *Les thèmes de la propagande delphique*. Paris: Librairie C. Klincksieck.

della Dora, Veronica (2009), "Mythological Landscape and Landscape of Myth: Circulating Visions of Pre-Christian Athos". In: Gary Backhaus & John Murungi (eds.), *Symbolic Landscapes*. Dordrecht & London: Springer, 109–131.

Demandt, Alexander (2002), *Über allen Wipfeln: der Baum in der Kulturgeschichte*. Cologne: Böhlau.

Demangel, R. (1926a), *Le Sanctuaire d'Athèna Pronaia (Marmaria) : Topographie du Sanctuaire* (École française d'Athènes : Fouilles de Delphes). Paris: Éditions de Boccard.

Demangel, R. (1926b), *Le Tumulus dit de Protésilas*. Paris: Éditions de Boccard.

Der Neue Pauly: Enzyklopädie der Antike. Ed. by Hubert Cancik (1996–2010). Stuttgart: Metzler.

Desnier, J.-L. (1995), *"Le Passage du Fleuve" de Cyrus le Grand à Julien l'Apostat. Essai sur la légitimité du souverain*. Paris: Éditions L'Harmattan.

Deubner, Ludwig (1932), *Attische Feste*. Berlin: Verlag Heinrich Keller.

Dewald, Carolyn (1993), "Reading the World: The Interpretation of Objects in Herodotus' *Histories*". In: Ralph M. Rosen & Joseph Farrell (eds.), *Nomodeiktes: Greek Studies in Honor of Martin Ostwald*. Ann Arbor: The University of Michigan Press, 55–70.

Dewald, Carolyn & Marincola, John (2006), "Introduction". In: Carolyn Dewald & John Marincola (eds.), *The Cambridge Companion to Herodotus*. Cambridge: Cambridge University Press, 1–12.

Dewing, Henry B. (1924), "Argonautic Associations of the Bosporus". *The Classical Journal* 19 (8), 469–483.

Di Cesare, Riccardo (2010) "Lo stereobate sotto il Partenone e l'Architettura H". In: Emanuele Greco (ed.), *Topografia di Atene: Sviluppo urbano e monumenti dalle origini al III secolo d.C. Tomo 1: Acropoli - Areopago - Tra Acropoli e Pnice*. Athens & Paestum: Pandemos, 96–101.

Dijkstra, Tamara M., van Rookhuijzen, Jan Zacharias & Kamphorst, Sjoukje M. (2017) "Investigating ancient Halos: Marking forty years of archaeological research on a city in Thessaly". *Bulletin Antieke Beschaving* (Babesch) 92, 145–158.

Dillery, John (1996), "Reconfiguring the Past: Thyrea, Thermopylae and Narrative Patterns in Herodotus". *American Journal of Philology* 117 (2), 217–254.

Dillon, Matthew (1997), *Pilgrims and Pilgrimage in Ancient Greece*. London & New York: Routledge.

Dinsmoor, William Bell Jr. (1980), *The Propylaia to the Athenian Akropolis. Volume I: The Predecessors*. Princeton: The American School of Classical Studies at Athens.

Domínguez Monedero, Adolfo J. (2013), "The Late Archaic Period". In: José Pasqual & Maria-Foteini Papakonstantinou (eds.), *Topography and History of Ancient Epicnemidian Locris*. Leiden: Brill, 445–470.

Dontas, George S. (1983), "The True Aglaurion". *Hesperia* 52 (1), 48–63.

Dörpfeld, Wilhelm (1885), "Der alte Athena-Tempel auf der Akropolis zu Athen". *Mitteilungen des kaiserlich deutschen archäologischen Instituts, athenische Abteilung* 10, 275–277.
Dörpfeld, Wilhelm (1886), "Der alte Athenatempel auf der Akropolis". *Mitteilungen des kaiserlich deutschen archäologischen Instituts, athenische Abteilung* 11, 337–351.
Dörpfeld, Wilhelm & Petersen, Eugen (1887), "Der alte Athenatempel auf der Akropolis. II. Baugeschichte". *Mitteilungen des kaiserlich deutschen archäologischen Instituts, athenische Abteilung* 12, 25–72.
Dörpfeld, Wilhelm (1892), "Der ältere Parthenon". *Mitteilungen des kaiserlich deutschen archäologischen Instituts, athenische Abteilung* 17, 158–189.
Dörpfeld, Wilhelm (1902), "Die Zeit des älteren Parthenons". *Mitteilungen des kaiserlich deutschen archäologischen Instituts, athenische Abteilung* 27, 379–416.
Draycott, Catherine M. (2011), "Funerary or Military Convoy? Thoughts on the Tatarlı Convoy Painting and Meaning of 'Graeco-Persian' Convoys". In: Lâtife Summerer, Askold Ivantchik & Alexander von Kienlin (eds.), *Kelainai-Apameia Kibotos: Stadtentwicklung im anatolischen Kontext. Akten des internationalen Kolloquiums, München, 2.-4. April 2009*. Bordeaux: Ausonius Éditions, 55–61.
Drews, Robert (1973), *The Greek Accounts of Eastern History*. Washington D.C.: Center for Hellenic Studies.
duBois, Page (1982), *Centaurs & Amazons: Women and the Pre-History of the Great Chain of Being*. Ann Arbor: The University of Michigan Press.
Dumortier, Jean (1963), "La retraite de Xerxès après Salamine". *Revue des études grecques* 76, 358–360.
Dusinberre, Elspeth R.M. (2003), *Aspects of Empire in Achaemenid Sardis*. Cambridge: Cambridge University Press.
Dusinberre, Elspeth R.M. (2013), *Empire, authority, and autonomy in Achaemenid Anatolia*. Cambridge: Cambridge University Press.
Eastwick, Edward B. (1864), *Journal of a Diplomate's Three Years' Residence in Persia*. London: Smith, Elder and Co.
École française d'Athènes (1991), *Guide de Delphes : Le Musée*. Paris: Éditions de Boccard.
Eckstein, Felix (1989), "Bosporos und Hellespontos bei Herodot". *Anadolu* 22, 317–27.
Edmonson, Colin N. (1964), "Κοίτη Ἀκταίωνος". *The Journal of Hellenic Studies* 84, 153–155.
Efstathiou, A., Malakasioti, Z. & H.R. Reinders (1991), "Een survey in het gebied ten noorden van hellenistisch Halos (Griekenland)". *PaleoAktueel* 2, 82–86.
Eibl, Kordula (2007), "H. G. Lollings Forschungen am Artemision in Nordeuböa 1877 bis 1883 – eine Auswertung der nachgelassenen Aufzeichnungen im Archiv des DAI Athen". In: Klaus Fittschen (ed.), *Historische Landeskunde und Epigraphik in Griechenland. Akten des Symposiums veranstaltet aus Anlaß des 100. Todestages von H. G. Lolling (1848–1894) in Athen vom 28. bis 30. 9. 1994*. Münster: Deutsches Archäologisches Institut, 227–267.
Elayi, J. (1978), "Le rôle de l'oracle de Delphes dans le conflit gréco-perse d'après «les Histoires» d'Hérodote: 1re partie". *Iranica Antiqua* 13, 94–118.
Elayi, J. (1979), "Le rôle de l'oracle de Delphes dans le conflit gréco-perse d'après «les Histoires» d'Hérodote (Suite)". *Iranica Antiqua* 14, 67–151.
Ellinger, Pierre (1993), *La légende nationale phocidienne. Artémis, les situations extrêmes et les récits de guerre d'anéantissement (Bulletin de correspondance hellénique supplément 27)*. Athens: École française d'Athènes.
Elsner, Jaś (2003). "Iconoclasm and the Preservation of Memory". In: Robert S. Nelson & Margaret Olin (ed.), *Monuments and Memory, Made and Unmade*. Chicago & London: The University of Chicago Press, 209–231.
Erbse, Hartmut (1992), *Studien zum Verständnis Herodots*. Berlin & New York: Walter de Gruyter.

Erskine, Andrew (2001), *Troy between Greece and Rome: Local Tradition and Imperial Power*. Oxford: Oxford University Press.
Evans, James Allan Stewart (1969), "Notes on Thermopylae and Artemisium". *Historia: Zeitschrift für Alte Geschichte* 18 (4), 389–406.
Evans, James Allan Stewart (1991), *Herodotus, Explorer of the Past: Three Essays*. Princeton: Princeton University Press.
Fabricius, Ernst (1926), review of "Das hellenische Thessalien: landeskundliche und geschichtliche Beschreibung Thessaliens in der hellenischen und römischen Zeit" by Friedrich Stählin. *Gnomon* 2 (1), 11–15.
Fairbanks, Arthur (1906), "Herodotus and the Oracle at Delphi". *The Classical Journal* 1 (2), 37–48.
Fehling, Detlev (1971), *Die Quellenangaben bei Herodot: Studien zur Erzählkunst Herodots*. Berlin: Walter de Gruyter.
Feifer, Maxine (1985), *Going Places: The Ways of the Tourist from Imperial Rome to the Present Day*. London: MacMillan.
Felsch, Rainer C.S., Kienast, Hermann J. & Schuler, Heinz (1980), "Apollon und Artemis oder Artemis und Apollon? Bericht von den Grabungen im neu entdeckten Heiligtum bei Kalapodi 1973 – 1977". *Archäologischer Anzeiger* 1980 (1), 38–123.
Felsch, Rainer C.S., Jacob-Felsch, Margrit, Hübner, Gerhild, Nitsche, Andreas, Salta, Maria & Ellinger, Pierre (1987), "Kalapodi: Bericht über die Grabungen im Heiligtum der Artemis Elaphebolos und des Apollon von Hyampolis 1978 – 1982". *Archäologischer Anzeiger* 1987 (1), 1–99.
Felsch, Rainer C.S. (ed.) (1996), *Kalapodi. Ergebnisse der Ausgrabungen im Heiligtum der Artemis und des Apollon von Hyampolis in der antiken Phokis. Band I*. Mainz am Rhein: Verlag Philipp von Zabern.
Felsch, Rainer C.S. (ed.) (2007), *Kalapodi. Ergebnisse der Ausgrabungen im Heiligtum der Artemis und des Apollon von Hyampolis in der antiken Phokis. Band II*. Mainz am Rhein: Verlag Philipp von Zabern.
Fentress, James & Wickham, Chris (1992), *Social Memory*. Oxford: Blackwell.
Ferrari, Gloria (2002), "The Ancient Temple on the Acropolis of Athens". *American Journal of Archaeology* 106 (1), 11–35.
Ferrill, Arthur (1966), "Herodotus and the Strategy and Tactics of the Invasion of Xerxes". *The American Historical Review* 72 (1), 102–115.
FGE = Denys L. Page (1981), *Further Greek Epigrams: Epigrams before AD 50 from the Greek Anthology and other sources, not included in 'Hellenistic Epigrams' or 'The Garland of Philip'*. Cambridge: Cambridge University Press.
FGrH = Felix Jacoby (1923), *Die Fragmente der griechischen Historiker*. Berlin: Weidmann.
Fingarette, Ann (1970), "The Marmaria Puzzles". *American Journal of Archaeology* 74 (4), 401–404.
Finkelberg, Margalit (2014), "Boreas and Oreithyia: a case-study in multichannel transmission of myth". In Ruth Scodel (ed.), *Between Orality and Literacy: Communication and Adaptation in Antiquity*. Leiden: Brill, 87–100.
Flory, Stewart (1987), *The Archaic Smile of Herodotus*. Detroit: Wayne State University Press.
Flower, Harriet I. (2013), "Herodotus and the Delphic traditions about Croesus". In: Rosaria Vignolo Munson (ed.), *Herodotus: Volume 1. Herodotus and the Narrative of the Past*. Oxford: Oxford University Press, 124–153.
Flower, Michael A. (1998), "Simonides, Ephorus, and Herodotus on the Battle of Thermopylae". *The Classical Quarterly* 48 (2), 365–379.
Flower, Michael A. & Marincola, John (2002), *Herodotus: Histories Book IX*. Cambridge: Cambridge University Press.
Fontenrose, Joseph (1969), "Daulis at Delphi". *California Studies in Classical Antiquity* 2, 107–144.

Fornara, Charles W. (1966), "The Hoplite Achievement at Psyttaleia". *The Journal of Hellenic Studies* 86, 51–54.
Forsdyke, Sara (2006), "Political history and political thought". In: Carolyn Dewald & John Marincola (eds.), *The Cambridge Companion to Herodotus*. Cambridge: Cambridge University Press, 224–241.
Förtsch, Reinhard (2001), *Kunstverwendung und Kunstlegitimation im archaischen und frühklassischen Sparta*. Mainz: Verlag Philipp von Zabern.
Foucart, Paul (1879), "Inscriptions archaïques de Thèbes". *Bulletin de correspondance hellénique* 3, 139–143.
Foucart, Paul (1918), *Le culte des héros chez les Grecs*. Paris: C. Klincksieck, Libraire.
Fowler, Robert (2003), "Herodotos and Athens". In: Peter Derow & Robert Parker (eds.), *Herodotus and his World: Essays from a Conference in Memory of George Forrest*. Oxford: Oxford University Press, 305–318.
Fowler, Robert (2006), "Herodotus and his Prose Predecessors". In: Carolyn Dewald & John Marincola (eds.), *The Cambridge Companion to Herodotus*. Cambridge: Cambridge University Press, 29–45.
Fowler, Robert (2013), "Herodotus and his contemporaries". In: Rosaria Vignolo Munson (ed.), *Herodotus: Volume 1. Herodotus and the Narrative of the Past*. Oxford: Oxford University Press, 46–83.
Franchi, Elena & Proietti, Giorgia (2015), "Guerra e memoria. Paradigmi antichi e moderni, tra polemologia e *memory studies*". In: Elena Franchi & Giorgia Proietti (eds.), *Guerra e memoria nel mondo antico*. Trento: Università degli Studi di Trento, 17–125.
Francis, E.D. & Vickers, Michael (1988), "The Agora Revisited: Athenian Chronology c. 500–450 BC". *The Annual of the British School at Athens* 83, 143–167.
French, David (1998), "Pre- and Early-Roman Roads of Asia Minor. The Persian Royal Road". *Iran* 36, 15–43.
Frickenhaus, August (1910), "Heilige Stätten in Delphi". *Mitteilungen des kaiserlich deutschen archäologischen Instituts, athenische Abteilung* 35, 235–273.
Friedman, Rachel (2006), "Location and dislocation in Herodotus". In: Carolyn Dewald & John Marincola (eds.), *The Cambridge Companion to Herodotus*. Cambridge: Cambridge University Press, 165–177.
Frost, Frank J. (1973), "A Note on Xerxes at Salamis". *Historia: Zeitschrift für Alte Geschichte* 22 (1), 118–119.
Frost, Frank J. (1978), "Troizen and the Persian War: Some New Data". *American Journal of Archaeology*, 82 (1), 105–107.
Funke, Peter (2004), "Herodotus and the Major Sanctuaries of the Greek World". In: Vassos Karageorghis & Ioannis Taifacos (eds.), *The World of Herodotus: Proceedings of an International Conference held at the Foundation Anastasios G. Leventis, Nicosia, September 18–21, 2003 and organized by the Foundation Anastasios G. Leventis and the Faculty of Letters, University of Cyprus*. Nicosia: Foundation Anastasios G. Leventis, 159–167.
Funke, Peter (2007), "Die Perser und die Griechische Heiligtümer in der Perserkriegszeit". In: Bruno Bleckmann (ed.), *Herodot und die Epoche der Perserkriege: Realitäten und Fiktionen. Kolloquium zum 80. Geburtstag von Dietmar Kienast*. Cologne: Böhlau Verlag, 21–34.
Furtwängler, Adolf (1893), *Meisterwerke der griechischen Plastik. Kunstgeschichtliche Untersuchungen*. Leipzig & Berlin: Verlag von Giesecke & Devrient.
Gabriel, Utta (2006), "Ein Blick zurück – Das fünfte Jahrtausend vor Christus in der Troas". In: Manfred Osman Korfmann (ed.), *Troia: Archäologie eines Siedlungshügels und seiner Landschaft*. Mainz am Rhein: Verlag Philipp von Zabern, 355–360.
Gammie, John G. (1986), "Herodotus on Kings and Tyrants: Objective Historiography or Conventional Portraiture?". *Journal of Near Eastern Studies* 45 (3), 171–195.

Gantz. Timothy (1996), *Early Greek Myth: A Guide to Literary and Artistic Sources*. Baltimore: The Johns Hopkins University Press.
Gardner, Ernest Arthur (1896), *A Handbook of Greek Sculpture*. London: MacMillan and Co.
Gauer, Werner (1968), *Weihgeschenke aus den Perserkriegen (Istanbuler Mitteilungen, Beiheft* 2). Tübingen: Ernst Wasmuth Verlag.
Gehrke, Hans-Joachim (1990), review of "Topographischer Bildkommentar zu den Historien Herodots: Griechenland im Umfang des heutigen griechischen Staatsgebiets" by Dietram Müller. *Gnomon* 62 (5), 385–393.
Gehrke, Hans-Joachim (2001), "Myth, History, and Collective Identity: Uses of the Past in Ancient Greece and Beyond". In: Nino Luraghi (ed.), *The Historian's Craft in the Age of Herodotus*. Oxford: Oxford University Press, 286–313.
Gehrke, Hans-Joachim (2003), "Marathon (490 v. Chr.) als Mythos: Von Helden und Barbaren". In: Gerd Krumeich & Susanne Brandt (eds.), *Schlachtenmythen: Ereignis – Erzählung – Erinnerung*. Cologne: Böhlau Verlag, 19–32.
Gehrke, Hans-Joachim (2010), "Greek Representations of the Past". In: Lin Foxhall, Hans-Joachim Gehrke & Nino Luraghi (eds.), *Intentional History: Spinning Time in Ancient Greece*. Stuttgart: Franz Steiner Verlag, 15–33.
Georges, Pericles B. (1986), "Saving Herodotus' Phenomena: The Oracles and the Events of 480 B.C.". *Classical Antiquity* 5 (1), 14–59.
Georges, Pericles B. (1994), *Barbarian Asia and the Greek Experience: From the Archaic Period to the Age of Xenophon*. Baltimore & London: The Johns Hopkins University Press.
Georgiadis, Nikolaos (1894), *Θεσσαλία*. Volos: Τυπογραφείο Ι.Ν. Δομεστίχου.
Giannopoulou, Nikolaos Ioannis (1925–1926), "Φθιωτικά. Α'. Χαλκοῦν προϊστορικὸν ἀγαλμάτιον ἐξ Ἅλου". *Ἀρχαιολογικὴ Ἐφημερίς* 1925–1926, 183–185.
Gilula, Dwora (2003), "Who Was Actually Buried in the First of the Three Spartan Tombs (Hdt. 9. 85. 1)? Textual and Historical Problems". In: Peter Derow & Robert Parker (eds.), *Herodotus and his World: Essays from a Conference in Memory of George Forrest*. Oxford: Oxford University Press, 73–87.
Giovino, Mariana (2006), "Assyrian Trees as Cult Objects". In: Paul Taylor (ed.), *The Iconography of Cylinder Seals*. London & Turin: The Warburg Institute & Nino Aragno Editore, 110–125.
Gnoli, Gherardo (1998), "Xerxès, Priam et Zoroastre". *Bulletin of the Asia Institute* 12, 59–67.
Goethert, Friedrich W. & Schleif, Hans (1962), *Der Athenatempel von Ilion*. Berlin: Verlag Walter de Gruyter & Co.
Goodwin, William W. (1906), "The Battle of Salamis". *Harvard Studies in Classical Philology* 17, 74–101.
Gould, John (1994), "Herodotus and Religion". In: Simon Hornblower (ed.), *Greek Historiography*. Oxford: Clarendon Press, 91–106.
Graef, B. (1902) in "Juni-Sitzung". *Archäologischer Anzeiger* 17, 86–87.
Grant, John R. (1961), "Leonidas' Last Stand". *Phoenix* 15 (1), 14–27.
Greco, Emanuele (2010), "Sulla Topografia di Atene: un'introduzione ai problemi". In: Emanuele Greco (ed.), *Topografia di Atene: Sviluppo urbano e monumenti dalle origini al III secolo d.C. Tomo 1: Acropoli - Areopago - Tra Acropoli e Pnice*. Athens & Paestum: Pandemos, 19–43.
Green, Peter (1996), *The Greco-Persian Wars*. Berkeley & Los Angeles: University of California Press.
Grethlein, Jonas (2009), "How Not to Do History: Xerxes in Herodotus' Histories". *American Journal of Philology* 130 (2), 195–218.
Grethlein, Jonas (2010), "Homer – die epische Erinnerung an ‹unvergänglichen Rum›". In: Elke Stein-Hölkeskamp & Karl-Joachim Hölkeskamp (eds.), *Erinnerungsorte der Antike: die griechische Welt*. Munich: C.H. Beck, 386–399.
Grundy, G.B. (1894), *The Topogaphy of the Battle of Plataea: The City of Plataea. The Field of Leuctra*. London: John Murray.

Grundy, G.B. (1897a), "Artemisium". *The Journal of Hellenic Studies* 17, 212–229.
Grundy, G.B. (1897b), "The Account of Salamis in Herodotus". *The Journal of Hellenic Studies* 17, 230–240.
Grundy, G.B. (1901), *The Great Persian War and its Preliminaries: A Study of the Evidence, Literary and Topographical*. London: John Murray.
Günzel, Stephan (2012), "Space and Cultural Geography". In: Birgit Neumann & Ansgar Nünning (eds.), *Travelling Concepts for the Study of Culture*. Berlin: De Gruyter, 307–320.
Habicht, Christian (1961), "Falsche Urkunden zur Geschichte Athens im Zeitalter der Perserkriege". *Hermes* 89 (1), 1–35.
Hadzisteliou Price, Theodora (1973), "An Enigma in Pella: The Tholos and Herakles Phylakos". *American Journal of Archaeology* 77 (1), 66–71.
Halbwachs, Maurice (1941), *La topographie légendaire des évangiles en Terre Sainte : étude de mémoire collective*. Paris: Presses universitaires de France.
Halbwachs, Maurice (1997), *La mémoire collective. Édition critique établie par Gérard Namer*. Paris: Presses Universitaires de France (second edition, first published 1950).
Hamilton, William J. (1842), *Researches in Asia Minor, Pontus, Armenia. Some account of their antiquities and geology*. London: Murray.
Hammond, N.G.L. (1956), "The Battle of Salamis". *The Journal of Hellenic Studies* 76, 32–54.
Hammond, N.G.L. (1973), *Studies in Greek History*. Oxford: Clarendon Press.
Hammond, N.G.L. (1988), "The Expedition of Xerxes". In: John Boardman, N.G.L. Hammond, D.M. Lewis, M. Ostwald (eds.), *The Cambridge Ancient History, Volume IV: Persia, Greece and the Western Mediterranean c. 525 to 479 B.C.* Cambridge: Cambridge University Press, 518–591.
Hammond, N.G.L. & Roseman, L.J. (1996), "The Construction of Xerxes' Bridge over the Hellespont". *The Journal of Hellenic Studies* 116, 88–107.
Hanfmann, George M.A. (1960), *Sardis und Lydien*. Wiesbaden: Verlag der Akademie der Wissenschaften und der Literatur in Mainz.
Hansen, William (1996), "The Protagonist on the Pyre: Herodotean Legend and Modern Folktale". *Fabula* 37, 272–285.
Hansen, William (2002), *Ariadne's Thread: A Guide to International Tales found in Classical Literature*. Ithaca & London: Cornell University Press.
Hansen, Mogens Herman & Nielsen, Thomas Heine (2004), *An Inventory of Archaic and Classical Poleis: An Investigation Conducted by the Copenhagen Polis Centre for the Danish National Research Foundation*. Oxford: Oxford University Press.
Harris, Diane (1995), *The Treasures of the Parthenon and Erechtheion*. Oxford: Clarendon Press.
Harrison, Evelyn B. (1966), "The Composition of the Amazonomachy on the Shield of Athena Parthenos". *Hesperia* 35 (2), 107–133.
Harrison, Evelyn B. (1981), "Motifs of the City-Siege on the Shield of Athena Parthenos". *American Journal of Archaeology* 85 (3), 281–317.
Harrison, Thomas (2000), *Divinity and History: The Religion of Herodotus*. Oxford: Clarendon Press.
Harrison, Thomas (2002), "The Persian Invasions". In: Egbert J. Bakker, Irene J.F. de Jong & Hans van Wees (eds.), *Brill's Companion to Herodotus*. Leiden: Brill, 551–578.
Harrison, Thomas (2003), "'Prophecy in Reverse'? Herodotus and the Origins of History". In: Peter Derow & Robert Parker (eds.), *Herodotus and his World: Essays from a Conference in Memory of George Forrest*. Oxford: Oxford University Press, 237–255.
Harrison, Thomas (2011), *Writing Ancient Persia*. Bristol: Bristol Classical Press.
Hart, John (1982), *Herodotus and Greek History*. London: Croom Helm.
Hartmann, Andreas (2010), *Zwischen Relikt und Reliquie: objektbezogene Erinnerungspraktiken in antiken Gesellschaften*. Berlin: Verlag Antike.

Hartog, François (1980), *Le miroir d'Hérodote: Essai sur la représentation de l'autre*. Paris: Éditions Gallimard.
Haubold, Johannes (2007), "'Xerxes' Homer". In: Emma Bridges, Edith Hall & P. J. Rhodes (eds.), *Cultural Responses to the Persian Wars: Antiquity to the Third Millennium*. Oxford: Oxford University Press, 47–63.
Haubold, Johannes (2013), *Greece and Mesopotamia: Dialogues in Literature*. Cambridge: Cambridge University Press.
Haussollier, Bernard (1878), "Inscriptions de Béotie (XXVI)". *Bulletin de correspondance hellénique* 2, 589–591.
Hauvette, Amédée (1894), *Hérodote. Historien des guerres médiques*. Paris: Librairie Hachette et Cie.
Hawkins, John David (1998), "Tarkasnawa King of Mira', 'Tarkondemos', 'Boğazköy sealings and Karabel'". *Anatolian Studies* 48, 1–31.
Hedrick, Charles W. Jr. (1993), "The Meaning of Material Culture: Herodotus, Thucydides, and Their Sources". In: Ralph M. Rosen & Joseph Farrell (eds.), *Nomodeiktes: Greek Studies in Honor of Martin Ostwald*. Ann Arbor: The University of Michigan Press, 17–37.
Heinrichs, Johannes (1987), "'Asiens König': Die Inschriften des Kyrosgrabs und das achämenidische Reichsverständnis". In: W. Will (ed.), *Zu Alexander d.Gr. Festschrift G. Wirth zum 60. Geburtstag am 9.12.86*. Amsterdam: Verlag Adolf M. Hakkert, 487–540.
Herbig, Reinhard (1928), "Archäologische Funde in den Jahren 1927–1928". *Jahrbuch des Deutschen Archäologischen Instituts* 43 569–635.
Hertel, Dieter (2003), *Die Mauern von Troia: Mythos und Geschichte im antiken Ilion*. Munich: C.H. Beck.
Heuck Allen, Susan (1999), *Finding the Walls of Troy: Frank Calvert and Heinrich Schliemann at Hisarlık*. Berkeley: University of California Press.
Hignett, Charles (1963), *Xerxes' Invasion of Greece*. Oxford: Clarendon Press.
Hill, B.H. (1912), "The Older Parthenon". *American Journal of Archaeology* 16 (4), 535–558.
Hirsch, Marianne (2012), *The Generation of Postmemory: Writing and Visual Culture after the Holocaust*. New York: Columbia University Press.
Hoepfner, Wolfram (2000), "Zur Tholos in Delphi". *Archäologischer Anzeiger* 2000, 99–107.
Hogarth, D. G. (1888), "Notes upon a Visit to Celaenae-Apamea". *The Journal of Hellenic Studies* 9, 343–349.
Hölkeskamp, Karl-Joachim (2001), "Marathon – vom Monument zum Mythos". In: Dietrich Papenfuß & Volker Michael Strocka (eds.), *Gab es das Griechische Wunder? Griechenland zwischen dem Ende des 6. und der Mitte des 5. Jahrhunderts v. Chr*. Mainz: Verlag Philipp von Zabern, 329–353.
Hölkeskamp, Karl-Joachim & Stein-Hölkeskamp, Elke (2010), "Einleitung: 'Erinnerungsorte' à la grecque – nochmals zu Begriff und Programm". In: Elke Stein-Hölkeskamp & Karl-Joachim Hölkeskamp (eds.), *Erinnerungsorte der Antike: die griechische Welt*. Munich: C.H. Beck, 11–16.
Holland, Tom (2005), *Persian Fire: The First World Empire and the Battle for the West*. London: Abacus.
Hollmann, Alexander (2011), *The Master of Signs: Signs and the Interpretation of Signs in Herodotus' Histories*. Washington D.C.: Center for Hellenic Studies.
Hölscher, Tonio (2010), "Athen – die Polis als Raum der Erinnerung". In: Elke Stein-Hölkeskamp & Karl-Joachim Hölkeskamp (eds.), *Erinnerungsorte der Antike: die griechische Welt*. Munich: C.H. Beck, 128–149.
Homolle, Théophile (1904), "Fouilles de Delphes : les découvertes de Marmaria". *Revue de l'art ancien et moderne* 15, 6–20.
Hornblower, Simon (2006), "Herodotus' Influence in Antiquity". In: Carolyn Dewald & John Marincola (eds.), *The Cambridge Companion to Herodotus*. Cambridge: Cambridge University Press, 306–317.

How, W.W. & Wells, J. (1912), *A Commentary on Herodotus*. Oxford: Clarendon Press.
Hude, Carolus (1927), *Herodoti Historiae. Recognovit brevique adnotatione critica instruxit. Editio tertia*. Oxford: Clarendon Press.
Hunt, W. Irving (1890), "Discoveries at Plataia in 1890. IV. Notes on the Battlefield of Plataia". *The American Journal of Archaeology and of the History of the Fine Arts* 6 (4), 463–475.
Hurwit, Jeffrey M. (1999), *The Athenian Acropolis: History, Mythology, and Archaeology from the Neolithic Era to the Present*. Cambridge: Cambridge University Press.
Hurwit, Jeffrey M. (2004), *The Acropolis in the Age of Pericles*. Cambridge: Cambridge University Press.
Huttner, Ulrich (1997), *Die politische Rolle der Heraklesgestalt im griechischen Herrschertum (Historia, Einzelschriften 112)*. Stuttgart: Franz Steiner Verlag.
Hutton, William (2005), *Describing Greece. Landscape and Literature in the Periegesis of Pausanias*. Cambridge: Cambridge University Press.
Huxley, George L. (1963), "Aeimnestos the Plataian". *Greek, Roman and Byzantine Studies* 4 (1), 5–8.
IG = *Inscriptiones Graecae*. Berlin: Berlin-Brandenburgische Akademie der Wissenschaften.
Immerwahr, Henry R. (1960), "Ergon: History as a Monument in Herodotus and Thucydides". *The American Journal of Philology* 81 (3), 261–290.
Immerwahr, Henry R. (1966), *Form and Thought in Herodotus*. Cleveland: Press of Western Reserve University.
In der Smitten, Wilhelm (1973), "Xerxes und die Daeva". *Bibliotheca Orientalis* 30, 368–369.
Ingold, Tim (2012), "Introduction". In: Monica Janowski & Tim Ingold (eds.), *Imagining Landscapes: Past, Present and Future*. Farnham: Ashgate, 1–18.
Instinsky, Hans Ulrich (1949), *Alexander der Grosse am Hellespont*. Munich: Helmut Küpper.
Instinsky, Hans Ulrich (1956), "Herodot und der erste Zug des Mardonios gegen Griechenland". *Hermes* 84 (4), 477–494.
Isaac, Benjamin (1986), *The Greek Settlements in Thrace until the Macedonian Conquest*. Leiden: Brill.
Isaac, Benjamin (2004), *The Invention of Racism in Classical Antiquity*. Princeton: Princeton University Press.
Isserlin, B.S.J. (1991), "The Canal of Xerxes: Facts and Problems". *The Annual of the British School at Athens* 86, 83–91.
Isserlin, B.S.J., Jonges, R.E., Karastathis, V., Papamarinopoulos, S.P., Syrides, G.E. & Uren, J. (2003), "The Canal of Xerxes: Summary of Investigations 1991–2001". *The Annual of the British School at Athens* 98, 369–385.
Ivantchik, Askold I. (1999), "Eine griechische Pseudo-Historie. Der Pharao Sesostris und der skytho-ägyptische Krieg". *Historia: Zeitschrift für Alte Geschichte* 48 (4), 395–441.
Jacoby, Felix (1913), "Herodotos". *RE Supplement 2*, 205–520.
Jacquemin, Anne (2000), *Guerre et Religion dans le monde grec (490–322 av. J.-C.)*. Liège: Sedes.
Jacquemin, Anne (2006), "Pausanias, la Perse et les Perses". In: Pascale Brillet-Dubois & Édith Parmentier (eds.), *Φιλολογία: Mélanges offerts à Michel Casevitz*. Lyon: Maison de l'Orient et de la Méditerranée, 277–287.
Jacquemin, Anne (2011), "Le sanctuaire de Delphes comme *lieu de mémoire*". In: Matthias Haake & Michael Jung (eds.), *Griechische Heiligtümer als Erinnerungsorte: Von der Archaik bis in den Hellenismus*. Stuttgart: Franz Steiner Verlag, 19–27.
Jameson, Michael H. (1960), "A Decree of Themistokles from Troizen". *Hsperia: The Journal of the American School of Classical Studies at Athens* 29 (2), 198–223.
Jameson, Michael H. (1961), "Waiting for the Barbarian: New Light on the Persian Wars". *Greece & Rome* (Second Series) 8 (1), 5–18.
Janni, Pietro (1984), *La Mappa e il Periplo. Cartografia antica e spazio odologico*. Rome: Giorgio Bretschneider Editore.

Janssen, Andreas Jozef (1957), *Het Antieke Tropaion*. Dissertation at R. K. Universiteit, Nijmegen.
Jeppesen, Kristian (1987), *The Theory of the Alternative Erechtheion*. Aarhus: Aarhus University Press.
Jochmus, A. (1954), "Notes on a Journey into the Balkan, or Mount Hæmus, in 1847". *Journal of the Royal Geographical Society of London* 24, 36–85.
Jones, Christopher P. (2001), "Philostratus' Heroikos and Its Setting in Reality". *The Journal of Hellenic Studies* 121, 141–149.
Judeich, Walther (1912), "Psyttaleia". *Klio* 12, 129–138.
Judeich, Walther (1931), *Topographie von Athen*. München: C.H. Beck'sche Verlagsbuchhandlung.
Jung, Michael (2006), *Marathon und Plataiai: Zwei Perserschlachten als »lieux de mémoire« im antiken Griechenland*. Göttingen: Vandenhoeck & Ruprecht.
Jung, Michael (2011a), "Methodisches: Heiligtümer und *lieux de mémoire*". In: Matthias Haake & Michael Jung (eds.), *Griechische Heiligtümer als Erinnerungsorte: Von der Archaik bis in den Hellenismus*. Stuttgart: Franz Steiner Verlag, 9–18.
Jung, Michael (2011b), "Wanderer, kommst du nach Sparta ...': Die Bestattung der Perserkämpfer Leonidas und Pausanias im Heiligtum der Athena Chalkioikos". In: Matthias Haake & Michael Jung (eds.), *Griechische Heiligtümer als Erinnerungsorte: Von der Archaik bis in den Hellenismus*. Stuttgart: Franz Steiner Verlag, 95–108.
Kahrstedt, Ulrich (1954), *Beiträge zur Geschichte der thrakischen Chersones*. Baden-Baden: Bruno Grimm Verlag für Kunst und Wissenschaft.
Kalpaxis, Thanassis E. (1986), *Hemiteles. Akzidentelle Unfertigkeit und „Bossen-Stil" in der griechischen Baukunst*. Mainz am Rhein: Verlag Philipp von Zabern.
Kaptan, Deniz (2002) *The Daskyleion Bullae: Seal Images from the Western Achaemenid Empire (Achaemenid History XII)*. Leiden: Nederlands Instituut voor het Nabije Oosten.
Kaptan, Deniz (2003), "A Glance at Northwestern Asia Minor during the Achaemenid Period". In: Wouter Henkelman & Amélie Kuhrt (eds.), *Achaemenid History XIII: A Persian Perspective: Essays in Memory of Heleen Sancisi-Weerdenburg*. Leiden: Nederlands Instituut voor het Nabije Oosten, 189–200.
Karo, Georg Heinrich (1910), "En marge de quelques textes delphiques (suite)." *Bulletin de correspondance hellénique* 34, 187–221.
Kase, Edward William & Szemler, George John (1982), "Xerxes' March through Phokis (Her. 8, 31–35)". *Klio* 64, 353–366.
Kelly, Thomas (2003), "Persian Propaganda – A Neglected Factor in Xerxes' Invasion of Greece and Herodotus". *Iranica Antiqua* 38, 173–219.
Keramopoullos, Ant. D. (1935), Ὁδηγός τῶν Δελφῶν. Athens: Ἡ ἐν Ἀθήναις ἀρχαιολογικὴ Ἑταιρεῖα.
Kienast, Dietmar (1995), "Die Politisierung des griechischen Nationalbewußtseins und die Rolle Delphis im großen Perserkrieg". In: Charlotte Schubert & Kai Brodersen (eds.), *Rom und der griechische Osten: Festschrift für Hatto H. Schmitt zum 65. Geburtstag, dargebracht von Schülern, Freunden und Münchener Kollegen*. Stuttgart: Steiner, 117–134.
Kienast, Dietmar (1996), "Der Wagen des Ahura Mazda und der Ausmarsch des Xerxes". *Chiron* 29, 285–313.
Kirchberg, Jutta (1965), *Die Funktion der Orakel im Werke Herodots*. Göttingen: Vandenhoeck & Ruprecht.
Kirsten, Ernst (1950), "Plataiai". *RE* 20, 2255–2332.
Kissas, Konstantin (2008), *Archaische Architektur der athener Akropolis. Dachziegel – Metopen – Geisa – Akroterbasen*. Wiesbaden: Reichtert Verlag.
Kledt, Annette (2004), *Die Entführung Kores: Studien zur athenisch-eleusinischen Demeterreligion (Palingenesia 84)*. Stuttgart: Franz Steiner Verlag.
Kolbe, Walther (1936), "Die Neugestaltung der Akropolis nach den Perserkriegen". *Jahrbuch des deutschen archäologischen Instituts* 51, 1–64.

Konecny, Andreas L., Aravantinos, Vassilis & Marchese, Ron (2013), *Plataiai: Archäologie und Geschichte einer boiotischen Polis (Österreichisches Archäologisches Institut, Sonderschriften 48)*.

Konecny, Andreas L., Boyd, Michael J., Marchese, Ronald T. & Aravantinos Vassilis (2008), "Plataiai in Boiotia: A Preliminary Report on Geophysical and Field Surveys Conducted in 2002–2005". *Hesperia* 77 (1), 43–71.

Konijnendijk, Roel (2012), "'Neither the Less Valorous nor the Weaker': Persian Military Might and the Battle of Plataia". *Historia* 61 (1), 1–17.

Kontorlis, Konstantinos P. (1972), *The Battle of Thermopylae*. Athens: J. Makris S.A.

Korres, Manolis (1994a), "The History of the Acropolis Monuments". In: Richard Economakis (ed.), *Acropolis Restoration: The CCAM Interventions*. London: Academy Editions, 34–51.

Korres, Manolis (1994b), "Recent Discoveries on the Acropolis". In: Richard Economakis (ed.), *Acropolis Restoration: The CCAM Interventions*. London: Academy Editions, 174–179.

Korres, Manolis (1994c), "The Architecture of the Parthenon". In: Panayotis Tournikiotis (ed.), *The Parthenon and its Impact in Modern Times*. Athens: "Melissa" Publishing House, 54–97.

Korres, Manolis (2003), "Athenian Classical Architecture". In: Charalambos Bouras, Michael B. Sakellariou, Konstantinos S. Stakos & Evi Touloupa (eds.), *Athens: From the Classical Period to the Present Day (5th century B.C. – A.D. 2000)*. New Castle: Oak Knoll Press, 2–45.

Kossatz-Deissmann, Anneliese (1978), *Dramen des Aischylos auf westgriechischen Vasen*. Mainz am Rhein: Verlag Philipp von Zabern.

Köster, August (1934), *Studien zur Geschichte des antiken Seewesens (Klio, Beiheft 32)*. Leipzig: Dieterisch'sche Verlagsbuchhandlung.

Kousser, Rachel (2009), "Destruction and Memory on the Athenian Acropolis". *Art Bulletin* 91 (3), 263–282.

Kowerski, Lawrence M. (2005), *Simonides on the Persian Wars: A Study of the Elegiac Veres of the "New Simonides"*. New York & London: Routlege.

Kraay, Colin M. (1976), *Archaic and Classical Greek Coins*. Berkeley & Los Angeles: University of California Press.

Kraft, John C., Rapp, Jr., George, Szemler, George J., Tziavos, Christos & Kase, Edward W. (1987), "The Pass at Thermopylae, Greece". *Journal of Field Archaeology* 14 (2), 181–198.

Kromayer, Johannes (1924), *Antike Schlachtfelder: Bausteine zu einer antiken Kriegsgeschichte. Vierter Band: Schlachtfelder aus den Perserkriegen, aus der späteren griechischen Geschichte und den Feldzügen Alexanders und aus der römischen Geschichte bis Augustus. 1. Lieferung*. Berlin: Weidmannsche Buchhandlung.

Kromayer, Johannes (1926), *Antike Schlachtfelder: Bausteine zu einer antiken Kriegsgeschichte. Vierter Band: Schlachtfelder aus den Perserkriegen, aus der späteren griechischen Geschichte und den Feldzügen Alexanders und aus der römischen Geschichte bis Augustus. 2. Lieferung*. Berlin: Weidmannsche Buchhandlung.

Kromayer, Johannes (1931), *Antike Schlachtfelder: Bausteine zu einer antiken Kriegsgeschichte. Vierter Band: Schlachtfelder aus den Perserkriegen, aus der späteren griechischen Geschichte und den Feldzügen Alexanders und aus der römischen Geschichte bis Augustus. 4. Lieferung*. Berlin: Weidmannsche Buchhandlung.

Kuhrt, Amélie (2007), *The Persian Empire: A Corpus of Sources from the Achaemenid Period*. Abingdon & New York: Routledge.

Kuhrt, Amélie & Sancisi-Weerdenburg, Heleen (1987), "Introduction". In: Heleen Sancisi-Weerdenburg & Amélie Kuhrt (eds.), *Achaemenid History II: The Greek Sources* (Proceedings of the Groningen 1984 Achaemenid History Workshop). Leiden: Nederlands Instituut voor het Nabije Oosten, ix–xiii.

Kuhrt, Amélie & Sherwin-White, Susan (1987), "Xerxes' Destruction of Babylonian Temples". In: Heleen Sancisi-Weerdenburg & Amélie Kuhrt (eds.), *Achaemenid History II: The Greek Sources* (Proceedings of the Groningen 1984 Achaemenid History Workshop). Leiden: Nederlands Instituut voor het Nabije Oosten, 69–78.
Kümmel, Hans Martin (1967), *Ersatzrituale für den hethitischen König* (Studien zu den Boğazköy-Texten 3). Wiesbaden: Otto Harrassowitz.
Kyriakidis, Nicolas (2010), "Erreurs à Delphes. La tholos de Marmaria au fil des interprétations". *Anabases* 11, 149–163.
Labarbe, Jules (1952), "Chiffres et modes de répartition de la flotte grecque à l'Artémision et à Salamine". *Bulletin de correspondance hellénique* 76, 384–441.
Lacy, Lamar Ronald (1984), *The Myth of Aktaion: Literary and Iconographic Studies*. Dissertation at Bryn Mawr College.
Lacy, Lamar Ronald (1990), "Aktaion and a Lost 'Bath of Artemis'". *The Journal of Hellenic Studies* 110, 26–42.
Lambert, Stephen D. (1997), "The Attic Genos Salaminioi and the Island of Salamis". *Zeitschrift für Papyrologie und Epigraphik* 119, 85–106.
Lane Fox, Robin (2008), *Travelling Heroes: Greeks and their Myths in the Epic Age of Homer*. London: Penguin Books.
Lang, Mabel L. (1984), *Herodotean Narrative and Discourse*. Cambridge, Massachusetts: Harvard University Press.
Langdon, Merle K. (2007), "Lolling's Topographical Work on Salamis". In: Klaus Fittschen (ed.), *Historische Landeskunde und Epigraphik in Griechenland. Akten des Symposiums veranstaltet aus Anlaß des 100. Todestages von H. G. Lolling (1848–1894) in Athen vom 28. bis 30. 9. 1994*. Münster: Deutsches Archäologisches Institut, 109–122.
Lateiner, Donald (1985), "Limit, Propriety, and Transgression in the *Histories* of Herodotus". In: *The Greek Historians: Literature and History. Papers presented to A.E. Raubitschek*. Saratoga: ANMA Libri, 87–100.
Lazenby, John Francis (1993), *The Defence of Greece 490–479 B.C.* Warminster: Aris & Phillips.
Le Roy, Christian (1977), "Pausanias à Marmaria". *Bulletin de correspondance hellénique, Supplément* 4, 247–272.
le Quien, R. P. F. Michaelis (1740), *Oriens christianus in quatuor patriarchatus digestus, in quo exhibentur Ecclesiae patriarchae caeterique praesules totius Orientis*. Paris: Ex Typographia Regia.
Leaf, Walter (1912), "Notes on the Troad". *The Geographical Journal* 40 (1), 25–45.
Leaf, Walter (1916), "The Military Geography of the Troad". *The Geographical Journal* 47 (6), 401–416.
Leaf, Walter (1923), *Strabo on the Troad*. Cambridge: Cambridge University Press.
Leake, William Martin (1821), *The Topography of Athens and the Demi. Vol. I. The Topography of Athens with some Remarks on its Antiquities*. London: John Murray.
Leake, William Martin (1824), *Journal of a Tour in Asia Minor with Comparative Remarks on the Ancient and Modern Geoography of that Country*. London: John Murray.
Leake, William Martin (1835), *Travels in Northern Greece*. London: J. Rodwell.
Leake, William Martin (1841), *The Topography of Athens and the Demi. Vol. II. The Demi of Attica*. London: J. Rodwell.
Lendering, Jona (2011), "De mythe van Thermopylae". *Lampas* 44 (1), 40–52.
Lenfant, Dominique (2002), "Pourquoi Xerxès détacha sa ceinture (Hérodote, VIII.120)". *Arta* 4, 1–7.
Lenfant, Dominique (2004), "L'amalgame entre les Perses et les Troyens chez les Grecs de l'époque classique : usages politiques et discours historiques". In: Candau Morón, José María, González

Ponce, Francisco Javier & Cruz Andreotti, Gonzalo (eds.), *Historia y mito: El pasado legendario como fuente de autoridad*. Malaga: Centro de Ediciones de la Diputación de Málaga, 77–94.

Lewis, David M. (1985), "Persians in Herodotus". In: *The Greek Historians: Literature and History. Papers presented to A.E. Raubitschek*. Saratoga: ANMA Libri, 101–117.

Liapis, Vayos (2011), "The Thracian Cult of Rhesus and the *Heros Equitans*". *Kernos* 24, 95–104.

LIMC = *Lexicon Iconographicum Mythologiae Classicae* (1981–1999), Zürich: Artemis & Winkler Verlag.

Lindenlauf, Astrid (1997), "Der Perserschutt der athener Akropolis". In: Wolfram Hoepfner (ed.), *Kult und Kultbauten auf der Akropolis. Internationales Symposion vom 7. bis 9. Juli 1995 in Berlin*. Berlin: Schriften des Seminars für klassische Archäologie der Freien Universität Berlin, 46–115.

Llewellyn-Jones, Lloyd (2012), "The Great Kings of the Fourth Century and the Greek Memory of the Persian Past". In: John Marincola, Lloyd Llewellyn-Jones & Calum Maciver (eds.), *Greek Notions of the Past in the Archaic and Classical Eras: History without Historians*. Edinburgh: Edinburgh University Press, 317–346.

Lloyd, Alan B. (2002), "Egypt". In: Egbert J. Bakker, Irene J.F. de Jong & Hans van Wees (eds.), *Brill's Companion to Herodotus*. Leiden: Brill, 415–435.

Lolling, H. Gerhard (1883), "Das Artemision auf Nordeuböa". *Mitteilungen des Deutschen Archäologischen Instituts, athenische Abteilung* 8, 7–23.

Lolling, H. Gerhard (1884), "Die Meerenge von Salamis". In: *Historische und philologische Aufsätze Ernst Curtius zu seinem siebenzigsten Geburtstage am zweiten September 1884 gewidmet*. Berlin: Verlag von A. Asher & Co, 3–10.

Longo, Fausto & Tofi, Maria Gaia (2010), "L'Areopago e le pendici. Quadro storico-topografico". In: Emanuele Greco (ed.), *Topografia di Atene: Sviluppo urbano e monumenti dalle origini al III secolo d.C. Tomo 1: Acropoli - Areopago - Tra Acropoli e Pnice*. Athens & Paestum: Pandemos, 209–218.

Lotfus, Elizabeth F., Feldman, Julie & Dashiell, Richard (1995), "The Reality of Illusory Memories". In: Daniel L. Schacter (ed.), *Memory Distortion: How Minds, Brains, and Societies Reconstruct the Past*. Cambridge, Massachusetts: Harvard University Press, 47–68.

Low, Polly (2011), "The power of the dead in classical Sparta: The case of Thermopylae". In: Maureen Carroll & Jane Rempel (eds.), *Living through the Dead: Burial and Commemoration in the Classical World*. Oxford: Oxbow Books, 1–20.

LSJ = Henry George Liddell, Robert Scott, Henry Stuart Jones & Roderick McKenzie (1940), *A Greek–English Lexicon*. Oxford: Oxford University Press (ninth edition, first published 1843).

Luce, John Victor (1998), *Celebrating Homer's Landscapes: Troy and Ithaca Revisited*. New Haven: Yale University Press.

Luraghi, Nino (2001), "Local Knowledge in Herodotus' *Histories*". In: Nino Luraghi (ed.), *The Historian's Craft in the Age of Herodotus*. Oxford: Oxford University Press, 138–160.

Luraghi, Nino (2013), "The stories before the Histories: Folktale and traditional narrative in Herodotus". In: Rosaria Vignolo Munson (ed.), *Herodotus: Volume 1. Herodotus and the Narrative of the Past*. Oxford: Oxford University Press, 87–112.

Lykoudis, Stylianos Emm. (1928), "Περὶ ἐξακριβώσεως χωρίου τινὸς τοῦ Ἡροδότου (Πολύμνια, 183) ἀφορῶντος εἰς τὴν ναυτικὴν ἀρχαιολογίαν". *Πρακτικὰ τῆς Ἀκαδημίας Ἀθηνῶν* 1928, 596–600.

Maass, Michael (1993), *Das antike Delphi. Orakel, Schätze und Monumente*. Darmstadt: Wissenschaftliche Buchgesellschaft.

Maass, Michael (2010), "Delphi 'monumental' – Prozessionsstraße, Schatzhäuser, Tempel". In: Elke Stein-Hölkeskamp & Karl-Joachim Hölkeskamp (eds.), *Erinnerungsorte der Antike: die griechische Welt*. Munich: C.H. Beck, 61–78.

Macan, Reginald Walter (1908), *Herodotus: The Seventh, Eighth, & Ninth Books with Introduction, Text, Apparatus, Commentary, Appendices, Indices, Maps*. London: MacMillan and Co.

Malacrino, Carmelo (2010), "L'*Eleusinion*". In: Emanuele Greco (ed.), *Topografia di Atene: Sviluppo urbano e monumenti dalle origini al III secolo d.C. Tomo 1: Acropoli - Areopago - Tra Acropoli e Pnice*. Athens & Paestum: Pandemos, 145–150.
Malkin, Irad (1994), *Myth and territory in the Spartan Mediterranean*. Cambridge: Cambridge University Press.
Malkin, Irad (2011), *A Small Greek World: Networks in the Ancient Mediterranean*. Oxford: Oxford University Press.
Mantel, Anne (1976), *Herodotus Historiën: Patronen en historische werkelijkheid bij Herodotus*. Amsterdam: Uitgeverij Adolf M. Hakkert.
Marinatos, Spyridon (1940), "Forschungen in Thermopylae". In: Archäeologisches Institut des deutschen Reiches, *Bericht über den VI. internationalen Kongress für Archäologie Berlin 21.-26. August*. Berlin: Walter de Gruyter & Co, 333–341.
Marinatos, Spyridon (1951), *Thermopylae: An Historical and Archaeological Guide*. Athens.
Marincola, John (2006), "Herodotus and the poetry of the past". In: Carolyn Dewald & John Marincola (eds.), *The Cambridge Companion to Herodotus*. Cambridge: Cambridge University Press, 13–28.
Marincola, John (2007), "The Persian Wars in Fourth-Century Oratory and Historiography". In: Emma Bridges, Edith Hall & P. J. Rhodes (eds.), *Cultural Responses to the Persian Wars: Antiquity to the Third Millennium*. Oxford: Oxford University Press, 105–124.
Marincola, John (2012), "Introduction: A Past without Historians". In: John Marincola, Lloyd Llewellyn-Jones & Calum Maciver (eds.), *Greek Notions of the Past in the Archaic and Classical Eras: History without Historians*. Edinburgh: Edinburgh University Press, 1–13.
Masaracchia, Agostino (1976), *Studi Erodotei*. Messina: Università degli Studi.
Mason, Hugh J. & Wallace, Malcolm B. (1972), "Appius Claudius Pulcher and the Hollows of Euboia". *Hesperia* 41 (1), 128–140.
Maurice, F. (1930), "The Size of the Army of Xerxes in the Invasion of Greece 480 B. C." *The Journal of Hellenic Studies* 50 (2), 210–235.
Maurizio, Lisa (1997), "Delphic Oracles as Oral Performances: Authenticity and Historical Evidence." *Classical Antiquity* 16 (2), 308–334.
Mayor, Adrienne (2000), *The First Fossil Hunters: Paleontology in Greek and Roman Times*. Princeton: Princeton University Press.
Mayor, Adrienne (2014), *The Amazons: Lives and Legends of Warrior Women across the Ancient World*. Princeton: Princeton University Press.
Mayrhofer, Manfred (1974), "Xerxès, Roi des Rois". In: Jacques Duchesne-Guillemin (ed.), *Acta Iranica. Commémoration Cyrus, Volume I: Hommage Universel*. Tehran & Liège: Bibliothèque Pahlavi, 108–116.
McInerney, Jeremy (1999), *The Folds of Parnassos: Land and Ethnicity in Ancient Phokis*. Austin: University of Texas Press.
Meier, Mischa (2010), "Die Thermopylen - "Wanderer, kommst du nach Spa(rta)"". In: Elke Stein-Hölkeskamp & Karl-Joachim Hölkeskamp (eds.), *Erinnerungsorte der Antike: die griechische Welt*. Munich: C.H. Beck, 98–113.
Mele, Alfonso (1955), "La battaglia di Platea". *Univerisità di Napoli: Annali della Facoltà di Lettere e Filosofia* 5, 5–41.
Meritt, Benjamin D. (1947), "The Persians at Delphi". *Hesperia* 16 (2), 58–62.
Meyer, Eduard (1954), *Geschichte des Altertums. Vierter Band, Erste Abteilung: Das Perserreich und die Griechen bis zum Vorabend des peloponnesischen Krieges*. Darmstadt: Wissenschaftliche Buchgesellschaft.
Meyer, Ernst (1956), "Thermopylen". *Mitteilungen des deutschen archäologischen Instituts, athenische Abteilung* 71, 101–106.

Mézières, M. Albert (1853), *Mémoire sur le Pélion et l'Ossa*. Paris: Imprimerie Imperiale.
Mierse, William E. (1983a), "The Persian Period". In: George M. A. Hanfmann (ed.), *Sardis: from Prehistoric to Roman Times. Results of the Archaeological Exploration of Sardis 1958–1975*. Cambridge, Massachusetts: Harvard University Press, 100–108.
Mierse, William E. (1983b), "Artemis Sanctuary". In: George M. A. Hanfmann (ed.), *Sardis: from Prehistoric to Roman Times. Results of the Archaeological Exploration of Sardis 1958–1975*. Cambridge, Massachusetts: Harvard University Press, 119–121.
Mikalson, Jon D. (2003), *Herodotus and Religion in the Persian Wars*. Chapel Hill: The University of North Carolina Press.
Milchhoefer, A. (1895), *Karten von Attika. Heft VII-VIII*. Berlin: Geographische Verlagshandlung Dietrich Reimer.
Miles, Margaret M. (1998), *The Athenian Agora: Results of Excavations Conducted by the American School of Classical Studies at Athens Volume XXXI: The City Eleusinion*. Princeton: American School of Classical Studies at Athens.
Miles, Margaret M. (2011), "The Lapis Primus and the Older Parthenon". *Hesperia* 80 (4), 657–675.
Miles, Margaret M. (2014), "Burnt Temples in the Landscape of the Past". In: James Ker & Cristoph Pieper (eds.), *Valuing the past in the Greco-Roman world: proceedings from the Penn-Leiden Colloquia on Ancient Values VII*. Leiden: Brill, 111–145.
Miles, Margaret M. (2016), "Birds around the Temple: Constructing a Sacred Environment". In: Jeremy McInerney & Ineke Sluiter (eds.), *Valueing Landscape in Classical Antiquity: Natural Environment and Cultural Imagination*. Leiden: Brill, 151–195.
Miller, Margaret C. (1999), *Athens and Persia in the fifth century BC: A study in cultural receptivity*. Cambridge: Cambridge University Press.
Minchin, Elizabeth (2016), "Heritage in the Landscape: The 'Heroic Tumuli' in the Troad Region". In: Jeremy McInerney & Ineke Sluiter (eds.), *Valueing Landscape in Classical Antiquity: Natural Environment and Cultural Imagination*. Leiden: Brill, 255–275.
Moggi, Mauro (1973), "I furti di statue attribuiti a Serse e le relative restituzioni". *Annali della Scuola Normale Superiore di Pisa. Classe di Lettere e Filosofia, Serie III* 3 (1), 1–42.
Moggi, Mauro (2007), "La battaglia delle Termopili: una sconfitta che vale una vittoria". In: Luigi Santi Amantini (ed.), *Il dopoguerra nel mondo greco. Politica, propaganda, storiografia*. Rome: «L'Erma» di Bretschneider, 3–39.
Moles, John (2002), "Herodotus and Athens". In: Egbert J. Bakker, Irene J.F. de Jong & Hans van Wees (eds.), *Brill's Companion to Herodotus*. Leiden: Brill, 33–52.
Molyneux, John H. (1992), *Simonides: a Historical Study*. Wauconda: Bolchazy-Carducci Publishers.
Momigliano, Arnaldo (1966), *Studies in Historiography*. New York & Evanston: Harper & Row Publishers.
Monaco, Maria Chiara (2010), "Il Tempio arcaico e il grande altare di Atena *Polias*". In: Emanuele Greco (ed.), *Topografia di Atene: Sviluppo urbano e monumenti dalle origini al III secolo d.C. Tomo 1: Acropoli - Areopago - Tra Acropoli e Pnice*. Athens & Paestum: Pandemos, 126–128.
Monaco, Maria Chiara (2015), "Atene e la memoria delle guerre. Appunti per una topografia dei luoghi". In: Elena Franchi & Giorgia Proietti (eds.), *Guerra e memoria nel mondo antico*. Trento: Università degli Studi di Trento, 153–175.
Montevecchi, Franco (1989), "A proposito di alcune burrasche e disastri navali avvenuti in Mediterraneo nell'antichità". In: Marta Sordi (ed.), *Fenomeni naturali e avvenimenti storici nell'antichità*. Milan: Vita e Pensiero, 22–34.
Mora, Fabio (1985), *Religione e Religioni nelle storie di Erodoto*. Milan: Editoriale Jaca Book.
Morris, Ian Macgregor (2000), "To Make a New Thermopylae: Hellenism, Greek Liberation, and the Battle of Thermopylae". *Greece & Rome* 47 (2), 211230.

Morris, Ian Macgregor (2007), "'Shrines of the Mighty': Rediscovering the Battlefields of the Persian Wars". In: Emma Bridges, Edith Hall & P. J. Rhodes (eds.), *Cultural Responses to the Persian Wars: Antiquity to the Third Millennium*. Oxford: Oxford University Press, 231–264.
Morton, Jamie (2001), *The Role of the Physical Environment in Ancient Greek Seafaring*. Leiden: Brill.
Moscovitch, Morris (1995), "Confabulation". In: Daniel L. Schacter (ed.), *Memory Distortion: How Minds, Brains, and Societies Reconstruct the Past*. Cambridge, Massachusetts: Harvard University Press, 226–251.
Müller, Dietram (1975), "Von Doriskos nach Therme: Der Weg des Xerxes-Heeres durch Thrakien und Ostmakedonien". *Chiron* 5, 1–11.
Müller, Dietram (1987), *Topographischer Bildkommentar zu den Historien Herodots: Griechenland im Umfang des heutigen Griechischen Staatsgebietes*. Tübingen: Ernst Wasmuth Verlag.
Müller, Dietram (1994), "Von Kritalla nach Doriskos: Die Persische Königsstraße und der Marschweg des Xerxesheeres in Kleinasien". *Istanbuler Mitteilungen* 44, 17–38.
Müller, Dietram (1997), *Topographischer Bildkommentar zu den Historien Herodots: Kleinasien und Angrenzende Gebiete mit Südostthrakien und Zypern*. Tübingen: Ernst Wasmuth Verlag.
Müller, Dietram (2004), "'Herodotus' Topography of Battlefields". In: Vassos Karageorghis & Ioannis Taifacos (eds.), *The World of Herodotus: Proceedings of an International Conference held at the Foundation Anastasios G. Leventis, Nicosia, September 18–21, 2003 and organized by the Foundation Anastasios G. Leventis and the Faculty of Letters, University of Cyprus*. Nicosia: Foundation Anastasios G. Leventis, 239–253.
Munro, John Arthur Ruskin (1902), "Some Observations on the Persian Wars (continued)". *The Journal of Hellenic Studies* 22, 294–332.
Munro, John Arthur Ruskin (1904), "Some Observations on the Persian Wars". *The Journal of Hellenic Studies* 24, 144–165.
Munro, John Arthur Ruskin (1926a), "Xerxes' Invasion of Greece". In: J.B. Bury, S.A. Cook & F.E. Adcock (eds.), *The Cambridge Ancient History, Volume IV: The Persian Empire and the West*. Cambridge: Cambridge University Press, 268–316.
Munro, John Arthur Ruskin (1926b), "The Deliverance of Greece". In: J.B. Bury, S.A. Cook & F.E. Adcock (eds.), *The Cambridge Ancient History, Volume IV: The Persian Empire and the West*. Cambridge: Cambridge University Press, 317–346.
Murray, Oswyn (1972), "Herodotus and Hellenistic Culture". *The Classical Quarterly* 22 (2), 200–213.
Murray, Oswyn (1987), "Herodotus and Oral History". In: Heleen Sancisi-Weerdenburg & Amélie Kuhrt (eds.), *Achaemenid History II: The Greek Sources* (*Proceedings of the Groningen 1984 Achaemenid History Workshop*). Leiden: Nederlands Instituut voor het Nabije Oosten, 93–115.
Murray, Oswyn (2001), "Herodotus and Oral History Reconsidered". In: Nino Luraghi (ed.), *The Historian's Craft in the Age of Herodotus*. Oxford: Oxford University Press, 314–325.
Mylonas, George E. (1961), *Eleusis and the Eleusinian Mysteries*. Princeton: Princeton University Press.
Mylonas Shear, Ione (1999), "The Western Approach to the Athenian Akropolis". *The Journal of Hellenic Studies* 119, 86–127.
Myres, John L. (1953), *Herodotus: Father of History*. Oxford: Clarendon Press.
Nagy, Gregory (1979), *The Best of the Achaeans: Concepts of the Hero in Archaic Greek Poetry*. Baltimore & London: The Johns Hopkins University Press.
Nauta, Ruurd (2007), "Inleiding". *Lampas* 40 (4), 258–262.
Nelson, Robert S. & Olin, Magaret (2003), "Introduction". In: Robert S. Nelson & Margaret Olin (eds.), *Monuments and Memory, Made and Unmade*. Chicago & London: The University of Chicago Press, 1–10.

Neumann, Birgit & Zierold, Martin (2012), "Cultural Memory and Memory Cultures". In: Birgit Neumann & Ansgar Nünning (eds.), *Travelling Concepts for the Study of Culture*. Berlin: De Gruyter, 225–248.
Nicolet-Pierre, Hélène (1992), "Xerxès et le trésor de l'Athos (IGCH 362)". *Revue numismatique* 34, 7–22.
Noack, Ferdinand (1927), *Eleusis. Die baugeschichtliche Entwicklung des Heiligtumes*. Berlin & Leipzig: Verlag von Walter de Gruyter & Co.
Nollé, Johannes (2006), "Beiträge zur kleinasiatischen Münzkunde und Geschichte 4–5". *Gephyra* 6, 49–131.
Nora, Pierre (1984–1992), *Les Lieux de Mémoire*. Paris: Gallimard.
Nunn, Astrid (2011), "Kelainai und seine Umgebung vor den Achämeniden". In: Lâtife Summerer, Askold Ivantchik & Alexander von Kienlin (eds.), *Kelainai-Apameia Kibotos: Stadtentwicklung im anatolischen Kontext. Akten des internationalen Kolloquiums, München, 2.-4. April 2009*. Bordeaux: Ausonius Éditions, 17–32.
O'Sullivan, James N. (1977), "On Herodotus 7.183: Three Sound Ships for Salamis". *Classical Quarterly* 27 (1), 92–94.
Obst, Ernst (1913), *Der Feldzug des Xerxes (Klio, Beiheft 12)*. Leipzig: Dieterisch'sche Verlagsbuchhandlung.
Olsen, Waldemar (1903), "Die Schlacht bei Plataeae". *Jahresbericht über das Städtische Gymnasium und die mit demselben verbundenen Real-Schule nebst Vorschule zu Greifswald für das Schuljahr 1901–1903*, 3–16.
Osborne, Robin (1996), *Greece in the Making, 1200–479 BC*. London: Routledge.
Osborne, Robin (2002), "Archaic Greek History". In: Egbert J. Bakker, Irene J.F. de Jong & Hans van Wees (eds.), *Brill's Companion to Herodotus*. Leiden: Brill, 497–520.
Pagel, Karl-August (1927), *Die Bedeutung des aitiologischen Momentes für Herodots Geschichtsschreibung*. Borna-Leipzig: Universitätsverlag von Robert Noske.
Papachatzi, Nikolaos D. (1974), *Παυσανίου Ελλάδος Περιήγησις: Ἀττικα*. Athens: Εκδοτική Αθηνών.
Papachatzi, Nikolaos D. (1976), *Παυσανίου Ελλάδος Περιήγησις: Βιβλίο 2. καὶ 3. Κορινθιακὰ καὶ Λακωνικά*. Athens: Εκδοτική Αθηνών.
Papachatzi, Nikolaos D. (1980), *Παυσανίου Ελλάδος Περιήγησις Βιβλία 7 καὶ 8: Ἀχαϊκὰ καὶ Ἀρκαδικά*. Athens: Εκδοτική Αθηνών.
Papachatzi, Nikolaos D. (1981), *Παυσανίου Ελλάδος Περιήγησις Βιβλία 9 καὶ 10: Βοιωτικὰ καὶ Φωκικά*. Athens: Εκδοτική Αθηνών.
Papadopoulou, Chryssanthi (2014), "Transforming the Surroundings and its Impact on Cult Rituals: The Case Study of Artemis Mounichia in the Fifth Century". In: Claudia Moser & Cecelia Feldman (eds.), *Locating the Sacred: Theoretical Approaches to the Emplacement of Religion*. Oxford: Oxbow Books, 111–127.
Papazarkadas, Nikolaos (2014), "Two new epigrams from Thebes". In: Nikolaos Papazarkadas (ed.), *The Epigraphy and History of Boeotia: New Finds, New Prospects*. Leiden: Brill, 223–251.
Parker, Robert (2004), "Sacrificing Twice Seven Children: Queen Amestris' Exchange with the God under the Earth (7.114)". In: Vassos Karageorghis & Ioannis Taifacos (eds.), *The World of Herodotus: Proceedings of an International Conference held at the Foundation Anastasios G. Leventis, Nicosia, September 18–21, 2003 and organized by the Foundation Anastasios G. Leventis and the Faculty of Letters, University of Cyprus*. Nicosia: Foundation Anastasios G. Leventis, 151–157.
Parker, Robert (2005), *Polytheism and Society at Athens*. Oxford: Oxford University Press.
Parker, Robert (2011), *On Greek Religion*. Ithaca: Cornell University Press.
Pasqual, José (2013a), "The Ancient Topography of Epicnemidian Locris". In: José Pasqual & Maria-Foteini Papakonstantinou (eds.), *Topography and History of Ancient Epicnemidian Locris*. Leiden: Brill, 65–199.

Pasqual, José (2013b), "The Classical Period (480–323 BC)". In: José Pasqual & Maria-Foteini Papakonstantinou (eds.), *Topography and History of Ancient Epicnemidian Locris*. Leiden: Brill, 471–505.
Patzek, Barbara (2006), "Troia und der Troia-Mythos im Bewußtsein der Griechen von der archaischen zur klassischen Zeit". In: Martin Zimmermann (ed.), *Der Traum von Troia. Geschichte und Mythos einer ewigen Stadt*. Munich: Verlag C.H. Beck, 57–70.
Pelling, Christopher (2007), "De Malignitate Plutarchi: Plutarch, Herodotus, and the Persian Wars". In: Emma Bridges, Edith Hall & P. J. Rhodes (eds.), *Cultural Responses to the Persian Wars: Antiquity to the Third Millennium*. Oxford: Oxford University Press, 145–165.
Pelzer, Erich (2003), "Waterloo (18. Juni 1815): Schlachtenmythos und Erinnerungssymbolik". In: Gerd Krumeich & Susanne Brandt (eds.), *Schlachtenmythen: Ereignis – Erzählung – Erinnerung*. Cologne: Böhlau Verlag, 143–164.
Penrose, F. C. (1891), "On the Ancient Hecatompedon Which Occupied the Site of the Parthenon on the Acropolis of Athens". *The Journal of Hellenic Studies* 12, 275–296.
Petropoulou, Angeliki (2008), "The Death of Masistios and the Mourning for his Loss (Hdt. 9.20-25.1)". In: Seyed Mohammad Reza Darbandi & Antigoni Zournatzi (eds.), *Ancient Greece and Ancient Iran: Cross-Cultural Encounters. 1st International Conference (Athens, 11–13 November 2006)*. Athens: National Hellenic Research Foundation, Cultural Center of the Embassy of the Islamic Republic of Iran in Athens, Hellenic National Commission for UNESCO, 9–30.
Philippson, Alfred & Kirsten, Ernst (1950), *Die griechischen Landschaften. Band 1. Der Nordosten der griechischen Halbinsel Teil 1. Thessalien und die Spercheios-Senke. Eine Landeskunde*. Frankfurt am Main: Vittorio Klostermann.
PMG: Denys L. Page (1962), *Poetae melici Graeci*. Oxford: Clarendon Press.
Pococke, Richard (1745), *A Description of the East, and Some other Countries*. London: W. Bowyer.
Podlecki, Anthony J. (1977), "Herodotus in Athens?". In: Konrad H. Kinzl (ed.), *Greece and the Eastern Mediterranean in Ancient History and Prehistory: Studies Presented to Fritz Schachermeyr on the Occasion of his Eightieth Birthday*. Berlin: Walter de Gruyter, 246–265.
Pohlenz, Max (1961), *Herodot: der erste Geschichtschreiber des Abendlandes*. Darmstadt: Wissenschaftliche Buchgesellschaft.
Pomtow, Hans (1912), "Die große Tholos zu Delphi und die Bestimmung der delphischen Rundbauten". *Klio* 12, 281–307.
Porciani, Leone (2001), *Prime forme della storiografia greca. Prospettiva locale e generale nella narrazione storica*. Stuttgart: Franz Steiner Verlag.
Porter, Barbara Nevling (2003), *Trees, Kings, and Politics: Studies in Assyrian Iconography*. Göttingen: Vandenhoeck & Ruprecht.
Poulsen, Frederik (1908), "Recherches sur quelques questions relatives à la topographie de Delphes". *Oversigt over det Kongelige Danske Videnskabernes Selskabs. Forhandlinger 1908*, 331–425.
Prandi, Luisa (1988), *Platea: momenti e problemi della storia di un polis*. Padua: Esedra Editrice.
Preißhofen, Felix (1977), "Zur Topographe der Akropolis". *Archäologischer Anzeiger* 1977 (1), 74–84.
Prentice, William Kelly (1920), "Thermopylae and Artemisium". *Transactions and Proceedings of the American Philological Association* 51, 5–18.
Pretzler, Maria (2007), *Pausanias: Travel Writing in Ancient Greece*. London: Duckworth.
Price, Simon (1985), "Delphi and divination". In: P.E. Easterling & J.V. Muir (eds.), *Greek Religion and Society*. Cambridge: Cambridge University Press, 128–154.
Price, Simon (2012), "Memory and Ancient Greece". In: Beate Dignas & R.R.R. Smith (eds.), *Historical and Religious Memory in the Ancient World*. Oxford: Oxford University Press, 15–36.
Priestley, Jessica (2014), *Herodotus and Hellenistic Culture*. Oxford: Oxford University Press.
Pritchett, W. Kendrick (1957), "New Light on Plataia". *American Journal of Archaeology* 61 (1), 9–28.

Pritchett, W. Kendrick (1958), "New Light on Thermopylae". *American Journal of Archaeology* 62 (2), 203–213.
Pritchett, W. Kendrick (1959), "Towards a Restudy of the Battle of Salamis". *American Journal of Archaeology* 63 (3), 251–262.
Pritchett, W. Kendrick (1961), "Xerxes' Route over Mount Olympos". *American Journal of Archaeology* 65 (4), 369–375.
Pritchett, W. Kendrick (1962), "Herodotos and the Themistokles Decree". *American Journal of Archaeology* 66 (1), 43–47.
Pritchett, W. Kendrick (1963), "Xerxes' Fleet at the "Ovens"". *American Journal of Archaeology* 67 (1), 1–6.
Pritchett, W. Kendrick (1965), *Studies in Ancient Greek Topography: Part I*. Berkeley: University of California Press.
Pritchett, W. Kendrick (1974), *The Greek State at War: Part II*. Berkeley: University of California Press.
Pritchett, W. Kendrick (1979a), *The Greek State at War: Part III: Religion*. Berkeley: University of California Press.
Pritchett, W. Kendrick (1979b), "Plataiai". *The American Journal of Philology* 100 (1), 145–152.
Pritchett, W. Kendrick (1982), *Studies in Ancient Greek Topography: Part IV (Passes) (Classical Studies 28)*. Berkeley: University of California Press.
Pritchett, W. Kendrick (1985a), *Studies in Ancient Greek Topography: Part V (Classical Studies 32)*. Berkeley: University of California Press.
Pritchett, W. Kendrick (1985b), *The Greek State at War: Part IV*. Berkeley: University of California Press.
Pritchett, W. Kendrick (1993), *The Liar School of Herodotos*. Amsterdam: Gieben.
Proietti, Giorgia (2012a), "La memoria delle guerre persiane in età imperiale. Il classicismo di Erode Attico e la 'stele dei Maratonomachi'". *Annuario della Scuola archeologica di Atene e delle missioni italiane in Oriente* 90, 97–117.
Proietti, Giorgia (2012b), "Memoria collettiva e identità etnica: nuovi paradigmi teorico-metodologici nella ricerca storica". In: Elena Franchi & Giorgia Proietti (eds.), *Forme della memoria e dinamiche identitarie nell'antichità greco-romana*, Trento: Dipartimento di Lettere e Filosofia Università degli Studi di Trento, 13–41.
Proietti, Giorgia (2012c) "Prospettive socio-antropologiche sull'arcaismo greco: la storiografia erodotea tra tradizione orale e 'storia intenzionale'". In: Elena Franchi & Giorgia Proietti (eds.), *Forme della memoria e dinamiche identitarie nell'antichità greco-romano*. Trento: Università degli studi di Trento, Dipartimento di filosofia, storia e beni culturali, 181–206.
Proietti, Giorgia (2014), "'Veri e falsi' nella memoria epigrafica di Maratona: il caso dell'epitaffio sul campo di battaglia". In: Angela Donati (ed.), *L'iscrizione e il suo doppio. Atti del Convegno Borghesi 2013*. Faenza: Fratelli Lega Editori, 165–182.
Proietti, Giorgia (2015a), "I Greci e la memoria della vittoria: alcune considerazioni sui trofei delle Guerre Persiane". *Hormos* 7, 148–175.
Proietti, Giorgia (2015b), "War and Memory: The Battle of Psyttaleia before Herodotus' Histories". *Bulletin of the Institute of Classical Studies* 58 (2), 43–54.
Purves, Alex C. (2010), *Space and Time in Ancient Greek Narrative*. Cambridge: Cambridge University Press.
Raaflaub, Kurt (2010), "Ulterior Motives in Ancient Historiography: What Exactly, and Why?". In: Lin Foxhall, Hans-Joachim Gehrke & Nino Luraghi (eds.), *Intentional History: Spinning Time in Ancient Greece*. Stuttgart: Franz Steiner Verlag, 189–210.
Radet, Georges Albert (1891), "Notes de géographie ancienne (1)". *Bulletin de correspondance hellénique* (15), 373–380.

Ramage, Andrew (1983), "Pactolus North". In: George M. A. Hanfmann (ed.), *Sardis: from Prehistoric to Roman Times. Results of the Archaeological Exploration of Sardis 1958–1975*. Cambridge, Massachusetts: Harvard University Press, 34–37.
Ramsay, W. M. (1887), "Antiquities of Southern Phrygia and the Border Lands (I)". *The American Journal of Archaeology and of the History of the Fine Arts* 3, 344–368.
Ramsay, W. M. (1897), *The Cities and Bishoprics of Phrygia. Being an Essay of the Local History of Phrygia from the Earliest Times to the Turkish Conquest*. Oxford: Clarendon Press.
Ramsay, W. M. (1920), "Military Operations on the North Front of Mount Taurus". *The Journal of Hellenic Studies* 40 (1), 89–112.
Rawlings, Louis (2007), *The Ancient Greeks at War*. Manchester: Manchester University Press.
Rawlinson, George (1880), *History of Herodotus*. New York: Scribner and Welford.
Ray, Fred Eugene Jr. (2009), *Land Battles in 5th Century B.C. Greece: A History and Analysis of 173 Engagements*. Jefferson: McFarland & Company, Inc., Publishers.
Rayet, Olivier & Thomas, Albert (1877–1880), *Milet et le golfe latmique: Tralles, Magnésie du Méandre, Priène, Milet, Didyme, Héraclée du Latmos*. Paris: J. Baudry.
RE = *Paulys Realencyclopädie der classischen Altertumswissenschaft* (1893–1980). Stuttgart: J. B. Metzler'sche Verlagsbuchhandlung.
Redfield, James (1985), "Herodotus the Tourist". *Classical Philology* 80:2, 97–118.
Rediadis, Periklis D. (1906), "Τὸ Ἡράκλειον τῆς ναυμαχίας τῆς Σαλαμῖνος". *Ἀρχαιολογικὴ Ἐφημερίς* 1906, 239–244.
Reicherter, K., Papanikolaou, I., Roger, J., Mathes-Schmidt, M., Papanikolaou, D., Rössler, S., Grützner, C., Stamatis, G., (2010), "Holocene tsunamigenic sediments and tsunami modelling in the Thermaikos Gulf area (northern Greece)". *Zeitschrift für Geomorphologie* 54, Supplement 3, 99–126.
Reinders, H.R. (1988), *New Halos, a Hellenistic Town in Thessalía, Greece*. Utrecht: Hes publishers.
Reitz-Joosse, Bettina (2016), "Land at Peace and Sea at War: Landscape and the Memory of Actium in Greek Epigrams and Propertius' *Elegies*". In: Jeremy McInerney & Ineke Sluiter (eds.), *Valueing Landscape in Classical Antiquity: Natural Environment and Cultural Imagination*. Leiden: Brill, 276–296.
Rhodes, Robin Francis (1995), *Architecture and Meaning on the Athenian Acropolis*. Cambridge: Cambridge University Press.
Richards, G.C. (1930), "The Hollows of Euboea". *Classical Review* 44 (2), 61–62.
Riegl, Alois (1928), *Gesammelte Aufsätze*. Vienna: Dr. Benno Filser Verlag.
Robert, Carl (1909), *Pausanias als Schriftsteller*. Berlin: Weidmannsche Buchhandlung.
Robert, Fernand (1939), *Thymélè : Recherches sur la signification et la destination des Monuments circulaires dans l'Architecture religieuse de la Grèce*. Paris: Éditions de Boccard.
Robert, L. (1935), *Villes d'Asie Mineure. Études de géographie antique*. Paris: Éditions de Boccard.
Robertson, N. (1976), "The Thessalian Expedition of 480 B.C.". *The Journal of Hellenic Studies* 96, 100–120.
Robertson, Noel (1982), "Hittite Ritual at Sardis". *Classical Antiquity* 1 (1), 122–140.
Robertson, Noel (1992), *Festivals and Legends: The Formation of Greek Cities in the Light of Public Ritual*. Toronto: University of Toronto Press.
Robertson, Noel (1996), "Athena's Shrines and Festivals". In: Jenifer Neils (ed.), *Worshipping Athena: Panathenaia and Parthenon*. Madison: The University of Wisconsin Press, 27–77.
Robertson, Noel (1998), "The City Center of Archaic Athens". *Hesperia* 67 (3), 283–302.
Rocchi, Maria (1980), "Serse e l'« acqua amara » dell'Ellesponto". In: *Perennitas: Studi in onore di Angelo Brelich*. Rome: Edizioni dell'Ateneo, 417–429.
Rollinger, Robert (1998), "Überlegungen zu Herodot, Xerxes und dessen angeblicher Zerstörung Babylons". *Altorientalische Forschungen* 25 (2), 339–373.

Rollinger, Robert (2003), Herodotus vii. Xerxes according to Herodotus". *Encyclopædia Iranica*, online edition (http://www.iranicaonline.org/articles/herodotus-vii) accessed on 20 October 2015.

Rollinger, Robert (2013), "Dareios und Xerxes an den Rändern der Welt". In: Boris Dunsch & Kai Ruffing (eds.), *Herodots Quellen – Die Quellen Herodots*. Wiesbaden: Harrassowitz Verlag, 95–116.

Romm, James (1998), *Herodotus*. New Haven: Yale University Press.

Romm, James (2006), "Herodotus and the natural world". In: Carolyn Dewald & John Marincola (eds.), *The Cambridge Companion to Herodotus*. Cambridge: Cambridge University Press, 178–191.

Rood, Tim (2006), "Herodotus and foreign lands". In: Carolyn Dewald & John Marincola (eds.), *The Cambridge Companion to Herodotus*. Cambridge: Cambridge University Press, 290–305.

Rood, Tim (2012), "Herodotus". In: Irene J.F. de Jong (ed.), *Space in Ancient Greek Literature: Studies in Ancient Greek Narrative*. Leiden: Brill, 121–140.

Rose, Charles Brian (1998), "Troy and the Historical Imagination". *The Classical World* 91 (5), 405–413.

Rose, Charles Brian (2003), "The Temple of Athena at Ilion". *Studia Troica* 13, 27–88.

Rose, Charles Brian (2006), "Auf mythengetränktem Boden – Ilion in griechischer, römischer und byzantinischer Zeit". In: Manfred Osman Korfmann (ed.), *Troia: Archäologie eines Siedlungshügels und seiner Landschaft*. Mainz am Rhein: Verlag Philipp von Zabern, 189–198.

Rosenberger, Veit (2003), "Reisen zum Orakel: Griechen, Lyder und Perser als Klienten hellenischer Orakelstätten". In: Markus Witte & Stefan Alkier (eds.), *Die Griechen und der Vordere Orient: Beiträge zum Kultur- und Religionskontakt zwischen Griechenland und dem Vorderen Orient im 1. Jahrtausend v. Chr.* Freiburg: Universtätsverlag, 25–57.

Rosenmeyer, Thomas G. (1982), "History or Poetry? The Example of Herodotus". *Clio* 11 (3), 239–259.

Rösler, Wolfgang (2013), "Ein Wunder im Kampf um Delphi (VIII 35–9) – schlagendstes Beispiel von Quellenfiktion durch Herodot? Kritische Retraktionen zum Herodotbild von Detlev Fehling". In: Boris Dunsch & Kai Ruffing (eds.), *Herodots Quellen – Die Quellen Herodots*. Wiesbaden: Harrassowitz Verlag, 241–253.

Rothberg, Michael (2009), *Multidirectional memory: remembering the Holocaust in the age of decolonization*. Stanford: Stanford University Press.

Ruberto, Antonella (2012), "La vittoria di Serse in Grecia. Problemi, testimonianze, ipotesi". *Klio* 94, 300–311.

Rutherford, Ian (2001), "The New Simonides: Toward a Commentary". In: Deborah Boedeker & David Sider (eds.), *The New Simonides: Contexts of Praise and Desire*. Oxford: Oxford University Press, 33–54.

Sabin, Philip (2007), *Lost Battles: Reconstructing the Great Clashes of the Ancient World*. London & New York: Hambledon Continuum.

Sacks, Kenneth S. (1976), "Herodotus and the Dating of the Battle of Thermopylae". *The Classical Quarterly*, 26 (2), 232–248.

Saïd, Suzanne (2012), "Herodotus and the 'Myth' of the Trojan War". In: Emily Baragwanath & Mathieu de Bakker (eds.), *Myth, Truth, and Narrative in Herodotus*. Oxford: Oxford University Press, 87–105.

Samiei, Sasan (2014), *Ancient Persia in Western history: Hellenism and the representation of the Achaemenid Empire*. London & New York: I. B. Tauris.

Sánchez-Moreno, Eduardo (2010), "El paso de Las Termópilas 2.500 años (y algunas ficciones) después". In: César Fornis, Julián Gallego, Pedro López Barja & Miriam Valdés (eds.), *Dialéctica histórica y compromiso social: Homenaje a Domingo Plácido*. Zaragoza: Pórtico, 1411–1436.

Sánchez-Moreno, Eduardo (2013a), "Communication Route in and around Epicnemidian Locris". In: José Pasqual & Maria-Foteini Papakonstantinou (eds.), *Topography and History of Ancient Epicnemidian Locris*. Leiden: Brill, 279–335.

Sánchez-Moreno, Eduardo (2013b), "Mountain Passes in Epicnemidian Locris". In: José Pasqual & Maria-Foteini Papakonstantinou (eds.), *Topography and History of Ancient Epicnemidian Locris*. Leiden: Brill, 337–359.
Sancisi-Weerdenburg, Heleen (1980), *Yaunā en Persai: Grieken en Perzen in een ander Perspectief*. Dissertation Rijksuniversiteit Leiden.
Sancisi-Weerdenburg, Heleen (1994a), "Xerxes vanuit Perzische optiek". *Lampas* 27, 194–212.
Sancisi-Weerdenburg, Heleen (1994b), "Xerxes en de plataan: vier variaties op een motief". *Lampas* 27, 213–229.
Sancisi-Weerdenburg, Heleen (1999), "The Persian Kings and History". In: Christina Shuttleworth Kraus (ed.), *The Limits of Historiography: Genre and Narrative in Ancient Historical Texts*. Leiden: Brill, 91–112.
Saporiti, Marta (2010), "Il santuario di Aglauro". In: Emanuele Greco (ed.), *Topografia di Atene: Sviluppo urbano e monumenti dalle origini al III secolo d.C. Tomo 1: Acropoli - Areopago - Tra Acropoli e Pnice*. Athens & Paestum: Pandemos, 159.
Sbardella, Livio (2000), "Achille e gli eroi di Platea. Simonide, frr. 10-11 W²". *Zeitschrift für Papyrologie und Epigraphik* 129, 1–11.
Schachter, Albert (1981), *Cults of Boeotia: 1. Acheloos to Hera* (*Institute of Classical Studies Bulletin*, Supplement 38.1). London: Institute of Classical Studies.
Schachter, Albert (1986), *Cults of Boeotia: 2. Herakles to Poseidon* (*Institute of Classical Studies Bulletin*, Supplement 38.2). London: Institute of Classical Studies.
Schachter, Albert (1994), *Cults of Boeotia: 3. Potnia to Zeus* (*Institute of Classical Studies Bulletin*, Supplement 38.3). London: Institute of Classical Studies.
Schama, Simon (1995), *Landscape and Memory*. New York: Alfred A. Knopf.
Scheer, Tanja Susanne (1993), *Mythische Vorväter: zur Bedeutung griechischer Heroenmythen im Selbstverständnis kleinasiatischer Städte*. Munich: Editio Maris.
Scheer, Tanja Susanne (2000), *Die Gottheit und ihr Bild. Untersuchungen zur Funktion griechischer Kultbilder in Religion und Politik* (Zetemata 105). Munich: C.H. Beck.
Scheer, Tanja Susanne (2003), "Die geraubte Artemis: Griechen, Perser und die Kultbilder der Götter". In: Markus Witte & Stefan Alkier (eds.), *Die Griechen und der Vordere Orient: Beiträge zum Kultur- und Religionskontakt zwischen Griechenland und dem Vorderen Orient im 1. Jahrtausend v. Chr*. Freiburg: Univertätsverlag, 59–85.
Schefold, Karl (1953–1954), "Weihgeschenke nach den Perserkriegen". Ἀρχαιολογικὴ Ἐφημερίς 1953–1954, 141–144.
Schliemann, Heinrich (1881), *Ilios. Stadt und Land der Trojaner. Forschungen und Entdeckungen in der Troas und besonderes auf der Baustelle von Troja*. Leipzig: F.A. Brockhaus.
Schliemann, Heinrich (1884), *Troja. Ergebnisse meiner neuesten Ausgrabungen auf der Baustelle von Troja, in den Heldengräbern, Bunarbaschi und andern Orten der Troas im Jahre 1882*. Leipzig: F.A. Brockhaus.
Schrader, Hans (1939), *Die archaischen Marmorbilwerke der Akropolis*. Frankfurt am Main: Vittorio Klostermann.
Schrijvers, Piet (2007), "De gevangenis van Socrates". *Lampas* 40 (4), 323–333.
Schudson, Michael (1995), "Dynamics of Distortion in Collective Memory". In: Daniel L. Schacter (ed.), *Memory Distortion: How Minds, Brains, and Societies Reconstruct the Past*. Cambridge, Massachusetts: Harvard University Press, 346–364.
Schulz, Fabian (2013), "Xerxes, Agamemnon und Hektor: Fehlentscheidungen und Fähigkeit zur Einsicht". In: Klaus Geus, Elisabeth Irwin & Thomas Poiss (eds.), *Herodots Wege des Erzählens: Logos und Topos in den* Historien. Frankfurt am Main: Peter Lang, 333–344.
Scott, Michael (2014), *Olympia and Delphi: The Spatial Politics of Panhellenism in the Archaic and Classical Periods*. Cambridge: Cambridge University Press.

SEG = *Supplementum Epigraphicum Graecum*. Leiden: Brill.
Sekunda, Nick V. (1988) "Persian settlement in Hellespontine Phrygia". In: Heleen Sancisi-Weerdenburg & Amélie Kuhrt (eds.), *Achaemenid History III: Method and Theory (Proceedings of the London 1985 Achaemenid History Workshop)*. Leiden: Nederlands Instituut voor het Nabije Oosten, 175–196.
Sementchenko, Lada (2011), "Sources of Maeander and Marsyas in Classical Texts". In: Lâtife Summerer, Askold Ivantchik & Alexander von Kienlin (eds.), *Kelainai-Apameia Kibotos: Stadtentwicklung im anatolischen Kontext. Akten des internationalen Kolloquiums, München, 2.-4. April 2009*. Bordeaux: Ausonius Éditions, 63–70.
Senior, Nassau William (1859), *A Journal kept in Turkey and Greece in the autumn of 1857, and the beginning of 1858*. London: Longman, Brown, Green, Longmans, and Roberts.
Settis, Salvatore (1967–1968), "Un « enigma » delfico: Pausania, la Tholos, il Phylakeion". *Annuario della Scuola Archeologica di Atene e delle Missioni Italiane in Oriente* 45–46 (new series 29–30), 355–372.
Shahbazi, A. Sh. (1985), "Iranian Notes 1-6". In: *Papers in Honour of Professor Mary Boyce* (Acta Iranica 25). Leiden: Brill: 497–510.
Shaw, P.-J. (2001), "Lord of Hellas, Old Men of the Sea: The Occasion of Simonides' Elegy on Plataea". In: Deborah Boedeker & David Sider (eds.), *The New Simonides: Contexts of Praise and Desire*. Oxford: Oxford University Press, 164–181.
Shear, T. Leslie Jr. (1982), "The Demolished Temple at Eleusis". In: *Studies in Athenian Architecture, Sculpture and Topography. Presented to Homer A. Thompson (Hesperia Supplements* 20). Princeton: American School of Classical Studies at Athens, 129–140 and 210–212.
Shear, T. Leslie Jr. (1993), "The Persian Destruction of Athens: Evidence from Agora Deposits". *Hesperia* 62 (4), 383–482.
Shrimpton, Gordon S. (1997), *History and Memory in Ancient Greece*. Montreal & Kingston: McGill-Queen's University Press.
Sidebotham, Steve (1982), "Herodotus on Artemisium". *The Classical World* 75 (3), 177–186.
Siewert, Peter (1972), *Der Eid von Plataiai*. Munich: C.H. Beck'sche Verlagsbuchhandlung.
Singor, Henk (2007), "Decline and Fall". *Lampas* 40 (4), 426–424.
Slatkin, Laura M. (1986), "The Wrath of Thetis". *Transactions of the American Philological Association* 116, 1–24.
Smid, T.C. (1970), "'Tsunamis' in Greek Literature". *Greece & Rome* 17 (1), 100–104.
Solmsen, Lieselotte (1944), "Speeches in Herodotus' Account of the Battle of Plataea". *Classical Philology* 39 (4), 241–253.
Sourvinou-Inwood, Christiane (1988), ""Myth" and History: on Herodotus III.48 and 50–53". *Opuscula Atheniensia* 17, 167–182.
Sourvinou-Inwood, Christiane & Parker, Robert (2011), *Athenian Myths and Festivals: Aglauros, Erechtheus, Plynteria, Panathenaia, Dionysia*. Oxford: Oxford University Press.
Spano, Giuseppe (1928), "Le rappresentanze di Artemis e Aktaion e l'Aphrodite di Doidalses". *Atti della reale Accademia di Archeologia, Lettere e Belle Arti* 10.
Spratt, T. (1847), "Remarks on the Isthmus of Mount Athos". *The Journal of the Royal Geographical Society of London* 17, 145–150.
Spyropoulos, Theodoros G. (1972), "Πλαταιαί" (part of "Ἀρχαιότητες και μνήμεια Βοιωτίας - Φθιώτιδος"). *Ἀρχαιολογικόν Δέλτιον* 27 (2), 318–319.
Spyropoulos, Theodoros G. (1973), "Ειδήσεις εκ Βοιωτίας". *Ἀρχαιολογικά Ἀνάλεκτα εξ Ἀθηνῶν* 6 (2), 375–395.
Squire, Larry. R. (1995), "Biological Foundations of Accuracy and Inaccuracy in Memory". In: Daniel L. Schacter (ed.), *Memory Distortion: How Minds, Brains, and Societies Reconstruct the Past*. Cambridge, Massachusetts: Harvard University Press, 197–225.

Stadter, Philip (2006), "Herodotus and the Cities of Mainland Greece". In: Carolyn Dewald & John Marincola (eds.), *The Cambridge Companion to Herodotus*. Cambridge: Cambridge University Press, 242–256.
Stählin, Friedrich (1924), *Das hellenische Thessalien: landeskundliche und geschichtliche Beschreibung Thessaliens in der hellenischen und römischen Zeit*. Stuttgart: Engelhorn.
Stählin, Friedrich (1936), "Thermopylen". *RE* 5a, 2398–2423.
Stefanini, Ruggiero (1977), "Giambattista Casti in Troy and Athens, 1788". *California Studies in Classical Antiquity* 10, 157–168.
Stein-Hölkeskamp, Elke & Hölkeskamp, Karl-Joachim (eds.) (2006), *Erinnerungsorte der Antike: die römische Welt*. Munich: C.H. Beck.
Stein-Hölkeskamp, Elke & Hölkeskamp, Karl-Joachim (eds.) (2010), *Erinnerungsorte der Antike: die griechische Welt*. Munich: C.H. Beck.
Steinbock, Bernd (2013), *Social Memory in Athenian Public Discourse: Uses and Meanings of the Past*. Ann Arbor: The University of Michigan Press.
Steiner, Deborah (1999), "To praise, not to bury: Simonides fr. 531P". *The Classical Quarterly* 49 (2), 383–395.
Steinhart, Matthias (1997), "Bemerkungen zu Rekonstruktion, Ikonographie und Inschrift des plätäischen Weihgeschenkes". *Bulletin de Correspondance Hellénique* 121 (1), 33–69.
Steskal, Martin (2004), *Der Zerstörungsbefund 480/79 der Athener Akropolis. Eine Fallstudie zum etablierten Chronologiegerüst*. Hamburg: Verlag Dr. Kovač.
Stissi, V.V., Agnousiotis, D., Efstatiou, D., Dijkstra, T., Heijmans, E., Kamphorst, S., Mamaloudi, I., Reinders, H.R., Rondiri, V., Stamelou, E., Rookhuijzen, J.Z. van, "Halos: Preliminary report of the 2013–2014 trial trenches at Magoula Plataniotiki". *Pharos* 21.2, 85–115.
Strasburger, Hermann (1951), review of "Alexander der Große am Hellespont" by Hans Ulrich Instinsky. *Gnomon* 23 (1), 83–88.
Strasburger, Hermann (1955), "Herodot und das perikleische Athen". *Historia: Zeitschrift für alte Geschichte* 4, 1–25.
Strasburger, Hermann (1972), *Homer und die Geschichtsschreibung*. Heidelberg: Carl Winter Universitätsverlag.
Strassler, Robert B. (ed.) (2007), *The Landmark Herodotus: The Histories*. New York: Anchor Books.
Strauss, Bary (2004), *The battle of Salamis : the naval encounter that saved Greece – and western civilization*. New York: Simon & Schuster.
Struck, Adolf (1907), "Der Xerxeskanal am Athos". *Neue Jahrbücher für das klassische Altertum, Geschichte und deutsche Literatur* 10, 115–130.
Stubbings, Frank H. (1946), "Xerxes and the Plane-Tree". *Greece & Rome* 15 (44), 63–67.
Summerer, Lâtife (2007), "Picturing Persian Victory: the Painted Battle Scene on the Munich Wood". *Ancient Civilizations from Scythia to Siberia* 13, 3–30.
Summerer, Lâtife (2008), "Imagining a Tomb Chamber: The Iconographic Program of the Tatarlı Wall Paintings". In: Seyed Mohammad Reza Darbandi & Antigoni Zournatzi (eds.), *Ancient Greece and Ancient Iran: Cross-Cultural Encounters. 1st International Conference (Athens, 11–13 November 2006)*. Athens: National Hellenic Research Foundation, Cultural Center of the Embassy of the Islamic Republic of Iran in Athens, Hellenic National Commission for UNESCO, 265–299.
Summerer, Lâtife (2011), "Die persische Armee in Kelainai". In: Lâtife Summerer, Askold Ivantchik & Alexander von Kienlin (eds.), *Kelainai-Apameia Kibotos: Stadtentwicklung im anatolischen Kontext. Akten des internationalen Kolloquiums, München, 2.-4. April 2009*. Bordeaux: Ausonius Éditions, 33–54.
Szegedy-Maszak, Andrew (1978), "Legends of Greek Lawgivers". *Greek, Roman and Byzantine Studies* 19 (3), 199–209.

Szemler, George John (1986), "The Great Isthmus Corridor, Delphi, Thermopylae: Centers of Resistance against Great Powers in North-Central Greece". In: Toru Yuge & Masaoki Doi (eds.), *Forms of Control and Subordination in Antiquity*. Leiden: Brill, 553–566.
Szemler, George John (1989), "„The Pass through Thrachis" – Her. 7,176,2". *Klio* 71 (1), 211–215.
Szemler, George John, Cherf, W.J. & Kraft, J.C. (1996), *Thermopylai. Myth and Reality in 480 B.C.* Chicago: Ares Publishers.
Tallis, Nigel (2010), "The Achaemenid Army in a Near Eastern Context". In: John Curtis & St. John Simpson (eds.), *The World of Achaemenid Persia: History, Art and Society in Iran and the Ancient Near East*. London: I.B. Tauris, 309–314.
Tarn, W.W. (1908), "The Fleet of Xerxes". *The Journal of Hellenic Studies* 28, 202–233.
Taylor, Martha C. (1997), *Salamis and the Salaminioi: The History of an Unofficial Athenian Demos*. Amsterdam: J.C. Gieben.
Terdiman, Richard (1993), *Present Past: Modernity and the Memory Crisis*. Ithaca & London: Cornell University Press.
Thalmann, Jean-Paul (1980), "Recherches aux Thermopyles". *Bulletin de correspondance hellénique* 104 (2), 757–760.
Thomas, Giorgos (2010), "Η αρχαία πόλη Αφέτες στον Πλατανιά του Πηλίου. Μία βέβαιη ταύτιση". *Θεσσαλικό Ημερολόγιο* 57, 3–14.
Thomas, Rosalind (1989), *Oral Tradition and Written Record in Classical Athens*. Cambridge: Cambridge University Press.
Thomas, Rosalind (2000), *Herodotus in Context: Ethnography, Science and the Art of Persuasion*. Cambridge: Cambridge University Press.
Thomas, Rosalind (2001), "Herodotus' *Histories* and the Floating Gap". In: Nino Luraghi (ed.), *The Historian's Craft in the Age of Herodotus*. Oxford: Oxford University Press, 198–210.
Thomas, Rosalind (2006), "The intellectual milieu of Herodotus". In: Carolyn Dewald & John Marincola (eds.), *The Cambridge Companion to Herodotus*. Cambridge: Cambridge University Press, 60–75.
Thompson, Dorothy Burr (1954), "The Persian Spoils in Athens". In: Saul S. Weinberg (ed.), *The Aegean and the Near East: Studies Presented to Hetty Goldman on the Occasion of her Seventy-fifth Birthday*. Locust Valley: J. J. Augustin Publisher, 281–291.
Thompson, Homer A. (1981), "Athens Faces Adversity". *Hesperia* 50 (4), 343–355.
Thonemann, Peter J. (2003), "Hellenistic Inscriptions from Lydia". *Epigraphica Anatolica* 36, 95–108.
Thonemann, Peter J. (2011), *The Maeander Valley: A Historical Geography from Antiquity to Alexander*. Cambridge: Cambridge University Press.
Thonemann, Peter J. (2014), "The wrong Croesus: Herodotus, the birth of history and some imaginative guesswork". *The Times Literary Supplement* 15 August 2014.
Tölle-Kastenbein, Renate (1976), *Herodotus und Samos*. Bochum: Duris Verlag.
Tölle-Kastenbein, Renate (1983), "Bemerkungen zur absoluten Chronologie spätarchaischer und frühklassischer Denkmäler Athens". *Archäologischer Anzeiger* 1983 (4), 573–584.
Tonkin, Elizabeth (1992), *Narrating Our Pasts: The Social Construction of Oral History*. Cambridge: Cambridge University Press.
Tracy, Stephen (2008), "Europe and Asia: Aeschylus' *Persians* and Homer's *Iliad*". In: Seyed Mohammad Reza Darbandi & Antigoni Zournatzi (eds.), *Ancient Greece and Ancient Iran: Cross-Cultural Encounters. 1st International Conference (Athens, 11–13 November 2006)*. Athens: National Hellenic Research Foundation, Cultural Center of the Embassy of the Islamic Republic of Iran in Athens, Hellenic National Commission for UNESCO, 1–8.
Travlos, John (1971), *Bildlexikon zur Topographie des antiken Athen*. Tübingen: Verlag Ernst Wasmuth.
Tripodi, Bruno (1986), "La Macedonia, la Peonia, il carro sacro di Serse (Herodot. 8, 115-16)". *Giornale italiano di filologia* 38, 243–251.

Tsantsanoglou, Kyriakos (2008), "Magi in Athens in the Fifth Century BC". In: Seyed Mohammad Reza Darbandi & Antigoni Zournatzi (eds.), *Ancient Greece and Ancient Iran: Cross-Cultural Encounters. 1st International Conference (Athens, 11–13 November 2006)*. Athens: National Hellenic Research Foundation, Cultural Center of the Embassy of the Islamic Republic of Iran in Athens, Hellenic National Commission for UNESCO, 31–39.

Tschira, Arnold (1940), "Die unfertigen Säulentrommeln auf der Akropolis von Athen". *Jahrbuch des deutschen archäologischen Instituts* 55, 242–264.

Tsirivakos, Elias (1967), "Μαγούλα". *Ἀρχαιολογικὸν Δέλτιον* 22, 146.

Tuplin, Christopher J. (1991), "Darius' Suez Canal and Persian Imperialism". In: Heleen Sancisi-Weerdenburg & Amélie Kuhrt (eds.), *Achaemenid History VI: Asia Minor and Egypt: Old Cultures in a New Empire* (Proceedings of the Groningen 1988 Achaemenid History Workshop). Leiden: Nederlands Instituut voor het Nabije Oosten, 237–283.

Tuplin, Christopher J. (2003), "Xerxes' March from Doriscus to Therme". *Historia: Zeitschrift für alte Geschichte* 52 (4), 385–409.

Tuplin, Christopher (2011), "Xenophon at Celaenae: Palaces, Rivers and Myths". In: Lâtife Summerer, Askold Ivantchik & Alexander von Kienlin (eds.), *Kelainai-Apameia Kibotos: Stadtentwicklung im anatolischen Kontext. Akten des internationalen Kolloquiums, München, 2.-4. April 2009*. Bordeaux: Ausonius Éditions, 71–92.

Tyrrell, William Blake (1984), *Amazons: A Study in Athenian Mythmaking*. Baltimore & London: The Johns Hopkins University Press.

Ulrichs, H.N. (1843), "Topographie und Inschriften von Tithora". *Rheinisches Museum für Philologie* 2, 544–560.

Unger, Eckhard & Weißbach, F.H. (1915), "Die Dariusstele am Tearos". *Archäologischer Anzeiger: Beiblatt zum Jahrbuch des Archäologischen Instituts* 1 (*Archäologischer Anzeiger* 30), 3–16.

Urry, John (2002), *The Tourist Gaze*. London: SAGE Publications (second edition, first published 1990).

Van Dyke, Ruth M. & Alcock, Susan E. (2003), "Archaeologies of Memory: An Introduction". In: Ruth M. Van Dyke & Susan E. Alcock (eds.), *Archaeologies of Memory*. Malden: Blackwell Publishers, 1–13.

van Opstall, Emilie (2007), "Onder de plataan". *Lampas* 40 (4), 314–322.

van Rookhuijzen, Jan Zacharias (2017a), "De 'archeologie van haat': mnemotopen van Perzische verwoesting in Griekenland". *Tijdschrift voor Mediterrane Archeologie* 57, 32–37.

van Rookhuijzen, Jan Zacharias (2017b), "Die delphische „Rolling Stones" und die imaginäre persische Belagerung von 480 v.Chr." In: Fabrizi, Virginia (ed.), *The Semantics of Space in Greek and Roman Narratives*. Heidelberg: Propylaeum, 55–68.

van Rookhuijzen, Jan Zacharias (2017c), "How not to appease Athena: A reconsideration of Xerxes' purported visit to the Troad (Hdt. 7.42-43)", *Klio* 99 (2), 464–484.

van Rookhuijzen, Jan Zacharias (2017d), "Lost in Cappadocia: A reconsideration of Xerxes' visit to Kritalla (Hdt. 7.26)", *Mnemosyne* 70 (2), 281–289.

van Rookhuijzen, Jan Zacharias (2017e) "Thetis in the Ovens: A reconsideration of Herodotus' topography of Magnesia". *The Journal of Hellenic Studies* 137, 24–41.

van Rookhuijzen, Jan Zacharias (2017f), "Where Aglauros Once Fell Down: The Memory Landscape of the Persian Siege of the Acropolis". In: Elena Franchi & Giorgia Proietti (eds.), Conflict in communities. Forward-looking Memories in Classical Athens. Trento, 27–68.

van Wees, Hans (2002), "Herodotus and the Past". In: Egbert J. Bakker, Irene J.F. de Jong & Hans van Wees (eds.), *Brill's Companion to Herodotus*. Leiden: Brill, 321–349.

van Wees, Hans (2004), *Greek Warfare: Myths and Realities*. London: Duckworth.

Vandiver, Elizabeth (1991), *Heroes in Herodotus: The Interaction of Myth and History*. Frankfurt am Main: Peter Lang.

Vansina, Jan (1961), *De la tradition orale : essay de méthode historique*. Tervuren: Koninklijk Museum voor Midden-Afrika.
Vansina, Jan (1985), *Oral Tradition as History*. Madison: The University of Wisconsin Press.
Vergunst, Jo (2012), "Seeing Ruins: Imagined and Visible Landscapes in North-East Scotland". In: Monica Janowski & Tim Ingold (eds.), *Imagining Landscapes: Past, Present and Future*. Farnham: Ashgate, 19–37.
Vermeule, Cornelius C. III (1995), "Neon Ilion and Ilium Novum: Kings, Soldiers, Citizens, and Tourists at Classical Troy". In: Jane B. Carter & Sarah P. Morris (eds.), *The Ages of Homer: a Tribute to Emily Townsend Vermeule*. Austin: University of Texas Press, 467–482.
Vignolo Munson, Rosaria (2009), "Who Are Herodotus' Persians?". *The Classical World* 102 (4), 457–470.
Vignolo Munson, Rosaria (2012), "Herodotus and the Heroic Age: The Case of Minos". In: Emily Baragwanath & Mathieu de Bakker (eds.), *Myth, Truth, and Narrative in Herodotus*. Oxford: Oxford University Press, 195–212.
Virchow, Rudolf (1892), "Über den troischen Ida, die Skamander-Quelle und die Porta van Zeitunlü". *Sitzungsberichte der Königlich Preussischen Akademie der Wissenschaften* 1892 (2), 969–982.
Visser, Margaret (1982), "Worship Your Enemy: Aspects of Cult of Heroes in Ancient Greece". *The Harvard Theological Review* 75 (4), 403–428.
Vollgraff, W. (1907–1908), "Notes on the Topography of Phthiotis". *Annual of the British School at Athens* 14, 224–225.
von Fritz, Kurt (1967), *Die Griechische Geschichtsschreibung. Band I: Von den Anfängen bis Thukydides*. Berlin: Walter de Gruyter & Co.
von Haehling, Raban (1993), "Furcht und Schrecken in Herodots Darstellung und Deutung der Perserkriege". *Klio* 75, 85–98.
Wace, Alan J.B. (1906), "The Topography of Pelion and Magnesia". *The Journal of Hellenic Studies* 26, 143–168.
Wace, Alan J.B. & Droop, J.P. (1906–1907), "Excavations at Theotokou, Thessaly". *The Annual of the British School at Athens* 13, 309–327.
Wade-Gery, H.T. (1933), "Classical Epigrams and Epitaphs: A Study of the Kimonian Age". *The Journal of Hellenic Studies* 53 (1), 71–104.
Walbank, F.W. (1950), review of "Alexander der Große am Hellespont" by Hans Ulrich Instinsky. *The Journal of Hellenic Studies* 70, 79–81.
Wallace, M.B. (1974), "Herodotos and Euboia". *Phoenix* 28 (1, *Studies Presented to Mary E. White on the Occasion of Her Sixty-Fifth Birthday*), 22–44.
Wallace, Paul W. (1969), "Psyttaleia and the Trophies of the Battle of Salamis". *American Journal of Archaeology* 73 (3), 293–303.
Wallace, Paul W. (1982), "The Final Battle at Plataia". In: *Studies in Attic Epigraphy, History and Topography. Presented to Eugene Vanderpool* (*Hesperia Supplements* 19). Princeton: American School of Classical Studies at Athens, 183–192.
Wallace, Paul W. (1984), "Aphetai and the Battle of Artemision". In: *Studies presented to Sterling Dow on his Eightieth Birthday* (*Greek, Roman and Byzantine Monograph* 10). Durham, USA: Duke University, 305–310.
Wallace, Paul W. (1985), "The Sanctuary of Demeter: The Site of the Victory at Plataia (479 B.C.)". In: Paul Roesch (ed.), *Colloques internationaux du CNRS « La Béotie antique » Lyon, Saint-Étienne 16–20 mai 1983*. Paris: Éditions du CNRS, 97–100.
Wallinga, H.T. (2005), *Xerxes' Greek Adventure: the Naval Perspective*. Leiden: Brill.
Walsch, R. (1836), *A Residence at Constantinople, during a Period including the Commencement, Progress, and Termination of the Greek and Turkish Revolutions*. London: Frederick Westley and A. H. Davis.

Walser, Gerold (1984), *Hellas und Iran*. Darmstadt: Wissenschaftliche Buchgesellschaft.
Walsh, John (1986), "The Date of the Athenian Stoa at Delphi". *American Journal of Archaeology* 90 (3), 319–336.
Walter, Uwe (2010), "Herodot und Thukydides – die Entstehung der Geschichtsschreibung". In: Elke Stein-Hölkeskamp & Karl-Joachim Hölkeskamp (eds.), *Erinnerungsorte der Antike: die griechische Welt*. Munich: C.H. Beck, 400–417.
Washington, Henry S. (1891), "Excavations by the American School at Plataia in 1891: Discovery of a Temple of Archaic Plan". *American Journal of Archaeology and of the History of the Fine Arts* 7 (4), 390–405.
Waters, Kenneth H. (1966), "The Purpose of Dramatisation in Herodotos". *Historia* 15 (2), 157–171.
Waters, Kenneth H. (1985), *Herodotus the Historian: His Problems, Methods and Originality*. London & Sydney: Croom Helm.
Waters, Matt (2014), *Ancient Persia: A Concise History of the Achaemenid Empire*. Cambridge: Cambridge University Press.
Wecklein, Nicolaus (1876), "Ueber die Tradition der Perserkriege". *Sitzungsberichte der königlich bayerischen Akademie der Wissenschaften. Philosophisch-philologische Classe* 1876, 239–314.
Weiskopf, Michael N. (2008), "The System Artaphernes-Mardonius as an Example of Imperial Nostalgia". In: Seyed Mohammad Reza Darbandi & Antigoni Zournatzi (eds.), *Ancient Greece and Ancient Iran: Cross-Cultural Encounters. 1st International Conference (Athens, 11–13 November 2006)*. Athens: National Hellenic Research Foundation, Cultural Center of the Embassy of the Islamic Republic of Iran in Athens, Hellenic National Commission for UNESCO, 83–91.
Wesenberg, Burkhardt (2004), "Ὀλοίτροχοι. Zur Verteidigung der Akropolis im Sommer 480 v. Chr. (Herodot 8,52-53)". In: Markus Janka (ed.), *Ἐγκύκλιον Κηπίον (Rundgärtchen). Zu Poesie, Historie und Fachliteratur der Antike*. Munich & Leipzig: K. G. Saur, 145–162.
West, Stephanie (1985), "Herodotus' Epigraphical Interests". *The Classical Quarterly* 35 (2), 278–305.
West, Stephanie (1992), "Sesostris' Stelae (Herodotus 2.102-2.106)". *Historia: Zeitschrift für Alte Geschichte* 41 (1), 117–120.
West, Stephanie (2013), "'Every picture tells a story': a note on Herodotus 4.88". In: Boris Dunsch & Kai Ruffing (eds.), *Herodots Quellen – Die Quellen Herodots*. Wiesbaden: Harrassowitz Verlag, 117–128.
West, William C. (III) (1969), "The Trophies of the Persian Wars". *Classical Philology* 64 (1), 7–19.
Westlake, H.D. (1936), "The Medism of Thessaly". *The Journal of Hellenic Studies* 56 (1), 12–24.
Whatley, N. (1964), "On the Possibility of Reconstructing Marathon and other Ancient Battles". *The Journal of Hellenic Studies* 84, 119–139.
Widdra, Klaus (1963), "Das Heroon des Phylakos in Delphi". *Marburger Winckelmann-Programm* 1962, 38–45.
Wiegand, Theodor (1904), *Die archaische Poros-architektur der Akropolis zu Athen, mit unterstützung aus der Eduard Gerhard-Stiftung der Königlich Preussischen Akademie der Wissenschaften*. Kassel & Leipzig: Verlag von Th. G. Fisher.
Wiegand, Theodor & Schrader, Hans (1904), *Priene: Ergebnisse der Ausgrabungen und Untersuchungen in den Jahren 1895–1898*. Berlin: Georg Reimer.
Wiesehöfer, Josef (1993), *Das antieke Persien: Von 550 v. Chr. bis 650 n. Chr.* Zürich: Artemis & Winkler.
Wiesehöfer, Josef (2004), "'O Master, Remember the Athenians': Herodotus and Persian Foreign Policy". In: Vassos Karageorghis & Ioannis Taifacos (eds.), *The World of Herodotus: Proceedings of an International Conference held at the Foundation Anastasios G. Leventis, Nicosia, September 18–21, 2003 and organized by the Foundation Anastasios G. Leventis and the Faculty of Letters, University of Cyprus*. Nicosia: Foundation Anastasios G. Leventis, 209–221.

Wilhelm, Adolf (1929), *Zur Topographie der Schlacht bei Salamis* (Akademie der Wissenschaften in Wien Philosophisch-historische Klasse Sitzungsberichte 211 (1)). Vienna & Leipzig: Hölder-Pichler-Tempsky.
Winter, Ludwig (1909), *Die Schlacht von Plataä*. Dissertation at Friedrich-Wilhelms-Universität, Berlin.
Woodhouse, William John (1898), "The Greeks at Plataiai". *The Journal of Hellenic Studies* 18, 33–35.
Woodward, Arthur M. (1910), "Greek inscriptions from Thessaly". *Liverpool Annals of Archaeology and Anthropology* 3, 145–60.
Wright, Henry Burt (1904), *The Campaign of Plataea (September, 479 B.C.)*. New Haven: Tuttle, Morehouse & Taylor.
Yegül, Fikret (2010), "Sardeis Artemis Tapınağı / The Temple of Artemis at Sardis". In: Nicholas Cahill (ed.), *Lidyalılar ve Dünyaları / The Lydians and Their World*. Istanbul: Yapi Kredi Kültür Merkezi, 363–388.
Yorke, V.W. (1896), "Excavations at Abae and Hyampolis in Phocis". *The Journal of Hellenic Studies* 16, 291–312.
Zahrnt, Michael (1971), *Olynth und die Chalkidier: Untersuchungen zur Staatenbildung auf der Chalkidischen Halbinsel im 5. und 4. Jahrhundert*. Munich: C.H. Beck.
Zahrnt, Michael (1996), "Alexanders Übergang über den Hellespont". *Chiron* 26, 129–147.
Zgusta, Ladislav (1984), *Kleinasiatische Ortnamen*. Heidelberg: Carl Winter Universitätsverlag.
Ziegler, Ruprecht (2007), "Zum Politischen Nachwirken der Perserkriegsidee in der Zeit der Zweiten Sophistik". In: Bruno Bleckmann (ed.), *Herodot und die Epoche der Perserkriege: Realitäten und Fiktionen. Kolloquium zum 80. Geburtstag von Dietmar Kienast*. Cologne: Böhlau Verlag, 151–168.
Zikos, K. (1905), *Καθορισμὸς τῶν θεσέων τῆς ἐν Πλαταιαῖς Μάχης. Étude historique sur la détermination des positions de la Bataille de Platées*. Athens: Spyridon Kousoulinos.
Zwingmann, Nicola (2011), "Erinnerungslandschaften und Identitäten in einer kulturellen Kontaktzone: Mythen und Denkmäler in Kelainai-Apameia Kibotos". In: Lâtife Summerer, Askold Ivantchik & Alexander von Kienlin (eds.), *Kelainai-Apameia Kibotos: Stadtentwicklung im anatolischen Kontext. Akten des internationalen Kolloquiums, München, 2.-4. April 2009*. Bordeaux: Ausonius Éditions, 93–116.
Zwingmann, Nicola (2012), *Antiker Tourismus in Kleinasien und auf den vorgelagerten Inseln. Selbstvergewisserung in der Fremde*. Bonn: Dr. Rudolf Habelt.
Zwingmann, Nicola (2013), "Überlegungen zur Zuverlässigkeit Herodots am Beispiel der Sesostrisreliefs in Ionien". In: Klaus Geus, Elisabeth Irwin & Thomas Poiss (eds.), *Herodots Wege des Erzählens: Logos und Topos in den* Historien. Frankfurt am Main: Peter Lang, 375–398.
Zwingmann, Nicola (2014), "Space, place and identity: Kelainai-Apameia Kibotos in Phrygia as an Anatolian case study". In: Tønnes Bekker-Nielsen (ed.), *Space, Place and Identity in Northern Anatolia*. Stuttgart: Franz Steiner Verlag, 157–173.

Index Locorum

Aelian
Varia Historia
2.14   56n64

Aeschines
In Ctesiphontem
116   245n742

Aeschylus
Agamemnon
192   98n248
653   98n248
1416   98n248

Eumenides
21   187
681-695   194

Persae
69-70   87n206
71   85n195
130-131   85n195
272-273   234
302-303   227
307   218
335   215n634
362   302n48
368   218
373   302n48
429   216
447-471   217
465-467   86, 228
482-484   254
483-495   239n725
495-507   98
722   87n206
723   83n186, 85n195
725   302n48
739-752   84n193
746   83n186
792-794   268
799   87n206
866   42

Septem contra Thebem
277   304n57
954   304n57

Alciphron
Epistulae
1.11.3   256n780
2.3.10   218n644

Alexis of Samos
fragment 1   274n848

Ammianus Marcellinus
Res gestae
22.8.4   61n89

Anthologia Graeca
6.217   133n356
7.141   285n889
7.666   86n203

Apollonius Rhodius
Argonautica
1.28-30   240n731
1.216   93
1.580-591   143n386
1.582   123, 124n330, 128n344
2.568   133n356
2.1140-1156   116n306

Appian
Mithridatica
149-152   190n549

Syriaca
75-77   162

Aristodemus
fragment
1   229, 237n720

Aristophanes
Acharnenses
20   95
80-82   240n730
82   20n96
85   20n96
709   106n277

Equites
785   223n661

Lysistrata
677-679   195n562, 195n567
931   240n730
1251   119n315, 137n365

Aristoteles
De ventorum situ et nominibus
2.17-18   98n248

Poetica
9   292n7
23   292n7

Arrian
Anabasis Alexandri
1.11   84n192
1.11.6   84n192
1.11.7-8   73n137
3.16.7-8   190n545
7.19.2   190n545

Athenaeus
Deipnosophistae
1.37   223n661
1.55   123, 128n345
7.87   279
8.7   242n738
13.31   274n848

Batrachomyamachia
159   304n57

Callimachus
In Delum
106-152   110n290
171-191   185n537

In lavacrum Palladis
113-114   256n781

Cicero
De divinatione
1.37   185
1.46   290n1

De natura deorum
1.115   296n23

De Oratore
2.350-360   5

Claudian
In Eutropium
2.257-263   45n28

Clidemus of Athens
fragment
1   194n560

Democritus of Abdera
fragments
162   192n553
299   12n51

Demosthenes
Adversus Androtionem
13   189

In Timocratem
129   190, 228, 308

De falsa legatione
163   114

Philippica 4
8   94

Περὶ τῶν πρὸς Ἀλέξανδρον συνθηκῶν
23   240n727

Dexippus
fragment
28a   190n549

Dio Chrysostom
Orationes
7   145
11.149   32n159

Diodorus Siculus
Bibliotheca historica
3.58.3   44n24
4.28.1-4   194n560
4.36.5-37.4   167
4.57.1   167n463
4.72.4   225n673
4.81.4   456n781
11.1.2   20n97
11.5-10   149n408
11.9.3-4   164
11.10   164

11.11.6 166n454
11.14 183
11.29.1 270
11.29.4 249n763
11.30.1 247
11.33.3 270n826
11.35.3 273n846
11.37.6 287n894
16.31.3-5 176
16.38.1 154
17.17.2-3 76n158
17.17.6 76n163
17.17.6-7 73n137
17.40.5-43.2 236n718
19.48.6-7 55
22.9.5 180n509, 185

Ephorus
fragment
48 279

Euphorion
fragment
30 226n675

Euripides
Andromache
16-25 129n347
1263-1269 131
1265 131, 144n391

Helena
766 147n400
1129 147n400

Iphigenia Aulidensis
705-707 128n344
1600 144n391

Rhesus
279 100
301-302 98n247
304 99
346 100
962-973 99

Troades
84 144n391
84-90 145n395
89 145

90 144n391

Galen
Quod animi mores corporis temperamenta sequantur
822 240n727

Hecataeus of Miletus
fragment 30 167

Hellanicus of Lesbos
fragments
127 87
169a 193n556

Hereas
fragment
3 98n248

Herodianus (Aelius)
Ἡ καθ' ὅλου προσῳδία
374 194n560

Περὶ Ὀδυσσεικακῆς προσῳδίας
133 161n438

Περὶ παθῶν
187 256n780

Herodotus
Histories
1.1 35
1.3-5 73
1.6 41
1.8 24n113
1.14 24, 56n66
1.19 210n613
1.28 41
1.29 12
1.29-1.30 23n110, 57
1.30 12, 59
1.47 202n588
1.49 26
1.52 26
1.53 42
1.60 190n549
1.65 202n588
1.67-68 163n442
1.70 275
1.72 41–42

1.75   41–42
1.84   57, 199
1.92   24
1.93   56n66, 57
1.131-132   74
1.133   20n96
1.138   97n240
1.165-167   106n277
1.168   239
1.174   104, 295n17
1.176   173n480
1.186   24
1.189   84n193, 85, 293n12
1.192   20n96
1.205   24
1.205-214   85
2.35   23n109
2.103   91
2.106   25, 91
2.116   292n4
2.143   202n588
2.156   216n639
2.182   275
3.26   29, 134, 147
3.35   97n241
3.48   293n11
3.50-53   293n11
3.60   236n718, 275, 295
3.117   293n12
3.123   275
3.136   23n110, 110
3.139   23n110
3.155   154n417
4.45   236n718
4.76   23n110
4.82   167n460
4.83   24
4.85   25, 81, 110
4.87-88   82
4.88   85, 275
4.89   24
4.90   25n123
4.91   25, 293n12
4.92   25
4.123-124   24
4.152   275
5.1   98n246
5.4   97
5.13   98n246
5.23   98n246

5.47   106n277
5.52   41–42
5.52-54   41n10
5.71   190n549
5.72   202
5.77   203
5.94   71n131
5.97   58
5.100   56n66
5.100-102   57, 200n582
5.102   57, 58
5.105   58
5.114-115   106n277
5.119   54n59
6.7-8   220
6.9   296
6.13   296
6.15   282
6.19   296
6.25   296
6.32   296
6.33   83n190
6.37   97n241, 209n610
6.44   65, 84n193, 104, 134, 147, 242n738
6.53   292n5
6.58   163n442
6.75   213, 268n823
6.91   268
6.94   58
6.105   190n547, 221, 299n34
6.108   248n761
6.116   280
6.118   24, 74
6.134   202n588
7.6   33n157, 74n147, 83
7.8.α   83n189
7.8.β   58, 83n189
7.10.β   83
7.10.γ   83
7.10.ε   65
7.11   58
7.20   109
7.22   104
7.23-24   101
7.24   96, 98n246
7.25   82n182
7.26   39-40, 42
7.27   55, 293n12
7.27-30   46
7.30   48

7.31 1, 51
7.32 57
7.33 73n142, 282, 287
7.33-34 78
7.34 82n184
7.35 84, 293n12
7.36 82n182, 295n18
7.37 57
7.38 46, 57
7.40-41 43
7.42 62
7.42-43 61
7.43 65, 67, 293n12
7.44 78
7.45-53 86
7.49 134, 268
7.54 84
7.55-56 86n201
7.57 57, 88
7.58 86, 92, 117
7.58-59 90
7.59 93, 240
7.60 94
7.75 90
7.89-99 119n315
7.100 95n233
7.101-105 95
7.105-106 94n230
7.107 98n246, 173n480
7.108-113 90n214
7.109 239
7.110 99
7.113 95
7.116 106
7.120 239
7.122-124 90n214
7.127 90n114
7.128 107, 111
7.129 108, 110–111
7.130 108
7.131 111, 199n579
7.137 20n96
7.139 190n548
7.139-144 31n152
7.140 178n502
7.141 267
7.148 178n502
7.150 292n8
7.166 274n846
7.169 178n502

7.172-173 111
7.173 109, 111, 114
7.174 73n142
7.175 137
7.176 136, 150, 154, 156
7.178 127, 147n398
7.180 97n240, 150n409
7.182 109
7.183 120, 122, 137
7.188 122, 132
7.189 127, 190n547
7.190 134n357
7.191 128
7.191-192 122
7.192 124, 147n398
7.193 134, 140, 143
7.196 115
7.197 97n240, 113
7.198-201 150
7.199 159
7.204 166n459
7.208 158, 166n459
7.212 154, 155n417, 161
7.215 158
7.216 158, 200n579
7.217 162n440, 200n579
7.217-218 161
7.218 162n440, 200n579
7.220 166n459
7.223 162
7.225 158, 162
7.227 166n454
7.228 163, 165, 168, 267
7.235 307
7.238 163n442
8.4 140–141
8.6 140–141
8.7 146
8.8 136, 140
8.12 136
8.13 136, 143, 199n579
8.22 138
8.24-25 166, 236
8.27-28 172–173
8.31 155
8.32-33 170
8.32 188
8.34 170
8.35 170, 185
8.36 186

8.38 177
8.39 177
8.41 31, 202
8.50 260n789
8.51 20n97
8.52 191
8.53 197, 201
8.54-55 207, 293n12
8.55 33n159
8.65 35, 213, 267
8.68 307
8.76 216, 222
8.77 222, 236, 297n30
8.83 216n635
8.86 230
8.88 230n689
8.90 138n371, 228
8.95 216n634, 217
8.96 233-234
8.98 33n159, 40
8.107 134n357, 237
8.108-110 85n134
8.114 245n743
8.115 33n159
8.115-117 98
8.117 85n194
8.118 98
8.120 239
8.121-122 214n632
8.129 199n579, 240
8.130 274
8.132 41n11
8.134 173
8.138 56n66, 111n292
8.144 35n168, 296
9.15 246
9.16 35, 246n747
9.19 249
9.20-24 249
9.25 250
9.26-28 246n749, 254n774
9.27 196
9.28-32 254
9.31 247
9.33 254n774, 264n804
9.35-36 264n804
9.37-38 74n147
9.39 249

9.40 247, 254n774
9.41 307
9.42 184
9.44-45 254n774
9.46-47 246n749, 254n774
9.48 246n749
9.49 254
9.50-51 257
9.51 246n747, 251
9.52 275, 251, 259
9.53 254
9.55 254
9.57 262
9.59 247
9.61 275, 259, 262n795
9.62 261, 263
9.63 260n792, 263
9.64 282
9.65 210-211, 247, 263, 260
9.69 48n35, 263
9.70 247, 245n742
9.72 254n774, 263n799
9.74 247n753
9.76 247n753
9.77 247n753
9.78-79 163n442, 245n743
9.80-81 247n753
9.82 247n753
9.83 269
9.85 269
9.89 83n190, 111n291
9.91 290n1
9.96 275, 274
9.97 275
9.98 138, 275–276
9.99 281–282
9.100 280–281
9.100-101 273
9.101 273n846
9.102 276, 281
9.103 281
9.104 274, 282
9.106 84, 276
9.107 282
9.108 57
9.114 82n184, 83–84
9.116 97, 283
9.117-118 286

9.118 199n579
9.119 97n240, 287
9.120 283, 285, 287
9.121 83
9.140 33n159

Hesiod
Opera et dies
504 98n248
547 98n248

Theogonia
245 130n352
497-499 186

Hesychius
Lexicon
γάργα 255n778
γόργυρα 255n778
ψύττα 218n646

Hierocles
Synekdemos
666.2 52

Historia Alexandri Magni
2.1 262n797

Homer
Iliad
1.221 113
1.349-51 135n359
1.398 135n362
1.611 308
2.303-329 55n60
2.353 65n104
2.494 264
2.497 248
2.681-685 116
2.682 114
2.695-702 282n879
2.717 123
2.753 109n282
2.820-821 64n99
2.836 86
2.845 87n206
2.869 282
4.276 113
4.383 248n761

4.508 308
6.86-95 78
6.136 130
6.297-304 69
7.84-91 71n132
7.202 64n100
7.242-243 306n64
7.435-441 134n359
7.478-82 70n127, 135n359
8.47-48 64n100
8.75 64n101, 308
8.170 64n101
8.207 64n101, 208
9.4 98n248
9.4-7 134n359
9.236-237 65n104
10.287 248n761
10.431-479 99
10.435 99–100
10.436-437 99
10.438-41 98n247
11.166 88n210
11.301 185n533
12.30 87n206
13.10-25 308
13.821-822 65n104
14.33 134n359
14.34-36 134n359
14.154 308
14.158-159 64n100
14.292 64n100
15.26-27 134n359
15.149-150 308
15.152-153 64n100
16.144 128n344
16.181 185n533
16.603-607 64n100
16.694 185n533
18.40 130
18.48 135
18.50 129
18.68-69 134n359
18.140 130n351
18.398-402 130
18.402 129
18.402-403 130
20.61-62 308
20.62 154n417
21.125 130n351

21.132 97n241
21.331-341 65
21.526 308
22.169-171 64n100
23.115-122 64n99
23.192-225 135n359
24.82 129

Odyssey
1.320 161n438
3.176-179 147n398, 148n402
4.1 144
4.435 130n351
4.500 147
4.844-847 221
5.52 130n351
12.61 25n122
15.231 185n533
22.385 144
24.80-84 71n132

Homeric Hymn to Demeter
96 210

Hyginus
Fabulae
116 148
180-181 780

Isocrates
Panathenaicus
42 293n10
193-195 195n565

Panegyricus
90 119n315
155 296n23
157 210n615
158-159 293n10

Philippus
148 165n453

Plataicus
58 269
59 266n809, 269
60 269
61 269

Isodorus of Seville
Etymologiae
6.3.3 298

Livy
Ab Urbe Condita
5.47 307n67
26.45 307n67
31.47 144n390
32.4 154
35.43 76n159
36.15 154
36.16-19 162
37.37.2-3 76n160
37.56 49n39
39.27 91
42.15 186, 188
42.63 296
44.6 109n282

Lucanus
Pharsalia
9.973 61n86

Lucian
Alexander
4 160n432

Lycophron
Alexandra
451 226
898-908 134n359

Lycurgus
Oratio in Leocratem
73 219n647, 223n661

Maximus
Dissertationes
5.1 56n66

Neanthes of Cyzicus
fragments
3 279
38 147n400

New Testament
Acta Apostolorum
17.19-34 193n557

Evangelium secundum Joannem
9.7 14

Nicetas Choniates
Historia
604-609 154

Nonnus
Dionysiaca
27.290 221n655

Ovid
Metamorphoses
3.155-156 255n780
6.392-400 44n24, 45n26
11.108-109 56n66
11.111-113 56n66
11.217-65 130n350

Pausanias
Periegesis
1.1.4 222n658, 232, 296
1.1.5 232
1.2.1 194n559
1.4.4 185
1.8.5 190n545, 298
1.13.7-8 106n277
1.15 195n562, 195n567
1.15.3 304n54
1.16.3 4n11, 298
1.17.2 195n565
1.17.4 195n562
1.18.2 197n573
1.20.4 190n545
1.24.2 114n300
1.25.1 273n843
1.25.2 195n567
1.27.1 189
1.27.2 208
1.28.2 190n547
1.28.5 193n556
1.28.6 193n555
1.28.7 193n557
1.31.1 238
1.32.6 253
1.32.7 299n34
1.34.2 285n889, 291n1
1.35.4-5 71n130
1.36.1 219n647, 223n661, 226–227
1.36.2 221
1.36.4 232
1.37.2 232n693
1.44.4 4n11, 268n823
2.5.4 297
2.14.5 214n632
2.21.4 268n823, 301
2.23.1 147n400
2.23.5 167n462
2.24.7 18
2.29.10 236n718
2.30.4 4n11
2.31.6 297
2.31.7 215n632
3.4.6 282n879
3.11.3 168n467
3.12.6 4n11
3.12.9 166n454
3.14.1 163n442, 166n454, 168n467
3.14.4 129n347
3.17.7-9 245n743
3.22.2 129n347
4.32.5 173
4.33.4 263n800
4.34.4 54n59
4.35.9 153n414
4.36.6 147n400, 217, 220
5.11.5 214n632
5.11.8 195n565
5.23.1-3 245n742
7.2.6 280n871
7.5.2-3 55n60
7.5.4 297
7.22.1 55n59
8.23.4 55n60
8.27.5 174
8.46.3 4n11, 298
8.54.6 221n655
9.1.1-2 248n761
9.2.1 247
9.2.2 271
9.2.3 257n783
9.2.5 270
9.2.6 266, 270n828
9.2.7 260
9.4.1 263n799
9.4.1-2 260n792
9.4.3 254, 264
9.4.4 247, 248n761, 264

9.19.7 55n60
9.24.1 116n306
9.25.9 4n11, 116, 268n823, 301
9.32.5 296
9.34.5 116
10.1.3-6 173
10.1.5 165n451
10.3.1-2 173
10.4.1 172n474
10.4.2-3 172n474
10.6.2 188
10.6.4 127
10.7.1 185
10.8.6-7 181n511
10.14.5-6 184
10.15.1 245n742
10.19.4-23.9 162
10.20-21 154
10.21.6 166n458
10.23 185
10.24.6 186
10.28.6 301n45
10.30.9 44n24, 45n26
10.31.7 91
10.32.2-7 187
10.32.8 175
10.33.8 172n474
10.35.2 296
10.35.3 174

Pherecydes of Athns
fragment
151 196

Philiades
fragment
1 165n452

Philochorus
fragments
67 208
105-106 200n583

Philostratos
Heroicus
8.1 71n130
17.3-6 99

Icones
1.20 45n26

Vita Apollonii
1.24 145, 147
4.23 165n452

Vitae sophistarum
1.494 240

Photius
Bibliotheca
72.39b 178n499, 229n684, 234
72.40a 178n499

Pindar
Vita Pindari
2.21 215n633

Pisander of Camiros
Heraclea
fragment 7 167

Plato
Phaedrus
229b-c 127n341
229d 193n557

Leges
12.953 12n52

Menexenus
245a 219n647, 223n661, 266

Pliny the Elder
Naturalis Historia
4.25 255n780
4.32 123
4.49 81n179
4.64 137n365
5.31 279n863
5.33 71n130, 71n132
5.119 120n320
5.141 81n179
9.5 130
12.5 55n60
16.44 55n59, 243n738

16.88 55n60, 285n889
16.89 44n24
17.38.2 53
34.69-70 298
35.172 59

Plutarch
Agesilaus
19.2 302

Alexander
15.4 73n137

Aristides
9.2 217, 218
9.3 84n194
11.2 247
11.3 257n783
11.3-8 262n797, 268
11.7-8 252
11.9 262n797
14.1 263
16.5 254
17.8 263n798
18.1 262n795
19.1 263n799
19.6 270n829
19.7 270n828
20.3 260n792, 266n809, 266n811
20.4 270n829
20.5 266n811
20.6 257n783
21.1 270n828
21.3-5 270n828
27.1 233n693

Cato Maior
13 161

De gloria Atheniensium
7 119n315, 223, 245n743, 273n842

De Herodoti malignitate
866a 149n408
867d-f 119n315
867f 139
870e 225
872f 270n826
873a 272n840
873a-b 266n809

Eumenes
8.5 43n17

Mulierum virtutes
27 47

Nicias
1.3 290n1

Pericles
13.5 190n545

Pyrrhus
34 106n277

Solon
8.4 233n704, 234
9.4 231n692

Sulla
15 176

Themistocles
1.3 197
8.2-3 136
8.4 139
9.1-2 138
10.6 227
13.1 228–229
13.2-3 97n240
15.1 213n630
15.3 214n632
16.1 235n708
22.1-2 223

Theseus
26.1 196
27.2 195
27.2-5 194n559
28.1 196

Polyaenus
Strategemata
6.53 100
7.15.5 162, 166n458

Polybius
Historiae
4.8.11 306n64
12.26-27 23n112
13.3.2-7 206n64
16.29.11 81n181, 86
16.29.13 79n170, 87n206
36.9.9 206n64

Priscian
De metris fabularum Terentii
24 93, 119

Procopius
De aedificiis
4.2 154

Pseudo-Apollodorus
Bibliotheca
1.2.7 130n352
1.4.2 44n24
1.9.1 87n206
1.9.19 143n385
2.5.9 92
2.7.6-7 167n463
2.8.1 167n463
3.4.4 256n781
3.5.1 100n252
3.12.7 225n673

Epitomae
1.10 201
1.16 194n558
6.7a-7b 147n400
6.11 147
6.15a-b 147n400

Pseudo-Plutarch
De fluviis
10 45
10.1 45n28

Ptolemy
Geographia
3.14.22 144n392
4.4.15 120n320
5.2.26 52

Quintus Curtius
Historiae Alexandri Magni
3.8.22 301n45

Simonides
PMG
26 149n408, 166, 268

FGE
5L 221
7 165n452
10 225
10-16 232
11 218n643, 225
12 214n632
13 165n452
15 270n829
83a-b 165n452

W²
3 119n316
6 215n633
7 215n633
17 266

Sophocles
Ajax
695 221
884 83n186

Odysseus Tyrannus
897 186

Trachiniae
684-704 167n462

Stadiasmus Maris Magni
10.3 120n320

Statius
Thebais
4.186 44n24
7.273-274 256n780

Stephanus Byzantinus
Ethnica s.v.
Ἀμαζόνειον 194n560

Ἀρτεμίσιον 137n365
Ἀταλάντη 218n642
Ἀφέται 141, 143
Ἐχελίδαι 228n683
Καθαρεύς 147n400
Κύδραρα 49n39
Κυχρεῖος 227n673, 227n675
Καλάτιβος 51n44
Τιθοραία 175n492
Φανοτεύς 172n474

Strabo
Geographica
2.5.22 81n179
3.5.6 129n347
4.1.7 25n120
5.8.17 49n39
7 fragments 14 and 15 111n294
7 fragment 35 104
7 fragment 52
8.6.2 147n400
9.1.13 234–235
9.1.19 225, 232n693
9.1.21 233, 238n721
9.1.9 225n673
9.2.30 296
9.2.31 248n761, 270
9.2.42 171n473
9.3.1 187
9.3.15 171n473
9.3.6 186
9.3.7 153n413
9.4.13 154n419, 167n461
9.4.14 167n460
9.4.16 154n419, 165n452
9.4.17 153n413, 168n468
9.5.15 124, 141
9.5.22 123, 126, 132
9.5.8 114
10.1.2 144n390
10.2.9 4n12
10.3.17 111n294
12.8.15 44n24, 45n26
13.1.1 61n86
13.1.11 86n203
13.1.22 79n170, 80, 81n179
13.1.27 68n114
13.1.29 72n135
13.1.30-32 71n130

13.1.31 66, 72n135, 283n881
13.1.32 72n135
13.1.33-34 66
13.1.36 66
13.1.42 68n114
13.1.51 64n99
13.4.5 59, 308
16.1.5 296n23

Suda
ἀλίπλαγκτος 221
ἀρτεμίσιος 137n365
Ἱππίας 221n655
Κέρκωπες 160n432
Σιμωνίδης 93, 119, 215n633

Theophrastus
Historia plantarum
2.3.1 53n52

De signis
fragment 6.35 98n248

Thucydides
Historiae
1.23 273n842
1.25 15, 134n357
1.100 96
1.126 190n549
1.132 245n742
1.134 245n743
2.67 20n96
2.71 267, 270n829
2.74 267
2.92 304n57
3.24 249, 252
3.58 267
3.59 269
3.68 262n795
3.92 168
4.8-4.38 220
4.57 20n96
4.76 172n474
4.102 96
4.103 96n239
4.108 96n239
4.109 102
5.52 168
6.70 304n57

7.1 63
7.54 304n57
8.102 283n881

Timotheus
Persae
72-78 237
141 43n19
196 223n661, 304n58

Tzetzes
Scholia in Lycophronem
50-51 167n461
175b 128
178 128
386 145n395
1095 145n395

Valerius Maximus
Facta et Dicta Memorabilia
1.8.10 144n390
2.10 298
5.3.ext.3f 193n557

Vibius Sequester
De fluminibus, fontibus, lacubus, nemoribus, gentibus
172 256n780

Virgil
Aeneis
1.469-473 99
2.21-24 220n650
6.124-155 55n62
6.183-211 55n62

Vitruvius
De Architectura
1.1.6 168n467
2.8.10 59

5.9.1 190n545
7.praef.12 179

Xenophon
Anabasis
1.2.13 45n28
1.2.5 24n117
1.2.7 43
1.2.8 43, 45n26
1.2.9 43n17, 45n26
1.8.16 290n1
2.4.13 24n117
2.4.24 24n117
3.2.13 219n647, 223n661
7.8.7 63n96

Cyropaedia
1.6.1 65n103
7.13 65n103
8.3.12 98n247

De republica Lacedaemoniorum
15.9 163n442

Hellenica
1.1.4 76n157
1.3.1 297
4.8.5 81n180
5.4.14 249n765
5.4.49 247
6.4.7 299n36
7.1.38 55

Oeconomicus
4.20 59

Zosimus
Historia Nova
5.5 154

General Index

This non-exhaustive index lists the main toponyms, personal names and concepts. Numbers in italics refer to maps.

Abai 118 (*4*), 155n420, 170–175
Abdera 12n51, 21 (*1*), 239–240, 243, 290
Abydos 21 (*1*), 60 (*3*), 61n89, 62, 68, 78–79, 81–86, 308
Accumulation (of narratives at mnemotopes) 14, 19, 89, 208, 226, 255, 272, 288, 291, 302
Achaea Phthiotis 113–114, 116
Achaemenid Empire and Achaemenids 16, 20, 24n115, 34n162, 42, 43n18, 54, 56, 59, 61n88, 69n121, 74, 76n155, 83n190, 85, 103, 105–106, 110, 178, 209, 294, 296n23, 301, 308n70
Achilles 61n88, 67, 71, 72n132, 72n134, 73n137, 89, 114, 116, 120n319, 128n344, 129n347, 131, 134n357, 134n359, 135n362, 185, 200n582, 236n718, 283, 293n9
Acı Göl 39 (*2*), 48–49
Acropolis of Athens 12, 33n159–160, 75, 175, 199–200, 203n595, 212, 214n632, 273n843, 296, 303, 305
– μέγαρον 191, 201–206, 208, 305
Aegina 20n96, 216n635, 236n718, 293n10
Afissos 118 (*4*), 125n330, 141–142
Agamemnon 55, 88n210, 139n375, 148n402
Agiokambos 118 (*4*), 125–126
Agios Giorgios (cape) 118 (*4*), 123n328, 124–125, 129n347, 131n353, 132–133, 141
Agios Giorgios (island) 215 (*6*), 217–218, 235, 236n717
Aglauros 189 (*5*), 197–201, 206, 214, 291
Agora of Athens 4n13, 16, 189–190, 195, 197n573, 212, 214n632, 254n777, 293n10
Agore 48n35, 60 (*3*), 86–87, 92, 290
Ahuramazda 74–75, 76n155, 84n192, 98n247, 209n611
Aianteia festival 215, 224
Aigaleos, Mount 218n642, 228–229, 235, 308
Ajax 71, 72n134, 73n137, 83n186, 89, 214n632, 218, 221, 224, 306n64
– the Lesser 147
Akanthos 91, 98n247, 105, 106n275, 107
Aktaion 255–257, 272

Alexander the Great 16, 55, 61n88, 71n131–132, 73n137, 76, 84n192, 236n718, 246n749, 262n797, 298, 301n45
Alexandroupoli 94
Alpenoi 118 (*4*), 150–151, 159
Alyattes 210n613
Amazons and Amazonomachy 181, 193–198, 200–201, 214, 291
Ambelakia 215 (*6*), 223n661, 225, 232n692
Ameinokles 134n357, 136
Amestris 96–97, 99
Amphiale, cape 234, 235n710
Amphiaraos 26–27, 291n1
Amphiktyons 152, 162, 165n452
– seats of 152, 153n413
Amphipolis 21 (*1*), 96, 98, 100. *See also* Ennea Hodoi
Anahitā 59, 69
Anaktoron *and* Telesterion of Eleusis 191, 210–213, 267, 296, 300
Anaphlystos 215 (*6*), 233
Anapodo (river) 258
Anaua 39 (*2*), 48, 52
Anavyssos 27, 233
Androkrates, shrine of 244 (*7*), 250–253, 255, 264, 267
Anopaia 147, 149, 158, 161–162, 165n450, 173n479, 282, 289, 306
Antandros 60 (*3*), 62–63, 66
Anthele 152–154
Antiochus III of Syria 76, 154
Apameia (Phrygia) 42, 45
Aphetai 124n330, 134, 137n367, 140–144, 148, 290–291
Aphrodite 74, 233n704, 274n848, 299n34
Apollo 24, 26, 42, 45n28, 47, 57n69, 74, 170, 173–175, 177–179, 181n511, 184, 186, 190n545, 192, 214n632, 238, 247n755, 260, 297–298, 301n43, 302, 308
– temple at Thebes 26
Arachova 127n342, 172n474
Arai 193

Araxes (river) 24, 85
Areopagus 189 (5), 191–196, 200–201, 206, 208, 288, 302
Ares 110n290, 191, 193–194, 231n692, 270n829, 301n43
Argiopion 262–263
Argonauts 61, 116, 125n330, 128n344, 134, 140, 143, 148, 290–291
Argos 18, 106n277, 165n451, 213, 260n792, 268n823
Artabanos 65, 78n169, 83, 86, 134, 207, 268
Artabazos 111n291, 240–241, 307
Artachaies, tomb of 21 (1), 105–108, 117
Artaÿktes 282–289, 292n8
Artemis 4n11, 58, 138n367, 139, 148, 173n482, 185, 222–224, 238, 255–257, 272, 298–299, 301
– temple at Anaphlystos 233
– temple at Artemision 136–138
– temple at Aulis 55n60, 139
– temple at Delphi 180n509
– temple at Ephesus 24
– temple at Mounichia 222, 237
– temple at Salamis 222n658
– temple at Sardis 58–59
Artemisia of Halicarnassus 138, 216n634, 231n689, 307
Artemision 21 (1), 118 (4), 306–307
– battle of 31, 93, 97n240, 99, 118–127, 134, 136–137, 140–143, 148, 199n579, 216n635, 222, 303
Asia. See Europe
Asklepios 181
Asopos (river)
– near Plataea 244 (7), 247–249, 257, 258n785, 272, 302
– near Thermopylae 152, 158–159, 161, 169
Asteris 220
Athamas 74, 86, 89, 114, 116–117, 301
Athena 5n13, 62, 74–78, 89, 136, 144n391, 167, 189n545, 190n549, 194, 196, 207–208, 210, 214, 239, 256, 267, 298, 299n34, 300–301
– Old Temple at Athens 189 (5), 190, 202–208, 305
– Parthenon 181, 189 (5), 190, 192, 195, 202–206, 228, 293n10
– sanctuary at Delphi 177–185, 192, 298, 302

– temple at Assessos 210n613
– temple at Itonos 114n298, 302
– temple at Phokaia 297
– temple at Plataea 260
– temple at Tithorea 175n492
– temple at Troy 67–70, 76n155, 298
– temple of Athena Nike 189 (5), 202n590, 214n632, 249n764
– temple of Athena Skiras 231–233, 243, 298, 300
Athens and Athenians 3, 13n51, 17, 20, 21 (1), 23, 30–31, 33n160, 35n168, 48n33, 53n52, 62n88, 57, 71n131, 73–74, 75n150, 77, 83, 85, 92–93, 95, 96n239, 97n244, 101n254, 109–110, 119n315, 120, 122, 127, 135, 136n363, 137n365, 139, 163, 172, 175, 177n497, 186, 188–197, 199–203, 205–215, 217, 220–224, 227, 231–234, 239, 245n742–743, 246n749, 247, 248n761, 249, 253n772, 254n774–775, 255n779, 259, 260n792, 261–263, 266, 268–270, 273, 281–282, 285–289, 291, 296, 298, 300, 302, 304, 306. See also Acropolis, Agora
Athos canal 21 (1), 56, 101, 102n259, 103–105, 107, 110, 117, 121, 236, 294
Athos, Mount 65, 84n193, 104n268, 134, 147, 242n738, 300n39
Attica 4n11, 21 (1), 27, 75, 159, 172, 191, 194, 195n565, 197, 210, 215–216, 223n660, 229, 233–234, 236–237, 240, 243, 268
Aulis 55n60, 139n375, 144
Autonoös 177, 179, 184, 185n533, 298
Avesta 54, 59, 128n343

Babylon 24, 75n150, 98n247, 296n23
Başmakçı 39n2
Bermion or Vermio, Mount 111, 112n295
Bethlehem 1, 14
Bigalı Kalesi 60 (3), 80–81
Black Sea 25, 61, 87n206, 89, 110, 134n357, 236n718
Bluebeard Temple 202n591, 205–206
Boeotia and Boeotians 4n12, 21 (1), 33n159, 75, 114n300, 116, 139n375, 159, 172, 203, 244, 247, 249, 254, 255n779–780, 257n783, 264, 268n823, 296, 302
Bolayır 87
Boreas 93, 98n248, 119, 127, 135, 190n547, 193, 298, 300–301

Bosporus 24, 25n122, 39 (2), 54n54, 82–83, 85, 275, 295n18, 308
Buddha 1, 7n25
Byzantine period 4n9, 52, 58, 156–157, 166, 253n771, 264n807

Cambyses 29, 85n197, 97n241, 147, 242n738
Çanakkale 60 (3), 61, 66, 68n113, 79, 81, 283
Cappadocia 39 (2), 40–41
Caria and Carians 2, 21 (1), 41n11, 51, 54n59, 138
Caves 16, 42, 45–46, 99, 118 (4), 123, 128n344, 129–133, 145, 173, 176, 177, 186–190, 198–199, 226, 299n34, 305–306
Celts 45n26, 154, 162, 166, 173n479, 180n509, 185–186
Cenotaphs 166, 271–272, 305
Centauromachy 181
Chalkis and Chalkidians 4n12, 119n314, 127n339, 144n390, 291n1, 203
Chalkotheke 189 (5), 204
Charadra 118 (4), 170, 171n474
Chili 145
Chiliadou 145
Cilicia and Cilicians 39 (2), 40n3, 41
Cilician Gates 39 (2) andn2, 41
Clustering (of mnemotopes) 13, 19, 134
Colchis 114, 116n306, 134, 140
Confabulation 18
Corfu *or* Kerkyra 15, 238
Corinth and Corinthians 214n632, 224–225, 231–232, 242–243, 297
Croesus 18n93, 24, 25n124, 26–27, 38, 42, 48, 50, 59–60, 85, 185
Ctesias 32, 178, 229n684, 235
Cybele 44n25, 58–59, 69, 278
– temple at Sardis 57, 60
Cycnus 154, 167
Cyrus the Elder 24, 41n9, 42, 60, 84n193, 85, 288
Cyrus the Younger 43n17, 43n19, 59

Daiva inscription 75, 178
Darius I 3, 24–25, 42, 46, 54n54, 55, 74n146, 76n155, 82–83, 85, 90n212, 93, 103–104, 110, 154n417, 205, 240n728, 275, 280, 294, 308. *See also* Thrones
Daskyleion 60 (3), 69n121, 70
Datis 24, 186, 301n45
Daulis (town) 118 (4), 170, 172n474

Delos 24, 61n88, 74, 127n341, 186, 239, 274
Delphi 12, 18n93, 21(1)21n100, 24, 27n128, 28n132, 47n32, 55n60, 56n66, 75, 83n187, 105, 118 (4), 127, 131, 135, 162, 169–170, 172, 175–179, 182, 214n632, 245n742–743, 255n779, 262n797, 270n829, 271, 298, 304–305, 308
– siege of 175, 177–188, 192, 195, 291, 300, 302–303
Demeter 106n277, 135n362, 213, 232, 266–268, 288, 296, 298–301
– temple at Anthele 152, 153n413
– temple at Argiopion 262
– temple at Argos 268n823
– temple at the Athenian Acropolis 212
– temple at Eleusis 175, 210–211, 213–214, 262, 264, 267n818, 268
– temple at Hysiai 244 (7), 247, 252, 263, 265–266
– temple at Kolias 233n704
– temple at Mykale (New Priene) 275–278, 280–281, 289
– temple on Paros 268n823, 301
– temple at Phaleron 296, 297n25
– temple at Plataea 117, 175, 210, 254–255, 259, 262–264, 268, 280, 305
– temple at Skiros 232n693
– temple at Skolos 247, 264
Denizli 49n39, 52–53
Dhema Gap 155
Dinar Suyu 42n15, 43, 45n26
Dinar 42, 44, 45n26, 46
Diokaisareia 52
Dionysos 36n175, 45, 97n240, 99, 130, 213n630, 267n818, 312n630
Dirphys, Mount 118 (4), 145–146
Doğanbey 278–279
Dorikos 21 (1), 22n103, 56n64, 92–95, 117, 230, 240, 308
Doris 118 (4), 155–156, 155n449, 170
Doro, cape 144–146
Drymos 118 (4), 170, 171n474

Eceabat *or* Madytos *or* Maydos 60 (3), 78, 80–81, 287–288
Egypt and Egyptians 12n49, 23n109–110, 24n115, 25–26, 29, 34n164, 75n150, 78, 85n197, 91, 134, 163, 242n738
Eïon 90n214, 91, 98, 100, 173n480, 239

Elaious 60 (3), 74, 87n204, 274, 283, 285n889, 287, 291, 296, 298, 300
Elateia 118 (4), 170, 171n474
Eleusis 21 (1), 171, 175, 189–191, 200, 210–214, 215 (6), 222, 229, 232, 235, 262n797, 264, 267–268, 276, 280, 296, 298, 300
Eleutheria festival 251n769, 266, 270–271
Enez 92, 94
Ennea Hodoi 21 (1), 74, 95–101, 117, 290
Ephialtes 121, 161–163, 169
Erechtheus 136n363, 196n568, 204, 207, 301
– temple of 189 (5), 191, 192n522, 202, 203n596, 208–209, 300
Eretria 118 (4), 146, 196
Erginos (river) 92
Erochos 118 (4), 170, 171n474
Erythrai 244 (7), 247, 248n758, 249–250
Etymology 45, 48, 52n47, 87n206, 98, 128–129, 133n356, 143, 148, 192, 240, 248, 251n767, 260n789, 263n800, 268, 286
Euboea and Euboeans 4n12, 21 (1), 118, 119n314, 119n317, 121, 124, 127n339, 134, 136–137, 139, 143–148, 168n468, 185, 218n642, 222n657, 291n2, 300n39
Eumenes II 43n17, 49n39, 51n43, 186, 188
Europe, opposition with Asia 30n146, 61–62, 73, 78, 83–84, 88–89, 138, 282, 285, 289. *See also* Hellespont
Evros *or* Hebros (river) 94, 98n246, 93

Faneromeni monastery 215 (6), 231n692, 232n692
Feres 94

Gaison 276–279
Gala Gölü 92
Gargaphie 244 (7), 250–259, 263, 265n807, 266n811, 272
Geraistos 144n390, 146, 148n402
Gonnoi 21 (1), 111–112, 118 (4)
Gorgopotamos (river) 167n460
Güllübahçe 277, 279, 282, 289
Gyndes (river) 84n193, 85

Halos 21 (1), 74, 89, 97n240, 113–117, 118 (4), 142n384, 291, 301
Halys (river) 39 (2), 40–42, 52, 60, 85
Hebros. *See* Evros
Hector 71n132, 72n135, 73, 88n210, 89, 306n64

Helle 116–117, 295
– grave of 86–89, 106–107, 117, 291
Hellespont bridges 78, 82–83, 85, 89, 234, 275n851, 286, 288–289, 294
Hellespont 39 (2), 40, 56, 60 (3), 61–63, 66, 68, 71n130, 72, 79n170, 81, 83–87, 89, 92, 97n244, 98, 105, 110, 117, 122, 134, 154, 230, 236, 238, 273n846, 282, 308
Hephaistos 130
– temple on the Athenian Agora 195, 293n10
Hera 263, 275, 287, 299n34, 301n43, 308
– temple at Phaleron 296
– temple at Plataea 244 (7), 251, 259–263, 266n811, 267, 299, 305
– temple at Samos 82, 85, 274–275, 297
Heracles 25n120, 72n135, 92, 140, 143, 149, 151–154, 160–161, 166–169, 181, 196n567, 291, 299n36
– island of 236n718
– shrine at Kynosarges 280
– shrine at Marathon 280, 304n54
– temple on the Aigaleos ridge 215 (6), 228, 234, 235n710
Herakleia Trachinia 152n411, 168
Hermes 93, 273n844
Hero and Leander 82n181, 86
Herodotus *passim*
– as a traveller 22
– relation to Anatolia 41, 50, 52, 60 (*see also Histories*)
Heros equitans 100
Hierapolis 39 (2), 44, 49–53
Hisarlık 60 (3), 66, 68–70
Histiaia 137
Histories
– aim 35
– and archaeology 34n164
– as a source of mnemotopes 20–24
– audience of 35
– date of 20
– eastern kings in 24–27
– history of scholarship 28–37
– iranological views of 32–33
– predecessors 35n169
– reception of 4n9
– sources 22–24, 28n134, 33n160, 35–36
– structure of 3, 31n151
Hittites 44n25, 47n34, 57n69
Hollows. *See* Koila of Euboea

Holy Land 1, 5, 299n36
Honaz 49
Hortensius 176–177
Hyampolis 118 (*4*), 155, 170, 171n474, 173
Hysiai 18, 244 (*7*), 247, 248n758, 251–253, 263, 271

Ida, Mount 52, 61–66, 77n164, 84n193, 89, 113, 134, 147, 242n738, 298, 300n39, 308
Ilissos (river) 93, 127, 190n547
İn Tepe 60 (*3*), 68n113, 71, 72n134
Inscriptions 5n17, 23, 25–27, 33, 36, 38, 40n4, 45n26, 48, 50, 51n41, 51n43, 58n73, 59, 74–75, 79, 85, 103, 124–125, 137–139, 166, 175, 178–179, 183–185, 187, 190n547, 198, 203, 204n599, 206, 212–214, 217, 218n645, 223n661, 224–226, 232, 245, 264, 266–267, 270–271, 275, 278–279, 294, 298–300
Iolkos 118 (*4*), 143
Ionia and Ionians 21 (*1*), 57, 74n146, 83n190, 122, 135, 138, 200n582, 234, 273–274, 276, 296
Iphigeneia 97n244, 139n375
Isthmus 102, 104n271, 105, 213n630, 214n632, 242, 245n742, 306

Jerusalem 7n24, 13–14, 16, 302
Jesus 1, 7n24, 13–14, 16–17, 302n46
Justinian the Great 82n185, 154

Kalamoi 39 (*2*), 274
Kalapodi 171n474, 172, 173n480, 173n482, 174
Kallatebos 2, 47, 51–56, 60, 110, 208
Kallidromos, Mount 118 (*4*), 155, 161, 171n474
Kamari 118 (*4*), 125–126, 133, 238
Kaphareus, cape 118 (*4*), 145–147
Kara Menderes (river) 66
Karaağaç Tepe 60 (*3*), 283–284
Karabel 20 (*1*), 25–26, 38
Kardie 60 (*3*), 86–87
Kastalian spring 177, 179, 184
Kasthanaia 118 (*4*), 122–125, 132–133
Katarrektes 42–45, 48, 290
Kaz Daği 63
Kelainai 39 (*2*), 40–48, 55, 56n66, 57, 60, 290–291, 294
Kelainos 44n25, 45
Kelebes 279

Keos 222–223
Kephisos (river) 155n420, 170, 171n474
Keramidi (river) 123–125, 133
Kerata, Mount 229
Keretapa 52
Kerkopes 158, 160–161
Kerkyra. *See* Corfu
Keyx 167
Kili 118 (*4*), 145
Kilitbahir 60 (*3*), 81, 82n181
Kimon 211n620
Kithairon, Mount 244, 249, 251, 256–257, 262–264
Kızılırmak (river) 40–41
Kleomenes 201, 202n592, 213, 268n823
Knossos 17
Kogamos (river) 51, 53
Koila *or* Hollows of Euboea 118, 121, 134, 136, 143–145, 147–148, 242n738, 291, 306
Kolias 233–234, 243
Kolossai 39 (*2*), 48–50, 52
Koruköy 60 (*3*), 87–88
Korykian cave 118 (*4*), 176, 186–188, 305
Kos 55n60, 186, 247n753
Kosmas, cape 215 (*6*), 233
Koukidis, Konstantinos 201
Koutsoumbou, cape 132
Krakari, cape 215 (*6*), 224
Kritalla. *See* Tiralla
Kychreus 225–227, 243
Kydrara 39 (*2*), 48–52, 56, 60
Kymi 118 (*4*), 145–146
Kynosoura 218n643, 222–227, 236–237, 243, 304–305
Kynossema 227
Kytissoros 114, 116n306, 117

Laodikeia 39 (*2*), 49n39, 52–53, 55
Leander. *See* Hero
Lefteri *or* Lefkari reef 120
Leipsokoutali 218
Leonidas 31, 148–150, 163–169, 245n743, 282
Leto 214n632, 238, 240
Lieux de mémoire 6–7, 8n28, 10, 11n48
Locris and Locrians 158, 170
Lydia and Lydians 2, 24n115, 26–28, 41, 43, 48, 50n41, 51, 52n47, 56–59, 62, 68n114, 92, 185, 200n582, 208, 210n613, 263n798, 307n66

Macedonia and Macedonians 33, 84, 89–90, 104, 107–108, 111, 114, 120, 296, 306
Macedonian mountain 110–111, 113, 199n579, 248, 281, 300, 306
Madytos 60 (3), 78, 80, 287–288
Maeander 2, 40, 42, 43n19, 43n21, 48, 49n39, 51–52, 277, 279n863
Magi 68, 70, 72–74, 77, 96–97, 100–101, 123, 127, 128n343, 133, 135n359, 135n362, 136, 240, 295, 301
Magnesia and Magnesians (Thessaly) 105, 118, 120, 122, 123n328, 125–126, 128, 131, 133, 134n359, 135–137, 140–141, 148, 300
Makri 241
Mal Tepe 68n113, 79–80
Malis and Malians 152, 158
Marathon, battle of 3, 11n46, 28n134, 30, 31n147, 37, 164, 190n545, 196n568, 205, 221, 222n657, 223n662, 224, 253, 260n792, 271n833, 293, 299n34, 304
Mardonios 33n159, 34n162, 116, 173, 174n486, 178n499, 184, 190, 211, 216n635, 234, 241, 244, 245n742, 246–248, 249n762, 254, 263, 268, 271, 296, 305, 307
Marmara, sea of 61, 89, 143n385
Marsyas (mythical figure) 42, 43n20, 44–47, 55n59, 61, 291
Marsyas (river) 43, 48n35
Masada 10, 14n60
Masistios 190, 249
Matakas 178n499
Mavri Troupa 176–177
Maydos. *See* Eceabat
Megara and Megareans 137n368, 211, 229, 245n743, 257n783, 269–270
Melampygos 118 (4), 158–161, 169
Melas (bay) 92
Melas (river) 92, 152
Meliboia 118 (4), 122–123, 132–133
Memnon 25–26, 91
Menelaos 55
Mesimvria 240–241
Midas 24, 44n25, 45–47, 56, 111n292, 308. *See also* Thrones
Miletus, battle of 220
Miltiades 221, 268n823, 301
Minos 17
Minotaur 97n244, 200
Mithra 74, 84n192

Moloeis (river) 262–263
Mounichia 215 (6), 222
– festival of 223–224
Mykale, Mount 274–278, 281, 282, 289
– battle of 40n5, 61n88, 82n184, 83, 248, 262, 273–275, 277, 280, 283, 289, 298–300, 302, 305
Myrmex 118 (4), 120–121, 124n330
Myrmidons 114, 116, 120n319, 134n359
Mysia and Mysians 52n51, 62, 71n130, 91, 109, 143
Mytilene 61n88, 71n131

Nağara, Cape 79
Neon 118 (4), 170, 171n474, 175
Nereids 74, 76n155, 84n192, 123, 128–133, 135–136, 148, 210, 298, 300–301
Nestor 1, 148n402
Nestos (river) 98
Nitocris (queen of Babylon) 24
Nymphs 93, 127, 129, 134n357, 135, 175n492, 187, 223, 255, 256n782, 263n800
Nysa 16n77

Oak Heads, pass of 244 (7), 249–250, 272
Oedipus 193
Oeroe (river) 257–258
Oiobazos 46, 97, 286–287
Oita, Mount 118 (4), 150, 154, 167, 168n468
Olympia 4n13, 12, 181, 214n632, 304
Olympus, Mount 21 (1), 108–113
Onochonos (river) 115, 116n304
Oreïthyia 93, 119, 127, 135, 136n363, 193
Orestes 163n442, 193
Ossa, Mount 21 (1), 108, 110–111, 118 (4)
Ottoman Empire and Ottomans 18n87, 52n47, 84n190, 223
Ovens 122–123, 129–130, 132–133, 135, 148

Pagasai 118 (4), 140–141, 143
Pagasetic Gulf 137n367, 140–143
Paktye 61 (3), 87, 117, 291
Pallene 241–242
Pamukkale. *See* Hierapolis
Pan 187, 190n547, 220–221, 227n678, 233, 299n34
Panathenaia festival 212
Pandrosos, temple of 204n597, 208
Pangaion, Mount 100

Panhellenism, Panhellenic 10n44, 11, 20n99, 35, 245, 268–269, 293n9–10, 299n35, 304
Panionion 274
Panopeai or Panopeus 118 (4), 170, 172n474
Parapotamioi 118 (4), 170, 171n474
Paris (Trojan prince) 64n99, 71
Parnassos, Mount 65, 118 (4), 170, 175n492, 176–177, 182, 184, 186–188, 263n800
Parnes, Mount 215 (6), 229
Parthenon. See Athena
Patroclus 64n99, 71, 73n137, 106n279, 135n359, 283
Pausanias (general) 245n742–744, 254, 270n829, 275
Pausanias (traveller) 1, 4, 11, 17, 23n109, 27n128, 44n24, 45n26, 54n59, 55n60, 71n130, 91, 106n277, 114n300, 116, 127, 129n347, 147n400, 153n414, 154, 162, 163n442, 165n451, 166n454, 166n458, 167n462, 168n467, 172n474, 173, 175, 180–182, 184–190, 193n555–557, 194n559, 195n562, 195n565, 195n567, 197n573, 208, 214n632, 217, 219n647, 220–223, 226–227, 232–233, 236n718, 238, 245n742, 245n744, 247, 248n761, 251n769, 253–254, 259–260, 262–264, 266, 268n823, 270–271, 273n843, 280n871, 282n879, 285n889, 291n1, 296–299, 301
Pedieai 118 (4), 170, 171n474
Pefki 137
Peisistratos and Peisistratids 73n140, 190n549, 191, 211, 298
Peleus 123, 128–132, 148
Pelion, Mount 65, 118, 122, 128n344, 300n39
Pella 100, 181
Peloponnesian War 35n168, 220
Peneios (river) 107–108, 110
Perama 4n12, 214 (6), 218, 228–229, 23n685, 235
Pericles 190, 202, 203n596, 204–206, 208–209, 211n620
Persephone or Kore 16n77, 210, 213, 232n693, 247, 262n797, 264, 267n818, 278, 281
Persepolis 16, 32n156, 33, 40n4, 54, 69n121, 74–75, 178, 294
Perserschutt 174
Phaleron 215 (6), 232–233, 296
Pharmakoussai 218, 235
Pheidias 4n13, 195, 200, 260n792

Pheme 273n844
Phocis and Phocians 20 (1), 75, 149, 154–158, 161–162, 165n451, 169–178, 185, 188, 296, 305
– wall of 118 (4), 149, 156–157, 162, 173n479
Phrixos 114, 116, 291
Phrygia and Phrygians 2, 24, 40–46, 48, 49n39, 51–52, 76n163, 91
Phylakos 177, 179–182, 184–185, 188, 298, 302
Pieria 110–111
Piraeus 194n559, 218n642, 222–224, 228, 229n683
Plataea, city of 21 (1), 175, 221
– battle of 21 (1), 30, 31n151, 33, 34n162, 111n291, 117, 166, 168n467, 174n486, 190, 195, 210–211, 216n635, 224, 244 (7), 244–275, 280–282, 288, 290, 293n9, 296, 298–300, 302–303, 305, 307
– island at 257–259
– oath of 206, 267, 297n26
Platania 118 (4), 125n330, 140–141
Pori. See Pouri
Poseidon 12, 72n135, 84n192, 92, 99n251, 108, 110, 137n365, 144n391, 147n398, 193, 207, 210n612, 214n632, 225, 232n693, 241–242, 245n742, 256n780, 269, 274n847, 293n10, 298, 301n43, 308
Postmemory 18n87
Potidaia 21 (1), 107, 110n290, 134, 199n579, 240–243, 306
Pouri, cape 118 (4), 124n328, 125, 132–133
Priene
– Old Priene 277–279
– New Priene 39 (2), 276–282, 289
Propylaea 189 (5), 192, 202n590, 204n597, 306
Protesilaos, grave of 76n162, 274, 282–287, 289n899, 291, 295–296
Psyttaleia 28n134, 215 (6), 216–224, 227, 235, 243, 304–305
Pythia 28, 184–185, 213, 267–268
Pythios 46–48, 55–57

Rhesus 98n247, 99–101
Rhoiteion 60 (3), 68, 71
Roads
– Royal Road in Anatolia 41, 56
– Royal Road in Thrace 91
Roman Empire and Romans 4n10, 5–6, 10, 43n17, 50n40, 51n43, 55n60, 61, 68n114,

86, 120n320, 123n325, 125n331, 130n350, 148, 154, 162, 166n454–455, 181n511, 214n632, 242, 255–256, 264n807, 270, 285, 298, 305, 306n64, 307n67

Sacred War (348 BCE) 173, 176
Salamis (island) 21 (*1*), 215 (*6*), 218n643, 222n657, 223, 225–227, 229, 232, 235–236, 244, 278n859, 294, 305
– battle of 30, 36n179, 43, 78, 85, 98, 110, 121, 126, 138, 147, 150n409, 154, 190, 206, 210, 213–237, 243–244, 267, 273n846, 274, 294, 298, 300, 302, 304n58, 305, 307
Salamis (mythical figure) 225
Salamis (town) 218n642, 223n661, 224, 226n674, 231n692
Samos 21 (*1*), 41n11, 82, 85, 220, 236n718, 274–275, 295, 296–297, 308
Sarayköy 49, 51
Sardis 2, 21 (*1*), 39 (*2*), 40, 41n10, 43n18, 46, 51–52, 56–60, 62, 65, 73, 78, 199–200, 282, 286, 306, 308
Sarıkavak 48, 52
Sarpedon, cape 21 (*1*), 92–93
Sarpedon (mythical figure) 92
Sassanids 16n74
Scamander 60 (*3*), 61, 63, 65–69, 89, 97n241, 99, 101
Scythia and Scythians 23n110, 42, 68n117, 93, 167n460
Seddülbahir 60 (*3*), 283
Seleucids 162
Semele 256
Sepias 21 (*1*), 74, 84n193, 118 (*4*), 121–136, 140, 144n391, 147–148, 210, 238, 242n738, 291, 298, 301
Sesostris 22n106, 25–26, 50, 91
Sestos 2, 21 (*1*), 60 (*3*), 62, 78, 80–84, 86, 199n579, 274
–siege of 273–274, 285–289, 306
Sigeion 60 (*3*), 71, 72n134–135, 73n140, 87n206, 283
Sivri Tepe 71
Skiathos 118 (*4*), 120, 136–137, 139, 146
Skiron 232
Skiti 123
Sklithro 123, 133
Skolopoeis 39 (*2*), 221, 248, 274–281, 289–290

Skolos 221, 244 (*7*), 247–248, 264, 272, 280, 290
Skyllias 136, 140–141, 142n384
Solon 23n110, 231n692
Soteria festival 186
Sousa 25n123, 32n156, 41n10, 55, 78, 207, 294, 298
Sparta and Spartans 4n11, 18, 20n96, 21 (*1*), 27n130, 35n168, 61n88, 95, 129n347, 148, 150, 156, 158, 161–169, 190n546, 213, 220, 245n743–744, 246n749, 247, 249, 253n772, 254, 259, 262–270, 273, 275, 281–282, 289, 299, 304–305, 307
Spatial densification 13, 19
Sphacteria, battle of 220
Stentor, lake 21 (*1*), 92
Stentor (mythical figure) 93
Stoa Poikile 181, 195, 293n10, 304n54
Strymon 102, 117, 239, 291n1, 294, 301
Sulla 190n549

Tatarlı, tomb of 42–43
Taurus mountains 39 (*2*), 39–40
Tegea and Tegeans 221, 245n742, 246n749, 247, 254n774, 262–263, 265n807, 269
Telesterion. *See* Anaktoron
Tempe valley 21 (*1*), 107–114, 117, 236, 294, 306, 308
Tethronion 118 (*4*), 170, 171n474
Teucrians 68, 91, 109
Thales of Miletus 41
Thebes and Thebans 21 (*1*), 26, 33, 60 (*3*), 163, 174, 244 (*7*), 246–248, 251n768, 252, 260n792, 262n795, 264, 269, 272, 278–279, 291n1, 301–302
– temple of the Kabeiroi 4n11, 116, 268n823
Themistocles 84n194, 138, 184, 215n634, 223–224, 297
– decree of 31–32
Therme 21 (*1*), 107–111, 120, 122
Thermopylae 21 (*1*), 137, 291, 305
– battle of 31, 33n161, 85, 91n132, 109, 118, 121, 147–158, 160n431, 161–162, 164–170, 199n579, 235, 245n743, 282, 288–289, 290n1, 300, 303, 305–306
– pass of 109n283, 113, 161, 164, 169, 302, 305, 306–307
Theseus 194, 196n567, 201, 232
– temple of 195

Thessaly and Thessalians 5n17, 21 (1), 33n157, 33n159, 89–90, 107–108, 110n285, 111, 113–114, 116–118, 123, 129n347, 131n355, 134n359, 149n406, 154–156, 158, 162, 166, 170, 172–173, 185n533, 210, 241, 285n889
Thetis 74, 76n155, 123, 128–133, 135–136, 148, 210, 291, 298, 300–301
Thrace and Thracians 25, 33n159, 37n185, 79n173, 86, 89–93, 95, 97–101, 119, 134n359, 136, 168n468, 238–239, 274, 282–283, 285n891, 287, 290n1, 294
Thracian Chersonesos 61, 79n173, 86, 274, 282–283, 285n891
Thrones 308
– of Darius 85, 308
– of Jamshid 16
– of Midas 24, 56n66, 308
– of Xerxes 78–79, 85, 86n201, 150, 154, 169, 190, 228–230, 234, 236, 243, 308
Tiralla *or* Kritalla 39 (2), 39–40
Tithorea 118 (4), 170, 171n474, 173, 175–176, 188, 305
Tmolos, mount 56n66, 59
Toponyms 47, 51, 52n51, 54n54, 87, 129, 132–133, 142n383, 161, 218n645, 231, 232n693, 238, 240n732, 248, 272, 281, 290–291, 294
Torbalı 25
Tourism 11–12, 17, 23, 61n86, 72, 119n317, 141, 148–149, 160, 165, 179, 192, 206, 209, 214, 230, 254, 270–272, 285
Trachis and Trachinians 118 (4), 150, 152–154, 157, 167–169, 308
Triteai 118 (4), 170, 171n474
Troad 5n17, 21 (1), 40n5, 60 (3), 61–63, 68n114, 68n117, 70, 71n128, 72–73, 77, 79n170, 113, 291, 308
Trojan War 4n11, 55n60, 61n88, 64–65, 71n131, 72n135, 73n138, 77–78, 89, 115, 135, 148, 220, 245, 263n799, 282–284, 292, 293n9–10
Troy 21 (1), 39 (2), 60 (3), 61, 63–64, 66–71, 73–74, 76n155, 76n162, 77–78, 87, 89, 91, 110, 116, 120n319, 129n347, 134n359, 135–136, 145, 147, 210, 216n635, 230, 264, 283, 285n889, 291, 293n9–10, 295, 298, 300–301. *See also* Trojan War
Tyre 236n718

Varvari, cape 223
Vasilika 4n12, 119n317, 143, 291n2
Velitsa 175
Veneto (Magnesia) 118 (4), 123, 129–133
Vermio. *See* Bermion
Vouliagmeni 215 (6), 238

Waterloo, battle of 1, 14

Xenophon 24n115–117, 42n16, 43, 45n26, 47n33, 55, 59, 63n96, 65n103, 76n157, 81n180, 98n247, 163n442, 219n647, 223n661, 247, 249n765, 290n1, 297, 299n36

Yaunā 33

Zeus 4n13, 45, 54n59, 63–65, 67, 74, 86n201, 98, 105, 113–114, 116–117, 120n319, 131, 135n359, 137n365, 160, 183, 186, 204n597, 208, 214n632, 224, 245n742, 270–271, 297–298, 300–301, 308
– temple of Zeus Laphystios 74, 113–114, 116–117
Zone 21 (1), 93, 238, 240–241, 290
Zoroastrianism 54, 73, 75n151–153, 84, 97, 128, 209, 239n724. *See also* Magi
Zoster, cape 237–238, 240, 243

www.ingramcontent.com/pod-product-compliance
Lightning Source LLC
Chambersburg PA
CBHW081823230426
43668CB00017B/2358